# A TO Z OF SPORTS CARS
## 1945-1990

# A TO Z OF SPORTS CARS 1945-1990

**BY MIKE LAWRENCE**

a-z sports cars page 4 patch

First published 1991 by
Bay View Books Ltd
The Red House,
25-26 Bridgeland Street,
Bideford, Devon EX39 2PZ

Paperback edition published 1996

Reprinted 1997
Reprinted 1998



Designed by Peter Laws
Typesetting and layout by Chris Fayers

ISBN 1 870979 81 8
Printed in Hong Kong

# FOREWORD

What is a sports car? Ask that question of a hundred enthusiasts and you'll get a hundred different answers. Nobody is going to argue that an MG TC, or a Porsche 959, is not a sports car but it's hard to find much similarity between them. Taking these two examples, performance does not make a sports car, nor a canvas hood, so what is the magic ingredient? All I can say is that if you find it, then bottle it and you will make a fortune.

When starting this book I tried to frame a definition of the ingredient, and I failed. I spoke to many of the motoring writers I respect the most and a consensus of their replies translated into an intake of breath and 'Don't envy you that problem, old lad.' I finally decided that a definition was impossible because it moves according to time and place; no Westerner would have called the Daihatsu Compagno a sports car but when it appeared the average Japanese, whose motor industry was still at a primitive level, perceived it as one. Few people associate Skoda with technical excellence, and few would regard its Felicia as a sports car in the Western perception of the notion; but if you were a Czech enthusiast in the 1950s, would you not have drooled over a Skoda Felicia? A fibreglass body on a VW Beetle chassis is not my idea of a sports car, but millions of Brazilians would disagree, and were not the first Porsches little more than Beetle specials?

Finally I decided that the only solution had to be a leap of imagination; to put oneself in a particular place, at a particular time, and try to imagine how one would see a particular car in the context of that time and place. Thus I have excluded the Jaguar XJS because nobody, least of all Jaguar, perceived it as a sports car; Jaguar's idea of a sports car was the E Type and the aborted F Type. In the same way, BMW's 1990 idea of a sports car was the Z1, not the 8-series although that is a much more powerful, competent and attractive car than most of the cars within these covers. One of my favourite cars is the Ford Sierra Cosworth but it is clearly a saloon for it races only in saloon car events.

Just as there is an overlap between what is a saloon car and what is a sports car, so there is a grey area between what is a sports car and what is a sports-racer. Nobody could confuse, say, a Group C car with a road car but, in the 1950s, the division was blurred because all sports racers had to be road legal and could, and many were, driven to and from the circuits. Some Jaguar C Types were bought for road use, *primarily*, but no Jaguar D Type was; Lotus offered a Ford-powered road version of the Eleven, and the Lola Mk1 could be driven on the road, but all were sold with racing as their primary function. In 1956 there was a spirited correspondence in *Autosport* in which expatriate Briton Ken Miles cited instances of lady owners of Ferrari Monzas using their cars to drive to the local market to buy veg. That was in California (of course) but it does not make the Ferrari Monza into a road car.

Some of the high performance American saloons of the 1960s have been included in some books on sports cars, but at their time of manufacture they were known as 'pony cars', 'personal cars' or, in retrospect, 'muscle cars'. To an American in the 1960s, a sports car was a Corvette, a Sprite, an E Type; not a Ford Mustang. It is true that the 1970 Boss Mustang had a 6.8-litre engine and 375bhp but when the Mustang appeared in 1965 the base car had a 101bhp 2.7-litre engine. A parallel situation exists with the Ford Capri; some factory racers had over 400bhp but the base Capri was the 61bhp 1300 model.

In some cases I have included cars from a sports car marque which I would not call sports cars, but they are there to keep the record tidy. In most cases I have signalled the fact, but it seemed to me that if I omitted, say, the Maserati Quattroporte, then it would give a false impression of the way Maserati was operating. I cannot imagine that a reader will object to extra information, especially when it helps to balance the history of a particular marque.

In the end, any selection of something as nebulous as 'sports cars', comes down to subjective judgement (or prejudice). Some marginal cars, such as the Invicta Black Prince and the EMW 321, have been included on the grounds that, for different reasons, both have an interesting story. The amount of space I have given each marque equally reflects my own prejudices; some makers, even failed makers, are interesting, and some are not.

One important point is that a replica, by definition, can be made only by the originator of a design or by someone licensed by the originator; thus, every Lamborghini Countach made by Lamborghini is a replica of the original design and the only AC Cobra replica currently made is the Autocraft MkIV—all other Cobra lookalikes are copies, for Autocraft is licensed. In fact, the best word to describe most unlicensed copies is *Doppelgänger*, which in Teutonic mythology is a spirit which has the appearance of something but lacks the substance.

When reading other people's selections, I've often fumed, Why has he omitted the Bandersnatch Hotspur? Or, How can he call the Snark Marbella a sports car? Now it's my turn to infuriate but, if the reader is happy with 90 percent of the contents, I will have achieved as much as I can reasonably hope for.

If anyone has additional information, corrections, or news of a marque I have missed, please write to me care of the publisher. It is always good to hear from fellow enthusiasts, and correspondents will be acknowledged in the second edition.

Mike Lawrence

Chichester, 1991

# FOREWORD TO THE 1996 EDITION

When this book was originally written we were in the middle of exciting times. Hardly a week seemed to go by without the announcement of a new sports car project. Manufacturers vied with each other to produce ever-faster cars. There were so many applications to own a Jaguar XJ220, for example, that a draw was held to decide who were the lucky applicants, and it was a raffle you could only enter by first laying down a deposit which, with tax, amounted to £57,500.

For various reasons motor cars were seen as a blue chip investment. The prices of classic cars soared and madness prevailed. Nobody asked even basic questions such as whether an Aston Martin DB4 convertible was really worth £200,000. There were 215 made, so for one to be worth so much there had to be more than 215 people in the world, each with £200,000 to spare, who would not be satisfied unless they owned a DB4 convertible. Although normal economics says that inflation is a bad thing, for some reason people embraced inflation when it involved cars.

In that atmosphere, some people thought that the ownership of a new Ferrari or Jaguar was a quick way to make a profit. Ferrari F40s changed hands for four times their list price. Against £900,000 for a Ferrari F40 (the seller had bought it, second hand, for £600,000 a few weeks earlier) the £634,500 asked for a new McLaren F1 seemed a regular bargain.

Then economic recession bit and the the bubble burst. There were bankruptcies, even suicides. The largest owners of classic cars became finance houses who had repossessed vehicles. Many of the new supercar projects folded, Lamborghini closed its works for a while and even Ferrari went on short time. Speculators who had joined the great Jaguar raffle suddenly got cold feet and some tried to get out of the deal. McLaren originally announced that it would make 400 F1s, but within months that figure was downgraded to 300 and production ended in 1996 with fewer than 100 made.

Along with the demise of ambitious projects such as Cizeta and Bugatti went many kit car makers. The information in this book is as accurate as I was able to make it to the end of 1990, and I have not attempted to discover which kit cars are still in production in 1996. There is no point. Most kit car projects consist of no more than body moulds and chassis jigs so they come out, are put away, or are sold on. I know of companies which are still apparently in the business of making cars who haven't made one for years (they do other work) but who will will dust off the jigs and moulds if you arrive at their door with cash.

While it lasted, the buoyant market gave rise to some extraordinary machines. For that much, future generations of enthusiasts will be grateful. We might also hope that such madness never grips the market again because it took cars away from people who loved them for their own sake and gave them to people who saw them only as a short cut to a quick profit. Enthusiasts love sports cars for the pleasure they give. That is true whether you can own a McLaren or the proverbial Beetle with a plastic body.

Mike Lawrence

Chichester, 1996

## ABARTH (I)

A problem unique to Abarth is trying to decide how many models were made: estimates range from 100 to 250 because hardly any two cars were alike and it is difficult to know at what point a type had undergone enough changes for it to be regarded as a new model.

**Abarths arrive for scrutineering at Le Mans, 1960**

Karl Abarth was born in Austria in 1908 but his family moved to Italy just after the First World War. He became a serious motorcycle racer in the late 1920s and developed into a world-class rider who was five times Champion of Europe. Since Italy was in need of sporting heroes to match German achievements, he was more or less adopted by the Fascists, who induced him to stay in Italy.

In October 1939, Abarth was severely injured in a race in Yugoslavia and when he was released from hospital he stayed in the country where he worked on engines. At the end of the War he turned to his old friend, Ferry Porsche, who employed him in his design studio. Abarth thus became involved with the Cisitalia project and when Cisitalia's patron, Piero Dusio, left Italy in 1949 Guido Scagliarini (a Cisitalia driver) persuaded his father to set up Abarth in business.

**Abarth 1100 Spyder by Boano, 1955**

At first he continued the Cisitalia competition programme, and then began making dual-purpose Tipo 204 sports-racing cars under his own name. These were not immediately successful, although Nuvolari won the last competition of his career, a hill climb, in an Abarth. From the beginning *Scuderia Abarth* made tuning accessories, mainly for Fiat engines, but Abarth silencers became available for many cars.

The 204 Berlinetta, which used a tuned Fiat 1100 engine in a bespoke chassis with Porsche-style trailing link torsion bar front suspension, came in 1950. Special editions of the Fiat 1100 followed, together with the odd prototype, and to drum up publicity Abarth turned to record breaking, with a great deal of success. It was not until 1955 that the company seriously began to build competition cars, introducing the Tipo 207 Spyder, with modified Fiat 1100 running gear and an open two-seat body by Boano. There is a story that the homologation minimum limit of 25 was achieved by building 13 cars and photographing them in front of a large mirror! The last of the 200 series cars was the Boano-bodied 215A coupé of 1956.

When Fiat introduced the 600 in 1956, Abarth began to make a 750cc version, which was followed by the 850TC (*Turismo Competizione*, not 'Twin Cam'). Fiat supplied part finished cars and, in return, received a great deal of publicity as they took thousands of outright and class wins (in 1972, Fiat put the number at 7,200). By degrees the engines were enlarged to one litre. As well as a dohc head there was one with cross-over pushrods rather like the BMW 328 engine. Many of these cars ran with the rear engine cover permanently open, supported on a tubular frame, and this improved cooling and acted as an aerofoil (long before anyone else twigged the virtues of this).

The Fiat 500 was not forgotten, but the Topolino conversion was never as popular because it was not much cheaper than the larger car. These were available with engines up to 689cc, and as well as the standard Fiat body there were special bodies by Zagato and Farina.

**Abarth Spyder by Zagato, 1957**

On the chassis of the Abarth-Fiat 600 Zagato essayed a very attractive coupé body in aluminium, with a distinctive 'double bubble' roofline to clear the occupants' heads. Most of these were sold with 750cc engines but some had different sized engines. There were even a few 'double bubble' cars with smooth roofs and some open cars. Nobody knows how many of these were made, estimates ranging from 600 to 1800, which shows the level of confusion surrounding Abarths. There was also a steel-bodied version, the Sestriere, with a smooth roof, and about 15 were made before Zagato and Abarth had a clash of temperament and the relationship came to an end.

Vignale, Viotto, Farina, Bertone and Allemano also built

**Abarth 850 coupé by Allemano, 1960**

bodies on this base, both coupés and spyders, but hardly any two were alike since the customer could select from a wide menu of engine options and, as each body was hand built, they could be altered to individual requirements. There were also some space-framed sports-racers using dohc one-litre engines.

In 1960 Karl Abarth's friendship with Ferry Porsche found a material expression in the Porsche-Abarth Carrera GTL; this had a Porsche 356B chassis, a dohc 1582cc Carrera engine, and a body by Abarth which was both significantly lighter (by over 300lb) than the standard Porsche body and much more slippery. These cars were capable of 135mph/215kmh and a later version with a 2-litre engine and disc brakes was capable of 140mph/225kmh. Most of the 18 made were used for competition and between 1960 and 1963 they were very successful.

In 1961 Abarth formed a relationship with Simca which

**Abarth 750 Zagato 'Double Bubble'**

followed the same pattern as that with Fiat: there were modified versions of the Simca 1100 saloon and special bodies on both front- and rear-engined Simca chassis. As with the Fiat cars there was a long menu of engine options, up to a dohc 2-litre version, so what began as the stodgy Simca 1500 finished up as a very attractive coupé capable of 143mph/230kmh. Most of these were actually made for competition but a few were seen on public roads. When Chrysler took over Simca in 1965 the relationship ended.

These affairs with other makers did not weaken the marriage with Fiat and there were rebodied Abarth versions of many of the larger Fiats from the 1100 to the 2300. When the 850 came along in 1964 this received the usual treatment: modified road cars and cars with special bodies. (Many people believe that the Fiat 850 engine derived from Abarth's own work on the Fiat 600, thus he finished up modifying a modified version of one of his own modifications!) By this time Abarth was also making its own dohc four-cylinder 1.3-litre and 1.6-litre engines, some of which found their way into Fiat 850 chassis.

Abarth also made a number of 'all-Abarth' sports-racers.

**Abarth Simca 1300, 1962**

Although some were very successful, others were ill-starred and, besides, motor racing was a financial drain because direct sponsorship was not permitted in Europe until 1968. Abarth became fairly ambitious and planned both a 3-litre Formula 1 engine and a 6-litre V12 unit to make an assault on the World (sports car) Championship. A lot of investment and work went into the latter but it was stillborn because a change in regulations imposed a 3-litre limit. The F1 engine was also stillborn.

**Fiat Abarth 1000 Spyder by Pininfarina, 1964**

These projects helped to weaken the company. In 1970 Abarth produced its last distinct model, the Scorpione, a mid-engined wedge-shaped coupé which used an enlarged Fiat 124 engine. That year Abarth also signed a contract to produce special versions of the Autobianchi A112, but by 1971 the company was in such a parlous state that Fiat took it over, retaining Karl Abarth as technical consultant. Fiat had already bought Ferrari and decided that Ferrari would look after racing, and Abarth would become the rallying arm of the company.

Karl Abarth, for so long his own master, soon found himself unhappy working for a large corporation with its bureaucracy and bean counters, so he retired and returned to Austria. The company developed the successful Fiat rally cars of the late 1970s and the equally successful Lancias of the 1980s, and in 1985 Fiat's rorty Strada 'hot hatch' was sold as the Strada Abarth 130TC.

## **ABS** (GB)

From 1986, Auto Build-up Services made a Lamborghini Countach copy to a high level of fit and finish. In 1990 an open version, the Monaco, was announced which like its sister was available with a choice of V6 and V8 engines.

**ABS Scorpion**

**ABS Monaco**

## **AC** (GB)

Founded in 1908, AC was taken over by the Hurlock brothers in 1930 and thereafter gained a reputation for a range of high quality sports cars which were made in small numbers. After the Second World War it marketed a 2-litre saloon and tourer with a decidedly old-fashioned specification and things looked bleak for the car building side of the company (AC's main work came from general engineering and the manufacture of invalid carriages) until it introduced the Ace, which was a refined version of a Tojeiro. The company continued to make variations of the Ace while also experimenting with a number of horizontally-opposed engines designed by Zdzislaw Marczewski. There were twins, fours and sixes, some air-cooled and some water-cooled, but although some of these engines were tested in cars, none saw production.

As the Ace began to show its age in the early 1960s it seemed as though it would fade away, but then Carroll Shelby had the bright idea of fitting a 4-litre Ford V8 engine into an Ace chassis, and so was born the AC Cobra. In various forms this kept the company active until 1973 when, again, it had no new product. It had taken over a mid-engined prototype (the Bohanna Stables 'Diabolo') but that took years to reach even limited production, as the AC 3000 ME, and even then it was never satisfactory. Other commercial interests kept AC alive until 1980, when it hit financial difficulties and was sold. In 1984, rights to the 3000 ME were taken over by AC (Scotland) Ltd (qv), a company which did not survive to see its second birthday. In 1988 this project was revived under the name 'Ecosse' (qv).

In 1980, Autokraft, a company based at the old Brooklands track in Surrey, acquired sole rights to the AC name and in 1985 was granted the right to use the Cobra name. Thus Autokraft became the only maker of Cobra replicas, and the Ford Motor Company, which owns the name 'Cobra', took steps to prevent unlicensed use of it. The Mk IV Cobra is listed under 'Autokraft'.

To complicate matters further, in 1986 Autokraft showed a new sports car which revived the name 'AC Ace'. The company's managing director, Brian Angliss, showed the car to Henry Ford II and in 1987 Ford and Autokraft became equal partners in AC Cars Ltd, with Autokraft itself remaining an independent company with a wide range of interests, including the restoration of vintage aircraft. In 1990 Ford announced that it no longer intended to pursue the new Ace but AC Cars Ltd developed the concept and sold a few cars. Unfortunately it was in financial trouble by 1996.

**Ace/Ace-Bristol, 1954-63. Prod: 226/466.** Racing driver Cliff Davis bought a Tojeiro chassis, fitted a Bristol engine, and had a copy of a Ferrari 166 *Barchetta* body made. After an extremely successful season on the tracks in

**AC Ace**

1953 the car was shown to the Hurlock brothers, who decided to put it into production (John Tojeiro received a £5 royalty for the first 100 cars). Its twin tube ladder frame and independent suspension by double wishbones and transverse leaf springs were pure Tojeiro (or Cooper, to be blunt) but AC's Allan Turner turned a pretty body into a stunning one. Initially, power was from AC's 1991cc straight-six engine (dating back to 1919!) which gave 80bhp in 1954 and 102bhp by 1958, but performance was brisk rather than startling. The Bristol engine was available from 1956 and, with up to 130bhp, top speed was 117mph/188kmh (0-60mph in 9.1 seconds). The Ace was very successful in production sports car racing on both sides of the Atlantic and was good enough to finish seventh overall, and first in class, at Le Mans in 1959.

In 1958, AC commissioned John Tojeiro to build a special 'Ace' which had a space frame, de Dion rear axle, and a body styled by Cavendish Morton. The works ran it only twice, at Le Mans where it finished second in class despite the rear suspension breaking up, and in the Tourist Trophy where it suffered cooling problems.

**Aceca/Aceca-Bristol, 1955-63. Prod: 150/169.** A fastback Ace, but with a wooden frame under its aluminium body (and all that means for the collector). As with the Ace, overdrive was an option and, from 1958, front disc brakes were fitted. In later Acecas and Aces the old Moss gearbox gave way to Triumph TR3 internals in an AC casing, which was a huge improvement. With an extra 115lb to carry the Aceca was not quite as nimble as the Ace, but the aerodynamics of its coupé body meant that top speed was about the same.

AC Aceca

**Greyhound, 1959-63. Prod: 80.** A four-seater Aceca which failed to catch on, perhaps partly due to the fact that the British market was not used to what was essentially a GT car on Italian lines. Most Greyhounds had Bristol units although a handful were fitted with AC and 2.6-litre Ford engines. With its greater weight the Greyhound was never a road burner, and its longer wheelbase and different weight distribution did nothing for its handling.

AC Greyhound

**Ace/Aceca 2.6, 1961-63. Prod: 47.** Ken Rudd used to win all the 2-litre sports car races in the South of England with his Ace. Peter Bolton won them in the North, and the two men never met on the circuits except when they were paired in a works car at Le Mans. Rudd ran a tuning shop and when he fitted a hot Ford Zephyr engine to an Ace it impressed the factory enough for it to be offered as an option. On the later cars the body was changed, especially at the front, and the Ace began to take on the looks which would become more familiar as the Cobra.

AC Ace 2.6 had revised nose

**Cobra 260/289, MkII 289, 1962, 1963-65. Prod: 75/51, 528.** It is the stuff of legend that Texan racing driver, Carroll Shelby, hit on the idea of shoe-horning the lightweight 260 cu in (4-litre) Ford Fairlane V8 into the Ace

AC Cobra 289

chassis. Shelby built a prototype in 1961 and production began in 1962. AC sent body/rolling chassis units (with disc brakes on all wheels) to America where they had the transplant and were sold as Shelby-AC Cobras. The MkII version kept the old chassis but had rack and pinion steering. AC did not launch the car in Britain until 1964 and made the 289 cu in (4.4-litre) engine the base unit for the home market.

**Cobra MkIII 289/427, 1965-68.** **Prod:** 27/348. The MkIII chassis was designed by Bob Negstadt of Shelby-American and Allen Turner of AC; the basic layout of the old chassis was retained but the main tubes were larger and set further apart, and coil springs replaced the transverse leaf arrangement. Cars with 289 cu in (4.4-litre) engines were sold in Britain and Europe while America took the 427 with a 7-litre engine, and this version, with its bulging wheel arches,

AC Cobra MkIII 289

is the favourite with the dozens of outfits who have built sometimes poorly engineered copies.

What can one say about this beast? Even customer cars had 390bhp and 475lb/ft of torque, which meant 0-60mph in 4.2 seconds and a top speed of 165mph/265kmh. It should be said, however, that very, very few drivers were capable of getting the best out of them, and there was far too much power for the crude chassis.

Variations on the theme included the Daytona coupés run by Dan Gurney in 1965, and a special works coupé styled by Allan Turner which ran, and crashed, at Le Mans in 1965.

**428, 1966-73.** **Prod:** 86. A long-wheelbase version of the Cobra MkIII which was usually fitted with the tamer 345bhp Galaxie engine. Frua styled and supplied the steel bodies, which looked not unlike their body for the Maserati Mistrale. Top speed was 140mph/225kmh, with 0-60mph in 5.9 seconds—fair figures for the day, but somehow the car's pretty looks did not get customers' hearts beating in the way that the Cobra could. Two styles were offered, a fastback (58 made) and a convertible (28 made) but these were Italian steel bodies, which means they were bio-degradable. Some cars have been converted into more glamorous, and valuable, Cobras.

AC 428, styled by Frua

**3000ME, 1979-84.** **Prod:** 82. Like the Ace, the 3000ME was a bought-in design. It was first shown by its creator, Bohanna Stables, in 1973 when it was fitted with an Austin Maxi engine/transmission. AC announced it would make it in 1974 but took five years to get it into production. When the car did arrive, power came from a transverse mid-mounted 3-litre Ford V6 engine driving through a special transmission, but performance was relatively disappointing (120mph/193kmh maximum), and its handling took a long time to sort out. As time went on its projected price increased, and when it finally did go into production it arrived in the middle of an economic downturn and it suffered by comparison to the Lotus Esprit. The project was eventually taken on by another company (A.C. (Scotland)) which made a further 30 examples.

AC 3000 ME had Ford V6 mid-mounted engine

**Ace.** First shown in 1986, the Ace was a front-engined 2+2 coupé with a Targa top. It had a steel monocoque with an aluminium body, and Ford-derived independent suspension all round. Ford Sierra/Scorpio four wheel drive was projected and is was expected that the customer would be able to specify either the Ford V6 engine or the Sierra Cosworth turbo unit.

**1986 AC Ace did not go into production**

With the latter engine, a top speed of over 140mph/225kmh was claimed, and a 0-60mph time of under seven seconds.

## AC (SCOTLAND) (GB)

In 1984 the rights to the AC 3000ME were bought by a Scottish businessman and the new company made 30 examples in ten months; good by AC standards but not so good for a firm which was geared to make 400 cars a year. In 1985 a replacement model, the 'Ecosse', was announced. This had a completely new body style, a 2.5-litre Alfa Romeo V6 engine, and a claimed top speed of 145mph/233kmh, but the company folded within a few weeks.

By 1988 a new company called 'Ecosse' (qv) had taken over the design.

## ACM (GB)

This kit car company's offering was the 'Bonito', which was originally built by the American firm, Fiberfab, and then manufactured by the associated German Fiberfab company. In 1982 the design was licensed to ACM but was soon sold on to another British firm, Seraph Cars Ltd (qv). The Bonito was a 2+2 coupé inspired by the Ford GT40, usually based on a VW floorpan with a number of engine options. Seraph Cars Ltd built a new backbone chassis and offered front-engined versions using Ford Capri or Granada or Rover V8 components, but the company folded in 1987.

**ACM Bonito was based on VW chassis**

## ACM (MC) *see* CENTAIRE

## ACURA (J)

The name under which some Honda models, including the NS-X sports car, are marketed in the USA. In 1990, one of the most prestigious cars to own in Japan was a Honda NS-X exported to America under the Acura name, complete with left hand drive, and then re-imported into Japan which, correctly, drives on the left.

**Acura NS-X**

## AD (GB) *see* AUTOMOTIVE DEVELOPMENTS

## ADAMO (BR)

Originally a maker of beach buggies, in 1978 Adamo began making fibreglass Ferrari Dino copies using VW Beetle running gear.

**Adamo GT of 1972 had no doors**

## HERB ADAMS VSE (USA)

A 1980s kit to turn a rusted first-series VW Golf, or any Scirocco, into a wedge-shaped open two-seater called the 'Jack Rabbit'. That name recalls one of the earliest of all sports cars, the Apperson Jack Rabbit speedster of 1907. Herb Adams was one of the team which revitalised Pontiac in the 1960s, and was a noted engineer in Trans-Am racing.

## ADAMS ROADSTER (GB)

In 1986 Dennis Adams, who designed both the Marcos and the Probe, began to market a traditionally-styled roadster with a ladder chassis, fibreglass body, and the running gear from the XK-engined Jaguar XJ6. It was usually sold as a turn key car, with a high standard of trim, and the company could provide a complete car or accept a donor car for conversion. Since the complete car weighed little more than a ton, with a 4.2-litre engine it could reach 125mph/200kmh.

## **AERO** (CS)

Aero was a Czech aircraft manufacturer which built light cars, always with two-stroke engines, from 1929. Its 955cc four-cylinder Type 30 of 1937 was a front wheel drive, 50bhp, close-coupled sports car of striking appearance and all independent suspension. A few were made after the War but production ceased in 1947.

**745cc Aero Pony, 1945**

## **AERO MINOR** (CS)

Aero Minor was a short-lived (1946-52) postwar Czech maker not connected to its compatriot 'Aero', although its cars shared such features as a two-stroke engine and front wheel drive. In fact the Aero Minor derived from the Jawa Minor, which had been refined during the war. A number of types were offered, all of which used a water-cooled two-cylinder 615cc engine on a backbone chassis, and some sports cars with their engines bored out to 744cc were made. In 1949 one of these won the 750cc class at Le Mans and in the Spa 24 Hour race, and the Le Mans success was repeated in 1950, but after that Czech cars were seen no more in Western motor racing.

## **AF** *see* AUTO FORGE

## **AFM** (D)

Former BMW engineer, Alex von Falkenhausen set up a small racing and tuning shop in Munich after the Second World War. His first products were BMW 328 specials but he made his name with BMW-based single seaters, the first of which was made in 1949. AFMs performed well in German F2 races and provided the chief threat to Veritas. On the back of its racing successes, in 1951 AFM made an attempt to market a four/five seat luxury coupé which used the running gear from the 60bhp six-cylinder 2.5-litre Opel Kapitän. Apparently it did not proceed beyond the prototype stage and soon afterwards von Falkenhausen returned to BMW.

**AFM 2½-litre coupé, 1951**

## **AGEA** (CH)

This odd-looking two seat fibreglass coupé was launched in Switzerland in 1954. The man behind the project was one Pierre de Tolédo and the car is sometimes referred to as the Agea de Tolédo. The square tube chassis frame accommodated a 721cc Crosley engine which was tuned to give, so it was claimed, 48bhp. Suspension was by Fiat 500 transverse leaf springs front and rear although the live rear axle was from the Fiat 1100. Most unusually, transmission was via a Lancia Ardea five-speed gearbox. Very few were made and the project had collapsed within a year.

**Agea de Tolédo 1955 coupé with 721cc ohc Crosley engine**

## **ALBAR** (CH)

From 1972, Al Barmettler produced a number of buggies and Beetle conversions. The 'Sonic' of 1982 was a futuristic wedge-shaped Targa-top car based on Beetle running gear. In 1985 it was joined by a 2+2 coupé (also called 'Sonic') which had

**VW Beetle-based Albar Sonic of 1982**

Albar Jet, 1982

a bespoke chassis, a mid-mounted VW Golf engine, and slightly more sober lines. It sold less well than the more outrageous version.

## ALDO (BR)

Since 1977, Aldo has been a highly successful maker following the usual Brazilian pattern: a fibreglass body on a VW floor pan. Its cars are sold under the name 'Miura'. At first coupés and sports cars were based on the Beetle chassis but in 1982 came the 'Targa', a coupé on the VW Passat floor pan. An open version followed in 1983 and the following year the similarly based 'Saga', in coupé or open form, joined the range, soon complemented by a 2+2 version. 1988 saw the X8, with the option of a 2-litre VW (Santana) engine, which could also be turbocharged, while those exported to the USA had 2-litre Ford engines. A further update, the 'Top Sport', followed in 1989.

Aldo Miura Targa, 1985, with 1588cc VW engine

## ALFA ROMEO (I)

Until the 1950s, cars were a relatively small part of Alfa Romeo's business, the main thrust being the manufacture of aero engines. In the late 1920s and early 1930s, however, largely thanks to the genius of Vittorio Jano, Alfa Romeo had won dozens of Grands Prix, ten of the twelve pre-war Mille Miglia races, and Le Mans four years in a row. Forget Bugatti, forget Mercedes-Benz—Alfa Romeo was the outstanding marque of the inter-war period. After the Second World War it concentrated on becoming a volume producer, but it wheeled out its 1938 Tipo 158 racers and, after failing on the first outing in 1946, won every Grand Prix these cars were entered in until mid-1951, when a new Ferrari finally beat Alfa's 13-year-old design.

In 1947 Alfa Romeo began limited production of a pre-war model as it struggled to recover with a factory which had been heavily bombed. In 1950 it showed its first postwar design, the 1900, which was intended for mass production. The company steered a course towards becoming a volume producer and by 1972 was making the small, popular and competent Alfasud, which was intended to be made at a rate of 1000 a day. The car was built in a new factory near Naples which was beset by incredible labour problems and this, even more than poor production engineering, poor quality and a tendency to rust, saw Alfa Romeo plunge into deep crisis.

In the early 1980s Alfa Romeo was reduced to fitting the Alfasud engine to a Datsun Cherry and passing off the bastard (called the 'Arna') as legitimate, while the Alfa Romeo 6 was one of the worst saloons made in the 1980s. With falling sales, the company was unable to invest to pull itself out of the spiral and the quality of the cars it was making was dubious. In 1987 it was taken over by Fiat and started on the way to regaining its lost reputation.

**6C 2500, 1947-52. Prod: 1,451.** As soon as Alfa Romeo was able to repair its war-damaged factory and begin production, it concentrated on this 1939 model while preparing its new cars. As the designation suggests, it had a six-cylinder, 2.5-litre dohc engine and a chassis that was pure Jano, with front suspension by coil springs and trailing arms and independent rear suspension by swing axles and longitudinal torsion bars. Several body styles were available, mostly executed by Touring, and all had right hand drive, like every other Alfa before them. The basic car used a 90bhp engine in a 118in wheelbase chassis, but the Super Sport (383 built) had 110bhp, a swb (106in) chassis and was good for 100+mph. The rare *Competizione* variant had 145bhp (125mph/200kmh) and one of these won the 1947 Mille Miglia, Alfa Romeo's eleventh and last win in the event.

Alfa Romeo 2500SS with Touring Superleggera body, 1951

**1900 Sprint/Super Sprint, 1954-58. Prod: 949/854.** Alfa's first mass-produced car, the 1900 saloon, arrived in 1950 and set the pattern for all the company's cars for some years: unitary construction, a dohc four-cylinder engine, a distinctly sporty feel, and poor detailing. It was not long before it received the attention of specialist coachbuilders (including the famous BAT series) but the first factory-generated special cars came in 1954. Touring styled the coupé, Pininfarina the cabriolet. The engine had grown to 1975cc with 115bhp, there was a five-speed gearbox and suspension was by coil springs, with double wishbones at the front and

Alfa Romeo 1900 Super Sprint

a live rear axle located by trailing arms and a triangulated link. Lovely style and up to 112mph/180kmh (SS Model); shame about the column change.

**Giulietta Sprint/Sprint Veloce, 1955-62. Prod: 24,083/3058.** Basically a smaller 1900 with similar construction and suspension but only 1290cc and 80bhp (90bhp on the Veloce). These were outstanding power outputs for the day

Alfa Romeo Giulietta Sprint Veloce

(compare them with the 70bhp for the Porsche 356 1300 Super) and even in standard form this pretty, Bertone-styled, two-seat coupé could top the ton. The Veloce was good for 110mph/175kmh, and both had handling to match.

**Giulietta Spyder/Spyder Veloce, 1955-62. Prod: 14,300/2,796.** This was an open version of the Sprint but with

Alfa Romeo Giulietta Spyder Veloce

floor change from the beginning. The designations had the same meanings: the Veloce had 90bhp to the standard Spyder's 80bhp. Like the closed car, there was no rhd until 1961 (yet no Alfa before 1950 had lhd!). Also like the coupés, most rotted away long ago.

**2000 Spyder, 1958-61. Prod: 3,443.** Really another version of the 1900 Super Sprint with the same 115bhp engine, and the same chassis, but given the '2000' designation to complement the new 2000 saloon range. Touring was responsible for the handsome 2+2 body; the gear lever was

Alfa Romeo 2000 Spyder, Touring bodied, had the 1900 Super Sprint's 115bhp engine

on the floor; and drum brakes were still fitted, although they were large Alfin drums. They were on the heavy side so a Giulietta was just as quick, and a lot more fun, from A to B. Steel disc wheels were standard—the only post-1950 Alfas with wires were factory competition cars or special models created by coachbuilders.

**Giulietta SS, SZ, 1957-62. Prod: 1366/200.** The ultimate Giulietta, with 100bhp which meant 120+mph. The

Alfa Romeo Giulietta SS was bodied by Bertone

Zagato's Giulietta SZ

SZ had a stubby, but smooth, body by Zagato and tended to be the choice of the serious competition driver. By contrast, the SS found greater favour at the kerbside with its startling Bertone body, which had massive overhang at both ends. It was claimed to be aerodynamically sound but it is noticeable that neither Alfa, nor anyone else, built another car which imitated its style.

**2600 Spyder, 1962-65. Prod: 2255.** By 1962, Alfa production was up from 1228 cars in 1951 to around 35,000 units (it would hit six figures in 1969); this was achieved by

The six-cylinder Alfa Romeo 2600 Spyder

cautious progress and niche marketing. The 2600 series followed the broad layout of its predecessors but had a 145bhp *six*-cylinder engine which was Alfa's first 'oversquare' unit. Another first was disc brakes and having decided to fit them, Alfa went the whole hog and put them on all four wheels. Basically a re-engined 2000, the extra power was welcome but although 125mph/200kmh was possible, nimble the car was not.

**Giulia Sprint, 1962-66. Prod: 42,889.** There were two distinct types of Giulia coupés; the 1962 car was an interim car and was actually a Giulietta given a new aluminium-block 1570cc dohc 'four'. Since it had only a single carburetter, and 92bhp, despite its bigger engine it was roughly the equivalent of the 90bhp Giulietta Sprint Veloce and like it was a 2+2. It came with front disc brakes (discs all round from 1966) and, like the Giulietta, with a nest of tinworm.

1962 Alfa Romeo Giulia Sprint had the new 1570cc engine

**Giulia Spyder/Spyder Veloce, 1962-65. Prod: 9250/ 1091.** This was the Pininfarina-styled Giulietta Spyder which, as usual, paralleled the Sprint coupé. Thus the Spyder had the new 92bhp 1570cc aluminium engine, and the Veloce had the twin-carburetter 112bhp version, which made it a very nippy little car indeed.

Giulia Spyder also arrived in 1962, styled by Pininfarina

**Giulia TZ (Tubolare)/TZ2, 1963-64, 1965-66. Prod: 120/50.** Alfa Romeo's successor to the SZ; the TZ designation stood for Tubular (its chassis) and Zagato. As this name implies, it was a special car with independent suspension all round by coil springs and double wishbones. As sold over the counter it had a 112bhp 1.6-litre engine but that was only the starting point because many of these cars

Alfa Romeo Giulia TZ (above) and TZ2 (below)

were used for competition and, fully tuned, these would top 150mph/240kmh. Of the 120 TZs made, ten had fibreglass bodies, which was something of a departure for Alfa Romeo and must have perplexed the *vermicelli.*

These cars were very successful in competition and when Porsche responded with the 904, Alfa Romeo made the TZ2 which was lower, and was competitive for a little longer.

**1300GT Junior, 1967-72. Prod: 92,053.** While the re-engined Giulietta masqueraded as the 'Giulia', most cars built under that name were hideous saloons disguising a super chassis and engine. From the new family came the 1300GT Junior, which was an swb four-seater with the 1290cc Giulietta engine and disc brakes all round. Bertone styled the body (the stylist was Giugiaro) but, true to form, these rusted. Power was up on the Giulia saloon, at 89bhp, and that meant 102mph/163kmh (0-60mph in 13.2 seconds). The real goody was the GTA (A = aluminium) which, with a 96bhp twin-plug head and much less weight, was a flyer. Alfa Romeo made 447 of them and the body doesn't rust!

Alfa Romeo 1300 GT Junior, 1969

**1300 GT Junior Z, 1969-72. Prod: 1,108.** This lovely little car proves that Zagato has had moments of lucidity within living memory. It was basically a lightweight special version of the 1300 Junior with slightly improved performance.

**Duetto, 1966-67. Prod: 6,325.** This simple body by Pininfarina has become a modern classic; a version was still in production in 1990, and looking hardly a day older. Under the skin it was a 109bhp Giulia which meant 116mph/186kmh and 0-60mph in 11.3 seconds and since it came in 1966 there were disc brakes all round. The name 'Duetto' was chosen after a competition in the Italian press but it was also known as the Giulia Sprint Spyder.

The 1966 Duetto, first of a long line

**33/2 Stradale, 1967-69. Prod: 18.** This was a road-going GT version of the car introduced as a 2-litre sports-racer in 1967 and which evolved into the 3-litre 33/3, winner of several important races in the early 1970s. The road car had the same large-tube light alloy 'H' frame, with extra stiffening at the front by a magnesium alloy casting and extra rear stiffening by sheet steel, and the legs of the 'H' were large enough to take the fuel tanks. Suspension was by coil springs and double wishbones at the front, coil springs, transverse links and radius arms at the rear, and the rear disc brakes were mounted inboard.

Two valve per cylinder heads were used (dohc naturally) and, aided by Spica indirect injection, this lovely little V8 delivered 230bhp, a phenomenal output for an engine of 1995cc. This was delivered via a six-speed gearbox and aided by light weight (just 1540lb) and a slippery, pretty coupé body by Scaglione, a top speed of 161mph/259kmh was claimed.

**1750 GTV, 1967-72. Prod: 43,965.** This brought together a new 1779cc dohc four-cylinder 118bhp engine and the 2+2 body from the 1300GT Junior, albeit with quad headlights.

Alfa Romeo 1750 GTV

**1750 Spyder Veloce, 1967-71. Prod: 8722.** Successor to the Duetto, but with the now-familiar chopped-off tail, this had the 118bhp 1750cc dohc 'four' and while the specifications on paper harked back to 1950 (same construction, suspension layout, etc) there had been constant updating. By the time it was introduced, mass-produced open sports cars at a reasonable price were becoming more and more rare.

1750 Spyder Veloce

**2000 Spyder Veloce, introduced 1970.** The ultimate expression of the 'Duetto' line; the basic chassis goes back to 1950 and the engine is a 120bhp 1962cc version of the aluminium block 'four' which was used in the 1962 Giulia range. For a time it sprouted nasty rubber bumpers, but in

1990 the factory gave it a new lease of life. A general facelift saw a new tail treatment and neat new bumpers, colour-keyed with the bodywork. By the end of 1990 it was the second oldest model available in the UK and with a top speed of a claimed 118mph/190kmh (0-60mph in 9.4 seconds) its performance was hardly electrifying. Still, there exist buyers who feel there is no substitute for the sheer personality of an Alfa Romeo.

2000 Spyder Veloce arrived in 1970...

...and gained rubber bumpers in the 1980s

**Montreal, 1971-77.** **Prod:** 3925. This was an attempt to build a supercar at a reasonable price which did not come off. The 'quad cam' fuel-injected 2593cc V8 engine was a road version of Alfa's briefly successful T33 sports-racer unit which fed its 200bhp through a five-speed ZF gearbox, but the chassis was from the Giulia 1750GTV (and that basically went back to 1950). Bertone's shape looked good, and the 137mph/220kmh top speed (0-60mph in 7.6 seconds) was promising, but Alfa Romeo was entering its years of crisis and decline. Most Britons and Americans found the driving position uncomfortable; the factory was torn by disputes, which delayed production; the engine was not properly prepared for series production; Alfa Romeo did not push the car; and 17mpg did not help after the 1973 energy crisis.

Alfa Romeo Montreal, 1971

**Alfasud Sprint, 1976-89.** This was not really a sports car by Alfa Romeo's standards but is included because the Alfasud range gave rise to some competition derivatives and the Alfasud itself was important in the company's history. The range was created to bring employment to southern Italy and was a complete departure from other models, indeed, Alfa Romeo encouraged the public to consider it a separate marque.

The most radical departure was a flat-four 'boxer' engine with single overhead camshafts. In the base model this was of 1186cc, although the Sprint had versions of 1286cc (76bhp, 1976-89), 1490cc (84bhp, 1979-86) and 1717cc (116bhp, 1987-89). All Alfasuds had front wheel drive, MacPherson strut front suspension and a beam rear axle suspended on coil springs and located by Watts linkages and a Panhard rod. The Sprint was styled by Giugiaro and was a 2+2 fastback coupé which, in 1.7-litre form, was good for 122mph/195kmh (0-62mph in nine seconds).

1976 Alfasud Sprint

**SZ Coupé, 1990.** The SZ is primarily a signal that Alfa Romeo is back in business as serious maker of serious cars although the Zagato body puts one in mind of the F1 team owner whose response to a new car was to ask his designer 'What were you smoking when you designed that?'

Alfa Romeo SZ coupé, 1990, by Zagato

Apart from the two-seat fibreglass body, which forms part of the unitary construction, most of the car comes from the

Alfa Romeo parts bin so the engine is a 206bhp version of the 3-litre dohc V6 from the Alfa 164 while floor pan, five-speed transaxle, and suspension come from the Alfa 75, with lower front wishbones, coil springs and transverse links, and a de Dion rear axle on coil springs and trailing arms. Alfa Romeo claims a top speed of 152mph/243kmh (0-62mph in seven seconds).

## ALLARD (GB)

Sydney Allard was a brave and forceful racing driver who admired American automotive engineering at a time when it was not fashionable in Europe. His cars reflected his personality and he began production in a small way in the late 1930s, with replicas of his Ford V8 trials special. After the War, there was a huge demand for new cars of any description and Allard clinched a deal, on very favourable terms, to buy Ford V8 Pilot engines originally ordered by the government for the war effort. This established him as a manufacturer and he was very successful (production peaked at 432 cars in 1948), until 1952 when restrictions on the home market were lifted and a lot of new models came on stream.

Allard production slumped despite the fact that Sydney won the Monte Carlo Rally in one of his cars, but then it has to be said that the company was still making what were, in essence, pre-war Ford specials. The company went into a decline which not even a micro-car, the 'Clipper', could resolve. From 1955 Allards were available only to special order and car production formally ended in 1960. Later, however, Allard marketed some hot Ford Anglias known as 'Allardettes'.

**K1, 1946-48. Prod: 151.** A new car in the immediate postwar era was always an event, but the K1 was a sensation. It was simplicity itself with a 106in wheelbase box section frame, transverse leaf and split axle i.f.s., a transverse rear leaf spring and live axle, and a two-seat body made of steel without a compound curve in sight. With a choice of an 85bhp 3662cc side-valve V8 Pilot engine, or a 95bhp 3.9-litre Mercury unit (which was basically a larger version of the same engine) it had an excellent power/weight ratio and terrific acceleration.

Allard K1 in the mountains

**L1, 1946-48. Prod: 191.** This was a K1 with wheelbase extended by 6in and another two seats: a car for the hairy-chested family man. Like the K1, many went abroad and, as was to become Allard practice, some went abroad without engine or gearbox. With a few exceptions, the two Ford V8s were Allard's works-fitted mainstay, but those were often modified. With the Ardun ohv conversion, for example, the Mercury engine would give 140bhp—and that was just the beginning. The basic rule is that if you lift the bonnet of an Allard, do not be surprised at what you find and, remember, it may have been there from day one.

Allard L1 had seats for four

**J1, 1947-48. Prod: 12.** A lighter, shorter (100in wheelbase), slimmer version of the K, built with competition in mind. The J1 was always intended to be limited to a run of 12 cars, and each one had the Mercury engine in a channel section frame. Although it was the third postwar Allard model to appear, its designation properly indicates that it was really the father of the line (it was almost a direct descendant from Allard's pre-war specials). J1s were very successful in the trials and sprints, which then formed the backbone of British motor sport.

Allard J1 had shorter grille

**M, 1947-50. Prod: 500.** Described as a 'drophead coupé' rather than as a 'four-seater sports car', there was some attempt at refinement in this model. However, the basic plot was similar to the L1, and it had the same 112in wheelbase. Coil spring

M type Allard, 1947

i.f.s. and hydraulic brakes appeared in 1949; a column gear shift (then considered desirable) was an option from 1948 and standard by 1950.

**P, 1949-52. Prod: 559.** A variation of the M, the P was a two-door four-seat 'saloon', but in reality was a tin-topped sports car and a close relation of the J1 trials car. In 1952, Sydney Allard drove a P to victory in the Monte Carlo Rally,

**Allard P, 1952, with Sydney Allard about to collect his trophy for winning the Monte Carlo Rally. Early cars had the full waterfall grille**

which then was the most important motor sport event in the world between the end of September and the beginning of April. Thus he became the only person in the event's history to win in a car of his own manufacture and, in doing so, he beat into second place a driver named Moss.

**J2, 1950-52. Prod: 90.** This was a Lotus Seven before its time: sheer automotive simplicity. It had the shorter (100in) wheelbase of the J1 but was still not a small car, for it had to accommodate husky American V8s (Cadillac was a favourite) which might be over 5 litres and come in highly tuned versions. To transmit that muscle onto the road a de Dion rear axle suspended on coil springs and located by radius arms was fitted. One peculiarity of the J2 was that the use of

**Allard J2 at work in 1950**

a Ford front axle meant a front track of 56in, while the track of the de Dion rear was only 52in, so they always looked as though they were 'crabbing', even when they were going in a straight line. A useful option for competition was a Halibrand differential with quick-change final drive ratio; Allard became the British agent for this device which has led to some writers to state that it was an Allard product. With the right engine, no contemporary sports car could match it off the line. It was a popular competition machine, being rugged and reliable, and one finished third at Le Mans in 1950 despite losing all gears bar top (third).

**K2, 1950-52. Prod: 119.** The K2 was a more civilised version of the K1, with integrated front styling. In common with all Allards from 1950 it had its swing front axles suspended on coil springs.

**Allard K2 of 1950**

**J2X, 1952-54. Prod: 83.** From the J2X all Allards with V8 engines had a new chassis frame built up from small diameter tubes, and there were parallel side members stitched together by plating. The de Dion rear axle, which was standard on this frame, was located by a Panhard rod. On the J2X there were Alfin drum brakes and the engine was

**J2X had slightly more angular nose than J2**

shifted 7in forward, which gave better balance and improved cockpit space. The cycle winged body was similar to the J2 (although a few had enveloping bodywork) and the J2X had wire wheels while most J2s had pressed steel wheels. Like the J2, most went to America where they were extremely successful in SCCA racing, but by 1954 had been overtaken by Ferraris, Jaguar C Types, and the like.

**M2X, 1951-52. Prod: 25.** This drophead version of the P was built on a 112in wheelbase version of the new X chassis with the usual choice of Ford, Mercury, Anything engines. It was distinguished by a radiator grill in the shape of an 'A' but by little else. Events had overtaken the Allard line, as the low production figure shows.

Allard M2X, 1951

**P2 Monte Carlo/Safari, 1952-55. Prod: 11/10.** A streamlined two-door saloon version of the M2X, the P2 had the same 'A' radiator grill and was built on the same 112in wheelbase chassis. The Safari was pure Monte Carlo to the windscreen and then it became a timbered shooting brake—Reliant was not the first to make a sporting estate car. What is a shooting brake with three rows of seats doing in a book on sports cars? It was basically a long wheelbase J2X—a sports car for the prolific family man.

Allard P2 Monte Carlo as offered at Earls Court motor show in 1952

**K3, 1952-55. Prod: 62.** As Allard sales began to slide, the company made a modern-looking sports car with full-width bodywork which bore comparison with such as the Nash-Healey. The K3 had the 'X' tubular frame, and, although the car looked like a two-seater, its 56in wide bench seat could take two adults and two children. Most went of America where the reaction was mixed; it was intended to be a civilised sporting tourer but details of finish and fit which were acceptable in a competition car, or at a time when customers had little choice, had stopped being little eccentricities and had become black marks. By 1954 annual Allard production had fallen from a high of 432 cars to just 36.

Allard K3

**Palm Beach 21C/21Z, 1952-55. Prod: 8/65.** When the mainstream cars started to dive in the market because of improved opposition, Allard turned to an 'economy' model using the Ford Consul (21C) or Zephyr (21Z) engines. They were smaller (96in wheelbase) versions of the K3 (without the de Dion axle) but the loss of size equated to loss of presence. The Consul-engined version, in particular, was a dog: it was feeble, undistinguished and expensive for what it was, the wonder is that eight people were daft enough to buy one when they could have had the infinitely superior TR2 for less outlay. The Zephyr-engined car was better, but it is difficult to think of a single reason for buying one in preference to an Austin-Healey 100 which cost about the same.

1952 Allard Palm Beach 21Z

**Palm Beach 21, 1954. Prod: 1.** Allard tried to fight back with a Palm Beach fitted with a 4.4-litre Dodge V8 engine. The production figure says everything.

**J2R, 1953-55. Prod: 7.** The fastest of all the Allards, this had the short wheelbase frame of the Palm Beach but with

J2R Allard, 1953

a de Dion rear axle (located by an A-frame), a full width body and a variety of engines, although the 5.4-litre Cadillac V8 was the favourite. Sydney Allard actually led the first lap at Le Mans in 1953 in one, but the race was won by a Jaguar C Type with proper aerodynamics, a space frame, and disc brakes.

**Palm Beach II, 1956-59. Prod: 7.** In 1956 Allard showed a very pretty, curvaceous body on the Palm Beach frame, still with the old swing axle front suspension, and fitted it with a Jaguar XK140 engine. On paper, it was promising

The Jaguar-powered 1956 Palm Beach II

but it was too little, too late, and only seven cars were built. They had various engines, in the Allard tradition, and at least one had a fastback coupé body, with a rear treatment that presaged the later Jaguar E Type. So ended Allard, not with a bang but a whimper.

## ALLARD (CDN)

Not connected to the original Allard concern, this company began in 1981 to make fibreglass copies of the Allard J2X powered by a Chrysler V8 engine.

Allard J2X2, 1984

## ALLISON (USA)

Introduced in 1980, this was a fibreglass MG TD body on VW Beetle floor pan with the 102bhp 1.7-litre VW-Porsche engine.

## ALLORA (GB)

A Lancia Stratos copy of the mid-1980s which was based on Lancia Beta running gear but suffered by comparison with the version produced by Transformer Cars (qv) at about the same time. Allora was soon in trouble but the project was revived as the Litton Corse (qv).

## ALMQUIST (USA)

A 1950s maker of fibreglass bodies to fit domestic chassis; by 1960 its range included bodies for the Renault 4CV and VW Beetle.

## ALPINA (D)

Since 1965, Alpina has modified and customised BMWs. Alpina has close links with the factory and is recognised by the German government as a manufacturer in its own right.

Alpina B7 Turbo Coupé, 1983, a modified BMW 6 Series

## ALPINE (F)

Jean Redélé, born in 1922, the son of a Renault dealer, was an engineer and a motor sport enthusiast. In the early 1950s he competed with some success in events such as the Alpine Rally and the Mille Miglia in a modified Renault 4CV saloon and he founded Société Automobiles Alpine in 1955.

The prototype car was little more than a two seat fibreglass coupé body, styled by Michelotti, on a Renault 4CV floor pan but with the option of a five-speed gearbox developed by Redélé and Claude Engineering. Redélé drove one in the 1955 Mille Miglia and so it was launched as the A106 'Mille Miles'. With one of these cars, Maurice Michy won his class in the 1956 Mille Miglia.

A version with a steel body, the A107, was made as a prototype but did not go into production but the A106 benefitted from new engines from the Renault Dauphine range. By 1957, A106s were being made at a rate of about two a week, and when production ended in 1960 some 650 had been built. 1957 saw the short-lived A108 cabriolet variant, 1959 saw the arrival of a tubular backbone chassis, and 1961 saw a 2+2 version and the aerodynamic Berlinette Tour de France.

**Alpine A106 Mille Miles, based on the Renault 4CV**

From the introduction of the sturdy backbone chassis, Alpines had Renault engines mounted behind the rear axle line in conjunction with Renault running gear. Naturally the specifications of Alpines changed as the products of the primary source changed, and Renault looked with favour on the little outfit which did so much to change its image. Thus 4CV components gave way to Dauphine parts and those, in turn, gave way to parts from the Renault R8. Naturally, from 1957, there were Gordini (qv) versions of the engines. Cars fitted with the Dauphine swing axle rear suspension became famous for the extraordinary attitudes which a skilled driver could assume in corners.

**Alpine A110, built from 1963 to 1977**

The big breakthrough came with the A110 of 1963, the car which established the classic Alpine shape. It started life with a 1108cc Renault R8 engine which gave all of 87bhp, but 1.25-litre, 1.3-litre and 1.6-litre units were also fitted (the 1.6-litre cars were most popular). By the time production ceased in 1977, a Renault 16 engine of up to 1.8 litres and up to 180bhp was used. These cars were particularly successful in rallying and among many glittering results, a 1-2-3 in the 1969 Alpine Rally stands out. From 1975 onwards, the A110 was tolerated rather than promoted and was mainly offered as a fairly mild road car. All flavours of the A110 were offered as cabriolets but the vast majority of buyers preferred the coupé. Some 8200 A110s were built.

In 1969, Alpine was making about ten cars a week and these were sold through Renault agencies with full warranties. By 1971, Alpine was officially nominated as Renault's competition arm, and the company became part of Renault in 1974 (it had suffered a sudden fall in sales following the energy crisis). The car which won Le Mans in 1978 was designated the Renault Alpine A442.

Meanwhile in 1971, when Alpine was still an independent company, it had introduced the A310 which became the main production car for the next 14 years. Its influence is still apparent in the Alpine-Renault GTA. Previously, Alpines had been fast but somewhat fragile two-seaters whose rugged approach to creature comforts could be easily forgiven in a rally but required some tolerance if they were to be used as road cars.

**1976 Alpine A310**

By contrast, the A310 took account of the passengers as well as the driver. Mechanically, it followed Alpine's established format with rear-engined layout and all-independent suspension in a backbone chassis. Compared with previous Alpines the body was long and wider—it was a genuine 2+2—and the styling was graceful rather than idiosyncratic. Initially power came from a 127bhp version of the 1605cc Renault R16 engine which drove through a modified Renault five-speed transaxle (originally made for front wheel drive). Suspension was by coil springs and double wishbones all round and brakes were discs at the front, drums at the rear.

This was a move up-market and as the company was not altogether geared for this it suffered some quality problems in the early days. As soon as the A310 was introduced, however, production went up to about ten cars a week for even with a 1.6-litre engine it would top 130mph/210kmh and sprint to 60mph in 8.1 seconds. In late 1976, this engine was replaced by the 150bhp 'PRV' V6 of 2664cc and this boosted top speed to 137mph/220kmh (0-60mph in 7.5 seconds). Disc brakes replaced the drums at the rear and production was increased even further. Late versions of this car had a number of detail revisions such as wider wheel arches, improved bumpers and a rear spoiler.

Renault replaced the A310 in 1985 but retained the overall mechanical and styling layout; the GTA was still a 2+2 fibreglass coupé based on a backbone chassis with a rear-mounted V6 engine, and the styling was recognisably related, but the car had been conceived by a major manufacturer and not a cottage industry company. One difference was that the fibreglass body had a lower drag factor and was bonded to the chassis, thus creating a semi-monocoque addition to the pressed steel backbone.

Although still bearing the name 'Alpine', the car was intended to be everything which a Renault should be, and that included having mass appeal. America was the main target market but that came to nothing when Chrysler bought

**Renault Alpine GTA V6 Turbo, 1986**

Renault's stake in American Motors and found that the GTA was too close to a Maserati-derived car which Chrysler had been planning. Thus the GTA did not cross the Atlantic.

The standard engine was 160bhp 2849cc version of the PRV V6, but a 200bhp turbocharged 2458cc unit was the option preferred by many for in this form the car would touch 150mph/240kmh and sprint to sixty in 6.3 seconds. The car was very responsive although at high cornering speeds the 39/61 weight distribution could be tricky. Enthusiasts should note that because Renault is not regarded as a great badge, second-hand GTAs can be wonderful value.

In 1990 Renault introduced a limited edition 'Le Mans' version with body bulges to accommodate wider wheels and in any colour the customer wanted, as long as it was metallic burgundy. The turbocharged engine gave 185bhp, slightly down on the original turbo, but it did come with a catalytic convertor so the performance figures were slightly down (146mph/ 235kmh, 0-60mph in 6.8 seconds) but such differences were really academic especially since development and the wider rear tyres had improved the car's handling.

## ALTA (GB)

From 1932, Geoffrey Taylor built small numbers of quite advanced sports and racing cars in his workshops in Kingston-upon-Thames. After the War, Taylor offered a 2-litre sports car for sale, and drawings appeared of a new enveloping body in the Italian style, but there were few takers and production ended in 1947. It was available as a sports car or sporting saloon, and its main feature was its alloy and aluminium dohc engine which, when blown, produced up to 180bhp. This had made it one of the fastest British sports cars of any size before the War, and although the chassis was fairly conventional, handling was good. Taylor was not terribly interested in road cars, however, and problems with supplies of materials saw him axe the line after only about 15 had been built. Thereafter Alta concentrated on building not very successful Formula 1 and 2 cars, and racing car engines, most notably for HWM, 1950-53, and Connaught, 1954-57.

## ALVIS (GB)

Alvis was founded in 1919 and, as a hungry young company, made its name with small-engined sports cars and light saloons, as well as through its pioneering front wheel drive and all-independent suspension. Alvis thrived and gradually moved up-market until in the late 1930s it was making cars which challenged Bentley but, along the way, it also became conservative. An aero engine division was started in 1937 and after the War cars became less and less important. There was little investment and development and the cars were pale shadows of the pre-war line. Some Alvis enthusiasts might argue for all, or most, of the postwar saloons it made for inclusion in a book on sports cars, but though graceful and slightly rakish, they were ponderous by comparison with the Alvis cars of the 1930s.

Alvis was bought by Rover in 1965, car production ceased the following year, and the company has since concentrated on armoured vehicles. In the late 1960s, however, Alvis built a mid-engined sports car powered by the 3.5-litre Rover V8 engine. Everyone who drove it raved about it but it was obviously too good for BL and it remained a prototype.

**TB14, 1949-50. Prod: 100.** Alvis' attempt to essay a really modern style coincided with the announcement of the Jaguar XK120—end of story. Underneath the ghastly bodyshell was a pre-war chassis with mechanical brakes, solid axles, and a four-cylinder pushrod 1892cc engine. In fact it was a warmed-over 1938 12/70 which was hard pushed to reach 85mph/135kmh. The 1948 London Show car had its headlights behind the radiator grill and a cocktail cabinet in one of the doors, but production models were spared these eccentricities.

**Alvis TB14, an unfortunate departure from tradition**

**TB21, 1951. Prod: 31.** This had the TB14 body, albeit with a traditional Alvis radiator, but the chassis and engine were new. Power came from a new 95bhp seven-bearing short stroke 2993cc straight six, which then became the only

**The 1951 TB21 regained the Alvis grille**

Last of the Ts, the TF1500 was not appreciated in its time but like all sports MGs was to become a sought-after car

409 AXT

**William Lyons' XK Jaguars had outstanding engines, looked beautiful and were great value for money, qualities that more than offset shortcomings their detractors looked for so diligently. The XK140 (right) had the lines first seen on the XK120, while the XK150 alongside is smoother and a little bulkier. Both cars are the rare Roadster models.**

**A quartet of late MGs, from an MGA 1500 in the foreground to a B roadster. Between them are a B GT and a C (right), identified by its 'power bulge'**

unit the company was to use for the rest of its life. Hydraulic brakes and coil spring i.f.s. were improvements and despite excessive weight the TB21 could nearly reach the ton. As with its ugly sister, build quality and 'badge' were plusses, but cost and style outweighed them. Current owners have saved a whale.

## AMC (USA)

The American Motors Corporation was formed in 1954 from Hudson and Nash and by 1959 it was in fourth place in the production league, with an ouput of just over 400,000 units. Its successful periods were achieved by AMC anticipating trends such as compact cars and, indeed, it made no 'full-size' cars after 1974.

A ploy which the smaller American companies frequently tried was the making of a sports car to give it publicity and presence at a relatively low cost. Nash tried it with the Nash-Healey, Kaiser with the Darrin and Studebaker with the Avanti. After a false start with an unsuccessful pony car called the Marlin in 1966, AMC bounced back with the Javelin fastback coupé in 1968. In the same year it also made a two-seat version, the AMX, which had a list of engine options up to a 315bhp 6.4-litre V8.

Almost as soon as the AMX was announced so AMC began to produce concept cars based on the floor pan. Thus 1968 also saw the one-off AMX-GT, with a fibreglass body and macho external exhaust pipes. This was followed by the AMX/2 of 1969, basically a full-size mock-up of a mid-engined coupé the shape of which was from AMC's own styling department and was chosen in preference to a submission by Giugiaro.

The AMX/2 then became the starting point for the AMX/3, which was prepared for possible production. AMC turned to Giotto Bizzarrini, who had become something of a specialist in the combining of American mechanical components and Italian flair, and he created a very stiff semi-monocoque with a central backbone and boxed sills and all independent suspension by coil springs and double wishbones. Disc brakes were fitted all round, the original body style was refined and BMW also had an input into the final design.

**AMX/3**

The first car was shown in 1970 and with the 6.4-litre V8, which had 340bhp but an incredible 430lb/ft torque at only 3,600rpm, the AMX/3 would top 160mph and sprint 0-60mph in under six seconds. By all accounts it handled as well as it looked, but when all the sums were done it was found to have a price tag of nearly $20,000 at a time when Ford had begun to sell the De Tomaso Pantera at $9,000. Thus the AMX/3 was axed after six had been made.

## AMERICAN SPEED SPECIALITIES

(GB) *see* CONTEMPORARY CLASSIC

## AMG (D)

AMG customises Mercedes-Benz models, makes dohc four valves per cylinder versions of Mercedes-Benz V8 engines and generally enjoys close links with the factory. It also makes the 'Hammer', a Mercedes 230CE saloon fitted with one of

**Mercedes-Benz 500SEC by AMG, 1984**

the modified engines and, with the 6-litre version, a top speed of 185mph/295kmh (0-60mph in five seconds) is claimed.

## AMORE (USA)

A kit car maker, in 1978 Amore introduced the 'Cimbria', a gull-wing coupé derived from Richard Oakes' classic 'Nova' (qv) on a VW Beetle floorpan. It later made its own tubular frame to take larger engines and, from 1981, this was marketed in Britain as the 'Eagle SS' (qv).

## ANADOL (TR)

This is the brand name of 'Ostosan Otomobil Sanaya', a Turkish car maker whose products were initially engineered by Reliant and which used Ford running gear. Anadol was established in 1966 and, in typical Third World style, its cars had a separate chassis and fibreglass body (hence the use of Reliant's expertise). A 1.6-litre coupé was offered from 1974 and remained in production until the late 1970s.

## ANTIQUE & CLASSIC AUTOMOTIVE (USA)

Anyone who knows the fringe car scene soon learns the coded messages of company names, and 'Antique & Classic'

**'SS100', 1981**

means fibreglass copies on proprietary running gear. Founded in 1972, this company essayed copies of the Frazer-Nash TT and SS100 on 1.6-litre VW Beetle chassis. By 1979 it was making inept Beetle-powered parodies of the Bugatti Type 35B, a 1931 Alfa Romeo, and a Bentley-ish pastiche which, even by the firm's standards, was pretty awful. In the late 1980s it was making reasonable imitation 'Jaguar XK120s' and 'SS100s', with a range of engine options from the Ford Pinto 'four' to Ford V8s.

## **APAL** (B)

An Apal two-seat coupé based on a Beetle chassis with a tuned (50bhp) 1.3-litre engine was offered from 1964, and later a 95bhp 1.6-litre Renault engine was used. Apal also made beach buggies and 'Jeeps' which were exported to 20 countries. In 1978 Apal made the 'Jet Corsa' which was a gull-wing coupé based on VW running gear. For many years it has also made, in kit and turn key forms, a close copy of the Porsche 356 Speedster with a fibreglass body on a shortened VW Beetle floor pan which has been sold in Britain as the 'TPC'.

**1983 Apal copy of Porsche 356 Speedster**

In 1990 Apal was also making the 'Francorchamps', a two-seat roadster with a detachable hardtop. The chassis was a three-part tubular steel affair and the body, which was principally notable for having six headlights, was of fibreglass and Kevlar. Running gear came from the Mercedes-Benz 190. As a quality, luxurious turn key car, the Francorchamps was available to special order only; with the standard 122bhp engine, a top speed of 128mph/205kmh was claimed but options included a 16-valve 160bhp engine or a 185bhp turbocharged version.

## **APOLLO** (USA)

A Californian sports car of 1962, the Apollo was designed by Milt Brown, styled by Ron Plescia, and the bodies, most of which were coupés, were made by Intermeccanica in Italy. In style it resembled a cleaner and longer MGB GT but, note, not even the MGB roadster had been announced when the Apollo was styled. Buick V8 engines of 3.5 or 5 litres were used in a tubular ladder frame with suspension and other components from the Buick Special. With the larger engine

**Apollo, 1962, available in 3.5- and 5-litre versions**

fitted, top speed was claimed to be 150mph/240kmh (0-60mph in 7.5 seconds) but the company was not sufficiently strong to advertise nationally, or establish a dealer network. To make matters worse, nobody thought very highly of the power unit—the Buick engine (which lives on as the Rover V8) was notorious for giving trouble—the bodies were expensive, and production ceased in 1964.

Intermeccanica then supplied the bodies to a firm in Texas, which used them to make a car called the Vetta Ventura (qv). Production of the Apollo was resumed in 1964 but this venture was dead by the following year. In all 88 Apollos (11 of which were convertibles) were made, together with 19 Vetta Venturas, but not all Apollos were delivered and some were quietly scrapped.

Trivia fans might like to know that an Apollo GT was the car driven by the 'baddies' in *The Love Bug*.

## **APOLLO** (USA)

Milt Brown and Ron Plescia, who were behind the first Apollo venture, returned in 1982 with a traditionally styled roadster called the 'Verona'. This looked like a first cousin to a Morgan yet was a distinct car in its own right. Available as a well-fitted turn key car, or a kit, the factory version had a 190bhp turbocharged 3.8-litre Buick V6 engine. In this form, 123mph/198kmh was claimed with the 0-60 dash being covered in

**Apollo Verona, 1983**

5.8 seconds. In the late 1980s the 'Verona' was manufactured in Germany under the name 'Warmouth' (qv).

## **AQUILA** (USA)

A 1978 VW-based kit car made by American Fiber Craft Inc. which seemed to have been inspired by the BMW M1. By

1980 Aquila

1990, when it was still in production, the lines had been changed so that it was more of a distinct car. By then a range of engine options was available, including Mazda, Porsche and small-block American engines.

## ARDEN (D)

Despite the very English name (Shakespeare's mum was an Arden) this is a German company which modifies the Jaguar XJ6 and XJ-S and offers a twin-turbo version of the straight six engine.

## ARGYLL (GB)

British turbocharger pioneer, Bob Henderson, created this hideous mid-engined coupé in 1976 and references to it, and its maker's ambitions, occasionally popped up in the press until the mid-1980s. It was intended for limited production, but even had it been attractive the high price tag was no inducement to buy. It had a box section chassis, Triumph 2500 all-independent suspension, and a Saab or a Rover V8 engine (both turbocharged and transversely mounted) driving through a five-speed ZF gearbox. A top speed of 150mph/240kmh was claimed for the Rover version, 130mph/210kmh for the Saab-engined variant.

Argyll Turbo GT

## ARISTA (F)

Originating in 1951 as the 'Ranelagh', these cars were based on the 850cc Panhard floor pan and were available until 1963 as a steel-bodied roadster, the 50bhp 'Sport', or a 42bhp 2+2 fibreglass coupé, the 'Passy'.

1963 Arista, with 850cc Panhard power

## ARKLEY (GB)

A clever fibreglass body kit introduced in 1970 to save rusted Sprites and MG Midgets. It recalled cars such as the Morgan yet remained a distinctive, modern, design.

Arkley, 1970

## ARNOLT (USA)

Stanley Howard 'Wacky' Arnolt started out as a football star and became a hugely successful industrialist who liked to race as a hobby. In 1952 he was taken by a pair of styling exercises on the Bertone stand at the Turin show, placed a large order and saved the *carrozzeria* from impending bankruptcy. Since the exercises were on MG TD chassis, Arnolt arranged for nude TDs to be shipped from Abingdon to Turin and they were then sold in the States as Arnolt-MGs.

About 100 MG-based cars had been made when, the following year, Arnolt was struck by the Bristol 404 chassis and the Arnolt-Bristol sold in the States at half the price of a 404. While the Arnolt-MG was a pretty car, the Bristol-based car

Arnolt-MG was built on the TD chassis

Arnolt-Bristol coupé, 1955

was an outstanding dual-purpose machine. This was a fine road car which could be parked with pride in any company, and, without modification, was very successful in SCCA racing. In 1955 and 1956, Arnolt-Bristols won their class in the Sebring 12 Hour race and competition success continued into the 1960s. Open cars came either as the 'Bolide' (stripped down, no hood) or 'Deluxe' (fully trimmed). Three coupé versions were made in 1955 but 12 cars of the total of 142 were destroyed in a fire. Production only ended when Bristol stopped supplying the basis in 1960.

## ARNOTT (GB)

In 1951, Daphne Arnott became perhaps the world's only female racing car constructor when, working with George Thornton, the manager of her family's garage business, she designed a 500cc Formula 3 car. It was made in small numbers but the marque achieved little success in racing, although it had better luck with a streamlined record breaker. A production sports car came in 1955 and two years later, there was a sports-racer and a racing GT car, both with Climax engines. The latter ran at Le Mans in 1957, its only race, but retired with a dropped valve; that failure wiped out the little company and Arnott ceased making cars. Superchargers had long been part of the Arnott business, and the firm made special kits to boost road cars.

**Sports, 1955-57. Prod: 7.** The Arnott used a ladder-frame chassis similar to the company's F3 car, with all-independent

Arnott Sports, 1955

suspension by coil springs and double wishbones, but in this case the engine was in front of the driver. The base engine was Austin A30 (three made), but other cars had Standard 10, Lea-Francis and Coventry Climax FWA units. The car was finished with a fibreglass body, similar to a proprietary shell later made by Rochdale, and it received a lot of publicity because it had been created by a woman. No reliable road test figures are available but a claim of 110mph/175kmh for the Climax-engined version seems reasonable. One of these cars was entered at Le Mans in 1955, but crashed during practice.

## ARNTZ (USA)

Late 1970s maker of a Cobra copy which had MGB front suspension, Jaguar i.r.s., and a wide range of engine options. It was available as a kit or turn key car, although production of the latter was strictly limited because under American law a company making no more than 250 examples of a model can escape the usual certification process.

## ASA (I)

A little-known Italian marque which had substantial backing from an enthusiastic industrialist. The real centre of interest, however, was the engine, which was originally a dohc four-cylinder 850cc unit built by Ferrari (no less) in 1958. Giotto Bizzarrini, designer of the Ferrari GTO, was responsible for the chassis and Bertone for the body. When it was first shown to the public it carried no badges, although everyone knew who had made it. By 1961 Ferrari had decided not to proceed further but to hand over the project to the right people: enter the de Nora family.

**Mille, 1963-67. Prod: approx 50-75.** The Mille was essentially a scaled-down 250GT with a tubular frame, coil spring and double wishbone front suspension and a live rear axle, also on coils. Disc brakes were on all four wheels (unusual for Italy at the time) and the Bertone body was

ASA Mille

available as either a coupé or cabriolet. The 1032cc engine produced 84bhp at 6800rpm, but just 66lb/ft torque at 5500rpm so although it was the world's most powerful road car for its size (it could top 115mph/185kmh) it had a decidedly peaky engine. By 1963, Ford 105E units were being tweaked to give similar output.

**Rollbar GT Spyder, 1966-67. Prod: see above.** The Mille never sold in sufficient numbers to make money, it was very expensive for the amount of car and performance the customer received. In 1966 ASA tried again, this time with a six cylinder 1.3-litre version of the engine (there was a 140bhp 1754cc version for export) and attempting to cut costs by having the body made in fibreglass. Like the Mille, it had a four-speed transmission with double overdrive but it too found few takers and the project folded in 1967.

## ASARDO (USA)

Built only in 1959, this was a small and light fibreglass coupé using a tuned (130bhp) 1.5-litre dohc Alfa Romeo engine and four-speed gearbox. Top speed was claimed to be 135mph/215kmh (0-60mph in 6.4 seconds) but its high price ($5875) was against it.

The 1959 Asardo 1500 AR-S

## ASC (USA)

Made by the American Sunroof Company in the late 1980s, the ASC McLaren was an open four-seater with 'European' styling (it seemed inspired by the Mercedes-Benz 450SL). The company emphasised the luxurious nature of the product, and virtually any extra was available as an option, so its sales literature stressed features such as stereo speakers in the head rests but not speed or acceleration. A 5-litre Ford V8 engine drove through either a five-speed manual gearbox or a four-speed automatic transmission.

ASC's 1990 Corvette ZR-1 featured lowered windscreen

## ASCORT (AUS)

This was a stylish 2+2 coupé body on a VW Beetle floorpan which was launched in Sydney in 1958. Although nothing was done to overcome the inadequacies of the base vehicle, the engine was mildly tuned and the body was well-made and trimmed. Not many more than a dozen were made before the project collapsed in 1960.

Ascort 1300 GT, 1959

## ASD (GB)

Bob Egginton's Automotive Systems Development first showed the Minim in 1984 as an advertisement for the company which restores racing cars and builds prototypes. A tube and sheet steel backbone chassis took a mid-mounted Mini engine/gearbox unit and a fibreglass body which was entirely practical, if a little boxy. It was much admired as an honest piece of engineering and public pressure saw limited production. It remains available but the company has never pushed it. ASD also produced the prototype Tripos (qv) and Maelstrom (qv).

ASD Minim, 1984

## ASHLEY (GB)

Keith Waddington and Peter Pellandine founded Ashley Laminates in 1954 to supply bodies for Austin Seven special builders and very successful they were, selling over 500 shells. Pellandine left to establish Falcon Shells, Pellandini and Pelland (qv). In the late 1950s, Waddington turned his attention to Ford specials with equal success and in 1958 Ashley marketed its own ladder chassis with coil spring suspension to take parts from Ford Ten donor cars and, of course, an Ashley shell. Development of the chassis allowed other engines to be fitted and one buyer fitted a tuned MGA unit which he claimed to be capable of 130mph, which made him a line shooter, a hero, or a lunatic.

The Sportiva, introduced in 1962, was a last-ditch attempt to reverse a falling sales graph and was a more practical variation on the theme: it could be bought in open or closed forms, with two or four seats. In the early 1960s, a combination of the Sprite, Mini, MoT test, and an upturn in the economy

Ashley Sportiva, 1962

hit the kit car market; it collapsed almost overnight in 1962, with Ashley among the victims.

That Ashley made a superior product may be gauged by the fact that, in 1960, Autocars Ltd of Israel bought the rights to an Ashley body for its Sabra sports car (a.k.a. Reliant Sabre) and in 1990, TA Developments showed a new Cortina-based kit car based on a lightly modified, but widened, Ashley shell.

## ASTON MARTIN (GB)

An Aston Martin prototype was built in 1914 but production did not begin until 1922. Despite a series of beautiful and successful cars, Aston Martin never established a sound financial basis. On the other hand, the name has so much charisma that there has always been somebody prepared to save it. In 1947, for example, the tractor and gear magnate, David Brown, bought the firm for £20,000 after seeing a small ad in *The Times*. Shortly afterwards he acquired Lagonda, mainly to obtain its new 2.6-litre straight six which had been designed by W.O. Bentley.

A series of admirable road cars followed supplemented by a competition programme which was generally inept; Aston Martins were designed for the classic races but spent most of their time running in British sprints. Despite that, in 1959 Aston Martin won at Le Mans (the field was the weakest for years) and won the World Sports Car Championship (thanks, in the main, to the genius of Stirling Moss). By 1972 the company was in the red to the tune of £450,000 and Sir David Brown sold it to Company Developments Ltd for £100. It was soon in trouble once more and was sold again in 1975; 1980 saw it change hands once more; and 1983 saw a brand new majority share holder. Finally, Ford took control in 1987, a move which enthusiasts viewed with a mixture of anticipation and anxiety.

**DB1, 1948-50. Prod: 15.** During the War, Claude Hill laid out a new box-section chassis with trailing link front suspension, a live rear axle and coil springs all round. Designated the 'Atom' this was fitted with a pre-war pushrod 2-litre engine giving 90bhp and a pretty, if conventional, four-seater aluminium body. It was underpowered and overweight, which explains why only 15 were made, but the potential of the chassis was demonstrated by a stripped down two-seater version with which St John Horsfall won the 1948 Spa 24-hour race.

The Aston Martin Atom (above) evolved into the 1948 DB1 (below)

**DB2, 1950-53. Prod: 410.** When the 105bhp Lagonda engine was mated to the 'Atom' chassis, and clothed in a body of timeless elegance, the result was the best car Aston Martin has ever made. In 1950 a DB2 came fifth at Le Mans and shared the Index of Performance, and then the cars scored a 1-2-3 in class in the Tourist Trophy. A lightweight version using the 125bhp 'Vantage' engine came third at Le Mans in 1951 which, even counting the marque's win in 1959, is surely its finest performance, for the DB2 was basically a road car. DB2s also won their class in the Mille Miglia in 1952 and 1953. Most were made as coupés but 49 were built as open cars. Some early cars, used by the works team, ran with the old 2-litre engine, and some had column gear changes.

Aston Martin DB2

**DB2/4 / DB2/4 MkII, 1953-55/1956-59. Prod: 566/199.** By the end of 1951 Aston Martin's competition efforts were concentrated on the DB3, an out and out sports-racer which, like most postwar Aston Martin competition cars was a conservative design, ineptly managed. Consequently, the DB2 was stood down as the company's main competition tool and was developed to become a more sophisticated road car. Bodies, which had grown an occasional rear seat, were built by H.J. Mulliner (all but 70 were coupés), and the 2.6-litre 'Vantage' engine was standard until 1954 when it was replaced by a 157bhp 3 litre unit.

**DB 2/4 (above) and 1956 DB 2/4 MkII (below)**

The MkII version of 1956 had a sharper rear wing line and was one of the very first cars to be made with a rear-opening 'hatch'. It could also be had in a notch-back hard top version (34 made) as well as a drophead (24 made). With a 178bhp version of the 3-litre engine top speed was 120mph/190kmh with 0-60mph achieved in 11.1 seconds.

**DB2/4 MkIII, 1957-59. Prod: 551.** A further revision to a successful theme, the MkIII had a grill recalling the DB3S competition car. It also had front disc brakes. Early models

**Aston Martin DB2/4 MkIII, 1957**

had 162bhp engines, with 178bhp units optional, but in 1958 this went up to 180bhp, with 195bhp as an option. Acceleration was much improved and other options included an overdrive or, perish the thought, automatic transmission. Sellers placing advertisments often call this car the DBIII, which is misleading for the DB3 was a sports racer.

**DB3S coupé, 1955. Prod: 3.** In 1954 Aston Martin tried running two coupé versions of its DB3S sports racer at Le Mans but they were slower than the previous year's less powerful cars. They had lower drag but lifted at speed and nobody in the works was smart enough to find that out before the race. The Le Mans cars were converted back to open spec but later three coupés were made for road use.

**DB3S coupé**

**DB4, 1958-63. Prod: 1103.** The first entirely new Aston Martin road car made after David Brown acquired the company, the DB4 was built on a new chassis (with coils and double wishbones at the front, coils and live axle at the rear), and a new dohc 3.7-litre straight six which delivered its 240bhp through a new four-speed gearbox. Touring of Milan provided the body style and its *Superleggera* style of construction, with aluminium panels on a thin tubular framework. It was a huge advance yet retained the flavour of its predecessors. Top speed was 141mph/226kmh, 0-60mph could be covered in 8.5 seconds (or better with the 266bhp 'Vantage' option which came in 1961 and, thanks to four wheel disc brakes, it was quicker from rest to the ton, and back to rest than any car in the world. A convertible was added in 1961 (a detachable steel

**1958 Aston Martin DB4 had Touring body**

hard top was an option) and the knowledgeable have detected five distinct series, which were not used by the factory, and were anyway minor facelifts. Most desirable of all is one of the 215 convertibles made.

**DB4GT, 1960-63. Prod: 75.** This was a DB4 Vantage with 5in taken from the wheelbase, two seats only, a lower roof line, faired-in headlights, and 302bhp from a twin-plug version of the engine. A smaller car, it was lighter than the standard DB4, but only by 175lb. It had no outstanding competition history but its road performance, 142mph/ 228kmh and 0-60mph in 6.4 seconds, was a different matter.

Faired-in headlights on the DB4GT

**DB4GT Zagato, 1961-63. Prod: 19.** Now revered as a great classic, thanks to a lot of hype, but few people thought that the Zagato was particularly special in its day, hence few were made. Its competition career was not outstanding even in the hands of the likes of Jim Clark, but 314bhp in a road car was not to be sniffed at. Although it was lighter (by 100lb) than the factory bodied DB4GT, at 2600lb it was no feather-weight; still, it had a more slippery shape and 153mph/246kmh and 0-60mph in 6.1 seconds were outstanding figures at the time—for a road car.

DB4GT Zagato

**DB5, 1963-65. Prod: 1021.** By the end of 1963 so many minor changes had been made to the DB4 that it deserved a new name. The faired-in headlights of the last DB4s were carried over, and the DB5 had a 282bhp 4-litre engine as standard. From 1964, a 325bhp 'Vantage' version was offered, but with an extra 440lb (over the first DB4) the additional power was needed. All but the earliest cars had an all-synchro five-speed ZF gearbox save for those who took the three-speed automatic option. The convertible (123 made) received the name 'Volante', which then became Aston's designation for its rag tops, and 12 cars were converted into sporting 'shooting brakes' (not 'estate cars', perish the thought) by Harold Radford.

Aston Martin DB5 Volante

**DB6, 1965-70. Prod: 1753.** The rot started to set in with the DB6 as Aston Martins increasingly became high speed carriages with a sporting ancestry; twelve years of constant development had seen improvements in luxury but hardly any in performance. In the DB6 the wheelbase was increased by 2in to give more room for the rear passengers but the chief external difference was the bobbed tail, and this actually gave a small increase in maximum speed. Beneath the skin, however, the *Superleggera* method of construction was abandoned and henceforward Aston Martins had aluminium outer panels on steel inner panels. Power and options were as for the DB5 but with the addition of a limited slip differential and, after 1967, power steering. The MkII version of 1967 had flared wheel arches and DBS style wire wheels. Some were fuel injected but today these are best avoided. Of the total, 140 were 'Volante' rag tops and six were Radford shooting brakes.

DB6 (above) and DB6 Volante (below)

**DBS, 1967-73. Prod: 857.** Built concurrently with the DB6, the new car had the older model's chassis with an extra inch in the wheelbase and 4½in added to the front and rear track, while rear suspension was by a de Dion axle on coil springs. There were the same options as on the DB6, and the chief difference was the new body, styled by William Towns, which looked very elegant with wire wheels before it started to sprout wheel arches and spoilers. Since Aston Martin was racing a V8 engine in a Team Surtees Lola (in every race it retired before David Hobbs, Surtees' partner, could drive), it was not hard to deduce why the engine bay was so large. Most cars were fitted with automatic transmission and three shooting brakes were made.

DBS was the last six-cylinder Aston Martin

**DBS V8 models, 1969-89. Prod: approx 2000.** The 5.3-litre dohc V8 engine arrived in 1969 and, taking a cue from Rolls-Royce, engine output was not disclosed (educated guesses have been made). Power steering was standard on all V8s, and it was necessary because they were heavy cars

1973 DBS V8 (above) and 1989 V8 Vantage Volante (below)

to drive and their dynamics were not wonderful. Even the carburetter version topped 145mph/233kmh (0-60mph in 6.2 seconds) but most had Bosch fuel injection (these engines were estimated to deliver about 360bhp); and the 438bhp 'Vantage' did 170mph/273kmh (0-60mph in 5.4 seconds). The 'DB' designation was dropped after David Brown sold the company in 1972, thereafter the cars were known as 'V8', 'Vantage' (from 1977, 320 made), 'Volante' (from 1978, 800 made) and 'Volante Vantage' (from 1986, 115 made). From the early 1980s, AM was bemoaning that it had lost direction and should be making a new DB4; we are still waiting.

**Zagato, 1986-87. Prod: 50 + 25 Volante.** With collectors prepared to pay silly money for limited edition cars, Aston Martin commissioned Zagato to build a new body on the Vantage chassis. The result was one of the most hideous shapes of recent times which wags soon dubbed the 'Aston Martin Sierra'. Still, there was a queue of people prepared to pay over the odds for an ugly tank with a chassis derived from a 1950s design and a lot of them burnt their fingers by doing so.

Aston Martin Vantage Zagato

**Virage, 1989 to present. Prod: 5 per week.** With the Virage, stylists John Heffernan and Ken Greenley proved that if you wish to create a car with stunning looks, you do not need to commission an Italian studio whose best work was done in the 1930s. Callaway Engineering of Connecticut was responsible for the four-valve cylinder heads on the old V8 and in the base form this meant 330bhp, 340lb/ft torque, a top speed of 157mph/252kmh and the ability to sprint to 60mph in 6.8 seconds. On paper the broad mechanical layout was similar to the previous cars but, in fact, everything had undergone subtle revision. Overall dimensions were close to the previous model as well, but it was slightly narrower while having much improve interior space. A two seat Volante version was announced in 1990 and it was joined by a 2+2 early in 1991.

Virage, 1990

## ASTRON (GB)

A short-lived (1984/5) kit car based on Ford Cortina components with 2+2 drophead bodywork.

## ATLA (F)

A fibreglass coupé with gull wing doors and a choice of Panhard or Renault 4CV engines, made only in 1958.

## ATS (I)

In 1961 Ferrari won the World Championship with a Ferrari-designed car for the first time since 1953—and many of the senior personnel promptly left. The reason was that Mr Ferrari had been intent on recognising an illegitimate son and Mrs Ferrari had retaliated by asserting herself in the works, and had irritated everybody. The dispute had been brewing for some time and within days of their leaving the defectors announced that they would be working for a new consortium whose aim was to beat Ferrari on the track and in the market place. The 1963 ATS Formula 1 car was a ghastly mess, one of the most inept racing cars ever, and its appalling performances did not help the road car.

**2500 GT, 1963-64. Prod: 12.** The work of Carlo Chiti, the ATS had a 2.5-litre sohc V8 which produced 210bhp in road form, 245bhp for competition. This was mounted amidships in a space frame and fed to a five-speed Colotti gearbox; in essence, it was a Ferrari Dino long before the Dino. It was a handsome car, with a body by Allemano. Top speed was claimed to be 160mph/255kmh but after the F1 car became the joke of the season few were prepared to trust the road car. Count Volpi, one of the early ATS backers, later attempted to revive the project under the name 'Serenissima', and failed and a further attempt by Moreno Baldi in 1970 was even more disastrous.

**ATS 2500GT, 1963**

## AUBURN (USA and AUS)

Since 1967, at least three companies, two in America, one in Australia, have marketed copies of 1930s Auburn roadsters under the name 'Auburn'. In addition there have been numerous other 'Auburn' kit cars, made without hi-jacking the original maker's name.

**Auburn 876 Speedster by California Custom Coach, 1988**

## AURORA (CDN)

Founded in 1977 but now, apparently, defunct, Aurora made a 'turn key' Cobra copy which had a space frame, fibreglass body and 5-litre Ford V8 engine.

**1982 Aurora GTX**

## AUSTIN (GB)

Founded in 1905, Austin became a power in the industry with the 1922 'Seven' and, although most of its products were dull, after its merger with Morris in 1952 it became the dominant partner in BMC, Britain's largest manufacturer. Other mergers followed but, although there were some inspired decisions along the way (the Austin-Healey 100 and the Mini), the company was ill-managed and it began to slide in the late 1960s. It threw away the sports car market and produced terrible cars such as the Allegro. The name was dropped in the late 1980s when it had become synonymous with all that was wrong with the British motor industry. Some late Sprites were badged 'Austin' (see Austin-Healey).

**A40 Sports, 1951-53. Prod: 3800.** In the immediate postwar period, Austin suffered the problems common to the rest of the British motor industry, including restrictions on the home market and shortage of materials but, to its credit, it was ready to try niche marketing. The Sheerline and Princess limousines, the A90 Atlantic, and the A40 Sports were all examples of this. The A40 Sports used a Jensen-built body, styled like a scaled-down Interceptor, on the chassis of the A40 Dorset saloon. There was a separate chassis with coil spring i.f.s., hydraulic brakes, and a 50bhp twin carb version of the four-cylinder 1200cc engine. Result: a car with no performance, no handling, and few sales.

Austin A40 Sports, 1951

## AUSTIN-HEALEY (GB)

The Donald Healey Motor Co had been making small numbers of sports cars, which enjoyed a high reputation, when, in 1952, Healey obtained a number of Austin components. From them he built a two-seater sports car which he took to Jabbeke in Belgium and recorded 117mph/ 188kmh. Then the car went straight to Earls Court and became the star of the London Motor Show. It was seen by Sir Leonard Lord, managing director of BMC, who promptly fell in love with it. Lord was an autocrat who did not bother with details like market research—what he thought went, a style of management which ultimately did BMC no good at all. Further, Triumph was showing a prototype which would become the TR2, and that looked as though it could be a threat to MG which was a BMC company. There and then Lord concluded a deal with Healey to take over the design and to retain his company as consultants on a long-term contract. A star was born.

**100/4 / 100M, 1953-56. Prod: BN1: 10,633; BN2: 2765; 100M: 1159.** A 2.6-litre four-cylinder Austin A90 engine, a simple chassis, coil spring and double wishbone front suspension, and a live rear axle sprung on semi-elliptics—the

Austin-Healey 100 (above) and 100M (below)

mechanical specification is ordinary, but the body was one of the loveliest ever made. With a top speed of about 103mph/ 165kmh, and 0-60mph in 10.3 seconds, the 100/4 also set new performance standards for a relatively inexpensive mass-produced sports car and soon buyers (mostly American) were queueing up to buy. The BN1 had three speeds, but overdrive on the top two gears; the BN2, introduced in 1955, had four speeds plus overdrive top; the 100M was a version of the BN2 with 110bhp instead of 90, two-tone paint and detail mods. The exhaust system caused excessive cockpit heat (never cured) and ground clearance was poor, but sometimes you have to suffer for style.

**100S, 1954-56. Prod: 55.** A rare variant intended mainly for racing with disc brakes front and rear (the first production car in the world to have them), aluminium body panels, and a 132bhp engine with an alloy cylinder head. Identity features are louvres and leather straps on the bonnet. With 126mph/202kmh, and 0-60mph in 7.8 seconds, there were not many cars which could live with it in a straight line but, like all big 'Healeys, the cockpit was fairly cramped and it was a heavy car to drive.

The rare 100S

**100/6, 1956-59. Prod: BN4: 10,289, BN6: 4150.** Styling changes included an elliptical radiator grill and a bonnet scoop, external door handles appeared for the first time and the windscreen no longer folded flat. Two extra inches in the wheelbase helped improve cockpit space, and most cars were made with an extra seat behind the driver, so the rare ones are the straight two-seaters. Those made up to 1957 (BN4)

100/6 with factory hardtop

performed much less well than the 'Four', because they were heavier and the new 2.6-litre 'six' gave only 102bhp which meant 102mph/164kmh and 0-60mph in 12.9 seconds. The

BN6, with 117bhp, saved the day; top speed went up to 111mph/178kmh and the 0-60mph time went down to 11.2 seconds.

**Sprite I, 1958-61. Prod: 48,999.** The much-loved 'Frogeye' was simple, basic and not particularly quick, but it was enormous fun and filled the spot in the market which MG vacated when it moved up-market. It made much use of Austin A35 components (the engine was tuned to give 43bhp) and had unitary construction. It barely topped 80mph/ 130kmh and 0-60mph took 20.9 seconds, but it won hearts everywhere, helped by its cheeky looks. Retractable headlights had been planned but were scrapped at the last moment for being too costly. There was no time to re-style the bonnet, hence the 'frog's eyes' which, with its radiator grille, gave it an endearing smile. Other indications that it was built to a price are the fact the boot did not open and there were no external door handles.

**First of the line: the 1958 Sprite**

**3000, 1959-68. Prod: MkI: 13,650; MkII: 5450; MkII Convertible: 6113; MkIII: 17,704.** As the name suggests, this version had a 3-litre engine, which gave 124bhp, and to cope with that, front disc brakes were fitted, which was oddly late considering that the 100S had discs all round in 1954. The MkII of 1961, had a new gearbox, triple SUs and 132bhp, but tune was difficult to maintain. In 1962, the body was subtly re-jigged, the two-seater option was dropped, the engine reverted to twin SUs and lost only one bhp; this was the MkII 'convertible'. The MkIII of 1963 had 148bhp, servo-assisted brakes, and a wooden facia; and was good for 121mph/ 195kmh (0-60mph in 9.8 seconds). In 1964, radius rods replaced the previous Panhard rod at the rear, which helped handling, which was never the 'Healey's strong suit. The model was axed in 1968; the official line was it was too expensive to modify an aging car to meet US safety and emission laws but the entry on the aborted '4000' tells a different tale.

**Austin-Healey 3000: MkI (top), MkII (middle), MkIII (bottom)**

**Sprite II, 1961-64. Prod: 31,665.** In MkII trim, the Sprite was restyled with more conventional, but less individual, looks, and a boot which opened from the outside. Front disc brakes were fitted and, in late 1962, the engine was enlarged to 1,098cc which gave a useful 56bhp but it was still no road burner: 85mph/136kmh, 0-60mph in 18.3 seconds. Like the MkI, it had detachable side screens and the doors had no external handles, hence no locks. The production figures suggests a drop in popularity but the badge-engineered MG Midget almost doubled the overall figure and, like the 'Frogeye', it gave thousands of enthusiasts the chance to own a real sports car. Since, for most buyers, it was their sole transport (not many people then could afford to keep a fun car for weekends) detachable hardtops were a popular option.

**The Sprite II of 1961**

**Sprite III, 1964-66. Prod: 25,905.** Basically this was a more civilised MkII, with wind-up windows and external

**1964 Sprite III (right) with its Midget cousin**

door locks. Handling was improved by replacing the original quarter-elliptical rear springs (and radius rods) with semi-elliptics, which located the rear axle more securely, and there was an extra 3bhp. With the MkIII, 90mph/145kmh was possible, and the 0-60 dash was down to the mid-teens. These figures could be beaten by many quite ordinary saloons, but on a winding road with the hood down, and one's heart's desire in the passenger seat, the Sprite gave many a young enthusiast a first taste of paradise. By one of those odd quirks of the 'classic car' market, Sprites now have cachet but the Triumph Spitfire actually outsold the Sprite and MG Midget combined.

**Sprite IV, V/Austin Sprite, 1966-69/1969-71. Prod: 14,350/8443.** The main difference was the 1275cc 65bhp engine, although performance was only fractionally improved. A permanently attached hood replaced the rather crude cover which had been on the Sprite from its inception. The MkV had some cosmetic 'improvements' such as new trim, black sills and Rostyle wheels. The ending of the agreement with Healey led the last 1022 cars to be sold as 'Austins', which was not a name to set the pulse racing. After 1971, it was left to the MG Midget to continue the model's life, which it did until 1979. Of course, British Leyland could have built a successor, and kept the connection with Healey, but its management had decided there was no future in sports cars. It was helped in its decision by the fact that BL did not have a modern engine in the pipeline which could either take it into the future, or meet the US emission laws which loomed on the horizon.

**Austin-Healey Sprite IV, 1966**

**4000, 1968. Prod: 3.** From 1964 Rolls-Royce supplied BMC with the 4-litre engine which powered the Vanden Plas R saloon. Donald Healey built three prototypes using this engine as a possible replacement for the 3000. The standard car was cut down the middle, and an extra six inches were added, and the ground clearance was increased to comply with U.S. headlight law. The car lost none of its looks but gained in cockpit space and, according to Healey, road holding was improved. Rolls-Royce essayed a dohc cylinder head which greatly improved the standard engine's 175bhp, so a truly fabulous car was within reach. It was all far too good for British Leyland and a great line died.

**Austin-Healey 4000, 1968, with R-R power**

## AUTECH (GB)

A late 1980s maker of a faithful copy of the Jaguar C Type with an aluminium body.

## AUTECH (I/J)

First shown in 1989, the Autech Zagato Stelvio AZ1 was a 2+2 coupé. There was a time when the name Zagato was synonymous with beauty but, in the 1980s, the once-great styling house had become an embarrassment—as if its styling for Aston Martin was not bad enough, Zagato emphasised its declining standards with the AZ1. Ugly beyond belief, a sorry mish-mash of styling gimmicks, the car was based on the platform of the 3-litre Nissan Leopard, a car normally available only on the Japanese market. This had a 251bhp V6 turbocharged engine, MacPherson strut front suspension, and independent rear suspension by diagonal arms and coil springs.

Autech is the specialist cars division of Nissan and it commissioned Zagato and, presumably, approved the drawings. Why Autech should do so remains a mystery since, from the mid-1980s, Nissan's in-house styling department had shown itself to be pretty competent. This beast had a claimed top speed of 155mph/250kmh and 0-60mph acceleration in 6.2 seconds. These are competitive figures if one is talking about a Sierra Cosworth, but here one is talking about a £64,000 car with no style or provenance. It was promised to limit production of the car to just 203 examples but one felt that Autech would never be pressured by that restriction.

## AUTOBIANCHI (I)

Founded as 'Bianchi' by Edoardo Bianchi in 1899, Bianchi mainly specialised in sports cars and sports saloons (Nuvolari

**Autobianchi Stellina, 1964**

Bianchina Special, 1965

once drove one in the Mille Miglia) but the company never became sufficiently strong to survive setbacks. Production ceased altogether between 1939 and 1957 when, under the new name of 'Autobianchi', the company began to make what were essentially customised Fiats. Fiat took control in 1963 and since then Autobianchi has made 'alternative' Fiats, mainly for the home market and, quite often, to test ideas for the parent company. Apart from some 'performance' versions of ordinary cars, Autobianchi offered the 'Stellina', a short-lived two seat sports version of the Fiat 600 in 1964, and the 1965 Bianchina was a cabriolet based on the Fiat 500. In 1975 the company became associated with Lancia and in 1990 made a luxury version of the Lancia Y10 saloon.

## AUTOBLEU (F)

This constructor built a pretty little coupé based on Renault 4CV running gear which was styled by Luigi Segre of Ghia. A cabriolet followed in 1955, and in the same year, Autobleu introduced a Boano-bodied coupé based on Renault Frégate running gear with the engine tuned by Carlo Abarth. After making 60 cars, the firm disappeared in 1957.

The rear-engined Autobleu Coupé, c1954

## AUTO CRAFT NORTHWEST (USA)

In 1968 this Oregon company made the MkIII, as a kit or a limited edition complete car built to customer's individual specifications. Two basic variants were offered, a rear-engined car using the drive train of the air-cooled 2.6-litre flat-six Corvair, or a mid-engined version which was offered with a choice of 5.2- or 6.8-litre Chevrolet V8 engines.

## AUTO FORGE (GB)

Introduced in 1987, the AF Sports was a kit car with a Lotus-style backbone chassis, all-independent suspension, a wide range of four cylinder engine options, and an aluminium body (with GRP wings) in the style of a 1930s sports car. A large range of engine options was suggested, including the Toyota and Fiat dohc units. Depending on the engine, up to 115mph/185kmh was possible but, although the car was widely admired, the firm folded in 1990.

## AUTOKRAFT (GB)

Brian Angliss' Autokraft company had included the restoration of AC Cobras among its wide portfolio of work. In 1980 Autokraft acquired the rights to the AC name and in 1987 became joint partner, with Ford, in AC Cars Ltd. The company also acquired all the original jigs for the Cobra and, in 1985, was given the right to use the Cobra name, which remains a Ford trade mark. Autokraft is thus the only licensed manufacturer of the AC Cobra.

**AC Cobra MkIV, 1980-present. Prod: approx 350 to the end of 1990.** By using the original jigs, Autocraft was able to continue production of the Cobra, and the chassis specification is the same as the Cobra MkIII. Times change, however, and since the original MkIII was in production, emission laws have stifled engine power outputs. The MkIV has had to keep pace since most of the production goes to America. In 1990, the MkIV, which met all US safety and emission laws, had a 225bhp 5-litre Ford V8 engine with catalytic convertor; this gave a 134mph/215kmh maximum and 0-60mph in five seconds. Some cars, however, have been converted by agents to take the full-blown 7-litre engine which restores the brute force of the Shelby cars.

## AUTOMOBILES LM (F)

First shown in 1986, the GMFSA SL coupé was still being readied for production at the end of 1990. A very sleek fibreglass coupé, which used the steel central section of the Matra Murena, it had a mid-mounted 200bhp 2.5-litre Renault V6 engine, as used in the Renault GTA. A top speed of 154mph/248kmh was claimed. The company also had plans for a version to use a 2-litre four-cylinder engine.

## AUTOMODA (USA)

In Italian, the name of this company means 'Autostyle', and it was one of a plethora of outfits which sprang up in the States in the late 1980s, hell-bent on converting a Pontiac Fiero into something which might pass as an import from Modena. In this case the conversion was more complicated than most since Automoda converted the base car into a 'Spyder'.

Automoda Spyder, 1990

## AUTOMOTIVE DEVELOPMENTS (GB)

Maker of the AD400, a 1984 fibreglass evocation of the open topped Ferrari Dino, with a front-mounted engine and Ford Cortina running gear. Few were sold and the project was soon passed on to another maker. AD also made a poor quality copy of the Cobra 427 and supplied bodies and chassis to Gravetti (qv).

## AUTO-POWER (GB)

Mike Broad's Auto-Power Services company announced the Magnum 427 in 1987, offering it complete or in kit form. Loosely based on the Cobra 427, and with some outward resemblance to it, the Magnum specification included a space frame, Jaguar suspension components and brakes and a single-skin plastic body shell.

## AUTO REPLICA (E)

Maker, since 1981, of the AR 50, a copy of the MG TD which, despite the fact it is a 2+2, is fairly convincing, due in no small part to having the right size wheels and tyres. It has coil spring and wishbone front suspension, a live rear axle, a 77bhp 1438cc Seat engine, and a top speed of 90mph/145kmh is claimed.

AR50 Roadster, 1985

## AUTOTUNE (GB)

Maker since the mid-1980s of the 'Aristocat', a Jaguar-based kit car with a fibreglass body which recalled the Jaguar XK

Autotune Aristocat

sports cars of the 1950s, but was seven inches wider to accommodate the running gear of the XJ6 or XK12. With modern running gear, it handled better, braked better, and was quicker than the original XKs; in fact with the V12 engine, claimed performance figures were 152mph/245kmh and 0-60mph in 7.1 seconds.

Autotune Gemini, 1988

Autotune also made the 'Mirage', a Marcos Mantis lookalike, in 1986 but this Cortina-sourced car, which used a tubular backbone chassis, appears to have enjoyed no better success than the original. In 1988 the company introduced the 'Gemini', a Ford Escort Mk1/2 based car with a fibreglass body which was a near copy of the Falcon 'Sports' body of the late 1950s.

## AUTO UNION (D)

A name for ever associated with a series of astonishing mid-

Auto-Union 1000SP, 1960

engined Grand Prix cars in the 1930s, Auto Union came about with the merger, in 1932, of Audi, DKW, Horch and Wanderer. The factories were all in Eastern Germany and, after the War, were nationalised and made cars under the name 'IFA', the blanket label for all East German makers. Two former DKW executives, however, restarted production in West Germany in 1950, using a pre-war DKW design, and the Auto Union 1000 was a sports DKW. In 1965 the Audi name was revived and DKW disappeared the following year.

**1000 SP, 1958-65. Prod: 6640.** This was a sports two-seater with a body designed by Bauer on a DKW 1000 chassis. It shared its parent's transverse leaf and lower wishbone all-independent suspension and front wheel drive and had front disc brakes from 1963. The 980cc three-cylinder two-stroke engine, which was also used by Saab, was tweaked to give 55bhp. That was not much but it was acceptable at that particular time and place.

## AVA (GB)

The AVA K1 was a kit car which appeared in 1986 and was out of the ordinary in that it had been designed in a wind tunnel (with a claimed cd of 0.295); its styling was similar to contemporary major manufacturers' 'concept' cars, and it had front wheel drive. Designed to take a range of engines, mainly Ford, with a notional 300bhp, a top speed of 170mph/274kmh was claimed. The AVA faded soon after its arrival but late in 1990 the concept was revived. In its new guise, the chassis and floorpan were made from 3CR12 stainless steel so the fibreglass body panels were unstressed while power came from any Ford Escort Mk3 engine. The revived marque was soon making its name in competition with the K1 RS version, which did away with details such as weather equipment.

AVA K1, introduced in 1986

## AVALLONE (BR)

Introduced in 1976, the Avallone was a reasonably accurate copy of the MG TF which used locally built Chevrolet chassis and running gear and a fibreglass body. In Brazil, 'Chevrolet' often means European GM cars such as the Opel/Vauxhall range marketed under the Chevrolet name, and in this case the source car was the Chevette. Engine options ranged from a 60bhp 1.4-litre 'four' up to a 150bhp 2.5-litre 'six' and the company was still active in 1990.

## AVANTE (GB)

A short-lived coupé (1982-86) originally based on a VW Beetle floorpan although a version with Golf GTI running gear was also made. The styling was original and handsome, with hints of the Corvette Stingray and the Ford GT40.

Avante coupé, 1984

## AVANTI II (USA)

After Studebaker closed its American branch in 1964, two enthusiastic dealers took over production of the Avanti coupé. An early (1966) improvement was the use of a 5.3-litre Chevrolet engine (5.7-litre in 1969) and Chevrolet engines have since been standard. Detail changes in the specification occurred as Federal laws required and in 1990 power came from a 175bhp fuel injected 5-litre engine driving through a three-speed automatic transmission which meant a top speed of 118mph/190kmh.

Annual production reached 100 cars in 1968, the company changed hands in 1982, made 276 cars in 1983 and, in 1985, offered a convertible version. Later that year the company ceased trading but it was revived under new ownership in 1986. A four-door 'Touring Sedan' on a longer wheelbase arrived in 1989.

1990 version of the Avanti II

## AVIOR (B)

This was a 1947 project for a new sports car with all-independent suspension (a Dubonnet front system and rubber springing at the rear). Coupé and saloon variants were also planned and if they had had the panache of the two seat prototype, they would have been handsome cars. The backers claimed that the four-cylinder 1930cc engine that would produce 70bhp, would be sourced in Britain, but it is hard to put a name to this profile. It seems that only the prototype sports car was made.

The still-born 1947 Avior

**The early Corvette had homely lines and was a boulevard cruiser rather than a sports car. A V-8 transformed its performance, and distinctive scalloped flanks helped give it sleek lines**

Above: Maserati's A6GCS cycle-winged spyder, built in tiny numbers 1947-51, a cramped 1952 two-seater with full-width bodywork, and this elegant A6G/2000 designed by Pinin Farina all used the same chassis. Early cars had a single ohc engine, this A6G/2000 had a twin-cam ohc unit

Right: Spain's postwar sports car, the Pegaso, was an indulgence by the ENASA national comercial vehicle company and director/designer Wilfredo P Ricart. This Z102 has restrained Touring lines behind its ponderous nose

M-180.080

Low Perspex screen and lack of embellishments such as bumpers hint at the competitions intentions for the Austin-Healey 100S. The bonnet strap is almost anachronistic, a large fuel filler cap behind the cockpit was in character, as were the bonnet louvres and the omission of hood and side screens

# B

## BADSEY (GB/ZA)

In the late 1970s Bill Badsey introduced the 'Racing Eagle', a two-seat Targa-top sports car which seemed inspired by the Fiat X1/9 but was based on BMC 1100/1300 running gear. Badsey found that the British market was not very receptive to the car (which apparently was very good) so he returned to his native South Africa and set up production there.

## BANDINI (I)

In 1947 Bandini built a sports car special using a tuned Fiat 500 engine in a tubular frame and was soon making small numbers of similar cars. By 1952 he was concentrating on the 750cc class which was popular in Italy. His cars had a Fiat-derived engine with twin overhead camshafts and front

**Bandini 750**

suspension by coil springs and double wishbones. Bandini enjoyed some success in Italian racing (he also made 750cc single seaters for a national class) but the key to expansion was success in America and no Fiat-based 750cc car could compete with Crosley-based specials. Even Bandinis with Crosley engines could not compete since they were built with rugged chassis for road racing whereas much SCCA racing was on airfield circuits. Bandini soldiered on until 1961 when he produced a front-engined Formula Junior which was obsolete when the first drawings were made.

## BANGERT (USA)

Short-lived mid-1950s maker of a simple ladder frame, which would take Ford suspension and which could be mated to

**Bangert, 1955, evidently an 'artist's impression'.**

an ill-favoured fibreglass body which parodied European sports-racers.

## b+b (D)

From the early 1970s, Rainer Buchmann's b+b studio specialised in customising cars to individual requirements. This work ranged from special paint jobs and interiors to reworked bodies such as a 'notch back' version of the Porsche 928. During 1978/9 the company built the CW311, a luxurious gull-wing mid-engined coupé with styling inspired by the experimental Mercedes-Benz C111. With a 375bhp 6.3-litre Mercedes-Benz V8 engine, a top speed of 200mph/320kmh was claimed (0-60mph in 4.5 seconds). It was made in very small numbers, each to special order, and the Isdera Imperator (qv) was based on the CW311.

## BBL (GB)

A short-lived fibreglass copy of the Lamborghini Countach which was marketed as the 'Primo' in the mid-1980s. The design was originated by GTD and used the same space frame as GTD's copy of the Ford GT40, usually with a Ford V8 engine mated to a Renault transaxle.

## BEAUFORD (GB)

Maker since the late 1980s of a 'nostalgia' car, apparently inspired by the Mercedes-Benz SSK, with Ford Cortina running gear. Astonishingly, a complete Mini body shell is used as the central section, disguised by a trunk shaped boot and by the bonnet panels.

**Beauford 1990. Spot the Mini doors**

## BEAUJANGLE (GB)

A Cam-Am style body on a shortened VW Beetle chassis, introduced 1972. Like many kit car projects it had a chequered

**Beaujangle was VW Beetle based—even the headlamps**

history and was last heard of in 1984 in the hands of a new maker.

## BECK DEVELOPMENT (BR/USA)

This was a range of Porsche copies (550 Spyder, 904 Carrera etc) on VW Beetle running gear. The machines were built in Brazil as turn key cars for Chuck Beck to sell in California in the 1980s.

**Beck 550 Spyder**

## BENTLEY (GB)

One of the most famous names in motoring history, Bentley was in deep financial trouble in 1930 and was taken over by Rolls-Royce, which marketed a new range as 'The Silent Sports Car'. After the War, the marque became a badge-engineered Roller, the choice of bookies rather than Owners, but in the late 1980s it once more bègan to assume an independent identity. The name 'Continental R' was revived on a new model early in 1991.

**Continental R, 1952-55. Prod: 207.** The fastest Grand Touring car of its day with a top speed of 120mph/195kmh. In some of Ian Fleming's books, James Bond had an even faster one, fitted with a Villiers supercharger (which negated the warranty). A Bentley R Type chassis (a.k.a. Rolls-Royce Silver Dawn) was fitted with a 4566cc straight six (4887cc on later models) but the superb body by H.J. Mulliner made this car distinctive. It was not a sports car but its 100+mph cruising speed made it the ultimate Grand Tourer: you could drive from London to Monte Carlo and arrive fresh enough to play the tables and the boot would hold a choice of evening gowns for m'lady.

**The inimitable Bentley Continental, admittedly not a sports car**

## BERKELEY (GB)

Berkeley of Biggleswade was Britain's leading maker of caravans in the 1950s, and pioneered the use of fibreglass in

**Berkeley Bandit: only two made**

their construction. Laurie Bond was a maverick designer who, apart from his motorcycle engined Minicar, had built a front wheel drive 500cc F3 car without suspension (the fat but tiny wheels, which were aircraft tail wheels, absorbed all the forces) and would go on to build a fwd Formula Junior car with a fibreglass monocoque in 1961. Berkeley built Bond's idea of an economy sports car; followed it with a popular three-wheeled version (some 2500 were made); then commissioned John Tojeiro to design a Ford 105-engined replacement, the Bandit. This promising little car was almost ready for production (two were made) when the caravan side of the business took a dive and Berkeley folded. Approximately 2000 four-wheeled Berkeleys were made.

**B60/B65, 1956-67, and 1961.** A tiny, pretty, car with fibreglass unitary construction and all-round independent suspension. In line with Laurie Bond's general thinking, it had front wheel drive via chains from a three-speed 'box on the early models, with four speeds on later cars. The B60 had a 332cc Anzani engine and the B65 had a 328cc Excelsior unit, preferable because it was more powerful; both were air-cooled two-stroke twins. It is not a coincidence that production was suspended in 1958, the year that the Sprite appeared.

**Berkeley B60/65**

**B90, 1958-59.** Berkeley's answer to the Sprite came either as a two or four-seater. This time the 492cc three-cylinder version of the Excelsior engine was used and performance was roughly the same as the baby 'Healey. But who wanted a tiny plastic car with a noisy two-stroke engine when the Sprite was practical, had a great name, and could be serviced in any high street? Incidentally, the type numbers (60, 65, 90) indicated the claimed top speed.

**1958 Berkeley B90**

**B95/105, 1959-61.** A further up-date with up to 50bhp from the high compression version of the four-stroke 692cc Royal Enfield 'Constellation' parallel twin. The chassis coped very well with this large increment in power which indicates that it was well conceived in the first place. The car was distinguishable from its less powerful sisters by its large rectangular grille and the fact it dispensed with the perspex headlight fairings. By the time Berkeley folded, however, the buying public had developed fairly sophisticated tastes, largely thanks to the Sprite and Mini, and bought such cars in preference to the much faster, but less comfortable, 'large-engined' Berkeleys.

**Berkeley B95/105, 1959**

## BERNARDET (F)

Designed by Marcel Violet, this was an unsuccessful attempt to build a small, open, three seater just after the War. The Bernardet had rakish lines and an original 'oversquare', water-cooled, side-valve, four-cylinder engine of 800cc cast from aluminium. This was mounted transversely and drove, through the front wheels, via a four-speed gearbox set in an independently-sprung chassis. If this sounds a little like the Mini, it should be remembered that the transverse engine/front wheel drive layout originated with DKW, it was the gearbox in the sump which made the Mini distinctive. The engine was enlarged to 848cc in 1947 and, two years later, was replaced by an air-cooled 750cc two-stroke engine, also built by Bernardet.

The project apparently had sound financial backing but it is still uncertain how many Bernardets were made; and the suspicion lingers that there might just have been a constantly uprated prototype which was hawked around motor shows in an effort to drum up interest in the project.

## BEUBHEUR (D)

In the late 1960s this company made a small number of fibre-glass coupés which used Porsche 356B running gear, with the engine tuned to give 75bhp.

## BEUTLER (CH)

When Porsche was struggling to establish its factory between 1948 and 1950, it was helped in no small measure by Beutler, a Swiss coachbuilding company. As a result, in 1957, Porsche supplied Beutler with complete Type 356 chassis and these were completed with a 2+2 two-door three box body and a false radiator grill.

**Beutler-Bodied Jowett Jupiter**

The car looked like a cross between a Borgward Isabella and a Lagonda 3-litre and it also used parts from the VW Beetle and Karmann Ghia. Beutler made about ten a year, and added a cabriolet version. 1960 saw a revised model, again in coupé and open forms, this time reminiscent of a Sunbeam Alpine, and Beutler also made a four-seat hard-top coupé which retained the 356 nose. The bodies were heavy and since the base model had only 60bhp perfor-mance was not sparkling. About sixty Beutler specials were built in all.

**Beutler special Porsche 356**

## BIOTA (GB)

The Mini engine/transmission unit has attracted many constructors but the problem all have found is the height of the lump. If it is mounted at the front, its height causes enormous problems in creating an attractive style. In 1968 John Houghton approached the problem by drawing a body with bold lines, the sheer confidence of which carried the style, and bringing in others to engineer the concept. The prototype attracted a lot of favourable attention but the originators were not geared up to cope with the enthusiastic response, and it took some time to get the concept right. Although the Biota was built to be a road car (four complete cars were sold to Holland), a specially prepared example gave its two drivers first and third overall in a British club hillclimb championship in 1972. That did not help the cause, however, and nor did the arrival of VAT in 1973; so few noticed when the project folded in 1976 after 30 cars had been built.

Biota, 1968

## BIRCHALL (GB)

This was a 1980s kit car based on the Clan Crusader, and engineered by Bob Luff, who was one of the luminaries of the Clan project. Unlike the original two seater, the Birchall McCoy was a 2+2 with front-mounted Mini or Metro running gear, and an estate version was also offered. In 1990, production of the range transferred to a new company, Wynes (qv).

## BITTER (D)

Erich Bitter sold Frank Reisner's Intermeccanica cars in Germany and he introduced Reisner to Opel, the upshot of which was the Intermeccanica Indra (qv). At the time Opel's image was undergoing a change for the better and, in 1969, the company produced a stylish exhibition car based on the Opel Diplomat floor pan. It was a hit at motor shows but was not a practical production proposition. However, in conjunction with Frua, the project was developed and the show car which appeared in 1972 was both practical and very pretty (it resembled the Maserati Khamsin which, coincidentally, appeared at the same time).

Erich Bitter pressed Opel to put the car into production but Opel was not prepared to do so under its own label. On the other hand, the Chevrolet-engined Diplomat (there was no Vauxhall equivalent) had been facing an uphill struggle against Mercedes-Benz in the market place and with unofficial help from Opel, Bitter was allowed to market the car under his own banner.

The Bitter CD was a 2+2 fastback coupé with a pressed steel body finalised and built by a small German coachbuilder, Baur. Front suspension was by coil springs and double wishbones, the de Dion rear axle was suspended on coil springs and located by radius arms and an A bracket, and disc brakes were fitted on all four wheels. With 230bhp from its 5354cc Chevrolet V8 engine, a top speed of 130mph/210kmh was possible (0-60mph in 9.9 seconds) and the car's finish and level of trim matched its performance and stunning good looks.

Its price and the fact that Baur could not make more than three bodies a week kept production figures down, but Bitter soon established a niche in the market and 493 had been built by the time the model was replaced in 1979 by the SC.

Bitter SC, on Opel Senator floor pan, 1982

Targa-top Bitter 'Roadster' Sports, 1985

The new car, also a 2+2 coupé, was based on the floor pan of the Opel Senator (Vauxhall Royale in Britain) with all-independent suspension, a 180bhp 3-litre straight-six engine and a choice of either automatic transmission or a five-speed manual gearbox. In 1983 Bitter offered an optional 210bhp 3.9-litre version of the engine which increased the 131mph

1989 Bitter Type III

of the 3-litre car to 143mph/230kmh and reduced the 0-62mph time of ten seconds to 7.6 seconds. A convertible was offered in 1984, then Bitter hit financial problems and ceased production for a time.

The marque was revived, and in 1987 introduced the Type III, a two seat sports car based on an Opel Omega (aka Vauxhall Carlton) floor pan which was sold in coupé or convertible forms. Front suspension was by MacPherson struts, the independent rear was by coil springs and trailing arms, disc brakes with ABS were fitted all round and the 3-litre straight six delivered its 174bhp through a five-speed manual gearbox or a four-speed automatic. With the manual gearbox top speed was 141mph/227kmh (137mph/220kmh with the automatic), and 0-62mph was achieved in 7.6 seconds (8.4 seconds with automatic transmission). By 1990 Opel's 201bhp dohc four valves per cylinder engine had been adopted and this increased top speed to 149mph/240kmh (or 146mph/235kmh with automatic transmission).

In typical Bitter style, the standard of finish and trim was outstanding and the cabriolet version was available with a hardtop. The bodies were built by Maggiora in Turin, and finished by Steyr Puch in Austria. A long wheelbase four seat version was introduced in 1989.

## BIZZARRINI (I)

Giotto Bizzarrini worked for Alfa Romeo and Ferrari (where he was responsible for the 250GTO) before he established his own company in 1962. At first he undertook subcontract work for other makers, most notably Iso and Lamborghini. His Strada of 1965 was basically a lightweight two seat Iso Grifo, made with the permission of Iso, but his small-engined Europa of the following year was a new departure as was the unsuccessful mid-engined sports racer, the P538. A GT version of the P538 was built for Iso but was not put into production. Despite having one of the most wonderful names with which any manufacturer has been blessed, his venture ended in 1969 (maybe Bizzarrini doesn't sound so quick in Italian). Bizzarrini became a freelance again and among his later projects were prototypes for American Motors and Iso.

**Strada, 1965-69.** This was Bizzarrini's version of his Iso Grifo A3C—the two cars were virtually identical but the Strada was over 400lb lighter, was lower by 3.5in, had skimpy trim and faired-in headlights. These are clues to the real difference, the Strada was intended for competition as well as the road and had 365bhp from its 5.4-litre Chevy engine. Unfortunately, it fell between two stools: it was not good enough to be a competition car and those who wanted a road-burner preferred the Iso Grifo, which was better equipped. In the USA it was sold as the Bizzarrini GT America.

Bizzarrini Strada, 1965

**Europa, 1967-69.** Looking like a miniature Strada, the Europa also fell between two stools. Its fibreglass body and its chassis seemed intended for competition but its unmodified 1.9-litre Opel engine produced only 110bhp. That was definitely not enough for the 2-litre class where Porsche and Alfa Romeo were active. The Europa had a steel platform chassis with independent suspension all round by coil springs and double wishbones, disc brakes on all four wheels, and was claimed to reach 128mph/205mph. Intended to broaden Bizzarrini's model range, it sold in tiny numbers and its failure hastened the marque's decline.

Bizzarrini Europa GT, 1967

## BJS (GB)

Maker of the short-lived Mistral 2+2 gull wing coupé announced in 1986. A kit car, it used Ford Cortina running gear.

## BLAKELY (USA)

Founded in 1972 by David Blakeley, the company first made the 'Bantam', a Ford Pinto-based kit car using a space frame

Blakely Bantam

Blakely Bearcat, 1976

and an attractive fibreglass body recalling typical 1930s sports cars without being a specific copy. This was followed by an improved model, the 'Bearcat' in 1973, and the 'Bearcat S', a 100mph car with a 2.3-litre Pinto engine, in 1976. By that time the company was concentrating on 'turn key' cars.

## BMC (USA)

A 1952 car from California which mated a two-seat fibreglass body to a Singer 1500 chassis. BMC stood for British Motor Car (the British Motor Corporation had then not been formed) which explains the apparently odd name for a car sourced by the Rootes Group. Originally intended to sell at a rate of 400 cars a year, the project actually lasted only a few months.

## BMW (D)

In the 1920s BMW made aero engines and motorcycles before beginning licensed production of the Austin Seven in 1929. The company's first original design arrived in 1934 and two years later it established its credentials with the 328, which was probably the best all-round sports car of its day. After hostilities ceased, the firm's major plant in the East was nationalised and eventually made the unloved Wartburgs. The Munich factory survived many calamities—at one time its main model was the Isetta bubble car—but in the mid-1960s the foundations of BMW's present success were laid with a series of well-made small saloons.

By the early 1970s, BMW was making some very desirable saloon cars which were very successful on the race tracks, and it also pioneered turbocharging in Europe with the 2002 Turbo which arrived in 1973, just before the energy crisis. Many people would argue for the inclusion of BMW 850I of 1990 in a book on sports cars but, like Jaguar, BMW has always been very clear about its own definition of a sports car.

**503, 1956-59. Prod: 413.** BMW's first postwar design was a four-seater GT car available as a coupé or convertible. The short-lived 3168cc V8 was fitted to the 501 chassis which, in turn, derived from the pre-war 326 chassis with torsion bar springing all round and independent suspension at the front. Styling was by Count Albrecht Goertz and the project was intended to announce that BMW was back in business, and to earn precious dollars. The column gear shift was not quite in keeping with the car's character and 115mph/ 185kmh top speed, and only left hookers were made, but the styling is timeless.

**BMW 503, 1956**

**507, 1956-59. Prod: 253.** Under the skin, this was broadly the same as the 503 but the wheelbase was shortened by 16in and power was up from 140bhp to 150bhp without losing the excellent low-range torque. Goertz was again responsible for the styling and this time he was less inhibited —BMW's first postwar two seater looks equally good as a coupé or as a rag top. Top speed was 124mph/200kmh (0-60mph in 8.8 seconds) but a higher rear axle ratio was available which would allow 135mph/ 217kmh. There was a floor gear change, and front disc brakes were fitted on some late cars. The engine and gearbox were also used in the Lago-Talbot 'America'.

**BMW 507 Sports, 1956**

**M1, 1979-80. Prod: 456.** Originally intended as an out and out racer, with a road version available to bump up the production figures for homologation purposes, the M1 fell victim to the company's shift of priorities as it decided to enter F1. March Engineering made a competition version which was a failure largely because BMW did not make enough cars to homologate it in the right category. Consequently most of its competition history was in the 'Pro-Car' series when Grand Prix drivers entertained the crowds after Saturday qualifying. It was a fabulous road car with a 277bhp dohc four-valves-per-cylinder version of BMW's 3.5-litre straight six, mounted amidships in a space frame with independent suspension all

**BMW M1 had 277bhp**

round by coil springs and double wishbones. Styling was by Giugiaro, rendered in fibreglass, and top speed was 162mph/260kmh with 60mph coming up in 5.5 seconds. From a commercial point of view, the M1 was an expensive failure, but lucky owners think differently.

**Z1, 1986-91.** The Z1 was originally built as a concept car, but public demand saw BMW put it into production. Under the fibreglass skin was a monocoque of steel and carbon composites with MacPherson strut front suspension and BMW's 'Z-axle' wishbone rear suspension. Power came from a 170bhp 2.5-litre engine which propelled the Z1 up to 136mph/218kmh with 0-60mph in 7.9 seconds. Most unusually, the doors slid down into the shell for access—a rare example of BMW employing a styling gimmick. It was horribly expensive in markets such as Britain (the same money would buy a Lotus Elan Turbo *and* a TVR S3) where most commentators found its steering and response disappointing, the engine inadequate and, all in all, rated the Z1 poor value for money.

Some German tuners, however, put more muscle under the bonnet; Richard Hamman, for example, would effect a transplant of the 315bhp 3.5-litre M5 engine. Late in 1990, BMW announced that it would cease production in 1991 when 8000 examples had been completed.

**1989 BMW Z1**

## BOCAR (USA)

Bob Carnes of Denver, Colorado, dreamed of being a top-notch sports car manufacturer. After a number of false starts (or prototypes if one wants to be kind) he announced the XP-4, which had strange styling and unpredictable handling. A replacement, the XP-5 of 1959, was better all round, but Carnes never made the big breakthrough.

Although the XP-4 spun like a top when leaned on, Carnes retained the short (90in) wheelbase for his replacement, but moderated the handling by replacing the Mercury V8 with the much lighter Chevrolet Corvette engine and using Kurtis-style beam suspension and trailing torsion bars. Quite a pretty car, it came in open or coupé forms and 12 were made. It performed reasonably well in competition without being a winner.

Bocar's second and last year of production, 1960, saw the XP-6 which was basically an XP-5 with 14in added to the wheelbase and a supercharger added to the 'Vette engine boosting output to 400bhp. Apparently it handled reasonably well while acceleration was phenomenal with 120mph coming up in 16 seconds on its way to a 170mph/273kmh maximum. The price tag of $11,700 limited its market, however, and few were sold. Carnes' swansong was an out and out sports-racer called the 'Stiletto', which was no more successful than the other cars.

## BOLIDE (USA)

A mid-engined coupé, the Can-Am 1 had a 5.7-litre Ford V8 engine. It was announced in 1969 but it is doubtful if any were sold.

## BOLWELL (AUS)

This is one Australian specialist car maker which nearly made it, for the products of the Bolwell brothers won wide-spread admiration for their style and engineering. One of the brothers' early successes was with a kit car, the Mk 7, which was a basic sports car with Holden components in a space frame. About four hundred were sold between 1967 and 1972.

**1972 Bolwell Nagari**

This was followed by the Nagari which was an altogether more ambitious project and was sold as a turn key car. It used Ford Falcon mechanicals (4.9-litre V8) in a backbone chassis, topped with a stunning fibreglass body which was available in GT form or as an open two-seater. With a 0-60mph time of a shade over seven seconds, a top speed of 130mph/210kmh, and road holding to match, the Nagari was a deserved success. Plans to sell it in America were thwarted by US emission and safety laws (including headlight height). Similar laws in Australia did not help and production ended in 1974 after about 140 had been made. Later the company turned its attention to industrial fibreglass products though the Ikara, a small sports car using a mid-mounted VW Golf engine, was shown in 1979—only ten kits were sold.

## RENÉ BONNET (F)

The partnership between René Bonnet and Charles Deutsch which had been so successful when they were in harness as DB (qv) came to an end in 1961; Deutsch went on to become a successful engineering consultant while Bonnet continued to make cars, but under his own name. Bonnet's neat little mid-engined Djet coupé used Renault components and was good enough to win its class at Le Mans in 1962 and 1963. The Djet was one of the very first mid-engined road cars; it has sometimes erroneously been compared to the Alpine-Renault, but that was *rear*-engined and, anyway, the thinking behind the car was recognisably DB. There was a tubular backbone chassis with independent suspension all round by coil springs and double wishbones and there were disc brakes on all four wheels. It was clothed in a very pretty and slippery fibreglass body and kerb weight was just 1350lb.

The usual engine was a 70bhp 1100cc unit but there was a 95bhp 'Gordini' option. With the standard unit, the car could reach the ton and return excellent fuel economy. To keep down weight, frills such as sound absorption material were ignored and that explains why more cars were used for competition than everyday motoring.

The firm made two other models, the 'Le Mans' and the 'Missile', but neither enjoyed the popularity of the Djet, being tamer and sold largely as road cars. Both also used Renault components but were front engined and had front wheel drive. Engine options on these ranged from 850cc to 1100cc and these cars had disc brakes only on the front wheels.

**1964 René Bonnet models: Djet IV GT (top), Le Mans (middle) and Missile (bottom)**

Bonnet also made some F2 and prototype sports cars which received backing from Renault. When these proved unsuccessful, Renault withdrew its sponsorship which left Bonnet in some difficulty. In 1964, Engins Matra, an aerospace company set on expanding into a new field, took over Bonnet and the cars were marketed under the name 'Matra-Bonnet'. The front-engined cars did not last long and production centred on the Djet. The 1966 model had an engine with a hemispherical cylinder head and was capable of 109mph/175kmh. The following year saw a 1255cc 105bhp version as well as a new 2+2 coupé which use a German Ford V4 engine. In the same year, Matra introduced its new '530' sports coupé and the Djet was dropped in 1968, and with it went the name 'Bonnet'.

## BORGWARD (D)

In the 1950s, Borgward occupied a place in the German car market roughly similar to Audi's today but it was ultimately destroyed by Carl Borgward, an autocrat who had created the company yet did not know when to change his style of management. In 1957 Borgward offered a 2+2 coupé, and cabriolet, based on the Isabella saloon, with a 1.5-litre engine, unitary construction, and a 95mph/153kmh top speed. Legend has it that the car was built to prevent Frau Borgward from buying a VW Karmann Ghia, which perfectly illustrates Herr Borgward's approach to building cars. The company also made some fine sports-racers, which never fulfilled their potential due to the lack of a proper programme, and an advanced dohc engine which was successful in Formula 2 in 1959. The Borgward group collapsed in 1961.

**Borgward Isabella Coupé, 1958**

## BOSCHI (RA)

In 1972, an Argentine racing driver called Boschi signed an agreement with Lotus to make the Seven under licence, and these examples of the Lotus Seven Series III were actually badged and sold as Lotuses. One could say, therefore, that there was no such thing as a Boschi, but how else does one list an obscure Argentine off-shoot of Lotus? For the first year of production, the 1.6-litre Fiat 125 engine was used but then was replaced by a 1.5-litre Dodge unit (the Hillman Avenger engine in Britain).

## BRA (GB)

A kit car launched in 1981, this was a copy of the Cobra 289 largely sourced from the MGB. A version with a Rover V8

**BRA Beribo**

**BRA Cobra**

engine was also offered and a Volvo-engined version was made in Denmark under the name Sommer Oscar (qv). BRA introduced a 2+2 'traditional' sports car (styled after the 1930s MG Midgets) in 1984 and that year also produced a copy of the Cobra 427. The company was still active in 1990.

## BRABUS (D)

A 1980s modifier and customiser of Mercedes-Benz models, including the 500SL. In that case Brabus could supply a 6-litre version which produced more than 400bhp and took the car's top speed to about 170mph/275kmh.

## BRADLEY (USA)

Bradley was a successful American kit car manufacturer between 1972 and 1982. The first car was a gull-wing coupé based on VW running gear which was noted for its ease of assembly, and 1,600 were made in the company's first four years. By 1981 it had diversified into VW-based models on the lines of the MG TD, 1955 Thunderbird, and Mercedes-Benz SS and 540K. Of special interest is the fact that Bradley offered some of its kits with electric power.

**Bradley GT was VW based**

## BRICKLIN (USA/CDN)

The story of Malcolm Bricklin's car uncannily parallels that of the later DeLorean. An ace American salesman conceives a wedge-shaped 'safety' sports car with gull-wing doors and a rot-resistant body. He embarks on a high profile publicity drive and persuades a foreign government to put up the money to

**Bricklin SV-1 at 1975 Geneva Show**

produce it and the government (in this case that of New Brunswick, Canada) does so in order to bring employment to a depressed area. The resulting car is very well received when shown as an exhibition model, and the advance order book is promising, but the first production versions are almost unsaleable. This is partly due to the complexity of the outstanding sales feature, the gull-wing doors, partly due to poor production engineering, and partly due to the fact that the newly recruited workers have no previous experience of the motor industry.

By the time the car hits the market, it costs significantly more than its projected price tag, which means that the production target will never be met. Further, because of the complexity of the design, and in particular the problem of adjusting the doors, labour costs rise and each car has so many faults to be rectified before they are saleable that the company loses money on each one. Although hailed by the press in prototype form, the disappointing quality plus horror stories about the occupants being trapped in the car when the doors refuse to open (in the Bricklin's case, they were electrically operated), kill the car's slender chance of survival. Before long cars are being heavily discounted and the entrepreneur requests more money from the government but, rather than throw good money after bad, this is refused and a year or so after the car is launched, it is dead.

The government loses a great deal of money ($23,000,000 in the case of the Bricklin) and the workers whom the project is supposed to help are made redundant. There are official enquiries and it emerges that the principal player has a history of unsatisfactory business practice (but he is unscathed and bounces back in other businesses). Later, the cars become a curious cult among collectors.

It is astonishing, but all these facts were common to both the Bricklin SV-1 and the DeLorean DMC-2. Bricklin, however, was personally bankrupted and nobody was able to film him with packets of funny powder. Further, the SV-1 was a much better concept, it was designed to sell on integrity, and apparently on the road it was something like a cross between a Jaguar E Type and a Chevrolet Corvette. In addition, the Bricklin's production target was realistic since there was very little on offer in its projected niche whereas the DeLorean was taking on the new generation of front-engined Porsches.

Later Malcolm Bricklin began to import the Bertone/Fiat S1/9 and the Pininfarina Spyder (formerly the Fiat 124 Sport) and, in 1985 he founded Global Motors which imported Yugo cars. In a curious twist to the story, he sold Global Motors early in 1988 and within a few months Global Motors (qv) announced that it was going to build a new 'international' sports car.

**SV-1, 1974 model. Prod: 780.** The SV-1 really did have strong claims to being a safety sports car: not only was the separate chassis very strong but there was a steel cage around the cockpit and behind the integral front bumpers were pneumatic rams to absorb impact. Of course, these features could be negated by the gull-wing doors—occupants could be trapped if the car inverted, or if the battery failed—but there were instances of people surviving very heavy crashes without a scratch. Many of the teething troubles stemmed from the material used to construct the body which, unusually, was of acrylic resin backed by fibreglass. It was prone to crack and about 25 per cent of all panels had to be rejected.

For the rest, it was a fairly conventional car with front suspension by coil springs and double wishbones, a live rear axle was suspended on semi-elliptic springs, and there were front disc brakes. 1974 cars had a 5.9-litre American Motors V8 engine which delivered its 220bhp through a Chrysler four-speed manual gearbox (144 made) or the more usual transmission was a three-speed automatic. With either method of juggling the cogs, top speed was 122mph/195kmh with 0-60mph in 8.5 second (manual) or 9.3 seconds (automatic).

**SV-1, 1975 model.** Prod: 2117. Although there was a '1976' model, this refers to 'model year' as Bricklin went into receivership in September 1975. After the 1974 model year, the manual gearbox option was dropped and both engines and transmissions were supplied by Ford. The new 5752cc V8 produced only 174bhp, and less torque, but maximum output in both areas came much lower in the rev range, so although top speed was slightly down at 118mph/190kmh, the 0-60mph dash time improved to 9.3 seconds.

## BRIGHTWHEEL (GB)

Originally a build-up specialist and an agent for Sheldonhurst, when the latter went into liquidation in 1986, Brightwheel took over the Sheldonhurst Cobra project, the chassis for which were made by the Rickman brothers. Ford Granada suspension was used and the Granada V6 was the favoured powerplant, although other units were available. Brightwheel was granted German TUV approval, exported turn key cars to Europe, and also made a copy of the Lamborghini Countach. The company collapsed in 1989 but the 'Cobra' was revived as the Cobretti (qv).

## BRISSONNEAU & LOTZ (F)

This company made a speciality of modifying the Renault 4CV and, in 1957, offered a two/three seat open car with a fibreglass body on a 4CV floor pan. Very few were made and the project was dead within the year.

Renault-based Brissonneau & Lotz, 1957

## BRISTOL (GB)

The origins of this company were in a partnership between the Bristol Aircraft Company and AFN Ltd, maker of Frazer Nash cars and the pre-war BMW concessionaire in Britain. Just after the War Bristol took possession of a number of BMW designs as war reparations. A conflict of philosophy split the partnership and AFN resumed Frazer Nash production using Bristol engines. By 1960 problems in the aircraft industry meant the money was not available to build a proposed dohc 3.65-litre engine and the car company became a private concern owned by Sir George White who, as chairman of Bristol Aircraft, had been partly responsible for creating it. Tony Crook, who was associated with Bristol from its earliest days, became a director and, in 1966, a partner. He has since become the proprietor and has concentrated on American-engined 'businessmen's expresses', a line which began in 1962.

**400, 1947-50. Prod:700.** The 400's box-section chassis derived from BMW 326, its aluminium body was based on the BMW 327/80, and the six-cylinder 1971cc cross-pushrod engine came from the BMW 328. However, all the elements went through Bristol's drawing office which substituted British thread sizes and made other minor adjustments, while the whole car showed the benefits of Bristol's aircraft-quality engineering. As produced by Bristol, the engine was under-powered with only 80bhp (it was regarded by BMW as obsolete). AFN wanted to use a 2.5-litre dohc straight six BMW had on the stocks, or at least tweak the 328 unit to give 120bhp, a fundamental difference which caused the split. Early 400s had three SU carburetters (some very early examples had only one carburetter) but these were soon replaced by three Solex carbs. The 400 had a top speed of only 94mph/151kmh but had excellent handling and one finished 13th from 303 starters in the 1949 Mille Miglia.

400, the first Bristol

Pininfarina started a trend when it created a handsome cabriolet body for the 400, and 17 examples were made.

**401, 1948-52. Prod: 650.** Introduced at the 1948 London Motor Show and at first for export only, the 401 retained

Bristol 401 arrived in 1948

the chassis and running gear of the 400 with its transverse leaf i.f.s. and solid rear axle suspended on torsion bars. Although Carrozzeria Superleggera Touring is often credited with the styling, in fact it provided only the base design (which anyway had some similarity to the Farina-bodied 400) and the final shape was arrived at by Dudley Hobbs after considerable work in Bristol's wind tunnel, something of a novelty in 1948. Hobbs' work included contour-hugging bumpers and flush press-button door locks while Touring's main contribution was the *Superleggera* construction, which it pioneered. Apart from a more modern appearance, the 401 was much roomier than the 400 while the weight was comparable.

**402, 1948-50. Prod: 20.** Announced at the same time as the 401, the same comments apply to this close-coupled four-seater cabriolet, although the chassis frame was slightly lengthened to re-locate the fuel tank. With the hood stowed the 402's lines were extremely elegant but when it was raised it gave the car a distinctly Teutonic look which ill became an essentially Italianate style.

Bristol 402, cabriolet sister of the 401

**403, 1953-55. Prod: 300.** An improved 401 and the car which Bristol could have built five years earlier. Despite a new crankshaft, camshaft and larger valves, the engine still gave only 100bhp, which was a long way short of its potential. A front anti-roll bar and Alfin brake drums completed the plot but falling production figures tell their own story. The main external difference to 401 was the silvered radiator grill and the few examples made in 1955 had 105bhp engines, like the 404 and 405.

Bristol 403 (behind) and the exquisite 404

**404, 1953-55. Prod: 40.** Built on the same short wheelbase as the Arnolt-Bristols, the 404 was a case of Bristol missing the boat, because few buyers wanted a two-seater costing twice as much as a Jaguar XK140, which out-classed it in every way. Engine options included a 125bhp version (at last) but even so the car's top speed was only 110mph/177kmh. Its body was among the most lovely of its time, with little tail fins echoing the huge fins on the Bristol 450 racing coupés, while the radiator grille shrugged off the BMW ancestry and was inspired by the leading edge of the wings of the ill-fated Bristol Brabazon airliner. Unfortunately the body was of aluminium on a pitch pine frame, and that is the weak element of those cars which have survived.

Using the same chassis, Arnolt (qv) made a much better car at half the price—and sold twice as many.

**405, 1954-58. Prod: 297.** Like most of the early Bristol range this car only just qualifies for inclusion in a book on sports cars. The 405 was basically a long wheelbase 404, although without the 125bhp engine option, and it is still the only four-door car the company has made. It was also the

405 was a four-door

first Bristol to have an opening boot and although some wood was used in the construction of its body, most was above the waistline so the problems of survival are potentially less severe than they are on the 404. A Laycock de Normanville overdrive was standard as were Michelin X radial tyres. Front disc brakes came in 1958 and a two-door cabriolet version (43 made) was also marketed up to 1956.

**406 Zagato, 1960-61. Prod: 7.** Bristol's last car to use the BMW-based engine, the standard 406 was an expensive, and rather staid, tourer. Although the engine was enlarged to 2216cc to improve torque, maximum output remained at 105bhp. On the other hand, the much lighter

Bristol 406 Zagato

Zagato 2+2 version which used a shortened chassis, and had a 130bhp engine, was good for 120mph/193kmh and was still a listed model when Jaguar unleashed the E Type at a fraction of the price.

Later Bristols, with big American engines, had much better performance (the 411 is the best of the bunch) but the 406 Zagato is the most exciting model the company made. Barring its disc brakes, it could have been ten years earlier but Bristol aspired to fill the gap vacated by the Crewe-built Bentleys, 'The Silent Sports Car', and was not interested in out and out performance.

*Postscript:* Since 1962, all Bristols have been built on the traditional chassis, continuously developed, with Chrysler V8 engines and automatic transmissions.

## BRITANNIA (GB)

Acland Geddes dreamed of making cars and, in 1957, he commissioned John Tojeiro to design a GT car. Unfortunately Geddes, who was related to the Dunlop empire, did not back his enthusiasm with efficiency, the project lacked direction and the car itself offered little for its £2400. It might also be added that Tojeiro had previously designed only racing cars and that, by 1957, the car market was demanding higher levels of sophistication than one designer working alone could achieve.

**Britannia GT outside the factory**

A tubular chassis with all-independent suspension, a 2.6-litre straight six Ford Zephyr engine given the full Raymond Mays treatment (say, 110bhp) and a reasonably pretty, but not exceptional, fibreglass body were the ingredients of Acland Geddes' dream car. No contemporary magazine subjected one to a road test (itself not a promising sign), so there is no reliable indication of its performance and competence. Had it sold for half the price, it might have found a niche in the market, alongside the Peerless/Warwick, and as an alternative to the Daimler SP250. The real wonder is that Geddes found six people who preferred his special to the cheaper Jaguar XK150S.

Britannia also made Formula Junior cars to boost its image but these were undistinguished, so the image was not boosted. When the receiver was called in 1960, Tojeiro himself bought some of the remaining Britannia FJ frames and components and marketed the car under his own name. They went no better for the change of name.

## BRUNNSCHMID AMD (D)

Founded in 1982, Brunnschmid specialises in converting and customising cars, especially Porsches.

**Brunnschmid AMD 1985 Porsche 935 Turbo**

## BRÜTSCH (D)

Egon Brütsch was a racing driver who essayed a number of prototypes during the 1950s, and some of his egg-shaped mini cars reached production under licence in Switzerland and France. In 1953 Brütsch showed a pretty two/four seat car based on the running gear of the Ford Taunus 12M Sport. It had a side valve engine of 1172cc (a famous size), offered in 38bhp or 46bhp versions, and a four-speed ZF gearbox in place of the three-speed Ford unit. The aluminium cabriolet and coupé bodies were to have been made at a rate of about one a week by Wendler of Reutlingen but the project collapsed.

**Brütsch 400, 1952**

**1172cc Brütsch-Ford, 1953**

**Brütsch V2, 1957**

It was later taken over by a company called Wacker, which offered the design with a revised body made of fibreglass. Few were made.

## BUBK (J)

Introduced in the late 1980s, BUBK's 'Le Seyde' was a Japanese 'nostalgia' car, which is to say a parody of the excesses of 1930s style on a modern chassis. In this case the base car was the Nissan 200SX, an excellent car in its own right, and handsome too. Why anyone would want to pay extra for a caricature of style on top of a terrific chassis is a mystery.

## BUCHANAN (AUS)

Nat Buchanan was an Australian pioneer of fibreglass bodies who made his mark with a shell to convert MG TCs into a 'modern' sports car. At the time that was not considered heresy, the shells sold well and competition successes blazoned the Buchanan name. Encouraged by this, Buchanan decided to market a small-engined sports car in 1958, but even as it was being readied for production the Austin-Healey Sprite came on the scene and stole its thunder—and sales.

The Cobra was a practical design with a good standard of finish, a useful boot, wind-up windows and, bearing in mind local conditions, a decent ground clearance. Unfortunately it was based on Standard Ten components in a bespoke chassis so, despite its low weight, it offered no advantage over a Sprite. Plans to market the car through Australian Standard-Triumph dealers came to nothing and the project was abandoned after just seven had been made.

## BUCKLE (AUS)

Australia's first home-grown postwar sports car was designed and marketed by Bill Buckle who drove one in competition with some success. In essence the Buckle GT was a fully assembled 2+2 based on Ford components. It featured a box section chassis, fibreglass body and a 2.6-litre straight-six Zephyr engine which meant it was good for 100mph/161kmh. Many, however, were fitted with the Raymond Mays conversion which made them fairly potent machines. Although the style was similar to any number of fibreglass bodies of the time (i.e. undistinguished), features included fold-down rear seats and electrically operated door locks.

It did not sell very well (only about 25 examples between 1956 and 1960), partly due to its high price, and Buckle lost heavily on the project. He was more successful with another enterprise, the importation of Goggomobil cars (qv), and the creation of the 'Dart' which was a Goggomobil floor pan fitted with a pretty two-seat fibreglass body.

## BUCKLER (GB)

Derek Buckler was inspired by the idea of bringing motor sport within the range of everyman by selling high quality, reasonably priced, kits. Not only was Buckler the father of the kit car, he was the first maker anywhere to sell space-framed sports cars (the company's last gasp was an advanced backbone chassis), while Buckler close-ratio gears were a standard fitting on all serious Ford specials, including early Lotus and Lola designs. A wide variety of frames were marketed (total production of all types was about 500) and when fibreglass bodies appeared, Buckler made frames to fit the better examples.

When karting arrived in Britain, it was natural for Buckler to embrace it since it was motor sport for everyman, and at first Buckler karts were very successful. By 1962 the Mini and Sprite had killed the kit car market and Buckler himself was in declining health. The company was sold but, without the inspiration of its founder, it soon went under. The following entries are representative of the Buckler range and both were sold as kits or exported as complete cars.

**MkV, 1949-62.** The first of more than a dozen Buckler designs was a versatile machine which won awards in trials, races, rallies, sprints and driving tests. Specification varied according to the customer's purse but could include Buckler close ratio gears, split axle i.f.s., a supercharger and an aluminium

Buckler MkV

body specially designed for it by another, loosely-related, firm. If a car was well finished Buckler would give the owner a bonnet badge but the number of badges issued has never been disclosed.

Available throughout the company's life, some MkVs were supplied complete and the first British car with a fibreglass body was a MkV in 1953. Buckler entered the prototype in races, rallies, trials, hill climbs, and driving tests (and used it as a road car), and he took over 200 awards. By the end of 1952, the day of the multi-purpose car was over. Why MkV for a first design? Buckler wanted to give the impression that it wasn't a first effort.

**Ninety, 1954-62.** A dual-purpose road/race car with a slippery body that pre-dated the first aerodynamic Lotus

Buckler 90 on the circuit

(the MkVIII), the Ninety was quite successful in club racing but Buckler's insistence on using Ford components, including wheels, cable brakes and split axle i.f.s., restricted its potential. Some cars were fitted with the Coventry Climax FWA engine and almost all Nineties used the 'official' body supplied by a shop next door. Later models included the DD1 and DD2, with de Dion rear suspension, and were intended to used proprietary fibreglass bodies. All Bucklers were noted for their high quality but that meant they could not compete with some of the gimcrack outfits which sprung up in the late 1950s.

## BUGATTI (F)

Although Bugatti is one of the most famous names in motoring history, it has to be said that its moments of glory on the race track were actually fewer than is widely believed and were typically because the company was building racing cars when nobody else was. Thus The Bugatti Type 35 became famous by beating other Bugatti Type 35s in a period when motor racing was in the doldrums. Bugatti's designs were usually derivative and old fashioned. They stir the blood of modern enthusiasts largely because they were so pretty but the legend is so much more powerful than the actual achievement, and Ettore Bugatti was adept at promoting his legend.

By the mid-1930s the greater part of Bugatti's business was general engineering. During the war it made prototype small cars (one of only 370cc) but these never saw production. The death of Ettore Bugatti in 1947 scotched further work on new cars (Jean Bugatti, his natural successor, had been killed in 1939) for the cars were sold on the maker's charisma.

After the founder's death the firm survived on sub-contract work but the marque was briefly revived in 1951 by Roland Bugatti. A short period of prosperity due to supplying defence contracts led, in 1956, to a radical mid-engined Formula One car (the Type 251) which was an unmitigated disaster. Defence contracts dried up and so work was abandoned on the Type 252, which was intended to be a sports car with a dohc 1.5-litre four cylinder engine. Later a V12 GT car (the Type 451) was proposed, but it had not progressed beyond preliminary drawings when the company was sold to Hispano-Suiza in 1963. Bugatti was later absorbed by the government-owned aerospace company, SNECMA.

In 1988 the dormant trademark was sold to an Italian entrepreneur who unveiled the EB110 GT, a four wheel drive supercar with a 550bhp V12 turbocharged engine. The EB112, a four-door saloon was shown in 1993, and that year Bugatti acquired Lotus. The cars did not sell in the market of the early 1990s (they might have done in the late 1980s) and the company collapsed in 1995.

**T101, 1951-56. Prod: 6.** Bugatti's last production model was really only a lightly modified Type 57, the most prized of all Bugatti road cars, which first saw the light of day in 1934. Thus the T101 had a dated specification with front and rear solid axles and suspension by semi-elliptical springs. A dohc straight eight engine of 3,257cc gave 135bhp unblown, or up to 200bhp if the optional supercharger was fitted; a five-speed gearbox was listed but all six cars built had a four-speed unit. Beautifully made and handsome, it

**Bugatti T101, 1951**

was also heavy (3200lb) and outrageously expensive, and not even widespread veneration for the marque could entice buyers.

**Bugatti EB110, 1993**

## BUGETTA (USA)

Introduced in 1968, this short-lived venture was a mid-engined 2+2 open fibreglass-bodied car with a 4.8 litre Ford V8 engine.

## BUG RIO (BR)

This company hardly needs an entry because the information is in its title! Bug Rio makes beach buggies in Rio de Janeiro and naturally uses a VW Beetle base, and it also makes a rather boxy Targa-top sports car on the same foundation.

## BUICK (US)

David Buick began making cars in 1903, and in 1908 his company became a founder member of General Motors. Buick became GM's mid-range marque and was quite often the division chosen to spearhead technical innovation (such as automatic transmission) and styling features. By the late

1980s the Buick range was largely conservative, so it was something of a surprise when, in 1988, it launched the Reatta. This two-seat coupé was based on the floor pan of the Buick Riviera saloon, and it more or less took over the market space vacated by the Pontiac Fiero (also a GM car), but it lacked the Pontiac's brio and the fact that a manual gearbox was not available speaks volumes.

**1990 Buick Reatta**

A 3.8-litre V6 engine was mounted transversely at the front and delivered its 165bhp to the rear wheels. Unlike the Fiero, unitary construction was used (with a front subframe) and the all-independent suspension was by MacPherson struts at the front with, at the rear, a transverse fibreglass leaf spring and both longitudinal and lateral arms. Disc brakes, with Teves ABS, were fitted to all four wheels and top speed was 124mph/200kmh (0-60mph in just under ten seconds). In 1990, a convertible was offered and this went some way to answering criticism about the car's style and interior.

## **BURLINGTON** (GB)

The 'Arrow', 'Beretta', and 'Dart' were '1930s style' sports cars using Triumph Herald/Spitfire chassis to be built from plans, although the company would supply its own chassis and body panels if required. In the early 1980s Burlington also marketed the 'Centurion', a coupé based on a Triumph Herald/Spitfire chassis, but the expertise required for the home builder to make compound-curve body panels meant

**Burlington Arrow, 1983**

it was never popular. In addition, Burlington originated the 'SS', a copy of the Morgan, later marketed as the Dorian SS. Burlington was founded in 1980, and was still active in 1990.

## **BUROCHE** (GB)

A Ford-based kit car of the 1950s which, unusually, had an aluminium body styled after a front-engined Ferrari Grand Prix car. Despite this, few were made.

## **BUTTERFIELD** (GB)

An unsuccessful 1961 attempt to market a two-seater coupé with tubular chassis, fibreglass body and Mini mechanicals.

# C

## CADILLAC (USA)

Founded by Henry M. Leland in 1903, Cadillac began by making simple single-cylinder cars. In 1908 it was one of the founder members of General Motors and quickly became the corporation's luxury badge. Apart from luxury cars, Cadillac became especially noted for its engines, and its first V8 arrived in 1915. In the 1930s the company produced cars with V12 and V16 engines—America was streets ahead of any other country in casting techniques and these were mass-produced and, by European standards, inexpensive.

After the Second World War Cadillac led the craze for fins and chrome but in more recent years the marque's styling has been notably restrained. In 1986 it launched a luxury two seater, the Allante, with a body styled and made by Pininfarina. In the manner of Mercedes-Benz, the Allante was a convertible supplied with a coupé hardtop. At first sales were disappointing, but in 1988 it received a larger and more powerful engine and revised suspension. This 4.5-litre fuel injected V8 was mounted transversely at the front and delivered its 200bhp to the front wheels via a four-speed automatic transmission. Construction was unitary (with a front subframe), the all-independent suspension was by MacPherson struts at the front while the rear layout employed a transverse fibreglass leaf spring with longitudinal and lateral locating arms, and disc brakes with Bosch ABS were fitted all round. Top speed was 124mph/200kmh and 0-60mph could be achieved in 8.9 seconds.

**The 1986 Cadillac Allante**

## CALIFORNIA ACE (USA)

Would you believe a 1980s Californian copy of the (late body style) AC Ace? In essence, this 'Ace' was an MGB with a fibreglass and Kevlar body.

## CALLAWAY (USA)

From the mid-1980s, Reeves Callaway made a turbo conversion for the Chevrolet Corvette which could be specified when a customer ordered his car from his local Chevy dealer, and it came with a full factory warranty (*see* Chevrolet Corvette). Callaway also made a Corvette-based car, the 'Sledgehammer' coupé, which had 920bhp from its enlarged and turbocharged engine. The prototype was officially timed at 254.76mph/409.91kmh, which made it the fastest road car ever, yet apparently it was sufficiently tractable to drive to work. It was not simply a case of adding large turbochargers, there was some subtle re-styling with particular care taken on aerodynamics; there was a six-speed ZF gearbox and selective ride control. Early in 1991 Callaway showed the Twin Turbo Speedster, based on the Corvette L98 with an 'Aerobody' convertible body and 450bhp V8.

Callaway was also responsible for the 'four valve' head used by Aston Martin.

## CAMBER (GB)

One of a number of cars which appeared in the 1960s using Mini components, the Camber was the work of George Holmes and Derek Bishop, who was boss of Heron Plastics and who had a garage in Camber Sands, Sussex. A fibreglass coupé body was mounted on a tubular frame, to which Mini subframes were bolted, and its roof was reinforced with sheet steel bonded into the plastic. It was a particularly well made car but the headlights of the first five cars completed were below legal height; the sixth was converted by the distributors, Checkpoint Ltd, and had cowled, square, lights.

A disagreement between the two men saw Holmes take over production after six had been made, and he renamed the car the 'Maya'. The Maya had a revised shell which met the law, final specification was chosen by the customer and options included rear seats. Holmes' death in a road accident spelled the end for production after a further six cars had been made.

**Maya GT**

## CAMDEN CARS *see* PARAMOUNT

## CANSTEL (AUS)

Over the years, the Canstel has been made by different companies and has come, gone, and returned again. Sold mainly in kit form in Australia, it bore more than a passing resemblance to the Lotus/Caterham Seven but its ingredients were a fabricated backbone chassis, Triumph Herald suspension (a

**Cobra 289, in right-hand drive form and carrying the appropriate AC badge. Elsewhere the car was presented as a Shelby or even Ford Cobra**

**Austin-Healey 3000, here in MkII form, was firmly in a British sports car tradition that was passing while it was in production**

Jaguar's E-type, on the other hand, was in the forefront of a new sports car generation. This is a Series 2 roadster with the classic twin-ohc straight six in 4.2-litre form

The Triumph TRs were robust and honest sports cars, which steadily became more refined. This TR4 has a modified TR3 chassis carrying a body designed by Michelotti. It was the first TR to have wind-up windows. A hard top slipped neatly onto the 'Surrey top' as a more rigid and weatherproof alternative to the usual soft top

live axle was optional), a fibreglass body, and a choice of engines (the Ford 1.6-litre unit was the most popular). The project folded in 1973 after 39 kits had been sold but it was revived in other hands in 1977. It was re-engineered to meet modern type approval requirements, while the cockpit made concessions to modern expectations of comfort and equipment.

## CAR (GB)

Classic Automotive Reproductions was an early 1980s outfit which would build a turn key copy of any exotic car the customer desired although most of the few made were 'Countachs' and 'Cobras' usually using Jaguar running gear. CAR also offered a copy of the Mercedes-Benz SSK which could be had with a variety of engines from the Rover V8 to the Jaguar V12.

**Rover V8-powered CAR, 1984.**

## CARISMA (GB)

Maker from the late 1980s of a 'traditional' sports car inspired by the SS100 and based on Ford Pinto running gear.

**Carisma**

## CARLTON (GB)

A kit car maker whose 'Carrera' was introduced in 1985 and combined style elements of the Datsun 280Z, the Ford Capri and the Porsche Turbo. Various engine options were possible, from Ford 1.6-litre to Jaguar XK units. In 1989 it was joined by the 'Acer', a Vauxhall-based copy of the Turner MkI Sports originally made by MC Cars. In 1990 Carlton was working on the C400, which was an evocation of the 1966 De Tomaso Pantera based on Ford Granada components and intended to carry a Rover V8 engine driving through a Renault transaxle.

## CAROUSEL (ZA)

From the late 1980s a maker of a 'shrunk' copy of an Aston Martin V8 using Ford Cortina suspension and a 3-litre Ford V6 engine in a ladder frame. The standard of trim was high and only complete cars were sold. Carousel also made a copy of the 1929 Mercedes-Benz SSK.

## CARTER CONVERSIONS (USA)

Despite the fact that the Pontiac Fiero was superior to the Ferrari Dino in several important areas, not to mention quality of build and reliability, in the late 1980s Carter Conversions began to practice plastic surgery on Fieros to turn them into Dino lookalikes.

## CATERHAM (GB)

Since 1973 Caterham has been the only authorised maker of the Lotus Seven, although the cars have always been marketed as Caterham Super Sevens. Along the way Caterham has had to fight off pirate versions of the Seven and has had some success in the courts.

Caterham began by taking over the Series Four model but, in 1974, when 38 cars had been built, the Series Four was dropped and the Series Three was revived. After that, the company did not look back and by 1990 had made over 3700 cars. In fact, the older the design became the more popular it was, and in the late 1980s it became a cult car in Japan, where hundreds were sold.

**Caterham Super Seven**

Those sold in Britain have been kit or component cars and, until 1990, the usual power unit was always Ford or Lotus Twin-Cam, and performance depended both on the type of engine, and its state of tune. With a 135bhp 1.71-litre version of the Ford 'Kent' engine, for example, it would sprint to 60mph in just over five seconds and reach a top speed of 112mph/180kmh.

The HPC model of 1990 used a version of the 2-litre 16-valve Vauxhall engine, with two twin-choke Weber carburetters in place of the normal fuel injection. This meant 175bhp, a top speed of 126mph/202kmh and 0-60mph in 5.2 seconds. Standard on this model was the de Dion rear suspension which had been an option since 1987, and this allowed the fitting of disc brakes all round.

While the Caterham had all the advantages of the Lotus original—terrific steering and chassis and phenomenal road performance—it also had all the drawbacks of the original, notably cramped cockpit, tiny fuel tank, primitive weather equipment, and hard ride. The difference is that back in 1957 a Lotus Seven was likely to be its buyer's only car whereas the Caterham increasingly became a fun car for fine weekends.

## **CAVALLO** (GB)

First shown in 1983, the Cavallo Estivo was a high quality component car with handsome and original styling. It had a four-seat convertible body and used the running gear from the BL 1100/1300. Hailed as an important new addition to the British kit car scene when it first appeared, its actual production life was short.

**CCC** *see* TRIPLE C

## **CDS** (D)

Car Design Schacht was established in the 19th Century but among its late 1980s products were customised and modified versions of BMW and Mercedes-Benz models.

## **CENTAIRE** (MC)

Announced in 1990, Monaco's only sports car was a stubby confection of unfortunate aspect. The basic specification followed current Group C thinking with a carbon fibre and aluminium honeycomb monocoque, and body panels of carbon fibre and Kevlar. It was launched to celebrate 100 years of the Automobile Club de Monaco, and intended to be a limited edition of about twenty cars, yet from the start it was surrounded by controversy. It was presented at the only press launch from which the press were excluded and its backers claimed that it would have a Lamborghini Countach engine but Lamborghini denied this.

## **CENTAUR** (AUS)

In the late 1950s and early 1960s, Tim Harlock built a small number of Centaur dual-purpose cars in Brisbane. They were in the Lotus Seven idiom with a space frame, aluminium body and, usually, a small Ford engine. At least one coupé was built and this had a Holden engine.

## **CENTAUR** (GB)

Centaur was the name under which a version of the Adams Probe was marketed by a company called Concept Developments between 1974 and 1978. Like the original Probe, it used Hillman Imp running gear and a monocoque made from a sandwich of plywood and fibreglass. It was later sold as the 'Pulsar'.

## **CENTAUR** (USA)

Introduced in 1980, this was a close copy of the 1936 Mercedes-Benz 500K special roadster. It was built on a GM frame with a 3.8-litre V8 engine and automatic transmission.

## **CG** (F)

Between 1967 and 1974 CG had a special relationship with Simca and made mid-engined fibreglass roadsters and coupés using Simca engines, from the 944cc unit to a supercharged version of the 1.3-litre engine. Production was tiny, less than one a week, and the firm never established more than a local reputation.

**CG coupé**

## **CHEETAH** (USA)

By 1963 Californian Bill Thomas had become the top Chevrolet tuning wizard but his thunder was being stolen by the Ford-engined Cobra. He therefore built a car to rival it and his Cheetah did more than rival the Cobra—it out-performed it. Despite the legend of the Cobra, one has to say this was not difficult since it is one of the most over-rated cars ever made.

The Cheetah was a coupé which appeared to be all nose and no body, largely because its 400bhp 6.1-litre engine was

**Cheetah gull-wing coupé—practically mid-engined**

set well back into the frame to give a 45/55 weight distribution, much the same as a mid-engined car. In fact the engine was so far back that the gearbox was attached to the differential by a universal joint, not a prop shaft. Most of the components, including the independent rear suspension (converted to coil springs) were stock Corvette parts. To judge by the car's performance on the race tracks, even when pitted against sports-racers, it had outstanding handling to go with its power, excellent traction and brakes.

Unfortunately, Chevrolet did not want to become involved and Thomas' attempts to build a hundred so they could be homologated came to nought (well, to sixteen). Thus, when Cheetahs were raced they were not pitched against Cobras and the like, but against the new breed of mid-engined British sports-racers, despite the fact that they were road-legal dual purpose cars.

In the 1980s the Cheetah received an accolade when an American company, Elegant Motors, marketed a copy of this extraordinary gull-wing coupé.

## CHEETAH CARS (GB)

Cheetah was a short-lived maker of copies of the AC Cobra, the Ford GT40 and the Lamborghini Miura in the mid-1980s. The 'Miura' was powered by a 1.6-litre Ford XR3i engine while the 'GT40' was a cut-price version usually using a Renault V6 or a Rover V8 engine, and Ford Granada components. Quality and panel fit were indifferent, and Cheetah pitched its cars too low in the market place. The company also made the 'Shamal' an original 2+2 coupé which would take Ford Cortina, Lancia Beta, or Alfasud components. All one can say about the styling of this is that Cheetah should have stuck to aping the work of professional stylists.

## CHEVROLET (USA)

Although Chevrolet was named for Louis Chevrolet, a racing driver, the company had little to do with the sport, or sporting cars, for the first forty years of its life. Chevrolets sold on value for money and not long after being founded in 1911 it was one of the most popular makes in America. Chevrolet's original partner, W.C. Durant, was the man who formed General Motors and, from 1917, the marque became GM's inexpensive arm. It was the third most popular make in America by 1920 and, in 1931, knocked Ford from the top spot for three years. Ford and Chevrolet vied with each other for the honour of making America's most popular cars for a number of years and, by 1939, Chevrolet had sold 15 million cars.

By the 1950s Chevrolet had the upper hand and factors other than sheer volume were at play. America was entering the fins and chrome era, where image was everything and dream cars proliferated at motor shows. America was also importing floods of British sports cars yet, by comparison with domestic products, they were slow and expensive: in 1948, an MG TC cost $1895 when a 100bhp 3.8-litre Ford V8 coupé cost just $1300.

Obviously buyers were looking for more than just value for money, but a car which combined European qualities with American value had to be a winner. In 1951, Harley Earl the head of GM styling instigated an idea for a sports car to be sold for about $1850, the price of a 1948 MG, but it would have a 150bhp engine. Thus the 'Vette was born, although it had a troubled start and was nearly axed early in its life.

It took some time to establish the Corvette's reputation in its home market, and it has never had a great deal of 'badge' value in Europe, yet the model introduced in 1984 is one of the most competent sports cars ever made and can hold its own in any company except some of the limited-production supercars.

All Corvettes have been left hookers, even the ZR1 which was an Anglo-American Project. You can believe that Britain has a special relationship with America when you see a Corvette with right hand drive. Why have we been deprived?

**Corvette, 1953-54. Prod: 3955.** The original car cost a lot more than the target and the big news about the Corvette was that it had a fibreglass body. This was then a new 'wonder material' which also slashed tooling costs (but it took Chevrolet a long time to get the door sealing right). Part of the increase

**1953 Corvette**

in price over the target was due to the need for a new, smaller, chassis. This followed normal Chevrolet practice, comprising an X-member frame with boxed sides. Coil spring and double wishbone front suspension was used, with a live rear axle suspended on semi-elliptics and to that extent it was similar to British sports cars. It departed from British practice in that the old 'Stove Pipe' 3.8-litre straight six delivered its 150bhp through a two-speed automatic transmission and everyone knew that was wrong for a sports car.

Only 315 Corvettes were delivered in 1953, partly due to difficulties in making the body, and partly because, to raise the model's image, it was sold only to selected customers. Its first full year of production saw only 3640 sold, a third of the target, and 1500 less than Chevrolet made. It was priced at $3490, which was in sight of the Jaguar XK120, yet was good for only 107mph/172kmh (0-60mph in 11 seconds) and the handling was not right.

**Corvette, 1955. Prod: 674.** The car began to improve in 1955 when Ed Cole's new 4.3-litre V8, with a three-speed

**1955 Corvette**

manual gearbox, was offered as an option. This was one of the 'milestone' engines of the American motor industry and in its first version, gave 195bhp. It was also lighter and had more torque than the old straight six, and performance improved to a top speed of 119mph/191kmh and 0-60mph in 8.7 seconds. This was more like a sports car, particularly since Zora Arkus-Duntov was able to make some chassis and suspension adjustments which greatly improved road holding and handling. Only 674 cars were made (all but six with the V8 engine) and the Corvette looked set for the axe until Ford brought out the two-seat Thunderbird, at which point Chevrolet needed a sports car.

**Corvette, 1956-57. Prod: 9806.** Having been given a stay of execution, the Corvette emerged as a new car. The chassis remained basically the same, but Arkus-Duntov made further improvements to the steering and handling, although

**1956 Corvette had new style**

the all-drum brake system was far from perfect. Power was increased, and tune options ranged from a basic 210bhp (1956) to 283bhp (1957); with the latter tune, the 'Vette topped 130mph/210kmh (0-60mph in 5.7 seconds) which put it in a very select class indeed. Better still, the body was completely restyled with a sensuous shape which both recalled some European cars yet was 100 percent American. The old two-speed automatic transmission remained an option but in 1957 buyers could have a four-speed manual 'box, a limited slip differential, a choice of rear axle ratios and a suspension and braking package for competition use. When Corvettes did appear on the circuits they gave very good accounts of themselves, and even scored 1-2 in class in the 1957 Sebring Twelve Hours.

**Corvette, 1958-60. Prod: 29,099.** From 1958 the Corvette began to sell around 10,000 units a year, although the new version was a retrograde step in some ways. The purity of the 1956 car's lines were lost under chrome and fashionable 'quad lights', and weight increased by 200lb; like so many other sports cars it was moving away from its roots

**1958 Corvette got quad lights**

and becoming more of a GT car. The least powerful cars had 230bhp and the highest state of tune was the 315bhp option of 1960 but, overall, they were not as fast as the 1957 model. Although a number of performance options were available, others became incorporated into the basic car so, in 1960 the suspension was uprated while retaining the same chassis and basic layout of the 1953 models. The 'Vette was successful in American racing and one finished 8th at Le Mans in 1960.

**Corvette, 1961-62. Prod: 25,470.** Although Chevrolet had been playing with a smaller and more advanced Corvette, the introduction of its important new Corvair saloon meant

**1961 Corvette**

that the Corvette was simply revised. William L. Mitchell, who had taken over from Harley Earl as GM's styling chief, did a clever update of the body which recaptured the essence of the '56 car and also made reference to the special 'SS' racing 'Vettes built in 1957. There was no change in the chassis, or the basic engine options, but in 1962 came a 360bhp option which meant 0-60mph in 5.5 seconds and that made any other mass produced sports car look slow—it was not even bettered by the 1968 Ferrari Daytona. For that you paid $5000 and received a car which was also practical, reliable and comfortable. Top speed, however, remained at about 130mph/210kmh because the body was not slippery and it was also wise to pay extra for the special brake linings.

**Corvette Sting Ray, 1963-67. Prod: 117,964.** The Sting Ray was an entirely new car: the chassis was a new ladder frame, with a wheelbase shorter by 4in, and rear suspension was independent by jointed half-shafts, lateral and radius arms, and a transverse leaf spring, while an anti-roll bar was fitted to the big-engined options. Brakes were improved, although they were still drums until 1965 when all-round discs were an option. But, of course, it was the body (still fibreglass) which caught the attention because it owed nothing to any other car (except a Bill Mitchell special) and, in either roadster or coupé form, it was stunning. An identity feature was the split rear window of the 1963 model.

Even the humble 5.3-litre engine delivered 250bhp; the big block 6.5-litre engine of 1965 gave 425bhp; the 7-litre version gave up to 435bhp (with 460 lb/ft torque), and that meant 140mph/225kmh and 0-60mph in 4.8 seconds. Twenty cars were fitted with a 7-litre engine which gave 560bhp.

Corvette Sting Ray, 1963

There was a long list of civilised options, up to air conditioning, and they were incredibly cheap. Although no Corvette has ever had finesse in its road manners, the worst thing about them was that few left their native land.

*There is a difference between a Sting Ray and a Stingray—it is not a printer's error.*

**Corvette Stingray, 1968-77. Prod: 339,651.** The Sting Ray had succeeded beyond anyone's dreams, and its replacement was launched simply as the 'Corvette' but 'Stingray' (one word) was added in 1969. The chassis remained as before but disc brakes were standardised, wheels were wider, a three-speed automatic arrived at last, and although the wheelbase remained the same, length increased by seven inches. New US laws were beginning to bite yet the Corvette had 'impact' bumpers which integrated with the body, unlike the monstrosities which appeared on cars such as the MGB. The base engine of 1968 gave 300bhp; that had dropped to 165bhp by 1975 but recovered to 210bhp by 1977.

1969 Corvette Stingray

As always there were a number of options. The 7440cc engine of 1970 was the biggest power unit; this peaked at 425bhp in 1971 but output had dropped to 270bhp by 1973. Not all buyers liked the new style but the T-bar top was innovative. Early cars were dogged by poor workmanship and the big block cars had cooling problems. Factors including strikes and the oil crisis affected production but nearly 50,000 were made in 1977. A sign of the times was that the roadster was axed in 1975, due to falling sales.

**Corvette, 1978-82. Prod: 212,235.** Chevrolet went a long way down the line to making a mid-engined replacement but settled for a Stingray with a smoother fastback body, although the 'Stingray' name was dropped. In terms of marketing success, that was not a bad decision because 1979 saw production peak at nearly 54,000. The days of raw power were over, however, and the base engine was the 5.7-litre V8 which gave just 185bhp in 1978 (there was a 220bhp option that year). Power peaked at 230bhp in 1980 and was

1978 Corvette

down to 200bhp in 1982. A 180bhp 5-litre engine was an option in 1980. By 1982 the only gearbox was a four-speed automatic. Even though the days of brute force were over, the hottest (230bhp) 'Vette with a manual box could sprint to 60mph in 6.5 seconds and, thanks to a more slippery shape, touch 130mph/210kmh.

**Corvette, Introduced 1984.** The first entirely new Corvette since 1963 featured a pressed steel backbone chassis with an additional tubular structure and new suspension. In place of coil springs the double wishbone front suspension

1984 Corvette

had a plastic transverse leaf spring; the independent rear, also with a plastic transverse spring, had upper and lower trailing arms, lateral struts from the differential to the hub carriers, and tie rods. The wheelbase was shortened by two inches, and the body was shorter by nearly nine inches, but cockpit and luggage space were increased; there was careful attention to weight saving, and a '4+3' manual gearbox (i.e. there was an electronically operated overdrive on the top three ratios).

At first it was offered only as a 'Targa top', but a roadster became available again in 1986 (another sign of the times). The 5735cc V8 started with 205bhp but by 1988 this had risen to 245bhp which, thanks to the car's clean shape, meant 151mph/243kmh and 0-60mph in six seconds. To control that, the massive ventilated disc brakes were fitted with an ABS system.

**Corvette Callaway Twin Turbo, 1985-present.** Although this was an add-on conversion, by Reeves Callaway, customers could specify it on the options list when

Corvette Callaway Twin Turbo, 1988

they ordered a Corvette from their local Chevrolet dealer, and the warranty remained valid. The engine was completely rebuilt and blueprinted before two Rotomaster Compact turbochargers were fitted but apart from magnesium wheels and badges, the rest of the car remained untouched which spoke volumes for its inherent competence. With the Callaway conversion maximum power was 382bhp, with a staggering 562 lb/ft torque at only 2500rpm. Maximum speed of the roadster was 176mph/283kmh but the coupé, being more aerodynamically efficient, went on to 187mph/300kmh and acceleration figures were comparable, 0-60mph in 4.6 seconds, 0-100mph in 11.3 seconds. Callaway showed a Twin Turbo Speedster in 1991.

*For further variants of the Corvette see 'Callaway' and 'Jankel'.*

**Corvette ZR-1, 1989-present.** The ultimate factory-built Corvette had a dohc four valves per cylinder 5.7-litre V8, developed by Lotus, which also reworked the suspension. This engine delivered its 380bhp through a six-speed ZF gearbox but the top ratio, at 0.49, was an overdrive. Although the maker's claim of 180mph/290kmh was doubted by British road testers, they still conceded at least 170mph/273kmh, and the 0-60mph time of 5.6 seconds was mightily impressive, even if it was slower than the Callaway Twin Turbo version. Not all road testers praised the Corvette's handling but the ZR-1 has been called one of the world's great chassis. Identity features of this model over the standard Corvette are a two inch wider body and a more rounded tail treatment.

Corvette ZR-1

High performance costs and although the original Corvette was intended to undercut the MG TC, to bring a ZR-1 into Britain in 1990 would have cost approximately £70,000. Even so, compared to anything which had 'i' at the end of the maker's name that was a bargain.

*Postscript:* The Corvette was America's first mass-produced sports car, and although it was slow to get off the ground, it helped strengthen and advance Chevrolet's image. On the back of the Corvette's success, Chevrolet launched the Camaro muscle car in 1967 and successive descendents of this further strengthened their postion. So successful was this exercise that Chevrolet's sister division in General Motors, Pontiac, took the concept even further. In turn, Pontiac's success led Chevrolet to make the Camaro more sporting and aggressive. The range introduced in 1981 contained some models, such as the 5.7-litre IROC-Z which was a desirable 140mph/225kmh 2+2 available as a coupé or convertible.

Chevrolet's 2+2 Beretta coupé, introduced in 1987, was a sporting compact with front wheel drive and lively performance and special versions won their spurs in the IMSA-GTO Championship in 1989 and 1990. Chevrolet's *sports* car, however, was the Corvette.

## **CHICAGOAN** (USA)

Introduced in 1952, the Chicagoan was a two-seat fibreglass sports car using Willys running gear. In 1954, the name was changed to 'Triplex' but production ceased that year after about 15 cars had been made.

## **CHIMERA** (AUS)

Built by Australian sports and racing car designer, Henry Nehrybecki, the Chimera was first shown in 1980. Two had been built by 1986, but the Chimera apparently was a chimera. A four seater coupé, it had a body made of aluminium and Kevlar on a space frame, all-independent suspension and a 3.8-litre V6 Holden engine with twin turbochargers.

## **CHRYSLER** (USA)

Walter P. Chrysler's first job was as a floor sweeper for a railway company and, on ability alone, he rose to become President of Buick and a vice-president of General Motors. His reputation as a manager was so high that he was hired by a bank to sort out several other motor companies and this led to him taking over two of them, Maxwell and Chalmers, in 1923. In 1925 the Chrysler Corporation was formed.

From the start, the cars were sold on refinement and value, and they quickly became extremely popular in the middle range of the market. In 1928 Chryslers finished third and fourth at Le Mans and the same year saw the launch of the Plymouth and De Soto marques which allowed the corporation to expand into the cheaper end of the market.

Chrysler was often associated with technical advances and while it remained the smallest of Detroit's 'Big Three', it was a long way ahead of number four. In 1958 it began to expand as a multi-national when it took a stake in Simca which became full ownership in 1963. The following year it acquired the Rootes Group and took a 15 percent stake in Mitsubishi in 1970.

After the 1973 energy crisis, Chrysler began to shed its

overseas branches which included facilities in Spain, Turkey, South Africa and South America. In the late 1970s Chrysler became a wounded giant which recorded huge losses. Its fortunes were turned around by Lee Iacocca who was hailed as a miracle worker and who responded by becoming Mr Instant Opinion.

The 'miracle' was not sustained and Chrysler was in trouble again in the late 1980s, by which time it had acquired Lamborghini. Television advertisements in the late 1980s stressed Chrysler's sports car links and featured a Lamborghini, the Dodge Stealth (aka Mitsubishi 3000GT) and the Dodge Viper which then was a much-publicised prototype under development.

In 1983 Chrysler introduced its first two seat car, the GS coupé. This front wheel drive model was available in a number of equipment levels, and was also sold under a number of names including Dodge Daytona. Many would say that only

**Chrysler GS Turbo 2, 1987**

the top of the range car, the 'Shelby', was a true sporting car. In this form it came with a five-speed manual gearbox (the three-speed automatic was not listed as an option) and 174bhp from a turbocharged four-cylinder 2213cc engine. It was good for 138mph/222kmh (0-60mph in 8.3 seconds).

The Chrysler TC by Maserati, first shown in 1985, consisted of a luxuriously trimmed two-seat convertible body on the chassis of Chrysler's K-series range, with a four-valves-per-

**Chrysler TC by Maserati, 1987**

cylinder turbocharged 2.2-litre 'four' which delivered 200bhp. It was difficult to understand why Maserati was cited on the badge—it had been a long time since the once-great Italian company had been spoken of with respect, so this must have been the idea of a marketing man. It did not merit an association with Maserati, but it was not entirely a lost cause since it would top 138mph/222kmh and sprint to 60mph in 8 seconds.

## CISITALIA (I)

In 1939, Piero Dusio, a former soccer star, set up a company called *Consorzio Industriale Sportiva Italia* to manufacture and sell a range of sports equipment. In fact it spent the War years making military uniforms, and a fortune, and in 1946 offered a single seater racing car. This was powered by an 1100cc Fiat engine and was unusual in that it had a space frame—it was the first series-built racing car to use this type of construction. Since the cars were relatively cheap, and the first postwar design to be available, they sold in fair numbers and Dusio persuaded some Swiss backers to finance a 16-car 'circus' where leading drivers would draw lots for a car and race it. This fell through after a couple of races in the Middle East, but individual cars enjoyed a great deal of success for many years.

Cisitalia followed the success of its single seaters with lightweight two-seat open and coupé competition cars and despite the handicap of a tuned Fiat engine of only 1100cc, the great Tazio Nuvolari nearly won the 1947 Mille Miglia in one (the time taken to dry a flooded magneto dropped him to second place). That year saw the first Cisitalia road cars and the commissioning of a GP car designed by the Porsche studio; it had a space frame, a mid-engined layout and four wheel drive but, by the time it was ready to race, Cisitalia was in financial difficulties and it remained a great *What if?* Dusio had over-reached himself, the GP car had taxed his resources and in 1949 he closed down his factories in Italy and moved to Argentina (the company was not actually bankrupted).

**202 Gran Sport, 1947-49, 1950-52. Prod: Coupé 153; Cabriolet, 17.** In essence, the Gran Sport was similar to any number of Fiat specials built just before, and after the War. Apart from the space frame, everything came from the Fiat 1100:

**Cisitalia 202 Gran Sport, 1947**

front suspension was by a transverse leaf spring and lower wishbones; the live rear axle was suspended on semi-elliptics; the drum brakes came from the 1100 as did the four cylinder 1089cc engine and four-speed gearbox. The engine was tuned to give 66bhp, which was a good figure for the day. What set the car apart was a superb body by Pinin Farina which bore a family relationship to the shape he had created for the Maserati A6/1500, but was even more sleek. On all sides it was hailed as a masterpiece, but lovely though it was the Cisitalia was a Fiat special which could barely top 100mph yet cost twice as much as a Jaguar XK120.

*Postscript:* When Dusio reached Argentina, he founded

'Autoar' which built cars based on the Willys Jeep, but bearing the Cisitalia badge. With a new backer, a remnant of the Italian firm was revived in 1950 under Dusio's son, Carlo, but production was spasmodic at first and American customers in particular were soon disenchanted. In 1952 the firm offered

**Cisitalia 847cc Coupé Tourism Special, 1963**

a new coupé with a fairly basic chassis, a de Dion rear axle, and a 160bhp 2.8-litre four-cylinder BPM marine engine. Although it was claimed to do 135mph/217kmh, making it one of the fastest cars in the world, it found few takers, for it simply did not have the élan of the original car.

An unsuccessful sports coupé version of the Fiat 1900 followed, and 1954 saw a customised Fiat 1100, with wire wheels and 70bhp engine, which sold about 100 examples. No cars were made between 1958 and 1961 but then Cisitalia came back with the rather pretty Coupé Tourism Special. This was really only a re-bodied Fiat 600, albeit with a choice of 750cc and 850cc engines. It wasn't a bad little car, but the badge had more weight than its competence could bear and, after a chequered history, the company finally folded in 1965.

## CITERIA (NL)

This promising Dutch project of 1958 was a handsome lightweight fibreglass two-seat hardtop. Power came from a 30bhp 600cc BMW flat-twin engine and suspension was independent all round. BMW's own 700 coupé which followed soon afterwards ruined the model's chances.

**1958 Citeria did not make production**

## CITROEN (F)

André Citroën began making cars in 1919, and these gained a reputation for being cheap and reliable. He made his big breakthrough with *Traction Avant* of 1934 which became more than a car, it became a symbol of France along with onions, the Eifel Tower, and that accordion which was always played in movies. Although it was to become a classic design, the cost of developing the car sent the company into bankruptcy and the Michelin tyre company acquired it. André Citroën died of cancer in 1935.

After the Second World War Citroën built cars as diverse as the 2CV and the DS 19, which is one of the few truly radical cars to have sold well. Citroën has never normally been associated with sports cars, but it surprised the world by announcing the Maserati-engined SM. In opinion polls about styling, this car regularly appears both on the 'Worst Ten' and 'Best Ten' lists of nominations.

**SM, 1970-75. Prod: 12,920.** Maserati supplied a 170bhp 2.7-litre dohc V6 (later seen in the Merak) and five-speed 'box; Citroën provided the hydro-pneumatic system which controlled the suspension, brakes and steering. It also supplied

**The Maserati-engined Citroën SM**

the body style with its six headlights, four of which swivelled with the steering wheel. A top speed of 140mph/225kmh was claimed, with 0-60mph coming up in 9.3 seconds, while the 3-litre fuel-injected version was even faster, although that was sold only with a three-speed automatic transmission. Only left hookers were made. Such a car seemed a good idea in 1970 but the 1973 energy crisis hit sales hard and when Peugeot-Talbot took over the company the SM was an early casualty.

## CIZETA (I)

Announced in 1989, the Cizeta Moroder was a massive (81in wide) mid-engined supercar with styling by Marcello Gandini, who was responsible for the Lamborghini Miura, Countach

**The 560bhp Cizeta Moroder, a victim of the 1990s market collapse.**

and Diablo. Its most unusual feature, however was its 6-litre V16 engine which was claimed to produce 560bhp. The car was predicted to reach 204mph/328kmh (0-60mph in four seconds).

## CK (GB)

Maker from the late 1980s of the GE 427, a Cobra copy which derived from the Gravetti GE 427 (qv). Since Bob Egginton of ASD was involved, the product was an improvement over the ill-starred original.

## CLAN (GB)

Colin Chapman changed the approach to racing and road cars by his own designs, and attracted a stream of like-minded individuals to work for him and inspired them to believe in themselves. Two such were Paul Haussauer and John Frayling, who worked on the Lotus Europa and thought they could see the next logical step. Chapman had his own views of how Lotus should develop, so Haussauer and Frayling founded a company to build the car they felt Lotus should have made. They attracted government grants to set up a factory in Washington, County Durham, and build the Crusader. Although this was nicely made, at £1400 it was a mite expensive for its performance so before long it was offered in kit form. When VAT was introduced in 1973 it damaged the kit car market and the final blow came in the same year when the OPEC oil crisis spread general panic.

**Crusader, 1971-74. Prod: 315.** Lotus nearly collapsed when it marketed the original Elite with its fibreglass monocoque but by the end of the 1960s the material was understood so an Elite for the 1970s was feasible. Clan used a Sunbeam Stiletto version of the Imp engine, mounted in the rear of a

**Clan Crusader, 1971**

neat, well finished and trimmed, two seat coupé (with seats for young children an option) which used a lot of other Stiletto components. Unfortunately, its performance on paper seemed modest for the price (100mph/161kmh top speed, 0-60mph in 12 seconds) but driving one was a different matter for it clung to the road and, indeed, was quite successful in competition. So much about the Crusader was right but it was a victim of circumstances which nobody could have foreseen.

## CLAN II (GB)

Despite having had its fingers burned by the DeLorean saga, the Northern Irish authorities gave backing to this attempt to revive the Clan Crusader in 1984. The born-again Crusader was distinguished from the original by having wider wheel arches and retractable headlights which gave it smoother nose lines but lost the car's idiosyncratic looks. Power came from the Imp engine, which was still in production for

**Clan II, 1987**

industrial use, and a model using the Alfasud engine and gearbox was also offered. The Belfast Clan promised much but, despite some success in rallying, the company folded in 1986 after about 40 cars had been made, including some for competition.

## CLASSIC AUTOMOTIVE REPRODUCTIONS *see* CAR

## CLASSIC CAR (D)

A late 1970s attempt to market cars based on VW Beetle running gear with fibreglass bodies originated by the American company, Antique and Classic (qv). If one was to be very charitable one might call them 'evocations' of classic designs, but a more realistic assessment is that they were nasty caricatures. The 4½-litre Bentley, Bugatti 35B, and SS100, were given this treatment. Apparently this company was a dead issue by 1980.

## CLASSIC FACTORY (USA)

Maker, from the 1980s, of copies of 1930s cars including Cord and Auburn and Mercedes.

**Classic Factory's '500K', 1988**

## CLASSIC MOTOR CARRIAGES (USA)

In the 1980s this maker claimed to be the 'world's largest

**'MG TD' by Classic Motor Carriages, 1982**

Classic Motor Carriages Tiffany in 1988

manufacturer of replicars and speciality automobiles'. Its MG TD copy and the Gazelle, evoking the Mercedes-Benz SSK were not very convincing but a VW-based version of the Porsche 356 Speedster, and the sports version of the same, were a different matter—at least on the surface. A Ford Cortina-based version of the Gazelle was offered in the UK for a short time.

## CLASSIC REPLICARS *see* REPLICAR

## CLASSIC REPRODUCTIONS *see* XK 120 Z

## CLASSIC SPORTS CARS (GB)

A company which, in the late 1980s, specialised in converting Datsun 240Z and 260Z into copies of the Ferrari 250GTO. A Rover V8 engine was an option. This nonsense was stopped by court order in 1989.

## CLEARFIELD (USA)

A short-lived maker of the mid-1950s which made fibreglass bodies for the likes of the Fiat Topolino and Crosley.

1956 Clearfield

## CLÉNET (USA)

An outrageous 'nostalgia' car at an outrageous price, the

Clénet Series I

Clénet was a two-seater with styling based on the Mercedes-Benz 540K (the cockpit area was MG Midget) which ran on a brand new Lincoln Continental chassis and drive train. A four-seater roadster was offered in 1979; the 1981 Series II was based on the Mercury Marquis; the 1982 Series III car had a 5-litre Lincoln-Mercury V8. Clénets were extremely expensive but came with every conceivable extra, and were made at a rate of about 125 units a year from 1976 until 1983 when the company ceased trading. The name and line were later revived by a former employee of the original company. In the wacky way of the copier, it was possible to buy a low-cost kit Clénet lookalike by the late 1980s.

## CLUA (E)

A short-lived (1958-59) attempt by a Spanish motorcycle manufacturer to produce an economy sports car. Looking a little like an MGB, the Clua Sports had a fibreglass body and a 497cc twin-cylinder motorcycle engine. Like most attempts to power a car with a motorcycle engine, it failed but about 100 examples were made.

Clua Sports, 1958

## CMC (USA)

In 1988, Corbett Motor Cars introduced the 'Countach 5000S', which was a fibreglass copy of a certain Italian car. For paupers, it could be built from a kit on a VW floor pan but the company made turn key cars using a variety of engines (Mazda rotary, Chevy V6 etc).

## COAST to COAST (USA)

In 1988, Coast to Coast Automotive Styling began to convert innocent Pontiac Fieros into something which suggested a styling heritage reminiscent of the top Italian design studios. In other words, its TR Fiero vaguely resembled a truncated Ferrari Testarossa.

## COBRETTI (GB)

A 1990 revival of the Brightwheel Cobra copy; the revised product was offered as the 'Viper'. It used Jaguar suspension and would take engine options from Rover V8 via Chevy V8 to Jaguar V12.

## COLANI (D)

Germany has spawned few kit makers, and that alone makes Colani unusual. Between 1964 and 1968 it offered a two-seat fibreglass body, in the style of contemporary sports-racers. It could be had as a coupé or a roadster and, naturally, used VW running gear.

## COLDWELL (GB)

Unsuccessful 1967-69 attempt to build a mid-engined Mini-based coupé. Six were made and the company later built some 2-litre sports-racers, which were not very successful.

Coldwell GT

## COMAHUE (RA)

An Argentine coupé introduced in 1968 which used the locally designed and built Torino sohc 3.8-litre straight six engine tuned to give 200bhp.

## COMMONWEALTH CUSTOM (USA)

Announced in 1980, the AR-1 was a mid-engined two seat coupé of ungainly aspect with a fibreglass body derived, at several removes, from the Ferrari 328, and with a pinch of the Ford GT40 thrown in for good measure. A modified General Motors V6 engine was used in conjunction with a ZF five-speed transaxle, and the company promised to tailor each car to the customer's requirements. It appears, however, that there were few, if any, customers.

Commonwealth Custom AR-1, 1980

## CONAN (GB)

A short-lived Lamborghini Countach copy of the mid-1980s notable for its use of a Lotus Esprit style chassis.

## CONDOR (D)

This 2+2 coupé was the final expression of the Trippel (qv) and Marathon (qv) lines and was made from 1957 to 1958. It had a steel backbone chassis, a fibreglass body, and all-independent suspension by swing axles and rubber in torsion. A three-cylinder two-stroke Heinkel engine of 677cc delivered its 32bhp through an all-synchromesh four-speed Getrag gearbox and a top speed of 80mph/130kmh was claimed. About 200 were made.

Condor S70, 1957, had 677cc Heinkel power

## CONNAUGHT (GB)

After the Second World War Rodney Clarke's Continental Cars garage had no new cars to sell but it was possible to circumvent the severe restrictions on the home market by buying rolling chassis. Thus Connaught sports cars were near-standard Lea-Francis 14 HP chassis with their four-cylinder 1767cc engines extensively modified by Clarke's partner, Mike Oliver, and bodies were built by Leacroft of Egham.

The first customer was Kenneth MacAlpine, who also commissioned Connaught to build F2 and F1 cars which handled superbly but were always let down by the lack of a competitive engine. Clarke was a brilliant innovator: he conceived a mid-engined GT car in 1950 (not built due to a lack of a suitable engine); he began work on a mid-engined monocoque F1 car in 1954 (not built because of the lack of a suitable engine); and he worked on such projects as an anti-lock braking system. Financial constraints hobbled his designs, and the activities of the Connaught racing team.

It should be noted, however, that the Connaught was the first British F1 car to win a Continental GP in the postwar era. Tony Brooks thrashed the works Maserati team at Syracuse in 1955. Alas, the entire project was dead by mid 1957.

**L2, L3, L3/SR, 1949-54. Prod: 6, 5, 5.** At first two models were offered, L1 and L2, but all six customers opted for the more powerful L2 which had up 102bhp as standard while up to 122bhp could be obtained. When Lea-Francis introduced torsion bar i.f.s in late 1949, the cars became known

Connaught L2

as L3s, but handling was inferior and only two were completed. Despite its beam front axle, and a chassis with the rigidity of a sponge, the L2 was a delight to drive although the cockpit was cramped. Despite appearances, boot space was virtually non-existent. When new, the L2 was good for 104mph/167kmh

(0-60mph in 11.9 seconds), which were excellent figures. Connaught sports cars achieved some minor competition successes. However, they were too expensive to sell well.

A stripped-down version, the L3/SR, was intended for the American market, but failed because it was expensive, poorly finished, and it was not particularly quick; only three were sold. When production formally ended in 1954 (it had actually ended years before) three remaining L3 chassis with Connaught-modified engines were sold on, but one has never been bodied.

Lea-Francis engined Cooper special

## CONTEMPORARY CLASSIC (USA)

From 1979, a maker of fibreglass-bodied Cobra 289 and 427 copies which used Jaguar suspension in a twin tube ladder frame with a choice of Ford V8 engines. An attempt to market it in Britain (as the 'Contemporary Cobra') in the early 1980s was unsuccessful but in 1990 it was imported by American Speed Specialities and sold as the Contemporary 427 SC.

## CONVAIR (GB)

A fibreglass 'special' body maker which essayed a kit car in 1958. It used a ladder frame, BMC series A engine and Minor (or A35) running gear, and Convair's not particularly handsome body. The venture ended within a year.

## COOPER (GB)

One firm which surely needs no introduction, Cooper concentrated almost exclusively on single seaters and bespoke sports racers but, in the early days, occasionally essayed a sports car. There was the one-off 'T4', basically an enlarged 500cc racer with an enveloping body and mid-mounted Triumph Twin engine. There was also an uncompleted prototype which was to have had a front-mounted JAP V-twin and some people even converted mid-engined Cooper 500 F3 cars to front-engined sports cars. In the end, only one Cooper sports car which could even pretend to be a dual-purpose machine saw series production.

**T6/T14/T21, 1948/1950/1952. Prod: approx 24.** The T6 was a front-engined sports car based on a similar chassis

Cooper T6 at Aintree, 1957

to the 500cc racers: independent suspension front and rear by top transverse springs and lower wishbones, joined together by a light but stiff chassis. The engine was mounted well back in the frame, which helped give it excellent handling and it was usually finished with a tight aluminium body and cycle wings. It was underpowered, however, and the T14 of 1950

Cliff Davis in a Cooper-MG at Castle Combe, 1953

was offered with a tuned MG engine. Some customers had their own bodies fitted and some used different engines. A second batch was made in 1952 and, before long, some Cooper-Bristol F2 cars were given sports bodies; most of these have been converted back to open-wheeled form for reasons not unassociated with current market value.

## COPYCAT (GB)

From the mid-1980s Copycat made a faithful Jaguar C Type copy using Jaguar components.

## CORBETT MOTOR CARS *see* CMC

## CORD (USA)

Built by Glenn Pray, who also made one of the cars which used the name 'Auburn', this was a 1964 revival of the great 1930s Cord 810/812. Gordon Buehrig, who styled the original car created a version which was about 80 percent of the original's size, hence it was marketed as the Cord 8/10. Like the original it had front wheel drive, this time by reversing the drive train of the Chevrolet Corvair. In 1968, it was taken over by another company which re-engineered it for rear wheel

**1965 Cord was scaled down**

drive. A Ford 4.8-litre V8 engine was standard fitting but a 7-litre Chrysler Magnum engine was optional. Production ended in 1972, by which time about 100 cars had been made.

## CORRY (GB)

In 1983 Ulster businessman Will Corry took over the assets of Davrian. The Corry Cultra was a modified Davrian with re-styled bodywork which was to few people's taste. A works car had a brief flowering of success in minor rallies but, after that, nothing more was heard of the Corry Cultra. The original (Davrian) concept, however, was revived as the Darrian (qv).

**Mid-engined Corry Cultra, 1983**

## CORSON (USA)

In the late 1980s, Corson was one of several American outfits which press-ganged Pontiac Fieros and made them look like something which resembled a Ferrari. In this case the Ferrari 512BB was the chosen victim and the cars were made in coupé or open form.

**1988 Corson**

## COSTELLO (GB)

In 1970, former saloon car racer, Ken Costello, began to install Rover V8 engines in MGB GTs and Roadsters. The result was a car which would top 128mph/206kmh, sprint to sixty in 7.8 seconds, and which found a steady trickle of sales. After a couple of years, British Leyland tried a Costello conversion, liked the idea, and promptly did everything it could to prevent Costello making more. In 1973, BL brought out its own version which, although generally considered inferior to the Costello car, undercut it in the market place, and came with a factory warranty. Costello converted over 200 cars before being forced out of business.

## COSTIN (GB)

In 1954 Frank Costin was working for the De Havilland aircraft company when his younger brother, Mike, sought his advice on an aerodynamic body for a special a friend of his was making. The friend was Colin Chapman, the special was the Lotus MkVIII, and so Frank became involved in motor racing. He designed a number of bodies for Lotus, introduced aerodynamics (as opposed to streamlining) to Formula 1 with his body for the 1956 Vanwall, and also designed bodies for Maserati and Lister.

In 1959 he collaborated with Jem Marsh to produce the Marcos (qv) and subsequently he designed a number of lightweight cars of outstanding aerodynamic efficiency, many of which used wooden monocoques. These included a prototype for TVR, the Costin-Nathan racing GTs, the Protos Formula 2 cars and the TMC-Costin (qv). In the late 1980s a financier tried to raise backing for a new Costin supercar which would have used a Cosworth DFV engine (Mike Costin is the 'Cos' of Cosworth) but although photographs of a model were issued, this project did not progress to a serious stage.

**Amigo, 1970-72. Prod: 9.** The Amigo typified Frank Costin's approach to motor cars: it was light, rigid, slippery and efficient, but little account was taken of the requirements of the market place. The monocoque was of plywood; front suspension was by a Vauxhall Victor pressed steel cross member with Vauxhall coil spring and double wishbones; rear suspension was by Victor live axle located by parallel leading links and a Panhard rod; the base engine was the 2-litre Victor VX4/90 unit and the same car provided the disc/drum braking system.

The Amigo was so efficient that with only 96bhp it would reach 137mph/220kmh (0-60mph in 7.5 seconds); by comparison the contemporary Ferrari Dino 246 needed 175bhp to reach 140mph (0-60mph in 8.0 seconds). With a tuned engine the Amigo could be really quick but it

**Costin Amigo, 1972**

cost £3,300 which put it on a par with the V12 Jaguar E Type. At that price, potential buyers wanted more conventional styling and items such as wind-up windows. Thus a car which was outstanding by any engineering standards was scuppered by the fact that most buyers prefer glitz to integrity.

## COVENTRY CLASSICS (USA)

A story for our time lies within this company's Z Jag Roadster, introduced in 1981, for it was an accurate copy

**Coventry Classics Z Jag Roadster, 1984**

of the Jaguar XK120 using the running gear of the Datsun Z series of sports cars. There was a time when the Japanese were great copiers.

## COVIN (GB)

Maker, from 1983, of kits to convert a VW Type 3 Variant or Fastback into a fibreglass 'Porsche' 911 Turbo. Porsche took

**Covin '911 Turbo' coupé, 1990**

legal action in 1985 and the result was a version with lightly revised body panels, which only a Porsche expert would spot. 1986 saw a version which used transversely mounted Ford engines (from the XR2 and XR3i) in a bespoke backbone chassis although the VW gearbox and torsion bar suspension was retained; a discreet radiator grill beneath the front number plate was the only giveaway. A cabriolet version was offered and a VW Beetle-based Porsche 356 Speedster copy was added in 1989.

## COVINI (I)

Covini began in 1978 with the manufacture of four wheel drive cross-country vehicles. In 1981 it showed a mid-engined GT car fitted with a 2.4-litre turbocharged VM diesel engine which delivered its 125bhp through a five-speed Lancia gearbox (a Lancia Gamma petrol engine was an option). This car had disc brakes and all-independent suspension. It appears to have faded soon afterwards.

## COX (GB)

First seen in 1967, the Cox GTM was a tiny mid-engined GT car using Mini running gear. Putting the engine behind the driver solved one of the problems inherent with cars using Mini components, its height, and the GTM was a very pretty car. It was based around a steel box section chassis, with modified Mini subframe, topped by a fibreglass body; it looked good, but it was difficult to build.

**Cox GTM, 1973**

The design's first years were marked by moves and company changes, but along the way it was improved in detail, and in 1990 was still in production by a company called GTM Cars, which seemed to be making a decent fist of it. GTM brought in Richard Oakes, of the Nova and Midas, the two lodestones of the kit car industry, and he did a top to tail rethink which was a lot more practical yet still managed to be a recognisable sibling of the original. The new/old car was known as the GTM Rossa and was available as either a roadster or a coupé.

## CREATIVE CARS (AUS)

In the late 1980s this outfit began converting the 1971-75 Toyota Celica into the 'Italia', an evocation of the Ferrari 308. If a customer favoured a more sober approach to engineering, it could supply the parts to convert a VW Beetle into a 'Porrera', which was a Porsche Carrera copy. Alternatively, the 'Poraga' had a Targa top.

## CRESPI (RA)

1969 saw the arrival of the Tulia GT, a fibreglass coupé which offered a choice of locally-sourced six-cylinder engines (e.g. Ford, Dodge, Chevrolet) in a conventional front-engined chassis. In the 1980s 4-litre Ford or 5-litre Chrysler were the engine choices, linked to a ZF gearbox. The handsome

**Crespi Tulieta GT, 1984, from Argentina**

Tulieta, introduced in 1975, came as a 2+2 GT coupé or convertible, both with fibreglass bodies, on locally-made Renault 6 chassis and with the 1.4-litre Renault 12 engine. Suspension was by torsion bars all round. Oddly, the Tulieta began life with drum brakes all round, though front discs arrived later.

## CROSLEY (USA)

Powell Crosley, a self-made millionaire, began making small simple cars powered by motorcycle engines just before the Second World War. After it he acquired the rights to a 722cc ohc four-cylinder engine originally commissioned by the US government. Between 1946 and 1952, Crosley made nearly 70,000 small cars (some as cheap as $299) before selling his diverse corporation to another company which ceased car production. By that time America had become affluent, and the American buyer wanted the fins and chrome which Detroit offered.

The engine, however, was still being made in 1990; it dominated SCCA Class H racing for decades and was even used by some European makers, such as Moretti and Bandini.

**Hot Shot/Super Sports, 1949-52.** **Prod: 2498.** America's first mass-produced sport car for many, many years; the only difference between the two models was that the Hot Shot had cutaway side panels and the 1950 Super Sports had doors. Both were tiny, ultra-light, not very fast, but a lot of fun—they were Sprites ahead of their time. Standard engines gave only 26bhp but tuning shops soon sold goodies and one in racing trim could deliver 55bhp, 75bhp if blown, and the good news was that they were virtually indestructible. There was a simple frame, a beam front axle on semi-elliptics while the live rear axle was suspended on quarter-elliptics. 1949-50 Hot Shots had Goodyear-Hawley 'spot' disc brakes, a first on a production car, but they were prone to seize and so were replaced by Bendix drums.

Crosley 722cc Super Sports, 1950

One of the first fibreglass bodies to be sold in America was made for a Crosley base and cars so finished were known as Wilro Skorpions.

## CSC (GB)

First shown at the beginning of 1953, the CSC 650 was one of several early-1950s attempts to market a lightweight sports car built on the lines of a two-seat version of a 500cc Formula 3 car. A tubular frame housed a vertical twin 650cc BSA gearbox which was modified to convert one of the four speeds to a reverse gear. The all-independent suspension followed Cooper lines, with transverse leaf springs and lower wishbones.

Since the kerb weight was only about 900lb, performance was quite brisk with 78mph/125kmh and 0-60mph in 17.6 seconds. The makers were nothing if not ambitious and announced that they had applied for an entry at Le Mans; that was wishful thinking, however, and since all contemporary photographs show the same number plate, it is likely that the car remained a prototype.

In 1955, the company tried again, this time using Austin A30 running gear in a tubular frame, topped off with a Rochdale fibreglass body. It is unlikely that any were sold.

## CUNNINGHAM (USA)

Briggs Cunningham, an American millionaire, was ambitious to win Le Mans and his cars came close several times (Cunningham himself was fourth in 1952 having driven 20 of the 24 hours). Had he succeeded it would have been a hugely popular win for his team combined style with sportsmanship—Cunningham was widely described as a 'sporting gentleman', the highest praise an Englishman can confer. In 1952, only bona fide manufacturers were allowed to run at Le Mans, so Cunningham laid down a run of road cars to qualify. The last Cunninghams ran at Le Mans in 1955, but that was by no means the last time a Cunningham-entered car ran there. The patron's finest hour came in 1958 when he skippered *Columbia* to win the America's Cup.

Cunningham C-1

1952 Cunningham C-4R sports racer

**Cunningham C-3. 1951-55.** **Prod: 27.** Based on the Cunningham C-2 sports-racer, which was theoretically available as a road car (brochures were printed but no cars were sold for the road), the C-3 was offered as a 2+2 coupé or a s.w.b. two-seater rag top (nine made) and both were styled by Giovanni Michelotti with bodies built by Vignale.

**Michelotti-styled Cunningham C-3 coupé, 1953**

Under the skin was a tubular chassis, with i.f.s by coil springs and double wishbones, a live rear axle (the C-2 had a de Dion system), and a 210bhp 5.3-litre Chrysler V8 engine which drove either through a Chrysler Fluid-Torque semi-automatic transmission or a four-speed ZF semi-automatic 'box. Handsome and quick (150+mph/240+kmh, 0-60mph in 6.3 seconds), the C-3 was also very expensive ($11,000+) which accounts for the low production, but in truth Cunningham was really only interested in racing. After building his own cars for five years, and failing to make a profit, under American law Cunningham was able to write off the total expenditure as a tax loss, something which explains why Lance Reventlow's Scarab project also lasted exactly five years.

## CURTANA (GB)

First shown in prototype form in 1990, the Curtana was the work of the Works Design Studio of Sheffield. It was a mid-engined open two-seat kit car with a difference: its styling was both original and extraordinarily striking—indeed it bore favourable comparison with many an Italian supercar. A tubular space frame accommodated an Escort Mk3 engine and all-independent suspension by coil springs and double wishbones.

**1990 Curtana prototype**

## CUSTOKA (A)

Introduced in 1971, the Custoka 'Hurrycan' was a 2+2 coupé

**Custoka Hurrycan of 1971 was VW based**

based on 1.6-litre VW Beetle running gear (the 1.7-litre VW-Porsche 'four' was an option); it had an original fibreglass body although the designer had obviously been smitten by the Ford GT40. The later 'Strato ES', was a fairly conventional fastback 2+2 coupé, which was shorter, narrower and marginally lighter, and less glamorous.

## CUSTOM DESIGN ASSOCIATES (USA)

Maker from the late 1980s of the 'GTF', an awkward evocation of the Ferrari GTB 308, front-engined because it was based on the Ford Pinto. A number of Ford engines could be fitted, from a 2.8-litre V6 to a 5-litre V8.

**1982 GTF by Custom Design Associates**

**The Lotus Six was Colin Chapman's first production car. The Seven (shown here), introduced in 1957, was a development of it and became Lotus' first popular road car**

**The Lotus Elite of 1957-63 had a drag coefficient of 0.29 to confirm visual impressions of aerodynamic efficiency. That figure was seldom matched 30 years later**

The Elan of the 1960s—this is a Sprint from late in that decade—was a pretty little car which started life as an open sports car and had become a GT car when production ended in 1973

**Caterham's Super 7 HPC marked a departure in 1990, for apart from very early Lotus suggestions that alternative engines such as the BMC A series unit might be fitted it was the first model in a 30-year-old series that was not powered by a Ford-based engine. Its 2-litre Vauxhall engine was rated at 175bhp in twin-carburetter form, and that was more than three times the power on offer in late-1950s Sevens...**

# D

## DAIHATSU (J)

Daihatsu's parent company began making internal combustion engines in 1907, three-wheeled vans in 1930, three-wheeled passenger cars in 1958, and four-wheelers in 1963. In 1967 Daihatsu was taken over by Toyota and has since maintained its own identity: dull.

**Compagno Sports, 1963-69.** The 'Sports' was not a European's idea of a sports car: it was a rag-top model in a range which included a saloon and an estate car (like the Triumph Herald) but the Japanese regarded it as a sports car in 1963 because there was nothing else around on their home market. All the range had separate chassis, with live rear axle suspended on semi-elliptics, and in 1965 front disc brakes were fitted. The first four-cylinder engines were 41bhp 797cc units but, in 1965, capacity was increased to 958cc. The sports version gave 65bhp, which was very respectable for an engine that size, and the car would top 90mph/145kmh.

797cc Daihatsu Compagno Sports, 1963

## DAIMLER (GB)

Founded in 1893 to exploit Gottleib Daimler's patents, Britain's oldest motor manufacturer was soon creating its own designs and before long had no formal links with the great German pioneer. The Prince of Wales (later Edward VII) bought a Daimler in 1900 and Daimler became the royal family's first choice for fifty years. The company, which had been taken over by BSA in 1910, found it hard to adapt to changed conditions after the Second World War, and saw its traditional market shrink. In 1954 Daimler moved down market with the small (2.5 litre) Conquest series of saloons, one of which, the 'Century', performed creditably in rallies and saloon car racing. The company then began to present a more sporting image but it was too small to survive as an independent and in 1960 was taken over by Jaguar.

**Conquest Century Roadster, 1954-55. Prod: 65.** Daimler's first sporting car since 1908, the Roadster fitted uneasily into the market: Daimler's image was hardly sparky, the styling was to few people's taste, and it was expensive. Under the skin it was pure Conquest, complete with 104in wheelbase, which explains the elongated shape and it weighed the same as the saloon, a portly 3100lb. Front

1954 Daimler Conquest Century Roadster

suspension was by wishbones and torsion bars, the live rear axle was suspended on semi-elliptical springs, while the straight six 2433cc engine was tweaked to give 100bhp and drove through a fluid flywheel and pre-selector 'box. Performance was hardly startling and although it has been called a '100mph' car, its true top speed was 89mph/143kmh and it took 19.7 seconds to reach sixty. On top of that it was thirsty (a driver was lucky to average 20mph) and the drum brakes were poor.

**Conquest Century Sports Coupé, 1956-57. Prod: 54.** The Sports Coupé had improved brakes and a third seat was placed across the back of the cockpit. Like the Roadster it had excellent luggage capacity and luxury items such as a power-operated hood and automatic chassis lubrication. Performance remained mediocre, although handling was quite good. At £1928 it was more expensive than a Jaguar XK150, which helps to explain its rarity.

**SP250, 1959-64. Prod: 2650.** Often erroneously called the 'Dart' (Dodge owned the name and stamped on the idea) the SP250 was distinguished by a splendid flexible 2548cc 'over-square' V8 engine which delivered 140bhp and gave the car lively performance (124mph/200kmh

Daimler SP250

maximum speed, 0-60mph in 8.8 seconds). Disc brakes all round were then still unusual. Two children could be carried, the standard of finish was high, options included a hard top, and at £1395 it was keenly priced. Unfortunately its fibreglass body was conceived in haste (or panic, as the end was in sight for Daimler) and its styling was controversial, and it never got prettier. Further, on early models the chassis was so flexible that some bodies cracked, which did nothing for their looks. Jaguar sorted out that problem with the improved 'B' model (April 1961) but the car never sold as well as it deserved. Daimler's image was partly to blame, for most of its products were then limousines. The SP250 was rarely raced in Europe, although it was quite successful in the States.

## DANKAR (BR)

In 1979 this firm introduced the 'Squalo' which was a mid-engined fibreglass coupé based on the mechanical components of the VW Passat. It had disc brakes on all four wheels and all-independent suspension by torsion bars. 'Squalo' actually means shark but the body was whale-like.

## DARDO (BR)

Built from 1981, this was a mid-engined, fibreglass-bodied Brazilian coupé which used a 1.5-litre version of a locally produced 1.3-litre Fiat engine.

## DARRIAN (GB)

After the Davrian concept had briefly passed into the hands of Will Corry (qv) production was revived again in North Wales by Tim Duffee. Instead of a simple fibreglass monocoque/body the born-again version (which reverted to the Davrian style) was reinforced with Kevlar. A roll cage was integral and this hinted at the key to the revival: the car was intended for competition. Darrians were fitted with a wide range of engines, up to an enlarged (2.2-litre) version of the dohc Hart F2 unit of the early 1980s. More to the point, they seemed capable of taking 250+bhp and were very successful in British club rallies.

## DARRIN (USA)

In the mid-1950s Howard Darrin, the man responsible for the striking lines of the Kaiser-Darrin sports car (qv), began to market fibreglass bodies for domestic products and also offered assembled cars. In addition Darrin built an open six-seat car on a DKW base and an extraordinary two-seat body on a Panhard chassis.

## DASH SPORTS CARS (GB)

In 1990 this company revived the Listair Dash (qv) which was a further development of the VW Beetle-based car which Peter Pellandine developed during his time in Australia and in Britain was known as the Rembrandt. Dash included Alfasud and Fiat-sourced kits among its options. The company also took over the MCA Sports 600 which was a small sports car, using Fiat 126 components originally designed by an Italian racing driver, Aurelio Bezzi. It was a sensible sports car for a young driver because although performance was not extraordinary, insurance premiums were low and 60mpg was claimed.

**1990 Dash 2 (above) and MCA Sports 600 (below)**

## DATSUN *see* NISSAN

## DAVRIAN (GB)

After structural engineer Adrian Evans had made a couple of open-top prototypes based on Hillman Imp running gear, he introduced the Davrian Mk1 in 1967. This car used Hillman Imp running gear in a stiff and light fibreglass monocoque/body. Like the specials, the first cars were open topped but in 1968 the little firm showed a fastback coupé, the 'Demon', which could take a variety of engines.

Two hundred kits had been sold by 1972 and by 1973

**A brace of Davrians**

there was a range of options which included VW Beetle and Mini engines. Most customers preferred the Imp engine, however, and there was a mix between buyers who bought the cars for road use (they were remarkably cheap) and those who wanted to race them. In 1974 a Davrian won the British Modsports Championship outright, and the marque then dominated the series for some years. The trouble was that the buying public began to regard them as racing cars, with a road version available, rather than genuine dual-purpose cars. Thus while Davrian went from strength to strength on the tracks, sales for road use tailed off.

In 1976 the company moved to Wales and, after it had made another 60 cars, it showed a new model, the Dragon, in 1981. This had a crisp, if bland, version of the established body together with the running gear of the Ford Fiesta, with disc brakes all round. It was primarily intended for road use and the Welsh Development Agency invested in the idea. Davrian expanded and took on new premises but sales did not back the optimism (there was a general turn-down in the economy) and early in 1983 the company folded, and the assets were acquired by Will Corry (see Corry).

## DAWB (GB)

Although only ever intended as a one-off, the DAWB deserves its place here because it is, quite simply, the finest special ever made. David Woods, a Belfast engineer, and Archie Bell, a Norton works rider, conceived it in 1955 and it was 13 years in the making. It was a strikingly handsome 2+2 GT coupé with a unique dohc straight-six air-cooled 1.5-litre engine mounted transversely over the front wheels. Its 150bhp was delivered via chains to a bespoke gearbox using Jaguar ratios which, in turn, drove the front wheels. Suspension was independent all round by double wishbones suspended by rubber bushes in tension.

The number of parts on the car which were sourced from other companies was tiny and amounted only to detail fittings such as instruments and door frames, for even the starter motor and the four-wheel disc brakes were specially made. As if all this was not enough, the steel body was made to Rolls-Royce standards.

It was quick and handled well but, having fulfilled his dream, Woods lost interest and started to build a boat. So, the DAWB, which today sits in the Belfast Transport Museum, covered little more than 1000 miles.

## DAX *see* DJ SPORTS CARS

## DAYTONA (USA)

Maker of the 'Migi', a fibreglass 'MG TD' body on a VW Beetle floorpan which was introduced in 1976 and by 1980 had become the most popular kit car in America. Like most cars of its type it was let down by its wheels which were pressed steel with 'wire-effect' hub caps. In 1982, the 'Moya' roadster joined the range and the company began to offer 'luxury' trim kits and wire wheels. It is not to be confused with another American firm of the same name which attempted to market a microcar in 1956.

1982 Daytona Moya

## DAYTONA CLASSICS (GB)

Mid-1980s maker of the '204GT', a Ferrari Dino copy using Lancia Beta components. Daytona Classics introduced a Triumph TR7 copy in 1989. Why anyone should want to do this at a time when real TR7s were still unloved remains a mystery.

## DB (F)

Charles Deutsch and René Bonnet were French enthusiasts who had once been promised a drive in a works car for the 1936 French GP (run for sports cars) and when that failed to materialize they set about making their own Citroën-based specials. Unfortunately, these were not ready until 1939, so although the two friends were able to run in a few events in France that year, the cars then had to stand idle for the next six.

**Early 1950s DB Panhard coupé**

In 1945, both the Citroën specials, one a 1.5-litre car the other a 2-litre, were placed in the first postwar race meeting, in Paris. Meanwhile a more advanced car was nearing completion. Work on this had been started clandestinely in occupied France during the war, at some risk to the two enthusiasts. 75bhp was claimed for the Citroën 11CV engine and suspension was independent all round, by torsion bars and wishbones at the front, and swing axles at the rear. Given the circumstances of its birth, the chassis specification was advanced, while the body was truly outstanding, a low, enveloping aluminium shell resembling in profile the later Porsche 550.

That car summarised the formula for all later DBs: low weight, low drag and a tuned production engine. In the partnership, Charles Deutsch was the theoretical engineer who had a natural instinct for aerodynamics, while René Bonnet complemented him admirably, being a pragmatic mechanical engineer. This combination of talents was to make DB pre-eminent among French makers of small-capacity sports cars.

DB made a number of Citroën-based single-seaters and sports cars on a distinctive forked backbone chassis until Deutsch and Bonnet discovered Panhard (qv), a discovery encouraged as Citroën proved difficult over the supply of parts. A prototype Citroën-based car intended for production was thus stillborn. In 1949, the friends formed Automobiles DB and, the following year, built a 500cc Panhard-based car for the new International Formula 3. It was an odd looking device with a hugh ground clearance and the engine mounted to the fore of the front wheels, as on the Panhard Dyna. About the only thing which can be said for it was that it was one of the best French 500cc F3 cars, which was no distinction at all, and it had a very varied single-seater career—there was even a supercharged 750cc version, which made it a F1 car which raced once, in the 1955 Pau GP (it finished 16 laps down), and it was finally resurrected for Formula Junior.

**Late DB Panhard coupé**

Concurrent with the first F3 car, DB turned its attention to sports-racers and while the single-seater had been outlandish, the sports cars were subtle. Many Panhard components were used, and the suspension was pure Panhard except that only a single transverse leaf was used at the front. As with the Citroën-engined DBs, the outstanding feature was the all-enveloping low-drag body.

DBs appeared at Le Mans from 1949 on, but they were not successful until the mid-1950s when they began to dominate the 750cc class in international events; there were numerous class wins at Le Mans, at Sebring, in the Mille Miglia and even an outright win in the 1954 Tourist Trophy, a World Championship event which was run on handicap. All the successful cars used Panhard components, although sometimes the partners made Renault-based cars.

At the 1952 Paris Saloon, DB exhibited a road-going coupé based on a box-section chassis using Panhard Dyna suspension front and rear. At first the engines in these cars ranged from a 30bhp 610cc unit up to a supercharged 850cc engine which gave 55bhp (from 1954). The first cars had aluminium bodies, but fibreglass shells were used from 1955, by which time front disc brakes were an option and engines of 1000cc and even 1300cc were offered. Customers had a great deal of choice in the final specification of their cars and DB developed an all-synchromesh version of the Panhard gearbox unit before Panhard did so. Over the years the bodywork changed, and became slimmer. Production of road cars was minute, and no reliable road test figures are available. Besides, since the customer chose from a menu, hardly any two DBs were alike.

In 1961 the two partners had a disagreement: Bonnet wanted to switch to a Renault-based car, Deutsch wished to stick with Panhard; and so they went their separate ways, thus ending a highly successful partnership. By an odd quirk of fate a 750cc CD-Panhard (CD = Charles Deutsch) won its class and came 16th at Le Mans in 1962, while in 17th spot, and also a class winner, was a 1-litre Bonnet-Renault. René Bonnet made cars under his own name and then was taken over by Matra. Deutsch became a successful engineering consultant.

## DE BRUYNE (GB/USA)

An American, John de Bruyne, bought the rights to the Gordon-Keeble and, in 1968, took space at the New York Motor Show to drum up business. On the stand were two re-badged Gordon-Keebles and a new mid-engined coupé which had a 5.7-litre Chevrolet engine, a five-speed transaxle, and a claimed top speed of 180mph/290kmh. That more or less concludes the story of De Bruyne.

## DEEP SANDERSON (GB)

Chris Lawrence made his reputation as an engine tuner, mainly of Triumph engines, and as the driver of a very successful Triumph-engined Morgan. In 1960 his firm, Lawrencetune, showed its first racing car, a VW-based Formula Junior car which had absolutely nothing to commend it (nor did a revised version a year later). Both were marketed as 'Deep Sandersons' because the backer of the enterprise was called Sanderson and Lawrence was a fan of the jazz musician Deep Henderson.

After failing with formula cars, Lawrence concentrated on sports cars. At the end of 1961 he showed a two seat fibreglass coupé body on a backbone chassis, with a Mini engine

**Deep Sanderson at practice, Le Mans**

behind the driver, and rear suspension by 'Lawrence-link' trailing arms. The few sold were mainly used in competition, then in 1963 Lawrence showed the 301GT, a more attractive updated derivative of which 14 were sold.

Deep Sandersons ran several times at Le Mans in the 1960s, always without success. The unsuccessful '501' of 1964 had tuned Mini engines front and rear, and the '303' coupé was built for Ford power. Lawrence was also involved in the abortive Jack Pearce F1 effort and the Monica GT car (qv), which both used Martin V8 engines.

## DEETYPE REPLICAS *see* WINGFIELD

## DE LA CHAPELLE (F)

A 1978 fibreglass copy of the Bugatti Type 55 based on a backbone chassis with BMW 3-series mechanical components and a choice of engines from 2 litres to 2.8 litres. In 1980 there was a longer wheelbase, and modern wheels and tyres made the car more competent on the road, at some cost in aesthetic aspects. In 1990 a 2+2 model was offered and, by that time, the De La Chapelle family had taken over the MVS coupé and had begun marketing it as the 'Venturi'.

**De La Chapelle Tourer and Roadster**

## DELAGE (F)

Louis Delage began making cars in 1905 but did not come to the fore until the 1920s when his company built some superb racing cars. In 1935 Delage was acquired by Delahaye and eventually the cars became badge-engineered versions of its step-parent's. In 1950 French government fiscal measures, designed to encourage mass production, dealt a body blow to all French hand-built car makers. In 1954 the company merged with Hotchkiss but this new group died the following year.

**D6, 1946-53. Prod: approx 250.** Delage attempted to re-enter the market after the War with a warmed-over version of its 1937 D-6, which had been designed by Delahaye. The short-stroke 3-litre engine, Cotal electric gearbox (four speeds forwards and reverse), and hydraulic brakes were pure Delage. Like all proper motor cars of the time, most were supplied

**Delage D6 3 litre at the Paris Salon in 1946**

as a bare chassis and the client chose his coachbuilder. It was available only with right hand drive—the popular reason is that rhd cars were safer when driving on the right over the Alps but this writer thinks the real reason is that, deep in their hearts, serious French engineers knew it was correct.

## DELAHAYE (F)

Delahaye could trace its roots back to a brick making factory founded in 1845. Emile Delahaye joined the firm twenty years later and by degrees he steered the company first towards steam, then gas engines. The first car was built in 1894 and by the late 1930s Delahaye had absorbed Delage (qv) and was making expensive high performance cars. Its range included a car with a V12 engine which was used in Grands Prix and international sports car racing (a Delahaye finished second at Le Mans in 1937 and in 1938, Delahayes were first, second and fourth).

Delahaye, then, was a serious constructor but that did not help it when, in 1950, the French government introduced fiscal measures which hit labour intensive firms, although part of the trouble was that all development work had been suspended during the Occupation so Delahaye was marketing pre-war designs. Things were not too bad in the immediate postwar years because there was a seller's market but production dropped from nearly 500 cars in 1950 to three in 1953. From 1951 Delahaye made a Jeep-like vehicle for the military and about 10,000 of these were made until 1955. Delahaye combined with the equally hard-pressed firm of Hotchkiss in 1954, and the revered name was used on trucks until 1956.

**T135, 1936-51. Prod: approx 2,000 including pre-war production.** In 1936 versions of the T135 won the Monte

**Delahaye T135 with Dubois body**

Carlo Rally, came 1-2-3 in the Marseille Grand Prix and second and third in the French GP, which was for sports cars. It was, therefore, a car with provenance and available in two and four seat versions. It had a 3.6-litre straight-six engine (which came in various states of tune, giving up to 135bhp), independent front suspension, a Cotal electrically operated eight-speed gearbox (four speeds in either direction) and massive 14in drum brakes which were cable operated. All were built with right hand drive, so export opportunities were limited, and all were presented nude with the customer arranging the body with the coachbuilder of his choice.

**T175, 1948-51. Prod: approx 150.** Delahaye's first post-war model was a revised T135 with a seven bearing, 4.5-litre version of the T135 engine which gave up to 140bhp. The old transverse leaf i.f.s. was replaced by Dubonnet coils, to the detriment of the handling, but the 175 had a de Dion rear axle and hydraulic brakes (at last). Long-chassis versions (T178 and T180) were sold with a single carburetter 125bhp engine, but these were both saloons. Cars in this series had left hand drive.

**Delahaye T175 on the 1951 Monte Carlo Rally**

**T235, 1951-3. Prod: approx 90.** From 1951 Delahaye made only one model which was an uprated T175 with 152bhp and was offered with a standard, modern, body made by both Antem and Letourneur et Marchand, though other bodies could be fitted.

**1951 Delahaye T235 by Saoutchik**

# DELKIT (GB)

A short-lived kit car maker of the mid-1980s. In 1984 Delkit marketed the 'Camino', a 2+2 coupé designed to take Ford Cortina components on a tubular backbone chassis. The Camino's styling was a little unusual and was the probable reason for its failure.

**The 1984 Delkit Camino used Cortina parts**

# DELLOW (GB)

When Ron Lowe mated a Ford Ten engine to an Austin Seven chassis, and clad it with a simple body made on the *superleggera* principle, he made a formidable trials car, and was soon asked to build replicas. His employer, Ken Delingpole, himself a trials driver, saw the potential and, worried by the prospect of losing his general manager, formed a partnership. Space was found at Delingpole's engineering works and production began.

Dellows were marketed as dual-purpose cars and sold well until 1952 when trials began to be dominated by drivers with bespoke specials, and restrictions on the home market were lifted so giving the buyer more choice. The decline set in during that year and, three years later, the project was taken over by Neville Nightingale. By then the concept's days were over, and Nightingale sold few cars, although production did not formally end until 1959.

**MkI/II/IIC/IIE, 1949-56. Prod: approx 250, including kits.** The earliest cars used scrap Austin chassis but

**Dellow MkI**

then Dellow made a similar frame using ex-WD rocket bodies. This illustrates the problems faced by small British constructors at the time—they were grateful for any material—but the quality of the metal was superb and Dellow chassis do not rust. At first marketed as a kit car, using the Ford 1172cc engine, Dellows were soon sold complete and Ford arranged for them to be distributed through selected agencies. Some were bought exclusively for road use and a firm of agricultural engineers bought Dellows for their mechanics because they could tackle remote farm tracks. They were also sold to farmers in South Africa and New Zealand. Coil springs and a Panhard rod replaced the Austin Seven-style quarter elliptics at the rear on the MkII. The 1955 IIC (built by Neville Nightingale) was an economy model using Ford Popular parts while the IIE, another Nightingale car, had full instrumentation and the 100E engine.

**MkIII/IV, 1952-55. Prod: 18.** The MkIII was a long wheelbase four-seater which was initially built to accommodate Ron Lowe's growing family. Unfortunately the revised weight distribution made the MkIII unsuitable for competition and, at £840, it was an expensive way to be cold and uncomfortable on the road. The MkIV was Ron Lowe's MkIII (which began life as a MkI, then became the prototype MkII) fitted with a 1508cc Ford Consul engine but, since Ford would not supply these units, it remained a prototype. Thus the Dellow MkIII and IV existed only as extensions of Ron Lowe's first car.

**MkV, 1953-55.** The last of the traditional Dellows, the MkV was a lightweight model with a slimmer body and the beam front axle suspended on coil springs instead of the traditional Ford transverse leaf. As usual there were no doors (they were an optional extra on all cars but cutting the holes spoiled rigidity) and this time the 1172 engine drove through a four-speed Morris gearbox. Its day, however, was long past and few were made although works driver Tony Marsh ran one in races, sprints and hill climbs as well as trials. Marsh built a special from Dellow MkV parts and this still exists, with a later fibreglass body, as a Marsh Special.

**The 1953 MkV Dellow**

**MkVI, 1957-59. Prod: 6.** A Neville Nightingale car with an enveloping body made from aluminium (not, as sometimes said, of fibreglass) on a ladder frame. Front suspension was by swing axles with coil springs and underslung semi-elliptic springs were used with the live rear axle. It was hoped to use the 105E engine which Ford had in the pipeline but when this was late in coming the MkVI was made with the elderly 100E unit. The result was a car which looked like a Ford Ten special, was under-powered, and was expensive for its performance and kerbside presence.

## DELOREAN (USA/GB)

In its anxiety to create jobs in Northern Ireland, the British government ignored advice, and common sense, and backed John Z. DeLorean, who had been touting his idea for a responsible sports car to any government which would listen. To have been successful it would have had to have sold more cars than every other model in its class was selling, yet it was billed as an 'exclusive' car. Its main selling points were really only gimmicks: gull-wing doors and a 'stainless steel body' which was really only a metal veneer over a plastic shell and stained easily. The car failed to match its projected price, fuel economy, and quality. The initial favourable reception soon cooled, financial irregularities within the company did not help matters and the project quickly fell apart.

One thing of particular interest is the number of points of similarity the DeLorean project had with the Bricklin (qv), which was also a wedge-shaped 'safety' sports car with gull-wing doors, and was also promoted by a dazzling salesman. The full story of DeLorean is told under 'Bricklin'.

**DMC-2, 1981-2. Prod: 8583.** With Lotus developing the independently sprung backbone chassis, which followed the broad layout of the Elan, and Giugiaro styling the body, the DMC-2 should have been a success, although perhaps not on the scale dreamed of by DeLorean. Some of the problems arose from his design parameters—the 2.8-litre V6 Renault engine overhung the rear wheels, and this caused indifferent handling, there were different sized tyres front and rear, the cockpit was very claustrophobic, and the car was overweight and a poor performer considering its $25,000 price tag.

Northern Ireland has no tradition of car building, but that would have been no problem with a car which had been engineered for mass production. Design associate Lotus had no expertise in this—on the contrary the quality of its own cars was then appalling. When cars reached America, they

**The ill-starred DeLorean**

needed $2-3000 spent on them to make them barely acceptable. Stories circulated of failures in the gull-wing door locking mechanism, and of trapped occupants. That did no good to the image of a car with a main selling point being occupant protection in a crash. Within a few months, the project was dead.

## DELTAYN (GB)

The maker of the 'Proteus', an open 2+2 sports car with Targa top which appeared in 1986 and disappeared soon afterwards. Suspension came from the Jaguar XJ and it was powered by a 3.5-litre Rover V8 engine. Much was made of quality features such as leather and walnut veneer but its odd styling won few converts. Deltayn seemed not to be put out by this failure and, in a bold move, decamped from South Humberside and reappeared in France at Magny Cours Technopolis (a fancy name for an industrial estate) under the name of the Parradine Motor Company (qv).

## DEMOCRATA (BR)

Announced in 1963, the Democrata was named because it was intended to be financed by public subscription. It was an elegant front-engined fibreglass coupé and was to have had a purpose-built 2.5-litre V6 engine. It is believed that only one car was completed and that had a Chevrolet Corvair engine.

## DEMOISELLE (BR)

Maker since 1980 of the Phantom SL, a boxy Targa-top 2+2 car based on the floorpan of the 1600cc VW Beetle.

**Demoiselle Phantom SL**

## DENZEL (A)

Although Austria bred Dr Porsche and the early cars of his son, Ferry, it has never been a major car making centre. Wolfgang Denzel tried to change that after the War when he began building some wooden-bodied sports four-seaters on war-surplus VW Kübelwagen chassis. Soon Denzel progressed to pretty little sports cars with VW engines with twin carbs. There was a box-section chassis, with tubular reinforcement, VW suspension was used and most had three-seater open bodies, although some had narrower two-seat bodies. In some markets, such as America, the cars were sold under the name 'W.D.'

At first many had engines linered down to 1100cc but by 1953 1.3-litre engines were usual. At 82.5in, the wheelbase was a foot shorter than the rival Porsche and the the car was

**A Denzel rallying in 1957**

lighter. Like Porsche, Denzel extensively modified the VW base unit and tweaked as much as 86bhp from a 1.5-litre version which translated into 105mph/170kmh and 0-60mph in 11 seconds.

In the mid-1950s Denzels appeared in some international rallies, and sometimes did well, but on the whole they were little known outside their native land. Whereas Porsche progressed beyond its 'Beetle Special' origins, Denzel never did, but then Porsche received a royalty on every VW Beetle, which did not harm its chances. By 1960 there was really no reason to buy a Denzel and the firm folded.

## DE PONTAC (F)

If a car's fate was decided on looks alone, the De Pontac would have been a runaway success because there was not much to touch it in the style stakes in 1956. Under the fibreglass body, however, was only a Citroën 2CV engine. It was bored out to 500cc (from the 425cc which was then standard), power was doubled to 26bhp, and a top speed of 75mph/120kmh was claimed. Production began in 1959 and customers could also specify Panhard running gear and/or floral patterned cloth incorporated in the bodywork! Despite these tantalising possibilities, few were made.

**De Pontac of 1956 had Citroën 2CV engine**

## DESANDE (GB)

First shown in 1980, the Desande Roadster was an evocation

**Desande Roadster, 1980**

(not a copy) of the Mercedes-Benz SSK with a 5-litre Chevrolet V8 engine.

## DESHAIS (F)

Although this 1950 open two-seater was a microcar, it was very pretty and looked like a grown up model. Its makers claimed that it was designed to be able to take any motorcycle engine, but details of how this was to be achieved have not survived. Just to get things rolling, Deshais offered three different two-stroke engines including a 6bhp 125cc unit which would propel the car to a blistering 31mph/50kmh—or so it was claimed.

Obviously more powerful engines would produce better results but like most projects which used motorcycle engines, this did not get off the ground.

**1950 Deshais: 125, 250 and 350cc engines were offered**

## DE TOMASO (I)

Alejandro de Tomaso was born in Argentina and made a small reputation as a racing driver in the 1950s, usually at the wheel of an OSCA. He settled in Italy and had the foresight to marry a very wealthy American lady, who sometimes co-drove with him in long distance events. He began making competition cars under his own name, and acquired companies including Maserati and Innocenti, the motorcycle makers Benelli and Moto Guzzi and, through his brother-in-law, control of the styling houses of Vignale and Ghia.

De Tomaso's own racing cars were unmitigated failures which tended to be embarrassingly inept copies of contemporary Coopers. In fact, the de Tomaso F1 cars were probably the worst cars of the 1961-65 formula and they had to beat some real dross to take that title. De Tomaso's road cars have not been entirely successful, although the cars have sometimes sold in quite large numbers. A common problem has been a lack of attention to detail.

**Vallelunga, 1965. Prod: approx 50.** De Tomaso had been threatening to break into the road car market for some time and had shown a number of prototypes which attracted little serious attention before this car appeared as a 1964 show car. It was an open two-seater with a pressed steel backbone chassis, with tubular subframes, and all independent suspension by coil springs and double wishbones. Unusually for the time it was mid-engined, with a 1.5-litre Ford Cortina engine.

**De Tomaso Vallelunga, 1965**

Apparently de Tomaso hoped that a major manufacturer would take over the design and, if it was not Ford, would substitute a similar small capacity four-cylinder engine. Nobody took the bait but the following year de Tomaso commissioned Giorgio Giugiaro, then working for Ghia, to design a coupé body and thus the Vallelunga was born. Unfortunately the chassis flexed in the area of the drive train and caused insoluble vibration problems, and the Vallelunga was quickly dropped.

**Mangusta, 1967-71. Prod: approx 400.** The Vallelunga chassis was re-engineered to take Ford's 4.7-litre V8 which delivered its 306bhp through a ZF five-speed gearbox, and there were disc brakes all round to cope with the claimed 155mph/250kmh top speed. At the same time, Giotto Bizzarrini had designed a mid-engined car for which Giugiaro designed a body; this project was stillborn but de Tomaso took over the body shape and so created the Mangusta ('Mongoose', an animal which the cobra—and Cobra?—fears). This time, people took notice because the Mangusta was stunning, and relatively cheap, and de Tomaso was in business.

The lovely lines, however, disguised a dog of a car: there wasn't enough passenger or luggage space, the driver's vision was severely restricted, and minimal ground clearance caused problems. There was worse to come, the chassis had flexed with a Ford Cortina engine, but with 306bhp, and 392lb/ft torque, the chassis *really* flexed which made for character building road holding; even had it been as rigid as granite the car's 32/68 weight distribution would have provided all the fun anyone could handle.

**De Tomaso Mangusta**

**Pantera, 1971-date. Prod: approx 10,000.** Having established himself as a manufacturer, de Tomaso decided to build a mid-engined supercar for America. Giampaolo Dallara designed a pressed steel unitary chassis (with 42/58 weight distribution, better than the Mangusta but still tail heavy) with coil spring and double wishbone suspension all round, with the rear layout further located by radius rods.

Power came from a 5763cc Ford V8 (made in Australia from 1980) which delivered its 330bhp (or as little as 250bhp in de-toxed form) via a ZF five-speed transaxle. In European trim it could touch 160mph/almost 260kmh and sprint 0-60mph in 5.2 seconds.

De Tomaso did a deal whereby Ford bought into de Tomaso Automobili (and Ghia) and distributed the Pantera through its Lincoln-Mercury network. The Pantera was more practical than the Mangusta, had Italian style, a Ford engine and a competitive price tag, so it should have been a winner. But it soon earned a reputation for rust, poor ventilation, poor quality, and unreliability. Ford was glad to drop it in 1974 when it was hit by the energy crisis and needed extensive work to meet new U.S. regulations. As part of the severance, Ford took over Ghia.

**De Tomaso Pantera GTS**

The Pantera has remained in production in small numbers. The GT5 had much wider wheels and add-on wheel arches, the more expensive GTS had 350bhp and a sensuous body with flared-in wheel arches; both had a huge rear wing as an option. Driver visibility was not good and you needed to be a body builder to drive one. One impressive statistic is that, with 330lb/ft torque, it was possible to accelerate from standstill to 160mph—260kmh in round terms—in top gear!

By 1990 de Tomaso had sold Maserati to Fiat and his only production car was the Pantera. The styling was revised by Marcello Gandini and the twenty year old design was updated with a front dam and a rear wing treatment which recalled the Ferrari F40. While previous Panteras had offered more presence than the list price would suggest, the price was almost doubled, and this made it much more expensive than far better cars such as the Mercedes-Benz 500SL or the Honda NSX. The Pantera had always been incompetent but had been undeniably stylish; when a company starts charging a serious price, one expects a serious car and that is something the Pantera never has been.

**Longchamp, 1972-89.** Along with the Pantera, de Tomaso launched the Deauville, a very expensive five-seater saloon by Ghia which was a shameless crib of the Jaguar XJ6. Most of the paper specifications were similar to the Pantera, with unitary construction, independent suspension and disc brakes all round, and the same 5.7-litre Ford V8, although this was front-mounted and drove through an automatic transmission. The Longchamp was a short wheelbase 2+2 version of the Deauville which was claimed to touch 150mph/240kmh and on which one could have a five-speed ZF manual gearbox.

**De Tomaso Longchamp**

It was not really a sports car, and nor were the GTS coupé and the cabriolet versions, but it is included to keep the record tidy and because it was used as the basis of the Maserati Kyalami (with the Maserati race-developed V8 'quad cam' engine) when de Tomaso took over the company and tried some badge engineering. Accurate production figures are not available but it is unlikely to have exceeded 600 cars of all types.

## DEVIN (USA)

Bill Devin marketed his first fibreglass body in 1952 when he took a mould from a friend's Scaglietti-bodied Ermini. Scaglietti later produced a similar shape for the Ferrari 'Monza' and Devin marketed his range of bodies under the name 'Monza'. These all shared the same basic shape but were available in sizes from a 78in wheelbase (for Fiats, Crosleys etc) up to 100in and some 3000 were to be sold. In 1958 Devin bought in chassis made in Belfast and the following year marketed a complete car, the SS, which was essentially a Cobra before its time. A cut-price VW-powered kit car came in 1960 but, as in Britain, the craze for kit cars was over by 1962.

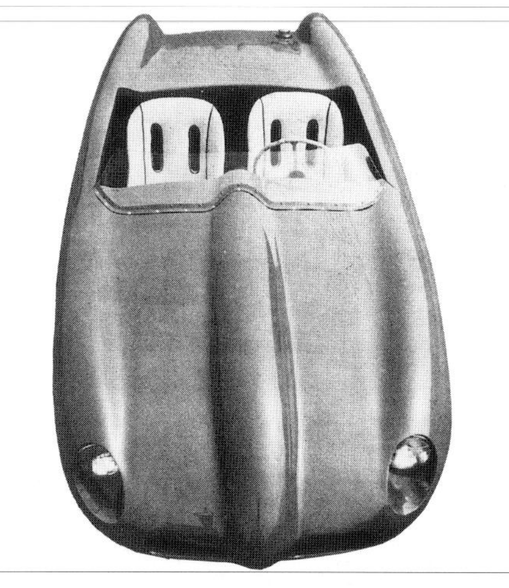

**Devin Type C body, 1955, for Panhard engines**

**SS, 1959-62. Prod: 15.** Based on a sturdy ladder frame made of 3in tubing, the SS had coil spring and double wishbone front suspension, a coil sprung de Dion rear axle located by twin radius arms, and a standard Corvette engine driving through a four-speed Chevy manual gearbox. Performance was sensational: 0-60mph in 4.8 seconds with a 130mph/210kmh maximum; but since there were plenty of tuning goodies for the Corvette engine that was only the starting point. The build and finish were outstanding, the chassis matched the power, and Devins were very successful in American sports car racing.

Unfortunately, Devin ran into problems with component suppliers and got his sums wrong. In the first year of production, he had to nearly double the price ($5995 to $10,000, more than the price of a Jaguar D Type) and that killed an outstanding car.

Devin SS, 1959

**D, 1960-62.** Compared to the SS, the 'D' was a bargain, a kit requiring a VW or Porsche donor car could be yours for $1495 or, built complete with new VW components, for $2950. The frame followed the broad outline of the SS but front suspension was by VW trailing links while the VW rear swing axles were suspended by coil springs and radius arms. Devin cleverly modified the 'Monza' style so the essence was retained even with a rear-engined car, and it was undeniably pretty. Unfortunately it cost about the same as an Austin-Healey 3000, but with mediocre performance and no weather equipment. In 1962 Devin offered the 'D' with a turbocharged Corvair engine but, at $4000, it found few takers.

Devin D, for VW or Porsche components

## DIAL (GB)

The 'Buccaneer' GT car first appeared in 1971 with a mid-mounted Ford Escort engine driving through a modified VW Beetle gearbox. A square-tube space frame took Triumph Spitfire front and rear suspension and the car was finished by an outrageous fibreglass body with gull-wing doors. With low weight and low drag, the Buccaneer was a rapid machine and with an 1100cc Ford engine was claimed to reach 120mph/193kmh and do the 0-60mph sprint in ten seconds. At least ten were built, for both road and competition use, but the company appears to have been a victim of VAT in 1973.

## DIAMANTE (USA)

Listed from 1978, this was a turn key 'nostalgia' car (styling was a mixture of 1930s Cord and Mercedes-Benz) with a 7-litre Cadillac engine.

1983 Diamante

## DIBA (CH)

In the early 1970s this company made a few examples of the 'GTC' which was a 2-litre Porsche 911 given a steel coupé body. It was a very handsome car and, with its long sloping nose and false radiator grill, it looked for all the world like a front-engined car; indeed, it had a touch of the Maserati Ghibli about it.

## DIVA (GB)

In 1962 Don Sim, one of the partners who made the Yimkin (qv), was with a new company, Tunex Conversions, when he designed the Diva GT. It was a compact little car with a pretty fibreglass body on a space frame, with independent suspension all round, disc brakes on the front wheels, and the choice of a variety of four-cylinder Ford engines. From the start it was offered in competition or road versions, the latter having upholstered seats and rubber engine mountings and so on. In the event, every one of the 65 buyers chose the competition version, although some cars were also used on the road.

Divas were phenomenally successful in the popular small engine GT racing class in Britain, one even won its class in the 1964 Nürburgring 1000 Km race, and later they were equally successful in Historic racing. To serve a changing market, Diva then made the Valkyr, a mid-engined coupé, but this was never as successful or popular. In 1967 rights to both cars changed hands but the new owner had withdrawn from the market by 1968.

Diva GT, 1964

## DJ SPORTS CARS (GB)

A mid-1980s maker of the 'Charger', a gull-wing fibreglass coupé showing Lotus Esprit influence, which was based on the VW Beetle floor pan and had been previously made by Embeesea Kit Cars (qv). It had a chequered career and was last heard of in 1987 under the name MDB Saturn (qv). By 1982, however, DJ had evolved its own Cobra copy which was marketed under the name 'Dax'; like so many cars of its type, this had a fibreglass body, a space frame chassis, and suspension sourced from the Jaguar XJ6 or XJ12. A wide range of engine options was available.

John Tojeiro, one of whose cars had formed the basis of the AC Ace, which evolved into the Cobra, became Technical Director of the company in 1985 and the Cobra copy was re-named the 'Dax Tojeiro' in honour of the grandfather of the Cobra. By 1988, Tojeiro had created a mid-engined space frame which became the basis of the Dax KVA40, a copy of the Ford GT40 using the KVA body.

**Dax Tojeiro**

**Dax KVA 40**

## DKW (D)

DKW had become well-known for its motorcycles long before it made its first car in 1928. This has a two-stroke engine, a characteristic which marked the company's cars and was of wooden unitary construction. Soon the marque's second distinctive feature, front wheel drive, was established. The make became one of the founders of Auto Union. After the Second World War the company was nationalised by the East German government and a DKW design became one of the bases of the projects that led to the IFA, the Wartburg and the Trabant.

In West Germany the DKW name was revived in 1949 *(see also* Auto Union) and pre-war designs were developed. This line found its ultimate expression in a range of front wheel drive cars with three-cylinder two-stroke engines of 900cc, give or take a little. The running gear and, sometimes, the floor pans of these machines became the basis for a number of sports and formula cars in the late 1950s. During 1957 and 1958 the factory itself made a small number of 'Monza' two-seat fibreglass coupés, with a 55bhp 980cc version of the engine, which was good for a claimed 100mph/161kmh. A Spyder version may not have progressed beyond the prototype stage.

**DKW Monza, 1957**

## DMG (RP)

The Philippines' first and (and only?) sports car was a fibreglass coupé on a VW Beetle floorpan called the 'Toro'. It was introduced in 1974.

## DMS (GB)

Dorset Motor Services made a Cobra copy using Ford Cortina components from the late 1980s. DMS also made a body kit to convert a Ford Capri Mk2/3 into something that looked a little like a shrunken Aston Martin V8 which was marketed under the name 'Bullitt'. A convertible was also available. In 1990 DMS made the 'Abingdon', a fibreglass copy of the MGA which used Ford Cortina running gear and offered a choice of engines up to the Rover V8.

**DMS Bullitt, 1990**

## DNK (GB)

By 1990 DNK was the maker of the 'Hornet', originated by Northern Kit Cars (qv). Still sourced from the Cortina, it had acquired a lift-out roof section and was sold as the 'Hornet II'.

## DODGE (USA)

The Dodge brothers were early shareholders in Ford and also built engines for the company. They began making cars under their own name in 1914 and in 1920 Dodge was the second most popular American marque. In 1928 Dodge became part of the Chrysler Corporation and became the 'second stage' marque, in other words it made low to medium priced cars, one step up from Plymouth.

The 1968 'Charger' was the first of a number of very powerful, and rapid, two-door saloons with a sporting edge. In 1970 the company began selling some Mitsubishi models under the Dodge name, although in 1987 Chrysler established the 'Eagle' marque to market most of these cars.

**Dodge Charger, 1968**

**Dodge Stealth, 1990**

**Dodge Viper concept car at the 1989 Detroit Show**

The Dodge 'Stealth' of 1990 was a sports coupé virtually identical to the Mitsubishi 3000 GT (qv) and the top of the range model with a 276bhp turbocharged engine was good for 160mph/255kmh and 0-60mph in under six seconds. In 1990 the company was preparing for production of the 'Viper', an aggressively styled front-engined sports car which, as the name suggests, was intended to be a latter day Cobra.

## DOFRAL (USA)

First seen in 1982, Dofral offered the 'Classic T' as a turn key car or as a kit. It was a fibreglass copy of the 1957 Ford Thunderbird which used the running gear of the Ford Pinto range.

## DOLO (F)

Introduced in 1947, the Dolo JB-4 was a streamlined coupé with a transparent Plexiglass roof and a narrow (35in) rear track. Suspension was independent all round by torsion bars and the prototype was shown with an air-cooled flat-four engine of 571cc which drove through the front wheels. The company also listed a model with a twin-carburetter eight-cylinder engine of 1143cc. A top speed of 87mph/140kmh was claimed but it is not known whether the car or the engine was ever built. Dolo attracted few, if any, buyers and did not reach its first birthday.

## DOME (J)

First shown in 1975, the Dome-O was a handsome wedge-shaped coupé which its four young creators hoped would give other Japanese makers a nudge and create cars of which motor enthusiasts could be proud. The name 'Dome' means 'children's dream'. A 145-bhp sohc 2.8-litre straight-six Datsun engine, as used in the 280Z, was mounted amidships in a steel monocoque and drove through a five-speed ZF gearbox. Suspension was independent all round by coil springs and double wishbones (or W. Wishbournes, as the catalogue had it) and Girling disc brakes were specified on all four corners. Apparently few were made but in 1980 a P2 version was offered, with a turbocharged version of the engine. Top speed was claimed to be 140mph/225kmh and 0-60 was said to be achieved in just over six seconds.

Precise details remain elusive and the company then concentrated on sports car racing, albeit with no great success. In 1989, however, it showed a new car, the Jiotto Caspita, which was as close to a road-legal Group C car as is possible to imagine. It had a carbon fibre monocoque, active suspension (including ride height adjustment) and power came from a version of the 3.5-litre, five valves per cylinder flat-12 F1 engine which Carlo Chiti's Motori Moderni concern designed for Subaru. This had been seen briefly, and unsuccessfully, in F1 in 1990 and in the Dome, it delivered its 450bhp through a six-speed gearbox. It was claimed that

**Dome-O at the 1978 Geneva Show**

the design used ground effect aerodynamics and would top 200mph/320kmh. Competition car practice was obvious in its specification, but was coupled with luxury, including air conditioning, electric windows and central locking.

## DOMINO (GB)

From the late 1980s Domino has made the 'Pimlico', a Mini-based fun car designed by Richard Oakes. Performance depended on the donor vehicle.

## DONKERVOORT (NL)

In the early 1980s Donkervoort made the 'Super Seven', and for the use of that name paid a royalty to Caterham Cars. In 1983 Donkervoort produced a car on strikingly similar lines which it called the Super Eight and this raised the wrath of Caterham Cars. The S8A of 1986 had independent rear suspension; the S8AT had a turbocharged 170bhp Ford engine. In 1988 Donkervoort introduced the S10, with revised styling, half-wheel-circumference front cycle wings and a 2.2-litre Ford engine, which could be turbocharged.

**Donkervoort Super Seven**

**Donkervoort S8A**

## DORAY (USA)

This was an odd three-seat roadster from 1950 which was basically an inept fibreglass Cord 810 body (the front had to be hinged to allow the wheels to turn!) on a Willys Jeepster chassis. Performance was mediocre and few, if any, were sold.

## DORIAN (GB)

In the late 1980s Dorian made the 'SS', a kit car which aped the Morgan and which had originally been marketed by Burlington (qv).

## DORSET MOTOR SERVICES *see* DMS

## DOUGLAS (GB)

From 1990 the Douglas Car company made the 'TF', a fibreglass evocation of the MG TF but with 2+2 seating. Two versions were offered, one based on the Triumph Herald/Vitesse/Spitfire, the other using Ford Escort and Cortina components. The TF was available as a kit or fully assembled.

**Douglas 'TF', 1990, a 2+2**

## DOVAL (USA)

In 1980 Doval showed the 'Shadow' which was an evocation of a typical 1930s sports car on a Ford LTD chassis. The body reflected the SS100, but it was not a copy and nor was it a cheap fibreglass shell. Doval actually recruited craftsmen from Aston Martin and Rolls-Royce, a fact which was reflected in both the car's quality and its price. Later Doval made a Cobra copy.

## DRAGONFLY (GB)

Like the Arkley (qv), this was a fibreglass body kit to replace rusted Sprites and Midgets. It had 'traditional' (1930s) styling and buyers had the option of buying a complete 'turn key' car. The Dragonfly was introduced in 1981 but was gone by 1986.

**Dragonfly Roadster, 1984**

## DREWS (D)

Between 1948 and 1951, the brothers Drews built about 150 special 2+2 cabriolet bodies on VW Beetle floor pans. The bodies were of steel and in profile resembled the first Jensen Interceptor, while the brightwork suggested American influence. Performance was about the same as the Beetle but at least one example was fitted with a hard top and a Porsche 356 engine.

## DRI SLEEVE (GB)

The Moonraker was a short-lived (1971 only) copy of the Bugatti Type 35 using Ford components but it was one of the more accurate Bugatti copies. The name 'Dri Sleeve' referred to a cover to protect the driver's right arm in bad weather (hand brake and gear lever were external) but, as they say in Vintage circles, 'If you can't stand the cold, get out of the Bug'.

**Dri Sleeve Moon-Raker**

## DUCHESS (USA)

Built from 1980, this comprised a plastic MG TD body on a VW floorpan. It was a 'turn key' car and one could buy front-engined examples with small Ford or Chevrolet units.

## DUESENBERG (USA)

There have been several attempts to revive one of the greatest names in automotive history, including some unlicensed copies. A 1947 effort fizzled out but in 1966 one was endorsed by Fritz Duesenberg, the son of Fred, one of the founders of the original company. It reached the stage of a single car with a modern chassis, a 7-litre Chrysler engine, and styling by Ghia. However, the financial backing evaporated.

**The Ghia-styled 1966 Duesenberg**

Subsequently at least two other companies have used the Duesenberg name and produced high-quality copies of the 1930s cars. A third company, sponsored by Fritz Duesenberg, has built stretch limos under the Duesenberg name.

## DUNHAM (USA)

In 1980 Dunham introduced the 'Caballista', an unspeakably vulgar two-seat fibreglass-bodied 'nostalgia' car using a Chevrolet Corvette chassis.

**1982 Dunham Caballista**

## DUROW (GB)

Available from the mid-1980s, the 'Deluge' was a nostalgia car of the sort popular in the States. There was no single recognisable model for its rakish lines. Like the Clénet it used the cockpit section from an MG Midget but the rest comprised Durow's own chassis, Ford Granada suspension and a fibreglass body.

## DUTTON (GB)

Dutton was a very prolific producer of kit cars, usually based on Ford Escort Mk 1 and 2 donor vehicles. Its wide range

**Dutton B**

**Dutton Phaeton S3, 1983**

**Dutton Melos**

**Dutton Legerra ZS**

included saloons, estate cars, and sports cars. The P1, a simple cycle-winged sports car on Lotus Seven lines (but not a crib) was introduced in 1970 and was usually fitted with BMC engines. It was replaced two years and nine cars later by the B-series and the Malaga, which had Triumph Spitfire front suspension and a wide range of engine options (nearly 900 kits were sold). The Phaeton was a developed version still in production in 1990. The Melos of 1981 was a Phaeton with 'traditional' styling (i.e. looking something like a 1940s sports car) while the Legerra ZS, introduced in 1986, had an enveloping body. In 1989 Dutton, which once claimed to be the world's most successful kit car maker in terms of kits made, sold on all its projects to other makers, retaining only the after-sales side of the business.

# E

## EAGLE (GB/USA)

Originally an American kit car design, although heavily influenced by the Nova (qv), the Eagle body was made in Britain from 1981. The SS/2, which had 'gull-wing' doors, could be either rear-engined (based on a VW floorpan) or front-engined, when Ford components were fitted to Eagle's own chassis. An open version, the 2 Plus, was also available. The 'M2', was an Anglo-German design with a multi-tubular backbone chassis, launched in 1987, usually with a front-mounted 2.9-litre Ford Scorpio engine. In the late 1980s, Eagle Cars took over production of the Dutton Phaeton.

Eagle SS/2

## EAGLE (USA)

Eagle was launched in mid-1987 as a new division of the Chrysler Corporation. Although its antecedants may seem clear in the company's official name, Jeep-Eagle, in fact it was one of the American-Japanese companies which sprang up in the late 1980s. In this case it resulted from the Chrysler Corporation's links with Mitsubishi, and the Eagle Talon was a sporting 2+2 coupé based on the Mitsubishi Galant and Eclipse ranges.

Eagle Talon TSi, 1990

The floorpan was fairly conventional, with MacPherson strut front suspension and an independent rear layout by trailing arms and an axle which was either 'dead' (on the front wheel drive cars) or 'live' (on the four wheel drive option). Buyers could choose from a menu of variants of a basic 16-valve four cylinder 2-litre engine, mounted transversely at the front, which delivered from 135bhp (fuel injected) to 195bhp (turbocharged) through a five-speed gearbox.

## EAGLE COACH WORK (USA)

Maker of 1980s copies of the Jaguar XK 120 and SS100 which featured fibreglass bodies on a bespoke chassis designed to take the running gear from the smaller American Fords.

## ECCO (USA)

Built from 1980, this car had a wedge-shaped coupé body on a shortened VW Beetle floorpan.

## ECOSSE (GB)

The English firm which relaunched the AC (Scotland) Ecosse with a turbocharged 2-litre Fiat engine in 1988, calling it the Signature.

Ecosse Signature, 1988

## EDWARDS (USA)

Sterling Edwards was a very wealthy individual who liked to relax by driving racing cars. He was not an ace but, backed by the best that money could buy, he acquitted himself fairly well on the West Coast until he retired from the sport in 1955.

In 1954 Edwards decided to build a road car for general sale. After a false start using a Kaiser chassis which proved too flexible (as he found out by racing it), he settled on a cut and shut Mercury chassis and a 5.5-litre Lincoln V8 engine giving 205bhp. Edwards was responsible for the elegant styling, which was inspired by a Virgil Exner design and was rendered in fibreglass. Two models were offered, both with four seats, a coupé and a convertible. The car won much praise for its styling, and performance was apparently good, but it offered too little for the asking price of $8000. The project ended in 1955, after just six cars had been built, and Edwards lost money on every one.

Edwards Hardtop, 1955: neatly styled

## ELABORATE MOTORS (USA)

In the late 1980s this American company began to import the Jaguar E Type lookalike body made by JPR in Britain, together with that company's space frame, and offered it with American Ford running gear from models such as the Pinto, Mustang II or Mercury Bobcat. Engine options ranged from the 2.3-litre Pinto 'four' to the small block V8s.

## ELEGANT MOTORS (USA)

From the late 1970s this company made a turn key car following the lines of the Auburn Speedster (and 2+2 Sports Phaeton) which used Jaguar XJ12 running gear. By the late 1980s it was also making copies of the Lamborghini Countach, Cord 812, AC Cobra, and Cheetah (1964 American car of that name, qv).

**Elegant Motors' 1976 856, not the only Auburn Speedster copy**

## ELITE (USA)

Late 1970s maker of the 'Laser 917', a ghastly parody of the Porsche 917 on a 1.6-litre VW Beetle chassis. This aberration was later made by Quint Enterprises (qv).

**Elite Laser 917, 1979**

## ELITE HERITAGE (USA)

From 1975, this company made turn key copies of the Duesenberg SJ and Speedster.

**Duesenberg II Royalton by Elite Heritage, 1981**

## EL-KG (D)

Horrid and (thankfully) short-lived fibreglass Bugatti Type 35 copy on a 1.6-litre VW Beetle chassis, built in the late 1970s.

## ELVA (GB)

In the early 1950s, Frank Nichols built up a garage business and was sufficiently successful to be able to indulge an ambition to go motor racing. He commissioned Mike Chapman to built him a car and the result, the CSM, was an 1172cc Ford-powered, cycle-winged sports car. It performed well enough to encourage Nichols, together with his mechanic 'Mac' Witts, to set about an improved version, which was christened 'Elva' (from the French *elle va*, she goes).

'Mac' Witts was the true creator of the car and he also designed the overhead inlet valve conversion for Ford 1172cc side valve engines which Elva marketed. The Elva Mk1 space frame followed the broad layout of the CSM (which, in turn, was very similar to the Lotus Mk6, as Colin Chapman was the first to point out), but Standard Ten front suspension replaced the previous swing axles and a simple semi-enveloping aluminium body completed the plot.

The Mk1 achieved some success in British club racing and perhaps two dozen were made. Further sports-racers followed and were particularly successful in America; they did not have the ultimate road holding of Lotus and Lola cars but they could be chucked about and were forgiving, virtues which appealed to the strictly amateur drivers in SCCA racing. In fact, although Elva did not have much of a presence in Europe, thanks to its American sales it was the company which came closest to Lotus in terms of cars made.

Further expansion came with the introduction of the Courier road car and in the early days of Formula Junior Elva was extremely successful, although it was soon overtaken by the likes of Lotus and Cooper. That hiccough apart, Elva seemed destined for long-term success but then the American importer was gaoled for financial irregularities and that wiped the company out.

The Courier project was sold to Trojan, and Nichols regrouped. His designer, Keith Marsden, produced some excellent mid-engined sports cars, good enough to be faked in the 1980s, and Nichols was able not only to persuade Porsche to provide him with engines (some later Porsche sports-racers bore marks of Elva influence) but also brought BMW into sports car racing. Elva was eventually absorbed by Trojan and made the production versions of McLaren Can-AM cars.

**Courier MkI/II, 1958-61. Prod: approx 700.** In Frank Nichols' own words, the ideal Courier owner should have a waterproof head and a pneumatic bum; it was really a built up special but it achieved a lot of competition success in production car racing on both sides of the Atlantic. It had a fibreglass body on top of a tubular frame, with coil spring and double wishbone front suspension and a live rear axle with coil springs and radius arms. Front disc brakes were standard and the engine was almost always the BMC series B unit. Apart from some early cars which used a Riley version, the Courier had the engine from the MGA and MGB, so during the model's life engine size ranged from 1489cc to 1798cc. Couriers were only sold abroad until 1960 when a lightly revised MkII version came along and the car became available as a kit on the home market.

**Courier MkIII/IV, 1962-68. Prod: approx 100.** These were the cars built by Trojan and they differed from the original in having a square tube frame. One of the criticisms of the car was a cramped cockpit, which Trojan solved by putting the engine further forward in the frame—

Elva Courier MkIII (top), MkIV Sports (middle) and MkIV coupé (bottom)

and promptly ruined the handling. This was rectified in the MkIV by putting the engine back in its original position. At the same time an independent rear layout by coil springs and double wishbones was adopted, and this allowed the option of rear disc brakes. Coupé versions were also offered, some with a Ford Anglia style rear window treatment, some with a fastback. Very few cars were made after 1965 and in the latter days the Ford Cortina GT engine was an option.

After Trojan ceased production an Elva specialist,Tony Ellis, created a version called the '3000' with a revised coupé body and a tuned 3-litre Ford V6 engine which gave it 130mph/210kmh and 0-60mph in around seven seconds. Ellis failed to put the car into production and the prototype no longer exists.

**GT160, 1965. Prod: 3.** Had this project come off, it would have changed Elva's history and, possibly, the history of the British specialist car industry. The idea was to take an Elva Mk7 sports-racer and clothe it in a GT body styled by Trevor Fiore (real name Trevor Frost, an Englishman) and built by Fissore in Italy. So far so good: the chassis was one of the best of its time, the 2-litre BMW engine was in the ball park, and Trevor came up with a stunning body style, as he so often did. It failed, however, and the reasons were manifold: Fissore underestimated the cost; the British government imposed swingeing import duties which further sent up prices; and the body was too heavy. Nichols was trying to go up-market when he might have tried a fibreglass GT body on the Elva 7 chassis and, today, he admits this is what he should have done. The GT160 remains, however, one of the loveliest cars of its time.

Elva GT 160, 1965, BMW powered

## EMBEESEA KIT CARS (GB)

The 'Charger' was a VW Beetle based gull-wing coupé kit which derived form the Siva Saluki (qv). Embeesea made it from 1977 until the mid-1980s when it was taken over by DJ Sports Cars (qv). The Charger II was a 2+2 version.

## EMERY (GB)

Only two constructors built cars to run in the first four World Championship formulae, 1950-65—Enzo Ferrari and Paul Emery. The difference between them was that Emery designed, physically built, and often drove his 'Emerysons'. Described by those who worked with him as a 'genius', Emery could turn his hand to any part of a car but he was always strapped for cash and some of his designs might have been better had he not had to rely on scrapyards. He once obtained five Aston Martin engines from the scrap merchant with the contract to take sub-standard stock; after that, all scrap Aston Martin engines were treated with a sledge hammer before leaving the works. Emery's biggest problem was that he was no businessman, and those who backed his projects found him impossible to deal with. Every so often he seemed to be on the verge of breaking into the big time, no more so than when he created his one road car, but although the GT showed enormous promise, the project folded when his financial backer suddenly died.

**GT, 1963. Prod: 4.** The Emery GT used a tuned Hillman

Imp engine mounted at the rear with the Imp gearbox inverted. A space frame chassis was used with all-round independent suspension by coil springs and wishbones, anti-dive at the front, anti-dip at the rear. The prototype had an aluminium body, and because it was constructed on an uneven floor one door sill was deeper than the other, so the doors were of different sizes (Emery's response was typical... "So what? You can't see both sides at once". The three other examples built had fibreglass bodies taken off the prototype and these were bonded onto the space frames. Although it was designed to be a practical road car the Emery GT was a natural racer and in 1963 John Markey won his class 15 times from 16 starts. That was not enough to save the project when the backer died. Later Emery built 12 highly tuned Imps with their roofs chopped down by four inches.

**Emery GT, 1963**

## EMW (DDR)

After the War the main BMW works at Eisenach was nationalised by the East German government and until 1955 production of the pre-war BMW 326 and 327 was continued alongside IFA saloon cars, to a pre-war DKW design (IFA was actually a nationalised union of several makers). The 327, a 2-litre cabriolet, was marketed as the EMW 321 but due to a shortage of high quality fuel the compression ratio was lowered and performance was poor. Until 1952 the company sold its cars as 'BMW' which caused the West German parent to request Western importers to put on a new badge and to file the letter 'B' on the engine block so that it looked like an 'E'. Few reached the West and most which did went to Finland.

**1955 EMW 321**

A dispute over the name and logo ensued in 1952 when the Bavarian works began production again and, naturally, laid claim to the BMW name since the initials stand for Bayerische Motoren-Werke. It was settled in 1955, in BMW's favour, and coincidentally the works was turned over to the production of Wartburg saloon cars. Until 1956 the works also made some very rapid F2 cars and 1.5-2-litre sports-racers which used dohc versions of BMW engines and which, after 1955, were known as AWE.

There is an intriguing 'What if?' in what is otherwise a grey story. At the 1949 Leipzig fair in East Germany, 'BMW' showed two new cars, both based on the pre-war 328. One, the 340S, was a low and handsome sports car, with an enveloping body which was as pretty as anything on sale in the world at the time. The other was an ultra-smooth coupé with fully enclosed wheels, the headlights set in a wide grille, and the fast-back hard top made of perspex. The cars exhibited all the flair people had come to expect of the pre-war BMW factory but East Germany was not the place in which to build advanced sports cars. Faceless commissars made sure that neither was put into production.

## ENGLISH CARS OF DISTINCTION (GB)

Country Classic Cars originated Jaguar XK and E Type copies, was taken over by Automobiles of Distinction in 1990 and that year underwent a name change. In 1990 it offered a range of five types, 'XK120/140/150' and 'Series 1/2 and 3 E Types', hand built to order and at very high prices. Appropriate Jaguar straight six or V12 engines were fitted, with the option of an original four-speed gearbox or a modern Jaguar five-speed 'box.

## ENIAK (RA)

In 1983 this Argentine furniture maker introduced the 'Antique', a 1930s style fibreglass-bodied two-seat sports car which seemed to have been inspired by the SS100.

**Eniak Antique, 1983**

## ENVEMO (BR)

Envemo specialised in tuning equipment for locally made Chevrolets and, in 1978, marketed a pretty, sharp-edged sports car using the 2.5-litre four-cylinder Chevrolet Opala engine. This was not a success and after 1980 the company concentrated on VW-based copies of the Porsche 356.

Cabriolet and coupé versions were made. Envemo products were marked out as they were so accurate that they won praise from senior Porsche personnel and were distributed in Germany by a Porsche dealer.

Envemo's 'Porsche 356'

## ENZMANN (CH)

A pretty, open, two-seat fibreglass body on a VW floorpan which was made as a turn key car between 1957 and 1970.

Enzmann, with curious hardtop

## ERA REPLICA AUTOMOBILES (USA)

This Connecticut company seems to have missed the point that it usurped a once-great name (ERA is now a division of the Jack Knight Group, building Mini Turbos). In the mid-1980s it made run-of-the-mill copies of the AC Cobra and Ford GT40. However, from 1986 ERA's 40s were remarkably faithful to the original GT40, with a slightly simplified monocoque (most GT40 copies were built around space frames) and accurate bodywork.

ERA Cobra copy, 1983

## ERMINI (I)

Pasquale Ermini was one of a number of constructors who made small numbers of Fiat-based sports cars in the 1950s. He tended to concentrate on the 1100cc class. In 1950 Piero Scotti won his class in the Pescara 4 Hours, the Tour of Sicily and the Targa Florio, but although Ermini made small numbers of such cars through the 1950s the marque never again reached such heights, usually being overshadowed by Stanguellini (qv). In 1953 Ermini showed a pretty 1.3-litre GT car with a body by Ghia but few, if any, were sold.

1954 Ermini 1.3-litre coupé, this one with Frua body

## EUROSPORT (GB)

From 1990, this company offered poseurs a golden opportunity to turn a perfectly respectable Triumph TR7 into a Ferrari F40 lookalike. It was still a Triumph TR7 under the fibreglass...

Eurosport TR40, 1990

## JIM EVANS (NZ)

A late-1980s Kiwi attempt to redress the fact that very few rhd Jaguar XK120s were made. Sourced from Jaguar MksVII-IX, the 'XK120' was a fibreglass copy of a Jaguar with a similar name.

## EVANTE CARS (GB)

Evante is an off-shoot of Vegantune, an established and respected engine tuner. This car, introduced in the mid-1980s, followed the original Lotus Elan in its styling and overall engineering. There were bulges and aerodynamic lips which the Elan never had, and the backbone chassis was made from steel tubes, not fabricated from sheet steel as the Lotus was. Vegantune was coy about its car's ancestry but had no reason to be so; the Evante was a reconstituted Elan which, with the right engine, was better than the original. It was also a practical car, with weather equipment, a decent boot and an optional walnut and leather interior package to go along with the (optional) carpets.

Evante in 1987

## EVERETT-MORRISON (USA)

Yet another company which offered a Cobra copy in the 1980s.

## EXCALIBUR (GB)

Introduced in 1986, and originally engineered around a VW Beetle floorpan, this Excalibur was a 2+2 fibreglass and Kevlar coupé inspired by the mid-engined De Tomaso Vallelunga. The few production models were sourced from the Ford Cortina, although the Granada/Capri V6 engine could also be used in this front-engined car. After an enthusiastic welcome (apparently the Excalibur's road holding was very good) little more was heard of it.

## EXCALIBUR (USA)

Brooks Stevens was a leading industrial designer and amateur racing driver whose taste in cars was distinctly European. Like Howard Darrin, he figured that the Kaiser Henry J chassis was an ideal base for a sports car and, again like Darrin, he thought that the ideal engine was the 2.6-litre Willys F-head straight six. The cars were outstandingly successful in SCCA racing (they could, and did, beat Jaguars and Ferraris) but Henry J Kaiser refused to put the design into production (it could have sold for $2000, a snip) and preferred Darrin's outlandish boulevard cruiser.

Stevens made just four examples of this Excalibur 'J'; of the three cars made in 1952-3, one had an Alfa Romeo 1900 chassis, but the two most successful cars had a Kaiser base. The Willys engine was tuned to produce 125bhp and was set well back in the frame, resulting in outstanding road holding. Styling was 'mid-Atlantic', with Stevens drawing his inspiration from British cycle-winged sports cars, and this seems to have been the stumbling block with Kaiser.

In 1958 Stevens built a fourth car, still on a Kaiser frame, this time with an enveloping body and a supercharged Jaguar 3.8-litre engine, and it won the SCCA National Championship outright. Had Henry J Kaiser possessed more foresight the history of the American sports car might have been very different.

From 1964 Brooks Stevens marketed high quality Mercedes-Benz SSK lookalikes. Until 1969, the car was based on a Studebaker Daytona chassis; later the base was Ford. A four-seater, the 'Phaeton', was offered from 1967, and in 1968 the company essayed a Bugatti copy which did not catch on. Excalibur was the first, and most successful, 'nostalgia' car maker, and despite high prices the cars have been made at the rate of about five a week. By 1990 the mechanical specification had changed, but if you are interested in that you are not the natural buyer of one of the great posemobiles.

1953 Excalibur J was Willys engined

Excalibur SS at Sebring in the late '60s

## EXOTIC DREAM CARS (USA)

A 1980s Californian company which made high quality copies of the Lamborghini Countach (including an open top 'Roadster') and various body kits to convert Porsche 911s into 'Speedsters' and '959s'.

# F

## FACEL VEGA (F)

Forges et Ateliers de Construction d'Eure et de Loire SA, or Facel, was founded in 1938 as a maker of machine tools for the aircraft industry. During the German Occupation it made gas generators for cars and after the War it diversified into a number of areas, including the manufacture of car bodies, mainly for Panhard and Simca. It also originated designs, built a one-off body on a Bentley chassis and built bodies for the Ford (France) Comète.

By 1954 most of the old French luxury car makers had gone, killed by a combination of fiscal measures and old fashioned designs, and Facel went against the trend with a car simply called the 'Vega' (the arrangement with Panhard had ended and the company had spare capacity). The Vega had a 4.5-litre De Soto V8 engine which usually fed its 180bhp through a two-speed automatic transmission, although a Pont-à-Mousson four-speed manual gearbox was an expensive option. Whatever the drive train, it was fitted to a tubular chassis frame with coil spring and double wishbone front suspension and a live rear axle on semi-elliptic springs. The chassis was topped by a handsome and luxuriously appointed four-seat body.

A total of 46 Vegas was sold in 1954 and 1955, but as the French economy grew stronger production was increased and it seemed that Facel would become an established feature of the automotive scene. Unfortunately, in 1960, Facel Vega introduced an original sports car, the Facellia, which was a disaster. By the end of 1962 the company was in the hands of a receiver. A survival package was put together but the cars produced under it were not successful and Facel was declared bankrupt in 1965.

**Vega and FVS, 1954-59. Prod: 357.** Originally called the Facel 'Vega', before long the company was called Facel Vega and the model was called the 'FVS'. The bare details are given above but during its production life larger engines were fitted and by the end there was a 325bhp 5.4-litre Chrysler V8 and a third ratio in the automatic transmission. In 1957 a brake servo was fitted and the following year disc brakes were an option. At the time, there were few cars in the world which would carry four people at 130mph/210kmh and none of them was as stylish or as well made as the Vega.

Facel Vega, 1954

**Excellence, 1958-64. Prod: 230.** Not a sports or even a sporting car, but included to keep the record tidy. The Excellence was a long wheelbase version of the Vega/FVS which originally had a 5.8-litre Chrysler engine and received a 6.3-litre unit in 1959. The trouble was that the 17ft long body was pillarless and contributed little to overall rigidity so the doors soon gave problems and it won few friends.

The four-door Facel Vega Excellence

**HK500, 1959-61. Prod: 500.** An uprated Vega/FVS but with the 360bhp 6.3-litre engine. Until April 1960, four wheel disc brakes were only an option. This perhaps highlights one of Facel's problems: it was long on style and power but short on the sort of detail which a company steeped in competition would have taken as read. For the same reason the seats were not right, so if a driver did press on he was likely to be thrown around the cockpit.

HK500, 1959

**Facel II, 1962-64. Prod: 184.** An uprated HK500 with sharper lines, better visibility and up to 390bhp. In this form

Facel II, an uprated HK500

it would top 150mph/240kmh (0-60mph in under eight seconds) and from the beginning there were servo-assisted disc brakes on all four wheels. In retrospect it may seem a mystery that it did not do better, but the chassis had not kept pace with the increase in power output and what was good enough for 1954 was not good enough for 1964.

**Facellia, 1960-63. Prod: 1258.** This was the car on which Facel pinned its hopes for expansion (it was making fewer and fewer bodies for other makers) but it brought down the company. In style it resembled a smaller, two-seat HK500. It was available as a hardtop coupé or a convertible, and the chassis followed established lines although, curiously, drum brakes were an option until 1961. The problem was the engine, a 1647cc dohc four-cylinder unit designed by former Talbot engineer, Carlo Marchetti, and built by Pont-à-Mousson.

For a start the car was expensive for a 1.6-litre sports car with no competition pedigree; it was heavy, performance was not outstanding since the 115bhp engine had a peaky power band, and the Facellia would only just top 105mph/170kmh (0-60mph in 11.9 seconds). There was no shortage of opposition on those terms. Worse, the engine was noisy and unreliable and soon earned a reputation for burning oil and pistons. The root cause was poor rigidity and cooling in the block, and Facel was not placed to sort out the problem quickly. The final cars were much better but by then it was too late.

**1960 Facellia 1.6 litre**

**Facel III/6, 1963-64. Prod: approx 1500/26.** Had this been the original package, it might have guaranteed Facel's success—it sold more in two years than all other Facel models (excepting the Facellia) did in eleven years. The Facel III was a Facellia with a 1780cc Volvo engine which with 108bhp gave almost the same performance as with the troublesome Pont-à-Mousson engine, but with excellent reliability. The weight of the Volvo engine meant that handling suffered, but since Facel Vega's clientele sought luxury and style rather than outright performance this was not a big issue.

**Facel III, 1963, had 1.8-litre Volvo engine**

The rare Facel 6 had a 150bhp BMC Series C engine similar to that used in the Austin-Healey 3000 but linered down to 2851cc. The unit was smaller to bring the car within a significant French tax bracket but its power meant that the performance of the car was much enhanced. Unfortunately it did not save the company.

## FAIRLEY (GB)

This was an unsuccessful 1950 attempt to market a five-seater convertible and a two-seater road/competition car using Jowett Javelin components.

## FAIRTHORPE (GB)

Founded by Air Vice Marshal Don 'Pathfinder' Bennett, Fairthorpe began production in 1954 with the 'Atom', a 'sporty' bubble car (a contradiction in terms if ever there was one) with hideous looks. Sports cars followed in 1956 and the Electron Minor was a 'pre-Sprite Sprite'. It was, however, let down by terrible styling, a Fairthorpe characteristic. Standard-Triumph mechanicals were not very exciting either but BMC would not supply components for rivals to the Sprite, Ford's small engines were still in the Stone Age and Standard's chairman was Air Marshal Lord Tedder. In 1965 Bennett's son, Torin, designed the equally eccentric 'TX' series and in 1970 this was established as a separate marque (qv).

In 1987 two Fairthorpe enthusiasts bought the old works and the remaining spares to offer a service to existing owners. When last heard of they were preparing a Ford Escort-based kit car to use a slightly modified version of the original body.

**Electron, 1956-65. Prod: approx 30.** A Fairthorpe ladder frame, a Microplas 'Mistral' fibreglass body usually sold to special builders, and a Coventry Climax FWA engine were the ingredients for the firm's first sports car. Performance was quite lively, and it was the cheapest car to use the Climax motor, but not many people wanted a car which could be easily mistaken for a Ford Ten special and which stood no chance in competition. Fairthorpe soon made its own body shell but that, too, looked like a Ford Ten special. Front disc brakes were fitted from 1957.

**1959 Fairthorpe Electron**

**Electron Minor, 1957-73.** **Prod: approx 500.** The economy version of the Electron got off to a good start and for a time sold at a rate of five a week, but then came the Sprite. Like the Electron it had a ladder frame and Standard 10 (later Herald) front suspension. A twin carb 50bhp 948cc Standard engine powered the early cars, the 63bhp 1147cc Spitfire version came in 1963 and the 75bhp 1.3-litre version was fitted from 1969; front disc brakes came in 1966. If the body was ugly in 1957, by the 1970s it had become a poor joke.

Electron Minor at showtime

**Electrina, 1961-63.** **Prod: approx 20.** A 2+2 Electron Minor with a roof, for the eccentric family man. Apparently eccentric family men were thin on the ground. Like all Fairthorpes it was sold complete or as a kit.

Not getting any prettier: the Electrina, 1961

**Zeta, 1960-65.** **Prod: approx 20.** Zeta was the name given to a much-publicised contemporary project to extract nuclear power from sea water. It failed, so it was an appropriate name to give this beast, which was an Electron fitted with a Ford Zephyr engine. With the right tweaks, up to 137bhp was available and the Zeta was fearsomely quick in a straight line, but to drive it a frontal lobotomy was desirable.

The Ford Zephyr powered Zeta, 1960

**Rockette, 1963-67.** **Prod: approx 25.** An Electron/Zeta chassis with the 70bhp Triumph Vitesse straight-six. Early cars had a central third headlamp, a bold innovation which did not catch on.

Fairthorpe Rockette, later model without central headlamp

**TX GT/S/SS, 1967-76.** **Prod: approx 50.** Torin Bennett's first car used a form of cross-over rocker arms in the rear suspension; it was called an innovation, but it had been developed by Arnott in 1957 and has reappeared at regular intervals ever since. This system made the wheels lean in, not out, when cornering and apparently it worked, as it had worked on the Arnott. Otherwise the car was the mixture as before, with a fibreglass body, Fairthorpe frame and, this time, a Triumph GT6 engine and gearbox. From 1969 the body was tidied up and became quite pretty. Some cars were made on the GT6 chassis, the TR6 engine was available on the SS, and into the 1980s it was still theoretically available with the 1.5-litre Triumph engine. By that time TX was established as a separate marque (qv).

Fairthorpe TX-SS

## FALCON (GB)

After Peter Pellandine split with Ashley Laminates, he set up his own company to make a wide range of fibreglass shells, one of which became standard on the Elva MkII and was revived in the 1980s as the Autotune 'Gemini' (qv). Falcon then began making a simple tubular frame to fit under its bodies and give a basis for special builders. For a time Len Terry (who later designed cars for Lotus, BRM, Eagle, Surtees and others) was employed to give advice to customers. There followed a kit car using the space frame which Terry had designed for his Terrier clubman's car, and a separate company, occupying the same premises, used this to make the Peregrine sports car.

In 1963 there was an attempt to establish the company as a regular constructor with the Falcon 515, which was styled by a Brazilian, T. Rohoyni. The pretty fibreglass body was bonded to a tubular frame designed to take Ford Cortina parts. It was offered as a complete car, but most of the 25 cars produced were sold as kits. For a time it looked as though Falcon was on its way to becoming a permanent part of the scene but it faded away in 1964 after its founder was seriously injured in a road accident. Peter Pellandine recovered, has since made kit cars in both Australia and Britain, and has been notable for his work on steam cars.

Falcon 515, 1963

## FALCON (GB)

From the mid-1980s, this company offered a Lotus Seven-type car but with 2+2 seating and based on Citroën Ami, Dyane or 2CV components; it was also available as a set of plans.

1990 Falcon

## FARUS (BR)

Established in 1981, this specialist maker followed the usual Brazilian lines in its car, with a fibreglass body (which could pass for a cousin of the Ferrari Dino GT4) and locally sourced engines. Until 1988 Farus made the mid-engined 2+2 ML 929 (with a 1.3-litre Fiat engine) while the TS 1.6 was similar but had a 1.6-litre VW Golf unit. A revised model (the Beta) using basically the same body was introduced in 1988 as a mid-engined two seat coupé or cabriolet. Like its forebears it had a backbone chassis, all-independent suspension and front disc brakes. It was available with VW or Chevrolet engines, both of 2 litres although, for export, a 2.2-litre Chrysler LeBaron Turbo unit was usual. In 2-litre form, a maximum speed of 124mph/200kmh was claimed; the 2.2-litre turbo version was naturally quicker and could accelerate 0-60mph in around seven seconds. In 1989 a front-engined front wheel drive four seat coupé, the Quadro, was introduced.

## FELBER (CH)

From 1974 until the 1980s Willi Felber made small numbers of sports cars and coupés based on proprietary chassis. He it was who commissioned the Panther Ferrari FF and its Lancia-based derivatives. In the late 1970s Felber offered the 'Excellence', which was available as either a coupé or a roadster. Its chief styling feature was a vertical radiator grille which looked like an inverted Bentley grille. Felber Excellences were basically re-bodied Pontiacs using the 225bhp 6.6-litre V8 engine and three-speed automatic transmission. Top speed was claimed to be 118mph/190kmh.

## FERA (BR)

This company introduced a copy of the Jaguar XK120 in 1981. It used a fibreglass body and a straight-six 4.1-litre Chevrolet engine.

Fera XK 4.1 HE, 1984

## FERGUS (GB)

Introduced in 1988, the Fergus 'Mosquito' was a well-made evocation of the 1930s Aston Martin Ulster. A fibreglass body was fitted to a box section frame with double wishbone and torsion bar front suspension, with decorative 'semi-elliptic' springs connected to the front dumb irons to give an air of authenticity. The period look was also aided by 18in wire wheels (modern wheels let down so many evocations of earlier cars). Power came from the 1.8-litre Rover B series engine which was also available in a Stage II 2-litre version.

## FERGUS (USA)

This was an unsuccessful 1949 attempt to market a sports car which used Austin A40 components and had a body styled on broadly the same lines as the Austin A40 Sports. How could it have failed?

## FERRARI (I)

Enzo Ferrari was a frustrated engineer (he flunked technical college) who became a fairly good racing driver, an adept politician and wheeler-dealer, and a very successful team manager whose *Scuderia Ferrari* was effectively the works Alfa Romeo team in the 1930s. After a split with Alfa, he set up his own workshop and built a couple of Fiat-based specials (called 'Auto Avia' for contractual reasons) which ran without success in the 1940 Gran Premio di Brescia (often erroneously called the 1940 Mille Miglia).

His company flourished during the Second World War and in 1947 he produced a new car under his own name. It was very successful in sports car racing, largely because it was the first postwar design. Ferrari's first attempt at a Formula 1 car, using a supercharged 1.5-litre engine, was less successful and it was not until he produced a 4.5-litre unblown engine that Ferrari was finally able to defeat Alfa Romeo (in 1951). It should be remembered that the Alfetta was by then 13 years old, so perhaps it was not as great an achievement as it might seem.

Ferrari dominated the next two seasons of racing but after that enjoyed only spasmodic success in F1, and then usually by employing English engineers; in fact until John Barnard joined the company in 1986 and produced a radical semi-automatic gearbox Ferrari had never, ever, introduced a new idea. On the contrary, it had been slow to adopt developments such as disc brakes and mid-mounted engines.

For the first twenty or so years of Ferrari's existence, road cars took second place to the firm's racing activities (but they funded it) although that changed in 1969 when Fiat bought the road car division (quietly) and half the racing team, leaving Ferrari to front the operation, which he did until his death in 1989. The road cars won an unparalleled reputation, but much of the credit rests with Pininfarina, which produced a long line of often breathtakingly beautiful bodies. These sometimes clothed fundamentally incompetent cars with such elegance that the shortcomings of the beast beneath have been forgiven; many owners have been in the position of a man besotted by a beautiful, exciting, but feckless temptress.

Until recently, Ferrari type numbers referred to the capacity of a single cylinder in the engine in cubic centimetres. When six-cylinder engines were introduced the designation referred to the engine size in litres and the number of cylinders (eg, Dino 246). Most early Ferraris followed racing practice and had right hand drive.

**166 Sport / 166 Inter / 166 MM, 1947-48/1948-53/1949-53.** **Prod:** 2/37/32. Ferrari commissioned Gioacchino Colombo to design a new car,

Chinetti at Le Mans in a 166, 1949

which had a sohc V12 engine suspiciously similar to a stillborn Alfa Romeo flat-12 with which Colombo had been associated. The first three cars (Tipo 125) were of 1.5 litres but the Tipo 166 had a 2-litre engine. Up to 150bhp was available (poor materials were a limiting factor on early Ferraris) and this fed through a five-speed gearbox, unusual at the time. Early Ferrari chassis were crude tubular affairs with coil spring and double wishbone front suspension and a live rear axle on semi-elliptics, but thanks to the engine 166s won everything in sight, including Le Mans and the Mille Miglia (hence the MM).

**195 / 212 Export / 212 Inter, 1950-53. Prod approx: 25/25/80.** Racing occupied most of Ferrari's attention, in particular he wanted to beat Alfa Romeo in the Grands Prix. The next 'road' cars to appear had enlarged engines: Tipo 195, 2341cc ('Inter', 130bhp; 'Sport', 150-170bhp); Tipo 212, 2562cc ('Inter', 130bhp; 'Export', 160-180bhp) but the original chassis was still used (with a longer wheelbase on the 212 Inter) and stylists produced a variety of bodies. The Tipo 195 was not very successful in racing but the 212, which ran in the same class, won a lot of events although it has to be said the opposition was negligible.

Ferrari 212 Inter, Alpine Rally 1953 (above) and an unbent 212 Inter L Berlina by Ghia (below)

**America 340/342/375, 1950-55. Prod:** 22/6/13. After Colombo's supercharged cars failed to beat Alfa Romeo in F1, Ferrari commissioned Aurelio Lampredi to design a 'long block' sohc V12. This began as a 3.3-litre engine and was gradually enlarged until, in 1951, it was running in F1 in 4.5-litre form. It also formed the basis of the 'America' sports car series, which retained the old chassis layout (with extended wheelbase), and a four-speed all-synchro gearbox could be specified, along with the non-synchro five-speed transmission. As before, body styles varied as did the engine size (340 = 4101cc, 280bhp; 342 = 4101cc, 230bhp, strictly a road car; 375

= 4522cc, 300bhp). Left hand cars were available. It is interesting that Ferrari works F1 drivers Farina and Ascari bought Jaguar C Types for road use, as did Fangio.

Ferrari 342 America

**250 Export, 1953-54. Prod: —.** Basically the last expression of the original theme, the 250 Export replaced the 212 series and used a long (96in) wheelbase chassis similar to the 212 Inter. However, power came from a linered-down 'long block' engine which, unusually for a Ferrari, was 'square' (68mm bore and stroke, 2963cc), and was rated at 210bhp. It is not to be confused with later 250s, which used Colombo's 'short block' design. As usual, there was no set body style but any number of Italian coachbuilders were happy to oblige.

**250 Europa, 1953-54. Prod: 17.** Until this model, all 'production' Ferraris had really been competition cars with road-style bodies and de-tuned engines. Actually, all Ferraris until the early 1960s were really specials although the parts were made in-house. The long wheelbase chassis had been used on the Tipo 375 America (chassis layout followed established lines although it was actually new). The model was intended for road use only, hence the long wheelbase, four-speed synchro 'box, and a mildly tuned (200bhp) 2963cc V12. A variety of bodies were fitted but few customers wanted a 'civilised' Ferrari.

250 Europa by Pininfarina

**250GT, 1954-62. Prod: 905 (all varieties).** This car marked the point when Ferrari edged towards being a volume producer. The chassis followed established practice and although it has become known as the 'long wheelbase' model, at 102in, it was 8in shorter than the 250 Europa. The engine was the 'classic' expression of Colombo's original design (73 x 58.5mm, 2953cc). Although there was a variety of body styles, by different coachbuilders, Ferrari was forging a relationship with Pininfarina which was to be mutually profitable. Disc brakes were fitted from late 1959 and the four-speed gearbox had overdrive after 1960.

1958 Ferrari 250GT by Pininfarina

**410 Superamerica, 1956-59. Prod: 38 (all types).** The replacement for the 375 America had a 340bhp 5-litre engine and was good for 135mph/217kmh with any body (Italian stylists had to look up 'aerodynamics' in a dictionary). The first fifteen cars had the 110in wheelbase chassis from the 375 America while the post-1957 models had the 102in wheelbase chassis from the 250GT. From 1958, a revised cylinder head raised the power output to 360bhp and over 155mph/250kmh could be seen. As the name implies, the car was aimed at America, but it did not sell well because it was incredibly expensive and, like all Ferraris of the time, was too temperamental to be a practical road car.

Ferrari 410 Superamerica, 1956

**250GT SWB, 1959-64. Prod 232 (all types).** The short (94.5in) wheelbase 250GT is rightly regarded as Ferrari's most perfect expression; and the reason is that it emerged at the time of transition when the production side was establishing sensible standards yet was still tied to racing.

250GT SWB (Scaglietti)

The chassis layout remained as before, but the shorter and stiffer frame endowed the car with outstanding road holding and balance. At last Ferrari used disc brakes, having been convinced by his English F1 drivers, Collins and Hawthorn—brakes had been a problem on many late 1950s Ferraris. It is hard to decide which is the most beautiful: the Scaglietti Berlinetta, the Pininfarina California Spyder, or the Pininfarina Lusso; here we are talking the Judgement of Paris.

**250 Lusso, 1962-65. Prod: 350.** Although the Lusso ('luxury') belongs to the 250GT SWB line, it was produced in sufficient quantity to deserve its own entry. For many Ferrari enthusiasts it is the ideal: it bears the signs of Ferrari's competition history (the rear axle location is from the GTO) but is a civilised, well-appointed road car of supreme grace. Unfortunately, the number of extant Lussos has diminished by the same number as fake GTOs that have appeared—there might be a connection here.

250GT Lusso

**250GT 2+2 / 330GT America / 330GT 2+2, 1960-63/1964/ 1965-68. Prod: approx 950/50/1000.** This was the line which saw Ferrari become a significant producer of road cars; the 2+2 had the same chassis as the lwb 250GT and the engine was warm rather than hot, rated at 240bhp. The 1964 'America' was an interim car using Ferrari's new 300bhp Tipo 209 4-litre V12, which was a new, longer version of the Colombo engine. A new five-speed gearbox replaced the four-speed unit in 1965, alloy wheels became standard with Borrani wires as an option, and new engine mounts reduced noise to soften the car's character.

250GT 2+2 (above), 330GT 2+2 (below)

**400 Superamerica, 1960-64. Prod 54 (all types).** The world wanted various forms of the 250GT, even if only a few who wanted one could afford one. In the face of this, and buoyed up by competition and commercial successes, Ferrari tried to milk the American market with a 4-litre supercar with a potential for over 160mph/260kmh, or so it was claimed. This used Colombo's sohc in its most stretched form (Ferrari had discarded the Lampredi 'long block' unit). Since America had strictly-enforced speed limits, there was no point in paying silly money for theoretical top speed; the Ferrari buyer wanted style and the 250 series provided that abundantly. To have succeeded, the Superamerica would have needed to have been more beautiful than any 250, and that it was not.

400 Superamerica

**250GTO, 1962-64. Prod: 39 (all types).** Derived from a prototype which had run at Le Mans in 1961, the GTO is today considered the most desirable of all Ferraris because it is a racing car which can be used on the road. A 250 Testarossa with a roof, 300bhp, a five-speed gearbox, and lighter than the 250SWB, the GTO was a formidable machine

250 GTO

on the circuits although technically, it was not legal because Ferrari did not build the 100 examples required for homologation. A 4-litre version was occasionally run by the works and 1964 cars were lower and wider, with a 'notch' back (like the 250LM). Giotto Bizzarrini and Piero Drogo also made some lightweight cars based on 250SWB components (the most famous of which was known as the 'breadvan') but these achieved little success. Today 250GTOs have an 'auction value' almost beyond belief.

**250 Le Mans, 1964-66. Prod: 32.** The first mid-engined Ferrari GT car. Most 250LMs were bought for racing, and were very successful, but they were viable road cars with enough luggage space for a weekend trip. According to Ferrari's own system of numbering, it should have been called the 275LM because it had a 3.3-litre engine, but Sig. Ferrari insisted it should have the '250' designation. The V12 engine was installed in a space frame with all-independent suspension and delivered its 320bhp through a five-speed transaxle. It was the last Ferrari which could be raced at the very top level (first and second at Le Mans in 1965) yet could be used on the road.

Ferrari 250 Le Mans

**275GTB / GTS, 1964-67. Approx prod: 940 (all types).** This was the 3.3-litre replacement for the 250GT series. Although the SWB Ferrari tubular frame could be traced back to the earliest days, contemporary racing practice could be detected in the all-independent suspension and the five-speed transaxle. The GTS (S = Spyder) convertible was intended as a road car, so had 260bhp, but the GTB (B = Berlinetta) coupé was a 'dual purpose' machine and had 280bhp. For serious competition work there was the lightweight 275GTB/C. Twin overhead camshafts appeared for the first time on a production Ferrari in 1966, boosting power to 300bhp, and these cars were designated GTB/4. There was no official Spyder version of the quad-cam but Scaglietti built ten convertibles for the American importer.

275GTB (above) and 275GTS (below), both 1965

**Superfast 500, 1964-67. Prod: 37 (all types).** Five litres, dohc, a claimed 400bhp (Italian horses), a not very successful body by Pininfarina, plus unprecedented levels of luxury—this led one writer to describe the Superfast as Ferrari's Bugatti Royale. The Royale wasn't much good either, but in its favour the 500's engine was special, being an amalgamation of the Colombo and Lampredi designs with a large input by (anonymous) design staff. That was not enough to make a notable car.

Ferrari Superfast 500, 1964

**330 GTC / GTS, 1966-68. Prod: 600/100.** The chassis for this series was basically from the 275GTB/S, but the capacity of the 'quad-cam' engine was up to 4 litres. There was no increase in power, at 300bhp, because the 330 was intended to be a 'softer' car, which explains the optional air conditioning. Still, 150mph/240kmh maximum speed and 0-60mph in seven seconds were impressive figures. The GTS convertible was slightly slower since it was heavier and less slippery, but its comparative rarity carries a premium in today's market.

330GTS, 1966

**365 California, 1966-67. Prod: 14.** This was the first of the 4.4-litre 'quad cam' cars and there are no prizes for guessing the target market. With a stunning body by Pininfarina on a longish (104in wheelbase) chassis, power steering and a high level of appointment, the California was more a successor to the 500 Superfast than to previous 'Californias', which were based on the LWB 250GT. Only one right hooker was made, and it has since been destroyed.

Ferrari 365 California, 1966

**365GT 2+2, 1967-71. Prod: 801.** Replacing the 330 2+2 was the largest and most luxurious Ferrari to that time. Although the wheelbase remained at 104in, overall length exceeded 16ft. Air conditioning and power brakes, windows and steering were standard, the rear seats would actually accommodate two adults, there was a large boot and there had even been attention to ergonomics (another word which Italian designers have to look up in a dictionary). Despite its goodies and consequent weight, it was no slouch (140+mph/225kmh, 0-60mph in 7.1 seconds), and it handled well. The single overhead camshaft 4.4-litre V12 gave 320bhp. Cromodora alloy wheels were fitted until 1968, when they were replaced by Daytona-style five spoke alloys, but Borrani wires were an option.

365GT 2+2, 1967

**365GTC / GTS, 1968-70/1968-69. Prod: approx 200/20.** An updated short chassis 330GTC given the 320bhp 4.4-litre version of the single overhead camshaft engine, which added nothing to performance but made for more relaxed driving due to improved torque. Like the 330 it was smooth rather than raunchy and was one of the first indications that Ferrari could make sensible road cars, for the fine performance and superb handling were allied to comfort and new levels of build quality. A two-seater, it was overshadowed by the much quicker Daytona, which explains its relative rarity, but then it was intended to be sophisticated and elegant rather than exciting.

365GTC, 1968

**Dino 206GT, 1967-69. Prod: approx 100.** Ferrari's small capacity V6 engine had been named for his son, who had made some input into the design before his death in 1956 (it was largely the work of the greatest of all Italian designers, Vittorio Jano). Long before the engine appeared, mounted transversely amidships, in the first 'baby' Ferrari, versions had enjoyed a long and successful competition career in F1, F2 and sports car racing. The 2-litre version in the Dino was rated at 180bhp and drove through a five-speed transaxle, suspension was independent all round and, thanks to light weight and low drag, 142mph/228kmh was possible (0-60mph in 7.1 seconds). Pininfarina's styling pointed the way for all mid-engined Ferraris, but the cockpit was noisy and luggage space was minimal. There was no Ferrari badge for the Dino was launched as a separate marque and Fiat built the engine. The traditional model designation changed: 206 stood for 2 litres, six cylinders.

Dino 206GT, 1967

**365GTB/4 'Daytona' / 365GTS/4, 1968-74. Prod: approx 1285/127 plus 20 Group 4 cars.** To call the Daytona the replacement for the 275GTB/4 is like calling Chartres Cathedral a building. It has become the stuff of dreams and it was the press, not the factory, which was responsible for the 'Daytona' nickname. It used the 275 chassis but had 352bhp from a 4.4-litre dry-sumped 'quad cam' engine, and with a slippery body this translated into 170+mph/275kmh (0-60mph in 5.9 seconds). Pininfarina's styling has made the car legendary (Rover's SD1 was influenced by it), but it was a brute to drive

365GTB/4 'Daytona', 1968

fast and even the 405bhp Group 4 versions achieved little because, despite aluminium bodies, they were overweight and their brakes were inadequate. Facts can spoil good myths.

**Dino 246GT / GTS, 1969-73. Prod: approx 2800/ 1200.** The first road-going Dino did not sell well, and few reached the obvious market, America. An uncomfortable and noisy 2-litre car with little luggage space was a no-no in the wide open spaces of the States. On the other hand, the 195bhp 2.4-litre version (also noisy and impractical) sold well despite the fact that it still did not have a Ferrari badge (some owners have since rectified the omission). Early cars had knock-off wheels but five-stud alloy wheels were fitted by mid-1970. The 246 GTS arrived in 1972, and although 'S' stood for 'Spyder' the car was not a convertible but a Targa-top. While lacking the ultimate performance of a Daytona (150mph/240kmh is hardly slow, however), a Dino could be quicker from A to B.

Dino 246GT, 1970

**365GTC/4, 1971-72. Prod: 500.** A short-lived but popular 2+2 which replaced both the 365GT 2+2 and the 365GTC and accounted for half of Ferrari's front-engined production in its short life. The chassis was similar to the Daytona's but a conventional five-speed gearbox replaced the Daytona's transaxle. Like all Ferraris it had a separate chassis (a very rigid tubular frame) because the Company does not build its own bodies, and this allowed at least two special bodies to be built on a 365GTC/4 base.

365 GTC/4, 1971

**365GT4 / 400i / 412i, 1972-75/1976-85/ 1985-88. Prod: 470/—/—.** Ferrari's replacement for the 365GTC/4 used that car's chassis, with a longer wheelbase. It had the luxurious appointments which marked its predecessors and Fiat was in charge so quality improved. In 1976 the model received a fuel-injected 4.8-litre 340bhp engine and automatic transmission became an option. Overall sales were not startling as Ferrari stopped selling its V12 cars in the States rather than compromise the engines to meet tougher emission laws, but that did not stop a few appearing on the 'grey market'. 1985 saw Bosch ABS and 4.9 litres; power remained at 340bhp but torque was improved.

Automatic transmission arrives: the 400i, 1977

**Dino 308GT4 / 208 GT4, 1973-79/1975-79. Prod: 2826/840.** As the type number indicates, this was a 3-litre car with a new 255bhp dohc V8 engine (the 177bhp 208 was a 'tax break' car for Italy). The 308 was quicker than previous Dinos (150+mph/240+kmh, 0-60mph in 6.4 seconds). It was more practical too, with +2 seating, but has become the nearest to a bargain used Ferrari. The reason is the Bertone body (the first time since 1953 that Pininfarina did not style a series Ferrari) which does not have the charisma of the Dino 246. Unlike the 246, the GT4 was badged as a Ferrari and the name 'Dino' was dropped from 1977.

Dino 308GT4 2+2, 1973

**365GT4BB / 512BB, BBi, 1973-76/1976-85. Prod: 387/1936.** A new multi-tube frame took the 380bhp dohc 4.4-litre engine, mounted amidships but in line, the all-independent suspension followed Ferrari's contemporary practice, and the Pininfarina studio surpassed itself. In 1976 the type was given a 5-litre engine with the same power but increased flexibility, a bib spoiler at the front, NACA ducts in front of the rear arches, and a new model designation. 'BB' stands for Berlinetta Boxer, the latter referring to the flat-12 engine, in which the pistons move away from each other, like boxers sparring.

Ferrari had used this configuration for some racing engines but this was the first road Ferrari that did not have a Vee engine. Fuel injection arrived in 1981 and a few, very few, Targa-tops were made. 188mph/302kmh was claimed by the

The classic early Ferrari lines, exemplified by a 225S of 1952

The 308GTB was widely regarded as a successor once removed to the classic 246. It was the first production Ferrari to have fibreglass bodywork, and the execution by Scaglietti was as impeccable as Pininfarina's lines

Left: GTOs were important cars in Ferrari history of the 1960s, as they are in Ferrari lore. This 1964 GTO was above all a competition car, one of a handful built and the last in Ferrari's line of front-engined V12 3-litre GT cars

**One car that really did qualify for a supercar label, the Ferrari F40, although within that definition it was difficult to place in a road or circuit car category. Even show cars had less than perfect finish in some details, but there was no denying the F40's 200mph plus capability**

factory, but this was queried by some motoring magazines; still, facts count for nothing with Ferrari, where ambience is all. Like other 12-cylinder Ferraris of the 1980s this model was not sold in the USA, which is not the same as saying that none were sold there because there is the border with Canada.

365GT4BB, 1973

**308GTB / 308GTS / 208GTB / 208GTS, 1975-81. Prod: —.** This was the true successor to the Dino 246 (the GT4 developed into the 2+2 Mondial) but it was never called a Dino. Pininfarina was in charge of styling and produced one of the most attractive shapes ever to emerge from the studio and considering Pininfarina's track record, that is saying something. The chassis was broadly the same as its predecessors, although the wheelbase was 8in shorter, and the 2921cc engine was dry-sumped. Models until 1977 had fibreglass body panels, which was a 'first' for a production Ferrari and a plus today since steel-bodied cars are prone to rust.

208GTB

**Mondial 8 / 3.2, 1980-85/1985-88. Prod: 2500/—.** Ferrari's replacement for the Dino GT4, the Mondial 8 shared that car's chassis but the wheelbase was increased by 4in to make this a true four-seater. It was significant in that it was Ferrari's first attempt to build a 'world car' and, to meet various governments' regulations, the 3-litre V8 was fitted with fuel injection, which brought power down from 255bhp in the GT4 to 214bhp, with a corresponding loss in torque. Still, 143mph/230kmh was claimed and, when the 240bhp quattrovalvole (four valves per cylinder) engine was introduced in 1982, it became an option. 1983 saw the introduction of a proper cabriolet, the first rag top Ferrari had made since the Daytona Spider. In 1985, the model received the 260bhp 3.2-litre engine.

Ferrari Mondial 8, 1980

**308i / 328GTB / 328GTS / 208GTB / 208GTS, 1981-88. Prod: —.** The less powerful fuel-injected engine which first appeared in the Mondial weakened the mid-range ability of the 308 and put 150mph/240kmh out of reach. The 1982 quattrovalvole 'clean' engine hiked power to 240bhp, increased torque, and restored the 308's performance. At the same time the 208, which had been struggling on the Italian market, was turbocharged. The 3.2-litre engine of 1985 brought power up to 260bhp with a useful increase in torque. By the time the 308 series was replaced in 1988, it had become easily the most popular model in Ferrari's history.

1981 308i (above) and 1985 328GTB (below)

**GTO, 1984-87. Prod: 200.** Built for Group B competition, which required a production run of at least 200 but was cancelled in 1986, the GTO was considered special enough to receive one of Ferrari's most famous model names. Designed at the factory, it resembled a 308GTB and used that car's engine; the difference was that the 3-litre V8 was mounted north/south rather than east/west and, with twin IHI turbochargers and Weber-Marelli electronic fuel injection, it pumped out a mighty

The 1984 Ferrari GTO

400bhp, with 366lb/ft torque at 3800rpm. It is easily distinguished by its high door mirrors, but less obvious is that the wheelbase is 4.4in longer, mainly to accommodate the different engine position. Ferrari claimed a top speed of 190mph/305kmh and 0-60mph in five seconds. 'Road' versions could have air conditioning and power windows.

**Testarossa, introduced 1984.** Another famous name was resurrected for the model which replaced the Berlinetta Boxer. Pininfarina was responsible for the body which, unlike most road Ferraris, was of aluminium save for the roof and doors. The shape was evolved in a wind tunnel with special attention paid to aerodynamic downforce, while the 'egg slicer' side grilles were claimed to increase cooling efficiency (the radiator was rear mounted). Larger overall than the 512BB (it was 78in wide), it followed that car's general chassis layout but was a little lighter (though still weighing 3660lb). The 5-litre V12, with four valves per cylinder and Bosch fuel injection, delivered 380bhp (and maximum 354lb/ft torque) to a five-speed transaxle. This car was good for 181mph/291kmh and 0-60mph in 5.3 seconds.

Testarossa Spyder, a non-standard conversion

**F40, introduced 1988.** Built to celebrate 40 years of Ferrari cars, the F40 was also designed to upstage the Porsche 959 and to be the world's fastest production car. In essence it was a GTO with different body panels, stripped of carpets and interior door panels, and it even had sliding Plexiglas windows to save weight. The engine was a short-stroke variation of the 3-litre quattrovalvole V8 with twin IHI turbochargers, and this gave 471bhp with 426lb/ft torque. In this form it was claimed to top 201mph/325kmh and reach 60mph in under four seconds. If this was a little tame, a factory kit with larger turbochargers and different camshafts could add a further 200bhp. Quintessentially it was an Italian supercar—most British F1 designers reckoned it was crudely engineered and some of them went off to try to do better.

F40, 1987

**348tb coupé/Targa, introduced 1989.** The big news in this range of models was that the engine was enlarged (to 3405cc) and was located longitudinally. This allowed the engine to sit 5in lower in the frame and significantly lowered the centre of gravity. The new chassis was claimed to be much stiffer than previous cars. The 348 was also wider than its predecessor because the radiator was taken from the nose and was replaced by a pair of side-mounted radiators. Despite the car's greater bulk there was an improvement in aerodynamics and the Cd dropped from 0.36 to 0.32. The 296bhp baby Ferrari was claimed to top 170mph/274kmh with 0-60 in 5.6 seconds—some baby.

Seen in isolation it was a magnificent car, but seen in context it was a disappointing (and portly) update of the 328, with some styling elements (the egg-cutter side grilles) carried over from more exotic models. Ferrari and Pininfarina did no more than go through the motions with this one, which one day may be seen as a mistake because other constructors, such as Honda, were making much better cars. The marque had charisma, but charisma has a sell-by date and in 1990 time was running out for Ferrari.

Ferrari 348 coupé and targa, 1989

**Mondial t coupé/convertible, introduced 1989.** Like the other V8 cars, Ferrari's four seater received the 296bhp 3405cc engine, which was mounted longitudinally in the frame although the radiator remained at the front. Along with the new engine came a completely new five-speed transmission, electronically controlled variable suspension, and a three-

1989 Mondial t coupé (above) and convertible (below)

position manual suspension selector. The external body revisions were less radical than its sister car but the interior was completely revised with much more passenger room and improved ergonomics. Top speed was 159mph/255kmh and the 0-60mph spring could be covered in 6.3 seconds.

Despite the many improvements, and a lower price than the 348, the Mondial was a slow seller, basically because it fell between two stools. It was not sufficiently practical to be used as a regular four seater, and was not as much fun to drive as the 348.

## FERRER (USA)

The first of the Ford GT40 copies, this had a fibreglass body with steel reinforcement and was built on a VW Beetle floorpan. Offered as a kit or a complete car, it was made only in 1965.

1965 Ferrer GT, VW based

## FIAT (I)

An old joke ran that in France the country owned the biggest car maker, while in Italy the biggest car maker... Fiat is a vast combine with incredibly varied interests. It was founded as a car maker by three wealthy young men in 1899 and went from strength to strength, helped in no small way by outstanding competition successes in the early years of the century. By the time Italy entered the First World War Fiat was also an established maker of commercial vehicles, aero engines and aircraft.

Most of Fiat's early cars were aimed at the middle of the market but a mass-produced car, the 501, introduced just after the First World War, saw Fiat on its way to becoming Italy's most popular make. In the 1920s it began to acquire other manufacturers and to establish manufacturing plants in other countries. Most of these were very successful (SEAT in Spain, Simca in France) but two attempts to establish a manufacturing foothold in Britain failed.

Fiat has continued its international policies with enormous success. It has absorbed a number of other makers (Abarth, Alfa Romeo, Autobianchi, Ferrari, Lancia, Moretti etc) and has established very successful branches in Brazil and India as well as supplying technology and designs to Eastern Europe which have led to such as Polski-Fiat, Lada and Zastava. So far as sports cars are concerned it should not be forgotten that as well as those models which have borne the Fiat badge, an army of small constructors have used Fiat components and these are to be found scattered throughout this book.

**8V, 1952-54. Prod: 114.** Most Fiats in the 1950s were utility cars built to satisfy mass hunger for the motor car. Against this background the arrival of the 8V was something of a surprise, but it seems that a group of Fiat engineers was given the opportunity to 'think aloud' and produce the sort of car they would like to see in production. The result had a V8 engine of 1996cc with pushrods operated by a single camshaft in the centre of the Vee. It was sold with 105bhp or 115bhp outputs and apparently even specialist tuners were unable to get more than 130bhp out of the unit.

The engine was set in a tubular chassis frame to which the steel body was welded to form unitary construction, and suspension was all-independent by coil springs and double wishbones. The four-speed gearbox had synchromesh on all gears, unusual at the time, and late cars had four headlights. Ghia, Pininfarina and Zagato built special bodies for the 8V and Siata used the engine for a model which easily outsold the Fiat version.

Fiat 8V

**1100 Transformabile, 1955-59. Prod: 571.** This odd looking little car was a two seat Fiat 1100TV (*turismo veloce*). Of unitary construction, it had coil spring and wishbone front suspension, a live rear axle suspended on semi elliptic springs, and a four-cylinder engine of 1089cc which produced 44bhp. Top speed was only 85mph/137kmh and sales were not stimulated by the car's looks—Pininfarina built the bodies but always denied it had anything to do with their styling. Despite its complete lack of distinction, the Transformabile was the direct forebear of an important line of sports cars.

Fiat 1100 Transformobile, 1956

**1200/1500/1500S/1600S, 1959-66. Prod: approx 43,000.** While Pininfarina denied having anything to do with the Transformabile, the great studio was unmistakably responsible for this line. Further, since Pininfarina built the bodies, and the series sold well, the model was an important factor in Pininfarina's expansion. The basis for the range was the Fiat 1200, which was an 1100

1959 Fiat 1200 (above) and 1963 1500 (below)

with the engine enlarged to 1221cc.

The 1200 had the 63bhp Gran Luce engine and would reach 90mph/145kmh, with 0-60mph in 19.1 seconds. When this version was introduced Fiat also launched the 1500S, which had a dohc four-cylinder engine of 1491cc developed from an Osca design. While Osca had achieved enormous competition success with the unit, Fiat kept the power output down to 80bhp, giving a respectable but not startling maximum speed of 105mph/170kmh (0-60mph in 10.6 seconds). The 1500S was distinguished from the 1200 by an air scoop on the bonnet and, from 1960, Dunlop disc brakes on the front wheels, while the 1200 retained drums throughout its life.

In 1963 the 1200 model was replaced by the 1500, which had a 72bhp 1481cc pushrod engine and front disc brakes. At the same time, the 1500S engine was enlarged to 1568cc and power increased to 90bhp. From 1965 the 1600S had a five-speed gearbox and disc brakes all round. Late cars had four headlights. Osca also built cars based on the 1500S/1600S.

**850 Spyder, 1965-73. Prod: 140,000.** Within a year of introducing the rather boxy 850 saloon, Fiat offered a pretty four seat coupé version and this Bertone-styled sports car on the same floorpan. Front suspension was by transverse leaf spring and lower wishbones, the independent rear was by coil springs and semi-trailing arms and the four cylinder 843cc 54bhp engine was mounted behind the rear axle line. Front disc brakes were standard, top speed was 87mph/140kmh and the 0-60mph time was 18.2 seconds. In 1968 the engine was enlarged to 903cc and performance improved to 91mph/146kmh (0-60mph in 15.6 seconds).

Fiat also sold tuned versions of the 850 saloon and coupé under the Fiat-Abarth label after the Abarth takeover.

The Bertone-styled 850 Spyder, 1965

**124 Spyder, 1968-85. Prod: approx 130,000.** Fiat dropped its 1500 and 1600S sports cars in 1966 when it introduced the 124 range of models (which lived on as Ladas, Polski-Fiats etc) and it was not until 1968 that the 2+2 sport version arrived. All had coil spring and double wishbone front suspension, and a live rear axle on coil springs located by trailing arms and a Panhard rod. Disc brakes were fitted to all four wheels and a five-speed gearbox was usual, although a three-speed automatic was optional. Five different engines were used during the model's life but all were four-cylinder units with twin overhead camshafts. Every car made had left hand drive.

The first version of the Spyder had a 96bhp 1438cc engine (the Spyder 1400) and this had a top speed of 102mph/164kmh (0-60mph in 12.6 seconds). In 1971 this was replaced by a 104bhp 1608cc unit which stayed in production for two years before being replaced in turn, for 1973 only, by an engine of 1592cc and 108bhp. This was the first of a new generation of engines and the forebear of all subsequent units fitted to the 124 Spyder.

The 1800 arrived in 1974 with an engine of 1756cc. For European markets this was rated at 118bhp (top speed 107mph/172kmh, 0-60mph in 10.5 seconds) but for America, where most cars were sold, it was rated at only 92bhp. This engine remained the standard fitting on European cars but to keep pace with US laws, cars for the American market were fitted with a 1995cc unit (Spyder 2000) in 1978, when power dropped to 80bhp.

In 1982 the power output of engines in the US models rose to 102bhp, thanks to fuel injection, and the same year a 120bhp turbocharged model was also offered. This was a

Fiat 124 Spyder, 1968

conversion developed for Fiat of North America by Legend Industries and was good for 104mph/167kmh (0-60mph in 9.4 seconds). For the American market there was also a short-lived 'Volumex' supercharged version which had similar output and performance to the turbocharged car.

In 1984 Fiat withdrew from the sports car market but the 124 Spyder continued in production built by Pininfarina and badged as a Pininfarina car in the same way that Bertone took over the Fiat X1/9. Production finally ceased in 1985.

Between 1968 and 1975 Fiat also built a four-seat coupé which had a longer wheelbase than the Spyder, while its engines ran in parallel to the open car. It was phased out after Fiat's sales in America went into a sharp decline in 1974.

**124 Abarth Rallye, 1972-75. Prod: 1013.** This was a 124 Spyder 1800 developed by Abarth for rallying and sold as an 'homologation special'. It had independent rear suspension, some body panels of aluminium and fibreglass, a permanent hard top and a built-in roll cage. Customer cars had 128bhp (these had a 118mph/190kmh top speed) but a few of the 1975 cars had an even more powerful 16-valve unit.

124 Abarth Rallye

**Dino Coupé/Spyder, 1966-73. Prod: approx 7500.** When Ferrari announced its Dino road car, Fiat announced cars with the same engine. This was before Fiat bought Ferrari and behind the collaboration was Ferrari's desire to sell the engine in sufficient numbers for it to be homologated for use in Formula 2.

The Coupé and the Spyder had steel bodies on a pressed steel floorpan, although the Spyder had a shorter wheelbase. Both had Bertone styling, with two doors and 2+2 seating. Front suspension was by coil spring and double wishbones and early cars had a live rear axle suspended on semi-elliptic springs and located by radius arms and a Panhard rod, similar to the 124 Spyder. The 1987cc dohc Dino V6 engine was front-mounted and delivered its 160bhp via a Fiat five-speed gearbox which was mounted in unit with it. Disc brakes were fitted to all four wheels.

Both models received a very favourable reception but sales were slow, at least by Fiat standards. The trouble was that the model was too expensive and complex for the humble badge it bore, and the Ferrari 206 Dino completely upstaged it even though it sold in only tiny numbers. The 2-litre Spyder could reach 127mph/205kmh (0-60mph in 8.1 seconds) but while these were excellent figures by most

Fiat Dino 2000 Coupé (above) and 2400 Spyder (below)

standards they were disappointing for a car with a Ferrari engine.

In 1969 the two models were extensively revised although styling remained unchanged. The 2418cc engine used the cast iron block from the Fiat 130, power increased to 180bhp and torque was improved by 17 percent. The Fiat five-speed gearbox was replaced by a ZF unit and the old live rear axle was replaced by an independent layout with coil springs and trailing arms. To accommodate the extra power, wider tyres and larger brakes were fitted.

Towards the end of the model's life, cars were built in Ferrari's works at Maranello which had become part of the Fiat empire in 1969.

**X1/9, X1/9 1500, 1972-89. Prod: approx 180,000.** The last sports car to be introduced with a Fiat badge, the X1/9 was not the first mass-produced mid-engined sports car (that was the VW-Porsche) but it became easily the most successful. Bertone convinced Fiat of the feasibility of the concept and also designed the Targa-topped body.

Built around a central pressed steel monocoque, the all-independent suspension was by MacPherson struts and disc brakes were fitted to all four wheels. On its introduction the X1/9 used the power pack from the Fiat 128 Rally, a sohc four-cylinder engine of 1290cc with an integral four-speed gearbox which was mounted transversely. This gave only 75bhp so top speed was only 99mph/160kmh (0-60mph in 12.7 seconds) but the same engine was used in cars for markets on both sides of the Atlantic. Handling and roadholding were both excellent but the car cried out for more power.

In 1980 Fiat installed a 1499cc engine and five-speed gearbox from the Ritmo/Strada. The new engine gave 85bhp in 'European form' but only 67bhp in American specification cars (75bhp after 1982 when fuel injection was fitted). Even in European trim, performance was not startling with a top speed of 106mph/170kmh (0-60mph in 11 seconds) and many enthusiasts regretted that even more power was not available because the chassis was very competent, as some competition versions proved.

Fiat ceased production of the X1/9 in 1982, at about the same time as it left the American market altogether, whereupon production was taken over by Bertone and the car was badged as such. Bertone sold a number of 'special editions' but changes on these were cosmetic.

Fiat Bertone X1/9 1500

## FIBERFAB (D)

This company was founded in 1969 to market American Fiberfab kits in Germany, but the formal links were broken in 1973. In 1975 the company began to make a Jeep-style vehicle of its own design. The original American Bonito coupé was taken over by a British firm in 1982.

Fiberfab Germany's Bonito, 1969

## FIBERFAB (USA)

Founded in 1965 to make fibreglass bodies for use on VW Beetle chassis, the company's first car was the Aztec, a coupé notable for its cheapness and ease of construction. In 1967 Fiberfab offered the Valkyrie GT, a mid-engine coupé with a tubular frame, all-independent suspension, disc brakes, a five-speed ZF gearbox and either a Ford or a Chevrolet V8 engine. Depending on the engine, a top speed of up to 180mph/290kmh was claimed (0-60mph was in a claimed 3.9 seconds) and a parachute for additional braking power was fitted! Offered between 1967 and 1969 at $12,500, it found few takers (a kit version used the Chevrolet Corvair engine).

1965 Fiberfab Aztec

Fiberfab's 500bhp Valkyrie came with parachute fitted

1982 Aztec

1969 Fiberfab Jamaican, V8 powered

Later came the Bonanza, Bonito, and another Aztec (a Ford GT40 copy), all based on VW running gear although non-VW engines could be specified. The 'Jamaican' was a front-engined car based on an MGA chassis but fitted with a 3.5-litre Buick V8 engine. By the late 1980s the company was concentrating on a VW-based copy of the Porsche 356A Speedster and the 'Speedster California', which was basically a customised version of the Porsche copy. Some of Fiberfab's bodies were also made abroad.

## FIBERSPORT (USA)

A short-lived (1953-54) sports car which was sold either complete or as a kit. It used a Crosley chassis and engine, a BMC four-speed gearbox and a fibreglass body. A top speed of 100mph/161kmh was claimed. Crosley production ceased in 1952 and the supply of components soon dried up, so the company made its own chassis.

## FIELDBAY (GB)

From the late 1980s a maker of the 'Magnum 427', a Cobra copy.

Fieldbay Magnum 427, 1990

## FILIPINETTI (CH)

Short-lived (1966-67) attempt to market a two-seater fibreglass coupé using the 1.6-litre air-cooled VW engine.

Prototype Filipinetti coupé

## FITCH (USA)

John Fitch was a Second World War fighter pilot and one of the first Americans to make a name in postwar European sports car racing—he was signed by Mercedes-Benz in 1955 to drive alongside the likes of Fangio and Moss. He made two attempts to become a sports car constructor, in 1949 and 1966, but both attempts failed because he misjudged the market. In between times he modified Chevrolet Corvairs so that they went like stink and had handling to match.

The first Fitch was a sensible attempt to build an American sports car before the Brits took over the market. His base was a modified Fiat 1100 chassis with a 2.2-litre Ford V8 and clothed with a simple body resembling the Crosley Hotshot. At $2850 it was keenly priced, and could out-perform an MG TC, but it failed to find many buyers largely because it lacked the cachet which the MG had, and production ended in 1951.

In 1966, and following the success of his modified Corvairs, Fitch tried to move up-market with a car powered by a 170bhp Corvair engine and a handsome body styled by Coby Whitmore, a commercial artist. By 1966 the Corvair had attracted the attention of Ralph *Unsafe At any Speed* Nader, which zilched that car's image. The $9000 price tag of the Fitch Phoenix did not help either so it never proceeded beyond the prototype stage.

## FLETCHER (GB)

Norman Fletcher was a boat builder who found business quiet at certain times of year so he took over the moulds of the Ogle SX1000 in order to take up the slack. Distinguished from the Ogle by a sharper tail and recessed front headlights behind perspex covers, the Fletcher could not be said to have been an aesthetic improvement on Ogle's plastic egg. It was originally produced for competition use, and ex-Cooper works driver John Handley enjoyed a lot of success in a Fletcher GT, which prompted the company to attempt to market a road-going version. Fletcher received an order for 30 cars from Switzerland but BMC, true to form, could not, or would not, supply the components. Thus the deal fell through and the project was abandoned after four had been made, all in 1967.

## FLINTRIDGE-DARRIN (USA)

This was a fibreglass two-seat sports car body styled by Howard 'Dutch' Darrin of Kaiser Darrin fame. It was built by Woodill (qv) on a DKW chassis in 1957 but production problems at Woodill, combined with consumer resistance to the 'Deek's' two-stroke engine, meant that only 15 were built.

## FORD (AUS)

Ford's Australian arm was founded in 1925, initially to fit locally made bodies to American Ford chassis. Until the 1970s, most models derived from the American parent, then came some models originated in Europe and some which derived from the Mazda range. In 1990 it announced its first sports car, the 'Capri', a 2+2 convertible with styling by Ghia.

A 1.6-litre four-cylinder Mazda engine was mounted transversely at the front and drove through the front wheels via a five-speed gearbox. It was available with an 82bhp fuel injected version (105mph/170kmh, 0-60mph in 11.5 seconds) or with a 134bhp turbocharged unit (124mph/199kmh, 0-60mph in 8.5 seconds). Suspension was independent all round by MacPherson struts, disc brakes were fitted at the front but were available as an option on the rear as well. To the disappointment of many, Ford decided not to sell the car in Europe, but it was marketed in America as the Mercury Capri.

## FORD (F)

Ford's French arm existed between 1947 and 1954 and was a hang over from a pre-war licensing deal with a company called Matford. All cars built by the company had a 63bhp 2.2-litre side-valve V8 engine and three-speed manual transmission set in an American-style chassis with coil spring and double wishbone front suspension, a live rear axle on semi-elliptic springs, hydraulic brakes and hypoid final drive. In 1951 the company produced the Comète, a very handsome

2+2 with coupé or convertible bodies built by Facel. On these cars a four-speed Cotal gearbox was an option and from 1954 buyers could specify a 3.9-litre version of the engine (which was related to the British Ford V8 and the Mercury V8). Simca acquired the company in 1954, and the V8 engine was fitted to the last Talbots after Simca had also bought that company.

**3.9-litre Ford Comète Monte Carlo, 1954**

## FORD (GB)

Ford's British operation began in 1911 in a former tramcar factory in Manchester. The plant assembled the Model T from components shipped from the States and by 1914 Ford was the largest maker in Europe. After the War Ford's popularity in Britain began to wane largely because other makers began producing cars which were specifically tailored to the market. Ford began work to rectify this and, at the same time, built a large plant in Essex. The first vehicle was completed at the Dagenham factory late in 1931 and the following year production of the Model Y, a specifically European design, set Ford back on its road to success.

Fords were sold on low price and good after-sales service and they were to be popular even in the 1950s despite the fact that the small cars were uneconomical and crudely engineered. Until 1959 all small Fords still had side valve engines and three-speed gearboxes but because the base models were simple, cheap and plentiful they became favourites with special builders and numerous companies marketed fibreglass bodies for them. The 1172 Formula, which was framed around Ford components was particularly important to the infant British motor racing industry—many designers cut their teeth on 1172 cars.

Ford's first modern small engine, the 997cc 105E of 1959, was to be fundamentally important to motor racing since versions tuned by the fledgling Cosworth company helped Lotus to dominate the international Formula Junior.

In 1961 the American parent company, which had always been the majority shareholder, took complete control of the British branch.

Until the 1960s Ford's image was worthy but dull, yet during that decade it embarked on a programme of motor sport which successfully embraced Formulae 1, 2, and 3 (through its tie-up with Cosworth), Indycar racing, sports car racing (with the Cobra and the Ford GT40), saloon car racing (the Anglia, Mustang and Lotus-Cortina), and in rallying. The company image was completely changed in a very short time.

Despite the fact that Ford (GB) has used motor sport as a very effective marketing tool, and has made some very sporty cars (the Capri RS3100, for example, was a serious piece of kit), it has never marketed a popular sports car. On the other hand, Ford has often lent a helping hand to small specialist makers and has thus had a profound influence on sports cars as well as the racing scene.

**GT40, 1966-72. Prod: 107 (31 road cars).** In the early 1960s Ford tried to buy Ferrari and when that fell through it set out to build a car which could win at Le Mans. The operation was based in Britain and Lola was chosen to fill a major role as Eric Broadley had already essayed an advanced mid-engined GT car which used a 4.7-litre Ford V8. The partnership was not altogether happy—too many Detroit empire builders were involved and Lola had to make too many compromises. For example, Broadley wanted to use aluminium for the monocoque, Ford insisted on mild steel. Broadley was right, the men in the executive suits were wrong.

Some writers list the GT40 as an American car, but in fact the cars were built by Ford Advanced Vehicles, which was a subsidiary of Ford of Britain (and when a GT40 did eventually win at Le Mans the French awarded it the prize for the highest placed British car). Beyond that, credit for the design is due to Eric Broadley, founder of Lola, and an expatriate Englishman, Roy Lunn. One might add that Eric's first design was for the 1172 formula in 1957—and is an example of how the building of Ford specials had a profound influence on British motor racing.

The GT40 was so named because it was 40in high. Suspension was independent all round, by coil springs and double wishbones, and on customer cars the engine was a 4.7-litre V8 which was dry sumped and gave up to 390bhp, which was delivered through a five-speed ZF gearbox (pre-production cars had a four-speed 'box). Performance depended on the rear axle ratio, and a works car achieved more than 200mph/322kmh at Le Mans. FAV built 107 GT40s at Slough, 31 being delivered for road use (cars tended to be converted for racing, and vice versa, while the GT40 served as the basis for the Mk2, which won the Le Mans race for Ford in 1966, and the later Mirage sports-racing car).

During the 1980s the GT40 became a popular model for kit car copies and while many of these were very accurate from the outside most had space frame chassis and used Renault transaxles which required a higher (by 4in) engine location and, hence, a higher centre of gravity. Among the

**Ford Mark 3, road version of the GT40**

exceptions were Safir and ERA Replica Automobiles, which used monocoques, and Mallock, who combined a space frame with a ZF transaxle to achieve the correct height.

**Mk3, 1967-69. Prod: 7.** Never 'GT40 Mk3', but plain Mk3, just as the related circuit machine was Mk2. The Mk3 was intended to be the definitive road car, with detuned 306bhp engine, effective silencers, interior trim and even luggage space. This car had a central gear shift, which meant that four could be completed as left-hand drive cars. Ford policy changes meant that 'production' did not even run to completing the first batch of 20.

**GT70, 1970-72. Prod: 4.** The nearest that Ford has come to making a popular sports car, the GT70 was designed for production with a steel platform, fibreglass body, all independent suspension and a mid-mounted engine. It was designed to take either four cylinder or V6 engines but had it gone into production it would have had the four cylinder 1.8-litre Ford Cosworth BDA unit. This very promising project was shelved when Ford hit a sticky patch in the early 1970s.

Ford GT70 styling prototype

**RS200, 1985-86. Prod: 200.** Unlike most other Group B rally cars, the RS200 was designed to be a practical two-seat road car which could be serviced in any country where Ford had outlets. Thus items such as door locks and glassware came from the Ford parts bin, as a matter of policy rather than expediency. It was designed by Tony Southgate and had a mid-mounted turbocharged 1803cc Ford Cosworth BDT engine which had been developed for the still-born Escort RS1700T. Power outputs began at 250bhp for road cars and rose according to how the car was to be used; by the end of 1986, works rally cars were producing 450bhp. Brian Hart later developed a 2.1-litre version which developed up to 650bhp for Rallycross use.

Central to the RS200 was a monocoque of steel, Kevlar and carbon fibre; suspension followed conventional competition practice, being independent by coil springs and double wishbones, and drive was to all four wheels via a five-speed gearbox and three viscous couplings. The road version had a top speed of 140mph/225kmh (0-60mph in 6.0 seconds) and buyers could have any colour they liked, provided it was white.

RS200, 1985

## FORD (USA)

The history of Ford is too complicated, and is anyway too well known, to call for review here. Although Henry Ford had made his early reputation in motor sport and in the 1930s Ford coupés had been very successful in national racing, the parent company was generally hostile to both motor sport and cars with sporting aspirations. It was something of a surprise, then, when Ford announced the Thunderbird in 1955, although it is less of a surprise when one recalls that Chevrolet had marketed the Corvette two years earlier.

The first Thunderbirds were two-seaters and were marketed as Fords. Although they were not out-and-out sports cars, they comfortably outsold the Chevrolet Corvette. After 1958 the T-bird transmuted into a separate division of Ford and the model name became a marque. At the same time they became overweight four-seaters which were 'personal' cars with no sporting pretensions.

In truth, the Thunderbird's biggest achievement was the fact that its presence in the market place meant that Chevrolet could not drop the Corvette, even though it wanted to after the first model's poor showing.

**Thunderbird, 1955-57. Prod: 53,166.** Ford's answer to the Corvette, and the European sports car invasion, was basically a parts bin special which was deliberately styled to emphasise its close relations. The 4.8-litre Mercury V8 would propel it to 115mph/185kmh. At $3000 it was very good value on a dollar per mph basis. It was quick in a straight line but did not like the wiggly bits; in fact its handling was pretty dire, but then it sold to people who were more interested in posing in a two-seater than driving one hard. By 1957 there were more powerful engine options and one, a 5.1-litre supercharged unit giving around 325bhp, was offered, and this was good for 125mph/200kmh (0-60mph in seven seconds).

1955 Thunderbird

## FRAZEN (USA)

Introduced in 1951, the Frazen was a two seat fibreglass-bodied sports car based on the chassis and running gear of the Kaiser Henry J. Available complete, or as a kit, all examples had the Kaiser 2.6-litre side-valve straight six. The Frazen's performance was mediocre, its styling was odd, its price was too high, and very few were built although it was still listed in 1962, long after Kaiser had disappeared.

## FRAZER NASH (GB)

Like many small sports car companies, the history of Frazer Nash was marked by crises. Founded in 1924 by Archie Frazer Nash, it only gained stability after it was taken over by H.J. Aldington in 1926 when the parent firm became AFN Ltd. Although they were built in tiny numbers, and were rather crude, Frazer Nashes gained an enviable competition reputation. At the end of 1934 AFN began to import BMWs which were marketed as Frazer Nash-BMWs.

After the War, this connection led to the BMW 328 engine becoming the basis of the Bristol unit (AFN was originally a partner in the Bristol project), and to Aldington springing some BMW engineers from prison in Germany. AFN made a small number of sports cars until 1957 when it concentrated on the importation of Porsche cars and those few cars are now highly prized (and sometimes faked). Porsche (UK) took over AFN when John Aldington, H.J.'s son, retired in 1986.

Should Frazer Nash be hyphenated? The marque name should never have a hyphen, but when dealing with the founder the answer is slightly more complicated. He was born in 1899 and was named Archibald Goodman Frazer Nash (not a hyphen in sight) but on 11th March 1938 he changed his name by deed poll and became Frazer-Nash. That is why the reference to the founder in the first paragraph has no hyphen because in 1924 he had no hyphen.

**High Speed / Le Mans Replica / Le Mans MkII, 1948-49/1950-52/1952-53. Prod: 4/25/8.** The basis of most postwar Frazer Nash cars was a tuned Bristol engine and gearbox in a twin-tube chassis with independent front suspension by transverse leaf and double wishbones and a live rear axle suspended on torsion bars. AFN first made two one-offs with enveloping bodywork until it made the stark, but very pretty 'High Speed' (aka 'Competition'). After finishing third at Le Mans in 1949, the model was renamed the Le Mans Replica. These cars dominated their class on British circuits and one even won the 1951 Targa Florio. The Le Mans MkII had a new chassis frame (called the 200 series) which retained the established layout but was about 100lb lighter.

Le Mans Replica on the 1953 Alpine Rally

Three single seaters were built using the 200 series frame, they were not very successful and two of them were later converted to Le Mans style sports cars, which was common practice at the time (many single seaters were made into sports cars to prolong their competition life). Unfortunately, because the Le Mans Replica is both simple and desirable, a fair number of fakes have been made.

**Cabriolet, 1950. Prod: 1.** Fritz Fiedler, a former BMW engineer who became the mainstay of Frazer Nash, was allowed to build a four seater 'dream car' on a lengthened Le Mans Replica chassis. Before the War, BMW had built some cars with very advanced aerodynamics, and lurking under the chrome and bulbous vulgarity of the Cabriolet were some of the ideas seen then. It was sold to a maker of liquorice allsorts, which is appropriate.

The one-off Frazer Nash Cabriolet

**Fast Tourer/Mille Miglia, 1949/1950-52. Prod: 2/11.** The specification of all postwar Frazer Nashes differed according to the buyer's wishes but this model was basically a

Frazer Nash Mille Miglia

Le Mans Replica fitted with an enveloping body and a less fierce engine. Although it was primarily intended for road use, it acquired the name 'Mille Miglia' after the prototype competed in the 1949 event. Although Frazer Nash covered itself with glory on the circuits its attempts to build road cars never took off, largely because of price.

**Targa Florio, 1952-54. Prod: 13.** The replacement for the Mille Miglia was named the Targa Florio in honour of the marque's victory in 1951, and it used the 200 series chassis of the Le Mans MkII. Like the Mille Miglia, it was intended for road use and had a fair degree of luxury. Two basic models were offered, the Gran Sport with 125bhp, and the Turismo with 100bhp. Unlike previous models, most Targa Florios had bolt-on wheels in place of the BMW-style discs with knock-off hubs, but some customers had wires and some had Le Mans MkII bodies.

Frazer Nash Targa Florio

**Le Mans Coupé, 1953-56.** **Prod: 9.** The first closed car Frazer Nash ever offered as a production model, the coupé was originally built for Le Mans and it obliged by taking the 2-litre class in 1953. In essence it was a Targa Florio with a hard top and slightly modified frontal treatment, but it was one of the smoothest looking cars of its day. Late cars had adjustable rear torsion bars.

Le Mans Coupé at Le Mans, 1954

**Sebring, 1954.** **Prod: 3.** A dual-purpose car for the road or track, with up to 140bhp from the ageing Bristol engine; and named because a 'Nash won the 1952 Sebring 12 Hour race. AFN had club racing in mind but one ran at Le Mans in 1955. One of the two cars had a de Dion rear axle and 'Dickie' Stoop enjoyed some success with it in British racing but an AC Ace-Bristol in the right hands usually had the legs of it.

1954 Frazer Nash Sebring

**Continental GT, 1956-57.** **Prod: 2.** AFN's history is typified by this car. The chassis was the forgiving '200' series frame, the engine was BMW's 3168cc V8, while the roof and doors came from Porsche. It was a very pretty car, bursting with pedigree but, alas, too expensive. In Britain it cost £3751 and, for that, you could buy a country cottage. A 'Continental' was shown at the 1958 London Motor Show and, with the Sebring, was a 'production' model for some years after. AFN made its last car in 1957 but, like a bespoke tailor, it would have run up a car had a customer so desired.

The V8 Continental GT, 1956

## FRICK (USA)

In 1953 Bill Frick made the 'Studillac' which entailed fitting a Cadillac engine in a Studebaker hardtop, the result being a car with a 125mph/200kmh top speed which would spring to 60mph in 8.5 seconds. Encouraged, he attempted to become a manufacturer in 1955. He designed a box channel chassis with coil spring and double wishbone front suspension and a live rear axle sprung by semi-elliptic leaf springs. Running gear was Cadillac and the Ferrari-like body was by Vignale. Production figures are unknown but it is likely that only the prototype was made.

The Vignale-styled 1955 Frick

## FROGEYE (GB)

Introduced in 1986, the Frogeye was designed to allow owners of rotting 'Frogeye' Sprites to reconstitute their cars without having to worry about tin worm. The 'restoration assembly' consisted of an accurate and high-quality fibreglass body, a fibreglass central monocoque and a tubular backbone. Geoffrey Healey, son of the original designer, was so impressed with the product that he became a consultant to it and a turn key version was offered. This had a 64bhp 1275cc 'A' series engine, front disc brakes, and a revised rear suspension layout by trailing arms sprung by rubber in torsion. The result was a car which comfortably out-performed the original, being good for 95mph/153kmh (0-60mph in twelve seconds).

## GALY (F)

This was a tiny coupé with a choice of a 175cc or 280cc rear-mounted engine. A handful were built between 1954 and 1957.

## GARDNER DOUGLAS (GB)

The GD was a late-1980s Cobra 427 copy using Jaguar suspension units on a tubular backbone chassis with a semi-monocoque body and the usual engine options (e.g. Jaguar V12, Ford V8 etc).

**Gardner Douglas GD427 (above) and chassis (below)**

## GATSBY COACHWORKS (USA)

A 1980s maker of 'nostalgia' cars, that is 'traditional' bodies mated to modern (usually Ford) chassis with V8 engines and modern refinements. None of the firm's models was a direct copy but the 'Griffin' recalled a late 1930s Alfa Romeo, the 'Cabriolet' seemed inspired by the Mercedes-Benz 540K, and so on.

**Gatsby Griffin, 1988**

## GATSO (NL)

Built in tiny numbers between 1948 and 1950 by Maurice Gatsonides, a top-line rally driver, the Gatso (or Gatford) was an astonishing 2+1 coupé based on Ford components. It had a strange 'aerodynamic' body made of Duralium and was built on aircraft fuselage principles, with three headlights and a perspex bubble canopy. Usually a 120bhp 3.9-litre side valve Mercury V8 engine was fitted but a 170bhp ohv version was an option (top speed with this was 112mph/180kmh). There was overdrive on all three gears.

**Gatso roadster—strange but true**

## GAYLORD (USA)

The Gaylord brothers were car enthusiasts who dreamed of creating their own sports car and, since their father had invented the bobby pin hair grip, they had no reason to think small. With styling by Brooks Stevens of Excalibur (qv) and a chassis designed by Jim Gaylord, the car had every amenity, including a hard top which, at the push of a button, would fold itself into the boot. It also had a useful performance.

First seen in 1955, the Gladiator had a tubular frame made from chrome molybdenum steel with coil spring and wishbone front suspension and a live rear axle. The prototype had a 5.4-litre 300bhp Chrysler V8 engine but the other three chassis (one was never bodied) had Cadillac V8 units of up to 350bhp. Regardless of engine, drive was through a Hydra-Matic gearbox modified to change up only at peak revs, unless the driver shifted the stick manually. At 4000lb it was no lightweight but it could reach 120mph/193kmh and accelerate

**1955 Gaylord Gladiator**

to sixty in under ten seconds. Handling was said to be good, although that was by American standards. At $17,500, a customer had every right to expect perfection and Jim Gaylord agreed; the quality of the first cars led to disputes with the German coachbuilders, there were recriminations and counter-claims, and the project was dead by 1957.

## GB RACING (GB)

From the mid-1980s this company made a Lamborghini Countach copy which was marketed as the 'GB 500S'. Like most of its ilk, it used a space frame chassis and the list of engine/gearbox options was extensive. To set it apart, GB advertised 'Koenig-style' (i.e. customised) panels.

**GD** *see* GARDNER DOUGLAS

## GE (GB)

The name under which the Gravetti GE427 (qv) was revived by an investment company after Gravetti folded in 1987. This was a short-lived arrangement and the company re-emerged as CK.

## GEMBALLA (D)

A customiser and modifier of cars which most enthusiasts would prefer in the state they left the factory. Among other offerings have been a customised Ferrari Testarossa, a two seat Porsche 928 convertible, and various versions of the Porsche 911 range.

**The 400bhp Gemballa Avalanche, 1985**

## GEMINI (GB)

Made by the Trevor Cook Motor Company from 1990, the Gemini was a Lotus Elan lookalike (but with fixed headlights) which used Vauxhall Chevette running gear in a ladder chassis.

## GENIE (GB)

1980s Ford Cortina-sourced kit car with 1930s styling.

**GENTRY** *see* RMB, SP MOTORS

## GEO (USA)

The marque name under which General Motors began to sell its small Japanese-American cars in 1990. The Geo 'Storm' was a 2+2 coupé which used various versions of the same Isuzu engine as powered the Lotus Elan; with the 125bhp dohc 1.6-litre engine a top speed of 123mph/198kmh was claimed (0-60mph in nine seconds). It was first shown in 1990, ahead of production in 1991.

## GEORGES IRAT (F)

Founded in 1921, this company specialised in sporting cars which were often technically advanced. It came close to collapse in 1935 but bounced back with a rakish front wheel drive sports car which used the 1100cc Ruby engine. Until the War it was made at the rate of about ten a week. During hostilities new designs were formulated and afterwards the company seemed ready to go into production with two advanced cars. Both had integral construction, all-independent suspension, bodies made from magnesium alloy, and 1100cc flat-four engines. One had front wheel drive, the other rear wheel drive (and a dohc version of the engine) but neither saw production and the firm folded in 1948.

**1948 Georges Irat—too advanced?**

## GETTY DESIGN (USA)

Late 1980s maker of the 'Vision', which was a Porsche 911 hacked about so that it finished up looking like a cabriolet version of the Porsche 959, a car which Porsche chose not to make.

**GF** *see* GITANE

## GFG (D)

Since 1984 GFG has made the 'Elisar', a high-quality evocation of the Mercedes-Benz 540K using Mercedes-Benz running gear.

**GFG Elisar, 1986**

## GHIA (I)

The famous Italian coachmaker had become known in America through the Dual-Ghia range, which was a collaboration between Ghia, Chrysler and Dual Motors, a Detroit trucking firm. These cars sold mainly to showbiz personalities and loopies. In March 1965 *Road & Track* featured on its cover a Ghia-bodied Fiat 2300 and Bert Sugarman of Los Angeles found true love. Sugarman managed to interest Ghia and Chrysler in his passion and this led to the Ghia 450/SS, which was a Plymouth Barracuda (235bhp, 4.4-litre V8, etc) in evening dress. The trouble was that the Plymouth was a $3000 car and the Ghia version was offered at $12,000 and there was little between them apart from the frock. So, handsome as it was, the Ghia 450/SS did not take America by storm.

**The 1965 Ghia 450/SS**

## GIANNINI (I)

Attilio Giannini's company was founded in 1920. Most of its work was engine tuning, particularly of Fiat units, including dohc conversions. After the Second World War Giannini went into partnership with Bernardo Taraschi and formed Giaur (qv) but by the second half of the 1950s was back on his own.

In 1963 Giannini formed a new eponymous company and began to market tuned and customised Fiats, just like Abarth—among the firm's initial range was an 850cc coupé based on Fiat 600 components. In 1965 this was replaced by another coupé based on Fiat 850 components, with the engine enlarged to 930cc. In 1969 Giannini fitted its 994cc engine to the Francis Lombardi 850 Grand Prix (aka OTAS Grand Prix) and sold it as the Giannini 1000 Grand Prix. OTAS also used Giannini engines in cars it sold under its own banner.

**1957 Fiat Giannini coupé**

**Giannini 1000 Grand Prix coupé, 1969**

1972 saw the 'Sirio', an odd looking 650cc two-seat sports car based on Fiat 500 parts. It did not find favour in the market place and soon afterwards Giannini once again concentrated on modifying Fiat saloons.

## GIAUR (I)

Giaur was a collaboration between Attilio Giannini, an engine tuner who also made cars under his own name (see previous entry), and Bernardo Taraschi who had taken over production of a maker of racing cars called Urania (GIAnnini and URania gave Giaur). Most of the company's cars were single seaters with small capacity engines but Giaur also made some basic (cycle-winged) sports cars which were road-legal although primarily intended for the race track. They were typically Italian in that the chassis was a simple, rugged, ladder frame and suspension was modified Fiat, with most of the attention devoted to the engine. Giannini produced sohc and dohc versions of the Fiat Topolino engine and Giaur also sold Crosley-engined cars in the USA, where they were blown off by locally made Crosley specials which had more advanced chassis and aerodynamics and which were honed to the tracks on which they raced.

**1953 Giaur with 750 Crosley engine**

**750cc dohc Giaur in 1954. A tiny car**

Giaur made no impact beyond a few domestic successes and it seems to have faded during 1955. A Giaur design was revived as the Taraschi Formula Junior car in 1958 and, in the first two years of the formula, it was second only to Stanguellini (qv) in terms of race wins.

## GILBERN (GB)

Gilbern was one of the very few car makers based in Wales and one of the few based anywhere to graduate from making kit cars to turn key vehicles. The name derived from the founders, GILes Smith and BERNard Friese, who was a German. From modest beginnings, the company grew steadily, and as it expanded had to seek capital from outside until, in 1968, it was taken over by Ace Holdings Ltd, also based in Wales. This company was then Britain's largest maker of slot machines and its owner wanted to be associated with a locally made sports car. When the company changed hands, Giles Smith left.

Friese left in 1969 when Ace Holdings became part of the Mecca group, a leisure company which, among other things, ran dance halls and organised the Miss World competition. Mecca inherited rather than sought a specialist car maker, which was essentially a detail in the ledgers and had to pull its weight to be justified to the share holders.

The majority of Gilberns were supplied in component form (i.e. a partly assembled kit requiring the owner to undertake only as much work as would escape purchase tax) but the coming of VAT in 1973 altered the position. Gilbern might have survived had it still been in the hands of enthusiasts but when difficult times arrived the parent company was not interested in seeing it through. Gilbern went into receivership in September 1973 and, despite efforts to save it, soon expired.

**GT, 1959-67. Prod: approx 580.** A handsome and practical 2+2 which was supplied with Coventry Climax FWA, BMC Series 'A' (948cc, with the option of a supercharger) or Series 'B' (1558-1798cc) engines. These were fitted in a multi-tubular frame which used Austin A35 front suspension and a BMC live axle sprung on coils. There was nothing startling about the style or specification but Gilbern's secret was to achieve a higher than average standard of finish, and satisfied owners spread the good news.

Gilbern GT, 1959

**Genie, 1966-69. Prod: approx 200.** The Genie had a beefed-up GT chassis, with MGB front suspension and rear axle, and front disc brakes, to take the 2.5- and 3.0-litre Ford V6 engines. The body was completely new, with sharp lines and more glassware, and was inspired by the Alfa Romeo Giulia Sprint GT. With the 3-litre engine, the Genie would carry four adults to 115mph/185kmh but uneven road surfaces would reveal loose dental fillings and the road holding was none too special.

1968 Gilbern Genie

**Invader, 1969-74. Prod: approx 600.** The Invader was an updated Genie which retained the broad body and chassis layout but had much improved trim and suspension. As before, there was a mixture of Ford and BMC components and options included overdrive and automatic transmission. It was updated in detail as the MkII in 1971, when a sporting estate car version was offered. The MkIII shown at the 1972 London Motor Show had a revised box section frame, Ford Cortina front suspension and a Ford (Taunus) back axle, and a 140bhp Ford V6.

Gilbern Invader

## GINETTA (GB)

Hundreds of small constructors have come and gone since 1957 so Ginetta's survival is unusual; that it remained solvent and was run by its founders until they retired in 1989 is remarkable. On top of that Ginetta styling has invariably been distinctive and attractive.

In the 1950s the Walklett brothers, Bob, Douglas, Ivor and Trevor, ran an agricultural engineering business in Woodbridge, Suffolk. They were all motor sport enthusiasts and Ivor built a special based on a Wolseley Hornet which, in retrospect, became known as the Ginetta G1. The brothers offered their first car, the G2, as a kit in 1957 and by 1962 the company had grown sufficiently for the brothers to abandon their agricultural engineering business and to move to new premises in Witham, Essex.

The talents of the four men complemented each other perfectly: Ivor designed the cars, Trevor styled them, Bob administered the company and Douglas ran the works. Ginetta moved away from kit cars to almost fully assembled cars in the 1960s, and also built some out and out racers. The company moved to larger premises in 1972 but returned to its old base after VAT was introduced. After that, the company became quite difficult to pin down: it made very few cars and all were fully assembled, yet unlike most small sports car makers Ginetta did not go bankrupt!

The company went through hard times in the 1970s but was helped by two things: it was unusually self-sufficient and by the time the market contracted it had sold so many cars that it was able to survive on spares and rebuild business. When kit cars enjoyed a revival in 1980, Ginetta entered the market with such success that by the late 1980s it had a new turn key car, the G32, on the stocks.

In 1989 the Walklett brothers were ready for retirement and sold their company, although Ivor stayed on as a consultant for an agreed period. The new company had sufficient financial muscle to submit its cars for Type Approval so that they could be sold fully assembled, and they were also marketed properly. One thing which the new owners did not buy was the secret of the name—only members of the Walklett family know why Ginetta was chosen and they are not telling.

Since there does exist some confusion over Ginetta type numbers, the 'missing' numbers appear in italics between the main model entries.

*G1—Ivor Walklett's Wolseley Hornet Special.*

**G2, 1957-60. Prod: approx 100.** This was one of the more sensible Ford-based kits—it gave a reasonably competent mechanic a chance to build a sports car in the Lotus Six idiom for about £250 (the basic kit cost £156). It was announced after Six production had ceased and before the Lotus Seven was announced and had a space frame chassis to which aluminium panels were attached, making for a rigid structure. There was a split axle i.f.s. conversion and the remote gear change was mounted on the dashboard.

Ginetta G2, 1957

**G3, 1960-62. Prod:—.** Just as the G2 had been a remarkably well-conceived kit so the G3 had a well-conceived body. The chassis was very similar to that of the G2 but the body came complete. Items such as wheel arches and the boot were built in, the doors fitted, there was a proper scuttle and the standard of finish was high, but the car was not everybody's favourite shape. The body was also sold separately.

**G4/G5/G6/G7 1961-69, 1981-present. Prod: over 500.** The car which put Ginetta on the map was first seen at the 1961 Racing Car Show in London. It was one of those concepts which are obviously right. An attractive fibreglass body with rear wings like the Lotus Eleven covered a space frame (the scuttle was bonded to the frame), there was coil spring and double wishbone front suspension, a live rear axle located by trailing arms and an A bracket, and a 997cc Ford 105E engine. Before long a complete kit was offered for £499, which was about the same as a Mini, although that was a fully assembled car and attracted purchase tax.

The Series II (1963) had carpets and revised rear bodywork which added 8in to the overall length and improved luggage capacity. A BMC rear axle replaced the Ford unit, offering a wider variety of ratios and saving 40lb. Among options were front disc brakes and a hard top.

The G4R (R for 'racing') of 1964 had disc brakes on all four wheels, a lighter body, and independent rear suspension by coil springs and double wishbones. The latter became a regular option for road cars.

Twenty years apart: 1961 G4 (above) and 1981 G4 (below)

The G5 (1964) was a G4 fitted with the 1498 cc Ford Cortina engine. This caused confusion so the designation was soon dropped and the model became known as the G4 1500.

The G4 Series III (1966) was a rationalisation of the design. There was a new square-tube space frame, which was stiffer yet easier to make, and Triumph Herald front wishbones were used. The windscreen was more sharply raked, there was a new front bumper treatment and pop-up headlights.

The G6 was a run of three Series I G4s modified to accept DKW engines at the request of a German customer.

The G7 was a prototype fitted with a Hillman transaxle, built to explore the effects of different weight distribution, particularly with hill climbing in mind.

In 1981 the G4 was revived in Series IV form, with the design revised to accept contemporary Ford components:

the 1600cc Kent engine was standard but 1300cc and 2-litre Ford engines were options. It was actually 3in longer and 2in wider than the Series III cars, and this made for a roomier cockpit. That was important since the car was offered as current model and not as a nostalgia vehicle or as a classic revival. Ginetta developed this into the G27 but the post-1989 management revived the G4 Series II as a 'reborn classic' primarily for the Japanese market.

*G8—an unsuccessful F3 car with a fibreglass monocoque.*

*G9—a projected F2 version of the G8.*

**G10, 1965. Prod: 6.** This car was intended to cash in on the idea of mating an English chassis and an American engine. It had a multi-tubular frame bonded to a fibreglass body which looked like an enlarged MGB roadster with a smoother frontal treatment. (MGB doors were used and proprietary doors do have a habit of imposing their personality on a whole car.) Suspension was independent all round by coil springs and double wishbones, there were disc brakes on all four wheels, and power came from a 4.7-litre Ford V8 engine which delivered its 270bhp via a Ford four-speed gearbox. 150mph/240kmh was claimed and nobody doubted it.

It was a promising car for SCCA racing and works driver Chris Meek had no difficulty in beating cars such as the AC Cobra in Britain. American orders were placed but since it had not been homologated in SCCA racing it had to face McLarens and Lolas—and that it could not do. American interest stopped there and then, orders were cancelled, and production remained at four fastback coupés and two open cars.

**G11, 1966. Prod: 12.** The G10 was re-engineered for the home market but with the MGB engine, gearbox and rear axle, which was suspended on coil springs and located by radius arms and an A-bracket. Great things were predicted for the G11 but BMC found major problems in providing doors. After a long delay 12 *left hand* doors arrived. With a supply line like that surrender is the only course and the model was dropped.

*G12—essentially a mid-engined G4, a 1966-8 sports-racing GT car which was successful in racing at a national level. Some cars were converted for road use, against the advice of the factory. It re-entered production in 1990 as a 'revived classic' primarily intended for Japan.*

*G13—not used for superstitious reasons.*

*G14—intended as a replacement for the G4, based on a tubular backbone chassis; it was not completed.*

**G15, 1968-74. Prod: over 800.** In terms of volume, this was Ginetta's most successful car, due in no small measure to the fact that it could be sold in partly assembled form on the home market. Introduced at the 1967 London Motor Show, the body of the G15 was built as a semi-monocoque bolted to a square tube ladder frame. Front suspension was from the Triumph Herald while the engine, transaxle and trailing arm independent rear suspension were from the 55bhp Hillman Imp Sport. Top speed was 95mph/153kmh (0-60mph in 12.9 seconds).

Few cars had been made when a Series II version was introduced. This had cosmetic improvements, and the radiator was mounted at the front (the car was not intended for competition but it was soon being raced, and cooling was better with a front radiator). The Series III of 1971 had minor improvements in trim and comfort and from April 1st 1973 (when VAT was imposed) all G15s were sold fully assembled. The main identity feature was Cosmic Mk2 alloy wheels with radial tyres.

Ginetta G15, 1973

*G16—a beefed-up open G12 (1968-69), designed to take engines from 2 litres.*

*G17—a Formula 4 single seater.*

*G18—a Formula Ford 1600 development of the G17.*

*G19—a Formula 3 car, started but abandoned.*

*G20—this designation was given to two projects which were planned but not made: a Formula 1 car which would have used the BRM V12, and a further development of the G12 which was to use a 3-litre Ford V6 engine.*

**G21, 1970-78. Prod: approx 150.** Looking not unlike a big brother for the G15, the G21 series was a second attempt to break into the middle ground of the sports car market, without relying on BMC for the supply of vital parts. The chassis was a tubular steel structure with pressed steel backbone centre section, while there was the usual coil spring and wishbone front suspension and a separate subframe

Ginetta G21

carried the rear suspension and final drive. As first shown, the G21 was available with a Ford V6 (i.r.s. with fixed length drive shafts acting as the upper lateral element) or a four-cylinder Ford engine (live rear axle located by twin rear trailing arms).

It was first shown in 1970 but did not go into production until 1972. The concept was engineered to use Ford components, but most of the line had the 1725cc Chrysler Rapier engine (79bhp; 112mph/180kmh, 0-60mph in 9.7 seconds) or a Holbay version badged as G21S (95bhp; 120mph/193kmh, 0-60mph in 8.5 seconds). Most G21s were sold fully assembled.

*G22—an unsuccessful Sports 2000 car.*

*G23—convertible based on G21, not produced.*

*G24—revised G21, not produced.*

*G25—mid-engined two seat coupé based on Ford Fiesta running gear, not produced.*

G25 prototype in 1984

*G26—four seat fastback kit car saloon based on Ford Cortina running gear.*

**G27, introduced 1985.** A development of the G4 with Triumph Vitesse front suspension and independent rear suspension using shortened Jaguar fixed-length drive shafts with Ginetta lower wishbones and radius arms. A wide variety of engines could be fitted, up to the 3.5-litre Rover V8, and while most cars were sold as kits the factory could supply fully assembled cars. A Mazda-engined car entered by the works and driven by Mark Walklett was very successful in British kit car racing.

*G28—a 'three box' 2+2 saloon kit car based on Ford Cortina running gear.*

*G29—a one-off sports-racer for British 'Thundersports' series.*

*G30—similar to G26 but with fixed headlights and higher bonnet line to take Ford V6 engines.*

*G31—similar to G28 but with pop-up headlights.*

**G32, introduced 1989.** In essence the G32 was a latter day G15, using the running gear from the Ford Fiesta XR2 with the standard 1.6-litre 110bhp fuel injected engine, or a special 1.9-litre 135bhp version. Like the G15 it had Type Approval, and was sold as a fully assembled car aimed squarely at the Toyota MR-2 market.

A box section steel chassis was topped by a fibreglass body which at first was offered only in coupé form, but a convertible was introduced at the 1990 British Motor Show. Front suspension was by coil springs and double wishbones, Fiesta front MacPherson struts were used at the rear, and disc brakes were fitted all round. In standard form this mid-engined car could reach 120mph/193kmh (0-60mph in 8.2 seconds) while the 1.9-litre car was capable of 130mph/209kmh (0-60mph in 7.3 seconds). Ginetta also offered a competition model which was a lightweight coupé fitted with a 1.6-litre turbocharged (ex-Fiesta) engine; in standard form this produced 133bhp but a 200bhp version was available.

1990 G32

**G33, first shown 1990.** In essence the G33 was a further development of the G27 but made as a fully assembled car. It had a completely new body and was offered with choice of a Rover V8 engines: a carburetter 145bhp 3.5-litre unit or a 3.9-litre fuel-injected version which produced 200bhp. Disc brakes were fitted to all four wheels. The prototype had G27 style suspension but production cars had suspension from the Ford Sierra Cosworth. With the more powerful engine, a top speed of 129mph/207kmh was claimed (0-60mph in 6.7 seconds).

G33 outside the factory in 1990

## GITANE (GB)

1962 was as bad a time as 1973 to launch a small GT car in Britain, for that year the kit car market collapsed. GF Plant Ltd of Wolverhampton could not have foreseen that when it launched the Gitane, which was a pioneer of a familiar pattern: a proprietary engine mounted amidships in a space frame and clothed with a fibreglass body. It used a 997cc Mini engine, gearbox, and suspension, but had wire wheels and disc brakes all round. Long-term plans envisaged using the Italian Giannini engine, but this Fiat-derived dohc unit was expensive, the styling of the car was not quite right, and the manufacturer's previous experience was making dumper trucks. It is therefore not surprising that the company folded within a year, after just six cars had been built.

**Gitane, 1962**

## GJM (AUS)

GJM introduced the 'Taipan' in 1986. It was a fibreglass-bodied Cobra copy which was claimed to be the only such car to surpass the awesome performance of the original Cobra 427—a 0-60mph time of just under four seconds was claimed. Power came from a modified 7.4-litre Chevrolet engine with twin turbochargers and to meet Australian emission laws which normally called for unleaded fuel, it was run on liquid propane gas.

## GLAS (D)

Glas was established in 1883 as a maker of agricultural equipment but in a diversification programme after the Second World War it introduced the Goggo motor scooter and then the Goggomobil micro car (qv). The Goggomobil was a huge success, in bubble car terms. Glas began to see itself as a mainstream manufacturer and introduced larger cars, one of which, the 1004, was notable for being the first European production car to use a toothed belt, instead of chain camshaft drive.

So far, so good Glas was an interesting newcomer on an upward curve, but it was to over-reach itself and try to operate on too many fronts. The range included a number of sporting coupés. In 1963 Glas showed two pretty cars, the 1300GT and the 1700GT. Both had 2+2 bodies by Frua with integral chassis, front suspension by coil springs and double wishbones, and a live rear axle on semi-elliptic springs, located by a Panhard rod. Unusually for the time both had disc brakes on the front wheels.

As the names suggest, one had a 1300cc engine, one a 1700cc unit and both had a single overhead camshaft cylinder head. The 85bhp 1300GT was capable of 98mph/157kmh (0-60mph in 12.5 seconds) while the 100bhp 1700GT could top 112mph/180kmh and sprint to sixty in 11.2 seconds. These were very respectable figures for the time, the cars were pretty, and they were competitively priced, but never successful. The problem was that Frua could not make more than five bodies a day and Glas' own production facilities were antiquated.

**1963 Frua-bodied Glas 1700GT (above) and 1965 2600GT (below)**

Despite these limitations Glas showed a new V8 coupé in 1965. Again the body was styled by Frua and looked something like those Maseratis which had Frua bodies; wags soon called them 'Glaseratis'. The steel platform was similar to the smaller Glas models but there was a de Dion rear axle on semi-elliptic springs and disc brakes were fitted all round. The sohc V8 engine (basically two 1300cc units on a common crankshaft) came in two sizes, a 140bhp 2.6-litre, and a 160bhp 3-litre, and the maker's claimed performance figures were impressive: the 2600GT could do 124mph/200kmh (0-60mph in 10.5 seconds); the 3000GT was good for 125mph/201kmh and would sprint to 60mph in nine seconds.

This was all good stuff but Glas was a small maker, with only about 1.5 percent of the West German market, and it was muscling in on Mercedes-Benz and Porsche territory. Glas did not have the infrastructure to support its ambitions and, in 1966, it was taken over by BMW. The new owner briefly put the V8 cars into production but, by 1967, the Glas name was no more.

## GLASCAR (USA)

An unsuccessful 1956 attempt to market a two-seat sports car using a tubular chassis, a tuned Ford V8 engine, and a fibreglass body bearing some resemblance to the original Chevrolet Corvette.

## GLASPAC (BR)

In 1980 this company introduced copies of the AC Cobra, powered by a 199bhp 5-litre Ford V8 engine.

## 162 GLASSFIBRE (GB)

This oddly named company began by making beach buggies and added the Jet coupé to the range in the early 1980s. This was a sharply-styled four-seater based on the VW Beetle which did not catch on. The company had gone by 1986.

## GLASSIC (USA)

Active from 1966, Glassic's first models were fibreglass copies of the Ford Model A roadster, using the mechanical components of the International-Harvester Scout. The company changed hands in 1972 and the new owners created a new chassis and a 200bhp 4.9-litre Ford V8 engine which made the car quite a road burner. Production increased dramatically and in 1975 the Model A was joined by the 'Romulus II', a copy of the Auburn Speedster, using the same Ford V8 and a three-speed automatic transmission. The following year the company changed hands again (*see* Total Performance), the models were extensively revised, Chevrolet V8 units were standardised, and other models based on the style of the Model B Ford were added.

## GLASSPAR (USA)

Between 1951 and 1955, Glasspar supplied fibreglass bodies to special builders, and made the body for the Woodill Wildfire (qv). The firm also built a tubular chassis which would accept a wide range of components from donor vehicles usually Mercury. It marketed a few complete cars under the 'Glasspar' name, notably the Ascot in 1955. This was a basic sports car in the Lotus Six idiom with a fibreglass body. Initially a Ford 2.75-litre industrial engine was used, but other engines were also tried. Glasspar folded at the end of 1955 and the Ascot died with it.

A 1953 Glasspar body

Glasspar Ascot, 1955

## GLENAULD (GB)

An early 1980s nostalgia car from Wales, which used Vauxhall Viva suspension and a 2-litre Ford engine. Its fibreglass body was dull which probably explains why the car did not catch on.

## GLOBAL MOTORS (USA)

In 1988 details emerged of a new open mid-engined sports car being planned in America by Global Motors, the Yugo importer which until the April of that year had been owned by Malcolm Bricklin, the man behind the Bricklin sports car (qv). The new owners began to drum up pre-launch publicity in much the same way that Bricklin had.

An international competition, which attracted more than fifty entrants, was set up to decide the styling. Suspension was to be independent all round, a composite materials transverse leaf spring was scheduled to be used at the back, and a number of engines were under consideration. The car was scheduled to appear in 1990...

## GOGGOMOBIL (AUS)

The German Glas company's most successful model was the Goggomobil, a small saloon which was introduced with a two cylinder two-stroke engine of just 250cc mounted at the rear. By 1958 it used front-mounted four-stroke 'twins' of 600cc and 700cc. Between 1958 and 1961 Bill Buckle, creator of the Buckle sports car, built a range of cars, all with fibreglass bodies, on Goggomobil running gear. Among the variants was the 'Dart', a pretty little sports car which weighed only 750lb. Top speed was only about 55mph/85kmh but acceleration was brisk. Buckle built about 5000 Goggomobil-based vehicles and then came the Mini...

## GOLIATH (D)

Carl Borgward's first motor company was founded in 1928 and specialised in three-wheelers and vans using engines of just 200cc. From 1934 it concentrated on commercial vehicles and built a Hansa-designed light truck (Borgward had taken over the Hansa company). Car production began again in 1950 and between 1951 and 1953 it made small numbers of an aerodynamic coupé version of its base model, the front wheel drive GP700, with a 24bhp two-cylinder two-stroke engine (and optional fuel injection). This was not normally a very reliable unit although it was used to take several records fitted in a three wheeled chassis.

The GP900, with a 40bhp fuel-injected 886cc version of the engine, came in 1955, and a few coupés were fitted with this engine. A flat four four-stroke engine of 1100cc arrived in 1957 and Goliath made some conventionally styled front

1953 Goliath GP700 Sport

wheel drive coupés using a 55bhp twin carburetter version of this engine (the unreliable fuel injection system had been dropped). They suffered from the poor reputation of the earlier cars and were marketed as Hansa from 1958 to 1961, when the Borgward group collapsed.

## GORDANO (GB)

Although it had an Italianate name the Gordano was named after Easton-in-Gordano, a village near Bristol. Before the war a group of Bristol enthusiasts had pioneered low-cost motor racing and after it they were largely responsible for the 500cc Formula 3. Walter Watkins, Robin Jackson and Dick Caesar from this group were the principals behind this project and backing came from Joe Fry, of the chocolate firm, who with Caesar had created a famous sprint special, the Freikaiserwagen.

The Gordano was advanced for its time, with all-independent suspension, a box section chassis and a Gordano-designed gearbox. A Cross rotary valve engine was the favoured power unit but it proved troublesome so the first car, a handsome sports car with cycle wings, was fitted with an MG YA engine. A second car had a 1.7-litre Lea-Francis unit and was fitted with an advanced coupé body with flush glass and push button door locks. Fry's death in 1950 saw the end of the project after just the two cars had been made.

Gordano, from the firm's 1948 catalogue

## GORDINI (F)

Amédée Gordini was an Italian who established a name for himself as a tuner and driver of Fiat cars in the 1930s. His exploits came to the attention of the Société Industrielle de Mécanique et Carrosserie Automobile, or Simca, which had been set up in France in 1934 to build Fiats under licence, and Simca offered him financial support to promote its name by using its products as the basis for his racing. By the time War broke out the relationship was well established, and Gordini-developed Simca saloons and sports cars were regular and very successful competitors at Le Mans from 1937 onwards.

This arrangement continued after the War until the two sides fell out over a question of policy in 1951. Thus began the six-year history of the Gordini marque, which was characterised by excellent design limited by severe financial constraints.

Gordini's first design as an independent was an F2 car fitted with what was basically a dry-sumped 2-litre straight six version of the 'four' he had designed for Simca. With

Gordini eight-cylinder 3-litre Le Mans car, 1953

'square' cylinder dimensions (75 x 75mm) and three twin choke Weber carburetters, it gave a decent 155bhp and was fitted into a lightweight ladder frame chassis with torsion bar suspension all round and a live back axle. This suspension, which Gordini was to use on all his cars, consisted at the front of a rhombus formed from single links with the longitudinal torsion bars located in the top of a cast cradle on which the suspension links were pivoted. The basic car was adapted for sports car racing, with 2-litre or 2.3-litre engines, and Gordini proposed to sell up to ten cars a year in 'Berlinette' or open form for road use. However, they were expensive and there were few, if any, takers.

In 1955 Gordini laid down a new 1.5-litre engine with an eye on the forthcoming Formula 2 and a road car with a 110bhp version was also mooted. Gordini went so far as to publish a leaflet giving details but it seems that none was made. Gordini struggled on until early 1957 when he went to work for Renault.

## GORDON-KEEBLE (GB)

John Gordon had been associated with the Peerless GT (qv) which on paper was a very promising project. That project failed, but before it did garage owner Jim Keeble showed Gordon a Peerless which he had modified for a customer, with a Chevrolet Corvette engine and drive train. Gordon saw the potential of this format and commissioned Bertone to create a body for it. Since it was a minor project Bertone threw it into the lap of a 21 year old trainee called Giugiaro.

When the Gordon-Keeble was first announced (as the 'Gordon') in 1960, it seemed the answer to many a motorist's prayer: space frame, Bertone body, Chevy engine and 140mph/225kmh potential. Had it been available from the moment it was shown it might have been a huge success but it did not see production until 1964. Even then it was an outstanding car and the best body maker of the time, Williams & Pritchard, was in charge of reproducing the body in fibreglass.

The Gordon-Keeble was inexpensive (£2798) for the specification, but it was priced too low to make money and the firm failed in 1965. It was revived as Keeble Cars two months later but never hit its stride since it then had a more realistic price (£4058). In 1968 production was taken over by another firm which intended to sell it in America as the 'De Bruyne' (qv).

**GK1/IT, 1964-65, 1965-67, 1968. Prod: 99, all types.** John Gordon had been associated with the Peerless GT and his second high performance four-seater was shown just as Peerless was fading away. The stunning Bertone body clothed a space frame which had a de Dion rear axle and disc brakes on all four wheels, and bore more than a passing resemblance to the Peerless (qv). Production cars had the 5.4-litre Chevy V8, which gave effortless and reliable performance, and the car won praise for its all-round competence. But with a realistic price tag it competed with the likes of Jensen and was knocking on the door of Aston Martin's market sector. In such company it stood little chance.

Gordon-Keeble was styled by Bertone

## GOZZY (GB)

In 1978, a Japanese owner of a Mercedes-Benz SSK commissioned Paul Weldon to make a copy of his car for daily use. Former F1 designer Len Terry engineered the project and the owner was so delighted with the car that he ordered another ten. About six were made for export to Japan, when the Anglo-Japanese relationship soured and the project faded.

## GP (GB)

Originally best known for its beach buggies, GP introduced the 'Centron' in 1971. Like all GP's cars it was based on a VW floorpan and had a fibreglass GT body with a rear deck recalling the one-off Ferrari 'breadvan' of the early 1960s. It was not a success but has frequently appeared under different names, made by other companies. GP's next attempt at a car rather than a beach buggy was the 'Madison' in 1980. This was based on either Ford Cortina or VW running gear and was styled by Neville Trickett as a witty pastiche of 1930s American roadsters, particularly the 1939 Packard, and a coupé version was also offered. The 'Talon' open two-seater based on a VW Beetle floorpan also came in 1980 (this originated in the USA—*see* Talon (US)). The 'Spyder' was also VW-based and was a copy of the Porsche 550 sports-racer.

GP Centron, 1971

GP Madison (above), and 1982 GP Spyder (below)

## GRAHAM AUTOS (GB)

A short-lived early 1980s constructor, responsible for the 'Royale', a fibreglass Morgan lookalike on a VW Beetle floorpan. Graham Autos also made the 'Rembrandt', originally the 'Pelland' (qv)) which later became the Listair Dash (qv) and in 1990 was made by Dash Sports Cars (qv).

## GRANTHAM (USA)

The Grantham was a Ford-based car with a fibreglass body, built by a company which was active 1953-57.

Grantham sports car, 1956

## GRANTURA (GB)

An unsuccessful 1968 attempt by the company which made TVR bodies (until 1970) to build a 'rival' two-seat coupé powered by a 3-litre Ford V6 engine. Called the 'Gem', it had independent suspension all round by rose-jointed double wishbones and disc brakes on all four wheels. Its originators hoped that it might become a production TVR, but although the chassis was promising the body was less so, and none was sold.

**Not pretty: the 1968 Grantura Gem**

## **GRAVETTI** (GB)

An early builder of Cobra copies, Gravetti was launched in 1983 with the GE427, which had a fibreglass body on a fairly basic ladder frame with Jaguar suspension. Although the quality of the chassis and body (supplied by Automotive Developments) was indifferent, Gravetti's marketing was excellent and it pioneered the 'Cob in a box', a complete kit ready to screw together and thus eliminating any problem associated with sourcing parts from donor vehicles. The company was launched publicly in 1986 and received favourable notices in some sections of the press; others, however, recorded reservations about its attitude and competence. The firm folded in 1987. The design was revived by an investment company, GE (qv) but this in turn was short-lived because the basic engineering of the car was poor. Some elements of the concept were revived by CK (qv).

## **GRÉGOIRE** (F)

Between the War J.A. Grégoire was associated with the Tracta, a sporting car which pioneered front wheel drive, and the fwd Amilcar 'Compound', which was made under Tracta patents. In 1945 he showed a lightweight saloon which became the basis of the Panhard Dyna although, after protracted legal battles, Grégoire never saw a franc. Attempts were made to market it in England (as the Kendall) and in Australia (as the Harnett) but both projects failed.

**The 1956 Chapron-bodied Grégoire**

In 1956, Grégoire showed a two seat convertible with a new water-cooled supercharged flat-four 2.2-litre engine which gave 130bhp and drove the front wheels through a four-speed gearbox with overdrive. Front disc brakes were standard and Henri Chapron designed and built the handsome bodies. Only ten were made before the marque folded in 1962 and each car was sold at a considerable loss. Later Grégoire dabbled with gas turbine and electrically powered front wheel drive cars, but somehow this adventurous and interesting engineer never made it into the main stream.

## **GREGORY** (USA)

Ben F. Gregory was a pioneering American advocate of front wheel drive who built fwd cars as early as 1920. In the mid-1950s he announced a 'safety' sports car which had styling combining European and American practice and a 70bhp Porsche engine placed forward of the front wheels. Mr Gregory announced that he would build up to 20 examples of his prototype but, it seems, nobody wanted one.

**1956 Gregory had front wheel drive**

## **GRIFFITH** (USA)

Jack Griffith imported TVRs into America, minus engine and gearbox, inserted a Ford V8 and slapped on his own badge. The result was quick but pretty lethal; an American writer, Rich Taylor, wrote *'there has never been a more dangerous production vehicle'*. That is no reflection on TVR as the Grantura was, after all, built for a 1.5-litre engine. This 'Griffith' is described in detail under TVR.

Griffith seems to have been one of those individuals who was smitten by the dream of building his own car, to the detriment of his bank balance, and he had the basic TVR chassis looked over by Frank Reisner's 'Intermeccanica' concern. The back axle was modified to take disc brakes ('four wheel disc brakes' was then a big selling point) and a 4.5-litre Plymouth V8 was specified. The chassis was topped by a very pretty coupé body, and about three dozen of these bodies, made of steel, were shipped to Griffith. In 1966 he ran out of cash and the Griffith story as such ended, although it continued as 'Omega'.

**Griffith, 1965**

## GRIFFON (GB)

Introduced in 1985, this was a kit car sourced from the Vauxhall Magnum/Viva with a fibreglass 'traditional' body derived from the American Witton Tiger, or 'Merlin' (*see* Thoroughbred, Merlin, and Paris Cars).

## GROUP SIX (GB)

Based on a VW floorpan, the idea in designer John Mitchell's mind was a CanAm *style* car for the road. It was offered as a body kit in 1973 and later that year a company began to make complete cars. A coupé was also offered but only a handful of either type was built.

## GSM (ZA/GB)

One of the few cars to originate in South Africa, the GSM was the work of Bob van Niekirk and Verster de Witt. After making a sound reputation at home, the partners set up a factory in England and the Delta was fairly successful in British club racing. The English branch was under-capitalised and collapsed, but van Niekirk returned to South Africa and found the capital to expand there. A new company was formed on January 1st, 1963 and a family car was planned but, in the meantime, the company continued with the 'Delta' and introduced the 'Flamingo', a 2+2 coupé version. Production is reputed to have peaked at five cars a week but the saloon never appeared and the company folded in 1966.

**Delta, Flamingo, 1958-66. Prod:—.** The Delta was simplicity itself, but none the worse for that. A tubular chassis was fitted with split axle i.f.s. and a Ford 100E live axle suspended on coil springs. Early cars had tuned 1172cc flathead Ford engines but as soon as the 105E became available that became the usual unit, although 1100cc and 1500cc Coventry Climax engines were also offered. Most were sold as open cars but a pretty coupé was also available. In Britain it was a victim of the kit car slump of 1961/2 although it was theoretically available until 1964. Production continued in South Africa and the Flamingo, with a Ford Taunus/Cortina engine, was introduced in 1963. The Flamingo was a luxuriously appointed coupé for which 120mph/193kmh was claimed. Work was continuing on a dohc cylinder head for the Ford engine when the firm folded.

GSM Delta

## GT DEVELOPMENTS (GB)

Originally an agent for the KVA copy of the Ford GT40, from the mid-1980s GTD built its own space frame chassis (which were usually fitted with Ford V8 engines driving through a Renault transaxle) and then built its own version of the GT40 body. A Lamborghini Countach copy, which used the same space frame as the GT40, was sold as a project to BBL (qv), which offered it as the 'Primo' before fading from the scene.

In 1987 GTD announced a copy of the Lola T70 MkIII, in turn key and 'modular format'. This road-going version of what was essentially a circuit car was again built around a space frame and was suitable for Ford, Chevrolet or Rover V8s. The GTD 40 MkII which came in 1990 was a refined version of the competition version of the GT40. It was designed by Ray Christopher; 5-or 7-litre Ford V8s were specified and the latter gave a claimed maximum speed of 150mph/240kmh and 0-60mph acceleration in 5.2 seconds.

GTD 40 (top), 1990 GTD40 MkII (middle), GTD T70, 1988 (bottom)

## GTM (GB) see COX

## GUANCI (USA)

Introduced in 1978, the Guanci SJJ-1 was a two-seat mid-engined coupé which looked a little like a Maserati Bora. It had all-independent suspension and a transverse turbo-charged Buick V6 engine which drove through a three-speed automatic gearbox. By 1980 a 220bhp Chevrolet V8 was fitted and the company was stressing the excellence of its seating (a bad sign for a sports car). Despite this, and dated styling, it was still in limited production in 1990.

**Guanci SJJ-1, 1985**

## **GUTBROD** (D)

Wilhelm Gutbrod made small-engined cars under the name Standard Superior between 1933 and 1935 and he tried again in 1949 with the Superior 600, a boxy two-seat coupé with a twin-cylinder two-stroke engine of 593cc which drove through the front wheels. There was a single tube backbone chassis with coil spring and swing axle rear suspension and a front layout by double wishbones, rocker arms, and inboard coil springs (note the specification and note the date). The engine was enlarged to 663cc and various other bodies were used, then in 1953 Gutbrod made a two-seat sports car which looked a little like a Jowett Jupiter and was capable of 87mph/140kmh. It received an enthusiastic response in America but, despite that, Gutbrod folded in 1954. Rights to the running gear were bought by the Norwegian backers of the Troll project (qv).

**Gutbrod Superior 600 cabriolet, 1950**

## HALCON (U)

Made in small numbers from 1978, Uruguay's best loved sports car was styled after the MG TD and used Ford Falcon components. This company also made a four-seater with a Chrysler V8 engine.

## HALDANE (GB)

A late 1980s Ford-engined fibreglass copy of the Austin-Healey 100M. It was based on a ladder frame, and normally the 2-litre Ford Pinto engine was used, although other four-cylinder engines could be fitted, and the suspension came from the Vauxhall Chevette. Whatever one thinks about cars of this ilk, at least the body could not rust—owners of real 'Healeys dream of bodies that do not rust.

**Haldane HD100**

## HATHAWAY *see* HS ENGINEERING

## HEALEY (GB)

In the 1930s Donald Healey was Technical Director of Triumph but after the War he set up a company in Warwick to make cars bearing his name. By 1949 the new marque was established, its style recognizable. Following the sensational debut of the Healey 100 at the 1952 London Motor Show, he entered an exclusive working agreement with BMC and when his existing commitments, including an agreement with Nash, came to an end in 1954 the Warwick factory was closed. While associated with BMC, however, his own workshop frequently produced competition cars based on Austin-Healey road cars (e.g. Sebring Sprite). When the Austin-Healey connection was terminated by British Leyland, he produced a new sports car in conjunction with Jensen. *See* Nash-Healey, Austin-Healey and Jensen-Healey.

**Healey-Duncan light sports two-seater, 1948, dubbed 'The Drone'**

**Westland Roadster, 1946-49. Prod: 64.** A four-seater rag top which mated a 2443cc Riley four-cylinder engine (which had camshafts high in the block to give a pushrod 'hemi' head) to a stiff box section chassis. Front suspension was by coil springs and trailing arms, coils also sprung the live rear axle, and there were hydraulic brakes. With a fairly slippery body and weighing only about a ton, the 90bhp (later 100bhp) Riley engine would propel it up to about 105mph/170kmh, which made it the fastest British four-seater of its time.

**Healey Westland Roadster, 1948**

**Elliott Saloon, 1946-50. Prod: 101.** Even faster than the Westland, with 110mph/177kmh possible—no contemporary four-seat closed car was quicker. Perspex windows saved weight and cut costs but owners today would rather they had been glass. In the 1948 Mille Miglia Donald Healey and his son Geoffrey finished ninth overall in a Westland, while Johnny Lurani and Giuglelmo Sandri won a Production Touring Car class in an Elliott. Like the Westland, some Elliotts were fitted with bodies by Duncan.

**Healey Elliott in the Butlin Rally at Clacton in 1950**

**Sportsmobile, 1949. Prod: 23.** The 2443cc engine was rated at 104bhp in this straight-sided and bulky model. The public reaction to an attempt to produce a more 'modern' line on the existing chassis can be judged by the length of production and the numbers made.

Sportsmobile found few takers

**Silverstone, 1949-51. Prod: 105.** A fine dual-purpose road and circuit car, the Silverstone had a short frame, an anti-roll bar at the front (very unusual for the time) and a simple but pretty body. With its gutsy engine and light weight, it would accelerate 10-107mph in top gear. A student persuaded his mother to buy one as a shopping car and then proceeded to make his name on the circuits. His name was Tony Brooks, later of Connaught, BRM, Aston Martin, Ferrari, and Vanwall. Production ended when the chassis became the basis for the Nash-Healey but some fakes have since appeared to make up the numbers.

A Healey Silverstone on the Stelvio in the 1953 Alpine Rally

**Tickford, 1951-54. Prod: 224.** Sharing the same basic style as the Elliott, Tickford's version was cleaner of line and better equipped (it even had a proper boot). This was achieved at the price of some middle-aged spread and some lack of agility, although it was geared lower to compensate and was still good for the ton. On the 'Tickford' glass, not perspex, keeps out the elements.

The 1951 Healey Tickford

**Abbot Drophead Coupé, 1951-54. Prod: 77.** As the Tickford was to the Elliott, so the Abbott Coupé was to the Westland Roadster. The line was recognisably related but sharper, and even with the rag top in place the Abbott kept its style, which is more than could be said for the Westland. Like the Tickford, it was a little portly and so had the lower gearing.

Healey Abbott Drophead Coupé, 1951

**G Type (aka Alvis-Healey), 1951-54. Prod: 25.** An all-British version of the Anglo-American Nash-Healey with the straight-six 3-litre Alvis TB21 engine (and four-speed gearbox) and a more restrained radiator grille. Since the Alvis unit produced the same 106bhp as the Riley engine, and the enveloping body was heavier, the G Type was never as nimble or as much fun as the Silverstone. Besides, the XK120 was faster, cheaper, and had more style and charisma.

1952 G Type Healey

## HEALEY MOTOR COMPANY *see* HMC

## HENSEN (GB)

This hideous coupé was first made in 1983 and was gone soon after. Designed by Hugo Henrickson, who had a proven track record in building kit cars, the company's one original design, the M30, used Ford Granada or Consul components. It had a hefty chassis and even those who had reservations about its bizarre looks conceded that it was well made and the handling was good. With a Granada V6 engine, a top speed of 125mph/200kmh was claimed and a 7-litre V8 version was planned. After a very few Hensen M30s had been made, the manufacturing rights to the design were taken over by Eagle Cars but it seems that company did not go ahead with production. In 1984 Hensen also offered a Cobra 427 copy.

## HERITAGE ENGINEERING (GB)

In 1985 this company produced a close copy of the Jaguar C Type, based on Jaguar running gear, with a fibreglass body and a space frame similar to the original. It followed that with a copy of the SS100, again Jaguar-sourced, but using a ladder chassis. In 1989 it introduced a copy of a 1958 'knobbly' Lister-Jaguar, using a space frame similar to the 'C Type'. Some of these cars were fitted with American V8 engines.

## HERITAGE MOTOR CARS (USA)

A 1980s maker of high quality 'turn key' copies of the Mercedes-Benz 500K and 540K.

**Heritage Legacy, 1990**

## HERON (GB)

In the late 1950s the arrival of fibreglass and a short-lived fad for building specials led to a spate of shells to convert old Ford and Austins into dream sports cars. One of the prettiest bodies was the Heron, designed for the Austin Seven chassis, and when the special-building market began to dip around 1961, Heron's owner, George Bishop, decided to follow some other body makers and create a whole car, using a wider version of his shell with a roof added. The prototype 'Europa' took nearly two years to make and when it appeared in 1963 it was offered, fully trimmed, for only £580. That was a bargain—too much of a bargain, in fact, for Heron lost money on each car made and the plug was pulled on the project the following year after only 12 had been made.

**Heron Europa, 1963**

The Europa's backbone chassis, with outriggers, was moulded into the body and this was a complication which contributed to the car's production costs and made repair difficult. Front suspension was by coil springs and wishbones while the rear end was Triumph Herald transverse leaf and swing axles, something which may explain its lack of success on circuits. It was, primarily a well-equipped road car but the lack of competition success, plus the fact it could still be mistaken for a Heron-bodied Austin Seven special, must have affected sales. The usual engine was the 997cc Ford 105E unit, although some cars had Ford 1500cc engines which gave a top speed of 115mph/185kmh. Peter Monteverdi, later a constructor in his own right, sold some in Switzerland under the 'MBM' label (qv).

## HISPANO-ALEMANIA (E)

From 1976 this company made a basic sports car on the lines of the Lotus Seven powered by local-made Ford or Seat engines. The company also made copies of the BMW 328 using modern BMW parts. The name means 'Spanish-German', and this came about in 1971 when the Spanish Porsche importer, Verne Ben Heidrich, commissioned Frua to build a coupé body on a VW-Porsche 914-6 chassis. It was intended to build a small number of replicas of this car but a dispute arose between Heidrich and Frua about the ownership of the rights to the design. After five years of legal battles. Heidrich won. By that time production of the VW-Porsche had ceased.

## HI-TECH (GB)

Maker of Ford GT40 copy, Hi-Tech was active in the late 1980s but was defunct by 1990.

## HMC (GB)

In 1990 this company showed the 'Healey MkIV' and the 'Silverstone', which were high quality turn key evocations of the Austin-Healey 3000 with a fibreglass body and a 3.5-litre Rover V8 engine fitted in a tubular backbone chassis. This had independent suspension and disc brakes on all four wheels. The two models were identical in essence but the MkIV had a more luxurious interior. This sounds like the answer to many a Healey-owner's prayer (a car with proper brakes, suspension, a decent cockpit and no body rust). Performance was markedly superior to the Austin-Healey with a claimed top speed of 140mph/225kmh (0-60mph in 5.6 seconds). Geoffrey Healey, son of Donald, endorsed the car, which was initially offered as a 'Healey', but a wrangle over the rights to the name (to which Jensen had claim) caused 'Healey' to be dropped.

## HOFSTETTER (BR)

The Hofstetter Turbo was made in small numbers from 1984. In style, this mid-engined gull-wing coupé had something of the Lamborghini Countach about it, but it was an original design, and rather better balanced than the Countach. Under the handsome body was a space frame, suspension was by coil springs with upper wishbones and lower transverse links at the front, while the rear layout had trailing arms and transverse links. Disc brakes were fitted all round and the engine was 2-litre VW Golf GTi with a Garrett turbocharger, which meant 173bhp, a top speed of 143mph/230kmh, and 0-60mph in a shade over seven seconds.

## HOLMAN & MOODY (USA)

This respected tuning specialist and race entrant was responsible for the Ford MkII sports-racing car in the 1960s, building them on GT40 bases supplied from the FAV plant in England. In 1990 it announced a 'MkIIA', faithful to the original but suitable for road use, assembled by some of the staff who built the 1966-67 cars, and carrying a very high price tag.

## HONDA (J)

Soichiro Honda made his money with a piston ring company, which he sold after the Second World War. He then worked on a number of projects, including a scheme to extract fresh water from brine, and built some motorised bicycles powered by small-ex-military generator engines. He then built his own 50cc two-stroke engines, which were clipped onto bicycles and, in 1948, built the first Japanese motorcycle to originate from only one maker. Honda exported his first motorcycles in 1957, and by 1962 was the world's largest manufacturer.

It is often said that the first Honda cars appeared in 1962 but Soichiro Honda and his brother built several racing specials in the 1920s; he won several races but retired from the sport after a frightening accident. Honda's first production cars were introduced in 1962 but they were not well received. The cars built throughout the 1960s were small by European standards but they did show evidence of advanced engineering. Honda entered Formula 1 in the 1960s, and although it hardly made a great impression, its aim was to use the exercise to train its brightest engineers, and the Civic of 1972 benefitted.

With that car Honda was on its way to becoming a major manufacturer whose products were preferred by Westerners above those of most other Japanese makers. Honda entered a technology partnership with British Leyland in 1979 and has since expanded into many other markets. By 1984 Honda was America's fifth largest maker, and by 1989 the Honda Accord was the single most popular model sold in the States. In terms of Japanese manufacturers, Honda is the fourth largest (but Toyota, Nissan and Mazda do not make motorcycles) while the achievements of its Formula 1 engines from the mid-1980s on are the stuff of legend. At the end of the decade it entered the 'supercar' category with the exemplary NS-X.

**S500/S600/S800, 1962-71. Prod:—.** The 500S was a tiny sports car with mechanical components clearly reflecting motorcycle practice. The box section chassis had all-independent suspension by torsion bars but the four-cylinder dohc 531cc engine delivered its 44bhp via individual chains to the two rear wheels—a strange mixture of sophistication (the engine and front disc brakes) and blacksmithery (the transmission). A top speed of 85mph/137kmh was claimed. All the cars built stayed in Japan.

In 1963 a coupé version was introduced and the engine capacity was increased to 606cc in the S600. This engine produced 57bhp and the S600 could top 90mph/145kmh—both remarkable figures for so small an engine.

The final expression of the line, the S800, was made from 1966. It had a 791cc version of the engine which revved to 8000rpm and gave 70bhp. Transmission was via a conical hypoid final drive. It was capable of close to 100mph/160kmh, with excellent handling, and some began to wonder how much longer cars such as the Sprite would survive. In fact it was too novel and complicated to threaten the Sprite, and it rusted very quickly, but it was a harbinger.

Honda S800 Sports (above) and Coupé (below)

**NS-X, introduced 1990.** It took Honda a long time to make a second sports car. When it did so, it was not a minicar to be pitched against the likes of the Austin-Healey Sprite, but a supercar which threatened Porsche and Ferrari. Honda managed to pull off the incredibly difficult trick of producing a thoroughly practical everyday car (you could teach your kids to drive in one) yet one which could reward the most skilled of drivers.

1990 Honda NS-X

Most of the car was constructed in aluminium, including the monocoque and the all-independent suspension by coil springs and double wishbones. The mid-mounted dohc 2977cc V6 engine delivered its 274bhp through a five-speed manual gearbox or a four-speed automatic. Top speed was 165mph/265kmh and the 0-60mph sprint could be covered in 5.8 seconds; these were not class-leading figures but most commentators thought that the NS-X's overall competence made the odd few miles per hour, or tenths of a second, irrelevant. In effect, Honda took a standing leap to the top of the heap.

## HOTCHKISS (F)

This old company picked up its handsome 1930s line of sporting cars after the Second World War, but allowed it to wither as development funds were squandered on a Grégoire saloon project and in the face of fiscal policies that were hostile to cars such as Hotchkiss's Grand Sport. A 3.5-litre straight-six was part of the conventional specification, and the only significant postwar innovation was the adoption of coil-spring i.f.s. There was a nod towards the 1950s in full-width bodywork. But early in that decade the car plant was closed and the attempt to restart car production in 1954 after a merger with Delahaye was short-lived.

**1949 Hotchkiss 686 Provence: sporting but not sports**

## HRG (GB)

HRG was a partnership between E.A. Halford, G.H. Robins and H.T. Godfrey, who had been the 'G' of 'GN', the most famous and successful of British cyclecars. The intention was to build a car for the sportsman, and production began in 1936. The simple, even dated, Meadows-engined HRG soon gained a reputation for being a good all-round car, equally at home on the road, the track, in trials or in rallies (in 1937 one finished second in its class at Le Mans). Since HRGs were hand built, and much more expensive than rivals such as MG, fewer than 40 had been made by 1939. By that time HRG had switched to Singer engines, which were modified with the co-operation of Singer. Apart from a single Triumph-engined car, shown at the 1938 London Motor Show, HRG was to remain faithful to Singer.

**In its element: an HRG fitted with a V8 Mercury engine trialling in 1953**

In the sellers' market of the immediate postwar period, HRG enjoyed some prosperity, and some international competition success (although a one-off Formula 2 car was an unmitigated flop) but its road cars did not keep pace with the times and sales slumped in 1952. When a replacement model appeared in 1955 it perhaps departed too far from traditional HRG values while not being radical enough to compete with new makers such as Lotus. Production ended in 1956 and HRG continued as a general engineering concern, later building some promising prototypes which might have revived the marque. Unfortunately, the death of the then owner in 1966 scotched any such plans and soon afterwards the company went into voluntary liquidation.

**1100, 1939-50. Postwar prod: 41 (total: 49).** HRG's small model shared the simple Vintage-style chassis (solid axles, cart springs, friction dampers, minimal rigidity) of the '1500' but was slightly smaller and had a 1074cc 44bhp sohc Singer Nine engine and Singer four-speed gearbox. Since HRG's 1500 model had nearly 50 percent more power for just 10 percent more money, it is a wonder that the 1100 sold at all.

**1500, 1939-55. Postwar prod: 126 (total: 138).** Although the 1500 had a top speed of less than 85mph/137kmh from its modified 1496cc 61bhp sohc Singer engine, it enjoyed a fair amount of competition success in the early postwar years, the apex being John Gott winning a Coupe des Alpes. A flexible chassis, solid axles and cable brakes speak of the 1930s as do the simple but superbly proportioned lines. Customers in the 1950s wanted sophistication (even Morgans were advanced by comparison) and all HRG could do was to offer the Singer SM engine and hydraulic brakes in 1953. Twelve examples of the 1953 1500 'WS' series were sold.

**John Gott's HRG 1500 on the 1951 Alpine Rally**

**1500 'Aerodynamic', 1946-7. Prod: 30.** Originally designed in 1939, this consisted of a 1500 chassis with an enveloping body by Fox & Nicholl mounted on outriggers. All left the factory as open two-seaters but the most successful in competition was Barrington Brock's, which had a coupé top. More expensive than the standard 1500, 'Aerodynamics' were often bought by types who would not have touched the basic car but they soon found the traditional HRG values: a combination of a flexible chassis and a rock-hard ride which tended to shake the body apart. Most of the cars have since been converted back to traditional 'Hurg' form, and are much the better for it.

HRG 'Aerodynamic' open two-seater in 1948

**1500 'Lightweight'.** An aluminium tube on wheels or, rather, three aluminium tubes, these were standard 1500s modified and lightened at Monaco Motors, Watford, by John Wyer. 'Lightweights' were class winners at Le Mans and in the Spa 24 Hours in 1949, although both successes were by default in thin fields and, because the cars were so rigidly sprung, they finished both races in a sorry state. As modified cars they do not appear separately in HRG's production lists.

**Twin Cam, 1955-56. Prod:** 4. After production dived to just six cars in 1952 work began on a new car. This took three years to finish and was a radical departure from HRG practice, with alloy wheels, all-independent suspension, a 1497cc Singer SM engine converted to dohc and rated at 108bhp, and Palmer aircraft disc brakes which were mounted on the wheels with the calipers operating on the inside of the disc. At £1867 it was expensive, the styling was not special, and nor in the perspective of its contemporaries was its specification.

Singer was interested in the engine conversion and at the 1955 London Motor Show exhibited a car with an iron version of the HRG dohc cylinder head, which suggests it was being seriously considered for production. It was, however, a victim of the Rootes take-over, as was HRG's 'Twin Cam' engine, because before long the Singer base unit was no longer available.

Twin Cam HRG, 1955

*Postscript:* Incredible though it may seem, some HRG 1500s have been made in Montevideo, Uruguay. Apparently local farmers favoured Singer cars in the 1950s and there is a ready supply of scrapped Singers. Most of these modern HRGs have been sold in America.

## HS ENGINEERING (USA)

In 1981 this company offered the Hathaway F/20 with a fibreglass body which combined elements of the Morgan and the BMW 328. Customers could buy a tubular steel chassis, which normally took Ford Pinto running gear, or the body could be used on any Triumph TR chassis. HS sold turn key cars and for a while the car was also marketed in Britain. The body later became the Hunter (USA).

## HUNTER (AUS) *see* J&S FIBREGLASS

## HUNTER (USA)

Originally the H. S. Hathaway F/20, a 1930s style sports car based on Triumph TR chassis. In 1987 the company was taken over by the British firm, Tripos R & D (qv); the intention was to build the products of both outfits in both countries and re-engineer the Hunter to take Ford components. By the end of 1990 such plans were suspended following the collapse of the project.

Hunter sports car of the mid-1980s

## HUTSON (GB)

Hutson took over production of the Naylor TF in 1986 (see Naylor). Although it maintained the Naylor philosophy of a quality hand-built product, it also made a component version marketed as the Mahcon TF.

## HYBRID (USA)

This late-1980s maker used the customised body originally made by its compatriot, AIR, for the VW-Porsche. That car's chassis was used while suggested power units were small-block American V6s or a Mazda rotary unit.

# I

## ILINGA (AUS)

An Australian attempt to create a world-class GT car ,the Ilinga AF2 of 1974 was handsome, well-engineered and properly developed. Tony Farrell, an Englishman, designed this 2+2 coupé with safety in mind. He used a box section chassis with three built-in roll bars, independent suspension all round, and foam-filled fuel tanks. It had an attractive two-door aluminium body. The 220bhp which its Leyland 4.4-litre V8 engine delivered was more than adequate to cope with power losses through weight, air conditioning, and the optional automatic transmission—top speed was around 125mph/200kmh.

Unlike many companies with such projects, Ilinga Pty Ltd set realistic production sights and even had a long-term plan for a successor. Unfortunately this was also designed to use the engine from the Leyland P76 saloon, which has become known as the 'Oz Edsel'. When Leyland's Australian operation collapsed at the end of 1974, the Ilinga project was doomed. Only two cars were made.

## IMPÉRIA (B)

Founded in 1906, Impéria specialised in medium-sized saloons and sports models which sold in relatively small numbers. In 1934 it began to build front wheel drive cars under licence, and soon its own designs were dropped to concentrate on these. In 1935 it merged with the other surviving Belgian car maker, Minerva. This company enjoyed a brief postwar revival when it marketed the TA8, a front wheel drive sports car using a four-cylinder 1340cc Amilcar engine, a three-speed gearbox (with the lever on the dashboard) and hydraulic brakes. About 100 of these had been made when, in 1950, the company concentrated on making Standard Vanguards and other vehicles under licence. When the agreement with Standard-Triumph expired in 1958, Impéria went into liquidation.

The Amilcar-engined Imperia TA8, 1947

## IMPERIAL SPECIALIST VEHICLES (GB)

Mid-1980s maker of the 'Jackal', a traditionally styled kit car which originally used Vauxhall Viva or Magnum components but was later re-engineered to accept Ford Cortina running gear.

## INNOCENTI (I)

Once upon a time, BMC products were so well thought of that makers overseas were pleased to make them under licence, among them Innocenti, makers of the Lambretta scooter. They sometimes added locally-styled bodies, such as the lovely shape Bertone essayed for the Mini. Innocenti became part of British Leyland (or whatever it was called that week) in 1972, but three years later BL pulled out, whereupon Innocenti joined the empire of Alejandro De Tomaso.

**C/Coupé, 1960-70. Prod: approx 13,000.** Underneath the crisp styling there lurked a Spridget, which makes some enthusiasts wonder whey the Italian could make such a pretty car and the British could not. Two styles were offered, a rag top by Ghia and a coupé styled by Osi. By the time production ended in 1970, only the 1.1-litre coupé was offered.

1960 Innocenti 950

## INSTITEC (RA)

An off-shoot of a government-owned aircraft company, Institec was an attempt to found an Argentine motor industry. It made a series of cars, trucks, vans and station wagons using a fwd two-stroke twin derived from a DKW design. It was a short-lived project (1954-55) although it was later revived as the Graciela, which was equally short-lived despite using the classic Wartburg engine. Institec's flagship was the hideous Justicialista Sports—details are sketchy, but its coupé body was of fibreglass and the 1.5-litre air-cooled engine was from Porsche.

Institec Justicialista Sports, 1954

## INTERMECCANICA (I/USA)

Frank Reisner, a Hungarian-born American, founded Intermeccanica in 1959 with the idea of bringing together the best elements of the Italian and American automotive industries. The company was involved in the making of the

The Ford GT40 was a genuine dual-purpose car, and while it seemed difficult to sell towards the end of the JW Automotive production run it has been an extremely popular replicar subject since the mid-1970s. This is one of the successful JWA-Gulf team cars in 1968.

Compared with the Countach, the de Tomaso was rather rough and ready with its big American V8 and variable build quality. However, it was a genuinely fast car and it was in production for more than 20 years, albeit sometimes erratically. This is a GTS, with 350bhp

Left: Lamborghini Countach seemed an improbable show car in 1971 but was transformed into a sensational road car by 1973. This 1975 car has the original Bertone lines little marred by practical additions such as the radiator cowls and NACA ducts. Later wide wheels and aerofoils did little to improve the car's astonishing good looks

Volante was the name used by Aston Martin for convertibles from the mid-1960s, and this 1978 V8 Volante was one of the most handsome

IMP, Apollo, Omega, and Vetta Ventura cars (qv) but it also made a number of cars under its own name. Among its other achievements was to make a number of Maserati and Ferrari road cars a little more practical by re-wiring them: taking out the pasta, it was called.

Intermeccanica's first car was the 'Italia' of 1956. This was an open two-seater similar in style to the Omega and was powered by a 4.7-litre Ford V8 engine. It was created when Reisner tooled up to make a steel-bodied version of the TVR Griffith which was called the Griffith Omega (qv). When this project failed Reisner was left with nearly 150 spare body/chassis units. He arranged for Ford to supply drive trains and marketed the cars himself, selling 500 in the first three years of production. In 1968, a convertible version, the 'Torino' was offered, with a choice of 5-litre or 5.7-litre engines. These continued to be successful and about a thousand V8-engined Intermeccanica cars were made, the last expression of the line being the IMX, with a lovely fibreglass coupé body.

The story of the company has many strands: there is Jack Griffith, maker of the TVR Griffith, whose story is told under 'Griffith' and 'Omega', and there is Erich Bitter, who sold Intermeccanica cars in Germany and who made an introduction to Opel. The upshot of this connection was the 'Indra' coupé, a steel-bodied car based on the floorpans of either the 2.8-litre Opel Admiral or the (Chevrolet-derived) 5.4-litre V8 Opel Diplomat.

**Intermeccanica Indra**

These sold especially well in Germany (and led Bitter to establish his own marque) but they were largely ignored in the target market, America. This was odd because, in top spec, the Indra was good for 150mph/240kmh and 0-60mph in about six seconds. In fact the style of the cars and their handling were widely admired, but before they could get into their stride American emission and safety laws began to bite. In 1975 the Turin office was closed and the company was re-located to California.

After the move the company prospered commercially but the zip went from its products and it made copies of the Porsche 356 Speedster on VW Beetle floorpans and a gross 'nostalgia' car, the 'La Crosse', which was based on Ford running gear with a 5.7-litre engine. Believed no longer active, Intermeccanica was a company which was exciting for a brief period but somehow failed to carry through its early promise.

## INTERNATIONAL RESEARCH MOTORSPORTS INC (USA)

A name like this perhaps evokes an F1 team or a major campaign at Le Mans. Wrong! In the kit car world one Golden Rule is that the grander the name the more mundane the product. In this case IRM was an outfit which modified Pontiac Fieros in the 1980s so that they looked as though they might be imports from Maranello. To be fair, the firm did carry out suspension work and offered turbocharged conversions, which is more than most such outfits attempted.

## INVICTA (GB)

Founded in 1925 by Noel Macklin and Oliver Lyle, Invicta used proprietary parts to make expensive high-performance sporting cars in small numbers. It had some local competition success with the 4.5-litre S Type of 1931, but folded in 1933. Macklin went off to make the Railton, using Hudson straight eight engines, and although the firm revived briefly it disappeared again in 1935. After the war there was a brief revival with the 'Black Prince'. Projected production was 250 a year but only 25 were sold in all. When Invicta finally folded in 1950 AFN bought the assets and found it had acquired components for hundreds of Black Princes. In the early 1980s the right to the name was bought by another company (see below).

**Black Prince, 1946-50. Prod: 25.** A luxury sporting car, the Black Prince was sold as a four-door saloon of markedly American style or, more usually, as a two-door drophead with traditional English styling. It was a very complex design with a twin-plug dohc straight six 3-litre Meadows engine which delivered 120bhp and drove through a form of constant velocity transmission. This rejoiced under the label of the 'Brockhouse hydro-kinetic turbo transmitter' and provided any ratio between 15:1 and 4.27:1, although it didn't much like reverse. Suspension was independent all round by torsion bars, brakes were hydraulic as were the built-in jacks, and both a radio and heater were standard. The trouble was that there were few takers for a radical new design which weighed nearly two tons, had only a 3-litre engine, and carried a price tag of £3890.

**Invicta Black Prince saloon, 1947**

## INVICTA (GB)

In the early 1980s this company bought the right to use the name 'Invicta' and offered an evocation of the pre-war car which was based on Jaguar running gear. The inevitable compromises which followed the use of different sized wheels and track dimensions meant that the result was a parody, lacking the cohesion of the original. Apart from the prototype few, if any, were made.

Invicta also essayed the 'Tredecim' (Latin for 'thirteen'). This was an evocation of the Jaguar XJ13, which some regard as the most beautiful sports-racing car ever built, even if it never proceeded beyond a single prototype. This appeared in 1984 but, again, was not quite right. It appears that only the prototype was made.

**1980s 'Invicta' (above) and 1984 Invicta Tredecim prototype (below)**

## INVICTA REPLICAS (GB)

This company, which offered a short-lived Cobra copy of the mid-1980s, clearly had not looked up the word 'replica' in a dictionary.

## IOTA (GB)

The men behind the Iota project were some of the founders of the 500cc racing movement, and Iota made a couple of dozen single seaters for this class which, in 1950, became the first International Formula 3. In 1951 Iota produced a prototype remarkable for being perhaps the world's first sports car with monocoque construction. Low and slippery, it had a mid-mounted 350cc Douglas flat twin engine, and the all-independent suspension (sliding pillar front, swing axle rear with radius arms and a transverse leaf spring) was mounted on tubular subframes. The prototype was well received by the press, was sold to an author, and saw regular service for several years.

**Iota**

In 1952 the first production model was shown, but for various reasons only one was made (this survives and is a very pleasant car to drive). It had a pretty body and a 350cc vertical twin Royal Enfield engine, reputedly giving 28bhp, which drove through a gearbox modified from four speeds to three with the odd ratio used for reverse. There was still i.r.s., chain drive and, naturally, no differential but the swing axles had given way to fixed-length drive shafts, and small coil springs mounted *in tension.*

## IPM (I)

IPM built a tiny GT coupé in 1960-61 with a mid-mounted two-cylinder 645cc Steyr-Puch engine. The company had strong connections with Intermeccanica (qv) and the car's body was styled by Frank Reisner. Only 21 were made.

## IRMSCHER (D)

First shown in 1988, the Irmscher GT was a well-proportioned, if bland, front-engined 2+2 coupé based on the floorpan of the Opel Omega/Vauxhall Carlton. The engine was enlarged to 3.6 litres to give 197bhp and drove through a special five-speed gearbox. Thanks to very low drag (a Cd factor of 0.273 was claimed) this meant a claimed top speed of 152mph/245kmh and 0-62mph in 7.9 seconds.

## IRONSMITH (USA)

A 1980s copy of the Bugatti Type 35, based on Ford running gear with a choice of engines from 2-litre 'Pinto' to small-block V8s. Like so many cars of its type the final effect was spoiled by modern wheels and tyres, small headlights, and dimensions dictated by the running gear.

## ISDERA (D)

The Isdera Imperator 108i was the creation of Eberhard Schulz, who had been an associate of Rainer Buchmann at b+b (qv) when he had created the b+b CW311. It was not surprising, then, that the Imperator was fairly close to that car and even used the periscope which replaced the more usual rear view mirror. The customer originally had a choice of Mercedes-Benz or Porsche V8 engines which promised the 0-60mph sprint in under five seconds. By 1990 the specification had settled and Mercedes-Benz engines, ranging from 3 to 6 litres, were offered in a tubular frame with independent suspension all round by coil springs and double wishbones. Bodies were of fibreglass. A Spyder version with a high T-bar and fussy styling behind it had presence but not, perhaps, line. By 1990 total production had reached about 24 each of the Spyder and Imperator.

Isdera Imperator

## ISO (I)

Motorcycle manufacturer Iso started the bubble car craze in 1953 with its 'Isetta', which was made under licence in Germany (BMW), France (VELAM), Spain (Borgward-Iso), and Brazil (Iso-Romi). Between 1955 and 1962 the firm made no more cars but then it came up with a design as far removed from a bubble car as it is possible to imagine, a four-seat GT car with a 5.4-litre Chevrolet engine. Iso cars were in production until 1974, when the company became a victim of a number of circumstances. The energy crisis was one factor but there were also financial and labour problems which had the effect of narrowing the price gap between Iso and makes such as Ferrari and Maserati. Thus an exciting mid-engined 5.3-litre two-seat prototype designed by Giotto Bizzarrini, the Varedo, did not reach production.

Then the founder, Renzo Rivolta, died and the firm was taken over by his son. The company was sold to an American refrigerator manufacturer but it was bankrupt in 1975. Another company, Ennezeta, was formed and, between 1976 and 1979, made a small number of Lele and Fidia models.

**Rivolta, 1962-70. Prod: 797.** This was similar in style to the Gordon-Keeble, but then both cars were styled by Bertone. Both had four-seat bodywork, a 5.4-litre Chevrolet engine (with up to 355bhp), disc brakes on all four wheels, coil spring and double wishbone front suspension and a de Dion rear axle. The Rivolta's platform chassis was the work of Giotto Bizzarrini, however, and the car fared rather better than the Gordon-Keeble. Despite its 142mph/228kmh top speed, and 0-60mph in eight seconds, it never had the cachet of Italian cars with more famous badges. Options included wire wheels, a five-speed gearbox, automatic transmission and air conditioning. The Fidia was in effect a four-door long-wheelbase version of the Rivolta, styled by Ghia and intended as a high-speed cruiser. After 1973 it was fitted with Ford V8 engines. 192 were built.

Iso Rivolta coupé (above) and four-door Fidia (below)

**Grifo, 1965-74. Prod: 504.** Using a shortened version of the Rivolta chassis, the Grifo had a splendidly aggressive shape, courtesy of Bertone. For the faint of heart there was the starter model with only 300bhp, which was good for 140mph/225kmh. For those with hairy chests there was a 365bhp, which was good for 161mph/260kmh and 0-60mph in seven seconds; for those with massive spheres, there was a 400bhp 7-litre version (90 were made) which meant nearly 180mph/290kmh—and the chassis coped well. From the early 1970s the nose was revised to improve air penetration and there

Iso Grifo, 1965

were flaps over the headlights, as on the Daytona. A lightweight version of this model was made by Bizzarrini, as the 'Strada', with Iso's approval.

**Lele, 1969-79. Prod: 317.** Intended as a replacement for the Rivolta, and using the same chassis, the Lele actually overlapped the Rivolta for nearly two years. Bertone was responsible for the body, which had something of the Dino GT4 about it. The Lele had all the usual luxury options but Ford engines replaced Chevrolet from 1973. Iso also made a special edition of the car called the 'Marlboro', after the cigarette company. This apparently odd link came about when both companies were involved as sponsors in one of Frank Williams' early F1 efforts under the name 'Iso-Marlboro'.

**Iso Lele**

## ISOTTA-FRASCHINI (I)

From its foundation in 1900, Isotta-Fraschini became one of the great names in the Italian automotive industry and for a time before the First World War it was Italy's most prolific maker. It became known for its luxury cars and high speed tourers (which were the *real* Gran Turismo cars) but by 1936 the company was making only trucks, and those were MAN designs built under licence.

After the Second World War Isotta-Fraschini attempted a comeback for at that time the world's motor industry was basically a blank piece of paper on which anyone could write his name. Its offering, the four-seat Tipo 8C Monterosa, was an advanced piece of kit: an sohc 3.4-litre V8 engine (production models were destined to have a 2544cc unit) was mounted at the rear of a platform chassis and drove through a five-speed all-synchromesh gearbox with overdrive top. Hydraulic brakes were fitted and the independent front suspension was by rubber in compression.

A number of coachbuilders offered bodies: Zagato essayed a sleek fastback streamliner, Touring made a more conventional closed car, and Boneschi built a convertible. Only six cars had been made when, in 1950, the Italian government liquidated the company to prevent its bankruptcy. Isotta-Fraschini passed through other hands and still existed in 1990, engaged in general engineering activities.

**Isotta-Fraschini 8C convertible**

## ISS (GB)

Short-lived mid-1980s maker of the 'Kestrel', a fibreglass evocation of the 1930s Riley Kestrel on a VW Beetle chassis which was available as a kit or complete car.

## ITALMECCANICA (I)

A rarity this, for it was an Italian-American hybrid made in 1950. A simple chassis, torsion bar suspension, a Ford V8 engine and a Farina body were the ingredients, and America was the target market, but only a tiny number were made and serious production never got under way.

**The 1950 Italmeccanica**

# J

## JAG

In 1950 John A. Griffiths tried to interest the public in a basic sports car using Ford V8 Pilot running gear in a simple tubular frame topped by a 'streamlined' body—a similar formula to Allard's. 1952 saw all such firms take a dive and JAG Cars of Thames Ditton folded. It was revived in 1954 as RGS Automotive Components Ltd which marketed a smaller version of the car using the Ford 1172cc flat-head four. Some MG-powered cars were also made and these achieved moderate success. RGS was not strong enough to weather the bumpy ride which followed the 1956 oil shortage, and expired. About 50 cars were made in all, and some chassis frames were sold to special builders.

## JAGUAR (GB)

William Lyons and William Walmsley set up Swallow Sidecars in 1922 in Blackpool and by 1927 had begun to offer special sporting bodies on popular chassis. The company moved to Coventry the following year and in 1931 marketed its first car, the rakish SS1 two-door sports saloon, which used Standard components (including that firm's side valve six-cylinder engines) in a special chassis. From the start SS offered West End style at East End prices. Though the company prospered, some sneered and called the cars 'Wardour Street Bentleys', or worse. Yet, as Jaguar, the company was to surpass Bentley's record at Le Mans.

After the Second World War, the company name was changed to Jaguar ('SS' had acquired unfortunate connotations). With a range of models using the remarkable six-cylinder dohc 3442cc 'XK' engine, Jaguar offered matchless value for money. It grew, took over firms such as Daimler and Coventry Climax, and then merged with BMC in 1967, when the group became British Motor Holdings. In turn this became British Leyland in 1972. During the 1970s the marque declined—indeed it came close to being axed. The appointment of John Egan as chief executive in 1980 saw a revival in fortunes and Jaguar again operated as a separate entity until in 1984 it was launched on the London Stock Exchange. Success continued but the company was still too small to survive as an independent and in 1989 was bought by Ford.

**XK120, 1948-54. Prod: 12,078.** When development of Jaguar's Mk VII saloon, which was to be the first to have the XK engine, took longer than expected, the company decided to drum up interest by cutting and shutting the chassis and fitting a two-seater aluminium roadster body. It was planned to sell only 240 but the car's looks, price and performance caused a sensation. For £998 Jaguar offered the most beautiful, and the fastest, production car in the world; a demand that might have been foreseen led Jaguar to re-engineer it with a steel body.

Apart from the initial batch of 240, serious production got under way in late 1949; with 120+mph/190+kmh top speed and 0-60mph in ten seconds, Jaguar's only problem was making enough. Since style carries all, buyers accepted the cramped cockpit, small luggage space, inadequate headlights and poor brakes. A fixed-head coupé was made from 1951, and its looks outweighed the claustrophobia. There was also a special performance version of the engine, with output increased from 160bhp to 180bhp. A drophead coupé was offered from 1953.

**1949 XK120 roadster (above) and 1953 drophead coupé (below)**

**C Type, 1951-53. Prod: 53.** Jaguar had raced the XK120 in 1950 but found it was too fragile in road races such as the Mille Miglia (the chassis flexed), and too slow for events such as Le Mans. The company therefore built a special car (XK120C) with a space frame, an aerodynamic (not 'streamlined') body designed by ex-aircraft man Malcolm Sayer, and a 210bhp version of the XK engine. Front suspension was by double wishbones and torsion bars, like the XK120, but in place of that car's semi-elliptic springs the live rear axle was carried by twin trailing arms, torsion bars and a Panhard rod.

The first three cars built became Jaguar's 1951 Le Mans entries, and one won at record speed. It was then offered as a 'catalogue' model and the first three World Champions, Farina, Fangio and Ascari, bought them as road cars, which

**The C Type, much copied**

suggests what they thought of Ferraris. Numerous other competition successes were achieved, most notably victory at Le Mans in 1953, where Jaguar's use of Dunlop disc brakes was decisive. Disc brakes had been around for a long time but that win proved them beyond question.

**XK140, 1954-57. Prod: 8884.** This was really an updated XK120, and roadster, coupé, and drophead coupé models were offered from the start, all on the familiar box section chassis. Power went up to 190bhp (210bhp for the Special Equipment model), overdrive became an option, and some late models had automatic transmission. New, heftier bumpers and fewer grille bars are identity marks and the cockpit was much roomier, partly due to the engine being moved forward 3in. The coupé had a smoother roof line and, like the drophead, an occasional rear seat. Top speed was about 130mph/210kmh and 0-60mph time was 8.4 seconds, with improved handling and brakes, and less tendency to overheat than its predecessor.

**XK140 fixed-head coupé**

**XK150, 1957-61. Prod: 9395.** Jaguar's last XK sports car was heavier and more refined, a 'soft' car by comparison to the XK120, so although it was the most competent of the line and, in terms of annual production, the most popular, it does not now attract the prices of the earlier cars. It was available in roadster, coupé and drophead versions, and automatic transmission became a popular option since most went to the States. It had disc brakes on all four wheels, one of the first cars in the world so equipped. Initially, power options were as the XK140 but the manual-only 'S' variant of 1958 had 250bhp. Later that year, all cars received a 3781cc engine which gave the base car 240bhp and the 'S' 265bhp. Since only 1466 'S' models were made this is now the most desirable, especially as the 3.8-litre version was good for 136mph/219kmh and 0-60mph in seven seconds.

**XK150 drophead (above) and fixed-head (below)**

**XKSS, 1957. Prod: 16.** Three Le Mans victories made the Jaguar D Type legendary but it only worked on fast, smooth tracks—the only one which ran in the Mille Miglia shook apart. Jaguar had a lot of surplus D Type parts and decided to dispose of them by building a version with full weather equipment, bumpers, etc. Construction was pure D Type: an aluminium central monocoque and a triangulated tubular front subframe which extended into the monocoque as a backbone; torsion bar and wishbone front suspension; and a live rear axle located by twin torsion-sprung trailing arms and an offset A-bracket. The XKSS also had the D's advanced aerodynamics, disc brakes, and a 250bhp dry sump 3442cc engine which made it the fastest (160mph/260kmh) and best-handling road car of its day. Alas, after 16 had been completed a disastrous fire at the factory killed it.

**XKSS, 1957**

**E Type 3.8, 1961-64. Prod: 15,490.** In essence the E was a productionised D Type, albeit with a rear tubular subframe to carry the new independent suspension: twin coil springs, fixed drive shafts and lower wishbones, and radius arms. When announced the E was the most beautiful car in the world (for about £2000!), and it became an icon of the 1960s. With 265bhp from the 3781cc XK engine, 145+mph/235kmh and 0-60mph in 7.2 seconds were possible; road testers actually exceeded 150mph but, for reasons which remain unexplained, customer cars could not quite match the speed of the cars supplied to the press...

With that performance, and style, few complained that the cockpit was cramped, the luggage space limited, the engine gobbled oil, or that the brakes were inadequate if the car was driven at its limit. It was available in roadster and coupé forms, and most sold in Britain were coupés. Few customers anywhere bought the roadster-based hardtop option. It was not then anticipated that rust would become a big problem.

E Type 3.8 roadster

**Lightweight E Type, 1962-64. Prod: 15.** E Types soon appeared on the circuits but were outclassed by cars such as the Ferrari 250GTO, which should have surprised nobody because the Jags were inexpensive, mass-produced road cars. John Coombs, a leading private entrant, instigated a development programme with his cars which received works assistance and led Jaguar to build special cars for selected buyers.

Each one differed but the menu included an aluminium monocoque and body panels; a five-speed ZF gearbox; an engine with an aluminium block, wide-angle 'D Type' cylinder head, and Lucas fuel injection; Dunlop alloy wheels; revised suspension geometry; improved brakes. Each car was essentially a works-built special, hand-made to the buyer's requirements. All, however, had power outputs in excess of 265bhp (outputs as high as 344bhp were recorded) and they have become regarded as the ultimate expression of a great line.

1963 Lightweight E Type

**E Type 4.2, 1965-68. Prod: 17,320.** The ageing XK engine was increased to 4235cc; power remained at 265bhp but torque was increased and mid-range pickup improved. Roadster and coupé styles were again listed, respective production figures being 9550 and 7770. Detailed refinements included more comfortable seats, radial tyres from 1966, and synchromesh on first gear—but the four-speed gearbox still won no prizes for smoothness. Most went to the States, but a larger proportion than hitherto stayed in Britain. At half the price of an Aston Martin, or a third of the price of the cheapest Ferrari, the E Type was surpassed only by the Lamborghini Miura in terms of presence, yet it would return 20mpg and could be serviced by even a village garage. The E Type's unbeatable formula has yet to be matched.

E Type 4.2 roadster

**E Type 4.2 2+2, 1966-68. Prod: 5600.** E Type style for the family man, although the extra 9in in length and raised roof line spoiled the car's looks, and for that reason it is cheaper than a two seater today. Like so many +2 cars, the rear seats were strictly for very young children, and the extra space was probably more useful for luggage; it was the only E Type in which two people could undertake a long tour without calling at a launderette every few days. Made only as a coupé, it was the only six-cylinder E Type available with automatic transmission (the re-engineered floorpan made it possible to fit a Borg-Warner automatic transmission).

**E Type 4.2 Series II, 1969-71. Prod: 18,808.** From about 1966 on, the Series I 4.2 began to receive modifications so that late cars were 'Series 1½'. Identity features of Series II

Series II E Type fixed-head (above) and 2+2 (below)

cars are open headlights and raised bumpers to meet US requirements but improvements included new switchgear, collapsible steering column, and twin electric fans. Power steering was an optional extra but automatic transmission remained exclusive to the +2. Weight increased over the years so these later cars had some performance shaved off, but 142mph/228kmh was quite fast enough for most people, and was better than the 125mph/ 201kmh the 179bhp de-toxed American version could manage.

**E Type Series III, 1971-75. Prod: 15,087.** The E Type's performance was restored by the first mass-produced V12 engine for over 20 years. The chassis from the Coupé +2 was used for the new 272bhp sohc 5343cc engine which meant that the old two-seat coupé was dropped. More brightwork, a veg-dicer grill, wider wheel arches and, usually, ungainly disc wheels are identity features and some of the reason why enthusiasts now prefer Series I cars (others being that a 142mph/228kmh top speed and 0-60mph in 6.8 seconds were not much to show for ten years of development). Nevertheless the engine was a gem, muscular yet silky, and let it not be forgotten that it formed the basis for a Le Mans-winning car, just like the immortal XK unit.

Although the styling bore the signs of a middle-aged spread, cockpit space was sensible, details such as ventilation were greatly improved, power steering was standard and automatic transmission was an option. It was a great car, but we are still waiting for the F Type.

**E Type Series III V12 roadster, 1971**

*Postscript.* The E Type was dropped in favour of the XJS, which has not been included in a book on sports cars. Among other reasons, the E Type was Jaguar's idea of what a sports car should be, and the XJS ran in (and won) the European Touring Car Championship, which makes it a touring car. Even the two-seat cabriolet variant introduced in 1985 was not a replacement for the E Type, although elsewhere in this book are entries for some of the firms (Arden, Lister, and TWR) which have used the XJS as the basis for interesting variants.

Jaguar's own proposed replacement for the E Type, logically dubbed the F Type, was built in prototype form and was tested in the late 1980s although Jaguar only admitted to the car's existence in mid-1990, after the decision had been made to scrap it. It was a handsome coupé bearing some resemblance to a Pininfarina concept car of 1979 and to the E Type, although it was shorter. Code-named 'XJ41', it had a 340bhp twin-turbo version of Jaguar's 3.6-litre straight-six engine and was based on the floorpan of the 1986 XJ6 saloon. The combination of the saloon car base and the extra plumbing required by the turbocharging system, plus essentials such as air conditioning, meant that the prototypes were overweight, and that consideration caused the idea of four wheel drive to be dropped quite late in the programme.

The weight of the car affected its acceleration, and it could not achieve its target of 0-60mph in around six seconds. By 1990, the idea that it might be brought in at under £30,000 had also proved false and the concept was abandoned by the new (Ford) management. The real problem was that its gestation period had been too long, for Jaguar's resources had been stretched by the new XJ6. In any case, JaguarSport (a partnership between Jaguar and TWR) had in the pipeline both the XJ220 and the XJR-15, two super cars which between them had enough charisma to fly the flag for Jaguar.

## JAGUARSPORT (GB)

From 1989 this company, a joint venture between Jaguar and TWR, marketed customised and modified versions of Jaguar road cars and built two supercars, the XJ220 and the XJR-15.

The XJR-15 came first in 1990 and was conceived as a road going version of the Jaguar R9R, which won at Le Mans in 1988. Although based on Tony Southgate's design, it was completely re-engineered to make road use a possibility and the body was styled by Peter Stevens, the outstanding stylist of the 1980s and responsible for the revised Lotus Esprit, the 1989 Elan, and the McLaren F1 supercar.

The 450bhp 6-litre V12 engine was mid-mounted (in a composite carbon fibre and Kevlar monocoque) and, following competition practice, it was a fully-stressed member which carried the rear suspension and six-speed gearbox. Its size was reduced from the 7-litre version used on the Le Mans so that it would not out-perform the heavier XJ220.

For the same reason, the XJR-15 was officially sold as a racing car (to 30 lucky people) for the Intercontinental Challenge. Only three races were run, and why did the car have pop-up headlights, indicators, bumpers, and a practical ground clearance? It was said at the time that any Group C car could be made road-legal but it is surely not a coincidence that it was easier to do on the XJR-15 than on any other.

The XJ220 which was first shown in 1991 derived from a prototype which some Jaguar engineers had made in their own time for the sheer love of it. It had an aluminium monocoque, a turbocharged 542bhp 3.5-litre V6 engine and was officially timed at over 213mph. Some potential customers, however, felt they had been cheated by the

**XJ220**

introduction of the XJR-15 and by the fact that the car had a V6 engine, not a V12. Whereas the XJR-15 was a racer which converted to a road car, the XJ220 was the reverse and won the GT class at Le Mans in 1993, only to be disqualified on a technicality.

## JAMOS (A)

This was a 1964 attempt to market a mini-GT car based on a Steyr-Puch chassis, which meant a dumpy fastback fibreglass body on the mechanical elements of a tuned Austrian-built Fiat 500. A top speed of 90mph/145kmh was claimed. It is doubtful if more than a handful were made.

## JANKEL (GB)

After Robert Jankel, founder of Panther Westwinds, sold his company he established Robert Jankel Design Ltd to build modified luxury cars, such as stretch limos and convertible Ferraris and Bentleys, sold under the marque name Le Marquis. In 1987 Le Marquis showed a new model, the 'Gold Label', and production (at the heady rate of two a year) began two years later. Under the aluminium convertible body was the running gear of a Bentley Turbo R, which gave a 154mph/248kmh top speed and 0-60mph in five seconds. It also meant that quality was assured since Jankel is the only maker to whom Rolls-Royce has released components, ever.

For paupers who could not lay hands on the quarter of a million pounds which Le Marquis required for its Bentley model, the company introduced a turbocharged two-door version of the Jaguar XJ6 which was sold as the Le Marquis XJ40 Coupé. Jaguar had planned a two-door version of the XJ6 but axed the project due to the cost of development.

In late 1990 Jankel showed the Tempest, a 200mph car based on the Chevrolet Corvette and like it available only with left hand drive. It was not marketed under the Le Marquis label but badged *Tempest by Robert Jankel*. The convertible Kevlar body (with a detachable hardtop as a standard item) combined elements of both the contemporary Corvette and the Stingray (spoiled by fussy intakes and side strakes) and was mounted on a Corvette XR-1 chassis. The engine, however, was a supercharged, water-injected, 6.7-litre GM V8 of a type developed in America for drag racing. This unit produced a massive 535bhp and, even more astonishing, 608lb/ft torque, which made it one of the most muscular engines ever let loose on the road.

That power was delivered through the Corvette's four-speed automatic or via a special version of the ZR-1's six-speed ZF manual gearbox and Jankel claimed a top speed of over 200mph/320kmh and 0-60mph in 3.3 seconds. Cars were made to special order and the level of trim and finish was exceptionally high, as on all of Jankel's cars. It was a sign of the times that even though it had a price tag of around £100,000 it was reasonably priced, for it was easily the cheapest of the 200mph supercars.

**Robert Jankel with the Tempest in 1990**

## J&S FIBREGLASS (AUS)

This Sydney-based firm began by making body shells for special builders and, in 1969, tried marketing complete cars just as any number of similar British and American firms had embarked on the road to oblivion. Bearing some similarity to the Heron Europa, the Hunter coupé was a two-seater dual purpose road-competition car. It had a tubular chassis, Holden running gear, and was much admired but it appeared too late which explains why no more than a couple of dozen were made.

The Hunter was designed by Len Moir and J&S made small numbers of his Moir-Renault (qv) sports car. Moir later designed some buggies and other off-road vehicles for J&S along with some fibreglass hardtops.

## JBA (GB)

Founded in 1982, JBA first offered the 'Falcon', a high quality Ford Cortina-sourced kit car with 'traditional' (1930s) styling which was a combination of MG and SS influences. JBA followed this with a conservatively styled four-seater Targa-top convertible based on the Ford Capril II. In 1990 the company was concentrating on the Falcon model in four-seater (Tourer) form and the two-seater Falcon sports.

**1989 Falcon Sports**

## JBM (GB)

Made between 1946 and 1948, the JBM was a light, basic, 'dual purpose' car with a very long wheelbase, a little like an Allard J2X. Powered by a modified 3.6-litre Ford V8 Pilot engine,

**The stark JBM, 1948**

tuned to give a claimed 120bhp, the car was assembled from reconditioned second-hand parts, mainly Ford, which meant it escaped purchase tax. At £750, however, it found few takers; perhaps buyers were put off by the starkness of the finish, the mechanical brakes, and the beam axle front suspension. A MkII version with i.f.s. and hydraulic brakes was planned but appears not to have been built.

## JC (GB)

Introduced in 1983, the 'Midge' was a 'traditional' sports car, based on the Triumph Herald/Spitfire chassis. The company sold sets of plans but could also provide a chassis frame to take Triumph components and the tricky bits such as scuttle, wings and bonnet (all made from thin 24swg aluminium on plywood). The later 'Locust' (guess what it looked like?) was a real D.I.Y. job, based on the Triumph Herald/Spitfire chassis, although J.C. could supply two frames to take Triumph or Ford Cortina running gear as well as aluminium on plywood body panels. In 1989 production of these models was taken over by T&J Sports Cars.

## JC COMPOSITES (GB)

A mid-1980s maker of the 'Wyvern', a 'traditional' sports car (MG TD influence was dominant) using the mechanical components from the Vauxhall Viva, Magnum or Firenza. It was re-engineered to take Ford Cortina components but did not survive to the end of the decade.

## JEFFREY (GB)

In the 1960s George Jeffrey built a car for the 750 Formula and then progressed to other cars for low-cost formulae. There was no intention to produce a road car until customers began to talk about running Jeffrey Clubmans cars on the road. George did not think this was a good idea, because the cars had not been designed for that, and so in 1971 he produced a bespoke car. The J4 was a sports car on Clubman lines with a space frame, fibreglass and aluminium body, Triumph Herald front suspension, Ford or Morris Minor rear axle and Mini steering. The customer specified the power unit, which was usually Ford and choices ranged from a 997cc Anglia unit to a bored-out turbocharged 1760cc Kent engine. The J5 of late 1972 was an improved version with a redesigned space frame to cope better with bumpy roads and to make assembly easier. Between 1971 and 1975, production was 30 J4s and 32 J5s.

## JEHLE (FL)

The Liechtenstein motor industry is Xavier Jehle. He made his reputation as the local 'Sbarro' and his twin-turbo version of the De Tomaso Pantera was claimed to do 189mph/304kmh and 0-60mph in under four seconds.

That was serious motoring but when Jehle made his own car in the late eighties, he called on the rich seam of fun which characterises Liechtenstein. Instead of taking the easy route, and building a pretty car, Jehle's Saphier was a wedge-shaped gull-wing coupé of utterly hideous aspect. His notional customers were offered a menu which started with a Beetle floorpan and Golf engine and spiralled upwards to monocoques, mid-mounted tuned 5-litre Ford V8s, and claims of wild performance.

Jehle Saphier (above) and V12 (below)

## JENSEN (GB)

Rather like Sir William Lyons of Jaguar, the Jensen brothers, Richard and Allen, made their names as stylists and with special versions of standard (and Standard) cars. From 1936 they marketed complete cars, while continuing to supply other manufacturers with bodies. After the War Jensens were made in small numbers until the firm touched a nerve with the Interceptor of 1967 whereupon production multiplied. The FF model had four-wheel drive and was the world's first production car to be fitted with anti-lock brakes. The 1973 energy crisis hit production, the Jensen-Healey project was disappointing, and the firm was liquidated in 1976. There was a revival in 1983 by the firm owning the rights to Jensen spares, which began making Interceptors, mainly for export, at a rate of about 30 a year. The new company promised a modern successor for launch in 1993.

**PW, 1946-51. Prod: 7.** A handsome car, and rather large, the PW was sold as a sports saloon. The PW was a heavy brute with coil springing all round (independent at the

Jensen PW saloon and drophead

front), hydraulic brakes, and a 130bhp 3.9-litre Meadows engine (which had terrible vibration at a point in the rev range). For the PWA of 1949 an Austin straight-six was specified. One PW was a drophead, with a powered hood, but only four of the seven cars made were actually sold. The PW was not a sports car, or even a sporting car, but it bred a line.

**Interceptor, 1950-57. Prod: 87.** The Interceptor was based on the PW chassis but the frame was shortened by 12in, rear suspension was by semi-elliptics and, curiously, early cars had hydro-mechanical brakes, although full hydraulics were soon back again. The engine was the 4-litre 'six' which powered the Austin A125 Sheerline, and the Interceptor was a high-geared, long-legged tourer which would cruise all day at 85-90mph. First offered as a convertible (25 made), a hard top model was added in 1952, when overdrive was fitted as standard. Jensen's association with Austin included making a scaled-down Interceptor body on the A40 chassis which was sold as the A40 Sports.

**The 1950 Interceptor convertible**

**541, 1954-59. Prod: 225.** One of the outstanding cars of its time, the 541 had a shortened Interceptor chassis, with a stunning body made of fibreglass. Although the material was then new to British car makers, the finish of the 541 has rarely been equalled, let alone bettered. Required to pull only 3165lb, the torquey Austin engine would propel the 541 to 115mph/185kmh in overdrive top (and take steep hills in its stride) but the lower gears were not entirely suitable. Servo-assisted brakes were fitted from the start, then late in 1956, the 541 became one of the very first cars to have disc brakes all round.

**Jensen 541, 1954**

**541R, 1957-60. Prod: 200.** A twin-carb 150bhp version of the Austin engine made for a 123mph/198kmh maximum speed with acceleration to match. Add to that the many virtues of the 541 plus improved ride (Armstrong dampers) and rack and pinion steering, and the wonder is that so few were sold. It was practical, well appointed and finished, and had a respected badge. The trouble was that Jaguar was making the 3.8-litre MkII saloon, which did everything the Jensen did but at half the price; the Jaguar also won races and, ultimate accolade, it was the wheelman's first choice for a getaway car after a bank job. Forget road tests, the choice of the wheelsman is always the most accurate barometer of competence.

**The 1957 541R had increased power**

**541S, 1961-63. Prod: 108.** Like so many other companies, Jensen eventually made a first class GT car into something a little more middle-aged. The 541S was wider and longer, had more room than the base car and was loaded with goodies such as a limited slip differential, a heated rear window and, unusually, seat belts. Buyers seem to have perceived it as a fast tourer rather than a GT car because most opted for the Hydramatic automatic transmission.

**Re-modelled nose on the 541S in 1961**

**CV8, MkI/II/III, 1962-63/1964-65/1965-66. Prod: 70/250/141.** The 541 chassis (which can be traced back to the 1946 PW) was fitted with a 6-litre Chrysler V8 and Chrysler's Torqueflite automatic transmission (a few had the manual 3-speed 'box). The fibreglass body was recognisably derived from the 541 but one of the prettiest cars of the 1950s

**Jensen CV8 styling found few admirers**

was turned into one of the ugliest of the 1960s. The MkI was good for 140mph/225kmh and the MkII was even quicker thanks to a 6.3-litre engine. It also had Selectaride rear dampers. The MkIII had improved brakes and equal-sized headlights.

**Interceptor, 1967-76.** **Prod (all types): 5577.** A Vignale hatchback body on the CV8 chassis seems to have been what the buying public wanted all along and production peaked at about 1200 cars in one year. Power-assisted steering came in 1969; the 1971 MkIII model had a 284bhp 7.2-litre engine, and this became the best-selling version; the SP version (105 made) had 330bhp, air conditioning, and a stereo. 1974 saw a convertible (267 made) and there was a coupé version of the convertible with a permanent hardtop (60 made). The Interceptor was a gas-guzzler, so was bad news in 1973, while the bio-degradable steel body can now be bad news for the collector.

1967 Jensen Interceptor

*Postscript:* 1987 saw a lightly up-dated model, the Interceptor S4. This had a 5.9-litre Chrysler V8 engine with a number of options of tune, and power outputs ranging from 185bhp to 243bhp. Naturally, performance depended on the engine option, but even with the 'cooking' engine 130mph/210kmh was claimed.

**FF, 1967-71.** **Prod: 327.** Three things militated against the FF: its price, early teething troubles, and the fact that the world was not really ready for four wheel drive. That does not detract from the excellence of the FF (Ferguson Formula) which also was the first car to have anti-lock brakes. This was the mechanical Dunlop Maxaret system, developed for aircraft, and the FF was the only car to use it. To house the transmission, the wheelbase was increased by 4in (all in the bonnet) and the model can be distinguished by twin cooling vents in the side panels (standard Interceptors had one).

The four wheel drive Jensen FF

A brave attempt at innovation by a small company, the FF will always have an honoured place in automotive history despite the fact that Mercedes-Benz has frequently made the spurious claim that it was the first company to offer an anti-lock braking system. It appears that Audi bought a Jensen FF and flogged it until it cried for mercy; as a result, Audi became committed to four wheel drive.

## JENSEN-HEALEY (GB)

By the late 1960s, Jensen needed a new product to guarantee its future and Donald Healey, whose contract with BMC/BL had expired, needed a new partner, so a marriage was arranged. With two great names behind the project it should have been a success, but the styling of the car was not thought to be worthy of Jensen or Healey, the Lotus engine that was used gained a reputation for being 'difficult', the 1974 energy crisis was no help and nor were ever more strict US Federal laws. In late 1975 Jensen went into voluntary liquidation, although a few cars were finished off in the 1976 model year.

**Jensen-Healey, 1972-76.** **Prod: 10,926.** The problem with the Jensen-Healey was that it was hard to think of a good reason for preferring one to the Triumph TR6. It showed no flair in its styling, the chassis (which used Vauxhall Viva suspension and steering) was competent but had no extra zing, and while the 120mph/193kmh top speed and a 0-60mph time of 7.8 seconds were good, they were not remarkable. The dohc, four valves per cylinder, 2-litre Lotus engine gave a respectable 140bhp—and a lot of trouble. As if that was not enough, potential buyers could not help but notice that the cars were prone to rust and road testers did not speak highly of the scuttle shake and rather crude hood.

Jensen-Healey

**Jensen GT, 1975-76.** **Prod: 473.** Donald Healey had severed his links with the company by the time this sporting

Jensen GT, 1975

estate car arrived, which explains why his name was not on it. Most of the base design's teething troubles had been solved by 1975 and all cars had a five-speed Getrag gearbox which had replaced the original Sunbeam four-speed 'box in 1974. Power windows and optional air conditioning added luxury but the car was not as roomy as the much cheaper MGB GT which, by contrast, had an excellent reputation as a practical and reliable sports car.

## JH CLASSICS (GB)

Maker from the 1980s of the 'DGT', a kit car using mainly Lancia components with a fibreglass body which was a copy of the Ferrari Dino. In the late 1980s an outfit offered a turn key version using Lancia components at a price for which real motorists could buy a Ford Sierra Cosworth 4x4.

JH Classics' DGT in 1989

## JIOTTO *see* DOME

## JL (F)

Introduced in 1980, this was a fibreglass parody of an MG TF based on a VW Beetle chassis.

The 1981 JL

## JOHNARD (GB)

An example of a type of car which flourished briefly in the late 1970s, the 'Donington' comprised a handsome Vintage-style fibreglass body on the lowered chassis from a modern Bentley. At the time there were many tatty and rusted examples of the steel-bodied Bentley MkVI (1946-52) which were fairly cheap to buy. Johnard refurbished the chassis, re-bodied it and sold it as a complete 'nostalgia' car with a claimed top speed of up to 140mph/225kmh (when based on the post-1959 Bentley S2 with a V8 engine).

## JOMAR (GB)

The name under which the first TVRs were sold in America.

## JOWETT (GB)

Jowett was founded in 1906 and for most of its life made worthy but dull cars. After the War, however, it startled the motoring world with the Javelin saloon which, by the lights of 1947, was a radical car which was very successful in rallies. Unfortunately it had severe teething troubles: the engine drowned in wet weather and was prone to blow its gaskets and run its bearings. By the time this had been corrected the day of the small niche producer was over, and the firm folded in 1954.

Outside the Jowett factory in 1951: Jupiter R1 (left) and a competition Jupiter

**Jupiter, 1950-54. Prod: 899.** Originally shown as the ERA-Jowett, this car had a tubular chassis drawn by a team headed by former Auto Union designer Eberan von Eberhorst. It was originally intended to be a simple, light car, but by the time the marketing men had had their say it was a portly three-seater (one bench seat) which was expensive to build and too expensive to sell in large numbers. Still there was torsion bar springing on all wheels (unequal length front wishbones, live rear axle), hydraulic brakes and a 60bhp 1.5-litre flat-four engine. There was also an incongruous column gear change and the styling was not to everyone's taste. The R3 competition version won its class at Le Mans in 1950 and 1952 and a standard Jupiter won the 1500 class in 1951. Some standard Jupiters were fitted with coupé bodies built by Pininfarina.

Jowett Jupiter on the 1953 RAC rally

**Jupiter R4, 1954. Prod: 3.** This was a short chassis Jupiter (but with semi-elliptic rear springs) clothed with a fibreglass body recalling the Ferrari 166 *barchetta*. At 1600lb it was 400lb lighter than its predecessor and had such novel features as overdrive and an electric fan which permitted a small radiator and, hence, a smaller frontal area. Top speed (with overdrive) was claimed to be 120mph/193kmh but by the time it was ready to go on stage, the show was over.

Jupiter R4

## **JPR** (GB)

From 1984 JPR made a Jaguar E Type 'lookalike' (i.e. not an exact copy); it was actually 8in wider than the E Type to accommodate the Ford Cortina rear axle, so what was lost in style was gained in luggage space. Most mechanical components came from the Cortina but JPR made its own chassis as well as frames for other kit car makers. In 1989 a 2+2 was offered together with versions to take components from a wide range of American, European, and Japanese donor cars.

The JPR Wildcat

## **JWF** (AUS)

In the late 1950s this company started to sell the 'Milano' fibreglass body for Austin Seven specials. Much was made of it being a miniature Ferrari Monza but one harbours the suspicion that it was a rip-off of one of the smaller shells made by Devin (qv). This suspicion grows when one knows that the Milano shell became available as a whole range to fit a number of wheelbases and track sizes—just like the Devin.

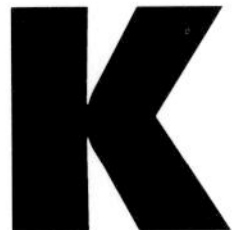

## KAISER-DARRIN (USA)

The Kaiser-Frazer Corporation was one of a number of new American manufacturers to appear after the Second World War and, with nearly 750,000 cars built in its ten-year history, it was easily the most successful. Howard 'Dutch' Darrin was a playboy and a gifted designer who had a series of coach-building firms between the wars and was used as a consultant by most American firms. He built his first fibreglass body in 1946 and used the same material for a sports car based on a Kaiser Henry J chassis in 1952. Kaiser put it into production in preference to Brooks Stevens' superior Excalibur J (qv) but the firm hit financial difficulties when defence contracts dried up at the end of the Korean War.

A conventional chassis, a Willys F-head 2.6-litre straight-six producing just 90bhp, and a three-speed automatic gearbox, made the Kaiser-Darrin a fairly sluggish car (0-60mph in 15 seconds, 98mph/158kmh max) but it was marketed on the strength of Darrin's fibreglass body. Its style did not meet all tastes, and it was unusual in having sliding doors and landau hood irons. Costing more than a Cadillac 62 or Lincoln Capri, the car sold slowly and some buyers felt the need to spend more on tuning equipment.

When Kaiser began to collapse, Darrin bought about a hundred kits and fitted a 5.5-litre 304bhp Cadillac V8 which propelled the car to 135mph/217kmh and 0-60mph in ten seconds. In this form, its muscle backed its looks, and some examples were raced quite successfully. A total of 435 cars were built, 1953-54. Later Darrin built fibreglass bodies for domestic chassis and essayed cars on DKW and Panhard chassis.

**The Kaiser-Darrin featured sliding doors**

## KAT (GB)

In the late 1980s Simon Saunders, an ex-Aston Martin stylist, marketed a multi-purpose vehicle based on the floorpan of the Ford Escort Mk4. Basically the customer decided his motoring needs and chose from a menu of ten body designs. Thus a plumber who wanted to cut a dash at the weekend could have a van or pick-up body on his Escort base during the working week and, come Saturday, fit a sports car body. All Escort engine options were available, including the 132bhp turbo which gave a top speed of 125mph/200kmh.

## KELLISON (USA)

Jim Kellison was a late 1950s maker of fibreglass bodies for the special builder and the best of these were very stylish indeed. Although most of Kellison's bodies were fitted to domestic chassis and specials, he also made a tubular chassis which would accept a wide range of running gear.

## KELMARK (USA)

In the late 1970s Kelmark introduced a two-seat fibreglass coupé influenced by the Ferrari Dino. The chassis was VW Beetle but the engine was the 1.7-litre VW-Porsche unit and a top speed of 125mph/200kmh was claimed.

**Kelmark GT MkIII, 1985**

## KESTREL (GB)

An early 1980s attempt to revive the Scorpion project (qv). The main differences to the original were Ford Cortina front suspension and a mid-mounted Alfasud engine and transmission.

## KIEFT (GB)

When the British steel industry was nationalised in the 1940s one of its young lions, Cyril Kieft, looked for new challenges and lit on motor racing. Financed by his own foundry business, Kieft designed a 500cc Formula 3 car which had little success (even when Kieft bought an advanced F3 design, the examples it made were so poor that the works driver, Don Parker, insisted on building his own).

In 1952 Kieft made the 650 Sports, which was based on the first Kieft Formula 3 car (ladder frame and conventional coil spring and double wishbone independent suspension); it had cycle mudguards, lights and a 650cc BSA vertical twin engine. It was one of several road cars built on Formula 3 lines but, like the others, it disappeared without a trace. The sole example went to Germany as a road car but although Kieft was ready to build more, nobody was interested.

Kieft made a central-seater sports racer in 1953 and, the following year, a De Soto-powered car for an American customer. Also in 1954 came a small sports car which had the distinction of being the first car to use the Coventry Climax FWA engine. It was perhaps the first car anywhere to have a single-piece fibreglass shell. This was offered to special builders but it seems that none took up the offer.

That year Kieft scored two fluke class wins in the World Sports Car Championship: at Sebring, which was effectively an American club race that year and in the Tourist Trophy (a Kieft was only finisher in its class). On the strength of that, Kieft was given a stand at the 1954 London Motor Show and, ever ambitious, offered one of its Coventry Climax-engined sports-racers as a 110mph road car. Nobody took it seriously; it was ill-finished and impractical with little leg room and no luggage space or weather equipment. Its chassis was a simple ladder frame with all-independent suspension by transverse leaf springs and wishbones, and this was no match for the Lotus and Cooper models which were soon using the FWA unit. It was offered for sale (at £1560) for some years but really there was only ever a stand at the Motor Show and a hastily cobbled show car.

When the steel industry was partly de-nationalised in 1954 Cyril Kieft went back to it and the company bearing his name passed into other hands. So far as car production was concerned this new outfit was a dead issue by the end of 1955 but, in 1960, the Kieft name was revived on a Formula Junior racing car. The only connection with earlier cars, however, was the name and the singular lack of success.

**Kieft 1100 sports, c. 1954**

## KILLEEN (GB)

Tom Killeen was a special builder who, in the 1950s and 1960s, essayed a number of designs which often incorporated unusual ideas but which never quite fulfilled their potential. 1953 saw the Killeen-MG, the world's third monocoque two seater (the first two were made by Iota—qv). Apart from the central structure, the rest of the car was pretty conventional, with coil and wishbone front suspension, a de Dion rear axle on quarter elliptical springs, an MG XPAG engine enlarged to 1,467cc and a slim two-seat body with cycle wings. It was entered in races but achieved no success.

In the 1960s Killeen designed a mid-engined coupé with a central monocoque, Hillman Imp running gear, a beam front axle suspended on torsion bars and de Dion rear axle. It was intended for production but it remained a prototype as apparently did every other Killeen design.

**The Killeen-MG**

## MIKE KING RACING (GB)

An early 1980s maker of a copy of the Bugatti Type 35.

## KINGFISHER (GB)

In an unsuccessful attempt to revive the Minijem (qv) in the early 1980s, Kingfisher Motors offered a 125bhp turbocharged version, could supply a complete car, and listed options which included a limited slip differential and a CB radio.

## KINGFISHER MOULDINGS (GB)

A short-lived maker of the 'Countess', a mid-1980s copy of the Lamborghini Countach on a VW Beetle floorpan.

## KITDEAL (GB)

Founded by Lee Noble, the company's first offering was the Ultima of 1985, a long and wide mid-engined car inspired by contemporary Group C sports racers. Components came from a wide variety of cars and the engine options were wide. This became the Ultima Shapecraft MkIII in 1987, with a revised body, and both versions were very successful in British kit car racing. In the late 1980s Kitdeal offered a copy of the Ferrari 330P4 with the Renault 30 V6 engine as the recommended power unit, and the popularity of this led to the Ultima MkIII being dropped in 1990. *See also* Noble.

## KODIAK (D)

First shown in 1986, and made in tiny numbers, like some other German supercars of the 1980s, the Kodiak F1 drew its inspiration from the Mercedes-Benz C111 prototype. The basic plot involved a fibreglass and Kevlar body, gull-wing doors, and a mid-mounted V8 engine. This could be from Mercedes-Benz or Chevrolet and the most powerful of four engine options was AMG's 380bhp version of the 5-litre Mercedes-Benz unit, which gave the F1 a top speed of 175mph/280kmh and 0-60mph acceleration in 4.9 seconds. Apart from its impressive performance, the Kodiak was designed to cosset its driver, so automatic transmission was an option and the luxurious cabin boasted no fewer than 22 loudspeakers for its stereo system. When the stereo system is a lead item in the brochure, you know you are in a landscape where compasses point to the west.

## KOENIG (D)

From the late 1970s Willy Koenig tuned and customised cars which most enthusiasts would give their eye teeth to own in their original form. These included cars such as the 700bhp twin-turbo Lamborghini Countach, and the 1,000bhp turbocharged Ferrari Testarossa, with revised styling, which was claimed to do 236mph/380kmh and take the 0-60mph sprint in 3.4 seconds. It was yours for a third of a million pounds, if you could get a Testarossa for Koenig to work on in the first place.

In 1990 Koenig offered a limited edition of 25 road-going versions of the Porsche 962 Group C car, so pre-empting Porsche's own plans to market a supercar based on the design. Each 'C62' closely followed the Porsche original, but was made by Koenig, and that meant an aluminium monocoque and carbon fibre and Kevlar body. Top speed was claimed to be 228mph/367kmh (0-60mph in 3.5 seconds) and the lucky customer with about £600,000 to spend got a fully civilized cockpit including air conditioning, as well as the performance. Of course, he also faced the possibility of drawing up at traffic lights alongside a Koenig Testarossa, a cheaper car which was marginally quicker...

**Koenig's 1000bhp Ferrari Testarossa, 1989**

## KOUGAR (GB)

A particularly adept kit car maker, Kougar introduced the 'Sports' in 1977. It was based on components from the Jaguar

**Kougar Sports (above) and Monza (below)**

S series saloons and was an original and well-engineered car with traditional styling and a fibreglass body. Although acceleration could be stunning with the right engine (the Rover V8 became an option in 1986), the Sports was a basic car without any weather equipment, let alone luxury items such as doors, bumpers, or luggage space. However, it attracted a dedicated band of enthusiastic owners.

In 1984 Kougar introduced the Ford-sourced 'Monza' which evoked, rather than copied, the Ferrari Monza and Testa Rossa of the 1950s; most of these have been sold abroad.

## KRIM-GHIA (USA)

In concept following similar lines to the successful Arnolt-Bristol, the Krim Car Import Company of Detroit commissioned Ghia to make coupé bodies on the chassis of the Fiat 1500 and the Plymouth Barracuda. Respective engines were modifed 860bhp Fiat and 245bhp Plymouth V8. This time the idea did not catch on, although Krim-Ghia models were listed 1966-69.

## KURTIS (USA)

From the late 1930s through to the late 1950s, Frank Kurtis was the most successful American racing car constructor. He built about 1100 midgets (including kits) which dominated that type of racing; on top of that were 128 Indycars and six successive victories in the '500', 1950-55. Kurtis began building road cars in 1948 to take up the slack in his workshop, for

**Kurtis Sports, 1949**

racing cars are seasonal. The chassis, with its Ford suspension, was designed to take any sort of American engine, so specification and performance varied widely—one car topped 142mph at Bonneville. Common to all, however, was a sleek body which Kurtis originally designed for a show car to advertise his speed shop. After 34 cars had been built the project was bought by Earl Muntz in 1950, and the story continues under 'Muntz'.

In 1952 Kurtis tried again with a new design, the 500KK which was basically a two-seater version of his Indycar, complete with beam front axle suspended on trailing torsion links. Intended as an inexpensive kit car, it was supplied with various wheelbases, depending on the engine the customer had in mind. The 500S, 'an Allard J2 with road holding', was a fully-built version, while the twelve 500X cars were competition models. They handled very well and were extremely rugged, but buyers wanted sophistication and style and only 52 were made up to the end of 1955.

**Kurtis 500S**

Since the world apparently did not want a simple aluminium body and cyclewings Kurtis tried to woo customers in 1954 with the 500M, which was a 500S chassis clothed with a rakish fibreglass body and fitted with a 5.4-litre Cadillac V8 or a 4.3-litre Ford V8. With the larger engine, a 135mph/217kmh top speed was claimed. It was strictly a poser's car (it succeeded in that, no question) and the model disappointed on the few occasions one was raced. Just 24 were made during 1954-55.

**1955 Kurtis 500M**

Central to the Kurtis story, and a possible topic for a PhD thesis, was the fact that, postwar, American racing split into camps. The sports car crowd was not impressed by Kurtis' track record—Kurtis was not sure what he had to do to please the sports car crowd. Making an effective and competitive machine was not enough. Perhaps he should have fitted tartan seat covers and added an 'i' to the end of his name.

## **KVA** (GB)

Ken Attwell built his first copy of a Ford MkIII for his own use

**The KVA GT40**

in 1982, and then started to produce kits before introducing the KVA 'GT40' in 1983. The KVA body was superb (at the time Attwell was a senior engineer at Ford's Swansea plant) and sets of body moulds were supplied to other copiers of the GT40 in Britain and abroad. The detail engineering was less well regarded, but by 1990 that had been sorted out with a new chassis. Ford suspension components were used, and there was a choice of engines (Renault V6, Rover V8, and small-block Ford V8) which drove through a Renault 25/30 transaxle.

In 1988 the company was granted the right to use the name 'GT40' on its cars. The cars cannot, however, be regarded as replicas since they have a tubular frame, Renault transaxle and so on.

# L

## LA DAWRI (USA)

In the late 1950s this company made awkwardly styled fibreglass bodies for special builders. It could also provide chassis frames which would accept a wide variety of (mainly domestic) running gear.

A 1961 La Dawri body

## LAFER (BR)

Lafer made the first, and most successful, of a genre of cars which have mated a fibreglass body in the style of the MG TD to a VW Beetle floorpan. Active since 1972, Lafer's first car, the 'MP', followed the MG lines closely (although the engine was at the rear, of course) while the 'TI' of 1978 had slightly smoother lines and a different nose treatment. A 1976 attempt to broaden the company's base by marketing a modern 2+2 coupé based on locally-made Chevrolet components, with a straight-six 4.1-litre engine, was a comparative failure. This 'LL' was an ill-proportioned car which needed an inch taken off here and a curve added there. It was dropped in the early 1980s.

Lafer exported its 'MG' cars to numerous countries. By 1983 a total of 3500 had been sold but then production fell away and in 1989 only 45 were built.

Lafer MP, 1977, after the MG TD

## LAGONDA (GB)

One of the great names of British motoring in the inter-war years, Lagonda was actually founded by an American, Wilbur Gunn, and was named for Lagonda Creek, Ohio. In the 1930s Lagonda replaced Bentley as the superior British sports car, it won at Le Mans in 1935 (a little luckily) and W.O. Bentley became chief designer soon after that. Its first postwar car was expensive and the firm collapsed in 1947, when it was bought by David Brown so that Aston Martin could use the engine. Aston Martin's success in the 1950s was mainly due to its use of this engine. There was a plan to market a range of Lagonda 'flag ship' cars using a dohc V12 engine. This was built and run in competition but had a fundamental design fault and was abandoned.

Lagonda remained a distinct marque until 1963 but thereafter models appeared only spasmodically. New owners revived the name in 1977 with a vulgar monstrosity which is included here only to complete the record.

**2.6 litre, 1948-53. Prod: 550.** Under the conventional and bulbous lines there beat a heart of gold, W.O. Bentley's 2.6-litre dohc straight-six, to be precise. This was fitted to a cruciform chassis which was advanced for the time, with all-independent suspension (coils and wishbones at the front, torsion bars at the rear) and inboard rear brakes. The original specification included a Cotal gearbox but production models had a conventional transmission with a column shift. The MkII of 1952 had built-in jacks and minor styling changes but, saloon or drophead, the Lagonda was too heavy to cause excitement and too expensive to sell well.

Lagonda 2.6-litre drophead, 1952

**3 litre, 1953-58. Prod: 430.** Under the skin the chassis was the same as the 2.6-litre car but this 1953 model had the 2922cc version of the engine and, with its weight, it needed it. Available as a two-door saloon (four-door from 1955) or a drophead, the 3 litre was a handsome car, with coachwork by Tickford. It did not sell well, largely due to its price and complexity and the fact that it barely touched 100mph/160kmh. It did however receive some cachet as the chosen transport of Prince Philip.

Lagonda 3-litre drophead, actress Kay Kendall at the wheel

**Rapide, 1961-64. Prod: 54.** Following the success of the Aston Martin DB4, Touring was again hired to style David Brown's next car. It was less successful with this one—somebody should have told Touring that if you wanted to copy a front-end treatment, the Edsel was not the car to copy! The Rapide had a platform chassis, a 3.9-litre version of the Aston Martin DB4's engine (but before Aston Martin), servo-assisted disc brakes all round, and a de Dion rear axle suspended on torsion bars. It found few takers when new and most buyers opted for automatic transmission, which speaks volumes for the way it was perceived.

The 1961 Rapide, unloved then but appreciated now

**'Lagonda', 1974-76. Prod: 7.** A great marque name became, in effect, an Aston Martin model name with this car, a long wheelbase four-door version of the Aston Martin DBS V8 which had originally been intended for a 1969 launch. 1974 was not a good year to re-launch a marque with a gas-guzzling 5.4-litre engine and the parent company anyway went into liquidation that year. The car also suffered from looking like a misproportioned DBS; all in all, it is hard to imagine the profile of the intended owner. It is now valuable because of its rarity—but it is rare only because few people wanted one in the first place.

The 'Lagonda' of 1974, rarely seen

**'Lagonda', introduced 1976.** Again 'Lagonda' was used as a model name rather than as a marque name. William Towns styled the angular body, which fitted on the DBS-derived chassis of the previous model. It was announced with an amazing electronic dashboard, which caused endless problems, and the first customers did not take delivery until 1978, by which time more conventional instruments were

1976 'Lagonda'

1989 'Lagonda'

fitted. The engine was a 5.3-litre V8. Top speed was limited to 143mph/230kmh and the 0-60mph time 8.8 seconds. The chassis had most of the virtues of the Aston Martin from which it derived so it was a wolf in warthog's clothing. A smoother, more rounded, body arrived in 1987. Surprising though it may seem, there have been periods when Lagondas have out-sold Aston Martins.

## LAKE (GB)

Short-lived mid-1980s maker of the 'Voyager', a kit car using Vauxhall Viva or VW Beetle running gear. In style it was a pastiche of 1940s sports cars.

## LALANDE (GB)

A brief 1984 resurrection of the G.P. 'Centron' kit car, before it became the MDB Sapphire.

## LAMBERT (F)

Lambert was a 'niche market' manufacturer from 1926 and among its products was a range of battery-powered cars built during the Second World War. In 1948 the company showed a new sports car, the 'Simplicia'. As its name implies, this was a fairly basic car—there was not even a starter motor since ignition was by magneto. It had a 1100cc ohv four-cylinder Ruby engine, which dated from 1920, and this came in a number of states of tune from a basic 36bhp up to a supercharged version which was good for 95mph/153kmh. Styling was usually distinctly pre-war (a few were fitted with enveloping bodies), brakes were mechanical and suspension was non-independent by quarter elliptic springs. In car-

Lambert 1100, 1952

starved France it sold reasonably briskly, and even had some competition success, but a combination of government fiscal measures and opportunities to buy more modern designs saw the company fold in 1952.

## LAMBORGHINI (I)

Legend has it that Ferruccio Lamborghini, a successful manufacturer of air conditioning equipment and tractors, bought a Ferrari and found it wanting. He took it back to Maranello and, infuriated by the haughty reception he received, vowed to make a better car. It's a good story which may be true, but long before he started his tractor business Lamborghini had built Fiat specials. Unlike Ferrari, Lamborghini kept away from the race tracks and, in place of competition pedigree, tended to offer cars with startling styling. They are fantasies for people who have never driven one because, in fact, most have been poorly made. Sig. Lamborghini lost interest in the 1970s when there was a downturn in the tractor market and sold control of the company to a Swiss watchmaker, Georges-Henri Rosetti.

Rosetti was soon suffering from a decline in business as the Swiss watch industry came under threat from Japanese makers of quartz watches, and in the late 1970s he sold part of his share in Lamborghini to a property developer called Leimer. It was not a good time to buy into an Italian company because industrial unrest was rife and this did not help the quality of the product. Then a proposed deal whereby Lamborghini would build production versions of the BMW M1 fell through. A number of packages were put together, and failed, then Rosetti and Leimer sold their share to two Germans: Hubert Hahne, a former racing driver, and a Dr Neumann. Hahne and Neumann soon sold the company on to an American, Zoltan Reti, and before long he put Lamborghini into receivership.

In 1981 the company was auctioned and was acquired by the Mimram family, who widened its base and had made it into a successful company by the time they sold it on to Chrysler in 1987. Most of Lamborghini's owners have faced a sudden down-turn in their main business and Chrysler was no exception; it was soon fighting for its existence against Japanese imports. How long it will feel it needs a branch like Lamborghini is anyone's guess.

Lamborghini began to supply Formula 1 engines in 1989 but these soon revealed that the company was not in touch with reality—it was only in touch with the type of buyer for whom style is everything and engineering competence comes a distant second.

**350GT/350GT '4.0', 1964-67. Prod: 120/23.** Lamborghini pitched its first car against the Ferrari 400 Superamerica and the Maserati Sebring. Giotto Bizzarrini designed the 280bhp 3.5-litre dohc V12 and the tubular chassis, which had all-independent suspension by coil springs and double wishbones. Styling was by Franco Scaglione, with improvements by Touring, but the end result was hardly stunning and doubtless contributed to the car's slow start. Sales picked up when word spread of the car's excellent handling and 150mph/240kmh top speed (0-60mph in 6.8 seconds) and by 1966 Lamborghini sales were eating into Maserati and Ferrari. Twenty three cars had the 320bhp 4-litre version of the engine and, from 1966, the original ZF five-speed gearbox was replaced by a Lamborghini unit.

Scaglione's extravagant 1963 350GT Veloce (above) evolved into the Touring-bodied 350GT (below) seen here at the 1965 Turin show

**400GT, 1966-68. Prod: 250.** Although this was outwardly similar to the 350GT, with quad headlights, Touring completely re-worked the body so no two panels were common. Mechanically similar to the 4-litre 350, the 400 was available as a 2+2 GT or as an open two-seater. Despite lacking competition history, this car put Lamborghini on the map because it handled and went so well (156mph/251kmh and 0-60mph in 7.5 seconds). At this end of the market, buyers are prepared to put up with noise and build quality they would not tolerate in a mass-produced hatchback.

The 400GT 2+2 of 1966

**Miura/S/SV, 1966-69/1969-71/1971-72. Prod: 475/140/ 150.** The Miura had no competition history but was a founder-member of the Supercar Club. Suspension was as before but the 4-litre engine was set transversely amidships in a fabricated platform chassis. The body was breathtaking, and still sets the standard for mid-engined cars but, alas, when the Miura approached its real top speed of *around* 165mph/261kmh (180mph was claimed) the front end lifted. This was because Lamborghini is a maker of male jewellery, not serious motor cars. The S model had 375bhp

Miura S on test in 1970

and could almost reach 180mph/290kmh while the SV, with 385bhp and wider track, could just about do it (with white knuckles, because front end lift had not been cured), and that version shaved the 0-60mph sprint to 6.3 seconds.

**Islero/S, 1968-70. Prod 125/100.** Basically this was a 400 GT 2+2 with similar suspension and a tubular frame, but improved in detail. The Islero had crisper lines, by Marazzi, with a notch back and retractable headlights, and the fittings began to match the price tag, with air conditioning and power steering and windows. The base model had 320bhp, the 'S' had twenty more horses and could just nudge 160mph/257kmh (0-60mph in 7.5 seconds). It benefited from the glamour of the Miura but its front engine and conservative styling made it ideal for the buyer who wished to be discreet.

Islero had retractable headlights

**Espada, 1969-78. Prod: 1217.** When Lamborghini introduced the Espada, Ferrari had yet to make a four seater. Maserati had made one in 1964, but the Quattroporte was more saloon than sports car, so only five years after introducing its first car Lamborghini set a trend with the Espada. Running gear was from the Islero, with 325bhp (350bhp in the Series II of 1970 and 365bhp in the 1972 Series III). Unlike the Islero it had a platform chassis, and a combination of an extra four inches in the wheelbase and moving the engine forward made for a genuine four seater which, in its ultimate form was good for 160mph/257kmh. The Bertone body looked good from some angles, ghastly from others, but since it was made from steel buying one now could be a painful experience.

The distinctive Espada in 1971

**Jarama/S, 1970-73/1973-78. Prod: 177/150.** By 1970 Lamborghini was ready for its second generation of cars. Giampaolo Dallara, who had guided the company through its first stage, left and was replaced by Paolo Stanzani. The last front-engined Lamborghini was basically a short wheelbase Espada with similar dimensions to the Islero. Since it had the Espada's fabricated steel chassis it was heavier than the Islero, but could match it in performance thanks to the 350bhp from the standard engine or 365bhp in the 'S' model. Like the Espada, automatic transmission was an option. The Jarama was a sensational performer but the beefy Bertone body lacked charisma.

The 1971 Jarama

**Urraco P250/P300/P200, 1970-79. Prod 520/190/66.** With the wind behind it, Lamborghini decided to tackle the Ferrari Dino. The Urraco was the Miura's younger brother, although the front and rear suspension was by MacPherson struts and lower wishbones, and the transversely mounted engine was a 220bhp sohc V8 of just 2463cc. Even so, the 2+2 Urraco was more powerful than the Dino and could outpace it. However, the small factory overestimated the problems of the popular end of the supercar market. It took two years to get the car into production and then the cockpit was wrong. The P300 had a dohc 3-litre engine and 265bhp but fitted uneasily in the market (it was felt not to be a 'real' Lamborghini and was too eccentric to attract, say, Porsche enthusiasts), while the 2-litre 182bhp sohc P200 was a lacklustre 'tax bracket' car for the Italian market.

Urraco P300

**Countach LP400/LP400S, 1974-79/1978-82. Prod 150/—.** First shown in 1971, the Countach was an instant sensation and has continued to be so ever since; its name, roughly translated, derives from a slang term for 'That's it'. The mid-mounted 4-litre engine was fixed in-line (the 'LP' designation stands for *Longitudinale Posteriore*) in a tubular frame and the five-speed gearbox was forward of the engine with the driveshaft then passing back through the engine sump. With 375bhp on tap the Countach was good for 170+mph/275kmh, with handling and brakes to match. The 'S' model of 1978 had wider tyres, modified suspension, the 'five pot' wheels which have become a Lamborghini trademark and, as an option, a high-mounted rear wing. The 2S of 1980 had an improved cockpit and instrumentation. The body was Bertone's finest.

Countach prototype (above) and early production Countach (below). Note changes in wheels, ducts and windows

**Silhouette, 1976-77. Prod: 54.** It was one thing for Lamborghini to be the cheeky interloper, it was another for it to retain its advantage, especially when it was going through a difficult patch. In fact the company was built on foundations of sand in that it could make concept cars in small numbers but had not learned how to make them in series. The Silhouette was a re-vamped, two-seat, Urraco P300, suitably stiffened to accommodate a Targa top (which usually leaked) and with a 265bhp 3-litre V8. Indifferent build quality, suspect reliability and poor ergonomics were all against it, as were Lamborghini's financial difficulties and the fact it could only sell in the States on the 'grey' market since it did not comply with US regulations. In the market it was less a silhouette, more a shadow.

Lamborghini Silhouette, 1976

**Jalpa, introduced 1981.** The Jalpa was basically a lightly reworked Silhouette with a 3.5-litre engine modified by the great former Maserati engineer, Giulio Alfieri. It had only an extra 5bhp, bringing the figure up to 270bhp, but maximum torque was up to 231lb/ft. The modified body style was to few people's taste but the cockpit was revamped and, by Italian standards, the ergonomics were quite reasonable.

The Jalpa on test in 1983

**Countach LP500/LP500S Quattrovalvole, 1982-85/1985-89. Prod—/—.** Although the Countach was the ultimate in male jewellery, sales were fairly slow due to the fact that the American market could not be served. That was put right with the LP500, which had a 5167cc version of the engine. Output remained at 375bhp (325bhp with US emission control equipment) but torque was improved. The opinion in the market place was that this was not enough so, in 1985, came the four-valves-per-cylinder 'Quattrovalvole' which pumped out 455bhp (425bhp in America) and was good for 183mph/295kmh (0-60mph in 4.9 seconds). The seating position is impossible, visibility is poor, and you need to be a weight lifter to drive one any distance, but it is paradise for poseurs.

Countach LP500, 1982

**Diablo, introduced 1990.** One of the main selling points of the Countach was the style and with the Diablo Marcello Gandini created a shape which had more presence than almost anything else on the road and which looked set to stay fresh to the end of the century and beyond. In isolation, it looks like nothing else, yet stand a Diablo alongside a Countach and the family resemblance is marked. That more or less sums up the Diablo: it was new, yet a logical development of the Countach. Their chassis were similar on paper but the Diablo had carbon fibre reinforcements, and while the Diablo's engine derived from the earlier car it was larger at 5729cc and power was increased to 492bhp (with 428lb/ft torque). Lamborghini claimed a top speed of 202mph/325kmh with 0-62mph in 4.1 seconds.

**Lamborghini Diablo in 1991**

## LANCIA (I)

Lancia is a little like Alfa Romeo in that it is difficult to equate the company's sagging image in the 1980s with the niche it once occupied, although happily that position has begun to change in the wake of improved production cars and considerable rally successes. This is as it should be because Lancia has long been noted for technical excellence and innovation: it was the first manufacturer, for example, to dispense with a separate chassis and use 'integral' construction, and that was in 1922 on the Lambda, which also had independent front suspension, a V4 engine and four-wheel brakes.

Vincenzo Lancia was a noted Grand Prix driver for Fiat in the early years of the century, but after founding Fabrica Automobile Lancia e Cia in 1906 he always kept racing at arm's length. Like a reformed alcoholic, he knew only too well that one could not go racing half-heartedly and that Lancia would be involved in heavy expenditure. This policy changed in the 1950s when Vincenzo's son, Gianni, committed Lancia to an ambitious competition programme, overseen by Vittorio Jano. Unfortunately the racing programme sapped the company's resources and, by mid-1955, Automobile Lancia was in desperate financial straits. The Lancia family sold their interests to Carlo Pesenti, who immediately curtailed racing and instigated a major modernisation programme. The Formula 1 cars passed to Ferrari, with Fiat financial backing.

Under Pesenti, Lancia's new chief engineer, Antonio Fessia instigated new models, but company policy put the emphasis on small cars, and small cars do not make as much profit as big cars. In the late 1960s sales fell and the company was in trouble again. In October 1969 Lancia, with its huge debts (£67 million), was taken over by Fiat for a nominal price (£670) and rationalisation took place.

The first 'Fiat' car was the Beta, which suffered terrible rust problems largely due to the use of inferior steel from the Soviet Union supplied in part payment for Fiat setting up the Lada plant. Unlike Volkswagen, which suffered similar problems in 1961 but managed to bury the story, Lancia did the honourable thing and bought back cars, but despite this honest gesture its reputation suffered.

For most of the period of Fiat ownership, Lancia has been Fiat's rally arm and has enjoyed considerable success. This has helped the marque regain the position it deserves, and its reputation.

**Aurelia B20-2500GT, 1951-58. Prod: 2568.** 1949 saw the announcement of Jano's Aurelia saloon, which had all independent suspension, inboard rear brakes, a four-speed transaxle and an ohv V6 engine of 1750cc. A GT version (B20) was introduced in 1951 with a slightly shorter wheelbase, an 85bhp 2-litre engine and a body styled by Pininfarina. By degrees the engine was enlarged until it reached 2.5 litres and 118bhp, and a de Dion rear axle was added in 1954.

It is difficult to put the Aurelia B20 into a modern perspective: one came second in the Mille Miglia in 1951, another came third in 1952, splitting the works Mercedes-Benz SLs—yet it was really only a forebear of the 'hot hatch'. It also won its class at Le Mans, scored a 1-2-3 in the Targa Florio and that is not to mention successes in rallies. All in all it makes the modern 'GT' car look like a cynical piece of marketing which such cars usually are.

**Lancia Aurelia B20 GT**

**Aurelia B24 Spyder and Convertible, 1955-58. Prod: 761.** A Pininfarina-styled two-seat open sports car (the difference between the Spyder and the Convertible was the level of the weather equipment), with the 2451cc version of the V6 engine and the de Dion rear axle.

**1955 Aurelia B24 Spyder. Convertible has quarter lights and different 'screen**

**Appia (coachbuilt) Series II/III, 1956-59/1959-63. Prod: 175/408.** These cars had special coupé or cabriolet bodywork by such as Pininfarina, Viotti, Zagato and Vignale, on the floorpan of the Aurelia's little sister. The Appia had a 1098cc ohv V4 engine (two thirds of the Aurelia's V6) which in Series II form gave 43bhp (53bhp in Series III cars). Like the Aurelia it had unitary construction and sliding pillar front suspension but other details were simplified: the four-speed gearbox was mounted behind the engine, there was a live rear axle, and the brakes were all outboard.

Appia Cabriolet by Vignale

**Flaminia Sport and Supersport, 1959-67. Prod: 525.** After the Lancia family sold the company to Carlo Pesenti, the first car from the new regime was the Flaminia. This had the 2.5-litre V6 engine, the de Dion rear axle and the four-speed transaxle, but the old sliding pillar front suspension gave way to coil springs and double wishbones and the form of the unitary construction was changed. The standard car was a Pininfarina-styled saloon and there were also 'coupés' (actually pillarless saloons), 'GTs' and convertibles, but the Sport and Supersport models were two-seat cars styled by Zagato. Front disc brakes were standard, some cars had a 2775cc version of the engine, and a few were made with units giving up to 175bhp, which meant over 130mph/210kmh.

Flaminia GT 2.8-litre (top) compares with the Flaminia Supersport Zagato (middle) and a dreadful 1960 effort by Raymond Loewy on the Flaminia Sport chassis (bottom)

**Fulvia Coupé/Sport, 1965-67/1967-76. Prod: 134,035/6170.** The coupé versions of the four-seat Flavia (with a flat-four engine) were styling variations rather than real sports cars, although they were more sporting than many another 'sports car'. They were short wheelbase versions of the front wheel drive Fulvia saloon range, with transverse leaf and lower wishbone front suspension and a dead rear axle on semi-elliptic springs with a Panhard rod. All the sports models had disc brakes on all four wheels. The front-mounted V4 engines ranged from 1216cc to 1298cc and a five-speed gearbox arrived in 1971. Some cars were bodied by Zagato with a lightweight shell (2600 made) and with this style Zagato boldly stated that it no longer wished to be regarded as a serious coach builder, for it was hideous...

1965 Fulvia Coupé (above) and Zagato Rallye 1.35 (below)

**Fulvia HF, 1966-72. Prod: 7102.** Lancia's standard Fulvia coupé body was pretty enough for anyone. The HF had a tuned engine and on the special Lusso models, intended for competition but prized by road drivers, aluminium body panels and plexiglass windows. Engine sizes varied between 1216cc (1966-68), 1298cc (1968-69) and 1584cc (1969-72) and with the latter there was up to 130bhp on tap. On the HF1600 Lusso, this meant 106mph/170kmh (0-60mph in 9.9 seconds) but the car's road holding and overall competence were sensational. Some 800 of the later 1.6-litre cars had the Zagato body (which meant up to 120mph/193kmh. The Fulvia series was the last of the real Lancias and had not a drop of Fiat blood in it.

Fulvia HF (above) and 1971 1.6 Sport Zagato (below)

**Stratos, 1973-75.** **Prod: 500 (including prototypes).** In 1970, just after Fiat had taken over Lancia, Bertone showed a mid-engined concept car using Lancia components. Cesare Fiorio, Lancia's competition manager, persuaded the company to take it seriously and in 1972 prototypes were made, and rallied. These used the 2.4-litre V6 Ferrari Dino engine. At first the car was unreliable but it was developed, won the World Rally Championship in 1975 and 1976, and was still competing in 1979, when a privateer won the Monte Carlo Rally.

It was a two-seat coupé built around a simple steel monocoque, with a fibreglass body, independent suspension all round by coil springs and double wishbones and four wheel disc brakes were fitted. To gain homologation, over 400 cars were made. The 'standard' cars had a 190bhp engine which fed through a five-speed transaxle (and meant 143mph/230kmh, 0-60mph in 6.8 seconds) but, of course, works cars had considerably more power, especially when fitted with four-valve heads and a turbocharger. It was cramped and claustrophobic, and Lancia took a long time to sell all the cars, but now these are desirable collector's items.

The desirable Stratos

**Beta Coupé/Spyder, 1973-84/1975-83.** **Prod: 111,801/ 9390.** Based on a shortened platform from the first 'Fiat' Lancia, this series of 2+2 front wheel drive cars had a 1367cc version of the transversely-mounted dohc Fiat-derived engine driving through a five-speed gearbox. Front and rear suspension was by MacPherson struts and lower wishbones, and disc brakes were fitted all round. Engine options included 1.6- and 2-litre versions; with fuel injection the 2-litre unit was good for 122bhp and there was 135bhp with the 'Volumex' supercharger. The HPE was a 'sports estate' version of the Beta.

Lancia Beta Spyder, 1975

**Monte Carlo, 1975-84.** **Prod: 7595.** This was a mid-engined two-seat coupé styled by Pininfarina, sourced from the Lancia Beta parts bin and originally intended to sell as a Fiat, a big brother to the X1/9 and, in fact, code-named the X1/20. Like the Beta series it had all-independent suspension by MacPherson struts and lower wishbones, but the standard engine was a 2-litre unit which gave 120bhp in European form and as little as 84bhp when sold in America, where it was named the 'Scorpion'. There was a removable roof panel and, although luggage space is always at a premium in a mid-engined car, in the Monte Carlo it was better than most.

For rallying Lancia used a highly developed version resembling the standard car only in name and broad outline, and this was built by Abarth, which had become the Fiat group's rally arm. Although the Monte Carlo looked the business, its performance was disappointing—even in European specification top speed was only 119mph/195kmh (0-60mph in 9.8 seconds) and road holding and grip were not all they should have been.

The mid-engined Monte Carlo, 1975

*Postscript:* In the mid-1980s Lancia built a superb four wheel drive Group B rally car based on the Delta hatchback. The engine was the work of ex-Ferrari designer, Aurelio Lampredi, and cleverly used a combination of supercharging and turbocharging. Transmission was by Hewland. Lessons learned with this car were applied to the Delta Integrale, a four wheel drive turbocharged hatchback which became Lancia's rally machine. It is a wonderful car, a sports car at heart, which is why it has to be mentioned even though it is only a hot hatch.

## **L&R** (D)

The German firm of Lorenz and Rankl made its reputation by marketing convertible versions of Ferrari GT cars, its rag top Testarossa being particularly successful. In the 1980s it also made a high-quality copy of the AC Cobra, which was unusual for having a 5-litre Mercedes-Benz V8 engine, and the 'Silver Falcon', which was an original design.

The Silver Falcon used the same chassis and Mercedes-Benz running gear as the Cobra copy and the styling was inspired by the Mercedes-Benz 300SL roadster, with a hint of the 300SLR sports-racer. It was, however, not a copy but an *evocation* of an era, and customers could specify either an aluminium body or one made from Kevlar. With the optional 279bhp 5.6-litre engine, a top speed of about 170mph/275kmh was possible.

## **LA SAETTA** (USA)

Between 1952 and 1955 this company built about 15 sports cars which used fibreglass bodies mated to shortened Ford or Chevrolet chassis with Hudson or Oldsmobile engines.

## **LATHAM** (GB)

A late-1980s maker of the F2 Super Sports, a kit car which used Triumph Dolomite components. The chassis consisted of a central composite fibre monocoque with tubular subframes front and rear, and the voluptuous fibreglass body, an open two-seater, seemed inspired by the Marcos Spyder.

## **L'AUTOMOBILE** (BR)

This was a typical Brazilian specialist car, comprising a VW floorpan and a fibreglass body. The company began with a copy of the 1931 Alfa Romeo Monza in 1978 but soon afterwards it added a modern 2+2 coupé, the 'Ventura'.

## **LEADER** *see* SYLVA

## **LEA-FRANCIS** (GB)

The Lea-Francis company was founded in 1895 to make bicycles, motorcycles and to undertake general engineering work and its first car appeared in 1904. Only three were made and in 1906 the design was taken over by Singer, which left Lea-Francis to concentrate on its other activities. Car making was revived in 1920 and lasted until 1935. There was another revival in 1937 which lasted until 1952. 1960 saw another attempt at resuscitation, abortive because the 'Lynx' sports car was a laughing stock.

**14HP Sports, 1947-49. Prod: 129.** Lea-Francis' 1767cc 72bhp four-cylinder engine layout was similar to the classic Riley, with camshafts mounted high in the block operating short pushrods. It was a willing engine which would propel the 2+2 Sports to about 85mph/135kmh. The car had excellent, predictable handling. Later models had independent front suspension in place of the beam axle and semi-elliptics, but many thought that this did not bring an improvement in handling. The Connaught L2 was based on the beam-axle chassis, the L3 on the i.f.s. model.

Lea-Francis 14hp Sports

**2½ litre Sports, 1950-53. Prod: 77.** A much undervalued car, the big Leaf sports had just over 100bhp, torsion bar i.f.s. and two decent-sized seats in the back. It was good for the magic hundred, and although it was a big car it had light and predictable steering, a crisp gear change, and could be chucked about with abandon. From 1952 hydraulic brakes were fitted.

Lea-Francis 2½-litre Sports

**Lynx, 1960. Prod: 3.** One of the great mysteries of motoring history is how anyone could have styled such a monstrosity; how someone else could see it and say, *We gotta*

The unfortunate Lea-Francis Lynx, 1960

*build it!*; then, when it stood complete in all its ghastliness, how someone could say, *Great! We'll take it to the Motor Show*; finally, how someone could say, *I think it would look good in mauve with gold brightwork.* That is what happened with the Lea-Francis Lynx, a 2/4 seat sports car which used a 2.6-litre Ford Zephyr engine in a tubular frame. Although production is listed at three, these were all prototypes. Nobody actually ordered one.

*Postscript:* The company kept going with general engineering work, and among its projects was an attempt to make a success of the Nobel (neé Fuldamobil) bubble car, which was a silly move after the introduction of the Mini. Some work was done on a large saloon to be powered by a Chrysler V8 engine, but this did not even reach the stage of a complete prototype. In 1962 the business end of the company was taken over by the components firm, Quinton Hazell Ltd, and rights to car manufacturing were bought by Barrie Price at the same time. In 1976 Price began work on a hand-built and expensive tourer using Jaguar running gear and recalling the style of 1930s Lea-Francis models. The first car was completed in 1980 and in 1990 the car was still available to special order.

**The Jaguar powered Lea-Francis**

## LEDL (A)

From 1973 Ledl's business centred on beach buggies, but it also made small numbers of the 'Targa', a mid-engined coupé with a 'Nova' fibreglass body (qv), independent suspension and disc brakes all round, and a transversely mounted 1.3-litre Ford engine. Front suspension was by coil springs and double wishbones while Ford Fiesta MacPherson strut front suspension was deployed at the rear.

Ledl has also made a particularly horrid fibreglass 'copy' of the Bugatti Type 35B (on a 1.2-litre VW Beetle floorpan) and an equally unconvincing '1929 Mercedes-Benz SS' (1.6- or 1.2-litre VW floorpan). In 1990 the firm concentrated on the 'AS', a Ford-based car which used the Nova-derived body. With Escort Turbo power, a top speed of just over 130mph/ 210kmh was claimed. By then it was making about two cars a week.

## LEGGATTI (D)

A late 1980s maker of a high-quality copy of the Ferrari Daytona Spyder based on the Chevrolet Corvette. Why anyone would want to take a car of the integrity and excellence of the Corvette and then spend a lot of money to convert it into a fake is beyond comprehension.

## LE MANS SPORTS CARS (GB)

A late 1980s maker of copies of the Jaguar C Type, D Type and XKSS using Jaguar running gear. Turn key cars were available.

## LE MARQUIS *see* JANKEL

## LEMAZONE (GB)

In 1985 Lemazone introduced the 'Pulsar', an unconvincing Porsche 911 Cabriolet lookalike which used VW Beetle running gear but the firm's own chassis. It did not last long.

## LENHAM (GB)

Lenham began to build small numbers of sports-racing cars in 1968, sold the Hamlen F Ford 1600 car in the early 1970s, and in 1976 introduced the Lenham-Healey. This had an extremely pretty fibreglass and aluminium body inspired by the Bugatti Type 35 but a distinct shape in its own right, which Lenham fitted to the renovated chassis of any of the large Austin-Healeys. At the time such cars were merely rusting old bangers, but when they became 'classics' supplies dried up.

**Lenham-Healey was a good looker**

## LEONARD (GB)

Lionel Leonard bought a Cooper-MG sports car chassis and fitted it with a copy of Touring's *barchetta* body for the Ferrari 166. This car (reg. JOY 500) was later sold to Cliff Davis, who in 1953 built a Tojeiro-Bristol (LOY 500) which became the pattern for the AC Ace. Leonard meanwhile built a car similar to his Cooper-MG which he called a 'Leonard-MG'. Some authorities maintain that he copied the Tojeiro but since the Tojeiro was a copy of the Cooper it is a very subtle point.

In 1954 Leonard offered copies of this chassis for sale and, for a brief spell, a fibreglass version of the *barchetta* body. This was one of the very first fibreglass bodies offered to the British special builder. To judge from the fact that it was advertised for only a few weeks it seems that few if any were sold. Several people bought chassis, however, and fitted their own bodies. Some of these, deliberately or mistakenly, have since been passed off as Tojeiros.

## LEONE (I)

A short-lived (1949-50) sports car in the typical Italian idiom. It used a tubular frame, and suspension and drive train came from the Fiat 1100. A 1200cc version was also offered but there were few takers.

## LEONTINA (I)

A faithful copy of the 1930 Zagato-bodied Alfa Romeo 1750GCS with a fibreglass body and contemporary Alfa Romeo components. It was first offered in 1975 but had gone by the end of 1976.

## LEOPARD (GB)

First shown in 1988, the Leopard Mirach was a car in the Lotus/Caterham Seven idiom. There was a fibreglass and Kevlar body and an enlarged (4-litre) Rover V8 engine which gave 250bhp. Maximum speed was claimed to be 150mph/240kmh with 0-60mph acceleration in five seconds.

## LESTER (GB)

Harry Lester built modified MGs just after the war and produced the first Lester-MG in 1949. It had a twin-tube ladder frame with an upswept front to accommodate the coil spring and double wishbone front suspension (from the MG Y Type saloon), the live rear axle (MG TA) was suspended on quarter elliptic springs, and the MG TC engine was linered down to 1087cc. The car was completed by a simple aluminium body with cycle wings. Two were built for the 1950 season and were fairly successful in British club racing. From 1951 an MG engine bored out to 1467cc was offered.

Most Lesters were bought for racing but Lester also made a fixed head coupé and some of these were exported. In 1955, keeping the broad original layout, Lester added independent rear suspension by a transverse leaf spring and double wishbones. A fibreglass coupé body was offered and at least one of these was built with a Coventry Climax FWA engine. By that time the cars were uncompetitive in racing but a tiny number were built for road use. The marque faded around the end of 1955.

Lester-MG at Trengwainton

## LE VICOMTE (CDN)

A 'nostalgia' car of 1977-79 which used Ford running gear including a 6.6-litre V8 engine.

Le Vicomte Renaissance

## LIBERTY SLR (USA)

A 'traditional' sports car with a fibreglass body made by Fiberfab between 1973 and 1976. It used Ford running gear and bore some resemblance to an Aston Martin Ulster.

## LIBRA CARS (GB)

In the mid-1980s this company made 'budget' Cobra copies based on Ford Cortina components. 'Cobra 289' and '427' bodies were offered and engine options began with a Ford 1300cc unit (just what the Cobra always needed) up to Ford V8s. The 427 'Cobra' was marketed as the 'King Cobra'; the firm seems not to have known that a 'King Cobra' was actually a Cooper Monaco fitted with a Ford V8 engine by Carroll Shelby—but nothing should surprise one about an outfit which made a Cobra copy with a 1300cc engine!

## LIGHTNING SPORTSCARS (GB)

A short-lived mid-1980s Ford Cortina-sourced kit car inspired by the Chevrolet Corvette Stingray.

## LIGHTSPEED PANELS (GB)

A kit car maker which brought out the 'Magenta', a 'traditionally' styled two-seater based on BMC 1100/1300

Lightspeed Magenta LSR, 1981

components in 1972. In 1978 this was followed by a version (Magenta LSR) which used Ford Escort running gear and then, in 1980, by the Mini-based Magenta Sprint. They were very basic cars (without even doors) and to widen its base in 1982 the company (now called Magenta Cars) was also making the 'Tarragon', a four-seater sporting estate using Ford Escort components. This company folded in 1986 and the sports car project was taken over by Motorspeed, re-engineered to take MGB parts, and marketed under the name 'Magic'. The following year Scorhill Motors took over the project and offered it as a Ford Cortina-based kit. And so it goes on...

**Magenta Tarragon**

## LIGIER (F)

Ex-rugby international Guy Ligier became a Formula 1 privateer after he hung up his studded boots. He was not exactly an ace and after he had had his fling he turned his attention to his business interests and to building competition sports cars. All Ligiers bear the 'JS' designation, in memory of Guy Ligier's friend, Jo Schlesser, who was killed in the 1968 French GP.

The one Ligier road sports model appeared in 1971 but in 1976 the company entered Formula 1 and soon devoted its efforts to that, and to micro cars at the other motoring extreme. In Formula 1 there have been odd periods of success, but for some years past the best one can say of Ligier is that it has survived, with a little help from its friends.

**JS2, 1971-77. Prod approx: 100.** The chassis of Ligier's road model was a pressed steel platform and the coupé body was of fibreglass. Its engine was the 3-litre version of the V6 which Citroën had developed for the SM, and this, with its five-speed transmission, was turned through 180 degrees to allow it to be mounted behind the driver. Servo-assisted disc brakes were fitted to all four wheels, which were independently sprung. The JS2 had a claimed top speed of 150mph/240kmh.

**Ligier JS2, 1975**

## LISTAIR (GB)

The Listair Dash arrived in 1986 and derived from one of Peter Pellandine's designs previously marketed as the Rembrandt. Engine options included the VW Beetle and Alfa Romeo 'boxer' units. The company was in trouble by 1988, and in 1990 the project was taken over by Dash Sports Cars Ltd (qv).

## LISTER (GB)

From the early 1980s WP Automotive modified the Jaguar XJ-S and sold the cars as Lister-Jaguars, thanks to an arrangement with Brian Lister, maker of the famous Lister-Jaguar sports-racer of the 1950s. With a 6-litre engine, up to 178mph/286kmh was claimed (0-60mph in 5.4 seconds). In 1989 Lister announced a run of 50 'Le Mans' models. The standard body was modified (the 'flying buttresses' at the rear were removed and there was a new frontal treatment). There was also a new gearbox, drive train and rear suspension. With a 500bhp 7-litre version of the Jaguar V12, a top speed of 200mph/320kmh (0-60mph in 4.4 seconds) was claimed. In 1990, Lister announced another limited edition, of 25 'Knobblies' (the affectionate nickname given to the 1958 production Lister-Jaguar sports racer).

**1984 Lister-Jaguar**

## LITTON (GB)

From the late 1980s Litton made an unconvincing copy of the Lancia Stratos based on Lancia Beta components and originally marketed under the name 'Allora' (qv).

## LMB (GB)

Leslie Ballamy became well known in the 1930s for his modifications to production cars, in particular his split-axle i.f.s. conversion for various beam axle Fords. In 1960 he designed a range of ladder-frame chassis, each using the swing-axle i.f.s., to take various proprietary fibreglass bodies, and to make life easier for Ford Ten special builders. It was also marketed as a complete kit using the EB (Edwards Brothers) 'Debonair' 2+2 GT shell. It was initially intended for the Ford 997cc 105E engine, but the Classic 107E engine became an option when it appeared. In common with most Ford-based kit cars which evolved from the special building craze of the late 1950s, the Debonair disappeared in 1962, but the chassis became the basis for the Reliant Sabre and the identical Autocars (of Israel) Sabra.

## LMX (I)

Made between 1969 and 1974, the LMX 2300 HCS used fibreglass coupé or convertible bodies on a forked backbone chassis. Suspension was independent all round by MacPherson struts (ex-Ford Zodiac MkIV) and there were disc brakes on all four wheels. The engine was the 126bhp German Ford 2.3-litre V6, and turbocharged versions developing up to 210bhp were available. There was a high level of trim. Only 43 were made.

**LMX 2300 HCS convertible, 1970**

## LOMAX *see* MUMFORD

## LOMBARDI *see* OTAS

## LORRAINE MOTOR RESEARCH (USA)

A late 1980s maker of a turn key Bugatti Type 59 copy powered by a tuned 2-litre Ford Pinto engine. One wonders where the 'research' comes in.

## LOTUS (GB)

The achievement of Colin Chapman, founder of Lotus, has yet to receive the credit it deserves. He built up a major force in motor racing from a lock-up garage; virtually founded the British motor racing industry; was more innovative in design than any other individual in automotive history; founded a production car company which has produced only classics; created an engineering consultancy which has no superior. Along the way, he designed the chassis of the Vanwall, Britain's first World Championship winner, re-designed the BRM P25 so that it could win races, and pioneered such developments as active suspension and aerodynamic ground effects. He also attracted like-minded engineers, and he employed and inspired many men who became important independent designers—it is no coincidence for example, that the principals of Cosworth Engineering met at Lotus. Chapman's road cars, however, frequently suffered from indifferent quality and reliability, and ironically it was only after his death in 1982 that Lotus began to live down its poor reputation. Yet his style of innovative thinking remains Lotus's strongest suit, which is why Lotus is in demand as a consultancy. After 1982, Lotus passed into other hands and Toyota became a minority shareholder for a time. Indeed Toyota was interested in buying the company but was discouraged by the British government. In 1985 Lotus was bought by General Motors, and in 1993 by Bugatti, which collapsed two years later.

**MkVI, 1952-56. Prod: approx 100.** After building a series of Austin and Ford specials Chapman essayed his first production car, the MkVI. It was a basic dual-purpose car, sold in kit form, which could be used for a wide range of motor sport: races, driving tests, hill climbs and trials. The MkVI had a space frame, a tight-fitting aluminium skin built by Williams and Pritchard, split axle (Ford) and coil spring front suspension, and a live rear axle on coil springs. Customers had a choice of engines and most chose Ford or MG. It had considerable competition success, the highlights being at Silverstone in 1954 when Peter Gammon's car beat Hans Herrmann's works Porsche 550 into third place (first place was taken by Colin Chapman in a Lotus MkVIII sports-racer).

**Colin Chapman in the first production Lotus MkVI, 1953**

**Seven Series I, 1957-60. Prod: 242.** A revamped, lower version of the MkVI, with a new space frame and suspension (based on the Lotus Eleven 'Club' sports-racer), hydraulic drum brakes and a choice of engines. BMC Series 'A' motors were favoured but the 1172cc Ford 100E engine

**Lotus Seven Series I, 1957**

was also offered. When a Coventry Climax engine was fitted the car became known as the 'Super Seven' and many of these also had wire wheels. A 'motorcycle on four wheels', the Seven had a hood (which leaked) and room for a collapsible tooth brush; but it was enormous fun, and had a Lotus badge. Cars on the home market had aluminium cycle mudguards while the export 'Seven America' had flowing fibreglass wings.

**Elite, 1957-63. Prod: 998.** Announced at the same time as the Seven, the Elite was Chapman's first GT car. While the Seven was basic, the Elite was a technical marvel, being the world's first car with unit construction in fibreglass. In the event, this proved costly to make and Lotus lost money on every one. Power came from the 1216cc FWE version of the Coventry Climax FWA which produced 71-95bhp, and several power options were offered throughout the model's life. Front suspension was by coil springs and double wishbones, and the independent rear was by 'Chapman struts', actually a modified MacPherson strut. Disc brakes were fitted all round, inboard at the rear. One of the prettiest cars ever, the Elite was quick (up to a 120mph/193kmh maximum with the twin carb FWE) and handled like a dream but was noisy and poorly made. Since the side windows were fixed, occupants could bake in hot weather.

The production figure, incidentally, is the official one; some surplus body shells found their way into private hands and other cars emerged. Subsequent attempts to build surplus shells into reasonable cars by using Ford or Lotus 'Twin Cam' engines have failed since the car's poise depended on the light weight of the aluminium Coventry Climax engine.

Lotus Elite Special Equipment arrived in 1960

**Seven Series II, 1960-68. Prod: 1350.** The Seven Series II had a new simplified space frame and lightly revised suspension geometry. Early British examples had aluminium cycle mudguards but the fibreglass wings from the Seven America soon became standard on all cars. The 997cc Ford 105E engine became available during 1960 and that soon became the most popular 1-litre engine. From 1961 the 1340cc Ford 109E was fitted to the Super Seven and later the 1.5-litre Ford Kent engine became the usual unit.

Lotus Seven Series II with 1.5-litre Ford engine

**Elan S1, 1962-64. Prod: incl. S2/3, 7895.** Lotus' first conventional road car, the Elite, almost bankrupted the firm; the Elan, however, was the making of it. In place of the fibreglass monocoque was a simple pressed steel backbone chassis, a long-established idea despite Chapman's attempts to claim it for his own. Each end was like a tuning fork: the front fork cradled the engine, the rear the final drive, and both carried the suspension, which was similar to the Elite although the wheelbase was slightly shorter. The fibreglass shell began as a rag top (a hard top was soon available) and featured pop-up headlights which were then something of a novelty. Lotus made its own engine, a 1588cc twin-cam on a Ford block (also used in the Lotus-Cortina) which was initially rated at 105bhp. A top speed of 115mph/185kmh and 0-60mph in nine seconds were respectable figures, but the real performance came from superb road holding and handling. Build quality, alas, remained problematical.

The S1 Elan

**Elan S2, S3, 1964-66, 1966-69. Prod: see Elan S1.** Although the Elan was always dogged by build quality problems, which was unforgiveable because it was not a cheap car, owners were prepared to tolerate that to experience the matchless handling. Besides it also had a lot of 'badge value' since Lotus was dominating motor racing in every major single-seater class.On the S2, centre-lock wheels replaced the previous discs, and there were a number of detail improvements. The majority of cars made were hard top. The S3 had a high final drive ratio together with a close ratio gearbox option. The 'SE' (Special Equipment) version had a 115bhp engine, close ratio gears and servo brakes.

Elan S3 Special Equipment had 115bhp engine

**The 911S cabriolet was a rare Porsche soft-top in 1980, based on the Targa which offered another route to fresh-air motoring. This car has 'sport equipment' aerodynamic add-ons, a front air dam and a large spoiler at the rear**

Timeless Morgan and in this case a very muscular one, a Plus 8 of the mid-1980s

A quartet of popular Triumphs: in the right foreground a Spitfire MkIII, alongside it a Spitfire 1500, which ended the Spitfire line, and behind GT6s MkI and III

Alfa Romeo built considerable numbers of sporting convertibles on 1900, 2000, Giulietta and Giulia bases, and like this Pininfarina-designed Giulia Spyder of the early 1960s they were invariably very pretty little cars

The six-cylinder MGC was criticised by road testers for poor handling and understeer, but enjoys a loyal following today

BMW's aggressive M1, a necessary road car spin-off from a racing programme. Achieving a homologation figure with it gave the Bavarian company a model in the supercar category

**Europa S1, 1966-69. Prod: all Europas, 9230.** Chapman's ambitions to build a mid-engined GT car were thwarted by the absence of a suitable powertrain until the Renault 16 arrived. Lotus bought in 78bhp versions of the Renault 1470cc engine and (fwd) transaxle, turned the engine through 180 degrees, and re-mated it to the suitably modified transaxle. The chassis was similar to the Elan, but rear suspension was by lower wishbones and transverse top links, similar to contemporary racing practice. The fibreglass body, which was bonded onto the chassis, was controversial for it looked like a squashed van. The 109mph/175kmh top speed and 0-60mph acceleration in 10.7 seconds were not outstanding figures, the cockpit was cramped and claustrophobic, rearward vision was poor and the windows did not open, but handling was to Lotus' usual standards. The first two year's production went to Europe, since Lotus wanted worldwide markets to match its worldwide fame; and exports to America began in 1968 with 88bhp 1565cc engines.

Lotus Europa S1, 1966

**Seven Series III, 1968-70. Prod: approx 350.** The Seven Series III had detail body revisions (which made it a little more civilised), Triumph Herald rack and pinion steering, front disc brakes and a Ford Escort back axle which gave a slightly wider rear track. The basic Seven could be bought with a variety of small Ford engines, but the Super Seven had the Lotus Twin Cam unit. It was the Series III which was put into production by Caterham Cars and which was subsequently copied by many unlicensed makers. With the hood up, you need to be an acrobat to get in; and if there's someone in the passenger seat, you'll become very close as a result.

Super Seven Series III Twin Cam, 1969: only 13 made

**Europa S2, 1968-71. Prod: see Europa S1.** The S2 was not available in Britain until 1969, and then it was usually sold in kit form to escape purchase tax (like most other Lotuses until 1974). It was not received with overwhelming enthusiasm, largely because it was underpowered, but then it was always intended to be a cheap car. Electric windows were a welcome improvement, since ventilation was poor, and the fibreglass body was now bolted, not bonded, to the chassis, which made repair very much easier. The cockpit remained tight since the two seats were divided by the deep backbone chassis, luggage space was laughable despite extra space behind the engine, and taller drivers could forget the Europa. People still bought them, though, because nothing at the price handled so well.

1969 Europa S2

**Elan+2, 1969-74. Prod: 5200.** An indication of where Lotus saw its future, as its name suggests, the Elan+2 coupé was for the Lotus enthusiast with a young family (just like Chapman). Wider, and with a longer wheelbase, it did not have the ultimate road holding of the base car but was still streets ahead of almost anything else. Like all Lotuses it had impeccable road manners, an excellent ride, and was easy on fuel. From the start it had the 115bhp engine. The 130+2S of 1971 had the 126bhp 'big valve' engine which meant 120mph/193kmh and 0-60mph in 7.5 seconds. From 1972 there was the 130-5, which had Lotus' new five-speed gearbox. A few were converted to rag tops after they left the factory. In keeping with its place in the market few were sold as kits, which meant better build quality from new, and by the time the +2 arrived, Lotus quality had improved a lot.

Elan 130+2S, 1973

**Elan S4, Sprint, 1968-71, 1971-73. Prod: see Elan S1.** The S4 had as standard equipment most of the features of the S3 'SE' such as servo-assisted brakes and the 115bhp engine; it also had wide wheel arches to accom-modate low-profile tyres. Lotus had taken to heart the many criticisms about quality, and made a big effort to put things right, so the general rule is: the later the car, the better its build. The most desirable of all was the 'Sprint' (1353 made) with two-tone paintwork and the 126bhp 'big valve' engine. Even among the Sprints there were prime cars—the few fitted with the new five-speed gearbox scheduled for the next generation of Lotus road cars. To the end of its life the Elan set the standard in road holding, and late models were capable of 120mph/193kmh and 0-60mph in 6.7 seconds—no wonder Mazda took the Elan as its criterion when building the MX-5.

Elan S4 Sprint is the most desirable

**Seven Series IV, 1970-73.** **Prod: approx 1000.** Lotus' changing priorities were reflected in this more 'civilised' and 'sophisticated' version of the Seven. It had the same basic layout as its predecessors but a new space frame, which was slightly longer and wider than before, front suspension derived from the Europa, and more positive location of the rear axle. Its fibreglass body was unstressed and it offered better weather protection and creature comforts.

In retrospect it has been perceived as the 'soft' Seven but that is unjustified; the fact that it sold more strongly than other Sevens shows how it was perceived in its own day. The shift of perception came when cars such as the Seven were no longer a motorist's sole car but had become a weekend runabout. That is the reason why the less practical but more macho Series III enjoyed a great revival in the 1980s when made by Caterham Cars.

Lotus Seven Series IV arrived in 1970

**Europa Twin Cam, 1971-75.** **Prod: see Europa S1.** At last the Europa received the power for which it was crying out, and the 105bhp Lotus-Ford 'Twin-Cam' engine transformed the car. Hand in glove with that went a much sharper look, achieved by cutting down the rear deck and the addition of alloy wheels. Even better was the 'Special' which came in 1972 with the 126bhp 'big valve' engine and an optional five-speed gearbox, which meant 121mph/195kmh and 0-60mph in 7.7 seconds. Since Lotus quality overall was improving year by year, and few Europas were sold as kits, the Europa is now a good buy, especially since it tends to be cheaper than a comparable Elan. Despite early shortcomings, the Europa was arguably the world's first practical mid-engined road car.

Europa Twin Cam Special was launched in 1972

**Elite S1, 1974-80.** **Prod: 2398.** Chapman had decided to move away from small sports cars, sold mainly in kit form, and go up-market. This was a shrewd move, since the imposition of VAT in Britain could have damaged Lotus. He could not, however, have predicted the panic that followed the 1973 OPEC oil crisis and this did affect Lotus sales, although 25mpg was good for a 124mph/200kmh car (0-60mph in 7.8 seconds).

The new Elite had a backbone chassis, coil spring and double wishbone front suspension, and independent rear suspension by coil springs, fixed drive shafts, lower wishbones and radius rods. It was powered by an all-new dohc 16-valve, 2-litre, four-cylinder, Lotus 907 engine (first seen in the Jensen-Healey) which delivered its 160bhp via a five-speed gearbox (in American trim it had 140bhp). A genuine four-seater, with reasonable luggage space, its hatchback styling was not to all tastes, but trim levels were high. The Elite 501 was the base car, the 502 was a de luxe version with air conditioning, a better stereo and so on. The 503 was a 502 with power assisted steering and the 504 was a 503 with automatic transmission. A problem was that Lotus had difficulty making a simple sports car properly; it was not up to making an 'executive' sports car properly.

Lotus Elite S1, 1974

**Eclat S1, 1975-80.** **Prod: 1299.** Lotus' second 'new generation' car was basically a fastback Elite and shared that car's chassis and drive train. The new style (which was to be refined and continued as the 'Excel') hardly reduced rear passenger space but Lotus liked to call it a 2+2, possibly to make the Elite seem larger. There were four levels of trim, 521, 522, 523, 524, which corresponded to the Elite 501, 502, 503 and 504. There was also an economy model, the 520, which had a skimpy interior, four-speed Ford gearbox, and steel wheels with only 5.5in wide rims. This did not catch on, however, and customers much preferred the more expensive models.

In America the Eclat was sold as the Lotus 'Sprint', not to be confused with the Eclat Sprint which was a 1977 version of the 520 or 521 with a lower rear axle ratio, white paint and black flashes. Lotus went through a period of building 'special editions'.

The Eclat was about 100lb lighter than the Elite and had a slightly more slippery body, thus it had a top speed of 129mph/207kmh and would cover 0-60mph in 7.9 seconds. As before, Lotus build quality lagged behind the demands of the market sector which the company had targeted, and early engines had relatively short lives before needing expensive rebuilds. The dynamics of the car on the road, however, were excellent and with the new generation Lotus set new standards of quality and finish for plastics bodies. The Eclat was not as rorty as an Elan, but then Chapman himself had reached middle age and his cars reflected his own tastes.

The four-seater Eclat S1, 1975

**Esprit S1/S2/S2.2, 1976-78/1978-80/1980-81.** **Prod: 994/980/88.** First shown as a prototype on a modified Europa chassis in 1972, the Esprit was launched in 1975 but did not reach production until mid-1976. Although mid-engined, with a wonderful, if wide, body by Giugiaro, under the skin it was recognisably the sister to the Elite and Eclat. It had the same engine and suspension layout on a pressed steel backbone chassis, but rear disc brakes were inboard and the five-speed transaxle was from the Citroën SM.

Early cars (S1) were not as quick as Lotus hoped—the works claimed 138mph/222kmh but *Autocar* could get only 124mph/200kmh with 0-60mph in 8.4 seconds, and other road test figures were similar. This suggests problems with the engine installation since the Esprit was slower than the Eclat. There were also vibration and cooling problems which were not sorted out until the S2 of 1979. This had a new camshaft, wider wheels, revised interior trim, and improved airflow to the engine bay with new collector ducts behind the rear side windows. Externally, the original blade front spoiler was replaced by an integrated wraparound spoiler. The S2 did deliver the performance for which Lotus hoped and was tested at 135mph/217kmh with 0-60mph in 8.0 seconds.

Esprit was styled by Giugiaro

In 1980 the Esprit became the S2.2 when it received the larger 2174cc Type 912 engine. This was a fairly extensively revised unit, still producing 160bhp but with improved torque.

**Elite S2.2, 1980-83.** **Prod: 133.** The main improvement was the 2.2-litre engine, which had more torque, and the five-speed Getrag gearbox which replaced the original five-speed Lotus gearbox with BL ratios. The system of badging the car (501, 502 etc) was dropped and customers

Elite S2.2, 1981

chose options in the usual way from a list in the catalogue. Detail improvements included different bumpers and there was a 'Riviera' special edition (the 'special' elements amounted to a sun roof and some badges).

**Eclat S2.2, 1980-85.** **Prod: 223.** All remarks about

Eclat S2.2 Riviera, 1981

the Elite S2.2 apply to the Eclat version, including the 'Riviera' special edition. It was still possible to buy a cheaper version with the Ford four-speed gearbox.

**Esprit Turbo, 1980-87. Prod: 1658.** Although the engine of the Esprit Turbo had the same capacity as the normally aspirated version it was more than just an engine with a Garrett AiResearch turbocharger bolted on. It was thoroughly re-worked and carried the designation Type 910. When the 210bhp Esprit Turbo appeared it set new standards for a car with such a small engine (148mph/238kmh top speed and 0-60mph in 6.1 seconds) yet such was the pace of progress in the 1980s that by 1985 Ford had made the Sierra Cosworth, which had a smaller engine yet similar performance.

The Turbo had a stiffer chassis, bigger bumpers, a new front spoiler, improved brakes, and larger wheels. The first 100 cars comprised a garish special edition in the colours of the sponsor of the Lotus Formula 1 team, Essex Petroleum.

For the 1985 model year there was a revised chassis with a new front section to carry new front suspension (still coil springs and double wishbones). By then top speed had risen

The 1980 Esprit Turbo

to 152mph/245kmh (0-60mph in 5.5 seconds) but that has never been the main reason why anyone would buy an Esprit Turbo; the reason is that nobody knows more about handling or road holding than Lotus.

**Esprit S3, 1981-87. Prod: 767.** The S3 had most of the improvements which had been incorporated into the Esprit Turbo. It also had a new rear suspension layout with lower

Esprit S3, 1985

wishbones, semi trailing arms and upper links which was incorporated into the Turbo and later adopted for the Excel when it replaced the Eclat. This model was capable of 134mph/215kmh and a 0-60mph time in 6.7 seconds.

**Excel, introduced 1985. Production to the end of 1990: 1972.** First sold in 1983 as the Eclat 'Excel' (to reduce the cost of type approval by carrying over Eclat certification), this car was an extensively re-engineered Eclat with softer body styling, a Toyota five-speed gearbox and Toyota brake components. (the use of Toyota components enhanced reliability). The rear suspension was revised along the lines of the Esprit S3, with lower wishbones, semi trailing arms and upper links. Top speed was 134mph/215kmh and the 0-60mph time was 7.0 seconds.

In October 1985 came the high compression 180bhp SE

1989 Excel had revised air dam and bonnet louvres

model, which was marginally quicker (135mph/216kmh and 0-60mph in 6.8 seconds), and the following year brought the SA, which also had the 180bhp engine but which used a four-speed ZF automatic transmission. 1988 brought minor modifications to the bodywork.

**Esprit S4, introduced 1987.** Giugiaro's earlier Esprit body, styled during his 'folded paper' period, was replaced by an in-house design submitted against stiff competition by Peter Stevens. He became an instant star and went on to style the 1989 Elan, the Jaguar XJR-15 and to work on the McLaren supercar project. The body had a low drag factor and it needed that to counteract an additional 500lb weight. The Esprit engine delivered slightly less power and torque than the equivalent

Esprit S4, 1991

unit in the Excel SE. Its 172bhp, delivered through a Renault GTA transaxle, propelled the Esprit S4 to 138mph/222kmh (0-60mph in 6.5 seconds) which were extraordinary figures for a normally aspirated 2.2-litre engine. Thanks to a more rigid chassis road holding was improved as well.

**Esprit Turbo, introduced 1987.** There was not a better chassis than the Esprit and the Turbo HC benefited from the new body, which was smoother and roomier. The base Turbo had up to 228bhp (European trim) which meant 150mph/240kmh and 0-60mph in 5.3 seconds. It was the only car on sale in Britain which would top 150mph, and sprint to sixty in under six seconds, and cost less than £30,000.

From May 1989 there was also the Turbo SE, which had 264bhp, and for this model Lotus was able to claim a top speed of 162.7mph/261.8kmh with the 0-60mph dash in 4.7 seconds. This put the Esprit SE in Supercar League Division

1989 Esprit Turbo

One, where it was the only player with a four-cylinder engine.

In 1990 Lotus built a run of special 'Club Sport' versions of the Esprit Turbo with larger brakes, a roll cage and engine modifications. As the roll cage implies, this variant was specifically intended for competition and followed on successes gained with an Esprit by Doc Bundy in American racing.

**Elan, introduced 1989.** Lotus had been threatening to make an Elan replacement for years, and prototypes of subsequently abandoned projects were tested in the early 1980s. Part of the trouble was that the Elan was a hard act to follow, but the car which was chosen to bear the name was generally welcomed as a worthy successor despite the fact that it had front wheel drive.

This was almost heresy—family cars had front wheel drive, sports cars had rear wheel drive, everyone knew that. Lotus broke the mould by using a patented interactive wishbone suspension on a floating front subframe. Road testers soon decided that it was quicker from A to B than virtually any other car and that torque steer was absent.

The chassis was a backbone affair, and the body was of composites (many people would call it fibreglass but in 1982 Lotus asked writers, very nicely, to use the term 'composites'.). The transversely mounted 1588cc engine was badged 'Isuzu

Lotus Elan SE, 1990

Lotus' since Lotus had made a significant input into the unit (made by a Japanese company in which General Motors was the largest shareholder). It was a dohc '16-valve' four-cylinder unit which produced 130bhp when fuel injected, 165bhp when turbocharged. In normally aspirated form top speed was 121mph/195kmh (0-62mph in 8.2 seconds) but the turbocharged SE model could top 136mph/219kmh (0-60mph in 6.5 seconds).

American-bound Elans had a longer nose (to accommodate US bumper laws) and people in the home market felt that this was an aesthetic improvement which might be nice to have. Lotus sternly refused this wish.

## LR ROADSTERS (GB)

In the early 1980s, before he hit the big time, Adrian Reynard designed a tubular backbone chassis for LR Roadsters and this formed the basis of fibreglass copies of the Cobra and Jaguar D Type marketed under the marque name 'Ram'. A stressed skin backbone chassis formed the basis of the Ram RT, a Jaguar-sourced copy of the Ferrari Daytona Spyder.

## LYNX (GB)

Starting in the early 1970s Lynx made rivet for rivet copies from original Jaguar drawings of the Jaguar D Type which were so faithful that, by changing the instrument panel, and a few other

Lynx D Type in 1988

details, an unscrupulous person could pass one off as the real thing (not that this has ever happened, Heaven forfend!). Sourced from the Jaguar E Type, and available as a kit or turn key car, the Lynx had the E Type's independent rear suspension whereas the D Type had a live axle. For those wishing to have creature comforts as well as performance (typically, about 155mph/250kmh and 0-60mph in 5.3 seconds), Lynx also made an equally fine copy of the Jaguar XK SS.

## MACHIAVELLI MOTORS (USA)

Founded in the mid-1980s by Bobby Henderson, who had finally had enough of the aggravation which can come from owning a real Ferrari, Machiavelli made evocations of contemporary Ferraris, usually based on Pontiac TransAm chassis and running gear. The dimensions meant they were not exact copies but the concept appealed and they sold by the hundred.

**A Machiavelli Motors creation in 1988**

## MAELSTROM (GB)

A 1986 kit car in the Lotus Seven idiom but with a distinctive wedge-shaped fibreglass body. Running gear was sourced from the Ford Cortina but the space frame was properly stressed and the rising rate front suspension was by double wishbones, rocker arms, and inboard coil springs. Although a promising project (Bob Egginton of ASD had engineered it) it quickly folded, but was updated and revived in 1990 by PACE (qv).

## MAGENTA *see* LIGHTSPEED PANELS

## MAICO (D)

Established in 1930, Maico was well known for its motorcycles when, in 1955, it joined a throng of German firms to produce small-engined economy cars to meet the demands of an impoverished but growing market. Its first models were based on those of another German maker, Champion, and had engines between 392cc and 452cc. Before Maico withdrew from the car market in 1958 to concentrate on motorcycles again it made a two-seat sports car using the two cylinder air-cooled 452cc (Heinkel) engine in an independently sprung backbone chassis. In 1957 this had rubber springing which, that year, was replaced by coil springs.

**Maico 500 Sport at the 1957 Frankfurt Show**

## MALLALIEU (GB)

Named for its founder who started to convert rusted Bentley Mk 6s into Vintage-style cars in 1972. D. Mallalieu died in 1975 but Mallalieu Cars Ltd was formed to take over the work and built 43 units before going into liquidation. The project was then taken over by The Abingdon Classic Car Company which offered two models, both convertibles with wire wheels, the 'Barchetta' and the 'Oxford', and for a time made them at a rate of about one a month. The number of derelict Bentleys, however, was limited; other firms began to convert them, and with price tags hovering around the £30,000 mark (in 1980) the Mallalieu could not survive.

**A Mallalieu Bentley**

## MALLOCK (GB) (MALLOCK RACING)

Arthur Mallock, an army officer and an engineer, built his first special before he was old enough to hold a driving licence. During the 1950s he became a well-known character on the British club racing scene with an Austin Seven special, and his career took off in 1959 when he began to race a Ford-engined special he called 'U2' (*you too can have a body like mine* ran the old Charles Atlas advertisements in which weaklings had sand kicked in their faces). The first U2 established the parameters for the Mallock line, which was still going strong in 1990: the space frame was very stiff, the bodywork was simple with cycle mudguards, and the live rear axle was carefully located.

Mallock's success has been due to his careful attention to detail in such areas as balancing spring rates and the torsional rigidity of his space frames. Soon after he started selling his cars they ceased to be dual-purpose machines and became specialist circuit cars, but that was the customer's choice, not Mallock's. Most Mallock U2 cars have been built for Clubmans racing but directly related designs (all front engined) have appeared in single-seater categories. Arthur Mallock's cause was helped by the driving skills of his sons, Richard and Ray, and in 1990 Ray Mallock Limited (qv) started to build cars.

**Mallock U2 at Zandvoort in 1981**

## MALLOCK (GB) (RAY MALLOCK)

Ray Mallock introduced his GT40 lookalike, the RML GT40, in 1991. Its high-quality fibreglass bodywork clothed a space frame, but unlike most other GT40 copies the RML car had a ZF gearbox instead of a Renault transaxle and this meant that the engine was four inches lower (like the original, which of course was in a monocoque chassis). The small-block 5-litre Ford V8 gave a claimed maximum speed of 180mph/290kmh.

## MALLORCA (E)

A basic (i.e. Lotus Seven-type) sports car, the '1800' was first offered in 1976. It had a platform chassis, fibreglass body, coil sprung independent suspension all round, and a 1.8-litre Fiat four-cylinder engine. The 'Valencia' of 1979 used a Ford 1.3-litre engine mounted amidships, yet with a front radiator. Most of the other components were Ford as by then Uncle Henry had set up a factory in Spain to produce the Fiesta.

## MANIC (CDN)

An aggressively styled fibreglass coupé of 1969, the Manic used a Renault 1.3-litre engine mounted amidships. There were few takers and the project was dead by 1971.

**Manic GT, 1970**

## MANTA (USA)

Founded in the early 1970s by the late Brad LoVette, Manta's first product was the Mirage, a mid-engined kit car which used a wide range of V8 engines in a machine which was styled after contemporary CanAm cars. The company followed this with the Montage, which was the first of many copies of the McLaren M6 GT car (originally an attempt to make a supercar based on McLaren's fabulously successful CanAm cars). Just two real McLarens were made, the project ending when Bruce McLaren was killed, but Manta made hundreds of copies of the body, which was usually based on the VW Beetle floor pan. Manta also made its own frame to take larger engines, in which case a Chevrolet Corvair transaxle was employed.

**1980 Manta Montage**

## MANTIS (GB)

Offered from 1965, this was a near copy of the Dennis Adams' extravagant 'Probe' body on a Beetle chassis which survived into the early 1980s. It is not to be confused with the Marcos Mantis which was also an Adams design.

## MARATHON (F)

A short-lived (1954-55) attempt to mate a revised version of the aerodynamic body of the unsuccessful German Trippel coupé with an 845cc Panhard engine and transaxle, moved through 180 degrees from its normal mounting, for this was a rear-engined car. Two models, both ugly, were offered: the Corsair (coupé) and the 'Pirate' (open sports). The company had the distinction of being the first maker in France to build a fibreglass body.

## MARAUDER (GB)

In 1948 some Rover engineers built a single-seater as a spare-time project; it received Rover's tacit approval and the car was still racing in 1990. In 1950 two of the team, Peter Wilks (the chairman's nephew) and George Mackie set up Wilks, Mackie & Co Ltd. and this company, better known for its 'Marauder' marque name (which echoed Rover's Viking longship badge) operated with the cooperation of Rover, which supplied components.

Based on the Rover 75, the 'A' had a lightly modified (80bhp) 2103cc engine while the '100', which was soon dropped, had a big-bore 2392cc three carburetter unit which gave 105bhp. Both engines were fitted in a cut and shut Rover 75 chassis which had slightly different rear suspension and a specially designed overdrive made by H&A Engineering. Though described as a sports car, because it had a rag top, it was perceived by the buying public as a touring version of the staid and respectable Rover 75, and that image, along with the three-occupant bench seat, could not have helped its cause. The last model made was a coupé, priced at £2000, which represented poor value for a 'sports car' with no sporting pedigreee.

It seems that Marauder was expected to become a design task force for Rover, which was then an exciting company since it was pioneering gas turbine cars, but production costs rose above an acceptable level (the design, anyway, had little to commend it) and the venture folded in 1952 after just 15 cars had been made.

**The Marauder's Rover parentage was evident**

## MARAUDER (USA)

A 1980s maker of copies of the Lamborghini Countach, Chevron B16, Ferrari 250GTO and 512, De Tomaso Pantera, Lola T70 MkIII, and McLaren M6 GT. Many of these copies were available on VW Beetle running gear and could use Marauder's own aluminium and steel monocoque although the cars more usually had American running gear.

Marauder also made the 'Di Napoli Coupé', a 'nostalgia' car, and the BR-X. This was styled after the Koenig version of the Ferrari Testarossa, and used the centre section of the Pontiac Fiero. Front suspension was from the Ford Pinto but at the rear was the independent set-up from the 1963-78 Chevrolet Corvette; power came from a 5.6-litre Chevrolet V8 driving through a Porsche 915 gearbox.

## MARAUDER (ZA)

An early 1970s basic sports car (i.e. in the Lotus 7 idiom) which was built on a space frame and used Ford Escort Mk 1/2 running gear.

## MARCADIER (F)

Once known as Fournier-Marcadier, this small French company made a trickle of mid-engined sports cars using Renault components from 1963 to 1977. After that its cars had Simca running gear in a backbone frame with all-independent suspension.

## MARCOS (GB)

In 1959 Jem Marsh, then of Speedex Accessories, and Frank Costin, who had just left de Havilland to become a freelance designer, combined to build a new small-engined GT car which they called 'Marcos' (MARsh + COStin). Although Costin was better known for his aerodynamic bodies for Lotus, Lister and Vanwall, he was trained as a structural engineer and had extensive experience of working on wooden military gliders during the Second World War. The first car was an ugly duckling but it received a lot of coverage in the national press because of its wooden construction; 'marine laminated ply' the publicity blurb claimed but, in fact, it was constructed from ordinary plywood. What was really revolutionary was the monocoque construction and at the 1960 London Racing Car Show Costin sketched its principles to a sceptical Colin Chapman—the Lotus 25 (the first of the modern monocoque F1 cars) was built along precisely the same lines.

After six cars had been made Costin left the project. Marsh carried on alone and the car was gradually modified. When Marcos decided to break into the American market in 1968 it abandoned the wooden monocoque because it did not comply with Federal laws and was also very difficult to repair although immensely strong.

Production had reached about ten cars a week when Marcos folded, in large part as cars shipped to America could not be sold due to new emission laws. It thus lost money on these cars and had to abandon its traditional British Ford engines. The heavy straight-six Volvo unit was the replacement but the car was then too expensive (and nose-heavy) to sell well and, already stretched financially by the expansion programme and the introduction of the Mantis four-seat coupé, the company went into liquidation.

For ten years Jem Marsh operated a business which serviced existing cars, then in 1981 he founded a new company, Jem Marsh Performance Cars, to resume production of the Marcos.

**GT, 1960-63. Prod: 29.** Conceived in Frank Costin's words as 'a dry Lotus Seven', the first car was a gull-wing coupé with cycle mudguards. Front suspension was by Triumph Herald coil springs and double wishbones, with revised geometry. The live rear axle was sprung on coil springs and located by parallel leading arms and a Panhard rod, and all suspension components were bolted directly to the wooden

**Marcos GT at Snetterton in 1963**

monocoque. The prototype had a side-valve Ford 100E engine, but production models used the new generation of Ford four-cylinder engines, beginning with the 105E. Front disc brakes were also fitted. Fibreglass nose cones came in various shapes, although none of them were pretty. The car's looks restricted its appeal as a road-going sports car but it was enormously successful on the circuits, especially in the hands of Bill Moss and a youngster from Scotland, name of Stewart.

**1800/1500/1600, 1964-66/1966-67/1967-68. Prod: 99/82/192.** Dennis Adams (see also the Adams Roadster) had been involved in updating Marcos and he created a stunning new fibreglass body which became a modern classic ('the heavyweight car', Frank Costin called it). The original plywood monocoque was retained but that this was basically a road car was evidenced by the 96bhp 1800cc Volvo engine. Performance was respectable with a 116mph/186kmh maximum (0-60mph in 8.2 seconds). Some early cars had a de Dion tube located by Triumph 2000 semi-trailing arms, but this had a sliding joint so the layout was really an independent system with the de Dion tube acting on behalf of lateral location.

When the Ford-engined 1500 and 1600 models came along Marcos reverted to a live back axle. These lacked the performance of the Volvo-powered cars (the 1600 could sprint 0-60mph in 11.4 seconds on its way to a maximum of 109mph/175kmh) but the use of Ford units kept the price down. Most sold in Britain were in kit form, like most Lotus Elans.

Marcos 1600

**Mini-Marcos, 1965-74. Prod: approx 700.** In 1964 an amateur racing driver called 'Dizzy' Addicot commissioned Paul Emery (*see* Emery) to build the 'Dart', an aluminium coupé body on a Mini-van floorpan, which had a slightly longer wheelbase than the saloon. However, only a new, or recently-made, chassis would have made the Dart viable and that, together with an aluminium body, would have proved too expensive and complex to sell to the typical impecunious enthusiast.

A sensible alternative was to use a glass-fibre body/monocoque with Mini components. One of those associated with the project, Jeremy Delmar-Morgan, took moulds from the 'Dart' and the result was marketed as the Minijem (qv). Another person involved was Jem Marsh, and he took the Dart as his starting point for the similar Mini-Marcos. Thus Marcos found itself making one of the most beautiful sports cars in the world, and one of the ugliest, for the Mini-Marcos looked like a squashed toad.

The light and low Mini-Marcos was a lively performer even with a standard engine, and it retained the Mini's excellent road holding. The little beast was successful both commercially and on the race tracks (one even ran at Le Mans, and finished) whereas the Minijem enjoyed a less successful career, largely because it was made by a series of one-product companies.

After Marcos folded in 1971 Rob Walker took over production, and in 1975 the project was sold to D&H Fibreglass Developments, which made a further 500 examples. The concept was continued as the Midas but, emphatically, that was not a redesigned Mini-Marcos but a new car using the concept of a fibreglass body/monocoque car with Mini components.

The Mini-Marcos

**3 litre/2½ litre/3 litre Volvo, 1969-71/1971/1970-71. Prod 80/11/250.** In 1969 Marcos abandoned the plywood monocoque and replaced it by a sturdy square-tube chassis frame which retained the same overall dimensions, suspension, and the Dennis Adams body. This move was partly in response to the demands of the American market, partly because it was cheaper to make a steel frame, and partly because by the 1970s the Marcos was seen mainly as a road car, although examples continued to be used in club racing. The 3-litre version had the 140bhp Ford V6 engine, the rare 2½-litre variant used a 150bhp Triumph TR6 unit, and the 3-litre had the large and heavy, but de-toxed, lump from the Volvo 164. All had overdrive top as an option.

Marcos 3 litre

**2 litre, 1970-71. Prod: approx 40.** The large-engined Marcos (according to Jem Marsh 'Marcos' is both the singular and the plural form) improved the company's fortunes and by 1970 the 'baby' of the range was a 2-litre model. This had an 85bhp Ford V4 engine and could be had with all the usual Marcos options such as alloy wheels and a sunroof but not, alas, with overdrive.

Marcos 2 litre came in 1970

**Mantis, 1970-71.** **Prod: 32.** The long and low four-seat coupé styling of the Mantis was also the work of Dennis Adams; it has always been a controversial shape but the car produced was not quite the car that Adams had on his drawing board—it was changed in deference to legal requirements and to please Jem Marsh. The tubular chassis was originally intended to take the Ford V6 engine but since that would have precluded American sales the 150bhp Triumph TR6 unit was used instead, US customers having to be content with 106bhp 'de-toxed' version. Front suspension was Triumph GT6 while the live rear axle followed established Marcos thinking. With the British-spec engine it was claimed to do 125mph/200kmh but the Mantis was never independently tested. It has been suggested that the Mantis led to Marcos failing but in fact the reasons were more complex.

1970 Marcos Mantis

**Marcos 1981 to 1990.** When the Marcos company was revived it offered kits, from very basic up to a few hours work away from being fully assembled. These had Ford engines (1600cc, 2-litre, 2.8-litre and 3-litre). There was a new front spoiler in 1984.

The Mantula, introduced in 1984, had the 3.5-litre Rover V8 engine and a revised nose treatment to eliminate high speed lift. In all important details these cars were identical to the Ford-engined machines and 'Mantula' was merely a model name for Rover-engined cars. With the 3.5-litre engine the Mantula would reach 137mph/220kmh (0-60mph in 5.4 seconds).

In 1986 Marcos introduced the Spyder convertible version of the Mantula (thus available only with a Rover engine). 1989 saw extensive revisions, including independent rear suspension by coil springs and double wishbones, inboard rear disc brakes, and 7in wide rear wheels. By this time the only engine listed was the 3.9-litre fuel-injected Rover unit and top speed increased to a claimed 150mph/240kmh. A by-product of the new rear suspension was an increase in boot size. In 1990 Marcos introduced closed and convertible versions using the dohc 2-litre fuel-injected Ford engine to meet Italian 'tax break' requirements.

The 1990 Marcos 2-litre Spyder

## MARLAND (F)

In 1970, this small French manufacturer began production of a fairly successful fibreglass coupé based on the running gear of the Renault 8. In late 1971 it marketed a 'traditional' sports car based on the components of Citroën cars using air-cooled flat-twin engines.

1970 Marland could take Renault engines from R8 Gordini to 1600

## MARLBOROUGH CARS (GB)

Mid-1980s maker of a 1930s style kit car with Morris Marina running gear. The unusual feature was that only the Morgan-like wings were of fibreglass. The rest of the body was of steel—who wants a potential rust trap when one is using the parts from an actual rust trap? Not many, is the answer, and not many were made.

## MARLIN (GB)

Introduced in 1979, the Marlin was a two-seater sports car with 'traditional' styling which managed to suggest a 1930s Alfa Romeo without being in any way a copy. The first hundred or so cars were built on Triumph Herald/Spitfire chassis, then in 1981 the company produced its own frame. Thereafter, three basic kits were offered, using components from the Triumph Herald/Vitesse, the Vitesse 2, or the Morris

Marina and, appropriately enough, the company demonstrator was fitted with an Alfa Romeo dohc 1750cc engine, which was listed as an option.

In 1984 the concept was re-engineered around Ford Cortina components but some owners have fitted the larger Ford V6 engines. A close-coupled 2+2 coupé, the Berlinetta, was offered from 1984 on a longer and wider chassis. The company was still active in 1990.

**Marlin Berlinetta, 1990**

## MARQUEZ (BR)

One of many Brazilian firms which mated fibreglass bodies, in open or coupé form, to a VW Beetle chassis. In this case it was the 1.6-litre platform, and the two seat 'GTM' was quite a pretty car. The company was active from 1978 but had gone before its tenth birthday.

## MARSONETTO (F)

The first car this company built was a fibreglass coupé using Panhard Dyna components, in 1958. In 1965 it introduced the Mars 1, a four-seat front wheel drive coupé with Renault 8 components, disc brakes, all-independent suspension, and a fibreglass body. It was replaced by the Marsonetto 1600 in 1967, another fibreglass four-seat GT car, this time using Renault 16TS components. Production ended in 1972.

## MARTINIQUE (USA)

First shown in 1981, this was a two-seat 'nostalgia' roadster which had a 3.2-litre BMW engine in a cast aluminium chassis.

**Martinique roadster, 1981**

## MARTLET (GB)

David Martin is a respected restorer of historic cars and, when money permits, a constructor of F Ford 1600 cars. These have been made in small numbers over the years and have been successful in club championships. In 1982 he essayed a basic sports car, the DM5, and by the end of the 1980s five had been completed. A 'motorcycle on four wheels', this had a space frame, fibreglass body and, usually, a Ford 1600cc engine. Coil spring and double wishbone front suspension derived from Team Martlet's racing experience and the live rear axle was located by radius arms and a Panhard rod. The appearance of a Lotus Seven copy was avoided. In 1987, Martin Short won the BRSCC Kit Car Championship with the prototype.

## MASERATI (I)

Between the Wars the Maserati brothers gained a first class reputation as suppliers of racing cars to the privateer. Their attempts to compete with the big boys at the highest level were often ingenious but the company never gained the financial or political muscle to play in the big league. At the beginning of 1938 the brothers were bought out by the Orsi industrial group, which was chiefly interested in the Maserati spark plug business. At the end of 1947 the surviving Maserati brothers had completed their service contract and went off to found OSCA (qv). They might have stayed but Omer Orsi, the owner's son, was pressing for the company to built GT cars and the Maserati brothers were interested only in racing.

For ten years the company which bore their name concentrated on competition cars for the privateer but a works-run version of the 250F Formula 1 car helped Fangio win his fifth World Championship in 1957.

When in 1957 the parent group was threatened with bankruptcy as a result of Juan Peron's overthrow in Argentina, where the Orsi family had considerable interests, Maserati turned its attention to road cars. There followed a line of cars which vied with Ferrari both in style and numbers sold, until Ferrari was bought by Fiat and made into a sensible manufacturer. In January 1968 Maserati entered into a cooperative deal with Citroën and, two months later, the French firm took a majority shareholding.

In turn, Citroën was taken over by Peugeot in 1975 and the new owner considered liquidating Maserati. Alejandro de Tomaso put together a rescue package with the aid of a government agency. The new management trimmed the workforce, gradually phased out the traditional designs and introduced the Biturbo saloon which, thanks to its famous name and relatively reasonable price tag, sold healthily (production peaked in 1984 at 6365 cars).

In 1984 Chrysler bought 5 percent of Maserati in return for a design contract for the American firm. This saw material expression in the 'Chrysler TC by Maserati'. In 1990 de Tomaso sold a 49 percent stake to Fiat.

**A6/1500, 1946-50. Prod: 61.** Maserati's first road car used a 1488cc sohc straight-six which derived from the 1936 supercharged dohc 6CM. It gave a modest 65bhp and drove through a four-speed gearbox to a live rear axle suspended on coil springs. The chassis was a simple ladder frame, and the coil spring and double wishbone front suspension derived from racing practice. Most cars had a timelessly elegant GT body by Pinin Farina but a few rag tops were built and Zagato made at least one body. Top speed was a claimed 95mph/

153kmh, which was probably optimistic, but the chassis was sweet. It was emphatically a road car and its few competition appearances were by private buyers.

Maserati A6 1500 by Pinin Farina, 1947

**A6G/A6G2000, 1951-54/1954-57. Prod: 16/61.** This series of cars used the chassis from the A6/1500 but the A6G had an engine enlarged to 1954cc, which meant 100bhp and a genuine 100mph/160kmh. Bodies from a variety of coachbuilders were available and there were occasional one-offs—it is difficult to find two identical cars. In 1954 Maserati built its first dohc engine for road-going cars and this produced 150bhp in standard trim, which translated into 118mph/190kmh and 0-60mph in 10 seconds. Although the chassis was now handling two and a half times the power of the original engine, it coped well.

A6G 2000 cabriolet by Frua, 1951 (above) and 1956 coupé by Allemano (below)

**3500GT/GTI, 1957-64. Prod: 2223.** Although Maserati won the F1 World Championship in 1957, the Orsi group's financial position caused it to withdraw from racing to concentrate on road cars and sports racers for private customers. The 3500GT made Maserati a significant producer of road cars and it was soon competing neck and neck with Ferrari. Designed by Giulio Alfieri, the best all-round designer of his day, the 3486cc dohc straight-six derived from the sports racing 350S unit and drove through a four-speed ZF gearbox (five-speed optional from 1960, standard from 1961). The chassis was recognisably the descendent of the A6/1500 but the live rear axle was suspended on semi-elliptics. Standard bodies were a 2+2 hardtop by Touring and a slightly shorter Vignale convertible, but there were some one-offs. Front disc brakes were optional in 1959, standard in 1960. Most cars had disc wheels but Borani wire wheels were a 1959 option. In 1961 the three Webers gave way to Lucas fuel injection and power went up by 15bhp.

Maserati 3500GT Coupé was Touring bodied

**5000GT, 1959-64. Prod: 32.** In 1957, its last season of racing, Maserati nearly won the World Sports Car Championship with its brutish 450S, which used the 4.5-litre dohc V8 originally commissioned for use in the Indianapolis 500. In 1959 a 330bhp 5-litre version was shoe-horned into a 3500GT chassis to make a road car which would touch 170mph/270kmh and sprint to 60mph in 6.5 seconds. Most were 2+2 coupés built by Allemano, but other coachbuilders also contributed bodies and at least one convertible was made. Three customers had full racing engines—the effect of these in a fairly crude chassis does not bear contemplation.

1959 Maserati 5000GT

**Sebring I/II, 1962-65/1965-66. Prod: 346/98.** The Sebring was basically a short wheelbase 1962 3500 GTI with a stylish 2+2 body by Giovanni Michelotti, who was then still with Vignale. Although the chassis was a little long in the tooth, the new style found favour. As the name implies, America was the target market, so options included air conditioning and automatic transmission. Without these power-wasters, the Sebring could top 135mph/215kmh (0-60mph in 8.4 seconds). The Series II had a 245bhp 3694cc engine and a few cars were fitted with a 255bhp 4014cc unit which made 150mph/240kmh possible. To cope with this extra performance disc brakes were fitted all round.

Maserati Sebring

**Mistrale, 1963-70. Prod: 948.** The Mistrale had an even shorter chassis than the Sebring and sheet steel reinforcements made it a more rigid structure. Engine options were the same as for the Sebring, although only a few had the 3.5-litre unit, and since the Mistrale was nearly 500lb lighter than the Sebring it was marginally quicker. Frua provided the elegant body, which was unusual in that it had a lifting tailgate; it was very similar to Frua's later body for the AC 428 and some panels were common to both. Serious production ended in 1968, in favour of cars with V8 engines.

Mistrale coupé (above) and Spyder (below)

**Quattroporte I, 1963-70. Prod: 679.** This was not really a sports car but is included to keep the record tidy and because it is an example of a type of car regularly essayed by sports car makers (the Lagonda was another example) and because its chassis was used as the basis for a number of sports cars. The Quattroporte ('four-door') was a five-seat saloon built on a tubular frame boxed for stiffness. A de Dion rear axle suspended on coil springs was fitted until 1966, when it was replaced with a live axle and semi-elliptics. The car had a 4136cc version of the V8 engine which fed its 260bhp through either a ZF five-speed 'box or a Borg-Warner automatic and would propel this ugly duckling (Frua is to blame for its looks) to 130mph/210kmh. In 1967 a 290bhp 4.7-litre engine was introduced.

1964 Quattroporte I

**Mexico, 1965-73. Prod: approx 250.** The Mexico was the first new sports model to use the V8 engine. It was a close-coupled four-seater which used the Quattroporte chassis, although it had the live rear axle a year before the Quattroporte. It was not significantly shorter or lighter than the saloon, and like its ancestor it had four wheel disc brakes and a five-speed ZF gearbox with a three-speed automatic option. With the 4.2-litre engine it was good for 150mph/240kmh, while the 4.7-litre version (an option from 1969) was quicker and would cover 0-60mph in 7.5 seconds. Despite these impressive figures, the Mexico did not sell well; in particular it received a cool reception in America, where buyers of expensive Italian cars wanted more style than Vignale's rather bland offering.

Maserati Mexico 4.7 litre

**Ghibli, 1966-73. Prod: 1274.** Perhaps the most stunning of all Maserati road cars, the Ghibli succeeded where the Mexico failed, on sheer style. They shared the same (ex-Quattroporte) chassis, although the Ghibli was 3.5in shorter in the wheelbase. The Ghibli was a two-seater, styled by Giorgio Giugiaro (who was then at Ghia) which looked equally good as a fastback coupé or in open form (from 1969, 125 built). Until 1970 the 330bhp 4.7-litre engine was fitted, but was then replaced by a 4.9-litre version which had only 5bhp more but produced a staggering 354lb/ft torque at 4000rpm.

Ghibli coupé, 1967

**Indy, 1966-74. Prod: 1136.** A 2+2 based on the Quattroporte chassis, slightly shortened but with wider track, the Indy completed Maserati's range for the late 1960s, and replaced the Sebring. It was said to have unitary construction, because the steel body was welded to the frame not bolted to it. As with its stablemates, the 4.1-litre engine was offered at first, the 4.7 came in 1970 (and that gave 156mph/250kmh, 0-60mph in 7.5 seconds) and 1973 saw the 4.9-litre version. Vignale styled the body, which bore some resemblance to the Ghibli but did not match it for sheer aggressive style. In some years the Indy outsold the two-seater.

1972 Maserati Indy

**Bora, 1971-80. Prod: 571.** Maserati had been relatively quick to embrace items like disc brakes and fuel injection, but its chassis engineering was conservative and it was a late-comer to the mid-engined club. Giugiaro's Ital Design studio created both the styling for the Bora and the steel unitary construction beneath it, while Alfieri was responsible for the layout and the all-round indpendent suspension by coil springs and double wishbones. The Bora was introduced with the 4.7-litre engine (4.9-litres from 1975) and, since Maserati was married to Citroën it had the French maker's 'no travel' braking system and hydraulic adjustment of pedal positions. Top speed was over 160mph/260kmh, with acceleration (0-60mph in 6.5 seconds) and road holding to match.

Maserati Bora, 1971

**Merak, 1972-83. Prod: 1832.** The Merak was a cocktail of existing parts and Maserati's answer to Ferrari's Dino. It had the 3-litre V6 (ex-Citroën SM) engine fitted to the Bora's chassis (and some body panels) and so 190bhp had to propel a car only 150lb lighter than the Bora, although a 220bhp 'SS' version came in 1974. It also began life with the Citroën SM instrument panel and steering wheel, which was a mite controversial. After the divorce, the oval instruments were replaced by proper Italian clocks and a new steering wheel. The Merak's handling and brakes were superb but top speed was 'only' 135mph/217kmh (0-60mph in 8.2 seconds). Until 1979 170bhp 2-litre 'tax bracket' versions were made for the Italian market.

1974 Merak SS had 220bhp

**Khamsin, 1974-82. Prod: 421.** To complement its new mid-engined cars Maserati created the front-engined Khamsin to replace the Ghibli and Indy. Styling was by Marcello Gandini (he of the Countach) at Bertone, and

Maserati Khamsin in 1975

Bertone was responsible for both the design and the supply of the unitary steel construction. Suspension was similar to the Bora/Merak, being independent all round by coil springs and double wishbones, rack and pinion steering was a new departure, and the Khamsin used Citroën hydraulic steering and brakes. Some owners found that the sensitivity of these components a little unsettling, as well they might—a Maserati should feel like a Maserati not like a Citroën. By contrast the interior was typically Italian: lousy ergonomics and poor ventilation. A 320bhp 4.9-litre engine was used (US buyers received a less powerful version) and with the manual 'box over 150mph/240kmh was possible.

**Quattroporte II, 1975-57. Prod: 5.** A child of the marriage with Citroën, this model used the 3-litre V6 which Maserati supplied for the Citroën SM, allied to Citroën transmission, front wheel drive, power steering and hydropneumatic suspension. In 1975 Citroën and Maserati divorced and the car was killed off when Maserati became bankrupt and was taken over by de Tomaso. Few people had shown any interest in it—all the Citroën elements meant it had no Maserati character, Bertone's bland body could have been on a Japanese import, and 190bhp was not enough for such a substantial machine.

Quattroporte II, 1975

**Kyalami, 1977-83. Prod: 150.** After Alejandro de Tomaso bought Maserati he introduced badge-engineering: the Kyalami was a De Tomaso Longchamps with light styling differences, but a 255bhp 4.1-litre Maserati V8 replaced the Ford V8. Ghia was responsible for the angular styling (which had heavy Jaguar and Mercedes-Benz influence), steel unitary construction was used, front suspension was by coil springs and double wishbones, and the independent rear used fixed driveshafts as upper links in combination with lateral lower links, radius arms and coil springs. In 1978, a 280bhp 4.9-litre version of the V8 was available as an option but even though the car was quick (147mph/237kmh, 0-60mph in 7.6 seconds) it found few buyers.

1977 Kyalami

**Quattroporte III/Royale, introduced 1977. Prod:—.** The last model with any claims to being a 'real' Maserati, this was a stretched Kyalami with styling by Ital Design which, depending on taste was either 'discrete' or 'dull'. You can take nothing away from that wonderful engine, though, and like the Kyalami it came in 4.1- and 4.9-litre forms. Also like the Kyalami, there were no Citroën components, so it was back to Low-Tech Italian Supercar country. Buyers liked it a little better than the Kyalami and it remained in production alongside the Biturbo. From 1985 only the 4.9-litre engine was being fitted and in 1987 it was re-named the 'Royale' and the level of luxury was increased.

Maserati Royale, 1988

*Postscript:* Maserati introduced the Biturbo saloon in 1981 with a 180bhp three-valves-per-cylinder dohc 2-litre V6 engine which, as the name implied, had twin turbochargers. It had unitary construction, front suspension was by MacPherson struts, the independent rear used coil springs and semi-trailing arms, and disc brakes were fitted all round. 1983 saw a four-door version, the 425, with a 2.5-litre engine. A two-seat Spyder, using the 2-litre engine, was introduced in 1984; 1985 saw the 420 and 420S which were 2-litre four-door saloons; in 1987 there was the 430, a four-door saloon with a 2.8-litre engine.

Biturbo Spyder, 1986

By 1990 there was a lengthy menu of models and Maserati was making three- and four-valves-per-cylinder versions of its V6 engine, although the practical difference between them was only academic. The 2-litre Spyder with the three-valve engine had a top speed of 140mph/225kmh (0-62mph in 6.2 seconds); with the four valve engine those figures improved to 143mph/230kmh (0-60mph in 5.9 seconds).

Of the 1990 range the only cars which merit a focus in a book on sports cars are the Spyder, the Karif and the Shamal. The Karif was a rather bland-looking 2+2 coupé with larger turbochargers and 285bhp from its 2.8-litre engine, which meant 150+mph/240+kmh (0-60mph in 4.8 seconds). Its road holding and handling were highly praised. The Shamal, introduced in December 1989, was promised as a new two-seat supercar but Maserati had little money so what actually appeared was a coupé which had a family resemblance to the Karif and was the work of Marcello Gandini. The overall layout was the same as on the rest of the range but the engine was enlarged to 3217cc and delivered its 318bhp through a six-speed Getrag gearbox. Maserati claimed a top speed of 'over 162mph'/'over 260kmh'.

## MATRA (F)

Engins Matra was primarily an aerospace company but in 1964 it took over René Bonnet's little concern and made the Djet coupé as the Matra-Bonnet. A Formula 3 car arrived in 1965, an F2 car the following year, and both were superb. Matra was taken over by Simca in 1969, so became part of the Chrysler empire. Jackie Stewart raced Cosworth-engined Matras in the Grands Prix in 1968-69, winning the World Championship in 1969 but this successful partnership ended when Chrysler refused to supply a Matra chassis for use with a Cosworth engine (which had 'Ford' writ large on the cam covers).

**Matra-Bonnet Djet 6**

Matra's efforts with its own V12 engine were much less successful in F1, but its sports cars won at Le Mans in 1972/3/4 and had many other successes. Peugeot bought the firm in 1978, and Renault acquired a controlling interest in 1983. Since it regarded Matra road cars as competitors, Renault turned the factory over to making the Renault Espace, which was a Matra design.

**M530A, 1967-73. Prod: 9690.** The M530A had one of those odd shapes which, every so often, emanates from France. Like it or loathe it, the M530 was certainly distinctive. Under the 2+2 fibreglass body was a sheet steel unitary structure, all-independent suspension and disc brakes all round. A 73bhp, 1.7-litre Cologne Ford V4 was mounted immediately behind the cockpit and the four-speed gearbox was behind the rear axle line, which meant that there was luggage space between the engine and rear wheels as well as at the front. It handled extremely well but was let down by its odd shape and lacklustre performance (95mph/153kmh maximum speed, 0-60mph in 15.6 seconds).

**Matra M530 SX**

**Bagheera, 1973-80. Prod: 47,802.** Named after the panther in Kipling's *Jungle Book*, the Bagheera was marketed as a Matra-Simca until 1979, when it became Talbot-Matra. Since Talbot was part of the Chrysler empire an 84bhp 1.3-litre Simca unit was fitted and performance was never startling (100mph/160kmh, 0-60mph in 12.3 seconds). From 1977, the 'S' model had an 1442cc, 90bhp engine, and 110mph,/177kmh. The fibreglass body was mounted on a space frame in such a way that it later led to chassis rot, the engine/gearbox was along the rear axle line, suspension was independent all round by torsion bars, and there were disc brakes on all four wheels. The car's most unusual feature, however, was its three seats: the driver sat behind the wheel as usual and, to his right, there was a pair of narrower seats.

**The three-seater Matra Bagheera**

**Murena, 1980-83. Prod: 10,613.** The Murena was a development of the Bagheera and retained the basic construction and the three-seat cabin but was substantially re-engineered. There was a new body shape with a cd of just 0.32, the torsion bar suspension was replaced by coil springs, the five-speed transmission which appeared on late Bagheeras was standard, and the customer had the choice of two engines. The base unit was a 1.6-litre (ex-Simca) engine, but there was the option of a 2155cc (Chrysler) lump with 118bhp and very good torque. In the desirable 2.2 form, the Murena would do 121mph/195kmh and sprint to sixty in 9.3 seconds, figures which were almost identical to the more expensive Porsche 924. As with the Bagheera, it was made as a left hooker only but five cars were converted to rhd.

**Matra Murena**

## MAVERICK (USA)

A fibreglass-bodied sports car based on a Cadillac chassis with a 5.4-litre V8 engine. Sixteen feet long with a wheel base of up to 128in, the Maverick was a fairly hefty car. It took two people at the front, with one behind, and could be supplied with one, two, or three doors. Seven were made between 1952 and 1955.

**1955 Mavericks**

## MAXTON (USA)

In 1990 Bob Sutherland, a well-known collector of historic cars, began to market two kit cars, both notable for the prettiness of their bodies and their low height. The 'Rollerskate' had an enveloping fibreglass body and was designed to take Mazda rotary engines. By contrast, the 'Mille Miglia' was a car in the Lotus Seven idiom but, emphatically, it was not a copy—for a start, it was much better looking. It was designed to take a six-cylinder Nissan 280Z engine, with a 220bhp supercharged option, and a five-speed Alfa Romeo transaxle.

## MAYA *see* CAMBER

## MAZDA (J)

The Toyo Cork Kogyo Co was founded in Hiroshima in 1920 to manufacture cork products, but was soon making machinery. By 1931 the company was making motorcycles and three-wheeled trucks and the latter were particularly successful; by the time war broke out about 75 Mazda light trucks were being made each week.

Half the factory was destroyed by bombing but limited production began again in December 1945. By 1948 200 three-wheeled trucks a week were being made; four-wheeled trucks were made from 1950 and the first Mazda car, with a 356cc engine, was launched in 1960. In 1961 Mazda signed an agreement with NSU to produce the Wankel engine and the following year it signed an agreement with Bertone. Both signalled ambitions: the one millionth Mazda was made in 1963, the second million was achieved in 1966, and the five million mark was passed in 1972. Of equal interest is the fact that Mazda produced its one millionth Wankel engine in 1978, thus proving that the concept could be made into a viable and reliable proposition, although in achieving this Mazda did come close to bankruptcy.

Ford USA has a 25 percent stake in Mazda and this has led to a number of joint efforts in some markets. In Australia, for example, Ford builds the Mazda 323 which is sold as the Ford Laser in Australia and Japan, and the Australian Ford Capri (Mercury Capri when sold in America) is also based on the Mazda 323.

**110S Coupé, 1967-72. Prod: 1176.** Mazda's first sports car was also its first Wankel-engined car, and it appeared almost simultaneously with the NSU RO80, which was infinitely more successful in the marketplace. The 110S was a front-engined car with rear wheel drive and a de Dion back axle. Its twin-rotor engine had a nominal capacity of 1964cc and when first marketed produced 111bhp, which meant a top speed of 115mph/185kmh. A five-speed gearbox was fitted from 1969 and in 1970 power was increased to 128bhp (124mph/200kmh top speed). All cars had front disc brakes and also the usual Wankel problems with high rates of engine component wear on the early cars.

**Mazda 110S Coupé, 1967**

**RX-7, 1978-85. Prod: 504,926.** After whetting appetites with the 110S Coupé, Mazda then employed the Wankel engine only in a series of small vulgarly styled saloons. After such cars, the clean svelte lines of the RX-7 came as a surprise and certainly helped to break down resistance to rotary power.

The twin rotor engine had a nominal capacity of 2292cc

and delivered its 105bhp through a five-speed gearbox, at least in all the models sold in Europe. Other markets were offered automatic transmissions. Cars sold in America were strictly two-seaters, those sold in Europe and Japan had additional 'child' seats which led to the RX-7 being allowed to race in saloon car events in Britain (it won the RAC Group One Championship in 1980). In Japan, the RX-7 was sold as the 'Savannah'.

**1978 Mazda RX-7**

Apart from the engine it was a conventional car, with front suspension by MacPherson struts and a live rear axle on coil springs located by lower trailing links, upper angled links, and a Watts linkage. Standard cars had front disc brakes, but discs were fitted all round on the top of range GSL model sold in some markets after 1981. In that year power was increased to 115bhp and there were detail cosmetic changes.

Meanwhile Japanese customers had a 130bhp version (sold in America as the GSL after 1981), and in 1983 a 165bhp turbocharged version which lifted top speed to 137mph/220kmh. In 1984, Americans had the option of the GSS-SE which had a nominal capacity of 2616cc and 135bhp. In Europe independent companies sold turbocharger conversions.

**RX-7, introduced 1986.** After the phenomenal success of the original RX-7, Mazda had a hard act to follow and perhaps relied too much on 'consumer clinics' and market research and not enough on gut reaction and flair. Thus the second generation car was styled in the Porsche vein and most commentators felt that it was a retrograde step since the RX-7 had its own niche.

The chassis was all new, however, with rack and pinion steering, MacPherson strut front suspension, and a complex independent rear layout using trailing arms (Mazda billed this as the 'Dynamic Tracking Suspension System'—an unwieldy name for a system that road testers agreed worked very well). The larger 2616cc engine was standard in Japan and America and in normally aspirated form this gave 147bhp while a turbocharged version produced 182bhp. This latter was badged as 'Turbo II' in all markets, even though only Japan had received 'Turbo I'.

**RX-7 in 1988 form**

Some European markets, including Britain, had cars with a normally aspirated engine of a nominal 2254cc which gave 148bhp (top speed 128mph/206kmh, 0-60mph in 8.4 seconds) while the turbocharged version in European trim gave 200bhp (which meant a top speed of 148mph/238kmh, 0-60mph in 6.7 seconds). Markets such as Britain received a standardised package specified by individual importers while the much bigger US market was offered a number of different packages.

In 1988, a two-seat convertible was offered, but in Turbo form only.

**MX-5, introduced 1989.** Also known as the 'Miata' or, in Japan, as the 'Eunos Roadster', the MX-5 was an unashamed attempt to build a Lotus Elan for the 1990s. A 1598cc dohc four-valve engine was set in line in an integral chassis/body and delivered its 118bhp via a five-speed gearbox. Front and rear suspension was by coil springs and double wishbones and there were disc brakes on all four wheels.

It was an immediate hit for it was practical, relatively inexpensive and extremely competent. Much of the credit for the super handling of the car was due to IAD, the British design consultancy, and the most commonly heard complaint was that the car could handle more power, so turbo conversions began to appear. The standard MX-5 had a top speed of 114mph/183kmh (0-60mph in 9.1 seconds).

Among specialist companies offering turbo MX-5s was Brodie Brittain Racing, which produced a version with the co-oporation of Mazda (UK), to be sold through Mazda dealers with a full Mazda warranty. A Garrett T25 turbocharger boosted power to 150bhp, an increase of 32 percent, but many would have been more grateful for the 54 percent increase in torque. Top speed increased to 130mph/210kmh while the 0-60mph dash was down to 6.8 seconds. The basic car was considered so competent that no chassis modifications were called for, although a limited slip differential was an optional extra.

**1990 Mazda MX-5 BBR Turbo**

**Eunos Cosmo, introduced 1990.** This 2+2 coupé appeared on American and Japanese markets in 1990 under the marque name 'Eunos'. It had a triple rotor engine of a nominal 3924cc which, fuel injected and turbocharged, developed 296bhp with 289lb/ft torque. It drove through a four-speed automatic transmission and claimed top speed was 155mph/250kmh (0-60mph in 5.1 seconds). Suspension was independent all round by coil springs and double wishbones and there were disc brakes on all four wheels.

## MBI(BR)

A short-lived (1962 only) two-seater sports car using locally made DKW components.

## MBM (CH)

Peter Monteverdi's first car company made small numbers of unsuccessful Formula Junior cars and small-engined sports-racers. In 1962 a few Heron Europas were sold under the name 'MBM'. In 1967 Monteverdi founded another company, this time bearing his own name (qv).

**1962 MBM Heron Europa**

## MC (GB)

In 1984 MC introduced the 'Acer' which was a near copy of the Turner Sports but with two extra seats for young children. A box section chassis originally took Vauxhall Viva/Magnum running gear but by degrees donor car options expanded to Ford Escort Mk1/2, Morris Marina and Datsun 120Y. By 1990 this was being made by Carlton (qv).

## MCA (D)

Between 1962 and 1964 this company made fibreglass-bodied cars on VW Beetle floorpans. Two models were offered, the Jetstar sports car, which had a tuned 1.2-litre VW engine, and the Jetkomet coupé, which used the 1.5-litre unit.

## McFEE (USA)

This was a mid-1950s sports car with a fibreglass body, multi-tubular frame, modified Fiat front suspension (transverse leaf spring and lower wishbones) and swing axle rear suspension with a transverse leaf spring. McFee offered cars with Crosley, MG, or Offenhauser engines. Few were sold.

## McLAREN (GB)

Bruce McLaren was an exceptionally gifted driver and engineer who made such an impression in his native New Zealand that his countrymen assisted him to race in Europe. He arrived in 1958, drove for the Cooper F1 team in 1959 and, at the end of that season, became the youngest driver ever to win a World Championship F1 race when he took the American GP not long after his 22nd birthday.

In early 1964 he set up his own racing team. At first this supplemented his main programme, which was with Cooper, but at the end of the following year it became his chief occupation. By the time Bruce was killed in a test session at Goodwood in 1970 his company had made cars which had won championships in Formula A/5000 and Grands Prix in F1, and had utterly dominated the lucrative Can-Am series.

The first of this line of sports racing cars was designed by Owen Maddock, who had just left Cooper, and was built by Elva (qv) which soon was given over entirely to building customer racing cars. In 1969 McLaren built the first of the modern 'supercars', the M6GT, which was a version of the successful M6B Can-Am car designed by Robin Herd (later of March Engineering) and Gordon Coppuck. It was of monocoque construction with coil springs, upper and lower lateral links and trailing radius rods while the rear layout was by lateral top links, lower wishbones, twin radius rods and coil springs. Power was from a Chevrolet V8 whose size and output depended on customer wishes.

There is some question over the numbers made – there were certainly two but it is possible that three or even four were made. McLaren's tragic death (before his 33rd birthday) caused the 6GT to be cancelled but because of its stunning lines it has since become a popular model to imitate.

Bruce McLaren did not live to see the incredible successes achieved by the team he founded but, given the foresight shown by the 6GT, it is wholly appropriate that in 1992 McLaren Cars announced a road-going, supercar, the F1. McLaren Cars is a sister company to McLaren International, the Formula One team.

The F1 was designed without compromise by Gordon Murray, who had been a Formula One star designer for much of his adult life; styling was the responsibility of Peter Stevens, whose work for Lotus and JaguarSport made him one of the most exciting stylists of his time. It was simply the greatest road car ever made. Unlike other supercars it could seat three people (the driver in the middle) and carry as much luggage as a Ford Fiesta.

Based on a carbonfibre monocoque, the car had a

**The McLaren M6GT**

normally-aspirated 6.1-litre dohc V12 engine made by BMW solely for the F1. Producing 627 bhp, and driving through a six-speed gearbox, this gave the F1 a top speed of over 230mph (0-60mph in 3.2 seconds) yet was perfectly tractable in city traffic. On the F1's launch it was said that no more than 400 would be made.

A competition version, the GTR, won at Le Mans on its debut in 1995, and McLarens also took third, fourth and fifth places. Production was due to end in 1996 with fewer than 100 cars completed.

The McLaren F1

## MCR PHOENIX (GB)

From the mid 1980s a maker of a GT40 copy which used the KVA version of the body and was available in a number of forms from basic kit to turn key car.

## MDB (GB)

In the mid-1980s, MDB took over production of the Charger, Charger 2+2, and Centron kit cars which it renamed, respectively, the 'Saratoga', 'Saturn', and 'Sapphire'. It was intended that the two 'Charger' derivatives should be re-engineered to use Ford Cortina components in a bespoke chassis but the company folded before that happened.

## MEAD AUTOMOTIVE (USA)

From the mid-1980s, Mead made a fibreglass copy of the 1957 two-seat Ford Thunderbird, based on the chassis and running gear of the 1971-80 Ford Pinto or Bobcat ranges.

## MÉAN (B)

Between 1966 and 1972, this company marketed mid-engined coupés and roadsters in kit form. The basic make- up was a space frame, a fibreglass body, all-independent suspension, and a wide choice of engines up to 2 litres.

## MECCANICA MANIERO (I)

Shown in 1967, the MM 4700 used Ford Mustang mechanical components with the 4.7-litre V8 engine. These were fitted to a square tube chassis with all independent suspension and a handsome coupé body styled by Michelotti but apparently the MM did not proceed beyond the prototype stage.

## MELKUS (DDR)

Melkus first became widely known in 1959, when it made Formula Junior cars using Wartburg (née DKW) engines. In 1969 it started production of a mid-engined fibreglass coupé using a tuned 1-litre three-cylinder two-stroke Wartburg engine and five-speed gearbox. In 1972 this was uprated with a 1119cc 70bhp version of the engine and in 1978 front disc brakes, previously an option, became standard.

Melkus RS 1000, 1970

## MERCEDES-BENZ (D)

Since this company founded the automobile industry, and grew into a massive corporation, it is impossible to do justice to its history in a few paragraphs. There is the story of Gottleib Daimler, there is the story of Carl Benz (they lived only 60 miles from each other and never met). There is the story of the early pioneering days, the story of motor sport before the First World War and the story of the company's revival after it. Mercedes-Benz SS and 540 models from the inter-war years are by far the most favoured models for modern creators of nostalgia cars.

In the post-1945 era the company first had to start again. Only 214 cars were made in 1946 but production reached 33,906 in 1950—Mercedes-Benz is emblematic of Germany's postwar economic miracle. German cars were barred from international motor racing until 1950 and the following year M-B resurrected a team of its pre-war cars and ran them in some races in Argentina. They were soundly beaten by a much smaller Ferrari but M-B was sufficiently encouraged to try a 'feeler' operation in 1952 sports car events with a team of 300SL coupés. In 1954 the company re-entered Formula 1 and, thanks to the genius of Fangio, it did not disgrace itself that year. M-B's postwar competition cars were actually not very special and all their most distinctive features (air flap brakes, straight-eight engines, desmodromic valves, inboard front drum brakes, enveloping streamlined bodies on Formula 1 cars) proved to be dead ends.

Mercedes did well for a very short time against indifferent opposition and then withdrew from racing for over 30 years. It concentrated its resources in other areas and there is no denying that its saloon cars benefited. By the 1980s the company had an enviable reputation for quality and reliability but none of its cars was exciting. Towards the end of the decade, however, it made a very successful comeback in Group C racing, at first with Sauber, and its new generation of sports cars combined technical excellence and were fun once more. Some people wondered whether the two facts were coincidental.

**300SL Coupé, 1954-57. Prod: 1400.** The original 300SL was created for the 1952 motor racing season and was primarily used to test the water prior to Mercedes-Benz making a full-scale return to competition. The exercise was successful and the model won Le Mans and the Carrera Panamericana, but there was no plan to put the car into production until the American importer ordered a thousand. Since the competition model had been sourced from the parts bin for the 300 series saloon cars, it was relatively easy to put the 300SL into series production. Further, its competition history, together with its famous gull-wing doors, ensured there was a ready market.

The gull-wing doors were necessary to maintain rigidity in the space frame, which was still a fairly unusual method of construction at the time. Power came from a dry sumped version of the 300 series sohc 2996cc straight-six engine, which was inclined on its side to reduce bonnet height. Most unusually for the time the engine was fuel injected, and it delivered its 240bhp through a four-speed gearbox. Front suspension was by coil springs and double wishbones while there were high-pivot swing axles at the rear. With a top speed of about 140mph/225kmh (0-60mph in 8.8 seconds) the 300SL was an outstanding performer but the swing axle rear suspension could induce vicious oversteer (partly overcome when low-pivot-swing axles were introduced). Despite this inherent limitation the 300SL gave a good account of itself in endurance events such as the Tour de France and the Mille Miglia.

Mercedes-Benz 300SL Coupé, 1954

**190SL, 1954-63. Prod: 25,881.** Like the 300SL, the 190SL was sourced from a saloon car, in this case the 180 series. It was styled to resemble the 300SL, which no doubt helped its cause in some quarters yet caused it to disappoint in others. It had a four-cylinder sohc engine of 1897cc which produced 105bhp. The chassis was an abbreviated floorpan from the 180 saloon with coil spring and double wishbone front suspension and a swing axle rear layout. Top speed was about 105mph/170kmh (0-60mph in 13.3 seconds) which was close to the contemporary Triumph TR series but the handling was more boulevard than race track. A factory hardtop was available.

190SL Roadster

**300SL Roadster, 1957-63. Prod: 1858.** On the classic car market the 300SL Roadster has traditionally been less highly valued than the coupé, yet it was a much better car. It was made because the cockpit of the coupé was claustrophobic and its doors, like all gull-wing doors, needed more space to open than conventional doors, which was a limitation in everyday use. As on the coupé most of the body was steel apart from the hinged panels (doors, bonnet and boot lid) which were of aluminium. The roadster retained the Bosch mechanical fuel injection, maximum power was increased to 250bhp and the 0-60mph time improved to 7.6 seconds.

The adoption of a low-pivot swing axle rear suspension layout improved the road holding and handling, but it still had room for improvement. Mercedes-Benz was slow to adopt disc brakes (the Not Invented Here syndrome?) and it was not until 1961 that they replaced the drums on all four wheels. A factory hardtop was an option.

300SL Roadster appeared in 1957

**230SL/250SL/280SL, 1963-66/1966-67/1967-71. Prod: 19,831/5196/23,885.** This series did not replace the 300SL and 190SL, for their day was over and an entirely new type of car was needed for the 1960s. They were not out and out sports cars like, for example, the Jaguar E Type, but they were sporting cars which were sufficiently fast, tough and competent to win several important rallies.

The parts bin which sourced this series was that of the second-generation 220 series, which first appeared in 1959. Thus these cars had an abbreviated pressed steel floorpan, front suspension by coil springs and double wishbones and a swing axle rear layout. All had fuel-injected sohc straight-six engines and there was an optional hardtop with a concave roofline—the 'pagoda roof'.

The 2308cc engine in the 230SL produced 170bhp, which meant it was good for around 120mph/190kmh (0-60mph in 10.7 seconds). All cars in the series were available with a four-speed automatic transmission but the manual 'box on the 230SL had only four gears. Disc brakes were fitted only to the front wheels.

Rear disc brakes arrived on the 250SL which replaced the 230SL in 1966. Although the engine increased in size to 2496cc, maximum power remained at 170bhp, with an increase in torque. The 280SL had an engine of 2778cc and power increased to 180bhp, with another useful increment in torque. From 1969 a five-speed ZF gearbox was an option. By the time that the 280SL arrived the car had taken on extra weight, so the 280SL's straight line performance (top speed 114mph/183kmh, 0-60mph in 9.9 seconds) was fairly close to the original 230SL, but the suspension was softer so it was not as much fun to drive.

1967 250SL Roadster, a special version with enlarged rear space

**R107-series cars, 1972-89.** The line which began with the 230SL may not have stirred the blood but they were very profitable. American buyers in particular responded to the build quality, comfort and style and the replacement cars carried the theme further. 'SL' stands for *sehr leicht* (very light); that had hardly been a true description of the old cars, but the new ones began with an extra 300-400lb (the lightest was 3550lb). They were not therefore agile cars and the change of mood was signalled by the fact that only automatic transmission was available. As before, a 'pagoda roof' hardtop was available and this shape was echoed by the boot lid. Suspension followed the broad outline of the earlier car but the swing axle rear layout was modified to become more on the lines of semi trailing arms.

To summarise the various SL Models:

350SL, 1970-80. Prod: 15,304. 3499cc sohc V8, 200bhp. Introduced as the baseline model for Europe.

450SL, 1971-80. Prod: 66,298. 4520cc sohc V8, 225bhp (Europe), 190bhp (US). Initially for the USA, by the end of the 1970s it was sold in other markets.

280SL, 1974-85. Prod: 22,598. 2746cc dohc straight six, 177-185bhp. A European car in the wake of the 1973 energy crisis.

380SL, 1980-85. Prod: 45,056. 3839cc sohc V8, 155bhp. The replacement for the 450SL on the American market, where its feeble performance led to a 'grey market' in European-spec cars.

500SL, 1980-89. Prod: 11,812. 4973cc sohc V8, 240bhp.

300SL, 1985-89. Prod: 13,742. 2962cc sohc straight six, 188bhp. Replacement for the 280SL with new engine.

420SL, 1985-89. Prod: 2148. 4196cc sohc V8, 218bhp. Replacement for the 380SL.

560SL, 1985-89. Prod: 49,347. 5547cc sohc V8, 227bhp. It was a sign of the times that the most expensive, and thirsty, individual model offered was the one which sold the best.

Shadowing the SL series was the SLC series, which were 2+2 fixed head coupés on a 14in longer wheelbase. These have been described as 'homologation specials' built by Mercedes-Benz for rallying. They had some success in endurance events such as 1978 Round South America Rally but cannot be classified as sports cars.

1980 500SL

**500SL, 300SL. Introduced 1989.** The 'SL' models had pursued a path towards bulk, weight, and breathlessness, but this series reversed the trend. And they did more than that, for they set new standards in terms of build quality, dynamics, and advanced safety features.

Common to all models was a body/chassis with outstanding aerodynamics—it was perhaps the first open production car ever made in which one could sustain 150mph without ear plugs, goggles, helmet or discomfort. Front suspension was by coil springs and double wishbones while the independent rear layout had, on each side, a semi-trailing arm with tie rod, upper transverse link, coil spring and anti-roll bar. An optional extra was a suspension level control system. Braking was by discs on all four wheels, with a Bosch anti-lock system as standard and with an anti-wheelspin system as an option.

All cars were two-seat convertibles but the hood was electrically operated and when down stowed itself under a body panel. A detachable hardtop could then be put in place and secured in a matter of seconds. A roll bar was fitted and owners could drive with it in position or retracted into the back of the cockpit area; in the case of an accident, however, the roll bar would snap into place in 0.3 seconds. Tiny occasional seats became an optional extra.

Mercedes-Benz offered a choice of five-speed manual or

four-speed automatic transmissions—at least those who drive on the wrong side of the road were offered such a choice. Right hand drive cars had to have the automatic transmission because M-B could not be bothered to engineer the manual 'box with the appropriate bias although, after America and Germany, Britain was the third largest market for the car.

Top of the range was the 500SL, which had a dohc 'four-valve' V8 engine of 4973cc giving 322bhp. With automatic transmission this would reach 157mph/252kmh (0-60mph in 5.9 seconds). The 300SL base model had a 2960cc sohc straight six which gave 188bhp; with automatic transmission this meant 138mph/222kmh (0-62mph in 9.5 seconds). Pitched between these the 1990 300SL-24 had, as the designation implies, a dohc 'four-valve' version of the 3-litre engine. Although this unit's 288bhp was close to the 500SL engine its torque was a long way short, which explains its top speed (with automatic transmission) of 146mph/235kmh (0-62mph in 8.5 seconds).

**The 1989 500SL**

## MERLIN (GB)

A 'traditional sports car', originally sold as the 'Witton Tiger' in the USA (see Thoroughbred). Two were imported into Britain in 1979 and this led to an agreement for the car to be made in Britain, by a company called Thoroughbred Cars. From 1980 it offered a chassis which would take post-1971 Ford Cortina components, and it also introduced a Plus Two model. This company seemed to be doing well but in 1984 it ceased trading. The model re-appeared, however, marketed by Paris Cars (qv).

**1980 Merlin**

## MESSERSCHMITT (D)

Just after the War, a German company called Fend produced an invalid carriage which, by degrees, grew into a microcar with two seats in tandam. Former aircraft manufacturers in Germany were forbidden to make aircraft and turned to other projects, in particular to the manufacture of microcars which, given the country's economic state, filled a need. Thus BMW (originally an aero-engine maker), Dornier and Heinkel all made vehicles and in 1953 Messerschmitt took over the Fend bubble car; it was noisy and felt unstable but was cheap and economical.

**TG500 Tiger, 1958-61. Prod: 250.** British enthusiasts noticed the Tiger when one won an important national rally and that is also reason enough for its inclusion here. It was a four-wheeled version of what was effectively a three-wheeled enclosed scooter, with a 493cc two-stroke 'twin' Fichtel & Sachs engine (the trikes had 175cc and 200cc engines). Its 20bhp drove through a four-speed non-synchro gearbox and the car was good for 75mph/120kmh; hence hydraulic brakes to tame it. Steering was via handlebars, and was direct, but that in a machine only 99in long and 48in wide made the TG500 ideal for competitive driving tests, which were a popular form of motor sport and tended to be included in rallies. It was not a vehicle for the faint hearted.

**Messerschmitt TG500 Tiger**

## METALEX (CS)

In late 1990 this Czech company reflected the new mood sweeping across Eastern Europe when it announced plans to build a two-seat sports car based on the running gear of the Skoda Favorit. Production was scheduled to begin in 1991 and 100 units a year were planned.

## METALINE (GB)

A short-lived Cobra 427 copy of the early 1980s. It followed the usual lines, with a space frame, fibreglass body, Jaguar suspension and the usual engine options.

## **METEOR** (USA)

A mid-1950s maker of fibreglass bodies and chassis frames which would take a wide range of domestic running gear.

## **METISSE** *see* RICKMAN BROS.

## **MEYRIGNAC** (F)

Made in small numbers from 1977, the Meyrignac was a handsome fibreglass coupé using an Alpine backbone chassis, with independent suspension and disc brakes all round, and a choice of either a 96bhp 1.6-litre Renault engine or a 150bhp 2.7-litre Renault V6.

1978 Meyrignac

## **MG** (GB)

The story of MG can make a strong man weep. The company was founded in 1924 by Cecil Kimber and, in essence, the first efforts were like that of many another hopeful new marque: a proprietary base (in this case Morris, 'MG' stands for 'Morris Garages') tinkered with and given a bit of style. MG's start was a little like Porsche's, in fact, and the marque's reputation was built in the 1930s when it established an instantly recognisable style and won laurels at the highest levels of international sports car racing. MG introduced sports cars, and motor sport, to a mass market—all in all, it was a marvellous success story.

MG was taken over by Morris Motors in 1935, and prospered. There was A Certain Unpleasantness, 1939-45, then America discovered MG. The American sports car buyer was prepared to put up with the Adoréd One's little ways and shortcomings.

In 1952 the Nuffield Group (which included Morris, MG, Riley and Wolseley) combined with Austin to form the British Motor Corporation. From that moment the rot set in as a new form of corporate mentality controlled its destiny. The story is told in the entries which follow but the summary is that MG had been an outstanding performer in overseas markets, with a reserve of goodwill which was the envy of every other manufacturer, but was allowed to die through management indifference and incompetence. To rub salt into the wounds, the revered badge was stuck onto tuned Austins, including the inept Metro Turbo and the even worse Montego Turbo.

MG also made 1250cc saloons and tourers of distinctly pre-war style between 1947 and 1953. In 1954 came the Magnette saloon which had an Austin chassis, Wolseley body and an MG grille, but it was still sufficiently distinct not to cause too much offence. In 1959, however, the MG badge was used for a variant of the Austin/Morris 'Farina' saloon, and from then on MG was used for the performance version of the corporation's saloons. In 1994 Rover Group was bought by BMW and the following year MG lived again when it introduced the MGF, a mid-engined sports car for the mass market. Its future seems brighter than for many a day.

**TC, 1945-49. Prod: 10,000.** This was the model which began America's love affair with the sports car despite the fact the fact it was slow and uncomfortable and came only with right hand drive. The secret was a vintage chassis (whippy frame, beam front axle) and a responsive little engine (the 54bhp, 1250cc XPAG). A driver had to pay attention to get the best from it; and if a car asks you to concentrate, before long you either love or hate it. Drivers fell in love with the TC despite a top speed of only 75mph/120kmh and a 0-60mph time of 22.7 seconds.

MG TC

**TD, 1950-53. Prod: 29,664.** After MG had established a bridgehead in America with the TC, TDs swarmed in—about 90 percent of all TDs were left-hookers. It was the

MG TD had steel wheels

recognisable descendent of the TC but its front suspension was independent, with coil springs and double wishbones. Allied to smaller and wider wheels this made the TD more manageable, and it was in its element on a winding road. Speed was never the TD's forté, it would just top 80mph/130kmh, with 0-60mph in 23.5 seconds. The rare TD MkII had 60bhp, but more power was also available via factory tuning kits.

**TF 1250/TF 1500, 1953-55. Prod: 6200/3400.** With cars such as the Triumph TR2 and the Austin-Healey 100 in the market place, MG needed a modern car. It had one on the stocks, but the BMC management insisted that it should soldier on with the 'classic' line. The TF was a smoother TD, with 57bhp; a bigger engine arrived in 1954, giving 63bhp, but that was not enough, as the falling sales figures showed. The TF 1500 was good for 85mph/ 137kmh (TF 1250: 80mph/130kmh) and acceleration was much improved, the 1500 covering 0-60mph in 16.3 seconds (TF 1250: 18.9 seconds). These make-weights are now the most sought-after of the line.

TF replaced TD in 1953

**A/A Coupé, 1955-59. Prod: 58,750.** The prototype was ready in 1952 but corporate accountants did not give it the green light until the TF was well past its 'best before' date. The A had a new rigid chassis with coil spring and double wishbone front suspension, a live rear axle hung on semi-elliptics, modern styling, and a 72bhp twin-carb version

MGA

MGA coupé

of BMC's 1492cc series 'B' engine. It added up to a car which recaptured MG's true spirit: cheap and cheerful but always fun. Performance figures were competitive for the time: 98mph/158kmh and 0-60mph in 15.6 seconds. The factory offered a detachable hard top and, in 1956, introduced a coupé version.

**A Twin Cam, 1958-60. Prod: 2111.** As the name suggests, this was an MGA fitted with a new 1588cc, 108bhp dohc engine. It was short-lived and unsuccessful. Top speed was over 110mph/177kmh (0-60mph in 9.1 seconds), it had disc brakes all round, and it looked good, with Dunlop centre-lock alloy wheels similar to those on the Jaguar D Type. The engine began as a dohc version of the series 'B' but gradually took on a life of its own; it was a good idea in principle but MG was not geared to mass-produce such a sophisticated unit. It needed high octane fuel or it detonated and the pistons could burn out. Such fuel was not always available. The engine also gobbled oil. Its reputation and its owners suffered, and sales dropped off when the word spread. MG managed to cure both problems by lowering the compression ratio, but by the time the cure was effected it was too late. MG dropped the model and its stack of spare chassis became the basis of the 'De Luxe'.

MGA Twin Cam had centre-lock wheels

**A 1600/MkII, 1959-61/1961-62. Prod: 31,601/8719.** The MGA 1600 had a slightly larger (1588cc) engine, 80bhp, sliding side screens and front disc brakes, which were all modest but welcome improvements. It could top the ton, just, and could reach 60mph in 15.6 seconds. A 'De Luxe' version, which had the Twin Cam chassis (but standard engine) was offered, to use up spare 'Twin Cam' chassis, and 82 of these were built. The 1600MkII had 86bhp from its 1622cc engine, and a higher rear axle ratio, which kept top speed just over 100mph/160kmh but brought the 0-60mph time down to 13.7 seconds. The 'De Luxe' version accounted for 313 units, and while the 'Twin Cam' has become the most desirable 'A', the Mk II 'De Luxe' runs it a close second, and is far less troublesome.

New rear lamp treatment for MGA 1600 MkII

**Midget Mk1, 1961-64. Prod: 25,681.** With this car MG became a badge on an Austin-Healey Sprite MkII (qv) but did not sell as well. It had all the virtues (and shortcomings) of the Sprite. Top speed was just 85mph/137kmh (0-60mph in 18.3 seconds) but the real point of the Midget was not to compete in the Traffic Lights Grand Prix but to wind along secondary roads with the top down. As on the Sprite, the engine was enlarged from 948cc to 1098cc late in 1962.

1961 Midget MkI

**B Roadster, 1962-67. Prod: 115,898.** This was the first original MG without a separate chassis. It derived directly from the 'A' (coil spring and double wishbone front suspension, semi-elliptics at the rear) and, naturally, it had front disc brakes. Its 95bhp 1798cc version of the series 'B' engine meant 103mph/166kmh and 0-60mph in 12.2 seconds, and overdrive was an option on the four-speed gearbox. Mechanically it was not startling, but its handsome body, styled in-house, was timeless—although each one came ready to succour Abingdon tin worms. From late 1965 the original three-bearing engine was replaced with a five-bearing version.

Early MGB Roadster

**Midget MkII, 1964-66. Prod: 22,601.** The MkII was a rebadged MkIII Sprite, still not quite as popular with buyers. Like the Sprite, it had a taller windscreen, wind-up windows, door locks, semi-elliptic rear springs, and an extra 3bhp. The new rear suspension (which replaced the old cantilever quarter elliptics and radius arms) improved handling.

1964 MkII Midget with wire wheels

**B GT, 1965-67. Prod: 21,835.** Styled with assistance from Pininfarina, the GT was close to being a sporting estate, although luggage space was limited if you wanted to see through the rear window and the small rear seat was suitable only for very young children. It was a clever adaptation which weighed only 160lb more than the roadster, so its performance was only fractionally inferior. Until 1990 it was markedly less expensive than the roadster on the second hand market, but the availability of a complete replacement shell that year changed the situation.

MGB GT arrived in 1965

**Midget MkIII, 1966-69. Prod: 13,425.** Not as popular as the equivalent Sprite in its day, the Midget now has more cachet in the second-hand—sorry, classic—car market which demonstrates a low level of thinking? Like the Sprite, the Midget MkIII had the 1275cc 65bhp engine and a permanently attached hood which replaced the rather crude canvas and tube affair of the early cars.

**B/BGT MkII, 1967-74. Prod: 218,870/91,207.** Detail refinements marked this model: synchromesh on bottom and Rostyle wheels (but wires were optional), while optional automatic transmission was a new departure. There was not much wrong with this car except that, from 1969, Datsun introduced the 125mph 240Z to America. MG had no answer to the Datsun, which became the fastest selling sports car in American history; in fact, to meet US emission laws, late MGBs sold in the States had only 82bhp and could barely top 90mph/145kmh. In de-toxed form 0-60mph took 18.3 seconds, which was pretty pathetic especially when the Datsun took only ten seconds.

The problem was deep-rooted: BL had no 'clean' engine on the stocks although it had had as much notice of the emission laws as anyone else. Further, EX234, a pretty front-engined car styled by Pininfarina which was scheduled to replace the 'B' in 1970, was axed just after the BL merger of 1968, when MG had to compete with Triumph and Jaguar for development money.

MkII MGB had revised grille

**C/CGT, 1967-69. Prod: 4552/4457.** This was an attempt by BL to fill the gap left by the Austin-Healey 3000

MGC Roadster, 1969

by shoe-horning a 145bhp 3-litre engine into the 'B'. There were numerous other modifications, including front suspension by wishbones and torsion bars. Contrary to popular belief the 'C' did not have the Healey's engine but used a seven-bearing unit which it shared with the Austin 3-litre saloon. Why such a heavy and inadequate lump was fitted, when the light Rover 3.5-litre V8 was available, remains a mystery.

Identity features were 15in wheels (the B had 14in wheels) and a power bulge in the bonnet. Although the 'C' was a brisk performer (120mph/193kmh, 0-60mph in ten seconds), it was nose heavy, unbalanced and unresponsive. Since most classic car buyers do not drive their cars hard the C has become something of a cult, but only because it is rare; and its is comparatively rare because it was not good enough to sell well first time round.

**Midget MkIV, 1969-74. Prod: 86,623.** With the Sprite becoming an 'Austin' in 1971, the Midget came into its own. As on the Sprite the main excitement came from new trim, black sills and Rostyle wheels. The vision of the new British Leyland management was not long in making itself felt, and in 1972 (are you ready for this?) the rear wheel arches were *rounded.*

1971 Midget MkIV (above) had squared rear wheel arches. From 1972 they were rounded (below)

**B GT V8, 1973-76. Prod: 2591.** Long after some tuning specialists, in particular Costello (qv), began to make a living by fitting the Rover V8 into MGBs, BL got the message and did the same with the BV8. Since the engine weighed only a few pounds more than the 1.8-litre 'four' the suspension did not have to be altered and the fine balance of the car was unimpaired. Although it could match the Datsun 240Z for performance (124mph/200kmh, 0-60mph in 8.6 seconds) and had much more 'badge', the car was not sold in the States—which drove another nail in the marque's coffin. Almost all were sold in Britain but the home market did not respond well to a relatively expensive car which was basically an eleven year old design (perhaps people thought that a new model *must* be waiting in the wings). There were, apparently, also engine supply problems since the Rover SD1 arrived in 1976 and was an immediate hit. The C has become a cult car because it is relatively rare, the V8 has become one because it is a fine motor car.

MGB GT V8, always chrome-bumpered

**B/BGT MkII 'black bumper', 1974-80. Prod: 52,907/12,915.** US safety laws were responsible for the increased ride height and ugly *fenders* of the 'black bumper' MkIIs. Early cars were justly criticised for handling deficiencies but from 1977 on they handled as well as 'chrome-bumpered' cars because MG got around to fitting anti-roll bars.

Half a million MGBs were sold but the marque was allowed to die despite the fact that it had essayed two replacement models: the EX234, axed in 1968, and the ADO21. The latter was a mid-engined coupé which would have taken BL's sohc E-series engines, the 1798cc 'four' and the 2227cc 'six', both of which were engineered for a transverse location and had five-speed gearboxes. In the end the rival Triumph TR7 was given the go-ahead, and with that decision MG was doomed.

MGB GT, 1976, with black bumpers

BL had severe labour problems, caused in no small measure by rotten management, so it closed down the MG works at Abingdon which had the best record of any BL plant.

**Midget MkV, 1974-79. Prod: 73,899.** To meet US safety regulations, the last expression of the Midget had huge plastic bumpers and increased ride height. The increase in ride height did not have to adversely affect handling, but it was allowed to through lack of development. US emission laws led to the use of the 1493cc Triumph Spitfire engine and gearbox, which was no bad thing since top speed exceeded 100mph/160kmh for the first time. In a rarely daring move, the rear wheel arches were squared off again. Its healthy production suggests that a proper replacement would have been welcomed but, naturally, the knuckle-dragging drongoes in charge of MG's fate could not see this and so the last genuine sports car for the masses was allowed to die.

MkV Midget: squared arches and black bumpers

*Postscript:* In 1985 BL (then called the Austin Rover Group) entered Group B rallying with a mid-engined, turbo-charged, four wheel drive car developed by Williams Grand Prix Engineering. It was badged as the MG Metro 6R4 and the body was vaguely Metro, albeit with front and rear aerofoils. It was a promising project (one finished third on its debut in the R.A.C. Rally) but was a victim of the ban on Group B cars early in 1986 when a series of serious accidents caused the FIA to take draconian action. Unlike the Ford RS200, which was developed with both Group B and road use in mind, the Metro 6R4 was unashamedly a competition car.

In the late 1980s, British Heritage began to market complete shells for the 'chrome bumper' B roadster, B GT, and the Sprite/Midget. As a result, many a rust bucket has been saved from oblivion and some cars have been built up from new.

## MICRON (GB)

The first Micron was completed in 1968 and had a plywood monocoque (à la Marcos) topped by a fibreglass coupé body with gull-wing doors. It had a mid-mounted Mini engine on a Mini subframe but with coil spring and double wishbone suspension. It appears never to have reached production.

## MID-AMERICA CORVETTE (USA)

This was a 1986 copy of the Corvette Grand Sport Coupé, a factory competition model of which just five were made in the early 1960s. Running gear was from the 1984 Corvette.

## MIDAS (GB)

Former Jaguar engineer Harold Dermott took over the Mini-Marcos project and sold about 500 examples. This gave him the expertise and financial stability to re-create the concept as the Midas which, while it shared Mini mechanicals and a fibreglass monocoque, was a completely new design. It was available in several levels of completion, from a basic kit to a virtually assembled car using new components throughout. Road testers raved about the Midas, it received constant development, and new models were introduced. The marque looked set to become a permanent part of the scene and complete cars were exported to countries whose Type Approval laws permitted it, but early in 1989 a fire destroyed the little factory and forced the company into receivership.

The project was sold to Pastiche Cars, which continued production in the face of financial problems in 1991, stressing servicing and the basic kit end of the market rather than the specification which was a few nuts and bolts away from a 'turn key' car. Harold Dermott became production manager on the McLaren 'supercar' project.

**Bronze, 1978-88. Prod: 350.** The Bronze was available with a variety of Mini-based engines. Few cars could match the Midas from point A to point B, if there were wiggly bits in between, and none could match it on a performance/economy basis. The fibreglass was of the highest quality and the special subframes were galvanized and filled with wax, making it a rot-free car—one could even order an exhaust system with a 25 year guarantee. Mini front suspension was used but the rear suspension had new trailing arms. Interior trim was up to the level of most mass-produced cars in its price range; all in all, it was a fabulous little car which had no close rival.

Midas Bronze

**Gold, 1985-89. Prod: 150.** The Gold used Metro components and, like the Bronze, was styled by Richard Oakes. It was improved in detail and was claimed to be the first production car to exploit under-car aerodynamics, achieved in consultation with F1 designer Gordon Murray who owned a Midas Bronze. A special 1.4-litre engine was available which helped overcome the car's only obvious weak point, a four-speed gearbox.

Midas Gold, 1985

**Gold Cabriolet, 1987-89. Prod: 15.** When the Cabriolet was announced it offered the world's best value in sports cars (which is some achievement for a company which made only one or two cars a week) although it was slightly restricted by its Metro running gear. It retained the torsional stiffness which helped all Midas cars handle so well. For winter use, a hard top clipped neatly in place and, hard top or rag top, it looked equally good. Since nothing in the car will rot, one can be kept going just as long as there is a replacement engine to fit every few years.

Midas Gold Cabriolet, 1987

## MIDDLEBRIDGE (GB)

Between 1988 and 1990 this Japanese-financed company took over production of the Reliant GTE, which was up-dated and re-engineered by Reliant to take the 2.9-litre Ford V6 engine. Unfortunately the price tag was too high, there were some production problems, and the firm did not have a sensible advertising budget. Middlebridge never

Middlebridge GTE, 1988

achieved its production target of five cars a week and it folded in 1990.

## MIKASA (J)

The 'Japanese Miracle' has not been without its casualties and Mikasa of Tokyo was one of a number of car companies which appeared in the 1950s but which did not survive. The Mikasa Sports was the first Japanese vehicle which could be called a sports car, even by a stretch of the imagination. Made between 1957 and 1961, it was a pretty little four-seater which showed the distant influence of the AC Ace although it was podgy rather than svelte. Like most Japanese cars of the time, it was designed with economy in mind and an air-cooled twin-cylinder engine delivered its 20bhp via a fluid torque converter to the front wheels.

## MINARI ENGINEERING (GB)

A 1990 two-seat sports car kit with modern styling. It had a fibreglass monocoque with a front tubular subframe which carried an AlfaSud engine, and other main components came from the same source.

**1990 Minari sports**

## MINIJEM (GB)

Test pilot and amateur racer Dizzy Addicot commissioned Paul Emery to build an aluminium coupé body on a Mini-van floorpan and he called the result the 'Dart'. It was obvious that aluminium was too expensive a material to sell to the typical impecunious enthusiast so the original was used to make fibreglass shells and these were marketed by Jeremy Delmar-Morgan as the Minijem. The 'Dart' was also used as the starting point for the similar Mini-Marcos since Jem Marsh had also been involved in the project.

Like the Mini-Marcos, the Minijem had a fibreglass monocoque with wooden floor reinforcement. Its light weight gave sparky performance even with a standard Mini engine, road holding was excellent, and Minijems scored some competition success. After the first change of ownership, in 1969, an improved MkII shell, which was painted and trimmed, was marketed—a wise move as some buyers had taken their cars on the road as soon as they would move under their own power and tatty Minijems did not help the cause. The second

**Minijem at Thruxton circuit in 1975**

firm, run by Rob Statham, eventually buckled under the financial strain of developing a VW-based sports car, the 'Futura'. Yet another change of owners saw a further improvement in the form of an opening rear window, but the mid-1970s saw the kit car market collapse in Britain and Minijem went in 1976. About 350 Minijems wer made by the project's various owners and, in the early 1980s, the project was revived yet again as the Kingfisher (qv).

## MIRAGE REPLICAS (GB)

A late 1980s maker of a copy of the Countach Quattro-valvole with a wide variety of engine options.

## MISTRAL (GB)

A mid-1980s kit car which seems to have barely got off the ground, the Mistral was a gull-wing 2+2 coupé sourced from the Ford Cortina.

## MITSUBISHI (J)

The roots of this company can be found in a shipping concern founded in 1870. It made its first car, based on a Fiat design, in 1917 but produced very few before it switched to making commercial vehicles. Buses and trucks were only a small part of the company's business, however, for the parent corporation also built ships and aircraft (including the Zero fighter).

Mitsubishi first built cars of its own design in 1959, and these were typical of contemporary Japanese cars, having engines of no more than 500cc. In 1964 the three former branches of Mitsubishi amalgamated to become one of the world's largest corporations with a very wide range of interests. The car division became independent in 1970 and the following year the Chrysler Corporation bought a 35 percent share.

Until the 1980s the company's products were sold under marque names such as 'Colt' and 'Lonsdale'. At about the same time as these names were dropped the company began to stress high performance, and its turbocharged saloons won a high reputation for their competence. Mitsubishi built a number of sporty coupés (such as the Starion and Eclipse), then in 1989 unveiled a sensational sports car which went into production in 1990.

**3000GT, introduced 1990.** Only four or five years before this car was announced, it would have been regarded as a Motor Show 'concept' or 'dream' car. Such was the pace of progress in the late 1980s that dreams could become reality and with a comparatively reasonable price tag. The 3000GT, badged in America as the Dodge Stealth, and in Japan as the Starion GTO, was a 2+2 which had four-wheel drive, four-wheel steering, anti-lock brakes, electronically controlled shock absorbers and retractable front and rear spoilers. There was even a control on the exhaust system which would reduce exhaust noise in built-up areas.

The dohc 'four-valve' 2972cc V6, mounted transversely in front of the car, was equipped with twin turbochargers and produced 300bhp. This meant a top speed of 160mph/ 260kmh (0-60mph in 5.4 seconds) and road testers found that the rest of the car's dynamics complemented such figures.

1990 Mitsubishi 3000GT

## MIURA *see* ALDO

## MODENA D&D (USA)

From the mid-1980s, Modena Design & Development made the 'Classic GT250', a turn key evocation of the Pininfarina-bodied Ferrari 250GT 'California Spyder' based on a Ford chassis with a 4.7-litre Ford V8 engine. The prototype was featured in the film, *Ferris Bueller's Day Off.*

1986 Modena Classic GT 250

## MOIR (AUS)

Len Moir was a young shoe salesman when, in 1959 he produced a tiny but lovely special which used Renault 4CV running gear in a tubular ladder frame topped by a sleek body, the central section of which was of steel and was load-bearing, but the front and rear sections were of fibreglass. As with the original Renault, the engine hung behind the rear axle line and it delivered its 21bhp via a three-speed transaxle.

The car caused quite a sensation when it appeared and pretty soon young Len was saved from the shoe shop. J&S put his special into production with an all-fibreglass body, and made 19, while Moir designed whole cars for J&S as well as fibreglass hardtops.

## MOMO (USA)

A short-lived Italo-American four-seat GT coupé introduced in 1971. Stanguellini made the chassis, Frua the body, and power came from a 5.7-litre Chevrolet V8 engine which fed its 350bhp through either a five-speed ZF gearbox or a three-speed automatic transmission.

1971 Momo Mk 1

## MONICA (F/GB)

The odd name for this project came from Monique, wife of Jean Tastevin, head of the CFPM railway wagon works. It was an attempt to build a French supercar but the engineering was mainly British. Chris Lawrence's Deep Sanderson concern was responsible for the chassis while the chosen power unit was a Martin V8, but an unknown engine did nothing to build an 'image' and production cars had Chrysler units, like many another high speed GT car.

Under the four-seat, four-door aluminium body was a space frame with sheet steel reinforcement, a 5.6- or 5.9-litre Chrysler V8, a five-speed ZF gearbox, and a de Dion rear axle. Some cars had automatic transmission and a two-speed back axle. The Monica never really caught the public's imagination and only 35 were made between 1971 and 1975. The project was then taken over by Panther Cars, who quickly forgot about it.

The Monica had four doors

## MONTEVERDI (CH)

Peter Monteverdi first attracted attention in 1960 when he launched the MBM Formula Junior car. This was not a success and nor were the other formula and sports cars which followed. A series of expensive luxury sports and GT cars bearing his name appeared in 1967 but although their styling was widely admired, and the marque seemed to be on the way to establishing itself, American Federal laws and the energy crisis of 1973 hit it badly.

In 1976, Monteverdi introduced the first of several luxurious 4x4 vehicles in the Range Rover idiom. The firm's final fling, in 1983-4, was the 'Tiara', a saloon based on Mercedes-Benz running gear. In 1990 Monteverdi bought the Onyx F1 team and announced he was to be chief designer. Monteverdi's previous F1 experience had been in the 1961 Solitude GP where he drove one of his MBMs fitted with a Porsche engine; he qualified last and retired after two laps. Onyx, which had been an F1 team that had been promising collapsed within a few months.

**375C, 1967-76. Prod:—.** Monteverdi supplied the tubular frame with coil spring and double wishbone front suspension and a de Dion rear axle, Chrysler the engine and drivetrain, and Pietro Frua the final styling to Monteverdi's sketches. The result was an elegant two-seater coupé which was joined by an open model in 1971. A choice of a 7-litre 375bhp or 7.2-litre 450bhp Chrysler V8 made for a well-handling car with a 150+mph/ 240+kmh top speed and, when the larger engine was fitted, a 0-60mph time of 6.3 seconds. Well made and well equipped, they were also very expensive, and it is doubtful whether production ever reached one a week. An extra 26in was added to the wheelbase to build a four-door version, the 375/4 limousine of 1971-77.

Monteverdi 375C coupé, late version with retractable headlamps (above), 1974 375/4 (below)

**375L, 1969-74. Prod:—.** This was a 2+2 version of the 375, and the extra cockpit length hardly spoiled the Frua styling. As with the base model, Fissore built the steel bodies and customers had the choice of a four-speed manual gearbox or three-speed automatic transmission. Engines were the same as in the two-seater but from 1973 American emission laws meant a 20 percent reduction in power. By that time, however, the figure was academic because very few were being made.

The 1969 375L

**Hai/450SS/450GTS, 1970-76. Prod:—.** This mid-engined supercar was perhaps the first sold anywhere. Monteverdi was responsible for the styling, which still looks good, but Fissore was responsible for its execution. As before, the chassis was rather basic (the suspension was much the same as on the front-engined cars) but the 450bhp 7-litre Chrysler engine, which was mated to a five-speed ZF gearbox, was claimed to give it a 169mph/272kmh top speed. As with all Monteverdis, equipment was lavish and air conditioning was standard.

Monteverdi Hai was mid-engined

**Palm Beach, 1975-77. Prod:—.** Another variation on the 375 theme, this had the shortest wheelbase of all and was sold only as a three-seater cabriolet. By the time it appeared, demand for the 375 series was falling away and Monteverdi was concentrating on production of luxury 4x4 vehicle in the Range Rover idiom.

*Postscript:* Between 1977 and 1984, Monteverdi made the Sierra, a 'baby 375' with a similar layout and the choice of only 5.2- or 5.9-litre Chrysler V8s. Since these had been stifled by US emission laws there was only 180bhp from the base

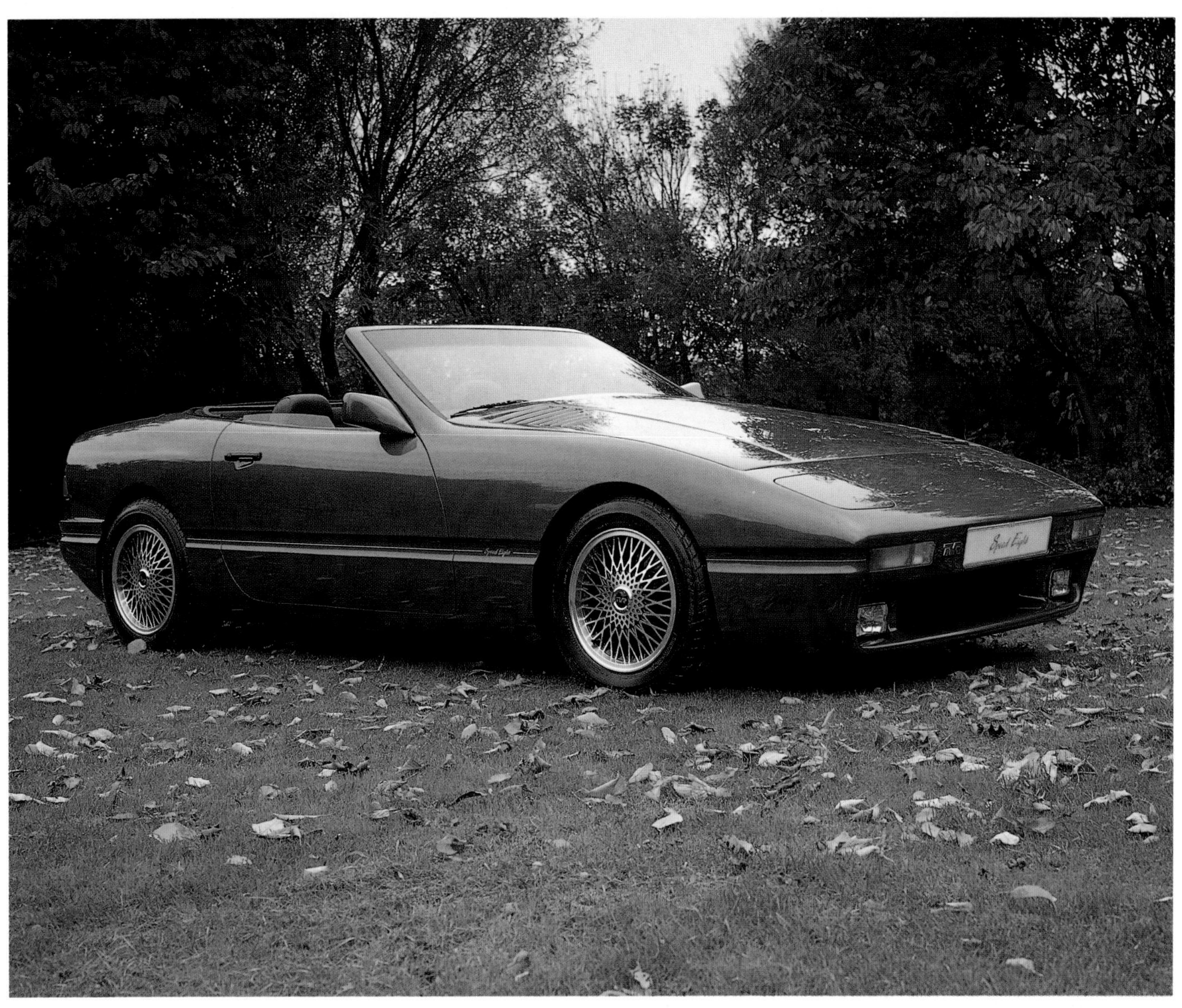

**TVR has built cars in an old tradition for more than forty years. Generally the pattern has been two-seaters with front-mounted engines and backbone space frames that do tend to restrict cockpit space. This is a Speed Eight from 1989**

The Honda NSX was a convincing entry in the supercar category as the 1990s opened, coupling real high performance with sophistication and exemplary build quality. Its looks turned heads, too...

With the G32, Ginetta re-entered the ranks of true constructors, moving out of the kit-car fringe again as the model received Type Approval. Outwardly, as well as in accommodation, it was a car in the Fiat X1/9 mould, but it used Ford components

In the MX5, or Miata, Mazda offered a relatively inexpensive sports car. It was refined and well-mannered, had performance that was no more than adequate for road use and just less-than-adequate for club-level racing

BMW Z1 originated as a concept car and was put into limited production for a few years when the company set aside supercar projects that sometimes seemed more worthy. An expensive fun car, it was best suited for use in countries with reliable sunshine records

Heading for its 40th anniversary: the Corvette model name was retained by GM through four decades of change, although this 1990s car was far removed from the original...

engine. The flair of the earlier cars was lost and in its place was a rather anonymous boxy four-seater (in saloon or cabriolet forms). More recently Monteverdi made the Tiara, a car derived from the Sierra but using various sizes of Mercedes-Benz V8 engines.

## MORETTI (I)

In 1925 Giovanni Moretti, then aged just 21, set up his own factory, specialising in racing motorcycle engines and the manufacture of three-wheeled commercial vehicles. In 1945 Moretti started to make small-engined four-wheel cars in small numbers (about one a week) until 1950. One thing which marked Moretti out was the fact that the company made its own engines and did not use Fiat components, which was the usual course for most small Italian makers. Thus Moretti's four-cylinder sohc engines should not be confused with the many Fiat-based units made for competition by constructors such as Stanguellini, Ermini, and Giaur.

Moretti's first model was the 'La Cita' minicar which had a front-mounted 14bhp vertical twin engine, first of 250cc, then of 340cc, in a tubular frame with hydraulic brakes and independent suspension by transverse leaf springs and lower wishbones. This was available as a saloon, a station wagon and a coupé. By 1950 the small sohc four-cylinder engine was ready and, in 600cc and 750cc versions, was fitted to a new backbone chassis, with independent suspension all round (on the sporting models). This was available with a variety of body styles, including a coupé.

**Very pretty mid-50s Moretti coupé (above) and 1961 Moretti 2300S coupé, Fiat engined (below)**

**Moretti Fiat 500 coupé, 1965 (above) and 125 Special, 1969 (below)**

1954 saw a wide range of Morettis which had power outputs from 27bhp (sohc two-bearing 750cc engine) to 51bhp (dohc three-bearing 750cc engine) plus a special 52bhp dohc 1.2-litre engine which was fitted into a coupé with styling by Michelotti. It sold mainly in America.

In 1957 Moretti made a special coupé body on a Fiat Nuova 500 but continued to offer a wide range of engines: there were 27bhp and 43bhp versions of the sohc 750cc engine, a 55bhp dohc 750cc unit, an 820cc sohc engine, and a 1-litre sohc version. Suspension was by coil springs and double wishbones and disc brakes were fitted to the front wheels of the most powerful model. Despite the wide range of engines, and models which included trucks, production was tiny—only 118 cars in 1958, for example, and hardly any two were alike. Obviously this state of affairs could not continue and from 1960 Moretti turned its attention to Fiats and dropped its original designs.

Most Morettis thereafter were actually new bodies on standard chassis—in fact after 1970 the company officially listed itself as a coachbuilder. Most notable of the sports Morettis was the 2.5-litre spyder made between 1960 and 1963; it was based on the running gear of the six-cylinder Fiat 2300 but the engine was enlarged and tuned to give 163bhp. Most models, however, were based on the smaller Fiats. In 1961 Fiat contracted Moretti to build special examples of its range and the subsequent vehicles were sold through Fiat agencies. The company was still active in 1990 when its range included off-road vehicles and convertible versions of such Fiats as the Uno and Regata.

## MORGAN (GB)

Morgan was founded in 1910 and is still a family business. Until 1936 it made only three wheelers (by 1923 it could boast it had built over 40,000) but the hot versions of these were formidable sports machines. Postwar the only Morgan trike had a water-cooled Ford engine and was pale by comparison to the 'Aero' and 'Supersports' models of the 1930s.

The Morgan 4/4 of 1936 was, to all intents and purposes, the model which Morgan was still making in 1990, and looks set to make for the forseeable future. The secret of this longevity is that production is restricted to about 500 cars a year; they are relatively cheap, but scarcity helps keep up their value, and most are now bought as fun cars. Modern owners, who tend to take them out only at weekends, are prepared to put up with the prehistoric ride, a spartan cockpit, scuttle shake, and a lower standard of build quality than is widely assumed. The marque attracts almost fanatical devotion from many owners and the main reason is the combination of a modern engine in a vintage chassis. This means the cars are responsive to the throttle and, since the flexing chassis is part of the equation, they can be chucked around and the tail hung out, with remarkable margins of safety.

**4/4, 1946-50. Postwar prod: 1084.** The chassis of Morgan's first four-wheeler was very similar to its water-cooled trikes: a simple tubular affair, with Z-section side members, independent front suspension by the old Morgan sliding pillars and coil springs arrangement, a live rear axle suspended on semi-elliptic springs, and worm and peg steering gear. That deals with Morgan's chassis for all its four-wheelers—it was a vintage chassis, indeed the front suspension was Edwardian, having first been used in 1910.

1950 Morgan 4/4

Most pre-war 4/4s had ioe Coventry Climax engines but in 1939 a special ohv 1267cc Standard engine was used in a few cars, mated to a Moss gearbox which was separately mounted. Although Standard had adopted a 'one-engine' policy (the Vanguard unit) in 1947, the 1267 was supplied to Morgan until 1949. Cable brakes and pressed steel wheels were also carried over from the 1930s. It was a relatively inexpensive car and was also a delight to drive, being more 'of a piece' than, say, the contemporary MG TA.

**Plus Four (Vanguard engine), 1951-55. Prod: 245.** Four inches were added to the wheelbase to accommodate the stock four-cylinder 2088cc Standard Vanguard engine, which delivered its 68bhp through a separately mounted Moss gearbox similar to the unit Jaguar used on the XK120. Performance was not shattering for a 2-litre car with an 86mph/138kmh maximum and 0-60mph in 17.9 seconds, but was better than the MG TD. The Plus Four had a hypoid rear axle and, a first for Morgan, hydraulic brakes.

From the end of 1953 there was a new body style, with a curved radiator grille, the front wings extended so they formed a front apron, and in place of the separate chrome headlights the units were flared into the body. Production of the Vanguard-engined car continued even after the TR engine became available because of engine shortages. The Vanguard engine, however, was also restricted, which explains why only 245 were built. In 1955 only a four-seater was offered.

Plus Four foursome drophead coupé, 1955

**Plus Four (TR engine), 1954-69. Prod: 3390.** The 90bhp 1991cc Triumph TR2 engine transformed the Plus Four. For 15 years Morgan received successive TR engines in parallel with the TR range, thus in 1955 power increased to 95bhp (TR3) and in 1962 it went up to 100bhp in the 2138cc TR4 version (increased to 104bhp in 1964). All engines drove through a separately mounted Moss gearbox, which was a weak point since the gearchange was slow and the synchromesh primative. With the TR2 engine the Plus Four was very nearly a 100mph car (top speed was 96mph/154kmh with 0-60mph in 13.3 seconds) and to cope with this, front disc brakes became an option in 1959 (when the body was slightly widened) and standard from 1961. With later engines, top speed went up to around 105mph/170kmh.

Plus Four 4-seater, 1959

**4/4 Series II/III, 1955-60/1960-61. Prod: 386/58.** The supply of Triumph TR engines was at first restricted, and this led Morgan to revive the 4/4, with the new styling and hydraulic brakes, with Ford's venerable side valve 1172cc 100E engine. Unlike the earlier 4/4, it shared the same 96in wheelbase with the Plus Four. With only 36bhp under foot, and a three-speed gearbox, performance was not the car's strong point. The gear shift was a push-pull affair mounted on the dashboard.

A major innovation was that the gearbox was mounted in unit with the engine, which became the practice on all Ford-engined cars (others had the separate Moss unit until mid-1972). From 1958, the high compression Aquaplane cylinder head was a factory option, and that increased power to 40bhp. The Series III of 1960 had the wider body and the new 54bhp 997cc ohv Ford 105E (Anglia) engine together with its splendid four-speed gearbox and a better remote gear shift. The economy Morgan still had drum brakes, and there was a +2 option. The fact that it sold reasonably well only goes to show that there is more to a sports car than power and performance.

4/4 Series II arrived in 1955

**Plus Four Supersports / Competition, 1960-69. Prod: 102.** Chris Lawrence, an engineer later associated with the Deep Sanderson and Monica projects, achieved a great deal of success in British club racing with a Morgan in the late 1950s, thanks to his modified engines as well as his driving skill. Morgan arranged for Lawrence to prepare a small number of TR engines every year. Lawrencetune balanced the engine, gas-flowed the head, and fitted a new camshaft, twin Weber carburetters and a four-branch exhaust system. These were fitted into Plus Fours which had lightweight aluminium bodies. All had wire wheels. An identity feature was an air scoop on the right hand side of the bonnet to clear the Webers. Most cars could reach 120mph/193kmh and the Supersports was basically the forerunner of the Plus Eight.

Plus Four Supersports

**4/4 Series IV/V, 1962-63/1963-68. Prod: 205/639.** The styling revisions introduced late in 1953 were expected to last five years, but apart from widening the bodies in 1959, they remain unaltered to the present day. The Series IV had front disc brakes and Ford's 60bhp 1340cc engine (from the Classic 315 saloon). This translated into 92mph/148kmh and 0-60mph in 10.5 seconds, which was a huge improvement on the Series II car. The Series V had the 1498cc engine from the Cortina GT, plus a new all-synchromesh Ford gearbox. The engine produced 78bhp in standard trim but factory tuning options could bring this up to 83bhp. Naturally, the normal Morgan virtues were present, as was the price to be paid for pleasure: cramped cockpit, little luggage space, poor weather equipment, and spine-jolting ride.

4/4 Series V 4-seater

**Plus Four Plus, 1963-66. Prod: 26.** Enthusiasts kept buying Morgans and suffering the leaks, the shaking bodies and the rock-hard suspension, but it was widely felt that the bubble had to burst. To be ready for that day, Morgan made a coupé on a Plus Four chassis with the TR4 engine. It was a major departure for the company because the body was in fibreglass and supplied by an outside contractor. To call the shape unfortunate is to put it mildly—it might have passed muster as a roadster but the odd 'bubble' top was a mistake. It was actually quicker than the traditional car (110mph/177kmh, 0-60mph in 12.5 seconds) but it found few takers; buyers who wanted a vintage chassis also wanted vintage style.

The Plus Four Plus in 1963

**4/4 1600/Plus Four, introduced 1967/ introduced 1988. Prod: 7000+ (to 1990).** Nothing changed on the chassis front; the specification was set with the Series IV of 1962. The 1600 had the new 1599cc Ford 'Kent' engine (the standard unit in Formula Ford 1600) which gave 74bhp. The 'Competition' version had 88bhp (102mph/

164kmh top speed and 0-60mph in 9.8 seconds) and this became standard after 1970. Buyers could specify an aluminium body at extra cost and, as the TR-engined Plus Four was dropped, the 4/4 became the only Morgan that could be supplied with the +2 body. The 96bhp Ford 1596cc CVH engine was fitted from 1982, when the 98bhp 1585cc dohc Fiat engine was also offered.

In 1988 the 2-litre dohc Rover M16 unit was introduced alongside the Ford crossflow engine (with Rover's 77mm longitudinal five-speed gearbox) and the 'Plus Four' name was revived for these cars. With 138bhp and impressive torque, the new Plus Four could reach 109mph/175kmh (the aerodynamics of a brick limited the maximum) but, more to the point, the 0-60mph time was down to 7.7 seconds. Customers were offered a choice of aluminium or steel bodies, wide or narrow running boards, and a four-seat version was available.

**Ford-engined 4/4 1600**

**Plus Eight, introduced 1968. Prod: 2500+ (to 1990).** When the four-cylinder TR engines neared the end of production, Morgan cast around for a replacement and found it in the 3.5-litre Rover V8. With its aluminium block and compact dimensions, this presented few installation problems and the only major change was adding 2in to the wheelbase. The other main innovation was the fitting of alloy wheels, while detail revisions included new bumpers, switchgear and instruments. The lightweight aluminium body was an option from 1975, but not the +2 body.

Over the years, power increased from 143bhp in 1968 to 190bhp from the 1985 fuel-injected version, while the chassis remained as it was laid down in 1935; it was, of course, inadequate for the power. Even the early cars exceeded 120mph/193kmh and did the 0-60mph dash in 6.5 seconds; late ones with fuel injection were good for 125mph/200kmh and 0-60mph in 5.6 seconds. A separately mounted Moss gearbox was fitted until 1972, when the Rover four-speed 'box was fitted, in unit with the engine; a Rover five-speed 'box was fitted from 1977, and rack and pinion steering was introduced in 1985.

**Morgan Plus Eight, 1968**

## MOSS (GB)

The first car offered in 1982 by this kit car maker was called the 'Malvern'. Malvern is the home of Morgan and there was much of the Moggie about this Triumph Vitesse-based 2+2, but Moss managed to avoid making it a copy, rather it was a parody. A two-seater 'Roadster' was also offered and by 1983 both models had the option of Ford components. In 1983 came the 'Mamba', which used either Triumph Vitesse or Ford Escort parts and had an oddly styled full-width fibreglass body. This was soon joined by the 'Monaco', best described as a tube on wheels with cycle mudguards. It was actually styled after an early 1950s Ferrari F1 car and, being light, was claimed to sprint to sixty in under six seconds with a 2-litre Ford engine, although many buyers fitted the more powerful Ford V6 unit.

By 1985 the company was doing well enough to move into larger premises but soon afterwards the factory was destroyed by fire and the moulds were lost. Production did not resume until 1986, by which time it had passed into the hands of Hampshire Classics. This venture lasted only until 1987 when the company folded; it was then taken over by three members of the Moss Owners Club who successfully resumed production but dropped the Mamba from the range.

**Moss Roadster**

**Moss Mamba of 1983**

## MOTORSPEED (GB)

The 'Magenta' (*see* Lightspeed Panels) was re-engineered by this company to take MGB components and called the 'Magic'. In 1987 the project was sold on to Scorhill Motors (qv).

## MR DEVELOPMENTS (GB)

This was an early 1980s revival of Dennis Adam's Probe concept but with some body changes. Based on a fibreglass monocoque, it used Hillman Imp running gear and was marketed under the name 'Pulsar'.

## MULTIPLEX (USA)

A two-seat sports car which came in 1952, and went in 1954 after just three had been made. Tuned Willys engines, an 87bhp F-head 'four' or a 124bhp 'six', and Willys running gear, were fitted to a tubular frame.

**Amazingly, only three Multiplex sports cars were made**

## MUMFORD ENGINEERING (GB)

In 1982 Mumford introduced the 'Musketeer', a three-wheeled sports car based on Vauxhall Viva running gear. 1984 saw a range of three models using air-cooled Citroën engines and marketed under the name 'Lomax'. All used Citroën chassis. The 223 was a Morgan-ish three wheeler based on the two-cylinder 2CV or Dyane; the 224 was a four-wheeled version of the trike; and the 424 was based on the four-cylinder Citroën Ami. In 1987 another firm took over production of the Citroën based cars and marketed them under the brand name 'Lomax'; the 'Musketeer' appears to have disappeared at the same time.

**Lomax in 1983**

## MUNTZ (USA)

Earl 'Madman' Muntz was a television manufacturer and high-powered salesman who made his name with commercials on American television just after the War. In 1949 he bought the rights to the Kurtis Sports as a means of promoting himself, and like-minded junior celebrities, and marketed it as the Muntz 'Jet'. The first 28 cars, built by Kurtis, were close replicas of the Kurtis Sports, complete with aluminium bodies and, with a 5.4-litre Cadillac engine as standard, performance was pretty lively.

In 1950, Muntz set up his own operation: he added 15in to the wheelbase, made it into a five-seater, replaced the Cadillac engine with the much heavier side-valve Lincoln V8, and used steel instead of aluminium for the bodies. It was still the fastest (108mph/174kmh), and quickest accelerating (0-60mph in 12.3 seconds) American production car of its time and it was exquisitely made. Despite its price (twice as much as a Cadillac), 394 were made, however, Muntz lost money on every one, and the plug was pulled in 1954 when some of his other business interests hit problems.

**1952 Muntz Jet, with five seats and Lincoln V8 power**

## MVM (GBG)

In 1956 Manor View Motors of Guernsey nearly became the Channel Islands' first motor manufacturer when it offered a small open two seater. It had a fibreglass body, ladder frame, all-independent suspension and a mid-mounted 325cc two-cylinder 2-stroke Anzani engine. Although a 325cc engine is not everyone's idea of a sports car unit, the Berkeley (qv) began with a similar engine. Unlike the Berkeley, this project did not progress beyond a few prototypes.

## MVS (F)

First shown in 1984, the MVS Venturi was a striking two seat coupé styled by Gerard Godfroy. A 197bhp 2.5-litre turbocharged Renault V6 engine was mounted amidships in a sheet steel backbone chassis with all independent suspension, at the front by coil springs and double wishbones, and at the rear by coil springs, twin radius arms and a lower lateral link. The chassis itself was engineered by Rondeau, the French racing car manufacturer (and Le Mans winner) so, rarely for a new marque, it arrived with a pedigree.

MVS discovered that the gap between a prototype and a production car can be large and it was not until 1987 that the first examples arrived on the market. The following year an open version was offered. In coupé form the Venturi was capable of 153mph/246kmh (0-60mph in 6.5 seconds) with road holding to match. Although both models were very well received, and praised for the quality and luxury of their finish, MVS was basically under-financed. It was not long before it folded but it was soon snapped up by a partnership between an investment company and the de la Chapelle family, maker of the eponymous Bugatti reproduction.

The new company expanded the capital base and implemented plans to build up to production of 500 units a year. Early in 1989 it introduced the Venturi 280, which had the 2849cc version of the engine but with a Garrett T3 turbocharger. Running with increased boost, the engine gave 260bhp but, more impressively, 298lb/ft maximum torque at only 1750 rpm, which may be a record for a turbocharged engine. This translated into a top speed of 168mph/270kmh with 0-60mph in 5.3 seconds (only a tenth shy of the Ferrari Testarossa, which was the firm's target).

**The MVS Venturi**

# N

## NACIONAL (MEX)

The pride of Mexico was introduced in 1949 but by 1951 only two had been made and, diplomatically, one of those was presented to the President. It was a two-seat sports car on a 4.5-litre Mercury chassis with a body shape which Farina might have made for Alfa Romeo around 1938, although the effect was spoiled by an excess of chrome. About 15 had been made when in 1952 the backers decided it was more profitable to sell Fiats.

## NARDI (I)

Enrico Nardi began his career as an engine tuner and special builder in the 1930s. He played a part in the creation of the Auto Avia 815, which was Enzo Ferrari's first car, and he was a co-driver on its debut in the 1940 Gran Premio di Brescia (often incorrectly called the 1940 Mille Miglia).

**1948 Nardi-Danese**

From 1947 Nardi made tuning equipment and accessories (Nardi steering wheels are still famous) and occasionally made cars as well. Between 1947 and 1951 there was a partnership with Renato Danese, and the handful of cars built during this time carried the hyphenated name, 'Nardi-Danese'. After 1951 'Danese' was dropped.

No Nardi could be called a production car as they were usually bespoke dual-purpose specials. Most were characterised by a multi-tubular frame (similar to a space frame but not properly stressed or triangulated) and had Fiat-derived front suspension by transverse leaf spring and lower wishbones and a live rear axle suspended on quarter-elliptic springs, again Fiat-derived. Engines included Panhard, BMW and Universal flat-twins, and Crosley and Fiat 'fours'.

**1953 Nardyna had fwd Panhard mechanics**

In 1951, Nardi made some unsuccessful mid-engined 500cc Formula 3 cars; the following year saw a Formula 2 car built with Lancia Aurelia components, and factory cooperation, which was never raced; and an incredible 'twin-boom' device ran with a predictable lack of success at Le Mans in 1954. The only large car Nardi built was a coupé made for the Chrysler Corporation with a body by Michelotti and a 350bhp Plymouth V8 engine. After that, Nardi abandoned cars and concentrated on tuning kits and accessories.

## NASH-HEALEY (USA/GB)

In 1949, Donald Healey was crossing the Atlantic on the Queen Elizabeth, in search of new markets for his cars, when he met George Mason, head of Nash-Kelvinator, whose problem was how to get an edge on Detroit's Big Three. Out

**1950 Nash-Healey (above) and 1952 model (below)**

of this meeting the Nash-Healey was born: there would be a new market for Healey, and a prestige car for Nash which would attract customers to showrooms.

The working arrangement was that batches of 125bhp 3.6-litre straight-six Nash engines, and three-speed gearboxes with overdrive top, were shipped to Warwickshire. There they were mated with Healey Silverstone chassis (a simple but effective ladder frame with coil spring and trailing arm front suspension and a live rear axle also suspended on coil springs). The ensemble was bodied by Panelcraft to a Healey design. 104 were sold in the first year, which was wonderful by Healey standards, dismal by Nash standards, so production stopped in 1951 and Pinin Farina was given the job of re-styling the car.

When it re-appeared, after a year's absence, it was available in coupé and sports versions. They were not particularly quick, despite an extra 10bhp—top speed was about 102mph/164kmh (0-60mph in 12 seconds)—but they were handsome and handled well. The trouble was that they were very expensive (shipping costs between America, Britain and Italy did not help), and Nash had other problems on its plate, like survival. Special versions prepared by the Healey works had some competition success, notably fourth at Le Mans in 1950 and third at Le Mans in 1952. In honour of this, a 'Le Mans' coupé with a longer wheelbase was offered in 1953, and one of these actually finished 11th at Le Mans that year.

The real problem was that, while the first cars were being prepared, Jaguar brought out the XK120, which cost about the same. Having the car restyled by Pinin Farina improved sales but although they were expensive Nash lost money on each one sold. Production ended in 1954 after a total of 506 cars had been built.

## **NAVAJO** (USA)

This was a three-seat sports car with a tuned side valve Mercury V8 engine giving 130bhp and a fibreglass body which was a close copy of the Jaguar XK120. The claimed 0-60mph time of 7.8 seconds was actually superior to the Jaguar, and claimed top speed was 125mph/200kmh, but few were sold during the car's production life, 1953-55.

**1953 Navajo, fibreglass bodied**

## **NAYLOR** (GB)

Naylor Bros was an established and respected company which specialised in the restoration of MGs. In 1985 it introduced the 'TF 1700', which was an authorized replica of the MG TF, a high quality turn key car with a body of steel panels on an ash frame. Allan Staniforth, originator of the 'Terrapin' (a Mini-based competition car), was involved on the technical side and the result was a car which looked like the MG TF but was better made, handled better, and had superior appointments. Power came from the 1700cc BL 'O' Series engine, which delivered its 77bhp via a BL four-speed gearbox. Front suspension was by BL coil springs and double wishbones while the live rear axle was sprung on coils and located by twin links and a Panhard rod. Bolt-on 'wire' wheels completed the effect.

The problem was that the price (£14,950 in 1987) made it unlikely that Naylor could sell enough cars to survive; a fully restored (real) MG TF cost less. Moreover, the Naylor had a top speed of only 94mph/151kmh (0-60mph in 12 seconds) and none of its rivals such as the Caterham Super Seven, Panther Kallista or Morgan Plus Four suffered from suspicions that they were copies. Road testers commented on the high standard of finish but also said that the chassis cried out for more than 77bhp—it was actually a fairly dull car to drive unlike a real TF.

By 1986 Naylor was in trouble. The original company went into liquidation and was baled out by Maurice Hutson, who eventually marketed the cars under his own name (qv).

**Naylor TF1700**

## **NECKAR** *see* NSU-FIAT

## **NELSON** (GB)

Introduced in 1990, the Nelson S350 was an originally styled basic sports car with a fibreglass body and cycle wings, which used a Rover V8 engine and Jaguar XJ6 suspension in a tubular backbone chassis.

## **NETHKEN ASSOCIATES** (USA)

A 1980s maker of budget copies of 1930s Duesenbergs, Packards, and the like, based on cars such as the VW Beetle and Ford Pinto.

## **NG** (GB)

NG was named for its founder, Nick Green, and was a pioneer of the post-VAT kit car. Its first model, the 2+2 TA, was inspired by the Aston Martin International and used MGB running gear in a cruciform tubular steel frame topped by a fibreglass body. The TC of 1982 was a two-seater inspired by the Aston Martin Ulster and while it was also sourced from the MGB it could take a Rover V8 engine. The TD of 1983 was a 2+2 version of the TC while the TF of the same year was a TC with flowing wings. It was also the first NG to have doors, although they became an option on all models by 1984.

NGs were widely admired for finish and engineering but the company had disappeared by 1989 (by which time it was possible to use MGB parts in a new MG body/chassis unit). The NG TA was made, briefly, by the TA Motor Company in 1987, when NG was listing only the TF. Then the entire range was taken over by Pastiche Cars and the cars were renamed. The TF became the 'Henley' and was re-engineered to use Ford Cortina or Sierra components; the TA became the 'International', and was re-engineered around Morris Marina/Ital components; the TC became the 'Ascot', to take MGB or Morris Marina parts.

**NG TC, 1984**

## NICHOLS (USA)

Late 1950s maker of a sports car using Panhard running gear in a tubular frame and topped by an aluminium or fibreglass body. Tuned Nichols-Panhards were quite popular for competition use.

## NIMBUS (GB)

A 1984 mid-engined kit car coupé which had something of the Clan Crusader in its styling. The body was of fibreglass, reinforced with Kevlar, and the centre section was a monocoque carrying Mini subframes front and rear. An Austin Metro engine/gearbox unit was usually fitted (a Mini engine was possible) and, with a 1.4-litre version, the works claimed a 122mph/196kmh top speed. By 1986 it had passed into other hands but faded soon afterwards.

**Nimbus coupé, 1984**

## NISSAN (J)

In 1933 the Tobata Imono industrial combine launched the Nissan Motor Company. This occurred after the parent company had acquired a small automotive corporation which included a company called DAT, then making small numbers of light cars. Thus Nissan came to make Datsuns, and the first exports were achieved within a few months of the formation of the new company. By the time Japan entered the Second World War production of all Nissan vehicles, including trucks, was approaching 20,000 units per annum. By then only the small models were sold as 'Datsuns', larger vehicles being sold under the Nissan name.

Production of pre-war models resumed in 1947 and in 1952 Nissan began making some Austin designs under licence. This collaboration was an important factor in Nissan's growth, and by the end of the 1950s the company was Japan's second largest car maker, producing over 77,000 units a year. Exports resumed in 1960 and the first overseas manufacturing subsidiary was established in Mexico the following year. Since then Nissan has established manufacturing facilities in Australia, the United States, and Great Britain. Most Nissans were marketed abroad under the Datsun name until 1983 when the name was dropped.

**D-3 Sport, 1952-57. Prod:—.** This little car was based on a pre-war design and its style was a mixture of MG and Singer roadsters. Its engine seems to have been influenced by the Austin Seven and was a side-valve four-cylinder unit of 860cc with splash lubrication. The similarity did not end there, for the car had a three-speed gearbox, 6 volt electrics and a beam front axle on a transverse leaf spring. The main differences were semi-elliptic rear springs, a worm-drive rear axle and 10in hydraulic brakes. One could say maybe that the car was overbraked since, with only about 29bhp, top speed was not much over 50mph/80kmh.

**Nissan D-3 Sport, 1952**

**S211, 1959-62. Prod:—.** This 2+2 convertible was the first of the Fairlady line of Nissan sports cars but only a brave, or foolish, man would have predicted the line's success on the strength of this car. It was an amalgamation of a fibreglass body, the chassis of the D-3 and the 1189cc four-cylinder ohv engine from the Type 310 Bluebird. With 60bhp, a top speed of 80mph/128kmh was possible—when it received a fourth gear. It was not a success even on its home market.

Nissan S211, 1959

**Fairlady 1500/1600/2000, 1961-69. Prod: approx 40,000.** Nissan's first serious attempt to make a sports car. Its style has been compared to the MGB, but it had first appeared at the 1960 Tokyo Motor Show nearly two years before the MGB entered production. It had a separate chassis and front suspension by coil springs and double wishbones, while the live rear axle was hung on semi-elliptic springs. The 1488cc engine produced just 71bhp at first, which meant only 95mph/153kmh and 0-60mph in 15.5 seconds. This was no match for British sports cars of similar size but the 1500 was very well equipped for its price.

In 1963 the engine was uprated to 85bhp but braking remained by drums all round. The 1600 came in late 1964 and had a 96bhp 1596cc engine, synchromesh on bottom gear, and front disc brakes. Finally, in 1967, came the Datsun 2000, which had a brand new sohc 1982cc four-cylinder engine producing 135bhp as standard. This was designed for the American market (the line was not sold in Europe) and its price, specification, and level of trim wiped out any reason to buy an MGB.

Nissan also made a series of 2+2 Silvia coupés which shadowed this Fairlady line.

Nissan Fairlady 2000, 1968

**240Z/260Z/280Z, 1969-78. Prod: 622,649.** The Datsun Fairlady Z (aka Datsun 240Z) was the car which established Nissan in overseas markets and saw off MG and Triumph in North America. It showed that Nissan had learned how to make a car with an up-to-date specification and lavish equipment at very reasonable prices, although its styling was not admired. To that end, the company engaged Count Albrecht Goertz (who had styled the BMW 503 and 507) and this proved to be an inspired decision.

Detail specifications and options differed from market to market but the model which left Japan had an sohc straight-six of 2393cc (there were 1998cc and twin-cam versions for the home market). The 2.4-litre engine typically produced 151bhp, delivered through a five-speed manual gearbox or a three-speed automatic transmission. Front suspension was by MacPherson struts, the independent rear was by Chapman struts, and disc brakes were fitted at the front.

With a top speed of 125mph/200kmh (0-60mph in 8 seconds), a high level of trim as standard (options included air conditioning), a low price, and new standards of reliability, the 240Z not only replaced the Austin-Healey 3000 but took sales from both the MGB and Jaguar E Type. It should be noted that the Austin-Healey had been forced out of America by new laws, yet the 240Z had to face the same regulations.

1973 saw the 260Z, which had a 139bhp 2565cc engine to cope with tighter emission regulations. A 2+2 version was also marketed and in many markets the line ended with these cars. In America, however, a 149bhp 2753cc engine with fuel injection was fitted from 1975 and this became the 280Z. Versions with dohc 'four valve' engines were available on the Japanese market.

Datsun 240Z, 1971

**280ZX, 1978-83. Prod: 414,358.** The replacement for the first-generation Fairlady Z range was styled in house but was longer and wider. The chassis was completely new, the rear suspension was by coil springs and semi-trailing arms, and the MacPherson strut front suspension was re-worked with lower lateral links and compliance arms in place of the previous lower wishbone.

The engine was from the 280Z and developed 135-148bhp, according to market, and disc brakes were fitted to all four wheels. The 280ZX was offered in two-seat and 2+2 forms and, from 1980, there was a T-bar roof. It was more luxuriously appointed than its predecessors and was thought to be much 'softer', yet sold at a much brisker rate. In 1981 a Turbo version was introduced with 180-200bhp and a top speed of 130mph/210kmh (0-60mph in 7.4 seconds). As before, the Japanese market received other engine options.

In 1983 the 280ZX was replaced by the 300ZX 2+2, which might be likened to an overweight, out of condition person in a designer track suit. It was not short of power, at least in the turbo version, and although it was still related to the 240Z in its styling, it was a million miles away in spirit.

**280ZX 2+2, 1980**

**200SX/Silvia, introduced 1988.** Although a 2+2 coupé, this model was the spiritual heir to the original 240Z, if only because it offered an extraordinary level of style, equipment, performance and competence for the money. As had become usual with most Japanese makers there were several distinct variants within the model range and individual importers chose particular packages for their markets. By taking away customer choice, save for a very limited choice of colours, the importer was able to supply cars immediately and was able to negotiate favourable terms with the parent company.

Thus Britain, where the 'Silvia' name was not used, received only the 200SX coupé, in its 173bhp turbocharged version and with the five-speed manual gearbox. Other markets had different type identification; Japan had the 'export' version (with tailgate) as the 180SX, and so on. Some markets had the four-speed automatic transmission, others received cars with a 133bhp normally-aspirated engine, there was a notch-back version badged as 240SX, and some markets received the convertible, which was available only with automatic transmission, at least in 1990. There were also different final drive ratios, and options included ABS, four wheel steering and a limited slip differential—but not all of these were available in all markets. While most engines had dohc 'four valve' heads, the American spec model had an sohc 'three valve' head on its turbo version.

Common to all cars, however, was a five main bearing four-cylinder engine of 1809cc mounted in line and driving

**The 1989 Nissan 200SX**

to the rear wheels. Front suspension was by MacPherson struts while the independent rear used lower wishbones, upper transverse links and diagonal struts. Disc brakes were fitted to all four wheels. In British specification (turbocharged, five-speed gearbox) the 200SX was good for 140mph/225kmh (0-60mph in 7.2 seconds) and it *felt* like a sports car.

**300ZX, introduced 1989.** When the new 300ZX reached Europe in 1990, *Autocar* hailed it as 'the first Japanese supercar' (that was a few months before the Honda NS-X arrived). Like the 200SX it was not so much a car as a menu and, again, not all markets received all versions. There were two-seat and 2+2 versions, a normally aspirated 227bhp engine and a 276bhp version with twin turbochargers, a five-speed manual gearbox and a four-speed automatic transmission, and versions with, and without, catalytic convertors and a T-bar roof.

All cars, however, had a front-mounted dohc 'four valve' 2960cc V6 engine with variable inlet valve timing in an integral body/chassis with multilink independent suspension all round. Nissan restricted top speed to 155mph/250kmh (0-60mph in 5.6 seconds) by fitting smaller turbochargers but, in turn, that improved the car's dynamics by reducing turbo lag. Despite having the very latest in technology (which normally has the effect of distancing the driver from the road) road testers were able to report that this was a 'back to basics' sports car.

**300ZX Turbo, 1989**

## NOBLE MOTORSPORT (GB)

Lee Noble founded Kitdeal (qv), which was eventually re-named Noble Motorsport. Apart from the Ultima kit car and the Ferrari 330P4 copy the company also made a copy of the Lotus 23 sports-racer under the name 'Noble 23'.

## NORDEC (GB)

An unsuccessful 1949 sports car which used a supercharged Ford 10 engine in a modified Ford 8 chassis with LMB split-axle independent front suspension. The body looked like a scaled-down Allard but the car was high, dumpy and expensive, and few if any were sold.

## NORTH AMERICAN FIBERGLASS (USA)

A maker of a Cobra copy in the 1980s.

## **NORTHEAST EXOTIC CARS** (USA)

A late 1980s maker of a Lamborghini Countach copy which was named 'Scorpion'. It was sold with a variety of V6 and V8 engines, in forms from basic kit to turn key car.

## **NORTHERN KIT CARS** (GB)

Introduced as a prototype in 1985, the 'Hornet' was an attractive, original two-seat coupé. A space frame carried Cortina running gear and a MkII version had a Targa top; the project was taken over by DNK in 1989.

## **NOTA** (AUS)

Englishman Guy Buckingham's Nota Engineering built over a hundred Clubmans-type sports cars and front-engined single seaters during the 1950s and 1960s, and sold some of its Clubmans cars for use on the road. The Type 4 (or 'Fang') of 1971 was the Sydney firm's one successful road car design (more ambitious projects were started but not completed) and it was offered for sale as a kit car in Britain in 1972. At £663, less engine, it might have enjoyed as much success in Britain as in Australia, but by the time it had become known, VAT and the OPEC oil crisis had thrown a spanner in the works.

Sold in kit form or fully assembled in Australia, the Type 4 used a space frame (with built-in roll bar), galvanised steel floor pan, aluminium lower body panels and fibreglass top panels. Front suspension was from the Hillman Imp while behind the two-seat cockpit was a complete Mini engine /gearbox/suspension unit in a Mini subframe. A Cooper S unit was favoured, but even with a bog standard unit performance was good, for the complete car weighed only 1064lb, and road holding, assisted by 12in wheels, was reputedly excellent.

In 1990 Nota was still making small numbers of specialist cars. Total production of the Type 4 was 105 but by 1990 Nota had made over 300 cars, including racers.

## **NOVA** (GB)

Designed by Richard Oakes, who was responsible for the Midas, the Nova was a rebodied VW Beetle. When introduced in 1971 it was arguably one of the most stunning shapes in the world and versions were made in Australia (Purvis 'Eureka'), America ('Sterling'), and Italy and South Africa ('Puma'). It was even copied and the 'Eagle' (qv) derived from the Nova via the 'Cimbria', made by Amore Cars in Milwaukee. The British version, however, had a chequered career and was owned by four different companies in its first seven years, and there have been others since then. It comes and it goes, but it was in production in 1990.

## **NSU** (D)

Like so many of the really long-established makers, NSU grew from non-automotive roots, in this case a sewing machine company founded in 1873. In 1905 NSU began to make the Belgian 'Pipe' car under licence but a year later introduced an original design. The company prospered, expanding into the manufacture of commercial vehicles and motorcycles, and, after the First World War made some successful small-engined competition cars. NSU suffered during the German depression of the 1920s, and through the activities of a speculator who ran into financial difficulties. For a time it had to abandon car production and then a 50 percent share was sold to Fiat. A complicated period followed, in which shares and control of the company changed hands, and NSU concentrated on motorcycles, although in 1934 it commissioned a car from Dr Ferdinand Porsche which was the recognisable ancestor of the VW Beetle.

Production of light motorcycles resumed after the Second World War but, save for mopeds, was discontinued in 1957. The company began production of a small car, the Prinz, in 1958 and the following year became embroiled in a dispute with Fiat over the use of the NSU name, for Fiat built cars in Germany under the names 'Neckar' and 'NSU-Fiat'. This was finally resolved in 1966, by which time NSU was a successful company making a model with the Wankel rotary engine, which had been under development since 1951. In 1969 NSU merged with Audi, which was part of the VW empire, and one of the company's designs was marketed as the VW K70, a disaster about which VW does not like to be reminded. When the advanced NSU Ro80 was dropped in 1977, the NSU name disappeared with it.

**Sport Prinz, 1959-67. Prod: 20,831.** Although the 2+2 Bertone coupé style looked the business, underneath was the chassis pan of the mundane NSU Prinz. The mid-mounted air-cooled 583cc sohc vertical twin (598cc from 1961) delivered its maximum output of 30bhp and 33lb/ft

**The VW Beetle-based Nova**

**NSU Sport Prinz**

torque through a four-speed gearbox. Front suspension was by coil springs and double wishbones while at the rear there were coil springs and swing axles, an arrangement much favoured by German makers of the period. The Sport Prinz had a top speed of 75mph/120kmh, with 0-60mph taking 27.7 seconds, so the introduction of front disc brakes in 1965 seems more a cosmetic touch rather than raw necessity.

**Wankel Spyder, 1964-67. Prod: 2375.** The world's first car to use the Wankel rotary engine had a single-rotor 50bhp unit, nominally rated at 1000cc although the actual capacity of the combustion chambers was 497cc (the discrepancy is explained by the fact that a Wankel unit has twice as many firing impulses as a reciprocating four-stroke engine). For the rest, the general specification was as the Sport Prinz but with only two seats and a rag top. Front disc brakes were standard and performance improved to 95mph/153kmh (0-60mph in 16.7 seconds).

Customers were promised vibration-free engines, but they were disappointed. In addition, the internal sealing problems which had delayed engine production for years (and which nearly bankrupted Mazda) meant that reliable engine life was little more than 10,000 miles, and then a major rebuild was called for. Customers and NSU learned lessons, but it was usually the customer who paid for the experience.

NSU Wankel Spyder was launched in 1964

*Postscript*: It is worth mentioning here the Ro80 because of the part it played in NSU's story and the development of the Wankel engine. Despite NSU selling a licence to Mazda to develop the Wankel engine, the Ro80 led the company to seek a partner, and that led to its ultimate demise.

The innovatively-styled Ro80 had a front-mounted 115bhp twin-rotor Wankel engine, nominally of 2 litres, which drove through a three-speed semi-automatic (with floor shift) gearbox to the front wheels, and was good for about 110mph/175kmh. It sold about a third of its total production in the first 18 months but then buyers discovered that, for all its many other virtues, the engine's shortcomings had not been completely cured. Later there was a cottage industry devoted to replacing the Wankel unit with Ford V4 or V6 engines.

## NSU-FIAT (D)

In 1930 Fiat established a branch in Germany to assemble cars for the local market. After the War the company continued to make Fiat-based cars and some special models were exported. It operated in much the same way as Fiat used Autobianchi to fill niches in the market and, indeed, the German company included some Autobianchi models in its range. In 1959 the marque name was changed to 'Neckar' to avoid confusion with 'the other NSU', but until 1966 cars were sold under both names.

Among other models, it marketed the Weinsberg, a two-seat coupé based on the Fiat 500 and, from 1961, the Jangst 770 Riviera Spyder and Coupé, which were based on the Fiat 600D but had striking bodies styled by Vignale. They were too expensive to sell well and production ended in 1964. Neckar production ceased in 1966.

NSU-Fiat Weinsberg 500 coupé, 1959

NSU-Fiat/Neckar Jagst 770 Riviera coupé, 1963

## NURBURGRING (BR)

A 1980s maker of the 'Phoenix', a fibreglass copy of the 1967 Mercedes-Benz 280SL roadster, using locally built running gear from the 2.5-litre Chevrolet Opala (known to Europeans as the old Opel Rekord C).

The fibreglass-bodied Nurburgring Phoenix in 1984

## NYVREM (GB)

The 'Nirvana' was an ugly two-seat coupé kit car using a space frame and Ford Cortina parts. It came in 1986 and vanished soon afterwards.

## O&C (GB)

O&C was originally Oldham and Crowther, a company which specialised in 'recreating' Jaguars. It moved into the kit car field in 1984 with the 'Sport', a car in the Lotus Seven idiom. Most unusually for a small manufacturer, it attempted a form of unitary construction. Versions were sold which could take components from Ford Escort Mk1/2, Morris Minor or Marina, and Toyota Celica—O&C claimed to be the first kit car maker to offer a car using a Toyota base. The 'Thruxton' was basically a 'Sport' with an ugly body kit (and weather equipment) which made a fundamentally decent car look like something which might haunt the worst dreams of the men who make Morgans. O&C might also have been the first kit car maker to sell a video tape to take the owner through the stages of assembly. However, it seems to have faded during 1987.

## OGLE (GB)

In 1954 David Ogle became one of Britain's first freelance industrial designers when he started to offer companies assistance with packaging and exhibition design and by 1959 his company employed four designers. In 1960 he launched the first of what was intended to be a range of cars, a move to publicise the studio which also reflected Ogle's own interest in cars and motor racing. Among other designs, it bodied a Daimler SP250 with a fibreglass shell which became the shape of the Reliant Scimitar coupé, and the studio afterwards became Reliant's first choice for its body styles for many years. Ogle made a small number of cars under his own name and it was in an Ogle SX1000 that he met his death in 1962. The company continued under Tom Karen and became established as one of Britain's leading design consultants.

**Daimler V8-engined Ogle SX250 shape became the Reliant Scimitar**

**1.5, 1960-62. Prod: 7.** Based on Riley 1.5 components, this four-seat coupé had a multi-tubular frame designed by John Tojeiro and a fibreglass body. Front suspension used Riley (ie Morris Minor) torsion bars, and the live rear axle was suspended on coil springs. The BMC series B engine came in the same state of tune as the Riley with twin carbs and rated at 68bhp but the car was a slow seller and was dropped after Ogle's death.

**Ogle 1.5, 1960**

**SX1000, 1962-64. Prod: 66.** A high quality and well-trimmed turn key Mini variant which demonstrated that a really capable designer could make a pretty car on this base despite the very high bonnet line. A strengthened Mini floorpan, Mini suspension, and a bonded fibreglass body completed the plot, and there was a choice of 997cc or 1275cc Mini-Cooper engines. In truth, it was less practical than a Mini, it was noisier and the boot did not open from the outside, but its main function was to bring the name of Ogle before the public and it did that more effectively than a multi-million pound advertising campaign. After 1964 the design was taken over and produced as the Fletcher GT (qv).

**The Mini-based Ogle SX1000**

## OMEGA (USA)

Jack Griffith's V8-powered version of the TVR started to hit consumer resistance as soon as word got around about its manifold deficiencies. Rather than give up he had the basic TVR chassis looked over by Frank Reisner's Intermeccanica concern. The back axle was modified to take disc brakes and the chassis was topped by a very pretty coupé body, which was something between a Lotus Elite and a Ferrari 250GTO.

About three dozen of these bodies, made of steel, were shipped to Griffith in America but, by 1966, he had run out of cash and the engineless cars gathered dust. Enter a company headed by Steve Wilder, technical editor of *Car and Driver.* Wilder was able to persuade Holman and Moody, the Ford tuning aces, to undertake assembly. Ford Mustang drive trains were used, with Ford 4.7-litre V8 power (a 5-litre Ford V8 was an option for 1968). What began as a Griffith then became an Omega. The cars did not sell, however, and Reisner was left with 142 rolling chassis in Turin in 1968. Thus the Intermeccanica 'Italia' was born (qv), and the 'Omega' name passed to GM.

## **OPEL** (D)

Opel built racing cars before the First World War, but when it became General Motors' German arm it became associated with worthy rather than exciting cars. Thus it was quite a surprise when Opel introduced a sleek little two-seat coupé in 1968 at a time when it seemed set on building a very staid image.

The GT was based on the Kadett Rallye floorpan, which meant front suspension by a transverse leaf spring and lower wishbones, with a live rear axle sprung on coil springs and located by radius arms and a Panhard rod. A 90bhp 1.9-litre engine gave a top speed of 115mph/185kmh (0-60mph in 12 seconds). A 60bhp 1.1-litre version was also produced—a sheep in wolf's clothing. Those who have driven the Opel GT are full of praise for its character but it was made only for those who drive on the wrong side of the road.

The GT sold strongly—103,373 were made in its short production life from 1968 to 1973—but no replacement was forthcoming.

**Opel 1900GT with headlamps raised**

## **OPPERMAN** (GB)

One of the many designs from the fertile mind of Laurie Bond, the Opperman minicar appeared in 1956. It had a fibreglass body on a fibreglass platform chassis, strut ifs and trailing arm independent rear suspension, and a rear-mounted 328cc Excelsior air-cooled vertical-twin engine. It was too crude to sell in any numbers and possibly only about 200 had been made (some as kits) by the time production ended in 1959.

**Opperman Stirling**

Before the company folded, however, it introduced the 'Stirling' which was a pretty 2+2 coupé with hydraulic brakes and the engine enlarged to 424cc (a Steyr-Puch 500cc unit was also tried). Top speed was claimed to be 70mph/112kmh but it cost as much as a Mini when that appeared in 1959 and few were sold.

## **ORSA** (I)

A short-lived revival (1973-76) of the mid-engined Siata Spring sports car, with Seat 850 (née Fiat 850) components and a body which parodied the MG TD.

## **OSCA** (I)

In 1938 the three surviving Maserati brothers, Ernesto, Ettore and Bindo, sold their eponymous company to industrialist Adolfo Orsi who used the firm's racing activities as a flagship for his group. After the War, the owner's son, Omer, took over the running of the company and was soon pressing Maserati to build road cars which would make money. A rift developed and in 1947, when their ten-year service contract was over, the brothers left Maserati to return to Bologna to start their own company. On 1st December, 1947 they registered Officine Specializzate per la Costruzione di Automobile - Fratelli Maserati SpA, which abbreviated to OSCA.

**Luigi Villoresi drives a 750cc OSCA in the 1956 Coppa d'Oro delle Dolomiti**

The talents of the three brothers were admirably complementary: Ernesto was the designer, Bindo the businessman and Ettore supervised the workshop, and they were united by their love of racing. Their company was tiny (there were never more than 40 employees) and their output was never any more than 30 cars a year.

Most of OSCA's production consisted of small-engined sports-racing cars, ranging from 750cc to 2500cc, and until advanced English chassis from Lotus, Cooper and Lola appeared they were very successful. A 1.5-litre OSCA won the 1954 Sebring 12 Hours outright, for example, and there were numerous class wins at Le Mans and in the Mille Miglia. OSCA also made a few single-seater racing cars.

The dohc 1.5-litre OSCA engine caught the attention of the former Ferrari designer Aurelio Lampredi, who was then at Fiat, and he arranged for Fiat to make a production version of it. Its power was deliberately kept in check and, with a single Weber carburetter, its 80bhp was a long way short of its potential. It was available from late 1959 in the Fiat 1500S (later in the 1600S) and stayed in production for six years.

**Michelotti's 1960 OSCA 1500 coupé**

In a reversal of the policy which led them to leave Maserati, *i fratelli* began to build GT cars using a tuned 1598cc version of the Fiat-OSCA engine which gave 140bhp. The chassis was pure Fiat apart from disc brakes on all four wheels and an optional six-speed gearbox. Like most Italian specialist GT cars of the period, these were more or less built to individual requirements and bodies came from Fissore, Vignale and Zagato.

**Zagato bodied this 1961 OSCA 1600 GT**

By 1963 the brothers were in their late sixties or early seventies, and maintaining the company had always been a struggle. That year they sold out to MV Agusta, which continued to make the GT cars in small numbers until 1967, though the last ones were offered with Ford V4 engines, which was a sad end to an illustrious line.

## OSPREY (GB)

An early 1980s 2+2 kit car styled after the Mercedes-Benz SS and using Ford Cortina components.

## OTAS (I)

Made by Francis Lombardi between 1969 and 1971, this coupé began life as a Fiat prototype based on the 903cc front wheel drive Autobianchi A112. Lombardi, however, built the body on the floor pan of the rear-engined Fiat 850 and sold it with the standard engine as the Francis Lombardi Grand Prix 850. Complete cars less engines were sold to Giannini which fitted its own engines, and dohc Giannini engines were sold to OTAS. A version with the 994cc Giannini engine marketed as the OTAS Grand Prix, and with the engine linered down to 820cc to bypass US emission laws it was sold as the OTAS 82 GP. Abarth also made a version, the Scorpione, which used a modified 1.3-litre Fiat 124 engine.

## OTTERCRAFT (GB)

A late 1980s evocation of the SS100, the Steadman TS100 used Jaguar XJ6 running gear and was sold as a high quality turn key car with a hand-built aluminium body. Like many other makers of similar cars, Ottercraft made subtle changes to the original proportions to accommodate the source-car's wider track and smaller, wider wheels. By careful attention to detail (such as the use of appropriately large headlights) the Steadman TS100 was much more successful than most.

# P

## PACE (GB)

In 1990 Performance Automobile Construction Engineers produced the 'Quadriga', a fibreglass copy of the Ferrari 328 (in coupé or Targa-top form) with Lancia Beta running gear. In 1990 the company also took over production of the Maelstrom sports car (qv).

Pace Quadriga (above) and Maelstrom (below)

## PACIFIC COACHWORKS (USA)

In 1980 Pacific announced a limited edition of 100 units of a 'nostalgia' coupé which used a turbocharged 3.8-litre Buick V6 engine.

## PACIFIC MOTOR SPORTS (USA)

This was one of the outfits which appeared in America in the late 1980s to turn Pontiac Fieros into parodies of Italian cars. Its 'Fiero Argenta' might have been mistaken for a shrunken Ferrari Testarossa—at a distance, in heavy fog.

## PANACHE (GB)

An early 1980s fibreglass evocation of the Lamborghini Countach based on the VW Beetle floor pan.

## PANHARD (F)

Just as it is useful to include an entry on Volkswagen because so many cars have been based on its chassis, so it is useful to list Panhard, whose products formed the basis of a fairly large number of mainly French specialist car makers. As in the case of VW, however, Panhard's own sporting offerings could be called sports cars only by a long stretch of the imagination.

Founded in 1891 as Panhard et Levassor, and derived from an even older company, Panhard made Benz designs under licence and became one of the most successful of the pioneer manufacturers. Between the wars it stagnated but its fortunes revived in 1946 with the Dyna saloon. This derived from an advanced 'people's car' designed by Francoise Grégoire and re-engineered by Panhard. Grégoire sued the company but received nothing from the courts, which was rough justice because Panhard was making what was recognisably his concept.

Much use was made of aluminium and the air-cooled flat-twin 610cc engine was mounted ahead of the front axle line. It drove the front wheels via a four-speed crash gearbox. Independent front suspension was by double transverse leaf springs, the 'dead' rear axle was sprung on torsion bars, the brakes were hydraulic and construction was unitary, with an aluminium body. Since so much aluminium was used the car was light, performance was surprisingly spritely for such a small engine, and road holding was excellent; the gearbox, however, was horrid, the car was noisy, and the unusual valve springing (by torsion bars) led to severe reliability problems in the early days.

By 1950 engine capacity had been increased to 745cc and the following year synchromesh was fitted to the top two gears. In 1952 Panhard offered the 'Junior', a two seat roadster. By that time, firms such as DB were already making sports, and racing, cars based on Panhard components. 1954 saw a new body style and a 845cc version of the engine as standard. In 1955 Citroën bought a 25 percent stake in the company, which by then was making about 10,000 cars a year. 1958 saw a steel body and over the next few years engine output was progressively increased, to as much as 60bhp in the 'Tigre' variant of 1961. The company was completely absorbed by Citroën in 1965 and two years later production ceased. Since Panhards were expensive and, by the 1960s, relatively crude, the real wonder is that the marque lasted so long.

Panhard-based cars enjoyed a fair degree of competition success and won the 750cc class at Le Mans no fewer than seven times between 1953 and 1962.

**Dyna Junior, 1952-55. Prod: approx 2000.** A two-seat open sports car which used a 40bhp 845cc engine (a 60bhp supercharged version was optional) in a box section chassis

Panhard Dyna Junior, 1954

with tubular cross bracing. It was an ugly brute but since it weighed only about 1500lb, performance was quite lively.

**24CT, 1964-67. Prod (all types): 24,962.** Panhard's last gasp was a further update of a design which had originated in the early 1940s. The 24CT was a 2+2 coupé, unmistakably styled by Citroën, with the 60bhp 'Tigre' engine and the all-synchromesh gearbox which had been introduced in 1963. Front disc brakes were fitted from 1965. It was claimed to be capable of 100mph/160kmh, which was probably optimistic, but 0-60mph took 22.3 seconds. Panhard also offered the 50bhp 24CD coupé and the 24B, which was a full four seater built on the same floorpan.

**Panhard 24CT, 1964**

## PANTHER (GB)

Bob Jankel was an engineer by profession and a special builder by inclination, so even when he went into the fashion industry he continued to build cars for his own pleasure. These attracted attention and potential buyers so in 1971 he sold his fashion business and founded Panther West Winds Ltd. His first car resembled a Vintage Rolls-Royce and this became the basis for the Panther J72, an evocation of the SS100. Despite a high price these cars sold steadily because they were superbly made, and through this reputation for quality Panther attracted customers who wanted restoration work or specialised coachwork.

1974 saw the FF, which used modern Ferrari running gear but which evoked the 1947 125S. This was joined the same year by the vulgar De Ville, powered by a Jaguar V12, which evoked the Bugatti Royale. Although the 1974 energy crisis hit many specialist makers, Panther was not affected because wealthy Arabs liked its products, which included customised production luxury cars.

The Jaguar-powered Lazer of 1975 was basically a sophisticate's beach buggy, with wedge styling and a high-mounted rear aerofoil, but did not go into production. 1976 saw two new models: the Rio was a Triumph Dolomite Sprint with a boxy, hand-built, body and a high level of trim which sold 38 examples; and the Lima which was a relatively inexpensive 'traditionally styled' sports car based on the floorpan of a Vauxhall Magnum which was soon selling at the same rate as Morgans.

The Super Six of 1977 was pitched at the opposite end of the market to the Lima. It was an open two-seat car with a mid-mounted 8.2-litre turbocharged Cadillac engine for which outrageous performance was claimed. Its name, however, derived from the fact that it had six wheels (i.e. there were four steerable wheels at the front), just like the Tyrrell Project 34 F1 car which had attracted so much attention but despite generating miles of column inches, only two were made.

**The 1977 Panther Super Six went over the top**

The general economic recession of the late 1970s and early 1980s hit Panther, and by October 1980 the company had gone into receivership. It was taken over by the Korean conglomerate, Jindo Industries. The new owners scrapped the entire range and at first concentrated on Panther's lucrative line of customised Range Rovers and Mercedes-Benz for the Middle East. When Panther cars were offered again, the bodies and chassis were made in Korea and were sent to Britain for finishing. The J72 was relaunched as the 'Brooklands', the De Ville was available to special order, and the Lima was re-engineered and became the 'Kallista'.

Panther was soon an established maker again and in 1984 showed a mid-engined coupé, the Solo, intended to be a relatively inexpensive car and to sell at the rate of 2000 a year, but when the Toyota MR-2 appeared Panther took a deep breath and decided to move the Solo up-market. The gestation period was long and it was not until late 1989 that the revised car appeared. In 1990 it was decided to axe the Kallista to concentrate on the Solo but a few weeks later, in the face of mixed reviews from the press, the Solo was also dropped.

**J72, 1972-80. Prod: approx 300.** As an evocation of the SS 100, the J72 did not quite come off, because

**Jaguar V12-powered Panther J72**

compromises with dimensions such as wheel size and back axle made it a rather vulgar parody. It was originally powered by a 3.8-litre XK engine but a V12 version was available from 1973, distinguished by large bulges in the sides of the bonnet. By 1975 the straight-six 4.2-litre engine was usual, and automatic transmission became the norm from 1976. Originally the car had a beam front axle but Jaguar independent front suspension was fitted from 1977.

It had the aerodynamic qualities of a brick, so even with the V12 engine top speed was only 125mph/200kmh. After the Korean takeover, the J72 was briefly revived as the 'Brooklands'.

**FF, 1974-75. Prod: 12.** Commissioned by the Swiss firm, Felber (qv), the FF was an evocation of the Ferrari 125S which used the running gear from the Ferrari 330GTC. It was exquisitely expensive and 1974 was not a good time to be selling expensive cars, which explains the low production. One car was made with Lancia components and front wheel drive.

The 1974 Panther FF

**Lima, 1976-81. Prod: 897.** Although Bob Jankel swore he would never stoop to use of fibreglass bodies, guess what the Lima's shell was made from? It needed to be because it cost just £4495 and was sold through Vauxhall agents. Under the 'traditional' styling was a Vauxhall Magnum floor pan and mechanical elements—a 108bhp sohc 2.3-litre engine, four-speed gearbox, coil spring and double wishbone front suspension, and a live rear axle with coil springs and radius arms. Acceleration 0-60mph was achieved in a fairly respectable 9.9 seconds but the top speed of 98mph/157kmh took ages to reach since the shape was as slippery as emery cloth. Cars built with the Vauxhall floorpan

1978 Panther Lima

had the torsional rigidity of a sponge and from 1979 Panther used Vauxhall running gear in a tubular frame.

For owners who were not satisfied with the basic performance, options included turbocharging and a version tuned by Bill Blydenstein, who was responsible for the successful Dealer Team Vauxhall saloon car racers.

**Kallista, 1982-90. Prod:—.** When Panther was revived the Lima was resurrected under this model name. This time the body was made from aluminium in Korea and shipped to England, while the running gear came from Ford. Front suspension was by coil springs and double wishbones and the live rear axle was suspended on coil springs and located by twin radius arms and a Panhard rod. Engine options ranged from a 91bhp 1.6-litre engine (for frugal poseurs) to 2.8- and 2.9-litre Ford V6s with either carburetters or fuel injection. On the big engined cars, automatic transmission was an option.

With the top spec engine and a five-speed manual gearbox, 0-60mph came up in 7.2 seconds and acceleration to 90mph was good, but then one hit a wall of air and progress was slow. The Kallista was built to a high standard of finish but let down by a cramped cockpit, proprietary parts and detail shortcomings. It was axed in mid-1990 as the company re-grouped following problems with the Solo.

1989 Panther Kallista

**Solo, 1990. Prod: 12.** First seen in 1984 as the prototype of a low-priced mid-engined coupé, the Solo was upstaged by the Toyota MR-2 and was re-engineered to take it up-market. When the car finally appeared in 1989 it had a monocoque made from aluminium honeycomb reinforced by carbon fibre, a body of composite fibres, four wheel drive (via a Ferguson system), ABS, all independent suspension and a 204-bhp Ford Sierra Cosworth engine. Although the original Ford XR3i-powered concept was intended to sell 2000 cars a year, the run for this one was said to be limited to just 100 examples.

There had been many false starts and broken deadlines so when the 2+2 coupé (actually the rear seats were an upholstered luggage space) was finally released to road testers in mid 1990, much was expected. Reports said that while the chassis was sound, the engine was under-powered and noisy. The car was tiring to drive but a muscular driver could go from A to B in a shorter time than in most of its rivals. It was felt that a potentially brilliant concept had been ruined—Panther obviously agreed as it axed the car after only twelve had been made.

Panther Solo, 1990: only 12 made

## PANTHER (I)

At first sight this little coupé was a typical Italian effort of the mid 1950s but actually it was radically different on several counts. Leaving aside the tubular chassis frame and all-independent suspension, the Colli body was of fibreglass—most unusual in Europe in 1954 and unheard of in Italy, a country which never bred a fibreglass automotive subculture. It also had front wheel drive, something which the Italians kept at arm's length longer than any other European nation. Finally, its twin cylinder, air-cooled ohc 450cc engine was a two-stroke diesel.

Panther appeared to have substantial financial backing because within a very short time a 12bhp 520cc water-cooled version of the diesel was offered, and this gave a top speed of 50mph/80kmh—or so it was claimed. For those addicted to speed there was an 18bhp 480cc four-stroke petrol version, four inches longer and a 2+2, which was good for 56mph/90kmh!

There was a great deal of publicity and talk of plans to build the car in San Marino, Argentina, Belgium and France (by Salmson no less). All this came to nothing, however, so San Marino has yet to become a centre of automotive excellence.

Unconventional in many ways: the 1954 Panther coupé

## PANTHER (USA)

A short-lived (1962-63) two-seat sports car with a fibreglass body and, unusually, the Daimler SP250 V8 in two states of tune, rated at 145bhp (Standard) and 190bhp (M).

## PARAMOUNT (GB)

Designed by a couple of enthusiasts in Derbyshire, the Paramount first saw the light of day in 1949 when it was shown as a luxury car with Alvis mechanical components. Since Alvis running gear would have made it prohibitively expensive, a simpler Ford-powered car was offered for sale. As such, its concept was excellent: it was well-made, well-equipped, keenly priced, and the design showed an unusual degree of thought in its execution. The prototype was a two-seater, but in production form it was offered as a two- or four-seat convertible, although only the latter was made. Since it relied on the Ford Ten engine performance was mediocre, but it was undoubtedly the best and most practical four-seat convertible within its price band. Had it reached serious production in 1950 it would probably have been a success, but the original makers spent too long trying to perfect the design instead of modifying it on the run.

By the end of 1951 it had passed to the separate, but related Meynell company, which modified the body style (most notably, the original's vertical radiator grille gave way to twin nostrils) but few were made. This second company essayed a very pretty two-seat sports car looking like a Frazer Nash Targa Florio with a BMW grille, but this remained a prototype. At the beginning of 1953 the original design passed to a third company, Camden Cars Ltd, and production was moved to Leighton Buzzard, but the price rose and Paramount had to compete with more modern and much cheaper cars which made it look distinctly old hat. The company folded in 1956 and the stock passed to Welbeck Motors which sold off the surplus of 26 cars at knock-down prices. A few chassis passed to another company which fitted proprietary bodies, in one case that of a Swallow Doretti, but the usual body was a Rochdale fibreglass shell.

**Ten/1½ Litre, 1950-56/1954-56. Prod: approx 72 (all types, including prototypes).** Paramount made its own underslung ladder frame to take Ford

Paramount 1½-litre convertible, 1954

components and topped it with an aluminium on ash body. The base engine was always the side valve 1172cc Ford unit (30 power-packed horses until 1953 when output was increased to 36bhp) and a three-speed gearbox, but a floor gear change was standard. Some cars had Shorrock or Wade superchargers. In 1954 the 1.5-litre ohv Ford Consul unit was an option, and this should have made the Paramount a more viable proposition with 73mph/117kmh top speed, but by then Ford was marketing its own convertibles. The Paramount with Consul engine cost £1009—the Consul convertible cost £808 and out-performed the Paramount in every important area: top speed, economy, and acceleration. It was also a modern design against the Paramount's 1940s styling.

## PARIS CARS (GB)

This company resurrected the Merlin kit car in 1986 (*see* Merlin *and* Thoroughbred).

## PARRADINE (F)

After Deltayn (qv) had failed with the 'Proteus' sports car, it moved to Magny-Cours in France and became the Parradine Motor Company. There it made the 'Pegasus', another car based on the running gear of the Jaguar XJ6/12 but with a body styled by Richard Oakes, who was responsible for the Nova and Midas. The two-seat convertible body was made from a mixture of composite materials and formed part of the car's semi-monocoque construction. The company emphasised the luxury of its trim (as well it might with a price tag of over £80,000) and with a tuned 360bhp version of the 5.3-litre Jaguar V12 engine, a top speed of 160mph/257kmh was claimed, with the 0-60mph sprint in 4.5 seconds.

## PASTICHE CARS (GB)

A company formed it the late 1980s which took over production of some of the better kit car projects including NG and Midas (qv).

## PBB (GB)

Basically, this project required a customer to buy a Lotus Esprit and take it to PBB Design in Bristol. They cut off the top, stiffened the remains, and handed back a rag top Lotus called the St Tropez.

## PEEL (GB)

At the time of writing Peel remains the only car maker the Isle of Man has bred, which is a conversation stopper if ever there was one. After making rather uninspired fibreglass shells, in 1962 it made a 50cc runabout ('a chair in a box on three wheels') which has a strong claim to being the smallest car ever made. In 1965 Peel came up with the Mini-based Viking.

A neat little 2+2 coupé, the Viking had a fibreglass body with an internal steel structure to which Mini subframes were attached. Beyond that, since the customer provided the engine/gearbox unit, the final specification varied. Originally it was called the Peel Trident Mini, but after two cars had been completed Bill Last's Viking Performance Co became the mainland agent and the name was changed to the Viking Minisport. Soon afterwards Last took over the TVR Trident and put that into production (*see* Trident) so the Minisport took a back seat. Only about 20 were made before production ceased in 1967.

**Peel Viking**

## PEERLESS (GB)

Bernie Rodger was a racing mechanic associated with a number of projects in the 1950s, none of which amounted to much, but he was one of the few individuals not connected to a motor manufacturer who had experience of building space frames. Consequently he was approached by two ex-racers, John Gordon (later of the Gordon-Keeble) and James Byrnes, to build an affordable 2+2 GT car. The prototype called the 'Warwick', was a pretty Italianate car but was considered too cramped. The production car was named the 'Peerless' after John Gordon's business, Peerless Motors.

**GT, 1957-60. Prod: 325.** A space frame with de Dion rear axle suspended on semi-elliptic leaf springs, proven and powerful TR3 running gear, including front suspension and front disc brakes—the make up of the Peerless was excellent. It was also reasonably priced (£1500 in Britain) and had room for a family and its luggage. Top speed was over

**Peerless GT, 1957**

110mph/175kmh, and 0-60mph could be covered in 9.8 seconds, which were very respectable figures at the time. One ran at Le Mans in 1958, the only four-seater in the race, and finished 16th overall. Public reaction was favourable, and sales of 2-3000 a year seemed feasible, but the company was under-financed and it was all over by 1960. After Peerless folded, Bernie Rodger modified the design and revived it as the 'Warwick' (qv), which was a short-lived venture. John Gordon left Peerless to start Gordon-Keeble, and the frame of that car looked suspiciously like that of the Peerless...

## PEGASO (E)

In the early 1950s Spain was ruled by a dictator, had a tiny motor vehicle industry and was desperately poor. Wilfredo Ricart, however, was wooed back to his homeland from Alfa Romeo to create 'jewels for the rich' because General Franco wished to convey the impression to the world that Spain was more advanced than it was. Hardly any two Pegaso cars were alike, they were very complicated, build quality was poor (although they were breathtakingly expensive), and they performed poorly on the few occasions they appeared in competition.

**Z102/103, 1951-58/1955-58. Prod: approx 125.** A problem with all Pegasos was that Ricart's racing background was too apparent. The Z102 engines were all dohc V8s of varying capacity (2.5, 2.8 and 3.2 litres) but with chain driven camshafts they were incredibly noisy. A supercharged version of the 2.8-litre engine was claimed to

2.5-litre Pegaso Z102B, 1952

Touring bodied the 2.8-litre Z102BS (Supercharged) Thrill (left) and Berlinetta (right) in 1953

1957 Pegaso Z103 4.5 litre by Serra. An output of some 300bhp was claimed

give 285bhp, but whatever engine the buyer chose, it drove through a five-speed *crash* gearbox. Z103 models, introduced in 1955, had new V8 engines of 3.9 and 4.5 litres, but with a single camshaft in the vee. By all accounts the Pegaso chassis was a delight, with torsion bar and double wishbone front suspension and a de Dion rear. However, finish was poor and Pegasos had no pedigree (the parent company built trucks) and were not able to gain one through any intrinsic excellence or competition success.

In 1990 Pegaso announced its intention to make a new batch of cars.

## PELLAND (GB)

Peter Pellandine, founder of Falcon Shells and maker of the Australian Pellandini, built a coupé with a steam engine in the mid-1970s, since he entertained hopes of breaking records for steam cars. In the late 1980s he put it into production as a conventional mid-engined sports coupé. It had a fibreglass body/monocoque and was sourced from various Alfa Romeos which used the 'boxer' engine originally designed for the Alfasud, although some Triumph GT6 components were used. With a 1.7-litre engine, a top speed of 130mph/210kmh was claimed. Late in 1990 Pellandine found backing for his steam power venture and the Pelland project was offered for sale.

## PELLANDINI (AUS)

After emigrating to Australia, Peter Pellandine (see previous entry) began making sports cars again and in 1973 announced a gull wing coupé based on either Mini or BMC 1100 mechanicals. It was remarkable both for its beauty and for the fact it remains the only car to have been made in Australia with a fibreglass monocoque. The front suspension used Mini uprights but was otherwise a coil spring and wishbone system unique to this car, and the independent rear layout was also by coils and wishbones. After seven coupés had been made, a roadster version was offered in 1974, but this remained a one-off.

For reasons which remain a mystery, the public did not

want the car, but in any case Pellandine soon received a grant from the South Australian government to develop a steam powered car. The car he created to test his engines in was a topless two seater, also with a fibreglass monocoque but this time using VW Beetle suspension. In parallel with the steam car, Pellandine also made a couple of VW-powered versions and these had the engines reversed so they were *mid-engined.*

After the initial panic of the energy crisis calmed down, the Souh Australian government withdrew its support of the steam project and Pellandine had great difficulty registering his VW version. He returned to England in 1979 and brought both projects with him. The 'Rembrandt' kit car made in Britain in the early 1980s was the VW-powered car (see Ryder) and the 'Pelland' (qv) became the basis for the steam car project.

## **PEREGRINE** (GB)

A peregrine is a rare breed of falcon, and this 1961 car was built in the premises of Peter Pellandine's Falcon Shells. It was based on the space frame originally designed by Len Terry for his Terrier Mk 2 Clubman's car. That was produced by an outfit which had taken over the design and it had undergone modifications which adversely affected its road holding. The Peregrine used a Falcon body shell, in open or hard top forms, and Ford Anglia running gear. The larger body, increased weight and impaired handling did nothing to further the splendid reputation of the Terrier. Very few were made during the car's one production year, 1961.

## **PERENTTI** (AUS)

Built by the Revolution Fibreglass Pty Ltd of Melbourne in 1983, the 2+2 Perentti coupé was first sold as a kit car but later was available fully assembled. It was based on a Holden van chassis, and used Holden components and running gear, with a choice of straight-six or V8 engines. The Perentti's styling showed the influence of the Chevrolet Corvette Stingray and the fibreglass body was reinforced by steel safety bars and a T-bar roof. The company also marketed a shell to convert a VW Beetle into a 'Ferrari Dino'.

## **PERRY AUTOMOTIVE** (GB)

In 1982 Perry began to make the 'Karma', a fibreglass copy of the Ferrari Dino which had been created by Custom Classics of California and, like so many American kit cars, was designed around the VW Beetle floorpan. In 1983 the British project was taken over by Richard Wooley's RW Kit Cars Ltd (qv), which continued to supply the Beetle-based car but also offered a Ford-sourced version. For a short time there was a front-engined variant but this was a failure, largely due to the fact that the engine had to be set too far back to fit under the sloping bonnet. The Ford version of the Karma took four- or six-cylinder engines, usually in conjunction with a Renault or Citroën transaxle, and used a mixture of Granada and Cortina components. RW's development work also saw the provision of two cramped rear seats. The car was exported to a number of countries.

## **PHILLIPS** (USA)

A turn key 'nostalgia' car styled after the Mercedes-Benz 540K, the Phillips 'Berlina' was basically a Chevrolet Corvette chassis surmounted by a fibreglass body. In 1979 a 'limited edition' of 500 cars was offered.

**1981 Phillips 'Berlina'**

## **PHOENIX** (D)

A late 1980s maker of a Cobra copy.

## **PHOENIX** (ET)

The only racing car to wear violet, which is Egypt's official racing colour, the Phoenix sports racer was actually the brainchild of British businessman Raymond Flowers, whose business interests in Egypt were threatened by political movements in the early 1950s. In 1956 a sports-racer appeared at the Reims 12 Hours race but did not start due, it was said, to sabotage. Since feelings about the Suez Canal were running high at the time, this may have been true.

The sports-racer used a Triumph engine in a Lister chassis but in 1955 Phoenix marketed the 'Flamebird', a two-seat coupé based on Fiat 1100 components. About 30 had been sold when Flowers had to quit Egypt in 1956, so that project died. Flowers brought his idea for a Phoenix minicar back to Britain and this appeared as the 'Frisky'.

**The Phoenix sports racer, 1956**

## **PHOENIX** (USA) *see* FITCH

## PIKE AUTOMOTIVE (GB)

A 1986 kit car maker of the 'Invader', a Morgan-like two-seater which used Ford Cortina and Sierra components. The 'Predator' was similar in style but was sourced from the Ford Granada and had the 2.8-litre V6 engine. A wide range of kits was offered, up to turn key cars, and the level of trim was high, but the company soon folded.

## PILGRIM (GB)

A kit car maker founded in the mid-1980s, Pilgrim was responsible for the 'Bulldog', sourced from the Morris Marina and with a rather unfortunate 'traditional sports car' fibreglass body. The 'Hawthorn' of 1987 was a 1950s style sports car with elements of the Austin-Healey 100 and AC Ace, and was also Marina-based. The 'Sumo' was a Cobra copy using Ford engines from 1300cc to 3 litres. Pilgrim was still active in 1990, by which time it was making a four-seat 'traditional sports car' sourced from the Ford Cortina, called the Pilgrim 'Family Tourer'.

**Pilgrim Bulldog (above) and Family Tourer (below)**

## PIPER (GB)

In the mid-1960s Piper was in the business of making small numbers of formula and sports-racing cars which were designed by Tony Hilder. George Henrotte, a former racing driver, commissioned Hilder to design a GT car, and this caused quite a stir when it was unveiled at the 1967 Racing Car Show in London. Tony Hilder's stunning body design was moulded on to a tubular backbone chassis with Triumph Herald front suspension and a live Ford rear axle. A separate

**Piper GTT, 1970**

firm, under Brian Sherwood, took charge of production the following year and the car was gradually developed, but it was still essentially an unrefined kit car. At first it was intended to take Ford, Hillman Imp or BMC Series 'A' engines, but after Sherwood took over production most cars had the 1600cc Ford unit. It was always offered complete but most early buyers bought the GTT as a kit.

Brian Sherwood died in 1970 and the company went into liquidation the following year. It was revived in the same year, however, and an improved version, the P2, was offered. It had a longer and more rigid chassis with the spring rates softened to improve the ride. Soon pop-up lights, tinted glass and sun roofs were offered and the car became quite luxurious. Eventually most were sold as complete cars, with quite a high price tag, but Piper was one of the marques which fell foul of VAT in 1973 and the economic uncertainty which followed the 1974 oil crisis. Production ceased early in 1975 after about 150 cars had been made, but the parent Piper company still flourishes and is well-known for its special camshafts and other tuning equipment.

## PLASTI-CAR (USA)

A 1954 attempt to build an economy sports car in open ('Rouge') or coupé ('Marquis') form using Renault 4CV components. A fibreglass body was usual, although the 'Marquis' could be had with an aluminium body.

## PLAYBOY (USA)

Another unsuccessful attempt to launch a new marque in America just after the war—97 Playboy three-seater convertibles were made, 1946-51 and the company's first name, Midget Motors, puts the car in perspective. Most had a 40bhp four-cylinder Continental Hercules-derived 1.5-litre engine, but some late cars had a Willys 2.2-litre engine, rated at 70bhp compared with the Continental unit's 40bhp. Both types drove through a three-speed manual gearbox.

**Playboy Convertible**

## **PODVIN** (F)

A licensed maker, since 1983, of the Sbarro copy of the BMW 328.

## **POLI-FORM INDUSTRIES** (USA)

A 1980s maker of copies of 1930s style coupés and roadsters.

## **PONTIAC** (USA)

Pontiac was launched as a division of General Motors in 1926 as a step up from the corporation's popular Chevrolet range. By the early 1960s the marque's image was fading and Pontiacs were regarded as stodgy cars. This position was rapidly changed, with much of the credit due to John Z. DeLorean, who was behind a series of cars with sporty style and engine options offering astonishing performance. Moreover, there were optional suspension packages which set new standards of roadholding and handling for mass-produced American saloons.

When Pontiac started to use the 'GTO' designation for its sportiest variants it attracted criticism from some sports car afficionados, but the respected American magazine *Car and Driver*, which is not noted for chauvinism, leapt to Pontiac's defence: 'with the addition of NASCAR road racing suspension, the Pontiac will take the measure of any Ferrari other than prototype racing cars...The Ferrari costs $20,000. With every concievable option on a GTO, it would be difficult to spend more than $3800.'

By 1970 Pontiac had established the 'muscle' car' as a feature of the American scene (Mustangs and Camaros were known as 'pony cars'), had attracted many imitators, and had established a distinct line of style which found ready acceptance on both sides of the Atlantic. Many would argue that some of these models, particularly some of the TransAm line, were really sports cars, but they were raced in saloon car classes (very successfully) and 1984 saw Pontiac's own idea of a sports car, the Fiero.

The Italian name was a clue to Pontiac's intentions but the actual design was carried out by an independent design studio, Entech of Detroit, while various General Motors divisions contributed components. In base form there was a mid-mounted transverse 92bhp 2.5-litre four-cylinder engine with the option of a four-speed manual gearbox or a three-speed automatic transmission, and this was good for 105mph/170kmh (0-60mph in 8.5 seconds). Front suspension was by Chevrolet coil springs and double wishbones, while the independent rear layout was by coil springs, Chapman struts, lower wishbones and tie rods.

Most unusually for a mass-produced car the Fiero was based on a space frame, so the body, which was of Enduraflex plastic, not fibreglass, was unstressed. This led to a number of companies making Ferrari lookalike bodies for the Fiero but there was nothing wrong with the car's original styling. Introduced in 1983 as a two-seat notch-back coupé it won praise for the overall package, but reservations were made about noise levels, the four-speed transmission and the car's ultimate handling. Pontiac responded to all these criticisms and soon offered a 140bhp V6 engine of 2837cc which boosted top speed to 120mph/193kmh (0-60mph in 7.7 seconds).

In 1984 the Fiero was chosen to be the pace car at the Indianapolis 500, which is an accolade. This car had a revised nose treatment and Pontiac built 6000 'Pace Car' replicas in 1984, making the nose standard for 1985. In late 1985 came a handsome fastback body, the GT; mid-1986 saw a five-speed (Getrag) gearbox; power dropped to 135bhp for the 1987 model year as a result of tighter emission controls; the suspension was revised for the 1988 model year, the model's final year of production. Although the Fiero was steadily improved, and became prettier, sales went down and only 19,596 examples were sold in 1987 compared to 67,671 in 1984. In time it will become regarded as a classic car.

**1987 Pontiac Fiero GT**

## **PORSCHE** (D)

At the end of the Second World War, surviving members of the design studio founded by Dr Ferdinand Porsche were operating from a disused timber mill in Gmünd, Austria, where they made and repaired agricultural implements, and renovated cars. Dr Porsche and some of his key personnel were invited by the French to advise on the Renault 4CV, and then were imprisoned on trumped-up war crime charges. His colleagues were released but Porsche was ransomed and the studio paid for his release by undertaking the design of an advanced GP car for Cisitalia.

In the meantime, Dr Porsche's son, Ferry, built a Volkswagen special (Ferdinand Porsche had designed the VW) which was sold to an enthusiast in Switzerland who was so delighted that he arranged for a magazine to road test it. As a result of an enthusiastic review a batch was made. In 1950 the Porsche studio returned to its Stuttgart headquarters in Germany. At first cars were built in a part of the Reutter plant and that company made the steel bodies (the first 50 cars, made in Gmünd, had aluminium panels).

One of the first 50 Porsches, hand made in Gmünd, Austria

The company grew and prospered, aided by an enviable record in sports car racing, although it should be noted that the successful sports racers were mid-engined while the road cars, betraying their Beetle heritage, were rear engined. Porsche was also aided by the fact that the company was able to negotiate a royalty on every VW Beetle made, and by licensing other manufacturers to use the famous Porsche synchromesh system which the studio had developed for the Cisitalia GP car it had designed at Gmünd.

The four cylinder mid-engined sports racing cars of the late 1950s won World Sports Car Championship events on occasion, despite having much smaller engines than their main rivals. In a time when most sports car makers (including Ferrari and Maserati) were special builders or special builders at heart, Porsches were made by engineers.

Porsche sports cars for the road gained high reputations despite the shortcomings inherent in the layout of the staple models. The 911 'family' in particular just went on and on, and towards the end of the 1980s the major faults had been ironed out. Other problems were looming, however, and as the 1980s ended Porsche sales fell seriously in some important markets, in part as the cars seemed over-priced.

As well as making cars under its own name, Porsche has a research division which acts as a consultant to the motor industry in general, and it was this division which undertook the TAG Formula 1 engine for McLaren. The Bosch engine management system was central to its success, however, which explains why, for the first time in its history, Porsche was able to compete at the cutting edge of motor racing for it has otherwise failed in its attempts to conquer Grand Prix and Indycar racing. The V12 Formula 1 engine which was supplied to the Footwork team from the beginning of 1991 was greeted with derision by other engine designers because it seemed to have no contact with the realities of Formula 1, and certainly did not impress in its first race meeting appearances.

As the company grew under Ferry Porsche, sons and nephews of his senior colleagues were appointed to important positions in the company. There is no suggestion that this was on grounds other than merit but the company became sensitive to this and reasoned that if it was perceived to be a hotbed of nepotism then it would not attract the right sort of bright young engineers from outside. The ruling dynasty deliberately fragmented and some members formed Porsche Design, an entirely separate operation which makes products such as sunglasses and sportswear and was one of the pioneers of the designer label.

**356, 1949-55. Prod: 7627.** This was a light and aerodynamic Beetle special and early cars had the Beetle's air-cooled 1131cc flat-four tuned to give 40bhp as opposed to 25bhp. It was not a road burner but although top speed was only 84mph/135kmh, it had outstanding road holding for its day. It was a rear-engined car (the gearbox was in front of the rear wheels, the engine behind them) and a steel platform chassis. Torsion bar springs were used, with trailing links at the front and swing axles at the rear, and brakes were cable operated until 1951.

The engine was soon reduced to 1086cc, so it could qualify for the 1100cc class, and in 1951 Porsche won the class on its first appearance at Le Mans. Also in 1951, a cabriolet version was offered and the following year saw the original split screen replaced by a one-piece screen.

Constant development saw the engine grow to 1287cc, 1290cc (in 1954), and eventually two 1488cc versions were offered: the 55bhp 1500 and the 70bhp 1500 Super. A batch of 20 lightweight roadsters went to America and established Porsche's name in competition, and these led to the 'Speedster' model with a lower windscreen and a basic cockpit, stripped for speed.

A line-up of 356s in 1952

**356A, 1955-59. Prod: 20,626.** The main changes on the second version of the 356, the model which really established the marque, were softer suspension, a steering damper, a new dashboard, and smaller wheels (reduced from 16in to 15in). A hardtop coupé version was added to the range. The 1290cc models (1300 with 44bhp, dropped in 1957; 1300 Super with 60bhp) tended to stay in Germany. The bread and butter models were 1600 (60bhp) and 1600 Super (75bhp) with a 'Speedster' for competition work or boulevard chic.

In 1953, Porsche introduced an entirely new dohc air-cooled flat-four for its sports racing cars, and de-tuned versions of this engine were used in the GS and GT 'Carrera' models of the 356. As versions of this engine came on stream, so Porsche road cars moved on from being Volkswagen specials. It is almost heresy to comment that until the mid-1950s all Porsche road cars were, in essence, no more than

Beetle specials, and so they continued until 1965. Introduced in 1955, as a 110bhp 1.5-litre car, the 120mph/195kmh Carrera had a 1.6-litre engine from 1958 (same power, better power curve) and 1958 also saw a Speedster with the new engine.

356A Carrera hardtop (above) and Speedster (below)

**356B/Carrera 2, 1959-63. Prod: 30,963/1810.** Porsche production mushroomed and the new range helped the image, with sharper styling—raised headlights, revised bonnet, larger rear window and new bumpers and wheel trims. It was sold only with 1.6-litre engines, and all models still had drum brakes, VW steering gear, and a four-speed gearbox, but the dohc Carrera 2, introduced in 1960, had 130bhp and greatly improved torque. It was in character that drum brakes were still used for the company has never been at the forefront of design.

The pushrod VW derived engined cars ranged from the 60bhp 1600, via the 1600 Super with 75bhp, to the 1600

356B

Super 90 which had 90bhp. All would top 100mph/160kmh but the base model (the 1600) was no dragster since the 0-60mph time was 14.5 seconds—but that was not bad for a Beetle special. Still, Porsche build quality, allied to its immense success in sports car racing saw another huge increment in production figures even though the rear-engine layout made high speed cornering in the wet a character building exercise.

**356C/Carrera 2, 1963-65. Prod: 16,668/2134.** Since Porsche was the last constructor to use drum brakes in Formula 1 it is not surprising that it took until 1963 to employ discs on road cars, but on these models they were fitted all round. Road manners were improved by a ZF steering system, and a compensating transverse spring calmed the swing axle and torsion bar rear suspension. It was standard on the Super and Carrera, optional on the 1600. Road holding remained marginal near the limit, however, but the combination of swing axles and a rear engine was hardly a sensible layout.

Porsche's biggest achievement has been to tame an inherently unstable design through constant development, but most manufacturers would perhaps have worked for an alternative in the first place. Just two pushrod engined models were offered: the 75bhp 1600 and the 95bhp 1600 Super but, as before, each model came with a choice of bodies or, rather, roofs.

356C convertible

**904 GTS, 1963-64. Prod: 100.** Many of the sports-racers which Porsche made in the 1950s were tractable road cars, and some were used as such, but the same could be said of any sports-racer of the time. The 904, however, was a true dual-purpose car, which won the 1964 Targa Florio and came second in the 1965 Monte Carlo Rally, which was run in heavy snow. Although Porsche already had its new six-cylinder engine in production, the 904 used the 2-litre dohc flat four in combination with a new five-speed transaxle. Unlike previous 'road' Porsches, the 904 was a mid-engined car, with a tubular boxed chassis and fibreglass body. Suspension was by coil springs with double wishbones at the front and transverse links and radius rods at the rear. Road versions had 155bhp (racing versions had 180bhp) which meant 150mph/240kmh and 0-60mph in 6.4 seconds.

**911/911L, 1964-68. Prod:—.** The 911 had a layout which was broadly similar to the 356: the gearbox was ahead of the rear wheels, the engine behind them, and springing was by torsion bars. The good news was that MacPherson struts were fitted to the front and the old swing axle rear suspension was replaced by a trailing arm system. A major departure was the use of full integral construction. Styling was deliberately similar, but although the 911 was 2.4in narrower, interior space was improved, making the 911 more a four seater than a 2+2.

The new 130bhp 1991cc flat-six engine was air cooled, and drove through the five-speed transmission first seen on the 904. Despite the fact it had only single overhead camshafts, the 911 was as quick as the 'quad-cam' Carrera 2. Weber carburetters replaced Solexes in 1966, a Targa top model came in 1967, and Sportomatic transmission in 1968.

Porsche likes to pretend that it originated the Targa top but this was actually originated by Toyota on its S800 (qv).

**1964 Porsche 911, first of the line**

**912/912E, 1965-69/1976-77. Prod: 30,300/ 2099.** The replacement of the 356 with the 911 saw Porsche move up-market and the 912 was introduced to cater for the sort of people who had bought the bread and butter cars such as the 1600 356. Thus it was basically a 911 fitted with the old VW-derived 90bhp 1582cc flat-four which drove through the old four-speed 'box, although the new five-speed transmission was an option. Levels of interior trim were lower than on the now-luxurious 911, and were more in line with the 356C.

Although much less powerful than the 911, the 912's lighter engine made for better weight distribution, and a top speed of 119mph/191kmh, and 0-60mph in 11.3 seconds, was good going for 2 litres in 1965. Over the years, the 912 received most of the up-dates of the 911, but not Sportomatic transmission because that would have sapped its strength. The model was dropped in 1969 but it was revived in 1976

**912 had four cylinders**

for America as the fuel-injected, but slightly slower, 912E. This was a marketing ploy for the 912E acted as Porsche's 'entry model' for the period between the 914 being dropped and the 924 being introduced.

**911S, 1966-69/1969-73. Prod: —.** This hot version of the 911 arrived with a high compression engine which gave 160bhp and ventilated disc brakes. From the end of 1968, fuel injection upped the power to 170bhp, which translated into 137mph/220kmh and 0-60mph in eight seconds. 1968 saw an extra 2.24in added to the wheelbase and flared wheel arches to take wider tyres; an option was gas strut front suspension. A 2.2-litre version of the engine arrived in 1969; power remained at 180bhp but the mid-range power curve was improved. A five-speed gearbox was standard but the semi-automatic Sportomatic transmission was not an option on the 911S in this period. A 190bhp 2.4-litre engine was fitted from late 1971.

**Flared wheel arches for the 1968 911S**

**911T, 1967-69/1969-73. Prod: —.** The quiet member of the family had a detuned, carburetter-fed 2-litre engine which usually delivered its 110bhp through a four-speed 'box, although five speeds and the Sportomatic were options. Ventilated brake discs were fitted from late 1968 and, in common with the rest of the range, the optional gas strut front suspension was dropped at the end of 1969. A 2.2-litre engine arrived in the same year but this was still the junior motor, having only 130bhp (which stayed the same for the 1971 2.4-litre version) and, hence, a top speed of only 110mph/177kmh, although 0-60mph was achieved in a respectable 9.1 seconds. No front anti-roll bar was fitted to this model but, like all 911s, it had loads of 'badge' and a noisy engine. It was dropped at the end of 1973.

**911T Targa, 1968**

**911E, 1968-69/1969-73. Prod: —.** This was the touring spec car, with fuel injection and a 155bhp engine. Front suspension was by Boge self-levelling hydropneumatic struts in place of the usual MacPherson struts and torsion bars, but these were dropped on all models in late 1969. In the main, the rest of the specification of this series matched the 911S, i.e. ventilated brake discs, longer wheelbase, flared wheel arches and, from 1969, a 2.2-litre engine. A five-speed transmission was standard but Sportomatic was an option. From 1969 Targa-topped models had a fixed wrap-round glass rear window, replacing the former 'zip-out' plastic section which usually leaked and increased engine noise to the cockpit. Power went up to 165bhp with the 2.4-litre engine of 1971. It was dropped at the end of 1973.

**1971 2.4-litre 911E**

**911, 1972-77. Prod: all models, 37,737.** Porsche's policy of constant development and revision was typified by the revival of the Carrera name. There were ever wider wheels, and wheel arches, more controllable handling, new bumpers (from late 1973) which met US impact laws and, unlike some bumpers these actually enhanced the type's lines. The Carrera was the first road Porsche to have the 2.7-litre version of the flat-six engine, which gave 210bhp. It also had an aerofoil on the engine lid which had been developed for the 911 Turbo which was then in preparation.

At the end of 1973, the model range consisted of the 911S, the 911SC, and the Carrera; all with 2.7-litre engines in various states of tune, starting with the 160bhp of the 911S. Three-litre engines began to be introduced in 1975, with the 315bhp RSR road/track car, and were standard by 1977. The American market received strangulated emission-controlled models.

**911 Carrera, 1974**

**911 Turbo, 1975-77. Prod: 2873.** One of the very first European turbocharged cars, the 'Turbo' was originally designated the Carrera 3.0. Its 260bhp was not exceptional, but the torque was phenomonal and Porsche decided that a special four-speed 'box was preferable to the usual five-speed transmission. 0-60mph in 5.2 seconds was even more impressive than the top speed of 156mph/251kmh. The car was quiet and tractable under most circumstances but there was serious turbo lag which, allied to the inherent instability of the rear-engined layout, meant it could be character building—especially on a roundabout in the wet—but the adoption of Pirelli P7 tyres made a huge difference.

Massive wheel arches, and the engine lid aerofoil from the Carrera, were identity features, while the interior was luxurious with leather seats, air conditioning and power windows. The chassis was made stiffer to cope with the power, indeed the car was so fundamentally re-engineered that, at Porsche, it was known as the 930 rather than a 911.

**1975 911 Turbo (right) with 1988 959**

**924/924S, 1976-85. Prod: 122,304/—.** Volkswagen/Audi commissioned the design of this car and Porsche duly raided the VW and Audi parts bins. Late in development, it was decided to market it as a Porsche and the 924 was duly hailed as the first front-engined water-cooled car from the marque, even though it was a blandly styled VW which completely lacked any presence. A 2-litre sohc fuel injected Audi van engine was persuaded to give 125bhp and was fitted in a 2+2 coupé with VW MacPherson strut front suspension and rear trailing arms sprung by transverse torsion bars.

Audi actually built the 924 and economy of scale made it the first 'bargain' Porsche for some time; it was still expensive for its performance—126mph/203kmh and 0-60mph in 9.5 seconds—but then the badge comes dear. Early cars had a four-speed transaxle (five speeds arrived in 1978) but some unfortunate examples had a three-speed automatic. Galvanised steel panels were a real plus and will ensure that there will be a lot of 924s around for a long time.

The 924S of 1985 had the 944's 'balancer shaft' engine and 163bhp. This increased top speed to 134mph/215kmh (0-60mph in 8.0 seconds) but since it retained the narrow, bland body it did not have the 944's visual presence although the price was not much less.

Meanwhile, the 924 Carrera GT was announced in 1980, as a supercar with competitions potential—hence the run was 400, sufficicient to qualify for Group 4 homologation. In 'normal' form this had a 210bhp turbocharged engine, but the racing variant (GTR) had 375bhp and the rally version (GTS) had 280bhp, while the works cars for Le Mans had 400bhp engines.

Porsche 924S, 1985

**911 Turbo, introduced 1977.** The sohc flat-six which began as a 1991cc unit reached 3.3 litres with this model, the increase in size being made largely to maintain performance in US-spec cars which were facing ever more severe emission laws. In European trim, however, this meant 300bhp, 160mph/260kmh top speed and 0-100mph in 12.3 seconds. To cope with this, brakes were uprated with cross-drilled ventilated brake discs and four-pot calipers from the mighty Porsche 917 sports-racer. Road testers still spoke darkly of the handling being interesting on wet roundabouts (how many spun the beast?) but it improved year by year. From 1977, the 'Turbo' was officially called the 'Turbo'. No cabriolet or Targa version was made until 1987, and a five-speed gearbox did not appear until 1989.

In 1990 a version appeared on the Carrera 2 platform. It shared most of the revised body panels of the Carrera 2 and Carrera 4 but was available only in fixed head form. It had even more power (320bhp) despite the fitting of the three-way catalytic convertor, and this meant a top speed of 168mph/270kmh and 0-60mph in 5.0 seconds.

The 1987 911 Turbo SE, a far cry from the original 911

**928 series, introduced 1977.** Aerodynamic it was, and efficient, but buyers of supercars like pizzazz and the 928 was short in that department. It had received a charisma by-pass yet it was an engineering masterpiece with build quality, reliability, and practicality which none of its rivals could match. Anyone who chose a Ferrari in preference announced either that he did few miles in it or had at least two so that one was on the road while the other was being serviced.

The 928's overall layout was similar to the 924 (which was actually designed later) but, in detail, they were chalk and cheese. Central to the plot was a superb fuel-injected sohc V8 of 4.5 litres. Smooth and torquey, it delivered its 240bhp at only 5500rpm and drove to a five-speed manual transaxle, through a twin-plate clutch, or a three-speed automatic. Coil springs all round were allied to double wishbones at the front, trailing arms at the rear, and road holding was exemplary. For those for whom 142mph/228kmh and 0-60mph in 7.5 seconds were not enough, the 300bhp 4.7-litre 'S' version of 1979 returned 152mph/245kmh and 0-60mph in 6.2 seconds (with the manual transmission).

The Series 2 model of 1984 had a four-speed automatic gearbox, derived from Mercedes-Benz, as standard (the five-speed manual was a no-cost option). Anti-lock brakes were standard. Power was increased to 310bhp, with slightly improved economy, and, with the automatic transmission, top speed was 149mph/240kmh with 0-60mph in 6.5 seconds.

The Series 3 was a USA-only car with a dohc 'four valve' 5-litre version of the engine, with Bosch LH-Jetronic fuel injection, and this increased power from the 234bhp of the Stateside 'S' version to 288bhp.

Europe received the 5-litre dohc 'four valve' engine in 1986, in the Series 4. Power was increased to 320bhp (316bhp in America) and with the manual gearbox Porsche claimed a top speed of 168mph/270kmh (not a figure reproduced by British road testers—*Motor* achieved 159mph/256kmh with the automatic transmission). Porsche also claimed that the 0-62mph dash could be achieved in 5.9 seconds (*Motor* achieved 0-60mph in 6.4 seconds). The Series 4 had a lower drag coefficient thanks to a larger rear spoiler and a revised nose section.

The V8 928

In 1989 a GT version was offered with 326bhp, stiffer suspension, wider wheels, a broader rear track and a claimed top speed of 171mph/275kmh.

**924 Turbo, 1978-83. Prod: 12,356.** Despite aggressive marketing, including a competition programme and a 'one type' race series, the 924 was not perceived in the same light as the 'classic' 911 series; worse, a new generation of hot hatchbacks increasingly challenged its performance figures. The turbo version, with 170bhp and greatly improved torque, set out to change that, until the 944 was ready. While 142mph/228kmh and 0-60mph in 6.9 seconds set serious parameters, the curiously anonymous styling was a handicap. Rear disc brakes replaced the drums of the 924 and there

1978 924 Turbo came with alloy wheels

were alloy wheels and a discreet spoiler around the bottom of the rear window.

**911, 1978-89. Prod: —.** With its burgeoning model range, and the need to build a 'world car' to meet different governments' requirements, Porsche rationalised the 911 series to the Turbo and the SC. The normally aspirated 3-litre engine meant it was good for 141mph/227kmh and 0-60mph in 6.5 seconds in European form (it was much slower in US spec). Servo-assisted brakes were standardised in 1979, the list of luxury options grew, and details such as headlight washers arrived in 1982. 1982 also saw the first genuine cabriolet since the 356 series was phased out. In 1984, the sohc flat-six engine was enlarged to 3.2 litres, and the SC became known as the Carrera.

1984 911 Carrera Targa (above) and 1986 911 Carrera Cabriolet SE (below)

1985 saw the SE (Sports Equipment) model which might be described as 'a Turbo without the turbocharger'. With 231bhp it was good for 144mph/232kmh and 0-60mph in 6.1 seconds. It was not, however, a success since it was considerably more expensive than the Carrera and was considered to be over-braked and over-equipped for the engine.

Every year brought detail improvements and, although Porsche was once set to kill off the 911 (it was kept because of its historical associations) it looks set to go on for ever. In 1989 the 911 metamorphosised into the 911 Carrera 2.

**944, introduced 1982.** Although obviously similar to the 924, the 944 had a great deal more presence thanks to a new nose treatment and wide wheel arches. In place of the 924's Audi van engine was a new in-line water-cooled four designed by Porsche; basically it comprised one bank of the 928's V8 although few parts were interchangeable. This 160bhp sohc 2.5-litre unit, with twin counter-weighted balancer shafts to overcome the vibration inherent in large capacity 'fours', made the car into a 'real' Porsche since its torque provided the 'driveability' one associates with the marque.

1984 944 Lux

The 944 Lux was also introduced in Spring 1982, and effectively ran to 1989 although the Lux designation was dropped in 1987. It resembled the 924 Carrera GT 'homologation special' with unobtrusive alloy wheels. The engine was rated at 163bhp (giving a 137mph/220kmh top speed). A five-speed manual gearbox was normal, and a three-speed automatic was optional.

1986 saw both the 944S and Turbo, both with wider wheels to the 928's five-hole design and both with similar performance below 100mph. The 'S' had a dohc 'four valve' head, and 188bhp. Although it was faster it was less flexible and the advantage was largely academic in real driving conditions.

A Cabriolet version was offered from mid-1988 and the same year saw the base 944 receive a 2.7-litre 162bhp engine (136mph/219kmh, 0-62mph in 8.2 seconds) while the 'S' was replaced by the 'S2' which had a 3-litre engine and 208bhp which translated into 149mph/240kmh and 0-62mph in 7.1 seconds.

**944 Turbo, introduced 1985.** Originally this version used the 2.5-litre sohc engine which, with a KKK turbocharger and a Bosch engine management system, gave 217bhp. By 1988 power had increased to 247bhp, which gave a top speed of 152mph/245kmh (0-60mph in 5.7

seconds). In Britain this was marketed as the 944 Turbo SE but designations varied from country to country and so did local specification.

A cabriolet version was offered as a limited edition in 1991.

944 Turbo arrived in 1985

**959, 1987-88. Prod: 200.** The 959 was originally designed for Group B competition, but by the time it was ready for production, Group B was dead and the 200 cars built became 'merely' a limited edition supercar, perhaps the most advanced road car ever built, and a pointer to future Porsches. The engine was a 2.9-litre flat six, with water-cooled dohc 'four valve' heads and twin turbochargers. It delivered its 405bhp, and maximum 369lb/ft torque, through a six-speed transaxle allied to a permanent four wheel drive system which had sensors to vary the torque split depending on conditions.

Performance was extraordinary, 190+mph/305+kmh and 0-60mph in 3.7 seconds, and to cope with that there were anti-lock brakes, competition style suspension (coil springs and double wishbones all round) with computer-adjusted ride height and even electronic monitoring of tyre pressures. The 'comfort' model had rear seats, additional sound insulation and air conditioning.

**911 Carrera, introduced 1988.** Although the style of the Carrera was identical to the 911 almost all the body panels were actually new. In the same way, the paper specification was similar to the earlier 911 but in fact it was all new and it finally really tamed the rear-engine layout of the line.

1990 911 Carrera 2 Cabriolet

In 1989 this heavily revised 911 was launched in the guise of the Carrera 4 which had permanent four wheel drive (31/69% split) and a 3.6-litre version of the flat-six engine. Power increased to 247bhp which meant a top speed of 156mph/251kmh (0-60mph in 5.2 seconds).

A two wheel drive version, the Carrera 2, arrived late in 1989 and was by a tiny fraction quicker than the four wheel drive car (158mph/254kmh, 0-60mph in 5.1 seconds). It was hailed as the best 911 yet made but road testers moderated the welcome with comments about road noise, the usual poor switchgear and ergonomics, and felt the need to point out that no matter how good a 911 becomes it will never compete in ultimate handling terms with a good mid-engined car.

Both two and four wheel drive ranges offered fixed head, cabriolet, and Targa-top versions. Available as an option on the two wheel drive version was the ZF Tiptronic gearbox (automatic transmission with additional manual shift) was available for a small cost in outright performance: it knocked about a second off the 0-60mph sprint time.

## PROBE (GB)

Dennis Adams made his mark with the body for the 1967 Marcos and to further promote his work designed the outlandish Probe 16 with his brother, Peter. It was originally intended to be a styling exercise rather than a serious production car but customers arrived bearing cheques and the Adams brothers built ten of them. It was not the most practical of designs, for one climbed into the Probe by lifting the roof and then adopted an almost horizontal position behind the steering wheel. The fibreglass monocoque housed a Hillman Imp engine on the prototype (Probe 15) but production cars (Probe 16) had a BMC 1800 engine mounted transversely behind he driver. Production was then taken over by a short-lived Scottish firm. The design was later revived by other outfits, first as the 'Centaur', then as the 'Pulsar'. A Belgian company also attempted to market the body on a VW floorpan.

Probe 15 in 1969

## PROCTOR (AUS)

Ted Proctor is a strong candidate for being the first to create an example of what was to become an almost universal model: the fibreglass body on a VW Beetle floorpan. When he showed his GT coupé in 1957 it received a very favourable press since its lighter weight and reduced drag meant a useful increase in performance but it suffered from being the first of its type and only three were sold. Then someone asked for a shortened version of the body on a ladder chassis fitted with VW suspension but a Porsche engine. This was successful in hill climbs and led Proctor to begin a short run of sports racers.

## PROTEUS (GB)

An off-shoot of 'Copycats' (qv), Proteus made convincing copies of the Jaguar C and D Types in the late 1980s. Bodies were made from a mixture of aluminium and fibreglass panels. Any Jaguar XK engine could be specified, so performance varied, but buyers could be assured that the car looked the part. In 1990 the company was working on a copy of the unique, exquisite Jaguar XJ13 which endeared itself to the writer on several counts: it is his ultimate dream car, the car was superb, and Proteus called it a copy, not a 'replica', which showed they were serious citizens.

**Proteus 'C Type'**

## PROVA DESIGNS (GB)

Listed from the mid-1980s, this Lamborghini Countach copy used a space frame designed by Kit Deal, Ford Cortina and Granada components, and a range of engines from the 2.8-litre Ford V6 up to the 5-litre V8.

## PULSAR *see* CENTAUR and PROBE

## PUMA (BR)

From its beginning in 1964, Puma was one of the most successful of Brazilian specialist car makers. It began with a coupé using Vemag components which is to say parts from a locally-made version of the three-cylinder two-stroke DKW. After about 135 cars had been made Puma changed to the VW Beetle floorpan because VW had taken over Vemag in 1967. There followed a series of original and stylish two-seat sports cars (GTS 1600) and coupés (GTE 1600) made on a 1.6-litre VW Beetle base. An attempt in 1973 to add Britain to the many countries which imported Pumas was scotched by Ford, which had registered the name.

Between 1973 and 1979 Puma made a number of front-engined 2+2 coupés called the 'GTB', using locally-sourced Chevrolet chassis and engines ranging from a 2.5-litre 'four' to a straight-six 4.1-litre unit. The company went under in 1985, mainly because it had rested on its laurels, but it was taken on by new management. Both VW and Chevrolet models were revived and continued until 1990, at least, but since development of the range appeared to have stopped nobody was placing serious money on Puma seeing the 21st century.

**1978 Puma GTS**

## PUMA (I)

A 1980s maker of a version of Richard Oakes' Nova (qv) fibreglass body with fixed headlights. The company offered a choice of VW Beetle and Alfasud engines.

**Puma GTV, 1984**

## PURVIS (AUS)

At the time of writing this company had made over 500 examples of the 'Eureka' since 1977, making it the most successful specialist sports car in Australian history. The Eureka was a re-styled version of Richard Oakes' famous 'Nova' body (qv) based on a VW Beetle floorpan. With the 1.6-litre engine a top speed of over 100mph/160+kmh was claimed. In the late 1980s, the company introduced a mid-engined open car called 'Free Spirit' which used Ford components.

## QUANTEK (USA)

Maker of the 'Vokaro', a doorless two-seat sports car on either the VW Beetle floorpan or the company's own frame. The 'Vokaro 4' was a 2+2 version and a number of small capacity engines could be fitted. The design was introduced in 1977 by Vopard Enterprises (qv) but in the late 1980s Quantek was established as a different company at the same address.

## QUANTUM (GB)

Announced in 1988, the Quantum was a four-seat coupé using Ford Fiesta running gear in a monocoque made from fibreglass and Kevlar. With a Fiesta turbo engine, top speed was claimed to be 140mph/225kmh (0-60mph in six seconds). Fully assembled cars could be supplied.

**1988 Quantum coupé**

## QUANTUM (USA)

Basically a rebodied and shortened Saab Sport (front wheel drive, three-cylinder two-stroke 50bhp 841cc engine) claimed to weight only 900lb. This sports-roadster was built in 1962-63 and sold through selected Saab dealers in America.

## RACECORP (GB)

Racecorp was founded in the 1980s to act as a service company to the motor racing industry, with particular emphasis on composite fibres. In 1990 the company offered the LA Roadster, a basic sports car in the Lotus Seven idiom which would take any Ford four-cylinder engine. Front suspension was by coil springs and double wishbones and customers had a choice of rear layout, the options being a live (Escort) axle with five-link location or an independent layout using Ford Sierra components.

## RAILTON (GB)

Funded by Noel Macklin, designed by Reid Railton (best known for his Land Speed Record cars) and built in the old Invicta works at Chobham, Railton was founded in 1933 and made an early Anglo-American hybrid. The chassis was always a lightly modified Hudson and the best examples used the splendid Hudson 4.2-litre straight-eight. After 1937 the firm lost its way when it tried going down market to increase sales. In 1940 it was sold to Hudson and had a brief revival after the War.

**Eight/Six, 1946-49. Prod: 16.** After the War Railton made up a number of cars from parts in stock at the old Hudson assembly plant at Chiswick. The Hudson Six was fairly ordinary but the flathead Eight was wonderful, being very smooth and torquey. All cars had hydraulic brakes and were 'Railtonised', which largely meant a smart body and stiffer springing. Unfortunately, government import restrictions meant that a new car would cost £4750 in 1948. 'Nuff said.

## RAILTON (GB)

A 1989 attempt to revive a famous name, the second coming of the Railton was given a thumbs down by those who saw

The 1989 Railton

it. The base of this £90,000 extravaganza was the Jaguar XJ-S. Styling was by William Towns but had nothing at all to commend it.

**RAM** *see* LR ROADSTERS

## RAPID (CH)

A mini sports car powered by a mid-mounted single cylinder 350cc MAG engine. Thirty-five were made in the car's only year of production, 1946.

## RAPPORTE (GB)

First shown in 1980, the Rapporte Forte was a luxurious four-seat convertible using Jaguar running gear and engines, from the 3.4-litre XK unit to the 5.3-litre V12. The wedge-shaped body was of aluminium on a steel inner structure, trim and equipment of a very high order and turbocharging was an option. Unfortunately, an economic recession is not the best time to launch an expensive new car and few were made.

## REAC (F)

Built in Casablanca, 1953-54, the REAC had an aerodynamic fibreglass body on a Panhard Dyna floorpan and was notable for having an odd turret top. Above the waist it looked as though it was ready for T.E. Lawrence to lead a desert uprising, below the waist it looked like an advanced aerodynamic design; the trouble was that the two halves were not in harmony.

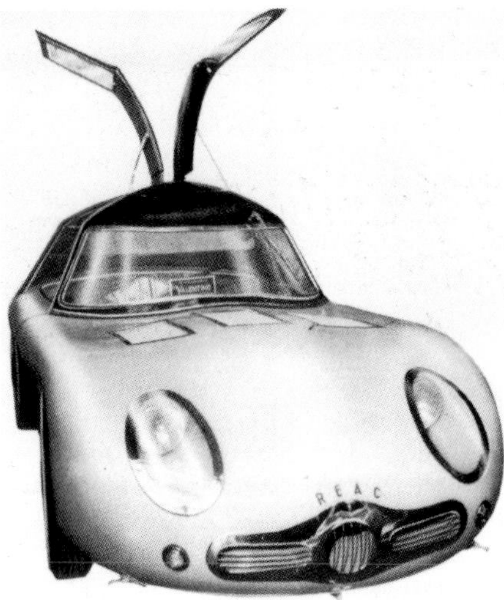


Gull-wing REAC-Panhard, 1953

## RED STALLION (USA)

An early 1980s copy of the Cobra 427 with a fibreglass body built by Jim Kellison, one of the most famous 1950s makers of bodies for specials, and a space frame designed by Paul Lamar, who had worked for Jim Hall's Chapparal team. Ford suspension was used, there was a choice of V8 engines, and one of the first buyers was Keke Rosberg, a man who knows a little about high performance motoring.

1979 Red Stallion 429

## REFLEX (GB)

A mid-engined kit car introduced in 1989. The fibreglass coupé body was fitted to a space frame and customers had a choice of Lancia Beta or Ford power units.

## REGAL T-BIRDS (USA)

A 1980s maker of a V8-powered copy of the 1955 Ford Thunderbird.

## REGIS AUTOMOTIVE (GB)

In the mid 1990s this company attempted to market the RAM 4S, a Cortina-sourced copy of the 1974 Lotus Elite. The Mohawk coupé of 1989 also used Cortina running gear in a sturdy tubular backbone chassis which allowed the fitting of larger engines such as the Rover V8. The 2+2 fibreglass body was made to a very high standard and, although it seemed inspired by the Lotus Excel, it was a distinct shape in its own right.

## RELIANT (GB)

From its foundation in 1935, Reliant specialised in lightweight three-wheelers. At first it made only vans, but a four-seater saloon, the Regal, was added in 1953. In the late 1950s it began to sell its expertise in fibreglass body manufacture and limited-series vehicle production to countries wishing to establish their own motor industries. From the first such collaboration, with Autocars Ltd of Israel, came the Sabra sports car, which was also sold as the Reliant Sabre.

After 1961 Reliant always had a sports car in its range alongside the three-wheelers which remained the company's staple product. The Sabre was something of a disaster, the Scimitar which replaced it established a good reputation, and the GTE 'sporting estate' acquired something of a cult status. The GTE was a clever piece of niche marketing and the small two-seat open car of 1984, the Scimitar SS1, should have been but was not. Reliant sold only a fraction of its projected 2-3000 cars a year and even a new body shape did not improve matters. Late in 1990 the company called in the receiver.

**Sabre, 1961-63. Prod: 100 complete 'Sabras' and 50 kits for Israel, plus 58 sold as Reliant Sabres.** Autocars of Israel bought the rights to Lesley Ballamy's ladder frame chassis and one of Ashley's fibreglass bodies (both originally designed for Ford-based specials) in order to make an instant sports car to sell to America. Reliant engineered the car with the 1703cc Ford Consul engine, an all-synchromesh four-speed ZF gearbox, and odd leading arm and coil spring front suspension. This arrived after the prototype, fitted with LMB split axle front suspension, failed to get out of the factory, its suspension having collapsed almost as soon as it was first driven.

Although well finished the Sabre was basically a ready-made Ford special which cost more than contemporary MGs and TRs yet could hardly top 90mph/145kmh. From 1962 the vulgar nose treatment was chopped and a GT version was offered. Apparently some of the Sabra kits were delayed at Israeli customs, and since Autocars was in no hurry to claim them they languished in a warehouse until being auctioned in the 1980s.

The four-cylinder Reliant Sabre of 1961

**Sabre Six SE2S, 1962-66. Prod: 77.** A much-improved car benefiting from the extra power provided by the six-cylinder 2553cc Ford Zephyr engine, which fed through either a Ford or ZF gearbox and gave a 110mph/177kmh top speed. The first 17 had the odd leading arm front suspension but those with TR4 double wishbones are to be preferred. Styling was improved, with rounded wheel arches and a chopped-off tail treatment, and all but two were GT models. Despite some competition success (first and second in class in the 1963 Alpine Rally) Reliant could not shake off the Sabre's kit car image, and since it cost only £30 less than an Austin-Healey 3000 the surprise is that any sold, let alone 77.

Sabre Six GT, 1962

**Scimitar SE4A, 1964-66. Prod: 297.** Reliant bought the rights to the handsome 2+2 coupé body which the Ogle design studio had first shown on a Daimler SP250 chassis. The pressed steel chassis was new but the running gear was the same as the Sabre Six until 1965, when the rear suspension was revised. Once that happened, the Scimitar became a fine car, with handsome looks matched by performance: 116mph/187kmh and 0-60mph in 11.4 seconds. Also in 1965 wire wheels were replaced by disc wheels and the ZF gearbox option was dropped.

1964 Scimitar SE4A

**Scimitar SE4B/SE4C, 1966-70/1967-70. Prod: 591/118.** A stiffer chassis and Ford's new 3-litre V6 engine further improved the Scimitar, which was now good for 121mph/195kmh and 0-60mph in ten seconds. The SE4C, an 'economy' version which had Ford's 2.5-litre V6 engine, found little favour. The popularity of the GTE caused Reliant to drop the coupé, which is still undervalued as a collector's car.

Scimitar SE4C, 1968

**Scimitar GTE SE5, 1968-75. Prod: 5127.** Reliant hit the jackpot when it asked Ogle to redesign the Scimitar as a sporting estate car. The idea of a sports estate had been around for a long time—there was the Allard Safari of 1952 and Tornado marketed an estate version of the Typhoon in 1959—but the GTE became the trend setter and the concept was copied by major manufacturers. The fact that Princess Anne became a GTE enthusiast did not damage its cause and for the first time Reliant found it had a chic car on its hands. Mechanically similar to the coupé, it had a new chassis with a longer wheelbase. It was a classic example of clever niche marketing—Tom Karen of Ogle did the work and deserves credit.

Scimitar GTE SE5

**Scimitar GTE SE6/SE6a, 1975-82. Prod: 543/3877.** The GTE concept was so right that having decided to replace it Reliant found it could do no better than make it larger. This was achieved by splitting the moulds and adding four inches to the wheelbase and three to the width. Together with this middle age spread came a new chassis which was softer in character, but the GTE retained its position as an ideal compromise between a sports car and family transportation. The SE6a version had a number of detailed improvements, including a stiffer scuttle to eliminate door sag, and larger rear brake drums. The Ford 2.8-litre V6 was introduced in 1979. Of special interest to the collector is that galvanised chassis frames were introduced in 1981.

Scimitar GTE SE6 came in 1975

**Scimitar GTE SE6b, 1982-86. Prod: 437.** The last expression of the GTE had a number of cosmetic improve-

Scimitar GTE SE6B

ments, a yet stiffer scuttle, and was 50lb lighter than its immediate forebear. A fall in demand for all large engined cars in the early 1980s saw production drop to 100/150 units a year and the range was axed in November 1986. The Bertone-designed SE82 project, a possible successor, had been shelved four years earlier. Later the GTE was revived by Middlebridge Scimitar Ltd ((qv), which bought the rights to it and the GTC, and Reliant undertook some re-engineering for the new owner. Despite the fact that Princess Anne was once again a customer, a high price tag did not help to sell cars and the new company went into receivership in 1990.

**Scimitar GTC SE8b, 1980-86.** **Prod:** 443. Another fine example of niche marketing, the GTC was one of the few four-seater rag tops available anywhere when it appeared in 1980. Ogle was responsible for the body, which retained the family look although that was becoming a little dated. A detachable hard top was available for winter motoring. Sales forecasts made in the late 1970s proved wildly optimistic as the car was launched at the beginning of a recession and never achieved the success it deserved. For the collector wanting a long-term investment, the GTC is the most desirable of all its family.

Scimitar GTC SE8B

**Scimitar SS1, 1300/1600, 1984-89.** **Prod:**—. Once more, Reliant predicted a trend, and with the SS1 it revived the classical formula for a popular sports car: two seats, rag top, good handling and simple (Ford) mechanicals. It should have been a runaway success, for it faced little competition in the market place at the time it was launched, but few people liked the fussy and dated lines by Michelotti. Some of the problems arose from the fact that Michelotti had

The 1984 Scimitar SS1

died before completing the design, and Reliant had committed itself so far that it felt it had to go ahead. Partly as a result of this panel fit was poor, as were many design details.

Worse, the car was underpowered: the 1300 was a snail and the 1600 could be humiliated by any number of hot hatches. Ford's fuel injected (XR3i) engine was the obvious solution but it would not fit under the bonnet, and the other obvious solution, the 2.9-litre Ford V6, was considered but not used. Annual sales were only a fraction of the predicted 3000 units. An opportunity had been missed, and a fine chassis with all-independent suspension was going to waste.

**SS1 1800Ti, 1986-89.** **Prod:**—. Because of long-term contracts with outside suppliers Reliant was unable to respond quickly to the almost universal dislike of the SS1 styling. But it was able to do something about the lack of power and under the bonnet of the 1800Ti (the 'SS' designation was dropped when Reliant entered European markets) was the turbocharged 1.8-litre engine from the Nissan Silvia, which is as sweet a turbo as any. With 135bhp, a top speed of 126mph/202kmh and a 0-60mph time of 6.9 seconds, the Scimitar took on a new lease of life and sales picked up immediately. The new engine demonstrated what a superb chassis there was under the skin, and it met USA emission laws. Distinguished from the Ford-engined cars by a black boot spoiler and alloy wheels, the car still met customer resistance due to its odd body.

Scimitar SS1 1800Ti, 1986

**SS2.** With styling by William Towns, this was a private commission by an American company, Universal Motors, who wanted a British sports car to sell. First shown in 1988, when it received a favourable reaction, it was likely to have had a Buick V6 engine and such goodies as air conditioning, but no cars had been made by the time Reliant went into receivership in 1990.

The 1988 SS2 concept car

**SST 1800 Ti/1400, 1990. Prod:—.** This was basically a restyled SS1 with another body by William Towns, this time commissioned by Reliant. It was generally thought to be not as pretty as the SS2 but still a great improvement on the original Michelotti effort. Since the body was much simplified it was easier to achieve good panel fit, but customers still found it too bland, especially since by 1990 there was a proliferation of open two seaters. The 1800Ti retained its exciting performance but the 'entry level' car with the 1.4-litre Ford CVH engine was considered disappointing. Top speed was only 98mph/158kmh (0-60mph in 12 seconds) and the engine was not sufficiently powerful to allow high-speed cornering when a car needs to be balanced on the throttle.

SST 1800 Ti, 1990

## RENAULT (F)

In 1898 Louis Renault, then aged just 21, made a car for his own amusement but some of his friends were so impressed by it that they asked him to build replicas. Within a matter of months a company was formed and dozens of customers had placed orders. That same year, 1899, saw Louis and his brother Marcel run in the Paris-Trouville race—and win the light car section. That and other competition successes helped establish the company, although Louis retired from the sport after Marcel was killed in 1903. A Renault won the first Grand Prix in 1906 but soon afterwards the company turned its back on competition for many years.

By 1913 Renault was the largest motor manufacturer in France, a position it has never lost. When the Second World War began Louis was loath to switch to military production since he was convinced the war would be short. He thus failed to contribute to the French war effort, but was soon forced to contribute to that of the Germans. This was held against him after Paris was liberated, as was his generally autocratic attitude to trade unions. He was imprisoned in September 1944 and was brutally treated by guards with old scores to settle against 'collaborators' and 'bosses'. Denied medical care, he died in October 1944, and his company was nationalised the following year.

Renault expanded in the 1950s and 1960s and became a major exporter as well as setting up overseas plants and entering manufacturing agreements with other companies. The company returned to motor racing in the 1970s and was particularly successful in Formula 2 and sports cars. In 1977 Renault entered Formula 1 with a turbocharged car and as this became more and more competitive other manufacturers were encouraged to follow suit.

Despite being a force in Formula 1 through its own team and, latterly, by supplying engines to other teams, Renault has only occasionally essayed performance cars for the road. It owns Alpine (qv) but the only sports car Renault has ever made entirely under its own name was the 5 Turbo 2 of 1983.

**5 Turbo 2, 1983-86. Prod: 3576.** Although this car had the name and something of the looks of the Renault 5, that was as far as it went. The Turbo 2 was a mid-engined two-seat coupé based on a 'homologation special' conceived for competition. This had aluminium panels and up to 250bhp whereas the road car had a steel body and a 160bhp version of the 1297cc pushrod four-cylinder engine. This engine (and its five-speed transmission) was basically the same as in the front-engined four-seat Renault 5 Gordini Turbo, but had been turned through 180 degrees.

The entire power train was fixed to a fabricated cradle which also carried the rear suspension. An abbreviated standard Renault 5 platform was used, with the usual torsion bar and double wishbone front suspension, while a coil spring and double wishbone layout was employed at the rear. Rear wheels had 7.5in rims (there were 5in rims at the front) and ventilated disc brakes were fitted to all four wheels.

With the standard 160bhp the car would reach 124mph/200kmh (0-60mph in 7 seconds) but that was only a starting point since Renault, through its Alpine arm, approved a number of tuning kits which increased power to between 180bhp and 240bhp. According to road test reports, the car's handling and road holding was easily able to cope with this power.

Renault 5 Turbo 2, 1983

## REPCO (AUS)

A GT car first shown in 1959, the Repco Dean was most notable for a very large rear window divided by a fin. Holden components were mounted in a tubular steel backbone chassis. The main object of the exercise was to draw attention to Repco and only a handful was made.

## REPLICAR (GB)

In 1979 Replicar (aka Classic Replicars) offered a ghastly copy of a Bugatti Type 35, following with a 'Type 43' and then a widely-praised fibreglass copy (made by Rawlsons of Dover) of the Ferrari 250LM. Like the 'Bugattis', this was based on a VW chassis and was available in two-seat and 2+2 forms. Replicar had little success with the car and by 1984 it had been taken over by K. Sharman & Co, but that did not last long either. Eventually the '250 LM' was taken on by Western Classics (qv) and completely re-engineered. In its brief life Replicar also offered a VW-based fibreglass copy of the SS100 imported from America.

Replicar 'Type 43' (above) and '250 LM' (below)

## REVOLUTION FIBREGLASS *see* PERENTTI

## RGS (GB)

In 1954 Dick Shattock, a noted special builder who was perhaps the first person in Britain to sell fibreglass bodies to special builders, revived the failed JAG project (qv) as the RGS. Some RGS bodies were also sold in America.

## RICKMAN BROS. (GB)

Originally the makers of Métisse motorcycle frames, which were immensely successful in racing and were even bought by police forces, Rickman turned to kit cars in 1987, starting with a range of 4x4-style vehicles which sold very well indeed.

In 1990 the company introduced the Métisse, a handsome 2+2 coupé based on a strong tubular backbone chassis and using Ford Sierra components. Since the Rickman brothers were serious engineers, this was an exceptional car. It could be delivered as a turn key car by any one of more than 20 Rickman agents and the car's excellence was emphasised by the fact that, almost as soon as it was announced, Ford offered direct assistance to the project.

1990 Rickman Métisse

## RINSPEED (CH)

A Swiss customiser and modifier, mainly working on Porsches.

Rinspeed R69, 1985

## RISING HOUSE MOTORS (USA)

In the late 1980s this company made an ill-favoured fibreglass copy of the Maserati T61 ('Birdcage') sports-racer on a VW chassis.

## RMB (GB)

Maker of the 'Gentry' kit car in the early 1980s. Its fibreglass body was a copy of the MG TF, on a Triumph Herald or Vitesse chassis. RMB followed that with the 'Heeley' (a copy of guess what?) but the company folded in 1987. However, the 'Gentry' was revived by SP Motors in 1989.

## RM CLASSICS (ZA)

A late 1980s maker of copies of the Lamborghini Countach and the Lotus Seven. As soon as the RM Seven was imported into Britain in 1990, Caterham Cars instigated legal action for use of the name 'Seven' and Westfield claimed infringement of copyright over the chassis (Caterham had successfully proceeded against Westfield in 1987 for exactly the same reason). The importer, Tiger Cars (qv), which had been assured that there would be no problems, lost heavily on the deal but responded by building the 'Six', which was a completely new design.

## RML *see* MALLOCK

## ROADSTER (BR)

First shown in 1981, the Roadster Victoria was a Morgan copy which used the running gear of the 1.6-litre VW Golf.

## ROARING '20s MOTOR CAR CO. (USA)

1980s maker of the 'Corsair', a V8-powered 1930s style roadster.

**Roaring '20s Corsair, 1983**

## ROBERTS MOTOR CO. (USA)

In the late 1980s Roberts began to convert perfectly respectable Chevrolet Corvettes into copies of the Ferrari Daytona Spyder. A couple of these were used in the television series *Miami Vice* but then Ferrari stepped in and offered a real car.

## ROBIN HOOD (GB)

In 1984 Robin Hood Engineering made a 'Ferrari Daytona Spyder' using Rover SD1 components and followed this with Daytona copies which were either Jaguar-based or built around a Triumph TR7. This was a case of ripping off the rich

**Robin Hood Jaguar-based RS Daytona Spyder**

**Robin Hood S7**

to sell to the poor. These cars disappeared after Ferrari began to take steps to protect its copyright. By 1990 the company was making the S7, a basic sports car which looked not unlike a famous car made by Caterham, but this used Triumph Dolomite components, and buyers had the choice of a space frame chassis or a monocoque made from mild steel.

## ROBLEY MOTORS (GB)

In 1990 this company took over production of the Leader sports car which had been created by Sylva (qv) and from 1985 had been made by Swindon Sports Cars (qv).

## ROCHDALE (GB)

Rochdale was easily the most successful of the dozens of companies which supplied bodies for British special builders in the 1950s and 1960s. It was founded in 1948 to make aluminium bodies for sports and racing cars, progressed to fibreglass shells in 1953 and then, in 1957, began to offer a chassis to make life easier for special builders using its bodies. In 1959 it showed the prototype of its radical fibreglass monocoque design, the Olympic, which enjoyed a nine-year production life, interrupted by a fire which destroyed the factory in 1961. In 1968, having sold over 1000 body shells, in addition to the Olympic, Rochdale decided there was more money in industrial fibreglass and changed direction.

**Rochdale 'Riviera' body on Ford running gear**

**Olympic, 1960-62. Prod: approx 150.** The Olympic was only the second car to be constructed entirely from fibreglass (the first was the Lotus Elite of 1957). Although lacking the cachet or sublime styling of the Elite, the Olympic had superior production engineering and would undoubtedly have sold in larger numbers had it not been for the fire at the factory in 1961. Available as a complete car or kit, the early Olympic used Riley 1.5 running gear although the live rear axle was suspended on coil springs. Thoroughly practical and safe (there was a built-in crash hoop), an Olympic is still a sensible buy for a collector with limited resources.

Rochdale Olympic in 1961

**Olympic II, 1963-70. Prod: approx 250.** Improved in detail with better access to the engine bay and third 'door' at the rear, the Mk II switched from BMC to Ford components. Base engine was the Cortina unit, the front suspension was changed from BMC torsion bars to Herald coils and double wishbones and there were disc brakes on the front. In 1968 Rochdale stopped supplying complete kits but, until 1972, still sold complete body/chassis units—about a hundred of these were sold.

Olympic II, 1963

## ROCKEFELLER YANKEE (USA)

A four-seat sports car with fibreglass body, a Ford V8 engine, and Ford suspension. A top speed of 100mph/160kmh was claimed. The company came and went in 1953.

## ROMANELLI (CDN)

An unsuccessful (1970) attempt to market an advanced sports car with a fibreglass body and a bespoke 6-litre V12 engine which was claimed to give 520bhp and, driving through a bespoke five-speed gear box, to give a top speed of 203mph/325kmh. It is difficult to assess how serious this project was, for the car never appeared.

## RONART (GB)

Basic, brutal, beautifully built, the Ronart W152 dates from 1986. It had a backbone space frame, aluminium body panels, Jaguar suspension and either a six-cylinder or V12 Jaguar engine. A serious piece of machinery, and one of the very few cars sold as kits which merit the term 'desirable'.

## ROYALE (USA)

From 1973, this company made copies of the Bugatti Type 35 and Mercedes-Benz SS on VW Beetle floorpans. Front-engined examples using Ford Pinto components were also listed and, in 1977, a plastic copy of the Bugatti Royale was made with GM running gear.

Lincoln-engined Royale Roadster

## R-SPORT (U)

In 1955 and 1956 the Uruguayan importer of Renault cars made a few dozen sports cars using Renault 4CV components in a locally-built chassis topped by a fibreglass body.

## RUF (D)

To call Alois Ruf a customiser of Porsches is to state the truth, but not the whole truth. Although Ruf does work on Porsches, his conversions are so extensive that the German government recognises him as a manufacturer in his own right, and his cars have distinct chassis plates. Ruf's conversion of the Porsche 911, for example, had its 3.2 litre engine bored out to 3.4 litres and, with twin turbochargers, produced a mighty 469bhp. This meant a verified top speed of just over 210mph/

338kmh (0-60mph in four seconds) which was better than the factory's 959.

1985 Ruf Porsche

## RUGER (USA)

Short-lived (1969-70) attempt by the famous gun maker to build a fibreglass copy of the 4½-litre Bentley using a 7-litre Ford V8 engine in a Vintage style chassis. The body shell was covered by naugahyde to give an 'authentic' fabric body effect and the 0-60mph time was claimed to be 7.7 seconds.

Ruger's Bentley copy, 1969

## RUSH (D)

'Rush' was the name under which, in the late 1980s, Jürgen Möhr sold copies of the AC Cobra and the Lotus/Caterham Seven. The 'Seven' could be had with a range of engine options including the Sierra Cosworth unit, with which the car was claimed to top 150mph/240kmh and sprint 0-62mph in 3.9 seconds. At the end of 1990 a tuned 280bhp version of this was announced which was claimed to be good for 169mph/272kmh (0-60mph in 3.7 seconds).

## RUSKA (NL)

This Dutch maker of beach buggies offered a fibreglass Mercedes-Benz SSK lookalike body on a VW Beetle floor pan in the late 1970s. In 1981 it offered a plastic Auburn Speedster body and, later, an SS100 copy.

The VW-based Ruska Regina Royal

## RVIA (USA)

From 1979 RVIA was the maker of the 'Sunrise', a nostalgia car with (distant) overtones of the 3-litre Bentley, using Ford V8 or Volvo four- or six-cylinder engines.

RVIA Sunrise roadster, 1983

## RW KIT CARS (GB)

In 1984 this company took over production of the 'Karma', an evocation of the Ferrari Dino, from Perry Automotive Developments (qv). It added to the range a new backbone chassis which allowed for a mid-mounted engine (previously VW running gear had been used). Front suspension was from the Ford Granada, there was a double wishbone layout at the rear, and a number of engine/transaxle options was offered. For a short time the company made a front-engined version of the Karma but this was not a success because the (Ford) engine had to be set too far back in the chassis in order to clear the low bonnet line.

## RYDER (GB)

In 1980 this company took over production of the VW-based Pelland (qv) and marketed it as the 'Rembrandt'. Ryder also made a Morgan-like car on the VW floor pan. By 1982 the 'Rembrandt' was being made by Graham Autos—but not for long.

# S

## SAAB (S)

As Saab's advertising constantly emphasises, the company is really an aircraft manufacturer—it was founded in 1937 with state backing to build defensive aircraft for the Swedish Air Force. Its first car, the 92, appeared in 1950 and used a DKW two-stroke engine, front wheel drive and an aerodynamic body. From the very beginning Saabs were successful in rallying, and its first victory occurred just two weeks after the marque was launched. Many major rally successes were scored until the end of the 1960s but in more recent years Saabs have become the choice of the professional person who wants something less bland than a BMW.

**Sonnet II/III, 1966-74. Prod: 10,219.** The first Sonnet was a concept car which did not reach production, thus Saab's first sports car was the Sonnet II. Launched with the American market in mind, it had a 841cc three-cylinder two-stroke engine which, thanks to a low pressure lubrication system, would run on ordinary pump fuel. From 1967 the 1.5-litre Ford V4 engine was fitted and this raised power from 60 to 65bhp. From 1970 the headlights retracted into the revised fibreglass body (Sonnet III). In the following year a 75bhp 1.7-litre engine was used and, thanks to a 0.32 cd, this version would top the ton. In 1973 American 'impact' bumpers were fitted but sales were never high enough for Saab to essay a successor.

Saab Sonnet MkIII

## SABER (USA)

Listed from 1977 to the mid-1980s, this was a coupé with a fibreglass body and bespoke chassis which used the running gear of the Opel GT.

1980 Saber GT

## SABRA (IL)

In order to publicise its new range of light cars made in conjunction with Reliant in 1961, Autocars Ltd of Haifa created a fully-made Ford special using an LMB chassis and an Ashley body. It was marketed by Reliant as the 'Sabre', and the full story appears under 'Reliant'.

Sabra prototype

## SAFIR (GB)

Safir is the only maker of Ford GT40 replicas; the others are copies or fakes. The first was built in 1981, and in 1985-86 Safir built a small series designated MkV. They then had the sole right to use the name GT40. The chassis numbers followed in sequence from the JW Automotive product. Safir revised the model and improved it in detail: the monocoque was made in zinc coated steel, for example, and the brakes were uprated; for the rest its specification was identical to the Ford MkIII. The Safir is not to be confused with the many copies, which tend to have space frame, not monocoque, construction.

The Safir MkV

## SAGA (F)

Introduced in 1980, this was a slightly scaled down copy of a Bugatti Type 55 sports car, using the four-cylinder dohc Alfa Romeo engine, in a choice of sizes, and Alfa Romeo running gear.

## SALMSON (F)

Car making was a side line for Salmson, whose main business was aero engines. However it had enjoyed great competition success with its small cars in the 1920s, until the arrival of the MG Midget fundamentally changed its market. From then on Salmson concentrated on small-capacity luxury cars and when it folded it had been making dohc engines longer than any other maker. In 1950 it made about 3,000 examples of a pre-war design but fiscal measures introduced by the French government saw sales dive, even though a new car was introduced in 1953.

Salmson's swan song was the 2300S, an Italianate two-seat coupé with a dohc 2.3-litre four-cylinder engine which delivered its 105bhp through a four-speed electromagnetically-operated Cotal gearbox. Although its chassis was conventional, and the engine lacked low-speed torque, it had excellent handling and performed well in national and international rallies. In 1955 it was joined by a convertible.

**Salmson 2300S coupé**

Lightly modified versions of the 2300S ran at Le Mans between 1955 and 1957 but without distinction. The end of the line came in 1957 when Salmson was taken over by Renault, by which time it had built 227 examples of its last car.

## SAM (PL)

In the classic movie *Casablanca*, Claude Raines' character was called 'Renault' and Sidney Greenstreet's was 'Ferrari'. Sam was a small sports car made in Poland between 1954 and 1956. A variety of engines were used in the twelve cars made, some were motorcycle units (Triumph, BMW etc), some came from cars such as Fiat, Lancia, and IFA. Even with the East-West barriers down, at the time of writing no sharper detail is available.

## SANDWOOD AUTOMOTIVE (GB)

This short-lived outfit of the early 1980s resurrected the practice adopted by all pre-war makers of quality cars of providing only a rolling chassis. It was a backbone affair which was fitted with an Alfasud engine, mounted amidships, with independent suspension all round.

## SANTA MATILDA (BR)

From 1977 this company offered a fibreglass 2+2 coupé using a locally built 4.1-litre straight-six Chevrolet engine in a Chevrolet floorpan.

**Santa Matilda SM 4.1 cabriolet and coupé, 1984**

## SBARRO (CH)

From 1971, Franco Sbarro has made a wide variety of exotic cars, each in small numbers. His first effort was a road-going coupé based on the Lola T70 Group 7 car, with a 5.4-litre Chevrolet V8. This was followed by the 'Tiger', a car whose styling was inspired by the Porsche 917, but which was powered by a 6.3-litre Mercedes-Benz V8, and the 'Stash' series of 2+2 mid-engined coupés and open cars, which all arrived in 1973.

**Mid-engined 6.3-litre Sbarro Tiger**

**1978 Sbarro Stash**

At first the Stash was offered with twin NSU Wankel engines or a supercharged VW K80 engine, but other cars in this family have been powered by six or eight-cylinder Mercedes-Benz engines. The Stash HS used a shortened and modified floorpan from the Mercedes 450SEL 6.9 and had all-independent suspension. Its 6834cc V8 engine delivered its 286bhp through a three-speed M-B automatic transmission, and gave a claimed top speed of 149mph/240kmh.

In 1973 Sbarro also produced a close fibreglass copy of the BMW 328 which, in standard form, was based on a reinforced BMW 316 floorpan but it was spoiled by having inappropriate wheels and tyres. In this form, a top speed of 112mph/180kmh was claimed but variants could be had which used other 3 Series floorpans and the 'America' version (based on the BMW 325) had a claimed top speed of 132mph/212kmh.

**BMW 328 copy by Sbarro**

Sbarro has also made copies of the Ford GT40 and some of these seem to have been confused with the real thing.

Apart from modified versions of production saloons, luxurious off-road vehicles and even electric cars, Sbarro has also made a copy of a Bugatti Royale (1979) with twin Rover V8 engines, and a copy of the Mercedes-Benz 540K (1981) with a 5-litre Chevrolet V8. Typical of Sbarro's extraordinary one-offs which draw the crowds at the Geneva Motor Show and drum up business was a tiny (10ft long) car which looked like a shrunken and smoothed Renault 5, but was powered by two Kawasaki Z1300 six-cylinder engines which gave a nominal 240bhp and meant that the car had a better power/weight ratio than a Porsche Turbo, Ferrari BB512 or Lamborghini Countach!

Since then Sbarro has operated as a constructor of 'one-off customised luxury vehicles according to plans discussed with its clients'. No two cars, therefore, are identical and the nearest thing to a production sports car made by the company in the late 1980s was the 'Challenge', a wedge-shaped coupé based on the Porsche 911, although other mechanical bases and chassis could also be specified. By 1990 the Challenge III was fitted with an enlarged (3.3 litre) Porsche engine which promised 180mph/290kmh for customers in a position to write a six-figure cheque.

**1985 Sbarro Challenge**

## **SCEPTRE** (USA)

A turn key 'nostalgia' car introduced in 1978, the Sceptre had a fibreglass body inspired by the Alfa Romeo 8C-2900, fitted to Mercury Cougar chassis. Power came from a 6.6-litre Mercury V8 engine and variants included a 2+2 and a coupé. Top speed was claimed to be 125mph/200kmh.

## **SCHEIB** (D)

1980s maker of a dreadful copy of the MG TD which used either VW Beetle or BMW running gear; a 'BMW 328' (with a BMW engine); a 'Mercedes-Benz SS' (on a Beetle floorpan); and a 'Mercedes-Benz 220S', although why anyone would want to copy that is a mystery.

**Scheib's '220S cabriolet', 1984**

## **SCHULZ** (D)

A 1980s modifier and customiser of cars from Mercedes-Benz.

## **SCM MOTORS** (USA)

A late 1980s outfit dedicated to taking new Chevrolet Corvettes (the company stressed that the Chevrolet warranty was unaffected) and converting them into 'Chevrolet Culebras'. These were high quality evocations of the Ferrari Testarossa but in open form.

## **SCORA** (F)

A two-seat coupé made between 1975 and 1978, it was mid-engined, with a choice of Renault 1.6- or 1.8-litre engines, which were transversely mounted. It had disc brakes, all independent suspension, and a five-speed gearbox.

## SCORHILL MOTORS (GB)

In 1987, this company took over production of the MFE 'Magic' (qv) and re-engineered it to take Ford Cortina running gear.

## SCORPIO (D)

A handsome fibreglass two-seat coupé with gull-wing doors, based on VW running gear and made between 1979 and 1981.

## SCORPION (GB)

The Scorpion was a neat mid-engined coupé which arrived in 1972, built by a company that was in difficulties the following year when it was hit by VAT. Designed by Tom Killeen, who was responsible for a number of specials, the first Scorpion had a tubular frame, all-independent suspension, 998cc Imp mechanicals, retractable headlights and gull-wing doors. Before the events of 1973, it seemed to have a good chance of survival since the Ginetta G15 and Clan Crusader were both doing well—it detracts nothing from a fine design that it was hurt by external circumstances. A revised version had a steel monocoque and another company was formed to press ahead but it failed in 1975. Later the design was available as the 'Mirage' kit car and since then it has emerged periodically under various other names.

1973 Scorpion coupé

## SCORPION (GB)

An early 1980s fibreglass copy of the MG TF based on a Triumph Spitfire chassis.

## SELTZER (USA)

Introduced in 1978, the Seltzer 'Willow' was a mid-engined kit sports car using a 2-litre Ford Pinto engine, with disc brakes all round, Triumph Spitfire front suspension and VW-Porsche rear suspension.

Seltzer Willow, 1980

## SEM (GB)

Designed by an ex-TVR engineer, and having something of the 1950s TVR Grantura about it, the SEM 'Saiga' was first shown in 1989. Under the rather unbalanced body was a space frame waiting to take Ford Cortina running gear.

## SERA (F)

Made in small numbers between 1959 and 1961, the Sera was a two seater, offered as a rag top or as a coupé, with a fibreglass body on a shortened Panhard floorpan.

The Panhard-based Sera, 1959

## SERAPH (GB)

The company was founded in the early 1980s by John Grossart, formerly chief design engineer of Girling, and Seraph's first car was the 'SS'. This had a mid-mounted Lotus Twin-Cam engine in a complex space frame, with equally complicated suspension, which was fine on the circuits but did not make for a practical road car. From this sprung the 115 and 215 models, the former using four-cylinder Ford engines, the latter a Ford V6—a top speed of up to 140mph/225kmh was claimed for this version. Front suspension was from the Ford Cortina, the live rear axle was located by double radius arms and a Panhard rod, and the space frame derived from the SS. A handsome fibreglass coupé body completed the plot. Road holding was said to be outstanding. Seraph also made a Ford-sourced version of the Bonito. The company was gone by the end of 1986.

## SERENISSIMA (I)

What is it about sports cars which makes people lose all reason? Count Volpi had become a laughing stock when his ambitious ATS Formula 1 team, which was set up to overthrow Ferrari, failed ignominiously. Many people would take up breeding budgies after that but no, in 1965 Volpi was throwing good money after bad as he revived the ATS road car (qv) under the name 'Serenissima' (the old name for the state of Venice). Most of the Serenissima GT was the ATS warmed over, but the engine was a major departure. In place of the single overhead camshafts of its forebear, there were new dohc heads and engine size was increased, with customers offered either a 300bhp 3-litre V8 or a 340bhp 3.5-litre version. A coupé with a new Ghia body was offered in 1968 but there were few takers. A Serenissima ran unsuccessfully in the 1966 Le Mans race and McLaren occasionally used a Serenissima engine in F1 that year, also without success. In 1970 the project was sold on, a revival was attempted, but it failed.

**Serenissima Ghia coupé, 1969**

## SETA (GB)

A gull-wing, wedge-shaped, fibreglass coupé body on VW Beetle running gear, made between 1976 and 1978.

## SHAMROCK (GB)

In 1955 the maverick Ulster designer Rex McCandless (designer of the Norton 'Featherbed' frame) unveiled a Ford-engined prototype which was intended to go into production as the 'Shamrock'. The prototype had been proven as a trials car in Ireland and it had a particularly interesting form of construction since the engine, gearbox and torque tube formed the backbone of the car. The only 'Shamrock' made in its final form, with an all-enveloping body, is on display in Belfast's superb transport museum—one can see why it did not succeed, it was too ugly and under-powered.

## SHAMROCK (IRL)

A short-lived (1959-60) fibreglass open four seater using the 1.5-litre BMC series 'A' engine.

**The 1959 Shamrock**

## SHARMAN (GB)

In 1984/5 this company briefly revived the Ferrari 250LM copy first built by Replicar (qv).

## SHAY REPRODUCTION (USA)

Maker, from 1978, of copies of Ford Model A roadsters and the 1955 Thunderbird, using modern Ford running gear.

**Shay 1955 Thunderbird copy, 1982**

## SHEEN (GB)

First shown in 1964, the Imperator, was a low and handsome two-seat coupé based on a Hillman Imp floorpan. The engine was offered in two states of tune. The standard car had a 70bhp engine, tuned by legendary Lotus mechanic Willy Griffiths, while a 105bhp 1147cc Paul Emery version was also available. Problems with component supply from Rootes meant only two were made, both with aluminium bodies.

## SHELBY (USA)

The foreword to this book explains why the Shelby Mustang is not covered in it and this entry simply refers readers to the foreword. The Mustang was a saloon car and not a sports car, because it raced in saloon car events and the Shelby Mustang was a modified saloon, like a Broadspeed Mini. Being a modified saloon does not downgrade it, indeed the author would prefer to own a Shelby Mustang to 90 percent of the cars within these covers...

**Shelby Mustang GT-350**

So that nobody can be in any doubt as to the car which has no place in this book, the most desirable Shelby Mustang the 1965/6 GT-350, is illustrated—after the 1967 model year the Mustang put on weight and inches, and by the 1969 model year it was positively porky. Along the way there had been interference by Ford (which wanted a slice of the lucrative 'add on' performance market) and by the American government through its emission and safety laws—in 1971 the most powerful Ford Mustang had 370bhp, three years later the most powerful Mustang had 105bhp but most had only 88bhp.

## SHELDONHURST (GB)

A shortened VW Beetle floorpan with a choice of fibreglass copies of the original Porsche and the 356 Speedster was offered in 1984. In the same year the company listed the 'Mongoose', a kit which originated in America and which cleverly combined the essence of a 1930s Ford coupé and the Lotus Seven. Sheldonhurst also made a Ford Granada-sourced Cobra copy and a Jaguar-based fibreglass copy of the XK120. The company folded in 1987 but the Cobra project was taken over by Brightwheel (qv) which had been a Sheldonhurst agent.

## SHELL VALLEY MOTORS (USA)

A 1980s maker of a Cobra 427 copy with a fibreglass and Kevlar body, a choice of Ford or Jaguar suspension and a range of V8 engine options.

## SIATA (I)

The Societa Italiana Applicazione Transformazione Automobilistiche was founded in 1926 by an amateur racing driver called Giorgio Ambrosini and, as the name implies, it tuned cars and sold performance equipment. Fiat products naturally received most attention and a particularly popular line was an ohv conversion for the Fiat Topolino.

In 1948 SIATA showed the 'Bersaglieri', a mid-engined three-seat sports car (with the driver in the middle) which had a tubular frame, a SIATA dohc four-cylinder 750cc engine largely made from aluminium, a two-speed rear axle, and independent suspension all round by coil springs and double wishbones. It appears that it did not reach production, or it sold only in tiny numbers, and the first popular model was the Amica. This was a handsome two seater with a full width body, available as an open car or a coupé, which used Fiat suspension on a tubular frame (independent front by transverse leaf spring and lower wishbones; quarter elliptics and a live axle at the rear) and Fiat 500 engines in various states of tune, including a 26bhp 750cc version. A special competition version of the Amica won the Italian Motor Racing Championship in 1948.

Siata Amica, 1950, had Fiat 500 power

1950 saw the little company link up with Fiat in one of the first examples of what became a regular Fiat ploy: a small company was encouraged to use Fiat components to fill niches which were too small and/or specialised for the giant. Thus came the 'Daina' which used Fiat 1400 running gear, again tuned and available in open or coupé forms, or with an optional 1.5-litre engine; and the following year saw the 'Rallye', a sports car which copied the MG TD, and which was also based on the Fiat 1400. The Daina and Rallye stayed in production until 1958. From 1951 SIATA had offered an optional five-speed gearbox of its own design.

1951 Siata Daina coupé with Farina body

Siata Rallye, 1951

Every sports car maker eyed the American market and in 1952 SIATA began to build cars with American engines. There was an Amica fitted with a 720cc Crosley engine, and a large coupé, the 'America', which used the Chrysler 'hemi-head' V8 in a tubular frame with independent torsion bar front suspension, and a de Dion rear axle. 1952 also saw a SIATA version of the Fiat 8V, with a Vignale body (with pop-up headlights, and available as a rag top or a coupé) and a five-speed gearbox which was sold as the SIATA 208 and stayed in production until 1955.

The Chrysler-engined Siata America

1952 Siata 208, based on the Fiat 8V

None of these cars sold in any great numbers and, apart from a minicar called the Mitzi, SIATA thereafter concentrated on building cars based on the Fiat 600 and Fiat 1100, with particular emphasis on the latter. From 1954 the company's main seller was the 1100-103 fastback coupé, which had the Fiat engine tweaked to give 52bhp. From then on SIATA built modified Fiats which sometimes had special bodies.

In 1959 SIATA joined forces with Abarth to form a new company called Siata-Abarth, but no joint-venture models came from this and the two marques continued to sell their own models. The arrangement ended in 1961 when SIATA became Siata-Auto, which tended to concentrate on the Fiat 1300 and 1500 models. Most Siatas thus made were tuned and modified versions of the standard four-seat saloon, but a very handsome GT body was also available.

The last Siata was the 'Spring' of 1968, a parody of the MG TD on a Fiat 850S floorpan which was available in various states of tune. It was one of the company's biggest sellers but the company folded in 1970. The Spring was revived by ORSA in 1973.

Siata Spring, 1970

## SIENNA CARS (GB)

A late 1980s manufacturer of Lamborghini Countach copies.

## SILHOUETTE (GB)

A two-seat fibreglass coupé of 1970, based on a VW Beetle floorpan. It featured an extraordinary interior finish called Velvetex, which was claimed to be waterproof and sound absorbent. At first made with conventional doors, a 1971 gull-wing version was called the 'Zagaroff', and three were exported to Italy. Twelve were made before the project folded in 1972.

1970 Silhouette

## SIMCA (F)

Founded in 1934 to make Fiats under licence in France, Simca soon began to establish a distinctive identity through a link with Amédée Gordini, whose heavily modified Simcas took five class wins at Le Mans before the War. In 1951 the first Simca-designed car, the Aronde, appeared (although its engine derived from the 1937 Fiat 508) and this sold over a million examples. On the back of this success, Simca bought a number of its rivals, including Talbot and Ford France, but Chrysler took a controlling interest in 1963. It was renamed Chrysler in 1976 and Talbot in 1979, after Peugeot took over. After 1981 not even this name survived.

**Eight Sport, 1948-56. Prod:—.** This was perhaps the most handsome car to be offered by a mass producer at the time, but then the coupé and convertible bodies were built by Facel Metallon under licence from Pinin Farina and closely resembled Farina's bodies for Cisitalia and Maserati. Originally its running gear was from the Simca-built Fiat 1100, but with a 50bhp high compression engine. One won its class in the 1949 Alpine Rally. In 1951 it received the running gear of the 1221cc Aronde, together with coil spring and double wishbone front suspension, and was restyled with more glass, wire wheels, a less curvy coupé body, a distinctly American grille and front bumper treatment, but the convertible was dropped.

Simca Eight Sport, 1950

**Aronde Océane, 1957-62. Prod: 11,560.** Perhaps best described as a two-seater rather than a true sports car, the Océane (aka Plein Ciel) was available as a coupé or a convertible. The big valve version of the 1290cc engine gave 57bhp but later cars had a revised five main bearing engine which gave 62bhp in 1961 and 70bhp in 1962. Its mechanical specification was fairly mundane but it sold on its mid-Atlantic styling, courtesy of Facel.

**Aronde Océane convertible, 1959**

**1000 Coupé, 1962-67. Prod: 10,011.** Simca's 1000 saloon was uglier than a car has a right to be, but Bertone waved a magic wand and transformed it into a crisp 2+2 coupé. The 52bhp four-cylinder engine would propel this little car to 90mph/145kmh, and disc brakes on all four wheels would bring it back to rest without fuss. An Abarth version with a 1.3-litre dohc engine was also available.

**Simca 1000 Coupé**

**1200S, 1967-71. Prod: 14,471.** This model had the shape of 1000 coupé with a stronger frontal treatment and louvres in the boot. The engine was enlarged to 1204cc and, with 85bhp, top speed increased to just over the 'ton' although this was stretching the chassis' capabilities. Like the 1000 coupé it was sold only as a left hooker, there was an Abarth version and, unfortunately, it was prone to rust.

**Revised frontal treatment for the Simca 1200S**

## SINGER (GB)

Singer moved on from bicycles and tri-cars to become a 'proper' car maker in 1905, went into receivership in 1908, was revived in 1909, and then soldiered on as a small-to-medium company with its own niche in the British motor industry. In 1933 it began to make sports cars and at first these did well. Then in the 1935 Tourist Trophy the works Singers all suffered steering failure and photographs of the crashed cars went around the world. This was a setback to the expanding company and sales dipped, but Singer survived.

After the War it revived its range, which was bland, and for a time it offered some sporting cars. These were short-lived and Singer decided to contest a market sector which Rover also targeted. Singer tried hard, it was one of the few British cars of the time with an overhead camshaft, and the 'Hunter' version of its base saloon was admired for its handsome bonnet mascot and metallic paint. Another variation broke new ground by being offered without a spare wheel because, it was said, the new breed of tubeless tyres was so reliable that there was no point in fitting a spare. A frivolous accessory, in the shape of a dohc cylinder head made in conjunction with HRG, did not see production.

At the end of 1955 Singer was taken over by the Rootes Group and was soon being sold as an up-market Hillman. The Singer name later appeared on Chrysler cars, but when it disappeared in 1970 the decision did not bring Singer owners rioting in the streets; by then it had become no more than a badge, and by the time it was dropped nobody wanted to wear the badge.

**Nine Roadster/Roadster 4A/Roadster 4AB, 1939-49/1949-50/1951-52. Prod: 2500/3390/1000.** A four-seat rag top with little to commend it, this model sold vigorously until 1952 simply because Singer was able to exploit a sellers' market. All had a 1047cc sohc four-cylinder engine which delivered a mighty 36bhp through a three-speed gearbox. During the model's life there were detail changes to the specification (some cars had overriders on the bumpers, for example) but the only significant move was on the short-lived Roadster 4AB when the old front beam axle gave way to coil sprung independent suspension. If anyone tells you that he was exceeding 70mph in one of these, he is shooting a line.

1946 Singer Nine Roadster

**SM Roadster, 1951-55. Prod: 3440.** The SM Roadster was a 4AB fitted with the short-stroke sohc 1497cc SM engine and hydromech brakes. 1953 saw a 58bhp twin-carburetter option and also its release onto the home market. Most desirable, and most rare, of all postwar Singers are the Bertone-bodied SM Roadsters which the American importer had created.

SM Roadster, 1951

Singer SMX failed to please

**SMX, 1953. Prod: 6.** A variation of the SM Roadster with smaller wheels, a staid enveloping style and, on some cars, a fibreglass body—this was the first time this material was used by a mainstream manufacturer in Europe.

## SIVA (GB)

Founded by Neville Trickett, between 1969 and 1976 Siva made a wide range of kit cars including buggies, 'Edwardian' cars, runabouts and 'Moke' style vehicles. 1971 saw the arrival of the S160 GT, a handsome and much imitated gull-wing coupé based on VW running gear. The following year, and not long before the energy crisis, saw the S530 GT which had a similarly styled body but it incorporated a monocoque and had a mid-mounted 5.3-litre Chevrolet V8 engine. In the circumstances it is not surprising that few were made. The handsome and futuristic Saluki coupé, based on VW running gear, came in 1973. There was a downturn in the market for kit cars and Siva folded three years later.

Siva S530 GT, 1972, with midships V8

## SIVA (I)

Maker between 1967 and 1970 of the 'Sirio', a mid-engined two-seat coupé using a tuned (130bhp) German Ford 20M V4 engine.

## SJ MOTOR ENGINEERS (GB)

From 1984 this company made the 'Milano', a handsome four-seat fibreglass cabriolet body designed to rescue the useable bits from rusted Alfa Romeo GTVs, of which there was no shortage. The body was inspired by Pininfarina's 1980 exercise on the Jaguar XJS. The 'Sportiva' of 1986 was a two-seat version of the 'Milano'.

## SKODA (CS)

Skoda was founded in the 19th Century and became one of Europe's largest armaments manufacturers. Car production began in 1923 but until the Second World War production figures were relatively small and never exceeded the 4452 cars of 1937. After the War the company was nationalised and became Czechoslovakia's main motor manufacturer; Skoda produced the bread and butter cars while Tatra made the prestige vehicles for the use of Party functionaries and the like.

During the postwar period, Skoda twice offered models which passed for sports cars behind the Iron Curtain: the 1100 Roadster of 1948 and the two-seat Felicia convertible

1961 Skoda Felicia convertible

One of two 1100cc Skoda 440s fitted with fibreglass bodies (by Karosa) in 1956 for national rallies

made between 1956 and 1964. Under their different bodies both cars were fundamentally the same: both had a backbone chassis, all-independent suspension by transverse leaf springs and swing axles, and a front mounted four-cylinder ohv engine. The 1100 Roadster had a 32bhp 1089cc engine, the Felicia had a 50bhp 1221cc version of the same design.

The requirements of the Communist regime meant that Skoda's engineers operated under severe constraints, but when allowed a little licence they could respond, as shown by the rally versions of their mundane saloons and by an advanced dohc 1100cc sports racer which was made in 1958.

## SKORPION (USA)

Made between 1950 and 1953 the Skorpion began as a simple two-seat body fitted to a lowered Crosley chassis. In this form it was available as a kit for $445, or complete for $1200. Soon customers could specify Morris Minor, Renault 4CV, or Ford V-8-60 engines, the latter being a 2.2-litre side-valve unit. The 'Super' of 1953 used a cut and shut Studebaker Champion chassis with a choice of Studebaker or Ford engines. The pick of the bunch was the Ford V8 in a Crosley chassis.

Odd looking 1953 Skorpion

## SKYLINE (USA)

Short-lived 1953 attempt to market a two-seat sports car using the Kaiser Henry J chassis and some of the lower body panels. Although the styling was not special, unusually for the time there were such safety features as seat belts, a padded dashboard and recessed knobs while, at a touch of a button, the hard top swung into the boot.

## SOMMER (DK)

In the early 1980s, O. Sommer A/S of Denmark combined with BRA of Britain, to re-engineer the latter's Cobra copy to take Volvo 240 Turbo running gear. The fully assembled result, the 'OScar', sold for a massive £24,000 in 1983.

Sommer OScar

## SORRELL (USA)

Late 1950s maker of chassis frames and fibreglass bodies designed to accept domestic running gear.

1956 Sorrell SR-100

## SORVA (F)

This firm was founded in 1969, and most of its output was beach buggies and conversions of mass-produced saloons. It did, however, essay the LM2, a two-seat open car or coupé based on a modified VW Beetle floorpan which was still in production in 1990.

## SOUTHEASTERN REPLICARS (USA)

Maker since 1977 of copies of cars such as the 1928 Stutz Black Hawk, the Cord 815E and the Auburn Speedster. These were based on contemporary American (mainly GM) floorpans and came with a high level of equipment. The Stutz Speedster was more faithful to the original, in that its chassis was a reproduction of the 1928 car, although the 'boat-tail' body was in fibreglass. With a 4.9-litre Ford six (a truck engine) it had a claimed top speed of 116mph/186kmh.

**Southeastern Replicas Speedster, 1980**

## SOUTHERN ROADCRAFT (GB)

From 1984 SR made a fibreglass Cobra copy and, in 1987, added the SR V12 Spyder. This was styled after the Ferrari Daytona Spyder and used Jaguar V12 components.

## SOUTH WEST REPLICAS (GB)

Founded in 1989 as a kit car build service, this company announced the Xanthos Type 90 in 1990. It was a faithful copy of the 1962 Lotus 23 sports-racer available as a kit or complete. There were a number of engine options up to the Lotus Twin Cam unit and, although mainly intended for kit car racing, a road going version was available.

## SOVAM (F)

Maker of front-engined, front wheel drive, fibreglass coupés between 1965 and 1968. The customer had a choice of Renault engines between 850cc and 1300cc (120mph/ 193kmh was claimed with the latter unit) and suspension was independent all round by torsion bars.

**Sovam 1300GS**

## SP MOTORS (GB)

This was the last known maker (in 1990) of the RMB (aka TM) Gentry, a kit car copy of the MG TF.

**SP Motors TM Gentry**

## SPARKS (USA)

An outrageous nostalgia car first shown in 1980; the Sparks was a 1930s roadster pastiche built as a turn key car and

**Sparks Turbo Phaeton, 1980**

was offered in a limited edition of 300. It was based on a Cadillac floorpan, built of steel, with a 6-litre V8 engine (turbocharger optional), and featured a rumble seat and a removable hardtop.

## SPARTAN (GB)

Founded in 1973 and still active in 1990, Spartan has been an immensely successful maker of kit cars—over 3500 examples have been sold in 25 countries and there is an enthusiastic owners' club. All have had the same basic 'traditional' styling, which was designed around the Triumph Herald chassis, and this used a combination of aluminium panels to form a 'semi-monocoque' central section, and fibreglass wings. A bespoke chassis was offered from 1974, and a 2+2 version came in 1975. Many different engines have been fitted but Ford units have been by far the most popular. The most recent cars were largely sourced from post-1971 Ford Cortinas.

Spartan Roadster

## SPEEDEX (GB)

A company created by Jem Marsh (of Marcos) in the late 1950s to service builders of Austin 7 and Ford specials. In 1960 it offered a space frame to take Ford running gear and most of the current proprietary fibreglass bodies, including the 'Scirocco GT' body made by Speedex itself. In the mid-1980s the 'Speedex' name was revived as the accessories branch of Marcos.

## SPIRIT MOTORS (GB)

A mid-1980s maker of a fibreglass Mercedes-Benz SS copy on a Beetle chassis.

## SPORTS CAR ENGINEERING (USA)

This company imported the Microplas Mistral body from England and sold it in the late 1950s as the 'Spyder'. It also made boxed and tubular chassis to go under the body. These would accept domestic running gear.

## SPORTS CAR SERVICES (GB)

Short-lived late 1980s maker of a Cobra copy.

## SPYDER (GB)

The greater part of Spyder's business has been the manufacture of replacement chassis for Lotus Elans and Europas and some people claim that these are superior to the original items. In 1985 Spyder announced the 'Silverstone' which was a basic sports car in the Lotus Seven idiom. It had a spaceframe chassis with a central fabricated backbone section, and integral roll bar, which had independent suspension all round by coil springs and double wishbones.

As with all cars of this type, performance depended on the power unit fitted. With what was described as a 'mildly tuned' dohc Toyota Celica engine, the works claimed a top speed in excess of 120mph/193kmh and a 0-60mph time approaching five seconds. One significant way in which the Silverstone differed from other cars of its type was that it had a lockable boot. Spyder built about forty cars between 1985 and 1988 but found that it was not making money at the price it was charging and dropped the car.

Spyder Silverstone, 1985-88

## SQUIRE (I)

An early 1970s maker of a copy of the SS100 which was built around the running gear of those American Fords (e.g. Mustang and Maverick) which used the Ford straight-six engine. Most cars went to the States.

## SQUIRE (USA)

Maker of a V8-powered 'nostalgia' car originally called the 'Doval', designed by Grand Prix Metalcraft. It had a Ford chassis, fibreglass body and MGB doors.

## SQUIRE SPORTS CARS (GB)

Introduced in 1984, this was a high quality turn key recreation of the rare, and breathtakingly beautiful, Squire sports car of the 1930s. It used Ford components until 1986 when the Alfa Romeo 105 engine was specified, but the body was built in the

The 1984 Squire

traditional manner with metal panels on a wooden frame. One of the best copies ever made, it has been built in strictly limited numbers and remains almost as rare as the original Squire.

## STANGUELLINI (I)

The father of Vittorio Stanguellini was the first person in Modena to own a car (reg: MO 1) and, given the fact that Modena is now synonymous with the motor car, it may come as a surprise to know that it was as late as 1910 when he bought it. The Stanguellini engineering company was founded in 1879 by Vittorio's grandfather and by the time Vittorio took over, in 1929, the family business included a Fiat agency.

Vittorio began to modify Fiats for competition, and was very successful. In 1938 he formed his own team, Squadra Stanguellini, and built a range of Fiat-based sports cars, often with very handsome aerodynamic bodies. For the rest of his manufacturing career Stanguellini concentrated on competition cars but just after the Second World War the company offered some road cars. In 1947 came a four-seat berlinetta, with a Bertone body and the tuned engine and running gear of a Fiat 1100 in a tubular chassis. It was also possible to order a 1.5-litre version of this engine. In 1948 a similar line was followed in a two-seat car based on the Fiat 750.

**A delightful Ala d'Oro Stanguellini sports racer**

By 1950 Stanguellini had made dohc ('Bialbero') versions of the 750cc and 1100cc Fiat engines; 60bhp was claimed for the smaller engine, 80bhp for the 1100, but it is likely that these claims were exaggerations—Italian horses at the time were usually not as strong as horses from other countries. These engines were available for road cars, and a few were built, but each was a bespoke car so few generalisations apply. Following competition practice the chassis were rugged rather than inventive (because there were a lot of road circuits in Italy with cobble stones, manhole covers and the like) and the usual specification included transverse leaf spring and lower wishbone front suspension with a live rear axle suspended on coil springs. The 750cc Bialbero road car was claimed to do 112mph/180kmh, the 1100cc version 120mph/193kmh.

Most Stanguellinis, however, were sports-racing cars which were successful in Italy but only rarely appeared abroad—in the 1950s entrants of small-capacity sports cars tended play in their own back yard, save for the odd trip to Le Mans. By the time such cars met more often on the international scene Lotus was in its stride and was dominating the 1100cc class.

**Stanguellini 1100 Berlinetta by Bertone, 1953**

Stanguellini received a second wind when Formula Junior was announced in Italy in 1957. This was a single-seater category using production engines and at first Stanguellini was very successful, going on to make more than 100 examples of its Fiat-based front-engined car. A Stanguellini won the first International Championship in 1959 but, from 1960, the British Formula Junior constructors were dominant. Stanguellini struggled on, making odd competition cars through to 1966. Thereafter it concentrated on tuning equipment and subcontract design for other companies.

**1957 Stanguellini Bialbero 750 Sport**

## STARDUST (GB)

An unconvincing 1990 plastic copy of the 'long nose' Jaguar D Type, using Ford Escort Mk1/2 components.

**Stardust 'D Type', 1990**

## STATUS (GB)

Brian Luff was an ex-Lotus man who also had a large input into the Clan Crusader. While working as manager of the Lotus Vehicle Engineering Division, he saw how the Seven had become more refined and expensive, and a far cry from the motorcycle on four wheels for the impecunious enthusiast it had been originally. He was in a particularly good position to form a judgement since he had been in charge of the design of the Lotus Seven Series Four.

Luff set out to fill the gap he saw in the market and his car had the usual recipe of a space frame and fibreglass body but, given his background, these were unusually well-engineered and well finished. Front and rear suspension was by wide track double wishbones with coil springs and the Mini engine/gearbox unit was mounted amidships. Originally it was planned to sell two bodies so that a customer could enjoy open air motoring in the summer and bolt on a GT shell for winter, but in the event only the open car was made. A hardtop was available from 1972 but, like so many projects, it was hit hard in the fateful year of 1973 and disappeared soon afterwards when about 20 cars had been made. Later the project was briefly revived and a four-seater GT car was announced, but was stillborn.

## STEADMAN *see* OTTERCRAFT

## STEANEY AUTOMOTIVE DEVELOPMENTS (GB)

Maker of the 'SN1', which was originated by the people behind the 'Charger' kit car (*see* Embeesea). The SN1 was offered in 1982 and was a fibreglass 2+2 coupé on a VW Beetle floorpan.

## STEERING WHEEL (USA)

A 1980s maker of a two-seat nostalgia car (inspired by the Mercedes-Benz 540K) which used a 5.7-litre General Motors V8 and was claimed to be able to top 130mph/210kmh. If anyone has ever achieved that it is likely to have been a real white knuckle job, but the point about such cars is that one does *not* do 130mph because at that speed one cannot be seen and admired by members of the lower classes.

**Steering Wheel Berlina Coupé, 1984**

## STERLING (USA)

Since the 1970s maker of the 'Sovran', a version of Richard Oakes' Nova body based on the floorpan of a VW Beetle.

**1980 Sterling Sovran**

## STEVENS (GB)

In 1977 Tony Stevens, formerly a stylist with Rootes, essayed the Sienna sports car on a Reliant Kitten chassis. It did not go into production but three years later he came up with a new design, using Kitten running gear in a bespoke space frame which was immensely strong and stiff. Front suspension was by coil springs and double wishbones, there was a live rear axle, and the engine and gearbox were set back in the frame for optimum balance. Some 40bhp from the Reliant 850cc engine does not sound much but it had been enough for the Frogeye Sprite, and the Cipher was lighter and more aerodynamic than the Frogeye. Road testers raved about its style, economy, performance and practability, and Reliant built two cars for evaluation, but decided it could not afford to prepare it for production.

Reliant decided instead to build a Ford kit car (the Scimitar SS1) and burned its fingers; in particular nobody liked the bodywork whereas everyone liked the Cipher. Later Stevens fitted Renault running gear and when last heard of was still looking for a backer to put his car into production; buyers deserve it.

**The Stevens Cipher**

## STIMULA (F)

Built by the same family as made the De La Chapelle (qv), this was a fairly accurate fibreglass copy of a 1932 Bugatti Type 55 roadster, introduced in 1978. Running gear was from the Opel Commodore, with a choice of 2.5- or 2.8-litre engines, set in a tubular and box section chassis. With the larger engine, a top speed of 124mph/200kmh was claimed.

Stimula 55 Series II

## STORM (USA)

A two-seat sports car which combined Bertone bodywork and a 250bhp Dodge V8 engine. It appeared in 1954 and it is likely that only the prototype was made.

## STORY (USA)

This was an unsuccessful 1950 attempt to market a sports car. Willys suspension was used on a bespoke chrome-molybdenum frame the rigidity of which was aided by steel body panels welded to it to form a semi-unitary construction. Low and handsome, its styling was Italianate and it used a tuned (113bhp) 2.2-litre Ford V8-60 engine with Offenhauser cylinder heads. A top speed of 105mph/170kmh was claimed, the first car made found a ready buyer and a four-seater was planned with torsion bar suspension and a choice of larger and more powerful engines. It seems, however, that production did not exceed the prototype.

The Story sports car of 1950

## STRALE (I)

Introduced in 1967, the Strale was a fibreglass coupé fitted with a 6.3-litre Chrysler V8 engine which, in tuned form, was claimed to give the car a top speed of 180mph/290kmh. Few, if any, were sold.

## STRAMAN (USA)

Since the late 1960s Richard Straman has specialised in cutting the tops from coupés to make rag tops. Provided that a car has only two doors, Straman will consider the project; his most famous conversion was a Ferrari Testarossa.

## STREET BEETLE (GB)

Guess what running gear lies under this late-1980s copy of a Porsche 356 Speedster.

Street Beetle's Chesil Speedster

## STROSEK (D)

A German customiser, working mainly with Porsches.

## STUDEBAKER (USA)

In 1852 the Studebaker brothers set up in business as blacksmiths and wagon makers and the firm's first (electric) cars appeared in 1902. By 1930 the marque was America's fourth largest seller behind Ford, Chevrolet and Buick. That pinnacle of popularity was never repeated, however, and after the Second World War the company engaged in niche marketing with particular emphasis on 'European' styling. Based in Indiana, Studebaker was distant from the components industry which was centred on Detroit, productivity at its main plant was significantly lower than at those of its rivals, the

The 1963 Studebaker Avanti

company was too small to engage in the price wars which occasionally flared, and in 1964 the American company folded. It was followed, two years later, by the Canadian branch.

In 1960 Studebaker introduced the Avanti, a four-seat coupé with a fibreglass body styled by Raymond Loewy whose other credits included the classic Coca Cola bottle. The chassis followed conventional American practice with a separate frame, wishbone front suspension and a live rear axle, but front disc brakes were specified for the first time on a mass-produced American car. The 4.7-litre V8 engine, which drove through a four-speed manual gearbox, could be had with an optional supercharger producing 240bhp (R1 model). By 1963 the 5-litre R3 was giving 290bhp and one of these achieved 170mph/273kmh at Bonneville, while a specially developed car reached 196mph/315kmh. When Studebaker closed its American arm in 1964, two enthusiasts took over the Avanti and, in 1990, it was still in production (*see* Avanti II).

## SUNBEAM (GB)

Sunbeam's first car was made in 1899 and from 1911 to 1925 Sunbeam was Britain's main, and often only, entrant in Grand Prix racing. Sunbeams ran at Indianapolis in 1921 and in 1923 Henry Segrave led home a Sunbeam 1-2-4 in the French GP. In 1920 Sunbeam amalgamated with Talbot and Darracq (which were British owned by then) and became known for quality touring and sporting cars. The group was in trouble in the 1930s and was taken over by Rootes in 1935. Between 1937 and 1953 no Sunbeams were made, although Rootes marketed touring versions of Hillman and Humber models under the name 'Sunbeam-Talbot'. After Chrysler bought Rootes in 1964 the Sunbeam name began to fade and it disappeared in 1974.

**Alpine, 1953-55. Prod: approx 3000.** This was really a two-seat body on a reinforced chassis from the Sunbeam-Talbot 90 MkII saloon. Thus it had coil spring ifs, a hypoid rear axle, and a high-compression 80bhp version of the 2.3-litre four which had first seen service in the Humber Hawk. It was heavy and a little breathless—more show than go, in fact, as its column gearchange indicated. Alpines were rallied extensively, with some success—a private entry saloon won the 1955 Monte Carlo Rally—but most of the success was due to the fact that Sunbeam employed world class drivers of the cut of Stirling Moss.

Alpine on the 1954 Alpine: Stirling Moss and John Cutts on the Stelvio

**Alpine I/II/III, 1959-60/1960-63/1963. Prod: 11,904/19,956/5863.** Under the pretty, rather feminine, skin was the floorpan of a Hillman Husky (and Commer Cob van). The MkI had an 83bhp 1.5-litre engine and front disc brakes and was good for nearly 100mph/160kmh. The MkII had a 1.6-litre unit and better trim and ride. The MkIII had a stiffer front end, telescopic rear dampers and servo brakes; a GT hardtop was available but while this was detachable, there was no hood. The Alpine was not a bad little car but it was derided by most sports car owners because it was perceived as being too pretty and lacking in machismo (it had wind-up windows, for Heaven's sake). The Brighton coachbuilder, Harrington, made about 400 2+2 coupé conversions on MkI and II Alpines and tuned versions were available.

1959 Alpine I

**Alpine IV/V, 1964-65/1965-68. Prod: 12,406/19,122.** Restyled with smaller tail fins, and with synchromesh on the bottom gear, the MkIV was still gutless and effete (automatic transmission was an option). The MkV had a 92bhp 1725cc engine, which meant a genuine 100mph/160kmh but it was not enough to change the image. Some cars become more interesting as time passes, however, and the Alpine is one of them; they are much cheaper than many of their contemporaries, although rust is a particular problem.

The 1592cc Alpine IV

**Tiger I/II, 1964-66/1967. Prod: 6495/571.** Carroll Shelby, he of the Cobra, was given the job of fitting the Ford 4260cc V8 to the Alpine IV and, wisely, he restricted it to the 'cooking' 164bhp version—after all the basis of the car was still the Hillman Husky. The result was a car with rack and pinion steering, a limited slip differential, and nearly double the Alpine's power, which meant 120mph/193kmh and 0-60mph in nine seconds. The Tiger I was available in Britain in 1965 but the Tiger II, with 200bhp 4.7-litre lump, was sold only in the States. The Tiger was not sufficiently different from the Alpine to do well, and it suffered from the Alpine's limp-wristed image, but it was a much under-rated car. With Chrysler taking control just as the Ford-engined car was being released, it is not surprising that its life was short.

1964 Sunbeam Tiger

## SUN CAR (F)

Introduced in 1980 and revised in 1984, the Sun Car Roadster was a 2+2 open car with 1930s styling which used front wheel drive and a 1397cc Renault engine and drive train. One was not forced back in one's seat when this beast was under way.

Sun Car Roadster, 1984

## SUNLIT (GB)

Short-lived (1983-84) attempt to market a fibreglass coupé body, of Italian origin, using components from the Fiat 500 or 126.

## SUPER TWO (GB)

A cheap (£99 on its introduction in 1960) and basic kit car consisting of a tubular chassis and a simple fibreglass body with cycle wings. Buyers added an old Ford engine and gearbox and stirred. About two hundred were sold in its five year production, and some were even completed. It was also known as the 'Bowden' and was made by Super Accessories.

## SUTOL (GB)

Late 1980s copy of the Lotus 23 sports-racer which usually used a four-cylinder Ford engine mated to a VW Beetle gearbox. It was intended both as a road car and for use in kit car racing.

## SVC (GB)

A basic kit sports car of the mid-1980s, the SVC Spectre had a fibreglass body on a space frame chassis with Ford Cortina components and was offered with engine options up to the 2.8-litre Ford V6.

## SWALLOW (GB)

The Swallow Coachbuilding Company (1935) Limited was created by William Lyons, but while his original firm, Swallow Sidecars, became best known for its cars which featured special bodies on standard chassis, and developed into Jaguar, Swallow Coachbuilding made only sidecars. In 1945, as part of Lyons' postwar expansion, it was sold to Tube Investments but in the 1950s the sidecar market declined. Frank Rainbow, an engineer with TI, was asked to design a sports car and ten months after the request the 'Doretti' was in production. For a newcomer it sold strongly, particularly in California, so much so that Jaguar told TI to choose

1954 Swallow Doretti (above) and the Sabre (below)

between marketing a rival or continuing to supply it with components. Although the Doretti made a profit in its ten months of production, it was not enough and TI chose to keep Jaguar happy.

**Doretti, 1954-55. Prod: 276.** Because the Doretti used Triumph TR2 running gear it is sometimes dismissed as a re-bodied TR2 with inferior performance, but it was as distinctive a car as, say, a TR-engined Morgan. A frame built from Reynolds 531 tubing was completed by a handsome body with aluminium panels on a sheet steel inner skin. As a hand-built, well-equipped 100mph/160kmh sports car the Doretti was a bargain despite limited boot space, a result of the haste in which it had been conceived, but fitted luggage came as standard and naturally it was made of leather as were most of the car's trimmings. A second model, a 2+2 called the 'Sabre', was much more practical and was ready for production (three were made) when politics killed the project. Triumph was prepared to take over production but that plan fell through when the company's chairman was seriously injured in a road accident.

## SWIFT (GB)

A short-lived early 1980s attempt to market a high quality 1930s style sports car. The Swift FJ 280 used a 2.8-litre Ford V6 engine in a multi-tubular backbone chassis and the body was entirely of aluminium. It was available in component form or fully assembled.

Swift FJ280

## SWINDON SPORTS CARS (GB)

In 1986 this company began producing the 'MPH' and the 'Brooklands' which were sold under the marque name 'Vincent' (after their designer and first builder, Martin Vincent and not to be confused with the contemporary builder of the Vincent 'Hurricane'). Both were fibreglass copies of the 1934 Riley MPH, but the Brooklands had cycle mudguards. There was a choice of Ford engines, front suspension was Triumph Spitfire and the live rear axle was Ford Escort. The company also took over production of the Sylva Leader SS in 1985. In 1991 the Vincent MPH and Brooklands were taken over by Dwornik Engineering.

## SYLVA (GB)

Jeremy Phillips, a structural designer, began marketing the Vauxhall-based 'Sylva Star' kit car in 1982. Two years later he revised it and called it the 'Leader' but although he sold about 70 kits of the two types, he felt that the real market was for a more basic car and so sold on the project, which became known simply as the 'Leader'. It was made first by Swindon Sports Cars and then, from the end of 1990, by Robley Motors.

Starting again from scratch, Phillips produced the Sylva Striker in 1986. This basic little car is intended for both road and competition and has scored numerous wins in the 750 MC's Kit Car series. It was joined by the 'Clubman's Mk4' in 1988; with an enveloping body and no weather equipment, this is intended primarily for competition, of the 'drive it to the circuit' sort.

Central to the Striker range was a sturdy space frame made of square tubing; on the Mk 2 front suspension was inboard

Sylva Leader (left), Striker Mk2 (below) and Striker Clubman's Mk4 (bottom)

by coil springs and rocker arms; on the Mk 3 it was coil springs and double wishbones using Vauxhall Chevette uprights; either system was available on the Mk 4; all had front disc brakes. A Ford live rear axle (with drum brakes) was suspended on coil springs and located by twin trailing and leading arms and a Panhard rod. Most customers have opted for 1600cc Ford cross-flow engines but Fiat units are a popular alternative. Some customers have fitted Rover V8 engines and one had a tuned Alfa Romeo Montreal unit. By the end of 1990, about 200 Strikers had been made, including 30 Clubman versions.

# T

## T&A SPORTS CARS (GB)

The maker of the 'Predator', a Jaguar-sourced Cobra 427 copy introduced in 1990 with a choice of fibreglass or Kevlar bodies and the usual engine options, such as Ford V8 or Jaguar V12.

## TA DESIGN & DEVELOPMENT (GB)

The TA Spirit was a basic sports car of 1989 using Ford Escort Mk1/2 components in a space frame, topped by an original and distinctive enveloping fibreglass body. In 1990, the company showed a prototype which used a modified and widened open 2+2 Ashley body (first shown in 1960) on a ladder frame fitted with Ford Cortina running gear.

## TAFCO (USA)

First offered in 1979, the Tafco Baronta was a two-seat coupé which was claimed to be the first road car to use ground effect aerodynamics. It was a luxurious, well-equipped car, which used Chevrolet running gear and was claimed to be capable of 150mph/240kmh. The steel body was first shown unpainted (a trick to upstage the DeLorean?) but despite bold claims made for its advanced aerodynamics it was ungainly, and its styling was of the 1960s.

## T&J SPORTS CARS *see* JC

## TALBOT (F)

Clement-Talbot was actually a British firm which started making cars in 1902. In 1919 it was taken over by Darracq, which was British-owned but based in France, and Darracq bought Sunbeam in 1925. Rootes bought the group in 1935 but Antonio Lago, a Venetian living in France, was able to buy Darracq and the Lago cars were badged as 'Darracq' in Britain and 'Talbot' in France. Postwar the Darracq name disappeared and the cars were variously known as 'Talbot', 'Talbot-Lago' and 'Lago-Talbot'.

From the moment that Lago took over in 1935, he instigated a competition programme which embraced Grand Prix racing as well as sports cars. Against the might of Mercedes-Benz and Auto Union Talbot stood little chance pre-war but the company played an important part in the immediate postwar period since it built an ideal privateers car—it was rugged and reliable and good enough to win three classic Grands Prix as well as a large number of lesser races.

A sports version won Le Mans in 1950, was second in 1951 and very nearly won again in 1952. It had a handsome lead over the works Mercedes-Benz 300SLs with little over an hour to go. After that Talbots disappeared from the results frame although cars continued to appear at Le Mans until 1957. Fiscal measures introduced by the French government dealt a body blow to the quality car industry and after 1950 Talbot production went into a steep dive. All such French makes were affected—Antonio Lago managed to hold on longer than most but there was no money for new models and so ambitious projects on the drawing board were still-born.

Simca took over the firm in 1959 and the name disappeared soon afterwards. Antonio Lago who had done so much to sustain French prestige died in 1961. It is an irony that three of the greatest French makers, Bugatti, Gordini, and Lago were Italian.

The Talbot name was revived in 1979 to badge those cars (ex-Rootes, Simca etc) which had been made by Chrysler prior to a takeover of the group by Peugeot. It was gross abuse of a great name.

**Record/Grand Sport 26CV, 1947-56. Prod: approx 750.** Dating back to 1936, the Record had a 170bhp version of Talbot's straight-six 4.5-litre engine with camshafts mounted high in the block. Independent front suspension was by transverse leaf springs and lower wishbones (long wheelbase models had coil springs), and hydraulic brakes were standard, as was a Wilson pre-selector gearbox. The Grand Sport was a short wheelbase version with 190bhp (220bhp from 1953) which made it, for a short time, the most powerful and fastest sports car in the world. A version won

**1947 (above) and 1953 (below) Talbot Lago Records. Hollywood actor Robert Stack is at the wheel of the earlier car, and the body of the later car is by Graber**

Le Mans in 1950 and came close to a repeat in 1952, and in single-seater form it won classic Grands Prix, beating works Ferraris and Maseratis. It was one of the few truly great cars

of the postwar era but the French government's fiscal measures saw production drop from 433 in 1950 to 80 in 1951 and then gradually fade away altogether.

**Baby 15CV, 1950-52. Prod:—.** This was an ill-judged attempt to break into the popular market with a 118bhp short-stroke four-cylinder 2.7-litre engine which escaped the swingeing taxes imposed on cars over 3 litres. Although intended as an economy model, it was a big car (112in wheelbase) which neither went nor stopped well, despite the fact that it had hydraulic brakes. The failure of this car helped the firm into receivership in 1951. When it was revived a few months later, all models, from the Record to the Baby, shared the same box section chassis with coil spring front suspension. This improvement in the chassis further overwhelmed an already inadequate engine. In 1952 a new model, the 'Quinze Luxe', was announced and this had the 1936 2.7-litre 'six'. Few, if any, were made.

**14CV/America, 1954-60. Prod: approx 80.** A derivative of the latter-day 'Baby' with the same basic chassis as the Record and Grand Sport, but shortened to a 98.5in wheelbase. At first this had a new 2.5-litre four-cylinder five-bearing engine which delivered its 120bhp through a ZF gearbox. The styling was potentially exquisite but was spoiled by having to accommodate proprietary parts (Vedette windscreen, Jensen 541 rear screen, etc). The 'America' had BMW's 2.5-litre V8, four-speed gearbox and instrumentation. It was good for 125mph/200kmh but the Germanic interior was at odds with the Franco-Italian style. A delight to drive, it was, alas, far too expensive. The trim level was poor with sliding windows and no inner door trim. Twelve of these were made and ten had *left hand drive* which shows how far Talbot had fallen. By 1959 Simca was in control and the last few cars (possibly one car) had the ex-Ford France 2.3-litre flathead V8—weep for the passing of a glorious marque.

**The 2.5-litre Talbot Lago America**

## TALON (GB)

Originally made in America (see below) the Talon became a model offered by GP (qv) in Britain. In 1988, the Talon was taken over by another maker and developed separately.

**Talon coupé**

Basically it was an open, doorless, fibreglass sports car body (with a hint of a Fiat X1/9) on a VW floorpan. Talon could also supply its own chassis to take VW components and in 1990 introduced a new space frame to take a mid-mounted Ford Fiesta engine and Fiesta running gear.

## TALON (USA)

A 1979 fibreglass coupé which was designed to cover a VW Beetle chassis; the body was taken up by GP (qv) in 1980, modified for the British market, and sold to Talon (GB) in 1988.

## TASCO (USA)

Tasco stood for 'The American Sports Car Company' and it was organised by some members of the then-fledgling Sports Car Club of America. Designed by Gordon Buehrig, who was famous for his work on the pre-war (and great) Cord range, it was based on a Mercury chassis. Features included an aircraft-style perspex canopy and front wheels which stood proud from the body and were enclosed by metal envelopes. Only the prototype was made (in 1948) because the market would not stand the price tag of $7500.

## TD 2000 (AUS)

A turn key MG TD copy introduced in 1986. The basic plot was a fibreglass body and a 2-litre Nissan engine with five-speed transmission. It was considerably quicker than the original and the standard of trim was high.

## TEAL (GB)

From 1984 Thistledown Engineering Automotives made one of the more convincing copies of the Bugatti Type 35, but that does not mean that the car would fool anyone with two points of IQ to rub together. The Teal was based on Morris Marina components and a four-seat version was also made.

**Teal 'Type 35', 1984**

## TECHNIC (GB)

A late 1980s maker of the '500 Spyder', a Beetle-based copy of the Porsche 550.

## TERRIER (GB)

In the 1950s Len Terry dabbled in club racing, joined Lotus and became Colin Chapman's right-hand man. In his spare time he made the Terrier Mk 2, with which Brian Hart not only won the 1172 Championship but also won almost every other race he entered. On paper it had a conventional specification, but the secret was the complicated, and very stiff, space frame with the body panels acting as a stressed skin.

Production of this car was taken over by another outfit and, like the Lotus Seven, it was offered as a road and circuit car. Unfortunately the new outfit tried to cut corners in making the cars and upset the careful thinking behind the design, which left buyers wondering why their cars were not as good as Brian Hart's. Terry washed his hands of the project and later Terrier cars had nothing to do with the firm which made the production Terrier Mk 2s.

There are postscripts to this brief story: the Terrier chassis was used by Falcon for its 'Sports' model (and also the associated 'Peregrine'); Brian Hart went on to become a top-line driver and engine designer; Colin Chapman was not pleased to see his chief designer's private venture beat Lotus cars on the track so Terry went on to design cars for Gilby, Shelby, Eagle, BRM and, for a time, Lotus again.

## TEVOG (D)

A 1980s builder of the 'Ledl', a version of Richard Oakes' Nova (but with conventional doors) which was built on a VW Beetle floorpan.

**Tevog Ledl AS 130 had 1300cc Ford power**

## THOROUGHBRED (USA)

The first kit car made by this firm, in 1975, was a rakish 'traditionally styled' sports car designed by an Englishman, Leonard Witton, who was resident in the States. Called the 'Witton Tiger', it was unusual in that it could be made with the engine at the back (VW base), or front. A wide variety of engines, up to small block V8s and Mazda rotaries, was fitted by customers. A V8-powered copy of the Mercedes-Benz 540K followed in 1980 and subsequent cars have included copies of the 300SLR sports-racer and the 300SLR coupé, a unique variant made by M-B in 1955. The 'Witton Tiger' was made in Britain as the 'Merlin' (qv).

**Thoroughbred Witton Tiger, 1980**

## THURNER (D)

The Thurner 'RS' was a fibreglass coupé made between 1970 and 1973. It incorporated components from the NSU TT1200.

**The Thurner RS**

## TIGER CARS (GB)

In 1990 Tiger Cars began to import a South African sports car, the RM7 (qv) and then discovered it contravened copyrights of both Westfield (qv) and Caterham (qv). However Tiger had two other projects in the pipeline and the first to be finished was the 'Six'. This was a basic cycle-winged sports car which used any Ford four-cylinder engine up to 2 litres, modified VW Golf uprights in cast wishbones, a coil sprung Ford Cortina live axle located by twin trailing arms and a Panhard rod, and VW Golf front disc brakes.

**Tiger Six, 1990**

The other project was a copy of the 'Ferrari 250LM' which had been originated by Replicar (qv), passed through other hands and had last been heard of as the LM164 made by Western Classics (qv). Tiger bought the rights to the body moulds, which were in two-seat and 2+2 form, and created an entirely new space frame. This time a mid-mounted VW Golf engine was used, mounted in line and mated to an Audi four- or five-speed gearbox. In order to give the right sound and ambience, the fuel injection was thrown away and was replaced by twin Webers. Golf double wishbone front suspension was used at both ends. The standard of finish and leather trim was high.

## TM (GB)

'TM' was the name under which more than one maker offered a copy of the MG TF sourced from Triumph 'separate chassis' donor cars.

## TMC COSTIN (IRL)

Designed by Frank Costin for the American-owned Eire-based Thompson Manufacturing Co, the TMC appeared in 1984. At first glance it could be dismissed as a Lotus Seven with an enclosed cockpit and boot space but underneath the ungainly body was a very ingenious space frame. Indeed, it was a major breakthrough in space frame design because it overcame the inherent problem of maintaining stiffness while providing conventional doors. From a side view the front module was essentially an oblong, there was a shallow triangle for the cockpit and a tall triangle for the tail section. The body was aluminium and fibreglass, front suspension was by coil springs and double wishbones, and the live rear axle was located by double radius arms and a Panhard rod.

Despite some competition success, high taxation in Ireland ruined its chances on the home market, poor quality scuppered an attempt to market it in Britain and a promising early response in Canada was not translated into sales. Total production was only 26, but if ever a design cried out for revival it is the TMC Costin.

TMC Costin, 1984

## TOJEIRO (GB)

John Tojeiro was essentially a special builder who provided components whereby customers could make dual-purpose road and track cars. One customer, Cliff Davis, was very successful in a Tojeiro-Bristol which had a body styled after the Ferrari 166 Barchetta. This car was taken up by AC and developed into the Ace which, by turns, became the Cobra, so Tojeiro has his slot in production car history.

This chassis (the basic kit could not be called a 'car') was a simple ladder frame with independent suspension by transverse leaf springs and lower wishbones. Buyers organised their own engines and bodies so no two cars were identical. The frame was suspiciously like the Cooper sports car, one of which was owned by Tojeiro's friend Brian Lister—not to beat about the bush, it was a straight crib and about the only distinctive thing was Tojeiro's use of alloy wheels made by Turner (qv)—Jack Turner's early cars were also cribbed from Cooper.

Tojeiro sports was made 1952-54

Perhaps 18 were made between 1952 and 1954—Tojeiro himself cannot remember—and since faking is easy, it has been done. Lionel Leonard (qv) also made a Ferrari 166 Barchetta-style fibreglass body and a frame similar to that used by Cliff Davis' Tojeiro-Bristol, and while it was a short-lived venture some of these frames may now have become absolutely genuine Tojeiros.

Tojeiro's attempts at more sophisticated sports-racing designs must be judged failures although he also designed the Berkeley Bandit and Britannia GT. The former was a very promising design but Berkeley folded before it could be put into production, the latter was priced out of its natural market. In the 1980s, after a long absence from the motoring scene, Tojeiro became involved with DAX, a maker of Cobra copies which changed its model name to DAX-Tojeiro in honour of the connection. Thus the grandfather of the Cobra completed a circle.

In 1990 Tojeiro announced that he had sanctioned the building of a single replica of each of his five pretty but unsuccessful Jaguar-powered sports racers of the late 1950s.

## TOMORROW'S CLASSIC (USA)

Founded in the late 1970s, and believed defunct in the next decade, this company began by making a faithful copy of the original Corvette. It was available with 100bhp or 155bhp versions of the straight-six engine which powered the real thing. In terms of power output, this was down on the original car but, of course, in the interim emission laws had been tightened. Tomorrow's Classic also made a fibreglass copy of the open four-seat Auburn Phaeton with a 5-litre Chevrolet V8 engine.

## TONTALA (AUS)

A 1955 attempt to market a fibreglass sports coupé using Holden mechanicals. It was offered as a turn key car, or as a kit, but it is unlikely that more than a couple were made.

## TORNADO (GB)

Having tried building a Ford special from parts provided by a maker whose advertising suggested it was a simple task, Bill Woodhouse decided that there must be a market for a really sensible kit. He not only marketed one but produced receipts to prove that he had made a complete sports car for under £200, including the cost of a donor car, and Tornado was on its way. It came close to becoming an established part of the scene, but hit cash-flow problems and withdrew voluntarily before forced to by circumstances.

**Typhoon, 1958-62. Prod: 400.** A simple ladder frame, coil springs at the rear, split axle front suspension, and a well-made but ugly fibreglass body which actually fitted the chassis—there was nothing complicated about the Typhoon. That appealed to special builders, who probably completed a higher proportion of these kits than any of their rivals. It was not the prettiest shell by any means, but Tornado made open models, a coupé, a four-seater version and even a sporting estate which pre-dated the Reliant GTE by years.

Tornado Typhoon going sideways

**Tempest, 1960-62. Prod: approx 15.** The basic plot was similar to the Typhoon but it was adapted to take more modern engines from Ford, BMC and Triumph. It also had rack and pinion steering and Triumph Herald front suspension and brakes.

Tornado Tempest

**Thunderbolt, 1960. Prod: 1.** Tornado got ambitious with this one and beefed up and widened the chassis to take the Triumph TR3A or Ford Consul engines. The only one built had the TR unit and although it was claimed to reach 108mph/174kmh it was also said to have been almost impossible to drive.

**Talisman, 1962-64. Prod: 186.** This 2+2 GT marked a new direction for Tornado since it was offered as a complete car as well as a kit. The ladder frame had coil spring suspension all round, with a live rear axle and Triumph Herald front suspension. A well-handling little car which promised much, it was comfortable, practical, and well-finished. At one point Colin Chapman considered taking it over and selling it as a Lotus, but he had financial worries of his own and that idea had to be shelved. Various Ford engines were offered in a range of tune from 55 to 85bhp. The name of the tuner was Cosworth, and thus the Talisman was the first road car to have a Cosworth engine.

Tornado Talisman had better looks

## TORNADO SPORTS CARS (GB)

From 1987, this company made a McLaren M6GT lookalike body which could be fitted on a VW Beetle floorpan or, if a V8 engine was chosen, the company could supply its own space frame. Tornado also made a copy of the Ford GT40.

Tornado Sports Cars' McLaren M6GT copy (above) and GT40 copy (below)

## TORO (RP)

The only sports car from the Philippines, this was a 1970s 2+2 fibreglass coupé based on a 1.3-litre VW Beetle chassis.

## TOYOTA (J)

For many years one perception of Japan was that it made shoddy imitations of superior Western goods. There was a fair amount of supporting evidence for this view, but Toyota was initially funded as the result of Sakichi Toyoda selling the rights to his improvements to weaving looms to a British company in 1929. At that time one hundred thousand pounds was a very large amount of money and it illustrates how much Toyoda's inventions were valued. The money was used to back Toyoda's son Kiichiro in a new venture, which was to build motor cars. After a couple of false starts Toyota Motor Company was formed in 1937 and before long was building General Motors designs under licence.

The new company's early years were not easy and, in common with some other manufacturers such as Nissan, Toyota was torn by industrial strife in the late 1940s and the early 1950s. This led to the resignation of Kiichiro Toyoda, who was replaced by his son, Eiji Toyoda. It took some time for car production to take off but in the meantime the company was helped by lateral deals, such as Toyota taking on the marketing of Esso petroil products from 1953.

Toyota built its first sports cars in the 1960s and then pulled back from making cars with personal appeal, possibly because they were commercial failures. In the 1970s Toyota made some superb engines, one of which became almost standard fitting in Formula 3, but although the production cars into which these engines were fitted bristled with fittings they were people movers, not drivers' cars. That did nothing to hamper the company's rise ever upwards until it became one of the world's Big Three. Then in 1984 Toyota showed it was capable of quality as well as quantity when it introduced the MR2, a sports car which gave every other maker pause for thought. It probably did more than any other model to change the popular perception of Japanese cars as being good value and reliable but nothing beyond that.

**S800, 1965-69. Prod: 3131.** This model was based on components from the Publica, which was then Toyota's small car range, and it is sometimes incorrectly referred to as the Publica Sport. Of unitary construction, it had a front-mounted air-cooled flat-twin engine of 790cc which delivered its 49bhp to the rear wheels via an all-synchromesh four-speed gearbox. Front suspension was by torsion bars and double wishbones and the live rear axle was suspended on semi-elliptics. Top speed was 97mph/156kmh but the company stressed that maximum cruising speed was 84mph/135kmh. All cars had a Targa top but since this was a year before Porsche perhaps it should be called a Toyota top.

**Toyota S800, 1969**

**2000GT, 1967-70. Prod: 337.** This car is familiar to millions as it featured in the James Bond movie *You Only Live Twice*, but that was a convertible made specially for the film—production models were all two-seat coupés. The 2000GT was originated by Yamaha, which has undertaken a lot of consultancy work for Toyota, especially on engines, and the aluminium body was styled by Count Albrecht Goertz, later responsible for the Datsun 240Z. It used a backbone chassis, with all-independent suspension by coil springs and double wishbones, which was clearly inspired by the Lotus Elan.

**Toyota 2000GT arrived in 1967**

Power came from a dohc straight-six engine of 1998cc which fed its 150bhp through a five-speed manual gearbox. The engine was actually a Yamaha-built version of the 2.3-litre sohc unit used in the Toyota Crown saloon.

Thanks to light weight and a slippery shape, a top speed of 137mph/220kmh was possible (0-60mph in 8.4 seconds) and examples performed well in production car racing in Japan. The 2000GT was not intended for series production—had that been so it would not have been made only with right hand drive because at the time the American market was crucial. The car was intended to test the water and to generate kudos for Toyota—it handsomely fulfilled both objectives.

**MR2, 1984-89. Prod: 166,104.** Like most Japanese cars of the 1980s, the MR2 was not so much a model but a menu from which an importer chose a package for its market.

**1985 Toyota MR2**

There were two basic engines, an sohc carburettered unit of 1453cc and a dohc fuel-injected '16 valve' engine of 1587cc which produced 118bhp or 143bhp when supercharged, an option which was available in some markets from 1986. Since there was a choice of a five-speed manual gearbox or a four-speed automatic, top speed of the MR2 ranged between 106mph/170kmh and 130mph/210kmh.

Common to all cars was independent front and rear suspension by MacPherson struts, with supplementary control arms, trailing arms and transverse arms at the rear. Disc brakes were fitted to all four wheels and no matter which engine was fitted, it was mounted transversely amidships.

It was a sports car for the 1980s, with superb handling and roadholding, a lively engine and terrific gear change. Not everyone liked the chunky styling but none could deny that the overall layout employed space wisely and that the cockpit was a model of ergonomics. In 1986 a T-bar roof was available in some markets.

**MR2, introduced 1989.** The replacement of a successful model is always a problem but Toyota made things even harder for itself by producing an entirely new design only five years after their original car was launched. As on the original model there was a range of engines but this time they were all of one size: 1998cc. They ranged from 119bhp dohc '16 valve', from the Camry saloon (maximum speed 124mph/200kmh, 0-62mph in 9.5 seconds), via a 158bhp version (similar to the Celica's engine) which gave a top speed of 137mph/220kmh with 0-62mph in 7.9 seconds, up to a turbocharged unit which produced 222bhp and gave the car a claimed 150mph/240kmh. A four-speed automatic transmission was optional on the normally aspirated cars but not in all markets, and the turbocharged version was sold only in Japan and America.

Overall the car resembled its predecessor but it was nine inches longer, an inch wider and lower. A T-bar roof was optional from the time of launch and the turbocharged version had ABS and power assisted steering.

With its larger dimensions, bigger engine, and greatly improved performance, the second generation MR2 moved the concept up a notch or two. Unlike many another car which has added inches and pounds, this one retained the nimbleness and zest of the much loved original.

MR2 in 1990

## TPC (GB)

The TPC Speedster was the 'British version' of the Apal VW Beetle-based copy of the Porsche 356 Speedster, introduced at the 1974 London Motor Show.

TPC Speedster

## TRANSFORMER (GB)

Maker of the HF 2000, a Lancia-based copy of the Lancia Stratos, notable for the accuracy of its bodywork; there were cases of owners of the real thing replacing damaged panels with those made by Transformer because they were cheaper and of better quality than the Lancia replacements. Transformer was active from 1986. In 1987 it introduced the 'SD 500' copy of the Ferrari 500 Mondial which had a de Dion rear axle and was sourced from the Alfa Romeo Alfetta or the GTV.

Transformer HF2000

## TRIAD (AUS)

Looking not unlike the original Lotus Esprit, the Sydney-built Triad coupé was first shown in 1984. A mid-engined two seater, it had a 2.8-litre Volvo V6 engine, all-independent

1984 Triad

suspension, a high level of trim and equipment, a body built of fibreglass and Kevlar, and a claimed top speed of 140mph/ 225kmh. It appears never to have gone into production.

## **TRIDENT** (GB)

The original Trident was a TVR with styling by Trevor Fiore. TVR then went through one of its many crises and the project was sold to one of its dealers, Bill Last, who was making the Peel Trident as the Viking Minisport. Although the Trident was one of the prettiest cars of its time, production never reached expected levels and the company folded in 1974 in the wake of both the energy crisis and the problems Trident faced in meeting new American regulations. It was revived with new backing in 1976 and died again in 1978.

**Clipper, 1967-74/1976-78. Prod: approx 225, all models.** Earlier Clippers had a TVR Grantura MkIII chassis, then Bill Last turned to an Austin-Healey 3000 chassis into which he put a 390bhp 4.7-litre Ford V8—the very thought of such a combination of brute force and ignorance is enough to bring tears to the eyes. It was marvellous in a straight line, less so when it came to stopping or turning corners, which is something of a handicap for a sports car. A convertible was offered, but most were coupés which had powered windows. From 1969 a modified Triumph TR6 chassis was used since production of the Austin-Healey had ended; detail body changes came in 1970; in 1971 the Clipper had a 5-litre Chrysler engine, but it was back to Ford (5.6-litre) for the marque's revival in 1976.

1969 Trident Clipper V8

Trident Venturer V6

**Venturer V6/Tycoon, 1969-74/1976-78/ 1971-74. Prod: see above.** This had the same basic style as the Clipper but the body was mounted on a modified TR6 chassis. The Venturer had the 134bhp Ford V6 Wessex engine and the Tycoon the 150bhp fuel injected TR6 engine, but this was really a stop-gap due to the fact that Ford engines were temporarily unavailable due to a strike. For the 1976 revival, Triumph i.r.s. was dropped in favour of a live rear axle. All in all, the Trident project was a waste of one of the most beautiful body styles of its day.

## **TRIDENT AUTOVET** (GB)

Early 1980s maker of the Project 400, a four-seat convertible kit car based on the styling of the Ferrari Dino.

## **TRIPLE C** (GB)

Late 1980s maker (aka CCC) of the 'Challenger', a fibreglass Jaguar E Type copy which used Ford Cortina running gear in a space frame, with the Ford V6 engine as an option.

## **TRIPLEX** (USA)

An unsuccessful attempt in 1954-55 to revive the Chicagoan sports car project with a one-piece fibreglass body. Almost any engine could be fitted but the chassis was basically designed for Ford V8s. As if two names were not enough, it was also sold as the 'Lightning'.

## **TRIPOS** (GB)

The R81 was a lovely and well-engineered basic sports car which looked as though its style had been inspired by an early 1960s Lotus single seater. A space frame designed by Bob Egginton carried Ford Cortina coil spring and double

Tripos R81

wishbone front suspension, and the coil sprung live rear axle was located by twin radius arms and a Panhard rod. The R81 was usually fitted with a 1.6-litre Ford Kent engine (the ohc equivalents were too tall to fit under the bonnet line of the early cars). The R81 stood head and shoulders above most similar cars.

In 1987 Tripos took over the American firm Hunter, which made a 1930s style sports car on Triumph TR running gear but the firm was soon in financial difficulties. At the end of 1990 the Tripos was not in production but that appeared to be a temporary situation.

## TRIPPEL (D)

From 1932 Hans Trippel had built amphibious vehicles, some of which were used by the German army. In 1950 he showed a two-seat coupé with a bulbous fastback body (which looked something like the later Saab 92) and a mid-mounted flat-twin 498cc Zündapp motor cycle engine. Few were made by the time production ended in 1952. The design was briefly, and equally unsuccessfully, made in France as the 'Marathon', with a Panhard engine.

## TRITON (GB)

First seen in 1963, the Triton was a special built by David Johnson-Webb, with a space frame, a front-mounted BMC 'B' series engine, bespoke suspension and a fibreglass hard top body. Johnson-Webb used it mainly for competition and, being very light, it was reputed to be capable of 140mph/225kmh. The Triton was built for its owner's pleasure but the project was taken over by a businessman who intended to put it into production as a road car. Two more were built but then the project folded.

## TRIUMPH (GB)

Triumph cars and Triumph motorcycles have a common ancestry, but while the firm's first car, a three wheeler, was made in 1903, the company's main business continued to be bicycles and motorcycles. In 1923 the Triumph Cycle Company offered a four wheeler, followed it with other models which made no great impact and then, in 1930, the car business was organised as the Triumph Motor Company, still a subsidiary of the motorcycle company. In 1936 the car division became independent and gained a reputation for middle-range sporting cars with a high level of equipment which were direct competitors to SS (later Jaguar).

However, Triumph went into receivership in 1939, and was absorbed by Standard during the War. By the end of the 1950s it had become the dominant partner, thanks to its sports cars. 1961 saw Standard-Triumph merge with BMC, and the Standard name disappeared in 1963. Triumph became a founder member of British Leyland in 1968, and flourished; indeed, for a time it was BL's favourite son, to the detriment of marques such as MG. Some of BL's problems arose from corporate infighting as protagonists of each marque under the umbrella struggled for identity and survival. Some spectacular mistakes by BL's management meant that by the early 1980s Triumph had lost its sports car market and this great name was only a badge on a British-built Honda.

**Roadster 18TR (1800)/TRA (2000), 1946-48/1948-49. Prod: 2501/2000.** A two-seater version of the staid, razor-edged, Triumph 1800 Saloon which was Roller style for country solicitors, the Roadster had an aluminium and ash body on a shortened chassis and the last dickey seat ever offered on a production car. The 18TR had Standard's transverse leaf spring i.f.s. but the TRA had a coil spring and double wishbone arrangement with, unusually for the time, an anti-roll bar; rear suspension was a live axle on semi-elliptic springs.

Power in the 18TR was courtesy of the Standard ohv 1776cc engine, which was also supplied to Jaguar, and it delivered its 65bhp via a four-speed box. In 1948, as the TRA, it received the 68bhp Vanguard 2088cc engine and *three*-speed transmission, larger brakes, a hypoid rear axle, and a stiffer frame. Top speed went up from 70mph/112kmh to a mighty 77mph/124kmh but the loss of a ratio meant it took over half a minute to touch sixty.

**Triumph 1800 Roadster, 1946**

**TR-X, 1950. Prod: 3.** An aerodynamic car with a stressed skin aluminium body, the TR-X was intended to replace the Roadster. It was basically a two-seater Standard Vanguard and it bristled with gadgets—electricity and hydraulics powered the overdrive, window, seats, hood and radio aerial. It even had pop-up headlights. The car weighed in at a hefty 2750lb but, with a twin carb 72bhp engine, it promised to reach 90mph/145kmh. By the time it was ready the Jaguar XK120 had made that look small beer and the start of the Korean War was used as an excuse to drop the project.

**The 1950 TR-X**

**TR2, 1953-55. Prod: 8628.** In the early 1950s Triumph could not help but notice that MGs were selling like hot cakes in the USA and Triumphs were not. When an attempt to buy Morgan failed, Triumph made its own prototype sports car, the TS20 (or 'TR1'), which was shown at the 1952 London Motor Show. The rear bodywork was not liked (especially when viewed alongside the Austin-Healey 100 which also made its debut at the show) and testing showed that the chassis was too flexible.

These problems were overcome and with a 1991cc 90bhp version of the Vanguard engine, but with a four-speed gearbox, the TR2 could reach 60mph in under 12 seconds, return impressive economy, and touch 103mph/165kmh (108mph/174kmh with the optional overdrive). It had a separate chassis, coil spring and wishbone front suspension, and a live rear axle on semi-elliptics. It was simple and practical and when American customers found they could buy a sports car which topped the ton for just $2500 they did so in large numbers and most did not mind that its handling was not all it should have been.

1953 TR2

**TR3, 1955-57. Prod: 13,378.** This was an improved TR2 which appeared in time to do battle with the new MGA. It was distinguished from the TR2 by a potato chipper grille. Options included overdrive on the top three gears, a tiny 'occasional' seat and, as on the TR2 from 1954, a factory hardtop. This was sold as the 'GT' package, and along with the hardtop came external door handles. Power went up to 95bhp but performance was slightly down due to an increase in weight as refinements were added. In 1956 the TR3 became the first mass-produced car with front disc brakes. TRs always had a he-man image, partly because of their chunky looks but mainly because of their very stiff suspension. This gave them a beefy feel but generated bump steer, which remained a perpetual problem.

TR3 in trouble

**TR3A/TR3B, 1957-62/1962. Prod: 58,236/3331.** Triumph was looking to replace the series by 1957 but since no replacement project had been satisfactory, this interim model was brought out and became a best seller. Externally distinguished by a wider grille, semi-recessed headlights and external door handles, it also had improved brakes and a luggage space behind the seats. Under the bonnet, the engine gave 100bhp but a 60lb increase in weight meant there was no improvement in performance. America got a 'B' model in 1961 with the TR4's all-synchro 'box and, mostly, the 2138cc engine. Earmarked for the TR4, this was still a 100bhp unit, but torque was improved. Of course, no owner at the time knew that one day the worst four letter word he would know would be 'rust'.

An important variant was the Italia 2000, which had a handsome GT body built by Vignale to a Michelotti design, and which was recognisably related to the later TR4. It was made between 1960 and 1962, and there remains some doubt as to the exact number built—estimates range between 150 and 329, although it is possible that even more were made.

TR3A shows its wide grille

**TR4/TR4A, 1961-64/1964-68. Prod: 40,253/ 28,465.** This was a rebodied TR3A with styling by Michelotti. The body accounted for the extra foot in overall length, the wider track helped handling, and there was useful luggage space. The cockpit was quite roomy and plush, but ride remained rock hard, continuing the TR's reputation as a macho car. One of the options, the 'Surrey' top, anticipated Porsche's Targa top. The 1991cc engine continued to be available but found few takers apart from those wanting to race in the 2-litre class.

The standard engine was the old unit taken out to 2138cc; power remained at 100bhp but torque was slightly improved. Top speed remained at 102mph/164kmh but 0-60mph acceleration improved to 10.9 seconds. The TR4A usually had coil spring and trailing arm independent rear suspension

TR4 on the 1962 Alpine Rally

(a few went to the USA with live axles) and this added about 100lb to the overall weight, so acceleration suffered, but as the engine was slightly tweaked (to give 104bhp) top speed went up to 109mph/175kmh.

An interesting variant of the TR4 was the 'Dove', a 2+2 (fibreglass) fastback coupé conversion executed by Harrington for Doves of Wimbledon. It was first shown as a prototype in 1963, and about 50 examples were made.

**Spitfire I/II, 1962-65/1965-67. Prod: 45,753/ 37,409.** Triumph's answer to the Sprite used a rugged backbone chassis frame, similar to the Triumph Herald but with a shorter wheelbase, and the four-cylinder 1147cc 63bhp engine from the Herald 12/50-plus. Like the Herald, it was styled by Michelotti and the hinged bonnet made maintenance easy. Quicker than the contemporary Sprite, and with front disc brakes, the Spitfire I was good for 90mph/145kmh (0-60mph in 16.5 seconds) but the transverse leaf and swing axle rear suspension left much to be desired. Wire wheels, hardtop and overdrive were available from late 1963. The Mk II had 67bhp, which knocked a second from the 0-60mph dash, and was better trimmed.

Spitfire I

**TR5 PI/TR250, 1967-68. Prod: 2947/8484.** Based on the TR4A but with Triumph's 2.5-litre straight-six engine.

TR5

Since this weighed about the same as the old 'four', and would fit the engine bay, it was a fairly easy transplant. It was also adaptable to the new US emission laws, so America received the carburetted 104bhp TR250, which had a top speed of 107mph/172kmh (0-60mph in 10.6 seconds), while other markets had the 150bhp fuel-injected model which was good for 120mph/193kmh (0-60mph in 8.8 seconds).

Comparative production figures show that the strangulation of the engine for the American market did not greatly affect sales, for about 75 percent of production crossed the Atlantic. Servo brakes and radial tyres were standard, as were horrid Rostyle wheels (wires were still an option). Early versions of the Lucas injection system could be troublesome.

TR250

**Spitfire III, 1967-70. Prod: 65,320.** A new 1296cc engine and 75bhp pushed top speed up to 100mph/160kmh (just) and brought the 0-60mph time down to 13.6 seconds. This increase in muscle, however, helped to highlight the shortcomings of the rear suspension. The high front bumper was adopted to meet American requirements while in the cockpit was a wooden fascia and a smaller steering wheel. Further refinements included wind-up windows and a permanently attached hood.

The Spitfire was a success story and, aided by its good looks and the Triumph badge, it consistently outsold both the Sprite and the Midget combined. While the Herald-derived rear suspension could be skittish, the car had the Herald's virtues: small turning circle, ease of access to the main components and decent luggage space. The separate chassis meant that replacement of body panels was easy. The Series III was the last Spitfire to have optional wire wheels.

Spitfire III had raised front bumper

**GT6, 1966-68. Prod: 15,818.** A Spitfire with a pretty coupé body which made it look like an undernourished Jaguar E Type. Power came from the 95bhp straight-six 2-

litre Vitesse engine and made it good for 105mph/169kmh (0-60mph in 12 seconds). Overdrive top was an option. In common with the Spitfire range, the standard of trim was good, but when adding the roof Triumph forgot about ventilation and so the cockpit had a nasty habit of misting up. It looked a good car on paper but putting the heavier and longer six-cylinder engine in the Spitfire chassis upset the balance of the car, and while the Herald-derived rear suspension was just about adequate for the Spitfire, on the nose-heavy and more powerful GT6 it was interesting...but stupid.

GT6 was launched in 1966

**GT6 MkII, 1968-70. Prod: 12,066.** The handling of the original GT6 was so bad that Triumph had to respond quickly. The revised rear suspension of the Vitesse MkII, with double-jointed half shafts and the transverse leaf spring acting as top wishbones, was grafted on. This transformed the car but it should have been done in the first place and, as a result, all GT6s have the reputation of the Series I clinging to them. Power was increased to 105bhp, which meant 112mph/180kmh and brisk acceleration (0-60mph in 10.1 seconds) in European spec cars, while American cars had 95bhp (the same as the Series I) and the car was badged the GT6+. Like the contemporary Spitfire the GT6 had a high front bumper but it also had improved cockpit trim and a decent ventilation system. Wire wheels and overdrive continued to be listed as options.

GT6 MkII, 1968

**TR6, 1969-76. Prod: 94,619.** The last of the true TR line, the TR6 was a rebodied TR5, the work of the German firm, Karmann. 0-60mph in 8.2 seconds and a maximum speed of 119mph/191kmh were outstanding figures for the time but America had the less muscular de-toxed version (0-60mph in 10.7 seconds, 109mph/175kmh). The engine was not the epitome of smoothness but things improved in 1973 with a new camshaft profile, which made it less lumpy at

Triumph TR6

the cost of a slight loss of power. An addition in 1973 was a small front spoiler and the following year there were black bumper guards to meet US impact regulations. Most buyers chose the new style disc wheels but wires were still an option as were hard top and overdrive. The TR6 was the last of the hairy-chested mass-produced sports cars.

**Spitfire IV, 1970-74. Prod: 70,021.** Revised styling with new nose and tail treatments, a new instrument layout (as on 'American spec' MkIII cars), and synchromesh on first gear kept the Spitfire ahead of the opposition. A higher rear axle ratio made the MkIV a more refined car but, in conjunction with increasing weight, scrubbed a little off its performance. The big news however, was revised rear suspension with the transverse leaf spring on a pivot which reduced roll stiffness

Revised styling for the Spitfire IV

and gave the car the handling it should have had all along. Cars for the US market were so strangled by emission laws that they would barely top 80mph/129kmh (0-60mph in 15.9 seconds) and power dropped to just 48bhp in 1972. To regain lost ground American cars received the 1.5-litre engine (and truly hideous 'impact' bumpers) in 1973, a year ahead of the European market. The problem was not American laws—every manufacturer had received ample notice of them—but the fact that BL's engines were past their 'sell by' dates and the company had no modern engine to offer.

**GT6 MkIII, 1970-73. Prod: 13,042.** The final expression of the line shared styling revisions with the Spitfire IV and, in 1973, its rear suspension layout. Cars for America lost power annually as new emission laws took hold and by 1972 had only 79bhp. Thus, while a European spec car was good for

112mph/180kmh (0-60mph in 10.1 seconds), the American version managed 95mph/154kmh (0-60mph in twelve seconds). Sales fell as a result and looked to fall off further as emission laws bit deeper. Since America was Triumph's main market, the model was axed at the end of 1973.

GT6 MkIII

**Stag, 1970-77. Prod: 25,877.** If ever a car should have been a winner, it was the Stag—there was nothing like it on sale anywhere—and it was keenly priced. For once, '2+2' meant what it said—the rear seats would accommodate mature adults with legs. Buyers had the choice of a rag top or a hardtop, and trim level was high. Unlike previous Triumph sports cars, the Stag had unitary construction. Front

The 1970 Stag

suspension was by MacPherson struts and the independent rear by coil springs and trailing arms.

Bickering inside British Leyland saw the obvious engine, the Rover V8, edged out and in its place came a 3-litre V8 (basically two 'Dolomite' slant fours grafted together) which was only used on the Stag. This produced 145bhp and meant 116mph/186kmh top speed (0-60mph in 9.3 seconds) but the problem was that the cooling system needed to be maintained very carefully. If it was not head gaskets were liable to go and, apart from inconvenience, they were expensive to replace. With the Rover engine it could have been a world beater.

**Spitfire 1500, 1974-80. Prod: 95,829.** Over the years the Spitfire put on weight and so the MkIV was not quite as nimble as the III, but this was redressed with the 1500, the last expression of the line, which was also the best in every respect. The 1493cc engine, which would also be used in the MG Midget, gave 71bhp in Europe (57bhp in America) so the magic 'ton' was, again, *just* possible in a 'European' car (0-60mph came down to 13.2 seconds). Handling was good, the engine was willing and the cars sold in Europe looked as Michelotti intended them to look, ie without the gross bumpers. One reason for the Spitfire's popularity had been its cheapness, since it shared so many parts with the Herald, Vitesse and GT6, but they had all long gone and, with them, economy of scale. In any case, a replacement was needed and BL was in deep trouble.

Last Spitfire was the 1500

**TR7, 1975-81. Prod: 112,368.** Triumph scored an own goal with its first new sports car for twelve years. Gone was the separate chassis; in its place was unitary construction, with MacPherson struts and a live rear axle. Gone was the chunky macho shape; in its place was an anaemic wedge and, until 1979, a roof with no rag top option. Gone too was the grunt, for the TR7 had a 105bhp 1998cc version of Triumph's slant-four (86bhp in America) and even in European spec top speed was only 110mph/177kmh (0-60mph in 9.1 seconds), so it was not as quick as the car it

TR7 drophead became available in 1979

replaced. To be fair, however, a TR7 could get from A to B quicker than a TR6.

Industrial problems beset it (it was built in the Liverpool plant, which had never made a sports car before), quality was indifferent, the promised 16-valve Dolomite Sprint engine never appeared, and the soft top did not appear until 1979 when the model's reputation was past saving. A five-speed box (and automatic) was optional from the end of 1976 and the four-speed 'box was dropped in 1979. By the time the last cars were made most of the problems had been solved—BL was five years too late but that was BL's way.

**TR8, 1980-81. Prod: 2497.** The car Triumph should have, could have, made in 1975; it had been in the air for years before that. Even as it was, it reached the market two years after its planned launch date due to BL's sorry state. It was basically a TR7 with the Rover 3.5-litre V8 (rated at 133bhp in the States) with small power bulges to accommodate the engine, and loaded with 'extras' including power steering; only automatic transmission and air conditioning were options.

Even in de-toxed form it was capable of 135mph/217kmh (0-60mph in 8.5 seconds) while the handful of cars made to British spec before the plug was pulled were really quick. Unfortunately workmanship was poor, the chassis flexed, and the brakes were not too special after a few hard applications. Despite that, handling was good and it had the TR7's excellent cockpit. All but a few went to the States (some TR7s have been converted to 'TR8s' in Britain) but it was too little, too late. BL management ineptitude killed a great marque and lost its most profitable market.

**TR8 drophead, 1980**

## TROLL (GB)

According to Norse mythology, Trolls are giants who command the hills, and that was the reasoning behind the name of this 1980s car, which was the natural heir of such marques as Buckler and Dellow. There once existed a category called 'motor sport' which implied a whole range of activities: hill climbs, trials, rallies and autotests with, perhaps, the odd race thrown in for good measure. No matter what the activity, the car was driven to the venue on public roads, and had to have a high degree of all-round competency. In the early 1950s this format was the centre of British national motor sport but as each branch became specialised it also became more professional. Recently, a yearning for purely amateur motor sport has seen a revival of events such as the old style trials.

The Troll came about through the enthusiasm of Peter James for traditional trialling, and after using modified production cars he essayed a bespoke machine in 1980. This combined the best elements of modern engineering with a proven format whose parameters had been laid down thirty years or more earlier. Peter James was successful, he had requests for replicas, and in 1986 a few Troll Mk 6s were made. One of the customers was a businessman and he was so delighted with his car that he began to put the project on a firmer footing. His decision was endorsed by the fact that in 1987 Troll not only won outright eight British classic trials but took the national championship as well.

The Troll Mk6B was a well-made basic sports car with a space frame, a body made from aluminium and fibreglass, coil spring and double wishbone front suspension and a securely located live rear axle. To take part in trials, ground clearance was eight inches yet journalists who drove the car on the road described its roadholding and grip as leech like.

**Troll Mk6B**

With 115bhp from a modified 1.7-litre Ford engine propelling a very light car, this was necessary, for the Troll would sprint to 60mph in a little over six seconds.

Available as a kit, or fully assembled, there was nothing quite like the Troll Mk6B available anywhere; it not only looked lovely (the 15in wire wheels helped) but it was a car of enormous integrity. Not many designs have been asked to be competent in so many different areas, and of those few have succeeded as well.

## TROLL (N)

Fun-loving Norway contributed this sporting coupé in 1957, for one year only. Rights to the 700cc two-cylinder two-stroke Gutbrod (qv) engine were bought and this water-cooled unit

**Fibreglass body of 1957 Troll**

was put in the front of a two-seat fibreglass coupé. Drive was through the front wheels, suspension was independent all round, and top speed was claimed to be 80mph/128kmh. Only five were made.

## TURNER (GB)

Jack Turner was a special builder who made a car for his own use and then was asked to make others—thus he became a manufacturer in a small way of business. As well as cars, he made alloy wheels and some engines, including a four-cylinder dohc 500cc unit, but he made no real impression until he decided to turn his back on racing and make road-going sports cars.

Ironically, these were more successful in competition than Turner's racing machines had ever been. The company grew to a point at which it needed to be restructured on a more professional level, and Jack became seriously ill. Without a management infrastructure to carry on, the company hit difficulties and went into voluntary liquidation in 1966. Turner survived his illness but chose not to return to manufacturing.

**Sports, 1951-52. Prod: 7.** An early kit car with lozenge-shaped twin tube ladder frame, all-round independent suspension by transverse leaf springs and lower wishbones, and alloy wheels (also used by Tojeiro). The chassis bore more than a passing resemblance to the Cooper sports car (just like the Tojeiro). Customers specified their own engines and bodies (just like Tojeiro); and most customers were local to Turner (just like whatsisname). An eighth chassis was made into an F2 car for John Webb (not the former Brands Hatch supremo) in 1953 and this was uprated to F1 spec in 1954. It was not a success, even in minor events and even when driven by professional racers.

**A30 Sports, 1955-57. Prod: 90.** The plot was a fibreglass body, a light tubular frame, with front suspension, hydro-mech brakes, engine and gearbox from the Austin A30, and a live rear axle suspended by trailing arms and torsion bars. With 80mph/129kmh and 45mpg, it was like the Austin-Healey Sprite before the Sprite. BMC thought so and refused to supply Turner directly, so he had to buy components from Austin dealers; this put the price up and restricted sales. Like all Turner sports cars, it was available in kit form.

Turner A30 Sports

**950 Sports, 1957-59. Prod: 170.** This was distinguished from its predecessor by vestigal fins and used the same chassis as the A30 Sports, but with fully hydraulic brakes and the 950cc A35 engine, which came with tuning options to five outputs from 34bhp to 43bhp. Some were fitted with the 75bhp 1100cc Coventry Climax FWA engine. Almost all were exported, mainly to the States and South Africa.

Turner 950 Sports had fins

**Sports, 1959-60. Prod: 160.** With a new body shell on the established chassis, this could be called a hand-built Sprite with strikingly good looks. Front disc brakes were an option, as were the Climax FWA and 1220cc 90bhp FWE engines, and a tuned Series A unit with twin carbs. It was successful in production sports car racing on both sides of the Atlantic and was the model which put Turner on the map.

1960 Turner Sports

**MkII/MkIII, 1960-63/1963-66. Prod: 150/90.** The tried and true chassis continued until the end of the Turner line although from 1960 the A30 front suspension was replaced by Triumph Herald coil spring and double wishbone units. The overall body shape remained, too, although the MkIII had a large bonnet scoop and elliptical

Turner GT and MkII Sports

tail lights. The big change was to Ford power for the base engines; Climax FWA and FWE units remained an option but most Turners used the Anglia, Classic and Cortina units.

**Turner-Climax, 1959-66. Prod: see above.** As mentioned, Climax engines were an option for all models from the 950 sports onwards, and were distinguished by the hyphenated name. The Climax-engined cars always had front disc brakes and wire wheels.

Turner-Climax FWA Sports, 1960

**GT, 1961-65. Prod: 9.** Designed by Turner as a fall-back should the sports car falter (which it never did) the GT was built only when an occasional order arrived. It had a fibreglass monocoque centre section with a steel floor pan bonded in, and square-tube sections front and rear. Triumph Herald front suspension and the usual Turner rear end completed the outline, while engines were either Ford or Climax. From some angles the GT was breathtaking, from others it looked decidedly odd, and it was not a particularly thrilling car to drive: its steering was vague and it was extremely noisy inside.

## TVR (GB)

TVR has had many escapes from oblivion, but the cars it has made have been so appealing that rescuers have been found. It all began in 1947 when Trevor Wilkinson founded a small garage business called Trevcar Motors in his home town of Blackpool, where Jaguar has its roots. Wilkinson's first car, an Alvis special, came a year later, and in that year Trevcar became TVR Engineering (TreVoR). In 1949 Wilkinson built a multi-tubular chassis, fitted components from a wide variety of (scrapped) cars, and a tight body with cycle wings, and the first TVR was born.

It was sold and that financed a second car, with a simpler chassis, which largely used Austin A40 components. That, too, was sold. A third car was made, for Wilkinson's own use, and by 1953 TVR was ready to market a kit car using proprietary fibreglass bodies, which were then appearing in Britain. A new tubular backbone chassis was designed in 1955 and, the following year, three competition sports cars went to America; all early TVRs which crossed the Atlantic were called Jomars, named for John and Margaret Saidal, the children of Ray Saidal, the first US importer. During 1957 the first of the now familiar GT coupés was made, pioneer of what was to become a familiar British type: a sporting GT car using a fibreglass body and proprietary components.

Arthur Lilley acquired the company in 1965, Martin Lilley became managing director, and the company name became TVR Engineering Ltd. This was retained through to the 1990s, although Peter Wheeler had taken over in 1982. Before the end of the 1960s the factory had settled down, and this was reflected in improved build quality. TVR survived by going for market niches, and filling them more competently than most, to the extent that in the 1980s it could claim to be the largest independent producer of sports cars in the UK.

**Grantura I, 1957-60. Prod: approx 100.** The first TVR sports cars had a smooth fibreglass body whose front and rear bodywork came from the same mould! Early TVRs were notch-back coupés (six built), and the first Granturas (in 1958) showed the unmistakeable influence of these cars: they were never formally styled, they just evolved. Under the skin was a tubular backbone frame with VW torsion bar and trailing arm independent suspension at both ends; engine options ranged from the Ford 1172cc side-valve unit to the MGA. As well as wide variations in mechanical specification, these early cars varied in other details for they were production-engineered on the run. Wire wheels were standard, as were drum brakes, but there was a long list of options and a few lightweight cars were built for racing. True to its roots, TVR sold these cars as kits in Britain.

TVR Grantura, 1958

**Grantura II/IIA, 1960-61/1961-62. Prod: approx 400.** Although by 1960 TVR faced many rivals for its niche in the market and the backstage moves by some of the investors in the company read like the script for a soap opera, it continued to make progress. It was helped by the quality of its fibreglass, the fact the Grantura was quieter than most cars in its class, and by continuous development.

Grantura IIA, 1962

Along the way, however, the car acquired about 100lb in extra weight, although the lightweight competition version remained an option. The 1588cc 80bhp MGA engine was usual but Ford and Coventry Climax units were optional. Rack and pinion steering was standard and the MkIIA had front disc brakes and the 1622cc 86bhp MGA engine. Although the car was finding acceptance, the company was in a mess and went into liquidation in 1962.

**Grantura III, 1962-64. Prod: approx 90.** Under new management production was slow to get into its stride, but the MkIII was a much improved car and was received enthusiastically by the press. There was a brand new chassis, also a multi-tubular backbone arrangement, and there was independent suspension all round by coil springs and wishbones. Although there were Ford and Climax options,

Grantura III, 1962

almost all cars had the 1622cc MGA engine or the 1782cc MGB unit. Both gave a 100mph/160kmh capability.

TVR's new priorities can be judged by the fact that most optional extras were comfort features, and the lightweight version was dropped. On the other hand, the works did enter a team of cars in selected events such as Le Mans and Sebring—and wished it hadn't, for the programme was a fiasco. All TVR cars built in this period stayed in Britain and were officially sold as kits to be assembled by selected dealers.

**Griffith 200/400, 1963-65. Prod: approx 300.** Legend has it that when the works TVRs raced at Sebring, they intrigued the American racing car entrant Jack Griffith, who saw them as a potential new 'Cobra'. Be that as it may, the first man to install a Ford V8 into a TVR was the British works driver Peter Bolton, who remembers it as a beast. When Griffith made an approach, TVR jumped at it and supplied body/chassis into which Griffith installed the 4727cc Ford V8, and four-speed Ford manual gearbox (automatic was an option). Griffith put his own badge on the cars when they arrived in America, which explains why some American writers often list it as a distinct marque.

Power ranged between 191bhp and 271bhp; even with the mild engine the car would top 140mph/225kmh (0-60mph in six seconds) while with a hot motor it would top 155mph/250kmh. The '200' cars were based on the MkIII, the '400' on the better-engineered TVR MkIV. Only 20 cars stayed in Britain, where some are still raced. While British TVR buyers would put up with the hard ride and patchy quality, American buyers (who were paying more) wanted better quality and better engineering and were not encouraged by such basic problems as a tendency to overheat.

TVR Griffith 200

There was another problem: when you replace an MG engine with a Ford V8 you get a *very* interesting change in weight distribution. When driven hard, the Griffith was unbalanced and fundamentally unsafe. The American writer David E. Davis summed it up: "[Griffith changed] it from a passive little car which did nothing wrong to a manic little car which did nothing right."

**Grantura MkIV/1800S, 1964-66/1966-67. Prod: 90/78.** Although the Grantura continued to be TVR's mainstay, the company essayed a number of prototypes. Most notably there was a lightweight and aerodynamically advanced coupé designed by Frank Costin, which was really not for TVR, and there was the lovely Trident (qv), which was taken over and produced separately. TVR was not set up to make either (it was going through a hairy period economically, and did not gain financial stability until the Lilley family acquired control in 1965). The 1800S was distinguished by its 'Manx' tail (with Ford Cortina tail lights); an MGB engine was standard, and a 115bhp version could be supplied on the MkIV. The other main differences were that the MkIV had steel wheels (wires optional), a larger fuel tank, better trim and an extended list of options which included a Sundym rear screen.

**Vixen S1/S2/S3, 1967-68/1968-70/ 1970-72. Prod: 117/438/168.** There was little to distinguish the Vixen from its predecessors apart from a new bonnet scoop. Under the new owners, however, the factory was able to

TVR Vixen S2

settle down and build the cars properly—quality, trim, and refinement improved. Although that brought a weight penalty, performance remained brisk (106mph/170kmh, 0-60mph in eleven seconds). Apart from the first 12 cars, which had MG engines, the Vixen line had the 1599cc Ford engine in 88bhp Cortina GT trim. The switch to Ford power and the fitting of steel wheels as standard (wires and alloys were options) helped to keep prices reasonable and the Vixen was a bargain at £998 as a kit or £1216 fully built. Since the Ford engine was lighter than the MGB unit there was no loss of performance despite a slight drop in power The optional brake servo became standard on the S2, which also had a longer wheelbase (90in, like the Tuscan SE), bolt-on (not bonded on) body panels, twin bonnet vents and Cortina MkII rear lights. The S3 had the 92bhp Capri version of the engine, and Zodiac side vents.

**Tuscan V8/V8SE, 1967/1968-70. Prod: 28/27.** TVR's new management decided to have another go at the 'Griffith' market. On paper, the Tuscan was a Griffith '400': it had the same engine options and the chassis was the same; the difference was that by 1967 the quality of the basic car, now called the Vixen, was a far cry from the 1963 Grantura. Unfortunately the American buyer, who had not seen a new TVR for some time, did not know this and had not forgotten the shortcomings of the Griffith. The original Tuscan fell like a lead balloon but TVR responded with a version with a longer wheelbase and a smoother body which presaged the 'M' series. Despite the car's improvements, its blistering performance, wider wheels, and competitive price (£2364 complete), there were few takers.

Tuscan V8

**Tuscan V6, 1969-71. Prod: 101.** While the V8 Tuscan was primarily intended for America, most of the cars built with the 136bhp 3-litre V6 Ford engine stayed at home. Fitting the V6 made for a good compromise because to drive the V8 cars quickly you either had to be very good, or have had a labotomy. The V6 car would have been better if the Ford gear ratios had been more suitable, yet with 125mph/200kmh top speed and 0-60mph in eight seconds it was a rapid, nimble and competent car—even if rough road surfaces would soon find any loose dental fillings. Since it cost only £1492 in kit form, it is surprising that there were relatively few takers.

Tuscan V6

**1300, 1971-72. Prod: 15.** TVR's economy model was a Vixen S3 fitted with the 63bhp Triumph Spitfire engine (and gearbox) but few wanted a Tivver which would barely top 90mph/145kmh. This is an interesting insight into the way buyers perceived the marque because Morgan has always been able to sell its 'slow' cars alongside models which for little more initial outlay will perform much better. Nine of the fifteen 1300s made had the old Grantura-style chassis, the last six had the new 'M' chassis which also appeared under the last Vixens. By that time TVRs had alloy wheels as standard.

**2500, 1971-72. Prod: 385.** The 2500 was another car which appeared in the interim period, but this time in a much more successful format. The designation referred to the 2.5-litre straight-six Triumph engine from the TR6, and the move was prompted by the increasingly severe US emission laws. TVR was determined to return to the US market and it regained a foothold with this model. More than half of the production run was exported, but the 104bhp version of the engine was pale by comparison with the 150bhp version the home market received. The US spec version was capable of 118mph/190kmh (0-60mph in ten seconds). Some of the last cars had the new 'M' chassis (see next entry).

TVR 2500, 1971

**Vixen S4, 1972-73. Prod: 23.** The last of the Vixen line was an interim car which used the new 'M' chassis under the old body. On paper, the 'M' chassis was the same as the l.w.b. (90in) Tuscan, but although tubular backbone construction was retained, it was an entirely new structure. It used round and square tubes, of two different gauges, and was stiffer than the old chassis despite being simpler and easier to build. The suspension was still by coil springs and double wishbones, with a slightly wider front track. Around this time, in 1971, TVR gained a lot of attention when it showed a prototype at the London Motor Show. There were two nude models draped over it but of greater historical interest is that it looked like a prototype for the 1974 Lotus Elite. Was this a missed opportunity for TVR?

**2500M, 1972-77. Prod: 947.** The first TVR to reflect the new management in every respect. From the beginning the 'M' chassis was used, coupled with a clever update of the old Grantura body which retained the essence of the shape but was longer, crisper and much roomier. In fact, it is one of the few shapes built by a small British maker which might reasonably have the tag 'timeless elegance' applied to it. As the designation implies it was a development of the previous 2500, which means the Triumph TR6 engine but, since most went to the USA with the de-toxed engine, few buyers saw the potential of the model. Production ended when Triumph stopped making the engine and, since the Ford V6 was not de-toxed, TVR withdrew from America for six years.

**3000M, 1972-79. Prod: 654.** While America received the de-toxed 2500M, the equivalent for British buyers was the identical chassis and body with Ford's 3-litre V6 in 138bhp Capri form. This meant 130mph/210kmh (0-60mph in 7.5 seconds) which were fair figures for the day, especially as the car was priced at only £2464 fully built. TVR's kit car days were almost over and 'M' models (save for the 1600) were factory-made; this was not only a shrewd move up-market but meant that the imposition of VAT in 1973 did not interrupt TVR's progress. Because of their light weight, and slippery shape, TVRs were also economical by comparison with the cars from whence their engines came, and this helped the company through the 1974 energy crisis.

TVR 3000M, 1978

**1600M, 1972-73/1975-77. Prod: 148.** The last TVR of which a significant number were sold in kit form—in fact the reason why the model was dropped in 1973 was the introduction of VAT. It was revived as the economy model TVR when market conditions dictated. The 1600M had Ford's 1588cc crossflow GT engine, which delivered 86bhp and was enough to give the car 105mph/169kmh and 0-60mph in 10.5 seconds, but of equal significance to buyers in those troubled times, it could deliver 35mpg on a cross country run.

**Taimar/Convertible, 1976-79/1978-79. Prod: 395/258.** The Taimar was a 3000M with a slightly restyled rear end to accommodate a hatchback. Thus, for the first time, a TVR owner could load the groceries or suitcases without pushing them over the seats. The Taimar was only sold with the 3-litre Ford engine and performance was the same as the 3000M. It took TVR over 20 years to come up with a convertible, which is odd considering so many of its recent cars have been rag tops. Again, it was based on the 3000M, but from windscreen back it was all new, and had a boot which opened. It did not, however, have wind-up windows but sliding sidescreens in detachable frames.

1978 Taimar

**Turbo, 1975-79. Prod: 3000M, 20; Taimar, 30; Convertible, 13.** In another sign of the ambitions of the new management, Broadspeed turbo conversions were offered on all three Ford V6-engined models. It was an image-building exercise rather than a mainstream car because 19mpg made many potential buyers take a deep breath. Still, it was Britain's first production turbocharged car and one of only a handful available anywhere, and it went like stink. With 230bhp under the bonnet, top speed was 139mph/224kmh and 0-60mph took only 5.8 seconds; further, it was a seamless conversion with none of the turbo

1976 Taimar Turbo

lag associated with many early turbo cars. The chassis remained unaltered, although wider tyres were fitted, so it still had a rock-hard ride, and the brakes were not as powerful as they might have been.

**Tasmin, introduced 1980.** With the Tasmin, TVR finally broke away from the Grantura, with an angular shape that reflected contemporary Italian thinking. It was built on an 'M' series chassis with the wheelbase extended by four inches. The independent rear suspension was by fixed length drive shafts and lower wishbones, Jaguar components being used. Originally launched as a two-seat coupé, within a year it was joined by a 2+2 coupé and a convertible, all on the same chassis. At first, Ford's 160bhp fuel-injected 2.8-litre V6 was fitted, and since that met US regulations, TVR began exporting to America again in 1983. The Tasmin was much more expensive than previous TVRs and the company made less luxurious version with the Ford 2-litre 'Pinto' engine.

TVR was taken over by Peter Wheeler in 1982. He wanted the cars to have more power and found it in the form of the Rover V8. This had another advantage—Arab customers would not buy a car with a Ford engine since Ford was proscribed because of its dealings with Israel.

In 1984 the name 'Tasmin' was dropped although it remained in use within the factory; the Ford-engined car was renamed the 280i (128mph/206kmh, 0-60mph in 7.8 seconds), and the 190bhp Rover version was marketed as the 350i (130mph/209kmh, 0-60mph in 6.3 seconds). Later that year came the 390SE, with a 275bhp 3.9-litre Rover engine (143mph/270kmh, 0-60mph in 5.7 seconds).

1980 Tasmin (top) 1986 400 SEAC (middle) and 1989 400SE (bottom)

In 1987, the Ford engine was dropped, and the range settled down with 3.5-litre, 4-litre, and 4.5-litre versions of the Rover engine. Apart from the unsuccessful Pinto-engined cars, which had four-speed gearboxes, buyers had a choice between five-speed manual 'boxes and for a while a three-speed automatic option.

1986 saw the 420 SEAC, which had a 300bhp 4.2-litre engine and was good for 150+mph/240+kmh (0-60mph in 5.6 seconds). It was the fastest TVR to date and SEAC stood for 'Special Equipment Aramid Composite'—Kevlar and carbon fibre were used in the car's construction.

Two years later the 400SE was introduced, with a revised body shape, a new interior and a 3943cc engine which produced 268bhp and gave 150mph/240kmh with 0-60mph in 5 seconds. By the end of 1989 the line had settled down to two models, the 400SE and 450SE. With the 4441cc 319bhp engine the 450 had a top speed of 155mph/250kmh (0-60mph in 4.7 seconds)—that was supercar performance, but at a fraction of the cost normally charged for it.

**S, introduced 1986.** With the 'Tasmin' series of cars TVR moved steadily up market and away from its roots. Peter Wheeler, the new owner, was concerned about this and in 1986 came the 'S', a design which cleverly captured the traditional TVR style. Its backbone chassis was similar to the 'Tasmin's' but with semi-trailing arm independent rear suspension. A two seat convertible, it was launched with the 2.8-litre Ford V6 engine and Ford five-speed gearbox. There were disc brakes on the front wheels, the standard of finish was high, and the hood was ingenious and easy to operate.

In late 1988 the model received the 2.9-litre Ford V6 engine and with some detail improvements in the chassis and trim it became the S2. The following year twin catalytic convertors were offered (S2C) and in 1990 the doors were redesigned (they became four inches longer) and long range driving lights were fitted under the front bumpers. This version was the S3/S3C. Road testers seemed to adore or dislike the 'S' but it undoubtedly filled a sizeable niche in the market since it was a real driver's car with sparkling performance (141mph/227kmh and 0-60mph in 6.8 seconds) at a reasonable price.

TVR S3C, 1990

**Tuscan, introduced 1988.** Originally intended as a road car, the Tuscan was made only as a competition model without type approval for road use. This did not prevent some buyers from exploiting loopholes in the laws of their countries and some were registered for road use. The tubular

TVR Tuscan Racer

backbone chassis was similar to the rest of the range, only the dimensions changed from model to model, there were disc brakes on all four wheels and suspension was by double wishbones all round. Power came from a 400bhp 4.4-litre version of the Rover V8 engine which resulted in a maximum speed of 165mph/265kmh (0-60mph in 3.7 seconds).

**Speed Eight, introduced 1989.** Originally the Speed Eight was intended as the eventual replacement for the 350i, but it was not received with overwhelming enthusiasm when first shown in 1989. A year was spent reworking the design and when the result was unveiled at the 1990 British Motor Show it had grown into a 2+2, the first convertible 2+2 in TVR's history. The backbone chassis was similar in concept to other TVR models, but a double wishbone rear suspension layout seen on the prototype was changed to fixed drive shafts and lower wishbones on production models.

A 240-bhp 3950cc version of the Rover V8 was used and TVR claimed a top speed of 144mph/232kmh (0-60mph in 5.7 seconds). A 286bhp 4.3-litre version was an option and, as on other models with the Rover engine, disc brakes were fitted all round. Production began in 1991.

**Griffith, introduced 1990.** The Griffith was designed to be the 'entry level' model to the range of cars with Rover engines. The body was entirely new, but much of the car, including the interior was sourced from the S3. The prototype had the trailing arm rear suspension from the S3 but Tuscan rear suspension was used on production cars when these began to appear in 1990. TVR claimed 240bhp from the 3.9-litre engine and this translated into 148mph/238kmh and 0-60mph in 4.9 seconds. TVR was particularly anxious that the power would be applicable to real driving conditions and the Griffith was claimed to be able to accelerate 30-70mph in 7.2 seconds in fourth gear.

The 1990 TVR Griffith

## **TWM** (GB)

A late 1950s maker of fibreglass body shells and chassis frames for the special builder, TWM also marketed a two-seat kit which used Austin A35 running gear. With the optional Downton Engineering version of the engine, it was claimed to be good for 100mph/160kmh.

## **TWR** (GB)

From the late 1970s Tom Walkinshaw Racing modified cars from Mazda, BMW and Jaguar. Hand in hand with these activities went a number of highly successful racing programmes, including Jaguar's Group C effort. In the late 1980s TWR Jaguar variants were marketed by a joint Jaguar-Walkinshaw company called 'JaguarSport' which was responsible for the Jaguar XJ220 and XJR-15 'supercars'.

## **TX** (GB)

Designed by Torix Bennett, son of the founder of Fairthorpe, some TX cars were sold under the Fairthorpe name but a separate company (Technical Exponents Ltd) was created in 1970 to market the 'Tripper'. Available complete or as a kit until 1978, the Tripper was a four-seat open car with a doorless fibreglass body which seemed inspired (if that's the word) by a beach buggy. The chassis was basically the same

TX Tripper departed in 1978

as that of the Fairthorpe TX GT, but suspension was from the Triumph GT6. The usual engines fitted were the Triumph Spitfire or Ford Cortina GT units, but options included the 2-litre or 2.5-litre Triumph straight-six. Too ugly to live, the Tripper's demise was a merciful release.

# U

## UIRAPURU (BR)

Originally called the 'Brasinca' when announced in 1965, this unsuccessful sports car was available in 1967 and 1968 in either open or coupé forms. Most of the running gear, including the 4.3-litre straight six, was sourced from locally made Chevrolet models.

## UNIPOWER (GB)

Originally commissioned by racing driver Roy Pierpoint, the first car was built by Andrew Hedges with an aluminium body. The project was then bought by Tim Powell, of Universal Power Drives, which made forestry tractors, and when the car went into production in 1966 it had a fibreglass body. Initially it sold quite strongly for a car of its type (50 road cars and 5 competition versions in the first two years) then the project changed hands. The new company, Unipower Cars Ltd, did not prosper and folded in 1970.

**GT, 1966-70. Prod: approx 70.** Widely regarded as one of the two best Mini-based cars ever made (the other is the Midas), the Unipower GT had its engine/gearbox unit in the back of its space frame, just ahead of the rear axle line. Suspension was independent all round by coil springs, the gear lever was mounted on the right hand door sill, and the fibreglass body was bonded on to the frame to create a rigid structure which contributed to the car's outstanding handling. 'Cooper' versions of the Mini engine were used, the 998cc version propelling the GT to 100mph/160kmh, while 120mph/193kmh was obtainable when the 1275cc engine was fitted.

The 1966 Unipower GT

## UNIQUE AUTOCRAFT (GB)

From 1981 this company built a Cobra 427 copy sold as the 'Python Roadster'. As with many such cars, Jaguar suspension was used together with a choice of engines.

## UNIQUE FABRICATION (USA)

A 1980s maker of fibreglass Cobra copies designed to take a wide range of proprietary suspension layouts as well as a choice of Ford or General Motors V8 engines.

## UNIQUE MOTORCARS (USA)

This was hardly an appropriate name for a company which was one of more than a dozen unlicenced copiers of the Cobra in the 1980s. This version used MGB front and Jaguar rear suspension in a square-tube chassis, with a choice of V8 engines.

## US FIBERGLASS (USA)

A fibreglass-bodied sports car of 1956 (only) which was available complete, or in kit form, with numerous engine and chassis options.

## US GULLWING (USA)

As the name suggests, this was a fibreglass copy of the Mercedes-Benz 300SL. Introduced in 1981 as a complete car,

US Gullwing's 300SL copy

it won praise for its accuracy: it had a space frame chassis, just like the original, and its 3.7-litre Chrysler straight six was mounted at a slant, again like the real thing. At about $40,000 when it appeared, it was even priced like the real thing. As for it being fibreglass, Mercedes-Benz had built at least one fibreglass 300SL with a view to production, but had abandoned it because it was not satisfied with its standard of finish.

## UVA (GB)

From 1982 the grandly named Unique Vehicle and Accessory Co Ltd has been one of the mainstays of the British kit car industry. Its first offering, the 'Bullet', was a wedge-shaped trike with a lift-up cockpit cover which originated in South Africa and, with the right motorcycle engine stuffed in the back, was claimed to be capable of 150mph/240kmh! Also in 1982, UVA offered the 'Montage', following an American copy (by Manta, qv) of the one-off McLaren M6 GT car but based on a VW Beetle chassis. By 1986 the range included the F33 Can-Am, which was a street-legal evocation of 1960s Can-Am cars (with a full roll cage) and was designed to take a V8 engine mounted amidships. UVA also made the 'Fugitive', a Baja-style roadster based on VW Beetle running gear.

**UVA Montage (top), F33 Can Am (middle) and Fugitive (bottom)**

# V

## VALIENTE (USA)

An outrageous two-seat open 'nostalgia' car of 1981; it had a fibreglass body, an enormous bonnet, and running gear and a 7.5-litre V8 engine by Lincoln.

## VANWALL (GB)

In 1990 a 'limited' edition of a new sports coupé that would revive the name of the 1950s Formula 1 team was announced. The car was based on a special Lotus which GKN (the current owner of Vandervell Products, the company which made the Vanwall) had commissioned as an exhibition/publicity vehicle in 1969. This was a Lotus 47 (the racing version of the Europe) fitted with a Rover V8 engine, five-speed ZF gearbox, wider wheels and uprated brakes.

## VAUGHAN (USA)

A very obscure outfit, which announced a sports car in 1954. There seems to be no record that a car was completed, let alone delivered, but one was shown. A 1.5-litre ohc V8 engine was plannned.

**Vaughan Super Sports with Ghia body was shown in 1954**

## VECTOR (USA)

An American supercar which popped up in reference books from 1980 as a 'real' car and even threatened to be put into production. A 5.7-litre Chevrolet engine, with twin turbochargers, was mounted amidships in an aluminium monocoque and delivered its 600bhp through a reversed Oldsmobile Toronado (originally front wheel drive) transmission. Front suspension was by coil springs and double wishbones, while the rear layout used a de Dion axle. Styling was spectacular, with gull-wing doors, and every conceivable extra was offered, including heated seats. Depending on turbo boost, speeds of up to 240mph/390kmh were *claimed* so, naturally, there were massive disc brakes all round.

**The 600bhp Vector**

Details of cars completed and sold remain in skeletal outline only, but then one would not expect one's tailor to divulge information about one's wardrobe—if something can be bought off the peg, like a Ferrari F40, it is too cheap to be of lasting value.

## VECTOR ENTERPRISES (USA)

A late 1980s copy of the 1984 Chevrolet Corvette for poor people who could not afford the real thing but who could stretch to a fibreglass body and a medium-sized GM donor car such as the Pontiac Le Mans or Chevrolet Monte Carlo.

## VEGA (USA)

In 1950 this sports car won a design competition organised by a motor magazine and three years later it appeared in the metal. It had a space frame skinned with an aluminium body, and a 2.2-litre side-valve Ford V8 engine. Production models were scheduled to have fibreglass panels and a range of engines including MG and Singer units, but it is doubtful if it reached production.

## VERITAS (D)

Just after the Second World War former BMW engineers Ernst Loof and Lorenz Dietrich combined with ex-Auto Union driver Schorsch Meier to build sports cars. This was no easy job in postwar Germany (in the American zone no car over 1000cc could be built) but they invited owners of BMW 328s to bring their cars for conversion to sports-racers and single seaters. They then moved to the French zone, where they could operate openly, and Loof designed a new engine based on the BMW 328 unit which was built by Heinkel. Perhaps this was too ambitious, for the firm folded in 1950 and Dietrich left. Loof, however, returned in the same year and, from a workshop under the main grandstand at the Nurburgring, made small numbers of cars through to 1953. Then he returned to BMW, which had just resumed car production. Although ultimately a failure, Veritas did more than any other marque to revive motor sport in Germany after the War.

**Meteor, 1948-50. Prod: 78 (all types).** This two-seater was based on the tubular frame of the special BMW which won the 1940 Brescia GP (sometimes wrongly, called the 1940 Mille Miglia). Power came from BMW 328 engines in various states of tune, and some even had roller bearings. Since Loof was a BMW man, and BMW had been streets ahead of other companies before the War when it came to aerodynamics on its competition cars, the Meteor had an enveloping body. Germany was not permitted to export complete cars but the contents of some crates of 'spares' imported into France bore a marked similarity to the Meteor.

Veritas Meteor at the 1950 Eifelrennen

**Dyna-Veritas, 1950-52. Prod: see above.** This is a really obscure motor car. It used a tubular frame and a 744cc flat-twin Panhard engine complete with Panhard gearbox and front wheel drive. The cabriolet bodies were designed by Veritas and built by Baur of Stuttgart. It was a nicely proportioned little car but it was only another Panhard special and few Germans had the cash to buy one.

1951 Dyna-Veritas

**Saturn/Scorpion/Comet, 1950-52. Prod: see above.** All of these cars had Loof's new seven-bearing 'square' straight six of 1988cc, although short-stroke 1.5-litre versions could be supplied and BMW 328 engines were also fitted. Between 98bhp and 147bhp was available, fed through a five-speed 'box (very unusual at the time), and although the old BMW frame was retained it had uprated brakes and a de Dion rear axle. The Saturn was a coupé, the Scorpion a cabriolet, and both had 102in wheelbases, while the Comet was a dual-purpose car on a 92.5in wheelbase. For the record, Loof also built a long wheelbase saloon/cabriolet, the Jupiter.

Veritas Saturn, 1950

## VERONAC (CDN)

From 1981 this company made high-quality and expensive copies of the Auburn Speedster, Cord 810 and various types of Duesenberg, including reproductions of one-off special bodies. The power unit was normally a 400bhp GM V8.

## VETTA VENTURA (USA)

Made in small numbers by the Vanguard Motors Corp of Dallas between 1964 and 1966, the Buick-powered Vetta Ventura was identical to the Apollo (qv) but outlasted it by a few months and was available only as a coupé.

1964 Vetta Ventura

## VEYRAT (F)

First shown in 1990 with a view to production in 1991, the Veyrat 630 VS was an open mid-engined two seater with styling following the prototype Pininfarina Mythos. Its construction followed contemporary competition car practice, with fully rose-jointed double wishbone and coil spring independent suspension all round, and a body combining aluminium and carbon fibre. Power came from a standard 200bhp 3-litre Alfa Romeo V6 engine, and since the prototype weighed only 1870lb acceleration was claimed to be *electrifying*. One day, perhaps, scholars may be able to probe the depths of such words and we may all gain as a result.

## VICTRESS (USA)

A mid-1950s maker of chassis frames and fibreglass bodies

1954 Victress

to enable the enthusiast to make open or coupé sports cars using almost any American car as a donor.

## VIKING (GB)

Claimed to have been inspired by the SS100, this project of the early 1980s required the eager punter to provide a Jaguar 'S' or XJ6, and a fairly large bag of gold. In return he would receive an ungainly 1930s-style two seater. It appears that few, if any, were so foolish.

## VIKING CARS (GB)

This boxy 2+2 coupé, which used Ford Escort Mk1/2 running gear, arrived in 1987 and seems to have departed soon afterwards.

## VINCENT (GB)

A 1980s maker of a fibreglass body kit, the 'Hurricane', to save rusted Triumph Spitfires and GT6s.

**Vincent Hurricane**

## VINCENT *see* SWINDON SPORTS CARS

## VINDICATOR (GB)

Introduced in 1990, the Vindicator SR was a low-cost sports car with an originally styled full-width fibreglass body, a Targa top, and Ford Cortina Mk 4/5 running gear. The same year Vindicator announced the 'Sprint', a basic sports car in the Caterham Seven idiom.

## VINLAND (IS)

Haraldur 'Harry' Magnusson came to England in 1959 with the aim of making his mark as a racing driver, but he committed himself to the 500cc Formula 3 at a time when it had become a lost cause. To support himself Harry worked for John Tojeiro (qv) as a welder and when he returned to Iceland in 1960 he was regarded as a man of some stature in local motoring circles. On the back of that Magnusson built a copy of the AC Ace (originally a Tojeiro design) but, to circumvent Iceland's tax rules, it was fitted with the 997cc Ford 105E engine and was sold as the Vinland 'Saga'.

Performance was mediocre by most people's standards but was more than adequate for Iceland's road system and 19 were made in the first year. In 1961 the veteran Indycar racer, Chuck Garfield, announced plans to import the chassis/body into California and fit an American V8 engine. The Cobra had not appeared in 1961 and the name 'Chuck Garfield' does not appear in Carroll Shelby's book on the Cobra.

Unfortunately for Garfield, before he could take delivery of the first chassis the Vinland project folded—there were simply not enough people in Iceland who wanted to buy an open sports car. Harry Magnusson later became one of the key men in Saab's rally programme. Some Vinland Sagas have been fitted with 4.7-litre Ford V8 engines and passed off as Cobras.

## VISCOUNT MOTORS (GB)

With a fibreglass body which vaguely recalled the lines of the Aston Martin Ulster, the mid-1980s 'TC' was designed to make a 'traditional' sports car from a rusted Triumph Herald but it suffered from direct comparison with NG's rival kit.

## VM (D)

A late 1980s maker of Lotus/Caterham Seven lookalikes marketed as the Rahman (105bhp 2-litre Ford engine) and the Seventy Seven (115bhp 2-litre Ford engine). In 1990 the company was working on an original design to be known as the 'Nardo'.

## VOLKSWAGEN (D)

Since so many cars in this volume are based on the VW Beetle, it would be odd if the model was not recorded. Dr Ferdinand Porsche believed in a 'people's car' and in 1931 began work on his Project 12, which was the Beetle's recognisable ancestor. He could not afford to make it himself but the motorcycle manufacturers, Zündapp, commissioned a design for a popular car, and three prototypes were made before Zündapp withdrew when the motorcycle market perked up. In 1933 another motorcycle maker, NSU, commissioned work on a car; more prototypes were made and then NSU decided to concentrate on its motorcycles, but further progress had been made.

One person who shared Porsche's dream of a cheap popular car was Adolf Hitler and in 1934 Porsche was invited to meet the German Chancellor to discuss such a project. Typically, Hitler was long on ideas and short on money, so Porsche was more or less ordered to proceed, and he had to use some of his own money to do so. Further, there was concerted opposition from other German car makers who did not like the idea of a cut-price car, but when Adolf said something was good everybody had to agree that, yes, it had its points.

Hitler laid the foundation stone for the Volkswagenwerk

in May 1938 and then announced that the car was to be known as the KdF-Wagen (*Kraft durch Freude* or 'Strength Through Joy'). The KdF-Wagen had a backbone chassis and pressed steel floorpan. Suspension was independent all round by torsion bars; there were twin trailing links at the front and swing axles at the rear. The engine was a rear-mounted flat-four air-cooled ohv unit, initially of 985cc, which gave 24bhp and drove through a four-speed gearbox. The first batch of 210 cars, the only ones made pre-war, had no rear windows but a louvred metal panel because that kept the price down. Incidentally, the 'Beetle' nickname first became popular in 1939.

During the War, the chassis was adapted to become the 1131cc Kübelwagen, a personnel carrier, and a four wheel drive amphibian, the Schwimmwagen. After the War these provided the materials for many a special builder, including Ferdinand Porsche's son Ferry. The factory was heavily bombed and the entire project was offered as war reparations to several countries, including Britain. Naturally the British motor industry saw no future in the Beetle but a British army officer, Major Ivan Hirst, did see the car's potential. With a small army contingent, he organised civilian labour and resumed production in August 1945. By the time the company returned to German administration at the beginning of 1948, production was running at about 600 a week.

The rest is history. The model was constantly uprated but Porsche's concept remained unchanged; and the fledgling Porsche company received a royalty on each car made. Thanks to Ferdinand Porsche's thinking, the Beetle was notable for three things: reliability, finish, and panel fit. Since these were not characteristic of most contemporary cars, the Beetle became very popular.

Beetle enthusiasts have made so many claims for the car that it should be said that it was sluggish, road holding was never good (a rear-engined car is inherently unstable), luggage space was poor, it was noisy and the interior was spartan, and the front-mounted fuel tank was vulnerable. The story was that Beetles did not rust, so why do you never see one made in 1960-61? VW used poor quality steel in that period but its PR department buried the bad news.

The Beetle became a cult car and all cult cars either have rounded lines, like a nursery toy (eg Citroën 2CV and Morris Minor), or have a cheeky 'human' face (eg Mini and Frogeye Sprite). The Beetle had both and so became a cult despite its many shortcomings.

A huge number of sports cars have been built using the Beetle chassis as a starting point and VW essayed a couple of cars on the same lines. The writer does not believe that they were sports cars, even by the lights of their time and place, but they are included here because if a rebodied Beetle can pass as a sports car in Brazil, a Beetle rebodied in Germany should be accepted. Later Volkswagen offerings such as the Scirocco and Corrado are pleasant, if bland, cars but Volkswagen's idea of what is a real sports car can be seen under 'VW-Porsche' or in the Porsche 924, originally a VW commission.

**1200 Karmann Ghia Coupé/Cabriolet, 1955-65/1957-65. Prod: 364,401/80,899.** Styled by Ghia in Italy, and built by Karmann in Germany, the VW Karmann

**Volkswagen 1200 Karmann Ghia Cabriolet**

Ghia was a 2+2 built on the running gear of the stock Beetle 1200, which meant the 34bhp 1192cc engine and a top speed of only 77mph/124kmh. If that seems dull, it should be remembered that the standard Beetle of the time was exhausted at 68mph/110kmh. The improved top speed came from better aerodynamics but, since the cars were heavier than the saloon, acceleration was slower and 0-60mph had to be measured with a diary, not an hourglass. The rag top version of 1957 was a neat conversion but the Beetle was no real basis for a sports car; its handling was never up to snuff, it had terrible oversteer when cornering hard, and its response to strong crosswinds was to seek the nearest ditch.

**1500S/1600 Karmann Ghia, 1963-65/ 1965-69. Prod: 42,563 (both types).** Based on the VW Variant rather than the standard Beetle, the second expression of the Karmann Ghia line had the larger engines (the 54bhp 1493cc version and the slightly more powerful and more torquey 1584cc unit). The styling was gross and there was no cabriolet version.

**1500S/1600 Karmann Ghia Coupé**

## VOLKSWAGEN-PORSCHE (D)

The very first Porsche was a VW special built by Ferry Porsche, son of the Beetle designer. By the late 1960s, Porsche had put such humble beginnings far behind it, but the historical links remained strong and, indeed, Porsche was a technical consultant to VW. In 1969 came the first public expression of that relationship, a mid-engined sports car (with Targa top) which was marketed under the names of both companies and was available with either a VW or a Porsche engine. This ploy did not work, Porsche buyers did not like the Beetle badge, and the companies' next collaboration was marketed as a 'Porsche' (924).

**914S/914SC, 1969-73/1972-75. Prod: 78,643.** This was more VW than Porsche since the 914S had the air-cooled flat-four engine from the VW 411; it was of 1679cc until 1972 when a 1795cc version was fitted. Many of the other components, including suspension, came from VW but there were disc brakes on all four wheels and a five-speed gearbox with a Sportomatic option. Despite awful styling and an inflated price tag it sold quite strongly in some markets, but not at all well in others such as Britain. The 914SC (lhd only) had a 1971cc engine and 120mph/195kmh was claimed, but that did not improve the beast's looks, lower the price, or erase the VW badge.

1973 VW-Porsche 914

**914/6, 1969-72. Prod: 3351.** Like the 914S, the 'Porsche' version (it had a 110bhp 911T engine) handled well but it still had odd looks and a high price tag. Performance was quite respectable for the time, with a top speed of 125mph/200kmh (0-60mph in 8.3 seconds) but few people wanted a car with a VW badge which cost more than a Jaguar E Type, and Porsche freaks shied away from a car which, although it handled better than a 911T, cost almost as much as a real Porsche. In fact, apart from badging, the only outward sign that this was the 'superior' version was Porsche wheels. Soon after its launch it was clear that it was never going to sell, and no rhd version was made.

VW-Porsche 914/6

**916, 1971. Prod: 20.** In an attempt to put some zip into the 914/6, Porsche planned a version with the 190bhp fuel-injected 911S engine. This had wider tyres, a top speed of 145mph/233kmh, and a fixed roof instead of the Targa top. It could have been a real road burner but Porsche read the sales figures which the 'affordable' cars were achieving and realised that, for all its merits, the more expensive 916 would bomb. The project was therefore cancelled before production had officially begun.

VW-Porsche 916

## VOLVO (S)

The frivolity which everyone associates with Sweden is epitomised by Volvo. Founded in 1926, it sells cars on the safety ticket yet has never pioneered an active safety measure (e.g. anti-lock brakes), for Volvos protect passengers *after* a crash. From time to time, however, Volvo has essayed a sports car but they have been joyless.

**P1900, 1956. Prod: 67.** In 1954 an arrangement with the American fibreglass specialist Glasspar (qv) resulted in a pleasant-looking two-seat sports car on a tubular chassis with PV444 saloon suspension, 1.4-litre 70bhp engine, three-speed gearbox and six volt electrics. This was first seen in 1955, and went into production in 1956. It did not take the world by storm and one of the first acts of newly-appointed chief executive Engellau was to axe the model.

Volvo P1900, 1956

**P1800/1800S/1800E, 1961-64/1964-68/1969-71. Prod: 6000/23,993/9414.** The overweight 1800 began life with a 100bhp version of the 1778cc 'Amazon' engine which would propel it to 107mph/172kmh (0-60mph in 13.9 seconds). Until 1964 Jensen assembled the cars. When assembly was transferred to Sweden power increased to 108bhp, rising to 115bhp in 1967 (115mph/185kmh, 0-60mph in 10.1 seconds). The cars had the usual Volvo characteristics: solid build, good brakes, and comfortable interior. It received an image boost it did not deserve when it featured in the television series *The Saint*, but the producers had really wanted Jaguar to supply an E Type.

Volvo P1800S, 1964

**1800ES, 1971-73. Prod: 8078.** Since the concept of a sports car was too exciting for Volvo's customers it was natural to turn the coupé into a 'sporting estate'. The result was actually too cramped to be a true dual purpose car although the rear passengers got a better deal than in most such types. As on all the earlier cars there were servo-assisted front disc brakes, but the engine was larger at 1958cc and power was up to 120bhp (112bhp in America).

Volvo P1800ES

**480ES/Turbo, introduced 1986.** The 480 had quite a pleasing and distinctive shape, but only Volvo would call it a sports car. Base engine was a 1.7-litre ex-Renault four giving 106bhp when injected, 120bhp with a turbo (which meant 120mph/193kmh and 0-60mph in nine seconds). Cornering power was good, thanks to an input by Lotus, but the steering was stodgy. It had the usual Volvo strong points, but the prayer of every true sports car enthusiast must be that he will never grow so old and feeble as to want one. In 1990 Volvo startled the automotive world by showing an open two-seat version and threatened to put it in production.

1990 Volvo 480ES Cabriolet

## VOODOO (GB)

The Voodoo was another promising British design which ran into the black hole of tax regulations in 1973. The chassis was designed by John Arnold, the body by Geoff Neale, and originally they had no plans other than to build a car each. The first one finished was displayed on the *Weekend Telegraph* stand at the 1971 London Motor Show; that led to requests to display it elsewhere and, before long, to promises of finance to begin production as a fully-finished, high-specification car.

At just 35in high, the Voodoo was one of the lowest closed cars ever built. Front suspension was Vauxhall HA Viva, and Imp units were used at the rear. Entry was by lifting the whole cockpit, assisted by gas rams. The second car to be finished was shown at the 1973 Racing Car Show in London and had a full-race 90bhp 998cc Imp Sport engine (production cars had a 70bhp unit). A combination of low drag and lightness made the claimed top speed of 115mph/185kmh with excellent fuel consumption seem realistic and it looked as though the Voodoo might succeed—but then came VAT. A kit version of the car was revived in the 1980s as the Cheetah Mirach using an Alfasud engine and gearbox.

The 1971 Voodoo

## VOPARD (USA)

Founded in 1977, this company first made the 'Vokaro', a doorless two-seater sports car on a shortened VW Beetle floorpan. That side of the business became a separate company, Quantum (qv), in the 1980s, while Vopard marketed a copy of the Ginetta G12 space frame topped by a body which recalled the McLaren M6GT.

Vopard Vokaro two seater and 2+2

# W

## WACKER *see* BRÜTSCH

## WARMOUTH (D)

From the late 1980s this German firm made a turn key version of the Apollo 'Verona'. It was not exactly like the American parent since Warmouth made its own multi-tubular chassis frame and, because it used BMW running gear, some of the dimensions were changed. The running gear was from the 5-Series, with the exception of Jaguar coil spring and double wishbone front suspension, and buyers had the choice of the 170bhp 2.5-litre unit, the 211bhp 3.5-litre engine, or a special equipment 250bhp version. Even with the 'cooking' engine top speed was 131mph/210kmh (0-62mph in 7.6 seconds). Some idea of the quality of this car can be gauged by the fact that in 1990 Warmouth was one of only a tiny handful of companies to which BMW was prepared to supply components.

## WARRIOR (USA)

Made by Vanguard Products, an air conditioner manufacturer based in Dallas, the 'Warrior' was a two-seat Targa-top sports car with a mid-mounted German Ford V4 engine. It was built for only one year, 1964.

## WARTBURG (D)

After the Second World War the motor industry in East Germany was nationalised under the IFA collective label. In 1956 the marque name 'Wartburg' was revived to apply to a new model based on the IFA F9 which, in turn, was based on a pre-war DKW design. These were made in the old BMW works at Eisenach—the town where the pioneer German maker Heinrich Ehrhardt had built Decauville cars under licence and marketed them under the Wartburg name, 1898-1904. BMW had also used the name in 1930 for a sports version of the Dixi, an Austin Seven built under licence.

**Wartburg Sport, 1958**

The IFA Wartburg had a three-cylinder two-stroke engine of 894cc which drove through the front wheels. Normally 40bhp was available but the company also made a 50bhp coupé, the Sport 313-1. It was a handsome car which had something of the Mercedes-Benz 190SL about it but, at the time of writing, exact production figures were still unobtainable.

## WARWICK (GB)

After the failure of the Peerless, the designer, Bernie Rodger, modified the concept and marketed it as the Warwick. Externally, the main differences were in moulded rain gutters and headlight treatment, but Rodger managed to shed about 80lb while creating a stiffer frame. Among other improvements were a revised dashboard and a one-piece forward-hinging bonnet. As with the Peerless, Triumph TR3 running gear, engine and gearbox (with overdrive on the top three gears) were installed in a space frame with a de Dion back axle suspended on semi-elliptic springs. The venture was under-financed, the car was not made to the highest standards, and production lasted only from late 1960 to late 1961.

Towards the end of the Warwick's short life a 3.5-litre Buick V8 engine (later taken over by Rover) was fitted to a prototype, but the intention to offer this as an option was not carried through. The idea of fitting a V8 engine into a space frame was picked up by John Gordon, one of the backers of the Peerless, and led to the Gordon-Keeble (qv).

An interesting variant was later built by Chris Lawrence (*see* Deep Sanderson, Morgan and Monica) from Peerless and Warwick components. Called the 'Peewick', it was Lawrence's idea of what the car should have been and had a new frame with a shorter wheelbase, lightly revised suspension and a Lawrencetune TR3A engine. A top speed of 135mph/217kmh was claimed. It remained a prototype.

**Warwick GT of 1960**

## WATFORD (GB)

One of a plethora of companies which between 1959 and 1962 offered a chassis frame and fibreglass body to convert a Ford Ten into the car of your dreams. A version called the 'Cheetah' had all-independent suspension, using Triumph Herald components.

## WATLING (GB)

Watling was one of the many British companies which in the late 1950s made fibreglass bodies for the special builder, alongside its boats and caravans. In 1959 the company began to offer a variety of kits using its bodies and a ladder frame chassis, which was available in two sizes to accommodate almost any running gear. Watling also supplied complete kits with Ford 1172cc or 105E (Anglia) engines but the car building side of the business folded in 1961, an early victim of the sudden down-turn in the kit car industry.

## WD see DENZEL

## WEINEM (CH)

From 1980 Weinem made a copy of the Cobra 427 which used a 5.7-litre Chevrolet V8.

## WELLINGTON (USA)

A fibreglass Mercedes-Benz SS lookalike with four seats and a range of small capacity engine options.

## WESTCHESTER FIBERGLASS (USA)

Chevrolet Corvettes made between 1968 and 1982 were decent enough cars but in the late 1980s some buyers passed them over to Westchester and received, in return, a 'New York Roadster' which had the style of a Ferrari Daytona Spyder. Under the skin, of course, it was still a Corvette.

## WEST COAST COBRA (USA)

This 1980s maker produced a part-assembled 'Cobra' kit using Ford components in a new chassis.

## WESTERN CLASSICS (GB)

In 1987 this company took over production of a copy of the Ferrari 250LM which had been originated in the early 1980s by Replicar (qv). Like the original it was designed to fit on a VW Beetle chassis but the company also listed a backbone space frame designed by Jago Fabrications. Offered as the 164LM (1.6 litres and four cylinders—that spells Ford) this version used Ford Granada suspension and a mid-mounted Ford CVH engine which could include the Escort Turbo version (135mph/217kmh and 0-60mph in under six seconds). Great things were forecast for this kit but it turned out to be a short-lived effort. In 1990 it was revived by Tiger Cars (qv) and re-engineered to take VW Golf components.

## WESTFIELD (GB)

In 1983, Westfield launched the Eleven, a fibreglass copy of Frank Costin's classic body for the Lotus Eleven, based on a space frame and using Sprite/Midget components. This was a great success and, in 1984, Westfield followed it withe the 'Seven' which was such a blatant copy of the Lotus/Caterham Seven that Caterham Cars took legal action—and, in 1987, won. Westfield agreed to modify its design and afterwards concentrated on the SE, which looked like a close relative of the Caterham Seven but was sufficiently different to avoid further action.

**Westfield Seven (above) and SEi (below)**

## WILRO see CROSLEY and SKORPION

## WIMILLE (F)

Jean-Pierre Wimille was an authentic hero of the French Resistance and, in the immediate postwar period, most people's choice as the greatest racing driver in the world. His advanced sports coupé first saw light of day in 1946 but there were understandable delays in getting it into production and only seven had been made by 1949, when Wimille was killed in a racing accident.

1948 Wimille prototype

Odd looking but very slippery, the Wimille began life with a Citroën 11CV engine but those built from 1948 had a 2.3-litre side valve Ford V8, a French cousin of the V8 Pilot engine. The chassis was a twin-tube affair with substantial cross-bracing to make a very rigid structure, front suspension was by coil springs and double wishbones, and the independent rear set-up was by coil springs and trailing arms. The engine was mid-mounted and although the maker of the four-speed rear-mounted gearbox was not acknowledged in the company's literature, it appears to have been an adaptation of the Citroën fwd unit.

The short bonnet contained the radiator, battery and spare wheel; the driver sat in the middle with twin passenger seats a little further back. Body features ahead of their time were the 'Venetian blind' rear window treatment (later popularised by the Lamborghini Miura), recessed door handles, and doors which extended into the roof-line. Production cars had the radiator in the rear, with air intakes just behind the doors, which allowed some luggage space. Even with only about 70bhp it was claimed that the car would top the ton, which speaks volumes for its aerodynamic efficiency.

## **WINGFIELD** (GB)

Since the early 1980s, Ford GT40 restorer Bryan Wingfield has made small numbers of very accurate copies of the Jaguar C and D Types sourced from the Jaguar E Type. In 1990 the company, which had become 'Deetype Replicas Ltd', showed a version of the one-off Jaguar XJ13.

## **WIZARD ROADSTERS** (GB)

Long established British VW Beetle specialist whose wide range of fibreglass bodies included an evocation of a 1930s Willys Coupe for street rodding.

Wizard Beetle Roadster

## **WOODILL** (USA)

'Woody' Woodill was a pioneer American kit car maker who claimed it was possible to make one of his cars in 14 hours, and apparently proved it. He bought fibreglass bodies from Glasspar and modified them, adding hinges, locks and so on. The chassis was engineered to take Ford parts, and some cars were sold complete, making them the world's first fibreglass-bodied production car.

Between 1952 and 1958, for an American with $2000 and a donor car, the Wildfire offered street-cred on the cheap, and if you wanted style without getting your hands dirty, you could buy one complete for $3260. Since the suspension and brakes were Ford, and the chassis was not the epitome of rigidity, you would not have wanted to race one against, say, a TR3 on a winding road but, for a time, they enjoyed immense prestige and appeared in three Hollywood movies. Exact production figures remain a mystery: Woodill estimated 300, Glasspar said it supplied less than 100 bodies.

Woodill Wildfire, 1956

## **WYNES** (GB)

From 1990 Wynes made the 'McCoy', which had previously been built by Birchall (qv).

1990 Wynes McCoy

## **XILLION** (USA)

In the late 1980s, Xillion began to convert Pontiac Fieros into something which could be mistaken for a Ferrari 328. Satisfied with this project, Xillion launched plans to convert Fieros into lookalikes of other mid-engined cars—and the civilised world was unable to stop it.

## **XR-6** (USA)

A *Hot Rod* magazine project, built to inspire its readers in 1964. An open two-seater, it had a tubular chassis, a slim angular body with odd cycle wings and a Dodge six-cylinder engine.

## **XTC** (USA)

XTC offered to convert a Pontiac Fiero into a customised Ferrari Testarossa, convert Plain Jane into Sophia Loren. Under the plastic surgery, the car was still a Fiero.

## **YANK** (USA)

A two-seat aluminium-bodied sports car offered with a Willys 2.2-litre four-cylinder engine in 1950. Top speed was 78mph/125kmh (about the same as the MG TD), but even with a modest $1000 price tag there were few takers.

## **YANKEE CLIPPER** (USA)

Offered between 1953 and 1954, the Clipper had a lightweight chassis which used mainly Ford running gear, including a 130bhp V8 engine, and was finished by a Glasspar G-2 fibreglass body. The car was low and mean but needed to be sold at a rate of ten a week to justify its price of $3400. The buying public, however, decided that this was too much to pay for something with a special builder's body and few were sold.

## **YIMKIN** (GB)

Yimkin Engineering appeared in the late 1950s as an engine tuning workshop, specializing in the BMC 'A' and 'B' series engines. In 1958 it started to make a basic 'clubman's' sports car to the usual recipe: a space frame, coil spring and double wishbone front suspension, a well-located live rear axle, and a skimpy body with cycle wings. About six were made, and most were used on both road and track, enjoying enough success on the tracks for a couple more to be built for Formula Junior. Yimkin folded when both partners married—a business which will support two enthusiastic bachelors will not necessarily support two families—but one of the partners, Don Sim, later bounced back with his Diva GT (qv).

# Z

## ZENDER (D)

Every so often Zender threatens the world with an original sports car design, but, in the end, it continues to make conversions and body kits. The main problem has been economic and so a series of promising prototypes have remained no more than that. The company's most recent prototype was the FACT 4, a mid-engined coupé in the Italian supercar idiom. It had a body and monocoque of carbon fibre and a twin turbocharged version of the 3562cc Audi V8 engine which delivered its 448bhp through a five-speed ZF gearbox. A top speed of 190mph/305kmh (0-60mph in 4.2 seconds) was claimed.

**Zender FACT 4**

## ZETA (AUS)

Lightburn of Adelaide was a diverse company whose activities included the assembly of Alfa Romeos for the Australian market. In 1963 it marketed a utility micro-car and followed with a sports version styled by Michelotti. The plot was a channel chassis, all-independent suspension, a fibreglass body and a mid-mounted 16bhp 500cc F.M.R. engine. Top speed was claimed to be 75mph but the Zeta Sports really belonged to the micro-car craze of the mid-Fifties rather than the Sixties, when the Mini and Sprite were on the scene. Neither model sold particularly well and the company ceased production in 1966 having made a total of about 350 cars, 48 of them the sports model.

## ZIGCLAIR (GB)

Late 1970s maker of a 1930s style kit car with a radiator that was suspiciously similar to the R-R trademark. A tubular chassis took modified Triumph Spitfire suspension and the usual engine was the MGB unit but very few were made.

## ZIMMER (USA)

In 1980, the well-known caravan maker, Zimmer, began to market a 'nostalgia' coupé, the 'Golden Spirit'. A bespoke coil-sprung chassis, which had a wheelbase of 142 inches, used Ford running gear including a 4.2 litre V8 engine. Like most nostalgia cars it was extravagent and outrageous, more for show than go.

## ZITA (GB)

First seen in 1971, the Zita ZS had a handsome, and well-trimmed, fibreglass body fitted to a VW Beetle floorpan. It was intended to offer a complete kit, with full trim, wiring and instruments, but only one further car was made before the project fell apart due to an internal disagreement among the partners who made it. It is possible that some further examples were made using Austin 1800 components in a bespoke chassis.

# INDEX TO MODELS

The alphabetical sequence means that this book is also an index to makes. This supplementary index is a guide to model names and to copies of cars that were originally built by major manufacturers. The copies are indexed under the name of the source model where this is a post-1945 car included in the book.

# INDEX TO PERSONALITIES

---

**Author's Acknowledgment**

The author wishes to express his particular thanks to Mike Cotton and Ed McDonough for their help

**Picture Acknowledgments**

The author and the publisher are grateful to the following for supplying photographs reproduced in this book: Nick Baldwin, Rob de la Rive Box, Peter Gowar, Haymarket Publishing Ltd (Archivist Christopher Balfour), David Hodges, R. Perry Zavitz

Thanks are also due for the supply of photographs to the following manufacturers:

ABS, Alfa Romeo, Aston Martin Lagonda, Beauford, Burlington, Caterham Cars, Curtana, Daimler-Benz, Dash Sports Cars DJ Sports Cars, Douglas, Evante Cars, FIAT, Fieldbay, Gardner Douglas, GTD, Haldane, Jaguar Cars, JBA, JH Classics, JPR, Lancia, Maranello Concessionnaires, Marlin, Midas, Minari, Morgan, PACE, Pilgrim, Porsche, Proteus, Rickman Bros, Robin Hood, SP Motors, Street Beetle, Sylva, Tiger Cars, Tornado Sports Cars, Transformer, Troll, Volvo, Wizard Roadsters, Wynes

Front cover photograph by Rowan Isaac

Special colour photography by Tim Andrew, John Colley, Paul Debois and Mick Walsh